D1028772

HILLS
Salt Fork of Arkansas
Cimarron
GLASS MTS
North
River
Grand R.
Verdigris River
Arkansas
Canadian
OSAGE PLAINS
River
Canadian
Washita
River
River
SHAWNEE HILLS
Kiamichi
WICHITA MOUNTAINS
ARBUCKLE MOUNTAINS
Muddy

HILLS
Salt Fork of Arkansas
Cimarron
GLASS MTS
North
River
Verdigris River
Grand R.
Arkansas
Canadian River
OSAGE PLAINS
Canadian
Washita
River
River
SHAWNEE HILLS
SAN BOIS MO
WINDING STAIR MOU
Kiamichi
KIAMICH
WICHITA MOUNTAINS
ARBUCKLE MOUNTAINS
Muddy

HISTORICAL ATLAS OF OKLAHOMA

FOURTH EDITION

OKLAHOMA
'07
CENTENNIAL
TM

Historical Atlas of Oklahoma

FOURTH EDITION

CHARLES ROBERT GOINS
& DANNEY GOBLE

Cartography by

CHARLES ROBERT GOINS AND JAMES H. ANDERSON

INTRODUCTION BY DAVID L. BOREN

UNIVERSITY OF OKLAHOMA PRESS : NORMAN

Also by Charles Robert Goins

(with John W. Morris) *Oklahoma Homes: Past and Present* (Norman, 1980)
(with John W. Morris and Edwin C. McReynolds) *Historical Atlas of Oklahoma,* 3rd ed. (Norman, 1986)
(with John Michael Caldwell) *Historical Atlas of Louisiana* (Norman, 1995)

Also by Danney Goble

Progressive Oklahoma: The Making of a New Kind of State (Norman, 1981)
(with James R. Scales) *Oklahoma Politics: A History* (Norman, 1982)
(with Carl Albert) *Little Giant: The Life and Times of Speaker Carl Albert* (Norman, 1990)
(with Ada Lois Sipuel Fisher) *A Matter of Black and White: The Autobiography of Ada Lois Sipuel Fisher* (Norman, 1996)
Tulsa! Biography of the American City (Tulsa, 1997)
(with David W. Baird) *The Story of Oklahoma,* 2nd ed. (Norman, 2006)

This book is published with the generous assistance of the Office of the President, University of Oklahoma; the College of Architecture, University of Oklahoma; and the Oklahoma Centennial Commission.

Library of Congress Cataloging-in-Publication Data

Goins, Charles Robert.
Historical atlas of Oklahoma / Charles Robert Goins and Danny Goble ; introduction by David L. Boren. — 4th ed.
p. cm.
Rev. and enlarged ed. of: Historical atlas of Oklahoma / by John W. Morris, Charles R. Goins, and Edwin C. McReynolds. 3rd ed. © 1986.
Includes bibliographical references (p.) and index.
ISBN 978-0-8061-3482-6 (hc : alk. paper)
ISBN 978-0-8061-3483-3 (pbk : alk. paper)
1. Oklahoma—Historical geography—Maps. 2. Oklahoma—History. I. Goble, Danney, 1946– II. Morris, John Wesely. Historical atlas of Oklahoma. III. Title.

G1366.S1M6 2006
911'.766—dc22
2006627733

Book design and page layout by Charles Robert Goins.

The paper in this book meets the guidelines for permanence and durability of the Committee on Production Guidelines for Book Longevity of the Council on Library Resources, Inc. ∞

Manufactured in Canada

3 5 7 9 8 6 4

Contents

Part V: Brand New State . . . Gonna Treat You Great

Illustrations

Tables and Graphs

Tables

Graphs

Preface

Exactly fifty years ago, the University of Oklahoma Press issued what was then something of a novel piece of scholarship: a *Historical Atlas of Oklahoma.* Nothing on its title page or amid its publication data identified it as a first edition of the *Historical Atlas,* perhaps because at the time it was so novel that there was little thought of future need for a subsequent edition. There must have been some who unthinkingly presumed that geography and history are, after all, two aspects of human affairs that are utterly impervious to change. The physical planet is not going to change. History lies entirely in the past, and that past is not going to change either.

So it might have seemed. But the fact that the press saw fit to offer two subsequent editions (one in 1976, the other in 1986) proves otherwise. The planet may not change, but what humankind does with and to and on this planet unceasingly does change. Humanity continues to make new history daily, just as humanity constantly needs to examine how that day came about. No wonder the *Historical Atlas of Oklahoma* would have to appear in a second edition and then a third, both cataloged as being revised and enlarged as well.

As much as this book owes to those earlier editions, however, we have come to see it as something more than another—a fourth—edition, even a revised and enlarged one. Its purpose and presentation are deliberately different. The initial release of this book is scheduled to coincide with Oklahoma's centennial year of statehood, in 2007. For that reason, this fourth edition aims to make its own special contribution to this state's year of commemoration and observances.

Because of that, it approaches both Oklahoma's geography and Oklahoma's history with considerably greater breadth and depth than did the earlier atlases. Offered in six distinct sections, it touches upon everything from the state's most elemental physical qualities to some of its most contemporary public practices. Soils, vegetation, wildlife, even tornadoes and other extreme weather events—each gets the attention it deserves as well as the cartography appropriate to showing it and the text necessary to understanding it. So too does the long history of human interaction with that physical environment, starting with the earliest known inhabitants and continuing with measured stride to Oklahomans who are now alive, who are still active, and who are destined to remain historically significant.

Only because we, as the co-editors, could draw upon the collective talents of seventeen outside contributors (each a respected scholar in her or his field) did we dare envision the charge that we imposed upon ourselves and assigned each of them: to produce a one-to-one match of geographical data with historical interpretation. If as volume editors we managed to achieve what we envisioned, it is only because so many others actually did it. They have our thanks, in measure far greater than their names' appearance with their work and inclusion in our list of contributors.

Our greatest hope is that our fellow Oklahomans will receive this book with a comparable sense of gratitude. We want this fourth edition of the *Historical Atlas of Oklahoma* to reflect well and thoughtfully upon the state that we both love and upon the people—all of the people—who love it as we do.

Acknowledgments

Anyone who has taken on an extended publication project, particularly one that invades one's life for several years, knows that you reach the end only by the efforts and cooperation of many others. It is no different with the development of the fourth edition of the *Historical Atlas of Oklahoma.*

From the very beginning, the idea of developing an enriched and updated fourth edition of the atlas with which to greet the centennial of the state of Oklahoma was met with encouraging approval from all we approached. John Drayton, director of the University of Oklahoma Press, and his considerate and patient staff very quickly encouraged us to proceed. Throughout the long effort ahead, Charles Rankin, editor-in-chief; Patsy Willcox and Emmy Ezzell, production managers; Kirk Bjornsgaard, acquisitions editor; and Steven Baker, assistant managing editor, were always available and most helpful when we called upon their advice and help. Sally Bennett, the copyeditor, performed a major accomplishment—if not a minor miracle—when she took the writings of nineteen contributors and brought an even flow to the vast range of subject material and style.

The authors approached this edition with a more comprehensive design concept than any of its predecessors'. Invitations were extended to seventeen outstanding researchers and practitioners, their strong attachment to Oklahoma already evident through the lives and works of all, to join us for this fourth edition. All accepted without hesitation, and for this confidence the authors are indeed indebted and grateful. We could not have developed this atlas without their research and analyses of the many complex layers of history that make Oklahoma unique.

The atlas took shape and substance within the walls of the College of Architecture. College staff members Deborah Snider and Kim Goodman provided day-to-day support for so many days that we all have lost count. Dean Bob Fillpot assisted with both funding and warm personal support—to say nothing of allowing us unlimited access to the college's copy machine, a lifesaver if ever there was one. Not to be forgotten are Linda Anderson, University of Oklahoma budget director, and Jamie Maddy, budget research analyst, who saw to it that we kept within budget. To all these we both extend heartfelt thanks.

Mere recognition that any atlas is primarily about maps leads us to recognize how much we are indebted to Jim Anderson. Not only is he a fine cartographer, but Jim, surely through some miracle, managed to survive all our many revisions and stay the course with us to the very end.

Curators with several museums and newspapers searched their files for specific illustrations. Special acknowledgment, however, must be made for the assistance of John Lovett, assistant curator of the Western History Collections, University of Oklahoma, for his superb knowledge in selecting and securing prints of photographs and posters for the atlas. Carolyn Hanneman, of the University of Oklahoma's Carl Albert Center, was also generous and helpful in locating elusive photographs. Special thanks are due Dr. Eric Lee, director of the university's Fred Jones, Jr., Museum of Art, and staff members Kim Moinett and Gail Anderson for their assistance in identifying some lovely museum pieces for our use and, more important, helping us locate copyright holders. Betty Price, director of the Oklahoma Arts Council, and her capable staff assisted us in locating data regarding art selections for the atlas, as did Debbie Roberts of the Oklahoma Indian Arts Gallery. We are indebted also to the Oklahoma Department of Transportation for providing generous access to their map files, and especially to Thom A. Renbarger for his knowledge and assistance.

It is as honorable as it is essential that we extend our gratitude to the two scholars, one a geographer, one a historian, who began this atlas more than forty years ago, in 1965. John W. Morris and Edwin C. McReynolds, like many before us, had a deep understanding of and affection for Oklahoma. For their pioneering work, all Oklahomans will forever be indebted, none more than we.

The development of this fourth edition was to a great extent driven by the excitement of the centennial of Oklahoma. This incentive was rewarded when the Oklahoma Centennial Commission made this atlas an official state centennial project. Thereupon, the commission provided a generous grant to assist the press in reducing the price of the atlas as much as possible—a real centennial gift to the citizens of Oklahoma. On their behalf we authors extend great appreciation to J. Blake Wade, executive director of the commission, and Lee Allan Smith, chairman of centennial projects and events, for their support, their encouragement, and their inclusion of this atlas among the many outstanding centennial tributes that the commission has sponsored.

With the strong support, effort, and encouragement that we received from so many, the authors are also deeply indebted to one person, without whom we could not have made this book a reality. That is why we pause to extend our special note of gratitude to President David L. Boren. Not only was he considerate enough to write our introduction, but from the very first he has been generous in providing funding for the book. By now, the citizens of Oklahoma are fully aware of their great, good fortune in having the enthusiastic support of President Boren and Molly Shi Boren for any number of educational, artistic, and historical projects. Their great love of Oklahoma is a blessing.

Finally, a loving word or two for Juanitta Goins, wife of one co-author and warm friend of both: over these last twelve months, she has given so much so selflessly so that we might at last bring many lose ends together and to closure. Saying just that takes us more than one word or two. No matter. There is no number great enough that we might say how much is due her. With her smiling, warm presence, her remarkable intelligence, her patience, and her persistence, Juanitta so transformed the day that we will just have to compromise and use four. But the four that she finally lets us say happen to be the same four that she most wants to hear.

This atlas is finished.

Charles Robert Goins, *Norman, Oklahoma*
Danney Goble, *Norman, Oklahoma*

Introduction

As Oklahoma marks the hundredth anniversary of its statehood, one could convincingly assert that no other state is as quintessentially American. Through its geography, people, and history, Oklahoma captures the essence of the spirit that defines our nation.

Geographically, it is one of the most diverse of all states. Its ecosystems range from the mountain streams of southeastern Oklahoma and the dense forests of the foothills of the Ozark Mountains to the short-grass prairies and deep rock canyons of western Oklahoma. Within its borders are the rugged Wichita Mountains in southwestern Oklahoma, with mountain meadows and prairies at lower elevations. There, bison from the Bronx Zoo and small numbers of longhorn cattle were introduced, to rebuild the herds of those animals, which were disappearing. Farther north, across the almost treeless prairies of the Panhandle—where major discoveries of fossilized dinosaur remains have been made—the earth is still indented by the hooves of thousands of cattle driven north across the famous trails to the railheads of the northern plains.

The state is divided by the Cross Timbers of blackjack oak, which run diagonally across it from southwest to northeast. In the northeast, the tallgrass prairie, never touched by a plow, remains a great sea of grass whose majesty has inspired poets and whose openness gave hope to pioneers who crossed it in their covered wagons. These weary travelers brought with them few possessions—but were sustained by grand dreams of a better future. Those who have experienced the beauty of the tallgrass prairie will forever have a better understanding of the courage of those who first came to the shores of America seeking freedom and a new beginning.

Oklahoma's varied landscape also includes many lakes, with more miles of shoreline than any other interior state except Minnesota. The wealth of diversity that is America can be seen not only in the distinctive geography of Oklahoma but also, and above all, in its people.

No other state has a richer American Indian heritage than does Oklahoma. The state has more tribes than any other. In western Oklahoma, the heritage of the Plains tribes—with their courage and skill as hunters—remains strong. From them has come our understanding that the arts are an integral part of life and not separate from it. The baskets and pottery as well as beaded wearing apparel that they used in everyday life are objects of beauty. Contemporary environmentalism and conservation in many ways have their roots in the reverence and respect for the land exhibited by the first Oklahomans.

The western tribes shared what is now Oklahoma with the eastern tribes, whose members were farmers and built permanent communities. Many of them were forcibly removed from the eastern part of the United States over what was called the "Trail of Tears." They built boarding schools and elaborate plantation homes and set up representative forms of government with three separate branches.

In addition to its Native American heritage, Oklahoma was early seen as a place of opportunity for African Americans recently freed from slavery. Tribal governments in the Indian Territory in the eastern part of Oklahoma granted African Americans a wide range of rights and participation. These emancipated pioneers often built communities of their own. The all-black towns and the dreams of their founders are eloquently described in an essay by writer Ralph Ellison, a native Oklahoman, which he titled "Going to the Territory."

Almost two decades before statehood, came the famous land runs in Oklahoma Territory, where thousands of men and women of all races lined up on the boundaries of tracts opened for general settlement. They waited for the gunshot that would signal that the race was on. Those who participated rushed to stake out acreages of farm- or ranchland or city lots, which would eventually become their own under federal law. Nothing in our national history more vividly symbolizes the United States as a land of equal opportunity. The historian Howard Lamar described this as a uniquely American event because it was a moment when ordinary people, not kings or queens or generals, knew that they were making history. In many ways, Oklahoma remains socially democratic. From the earliest days, men and women have been judged by their abilities and by their integrity rather than by the wealth or prestige of earlier generations in their families.

Close enough in time to the frontier and challenged by an often harsh environment (from droughts to tornadoes), Oklahomans have been defined as both rugged individualists and neighbors who help care for each other. Individualism and commitment to community have come together to shape Oklahoma.

Nowhere is the American spirit more alive and well than it is in Oklahoma. This fourth edition of the *Historical Atlas of Oklahoma* helps explain why and how that spirit was nurtured.

David L. Boren,
President of the
University of Oklahoma

Oologah Lake, northeast of Tulsa. (Photograph by John Elk III, courtesy of Elk Photography)

Part I

Native Oklahoma

Adopted in 1925, the Oklahoma state flag features peace symbols from Indian culture (the peace pipe) and Anglo-American culture (the olive branch).

1. OKLAHOMA—HEARTLAND OF AMERICA *Charles Robert Goins*

On Saturday, November 16, 1907, President Theodore Roosevelt signed a proclamation establishing Oklahoma as the forty-sixth state of the United States. This proclamation officially joined the "Twin Territories"—Indian Territory and Oklahoma Territory—into a brand new state. Beginning in 1866, with revised treaties following the Civil War, American Indian rights to lands in Oklahoma that had been set aside as homelands by the U.S. government began eroding and dissolving as a result of the invasion of these lands by non-Indian people, through settlement by land runs, land lotteries, and finally allotment of individual tribal lands. Following the Land Run of 1889, the U.S. Congress, on May 2, 1890, passed the Oklahoma Organic Act, establishing the formation of Oklahoma Territory. The U.S. Census of 1890 indicated that the new Oklahoma Territory had a population of 78,475, and what remained of Indian Territory had a population of 180,182—giving the Twin Territories a combined population of 258,657.

By 1900, the combined population of the two territories had more than tripled (to 790,391 people), and excitement was growing over the possibility of statehood. On June 16, 1906, President Roosevelt signed the Oklahoma Enabling Act, which provided for the creation of a single state from the "Twin Territories." This act called for a convention to be convened in Guthrie to draft a constitution for the proposed state. This convention was to comprise 112 members: 55 from Indian Territory, 55 from Oklahoma Territory, and 2 from the Osage Reservation. The Enabling Act also required that, as part of the statehood process, an up-to-date population census be taken. On June 20, 1907, the president directed that a census be taken as quickly as possible and that this census reflect the population of both territories as of July 1, 1907. This census indicated the following: Indian Territory had a population of 681,115 and Oklahoma Territory had a population of 733,062, yielding a total population of 1,414,177 for the new state.

Delegates to the convention were elected on November 6, 1906, and met for the first time on November 20, 1906. By September 17, 1907, the work of the convention had been completed, and the proposed constitution was submitted to the two territories (to an all-male electorate); it was ratified by a vote of 180,333 to 73,059. Included at the time of voting on the new constitution was an amendment that, if passed, would prohibit the sale of alcohol within the new state. This amendment passed by a vote of 130,361 to 112,258.

Geographic Profile of Oklahoma

Oklahoma is situated between 33°41′ and 37° north latitude, which places it at about the same latitude as countries such as Algeria, Israel, Iraq, Afghanistan, central China, and southern Japan. It is between 94°29′ and 103° west longitude; only Canada and Mexico share a similar longitude, while all of South America lies east of Oklahoma.

Oklahoma is the twentieth-largest state in area in the United States, having a total area of 69,898 square miles, of which 1,231 square miles are lakes, reservoirs, and ponds each having an area of forty acres or more. Oklahoma is about 18,000 square miles larger than England but three times smaller than France. The U.S. Census of 2000 has the population of Oklahoma at 3,450,654.

Selected State Symbols and Emblems

Animal	American buffalo (bison)	1972
Bird	scissor-tailed flycatcher	1951
Fish	white bass/sand bass	1974
Floral	mistletoe	1893
Flower	Oklahoma rose	2004
Grass	Indian grass	1972
Rock	rose rock	1968
Soil	port silt loam	1987
Song	"Oklahoma!"	1953
Tree	redbud	1971
Wildflower	Indian blanket	1910

CANADA
1500 Miles
1000 Miles
500 Miles
Seattle
Minneapolis
LAKE SUPERIOR
LAKE MICHIGAN
LAKE HURON
L. ONTARIO
LAKE ERIE
New York
Chicago
Pittsburgh
Washington, D.C.
San Francisco
Denver
Los Angeles
OKLAHOMA
Memphis
Atlanta
Houston
Miami
ATLANTIC OCEAN
PACIFIC OCEAN
MEXICO
GULF OF MEXICO
CUBA
Miles
0 100 200 300 400
0 100 200 300 400 500
Kilometers
110°
100°
90°
80°
70°
45°
35°
25°

2. GEOMORPHIC PROVINCES

Essay by *Kenneth S. Johnson*

A geomorphic province is a part of the Earth's surface where a suite of rocks with similar geologic character and structure have undergone a similar geologic history, and where its present-day character and landforms differ significantly from those of adjacent provinces. As used here, the term is considered similar to "physiographic province."

Most of the outcrops in Oklahoma consist of horizontal or gently dipping sandstones, sands, and shales of Pennsylvanian, Permian, Cretaceous, and Tertiary age (see Topography and Principal Landforms, map 3). Some of the sandstones (mainly in eastern Oklahoma) are well indurated (cemented), but sandstones in most other parts of Oklahoma are not well indurated and are not very resistant to erosion; thus, much of Oklahoma consists of gently rolling hills and broad, flat plains. Elsewhere, buttes, cuestas, escarpments, and high hills are capped by erosion-resistant layers such as indurated sandstone, limestone, or gypsum, which are interbedded with shales and nonresistant sandstones.

Among the more impressive geomorphic provinces in Oklahoma are the several mountain belts and uplifts of the south and northeast. In the southern third of the state, well-indurated rocks have been folded, faulted, and uplifted to form the Wichita, Arbuckle, and Ouachita Mountain ranges. The resistant rock units, the complex geology, and the mountains and high hills of these three provinces contrast sharply with Oklahoma's typical rolling hills and broad plains. In the hilly, wooded area of the Ozark Plateau and the Boston Mountains in northeastern Oklahoma, streams and rivers cutting down into resistant limestones and sandstones have locally created sharp relief.

One of the more striking characteristics of rocks and landforms in central and western Oklahoma is their red color. This results from a thin coating of oxidized iron minerals (mainly hematite) that coats or stains individual grains or particles of the rock. The red color is noted in the names of some of the geomorphic provinces, such as the Central and Western Red-Bed Plains.

Several geologic processes (glaciation and volcanism) that normally create distinctive landforms are not applicable in Oklahoma. Glaciers did not reach or cover any parts of Oklahoma during the ice ages of the Pleistocene Epoch. Continental glaciers extended only as far south as northeastern Kansas. Volcanic peaks and their typical shapes also are lacking in Oklahoma. The nearest volcanoes are 1,050 miles west of the Oklahoma Panhandle, in New Mexico and Colorado, although a basaltic lava flow extruded from a volcano in Colorado did reach into Oklahoma at Black Mesa.

When Pleistocene glaciation reached its maximum extent, about 18,000 years ago, ice covered nearly all of Canada and much of the northern United States. Because so much global water was tied up in glacial ice, sea level was about 200 to 400 feet lower around most of the continent and the shoreline was farther seaward than it is today. The lower sea level exposed a land bridge, called Beringia, in the Pacific Northwest, across what is now the Bering Sea. This land bridge connected Siberia to North America and allowed humans to migrate from Asia into Alaska. About 12,000 years ago, as the last continental ice sheet was melting from western Canada, an ice-free corridor opened that enabled Paleo-Indians to migrate southward through Canada and move across the Americas.

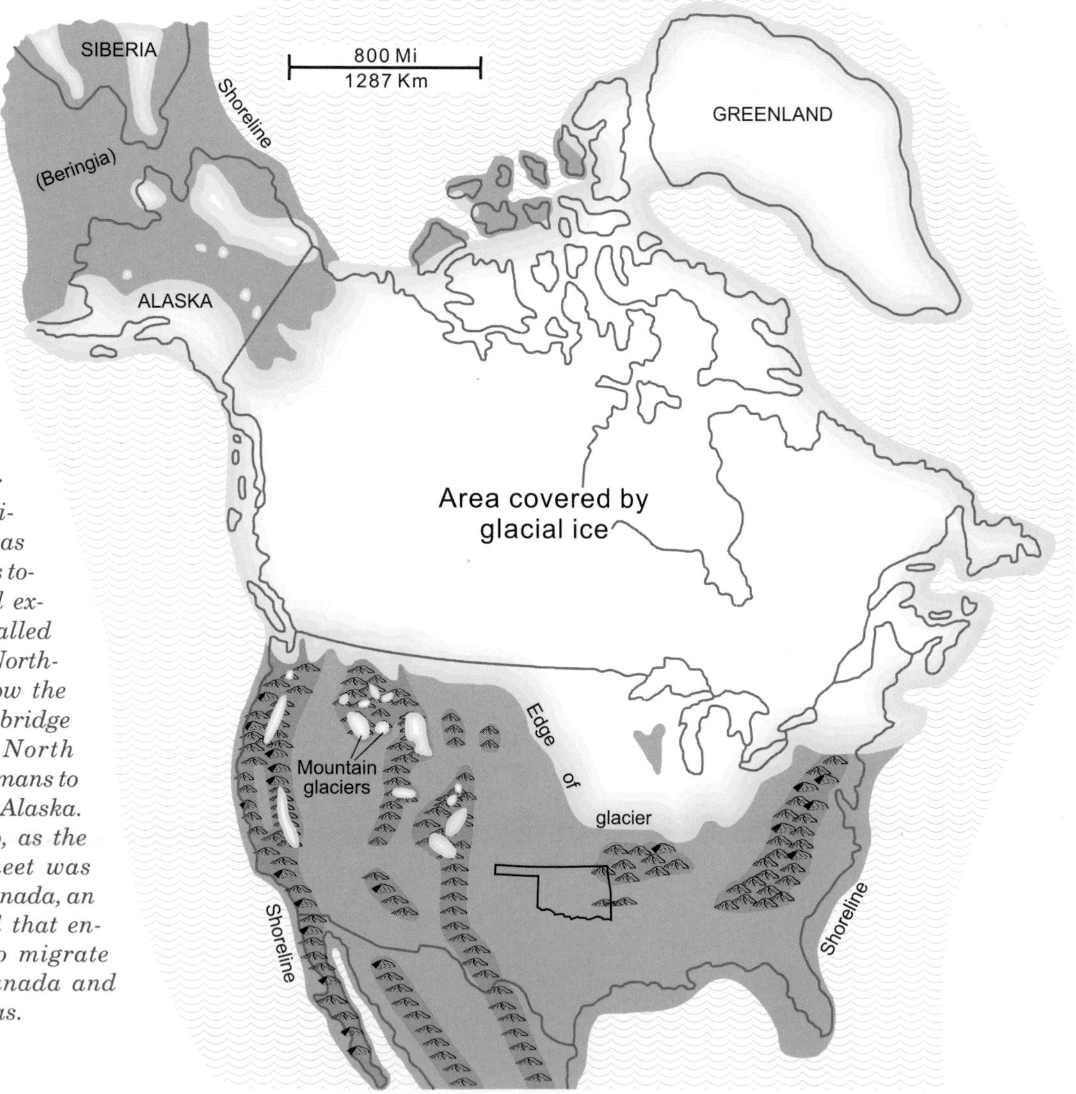

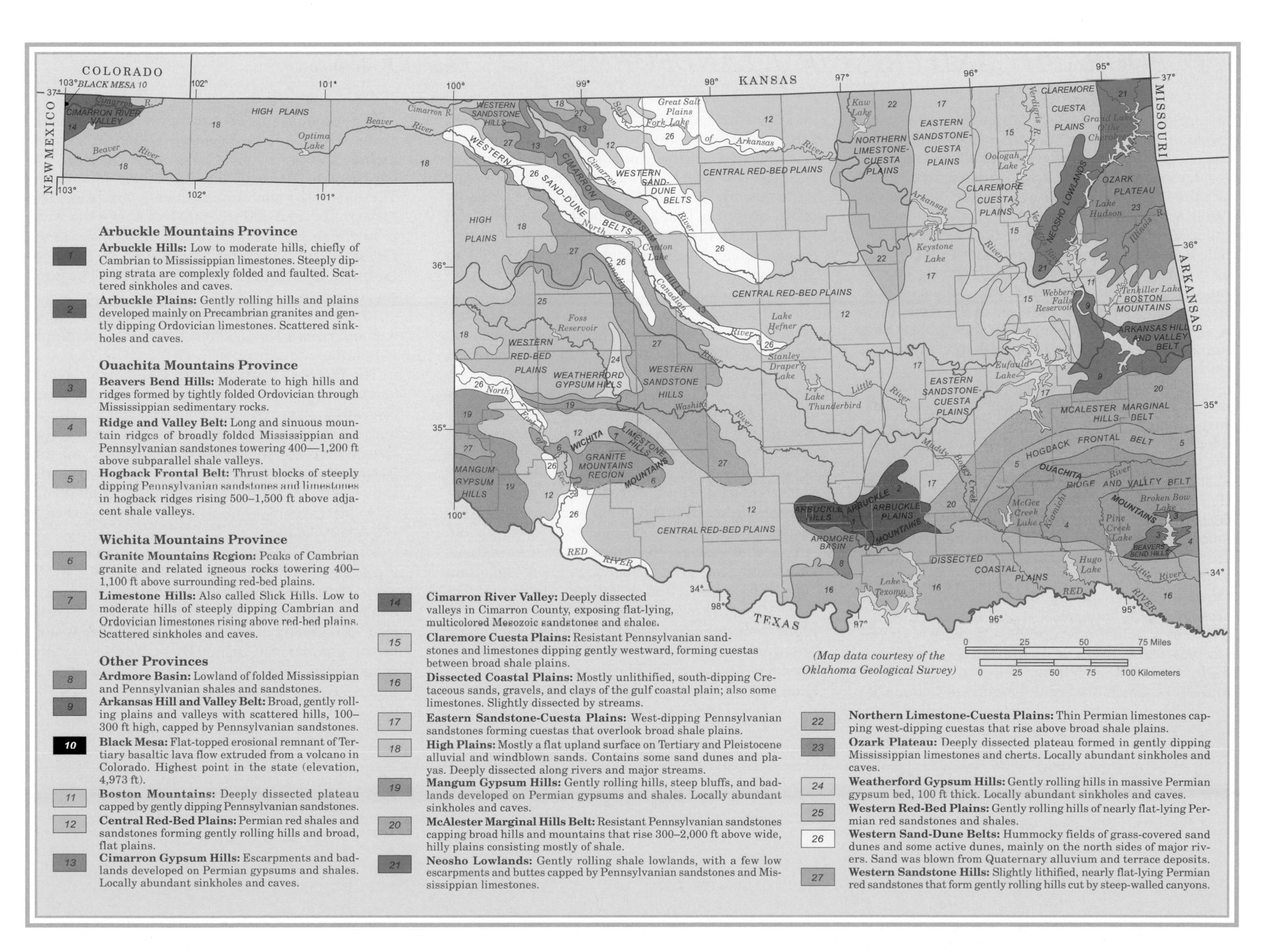
COLORADO
KANSAS
MISSOURI
ARKANSAS
TEXAS
NEW MEXICO
BLACK MESA 10
CIMARRON RIVER VALLEY
HIGH PLAINS
WESTERN SANDSTONE HILLS
WESTERN SAND-DUNE BELTS
CIMARRON GYPSUM HILLS
CENTRAL RED-BED PLAINS
NORTHERN LIMESTONE-CUESTA PLAINS
EASTERN SANDSTONE-CUESTA PLAINS
CLAREMORE CUESTA PLAINS
NEOSHO LOWLANDS
OZARK PLATEAU
BOSTON MOUNTAINS
ARKANSAS HILL AND VALLEY BELT
WESTERN RED-BED PLAINS
WEATHERFORD GYPSUM HILLS
MCALESTER MARGINAL HILLS BELT
HOGBACK FRONTAL BELT
OUACHITA RIDGE AND VALLEY BELT
OUACHITA MOUNTAINS
BEAVERS BEND HILLS
WICHITA GRANITE MOUNTAINS REGION
LIMESTONE HILLS
WICHITA MOUNTAINS
MANGUM GYPSUM HILLS
ARBUCKLE HILLS
ARBUCKLE PLAINS
ARBUCKLE MOUNTAINS
ARDMORE BASIN
DISSECTED COASTAL PLAINS
RED RIVER
(Map data courtesy of the Oklahoma Geological Survey)
0 25 50 75 Miles
0 25 50 75 100 Kilometers
Arbuckle Mountains Province
1 Arbuckle Hills: Low to moderate hills, chiefly of Cambrian to Mississippian limestones. Steeply dipping strata are complexly folded and faulted. Scattered sinkholes and caves.
2 Arbuckle Plains: Gently rolling hills and plains developed mainly on Precambrian granites and gently dipping Ordovician limestones. Scattered sinkholes and caves.
Ouachita Mountains Province
3 Beavers Bend Hills: Moderate to high hills and ridges formed by tightly folded Ordovician through Mississippian sedimentary rocks.
4 Ridge and Valley Belt: Long and sinuous mountain ridges of broadly folded Mississippian and Pennsylvanian sandstones towering 400—1,200 ft above subparallel shale valleys.
5 Hogback Frontal Belt: Thrust blocks of steeply dipping Pennsylvanian sandstones and limestones in hogback ridges rising 500–1,500 ft above adjacent shale valleys.
Wichita Mountains Province
6 Granite Mountains Region: Peaks of Cambrian granite and related igneous rocks towering 400–1,100 ft above surrounding red-bed plains.
7 Limestone Hills: Also called Slick Hills. Low to moderate hills of steeply dipping Cambrian and Ordovician limestones rising above red-bed plains. Scattered sinkholes and caves.
Other Provinces
8 Ardmore Basin: Lowland of folded Mississippian and Pennsylvanian shales and sandstones.
9 Arkansas Hill and Valley Belt: Broad, gently rolling plains and valleys with scattered hills, 100–300 ft high, capped by Pennsylvanian sandstones.
10 Black Mesa: Flat-topped erosional remnant of Tertiary basaltic lava flow extruded from a volcano in Colorado. Highest point in the state (elevation, 4,973 ft).
11 Boston Mountains: Deeply dissected plateau capped by gently dipping Pennsylvanian sandstones.
12 Central Red-Bed Plains: Permian red shales and sandstones forming gently rolling hills and broad, flat plains.
13 Cimarron Gypsum Hills: Escarpments and badlands developed on Permian gypsums and shales. Locally abundant sinkholes and caves.
14 Cimarron River Valley: Deeply dissected valleys in Cimarron County, exposing flat-lying, multicolored Mesozoic sandstones and shales.
15 Claremore Cuesta Plains: Resistant Pennsylvanian sandstones and limestones dipping gently westward, forming cuestas between broad shale plains.
16 Dissected Coastal Plains: Mostly unlithified, south-dipping Cretaceous sands, gravels, and clays of the gulf coastal plain; also some limestones. Slightly dissected by streams.
17 Eastern Sandstone-Cuesta Plains: West-dipping Pennsylvanian sandstones forming cuestas that overlook broad shale plains.
18 High Plains: Mostly a flat upland surface on Tertiary and Pleistocene alluvial and windblown sands. Contains some sand dunes and playas. Deeply dissected along rivers and major streams.
19 Mangum Gypsum Hills: Gently rolling hills, steep bluffs, and badlands developed on Permian gypsums and shales. Locally abundant sinkholes and caves.
20 McAlester Marginal Hills Belt: Resistant Pennsylvanian sandstones capping broad hills and mountains that rise 300–2,000 ft above wide, hilly plains consisting mostly of shale.
21 Neosho Lowlands: Gently rolling shale lowlands, with a few low escarpments and buttes capped by Pennsylvanian sandstones and Mississippian limestones.
22 Northern Limestone-Cuesta Plains: Thin Permian limestones capping west-dipping cuestas that rise above broad shale plains.
23 Ozark Plateau: Deeply dissected plateau formed in gently dipping Mississippian limestones and cherts. Locally abundant sinkholes and caves.
24 Weatherford Gypsum Hills: Gently rolling hills in massive Permian gypsum bed, 100 ft thick. Locally abundant sinkholes and caves.
25 Western Red-Bed Plains: Gently rolling hills of nearly flat-lying Permian red sandstones and shales.
26 Western Sand-Dune Belts: Hummocky fields of grass-covered sand dunes and some active dunes, mainly on the north sides of major rivers. Sand was blown from Quaternary alluvium and terrace deposits.
27 Western Sandstone Hills: Slightly lithified, nearly flat-lying Permian red sandstones that form gently rolling hills cut by steep-walled canyons.

3. *TOPOGRAPHY AND PRINCIPAL LANDFORMS*

Essay by *Kenneth S. Johnson*

The topographic features of Oklahoma's surface can be visualized by means of contour lines, which are lines of equal elevation above sea level. Oklahoma's overall topographic surface slopes down toward the east: the highest elevation in the state (4,973 feet) is on Black Mesa, in the northwestern corner of the Panhandle; the lowest elevation (287 feet) is where Little River flows into Arkansas, about twenty miles north of the southeast corner of the state. Therefore, the land surface slopes down to the east and east-southeast at an average of about 9 feet per mile; the slope ranges from about 15 feet per mile in the Panhandle to about 4 feet per mile in central and eastern Oklahoma.

The topography or landscape of Oklahoma is defined by its mountains and streams. The mountains consist mainly of resistant rock masses that were folded, faulted, and thrust upward in the geologic past, whereas the streams continue to erode the less-resistant rock units and lower the landscape to form hills, broad valleys, and plains throughout most of the remainder of the state. The three principal mountain ranges (Wichita, Arbuckle, and Ouachita) occur in southern Oklahoma, although mountainous and hilly areas extend across many other parts of the state as well (see Geomorphic Provinces, map 2, for landscape features).

The term "relief" refers to the difference in elevation between hilltops or mountain summits and nearby lowlands or valleys. Relief in the Wichita Mountains, which are located mainly in Comanche and Kiowa counties in southwestern Oklahoma, ranges from about 400 to 1,100 feet. The highest elevation in the sparsely wooded Wichita Mountains is about 2,475 feet, on an unnamed peak in the northwestern corner of Comanche County. Nearby is Mt. Scott, the best-known peak in the Wichitas; its summit (2,464 feet), which can be reached by car or bus, commands a spectacular view of the Wichita Mountains.

The Arbuckle Mountains lie within an area of low-to-moderate, sparsely wooded hills in Murray, Johnston, and Pontotoc counties in south-central Oklahoma. Relief in the area ranges from 100 to 600 feet, and the highest elevation (about 1,419 feet) is in the West Timbered Hills, in western Murray County. Although the relief in this mountain area is low, it is still impressive because it is six times greater than that of any other topographic feature between Oklahoma City and Dallas, Texas.

The Ouachita (pronounced "wa-she-tah") Mountains of southeastern Oklahoma and western Arkansas make up a curved belt of forested ridges and subparallel valleys. Resistant beds of sandstone, chert, and novaculite form long, sinuous mountain ridges that rise 500 to 1,500 feet above adjacent valleys that are formed in easily eroded shales. The highest elevation is 2,666 feet, on Rich Mountain. Major prominent ridges within the Ouachitas are known locally as the Winding Stair, Rich, Kiamichi, Blue, Jackfork, and Blackjack mountains.

Other mountains are scattered across the Arkansas River valley of eastern Oklahoma. These include the Sans Bois, Cavanal, Sugar Loaf, Poteau, Beaver, Hi Early, and Rattlesnake mountains. These forested mountains typically are broad features that stand 300 to 2,000 feet above the wide, rolling plains. The largest mountainous area in the region is the Sans Bois Mountains, in northern Latimer and southern Haskell counties. The highest summit is Sugar Loaf Mountain, in northeastern Le Flore County; it has an elevation of 2,568 feet and rises about 2,000 feet above the surrounding plains.

The Ozarks of northeastern Oklahoma are best described as a deeply dissected, forested plateau consisting of nearly flat-lying limestones, cherts, and sandstones. The area embraces parts of the Ozark Plateau, the Brushy Mountains, and the Boston Mountains. Relief in the Ozarks typically is 50 to 400 feet, and the highest elevation (about 1,745 feet) is on Workman Mountain, in southeastern Adair County.

The Glass Mountains is an area of "badlands" topography in north-central Major County, in the grasslands of northwestern Oklahoma. It is a misnomer to call them "mountains"—they are, however, prominent mesas, buttes, and escarpments in the Cimarron Gypsum Hills. The local relief ranges from 150 to 200 feet, and the highest elevation is about 1,585 feet.

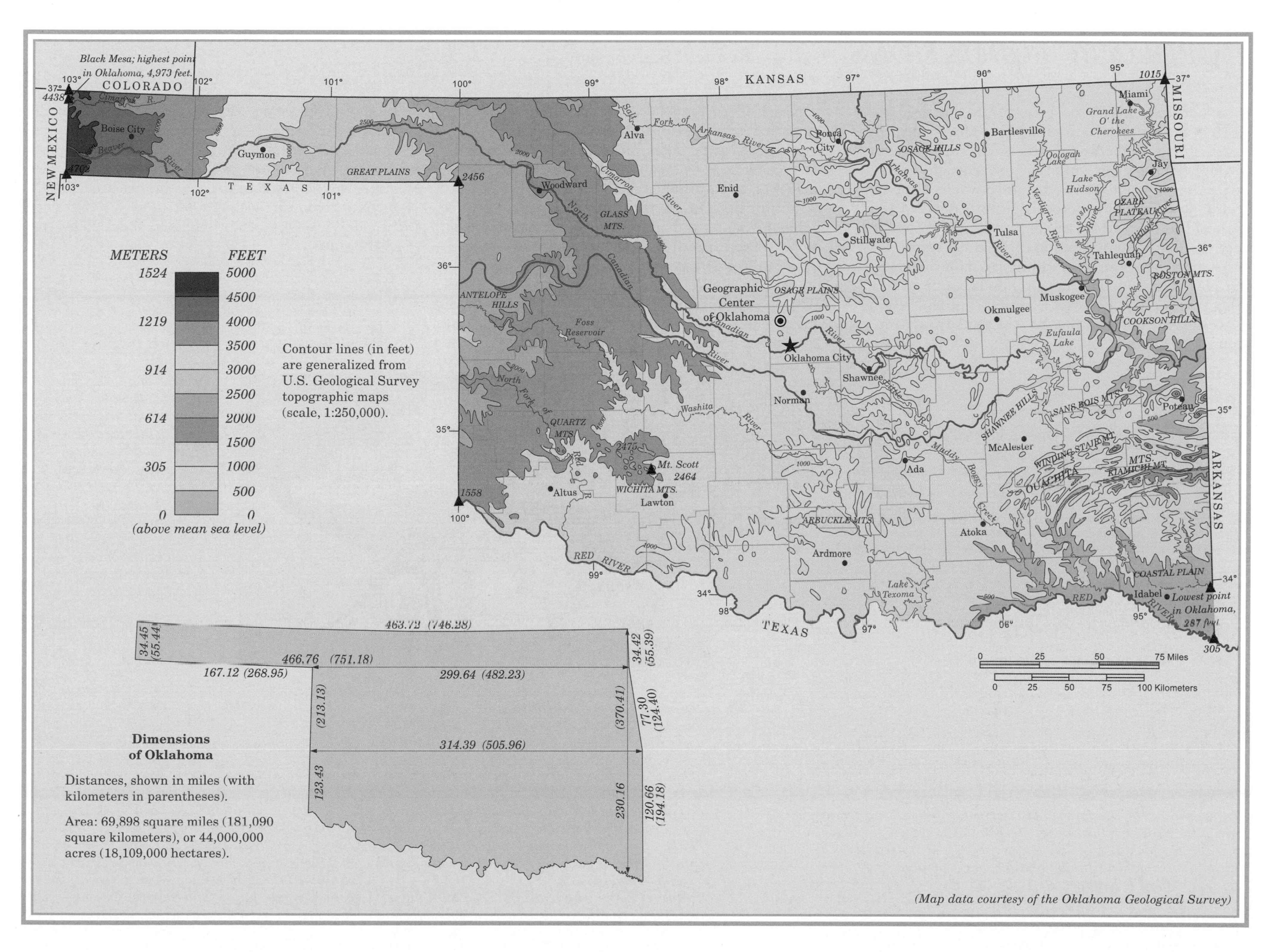
Black Mesa; highest point in Oklahoma, 4,973 feet.
COLORADO
KANSAS
MISSOURI
ARKANSAS
TEXAS
NEW MEXICO
METERS
FEET
(above mean sea level)
Contour lines (in feet) are generalized from U.S. Geological Survey topographic maps (scale, 1:250,000).
Geographic Center of Oklahoma
Oklahoma City
Boise City
Guymon
Woodward
Alva
Enid
Ponca City
Bartlesville
Miami
Tulsa
Stillwater
Tahlequah
Muskogee
Okmulgee
Shawnee
Norman
McAlester
Ada
Poteau
Altus
Lawton
Mt. Scott 2464
Ardmore
Atoka
Idabel
Lowest point in Oklahoma, 287 feet
GREAT PLAINS
GLASS MTS.
ANTELOPE HILLS
QUARTZ MTS.
WICHITA MTS.
ARBUCKLE MTS.
OSAGE PLAINS
OSAGE HILLS
OZARK PLATEAU
BOSTON MTS.
COOKSON HILLS
SHAWNEE HILLS
SANS BOIS MTS.
WINDING STAIR MT.
OUACHITA MTS.
KIAMICHI MT.
COASTAL PLAIN
Grand Lake O' the Cherokees
Oologah Lake
Lake Hudson
Eufaula Lake
Foss Reservoir
Lake Texoma
RED RIVER
Miles
Kilometers
Dimensions of Oklahoma
Distances, shown in miles (with kilometers in parentheses).
Area: 69,898 square miles (181,090 square kilometers), or 44,000,000 acres (18,109,000 hectares).
(Map data courtesy of the Oklahoma Geological Survey)

4. GEOLOGIC FORMATIONS

Essay by *Kenneth S. Johnson*

A geologic map shows those rock units that crop out in an area or that are mantled by a thin veneer of soil. Oklahoma's bedrock units are of Precambrian through Tertiary age, and they are overlain locally by Quaternary-age sediments laid down by streams and rivers that flow across the state toward the east and southeast. An understanding of the character and age of outcropping rocks is necessary for assessing petroleum reservoirs, local mineral deposits, potential construction problems, engineering properties, and groundwater-aquifer characteristics, as well as for determining how to remedy environmental problems.

Nearly 99 percent of all outcropping rocks in Oklahoma are of sedimentary origin, deposited in ancient seas, deltas, lakes, and rivers. The remaining outcrops (about 1 percent) are divided among igneous rocks, mainly in the Wichita and Arbuckle Mountain ranges; metamorphic rocks in the eastern Arbuckle Mountains; and mildly metamorphosed rocks in the core of the Ouachita Mountains.

Rocks of every geologic period crop out in Oklahoma. Rocks of Permian age are exposed at the surface in about 46 percent of the state. Other extensive outcrops are rocks of Pennsylvanian age (in about 25 percent of the state), Tertiary (11 percent), Cretaceous (7 percent), Mississippian (6 percent), Ordovician (1 percent), or Cambrian (1 percent); Precambrian, Silurian, Devonian, Triassic, and Jurassic rocks each are exposed in less than 1 percent of the state. Not included in these estimates are the Quaternary river, terrace, and lake deposits that overlie older, pre-Quaternary rocks in about 20 percent of the state.

Bedrock geology is generalized from Miser's (1954) *Geologic Map of Oklahoma* (scale, 1:500,000). Mapping of Quaternary alluvium and terrace deposits is generalized from the nine hydrologic atlases of Oklahoma prepared cooperatively by the Oklahoma Geological Survey and the U.S. Geological Survey.

Era	Period		Major biologic events		Millions of years ago
CENOZOIC	Quaternary		First humans		0
	Tertiary		Mammals become abundant		2
MESOZOIC	Cretaceous	Late	Flowering plants abundant		65
		Early	First flowering plants	"Age of Dinosaurs"	100
	Jurassic		First birds		140
	Triassic		First dinosaurs/ first mammals		200
PALEOZOIC	Permian		Mass extinction of most marine invertebrates		250
	Pennsylvanian		Major coal-forming swamps		290
	Mississippian		First reptiles		330
	Devonian		First amphibians		365
	Silurian		Early land plants		405
	Ordovician		Early fish		425
	Cambrian		Trilobites/shelled animals		500
PRECAMBRIAN			Early life-forms without shells		570

Acrocanthosaurus lived about 110 million to 100 million years ago, during the Early Cretaceous epoch. The Cretaceous is the last period in the Mesozoic era known as the "Age of Dinosaurs." The dinosaurs—along with flying reptiles, many swimming reptiles, and giant clams—disappeared at the end of the Cretaceous period.

Acrocanthosaurus relied on its tremendous jaws to capture and tear apart prey such as this Pleurocoelus. Fossil remains of both Acrocanthosaurus and Pleurocoelus have been found in the Antlers Formation of southeastern Oklahoma. (Illustration by Karen Carr, courtesy of Fort Worth Museum of Science and History)

Dinosaurs in Oklahoma

The "Age of Dinosaurs" included the Triassic, Jurassic, and Cretaceous periods of geologic time (the Mesozoic era). Although giant plant- and flesh-eating dinosaurs roamed freely over all parts of Oklahoma, their fossil remains are preserved only in the southeast and in the Panhandle (these are the only parts of the state where rocks deposited during the Mesozoic era are still present). Bones and footprints are the common types of dinosaur fossils found in Oklahoma.

Most of Oklahoma was above sea level during the Triassic and Jurassic periods, when footprints and bones were left in sediments (now rocks) in the western part of the Panhandle. Later, during the Cretaceous period, dinosaurs in southeastern Oklahoma lived (and are now fossilized) in ancient deltas that bordered the ancestral Gulf of Mexico.

Among the dinosaur fossil bones found in Oklahoma are those of plant eaters such as Stegosaurus, Apatosaurus, Diplodocus, and Pentaceratops and flesh eaters such as Saurophaganax, Acrocanthosaurus, and Deinonychus. These dinosaurs are among the largest and/or most ferocious beasts that ever roamed the surface of the Earth.

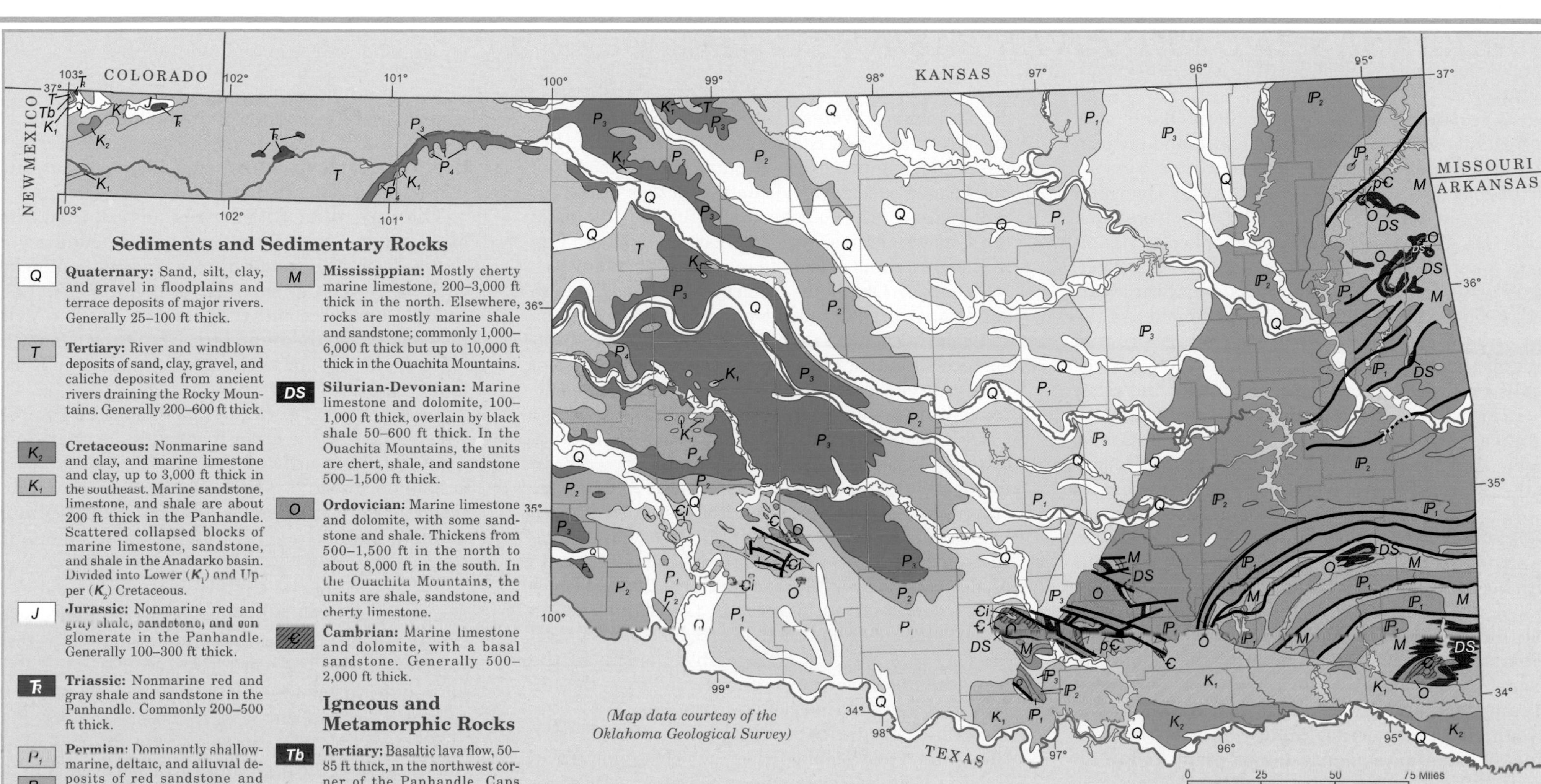

(Map data courtesy of the Oklahoma Geological Survey)

Sediments and Sedimentary Rocks

Q **Quaternary:** Sand, silt, clay, and gravel in floodplains and terrace deposits of major rivers. Generally 25–100 ft thick.

T **Tertiary:** River and windblown deposits of sand, clay, gravel, and caliche deposited from ancient rivers draining the Rocky Mountains. Generally 200–600 ft thick.

K_2 / K_1 **Cretaceous:** Nonmarine sand and clay, and marine limestone and clay, up to 3,000 ft thick in the southeast. Marine sandstone, limestone, and shale are about 200 ft thick in the Panhandle. Scattered collapsed blocks of marine limestone, sandstone, and shale in the Anadarko basin. Divided into Lower (**K_1**) and Upper (**K_2**) Cretaceous.

J **Jurassic:** Nonmarine red and gray shale, sandstone, and conglomerate in the Panhandle. Generally 100–300 ft thick.

Ʀ **Triassic:** Nonmarine red and gray shale and sandstone in the Panhandle. Commonly 200–500 ft thick.

P_1 / P_2 / P_3 / P_4 **Permian:** Dominantly shallow-marine, deltaic, and alluvial deposits of red sandstone and shale. Outcrops of white gypsum are conspicuous, and thick salt deposits are widespread in the subsurface in the west. Generally 1,000–6,500 ft thick. Divided into Lower (**P_1** and **P_2**) and Upper (**P_3** and **P_4**) Permian. The lower part of P_1 is mostly marine red sandstone and shale, with some thin beds of limestone.

IP_1 / IP_2 / IP_3 **Pennsylvanian:** Dominantly marine shale, with interbedded sandstone, limestone, and coal. Thickness is commonly 2,000–5,000 ft but much greater in the Anadarko basin (16,000 ft thick), Ardmore basin (15,000 ft), Marietta basin (13,000 ft), Ouachita Mountains (15,000 ft), and Arkoma basin (18,000 ft). Thick conglomerates are present near the Wichita and Arbuckle Mountain ranges. Divided into Lower (**IP_1**), Middle (**IP_2**), and Upper (**IP_3**) Pennsylvanian.

M **Mississippian:** Mostly cherty marine limestone, 200–3,000 ft thick in the north. Elsewhere, rocks are mostly marine shale and sandstone; commonly 1,000–6,000 ft thick but up to 10,000 ft thick in the Ouachita Mountains.

DS **Silurian-Devonian:** Marine limestone and dolomite, 100–1,000 ft thick, overlain by black shale 50–600 ft thick. In the Ouachita Mountains, the units are chert, shale, and sandstone 500–1,500 ft thick.

O **Ordovician:** Marine limestone and dolomite, with some sandstone and shale. Thickens from 500–1,500 ft in the north to about 8,000 ft in the south. In the Ouachita Mountains, the units are shale, sandstone, and cherty limestone.

Ꞓ **Cambrian:** Marine limestone and dolomite, with a basal sandstone. Generally 500–2,000 ft thick.

Igneous and Metamorphic Rocks

Tb **Tertiary:** Basaltic lava flow, 50–85 ft thick, in the northwest corner of the Panhandle. Caps Black Mesa.

Ꞓi **Cambrian:** Outcrops of granite, rhyolite, and gabbro in the Wichita Mountains and rhyolite in the Arbuckle Mountains. Formed from magma about 525 million years ago; nearly 20,000 ft thick.

pꞒ **Precambrian:** Granite and gneiss (a metamorphosed igneous rock) crop out in the Arbuckle Mountains, and granite crops out in a small area in Mayes County (in the northeast). Formed about 1.4 billion years ago, these are the oldest outcropping rocks in Oklahoma.

(Symbols)

Geologic contact

Fault; dotted where concealed by quaternary sediments

Geologic Hazards in Oklahoma

Earthquake damage is low in Oklahoma. The state experiences an average of about 50 seismic events each year that are recorded on sensitive instruments; typically, only one tremor per year is felt by humans. Landslides occur mainly in the eastern third of the state, owing to wetter climate, higher relief, and steeper slopes in the region. Expansive soils typically are those with clay minerals that shrink and swell as water is added or removed. Major floods can occur along the floodplains of any of the state's principal rivers and streams. The term "karst" refers to sinkholes, caves, and other subsidence features that form where water-soluble rocks (limestone, dolomite, gypsum, or salt) are partly or totally dissolved. Radon is a carcinogenic, radioactive gas given off during the natural decay of uranium in rocks: only about 7 percent of the counties in Oklahoma have a locally moderate or locally moderate-to-high potential for radon emissions. Solid and liquid industrial wastes must be disposed of in rock units that can ensure containment of the waste and that prevent migration of leachate into the human environment. Mining activities from both underground and surface mines pose additional problems, including barren waste dumps, flooding of active mines, acidic or toxic leachate contaminating local water supplies, collapse or subsidence of the land's surface, and instability of high walls and quarry faces.

5. *ARKANSAS AND RED RIVER BASINS* Essay by *Bruce W. Hoagland*

Rivers are an important component of Oklahoma's natural history, political development, and modern economy. For early settlers, rivers were a corridor for the movement of people and material. Overland trails across Indian Territory followed rivers such as the Canadian. Early forts were supplied by steamboats on the Red and Arkansas rivers. However, cattle trails from Texas to Kansas found the west-to-east-flowing rivers to be an impediment. As the two territories matured to statehood, rivers and streams became political boundaries. The Red River is still a contentious interstate boundary, and other rivers form part of the boundaries of several modern counties, such as Cleveland, Ellis, Haskell, Osage, Sequoyah, Tillman, and Woods. Today, the McClellan-Kerr Arkansas River Navigation System provides an outlet to world markets for Oklahoma goods.

Oklahoma rivers pass through a variety of natural environments as they traverse the state. Streams with headwaters in New Mexico and Colorado carry snowmelt east in the spring. Much of this water is lost to evaporation as these streams flow onto the semiarid Great Plains. In general, the amount of stream discharge and the number of perennial streams increases from west to east in Oklahoma. Stream flow can increase rapidly after storms, visiting disaster on residents downstream. Today, although flooding still occurs, floodwaters are restrained by a number of federal dam-building programs.

Many visitors to Oklahoma notice the sandy stream channels— the product of Oklahoma's sandstone surface geology and materials washed in from farther west. In western and central Oklahoma, red sandstone and shale from the Permian period erode into red clay soils, giving lakes and streams a characteristic muddy-red color. Over time, sand has been scooped out of streambeds and deposited by southwest-prevailing winds on the north side of rivers, forming the large sand dune fields that are characteristic of western rivers. Water quality of Oklahoma streams is affected by the gypsum deposits of western Oklahoma. Water passing through this region dissolves salts and carries them downstream. For millennia, the process of flooding and evaporation has formed extensive salt flats—such as the Great Salt Plains of the Salt Fork and Big Salt Plains of the Cimarron River—along western streams. Life in these streams is well adapted to high salinity.

In eastern Oklahoma, yellow-gray Pennsylvanian sandstones prevail, and streams and lakes lose the red coloring. On the Gulf Coastal Plain of southeastern Oklahoma, floodplain soils are composed of pale-gray clay and silt soils that have developed after centuries of deposition from upstream sources.

Oklahoma lies entirely within the Mississippi drainage basin. The Red and Arkansas rivers, two major tributaries of the Mississippi River, drain the state. The headwaters of the Red River are located in Deaf Smith County, Texas. The river flows along the southern border of Oklahoma from Harmon to McCurtain County. The confluence of the Red River with the Mississippi River is in Louisiana, though much of its water has been diverted by flood-control projects into the Atchafalaya River basin. In the past, the Red River has been referred to as the Rio Rojo and the Red River of Natchitoches.

Several tributaries of the Red River flow through the state. The Washita River, which originates in Roberts County, Texas, enters Oklahoma in Roger Mills County. It joins the Red River to help form Lake Texoma and was recognized as the boundary between Bryan and Marshall counties. The Washita's meandering course through the state is impeded by the Arbuckle Mountains, which it breaches at Big Canyon in Murray County. The word Washita is derived from the Choctaw words "oua" and "cito," meaning "big hunt."

The Arkansas River headwaters are located near Leadville, Colorado. The river flows over the Great Plains and enters Oklahoma in Kay County. Its confluence with the Mississippi River is in Desha County, Arkansas. The river has been repeatedly diverted over the years for irrigation projects in Kansas and Colorado. Coronado dubbed it the St. Peter's and St. Paul's River during his 1540 expedition. French trappers named it the Arkansas after tribes living along its banks.

The Canadian River rises near Raton, New Mexico, and enters Oklahoma as the boundary between Roger Mills and Ellis counties. Its confluence with the North Canadian River helps to form Lake Eufaula, and it becomes the boundary between McIntosh and Pittsburg counties. Early Spanish maps labeled the Canadian as the Rio Colorado. The Kiowa and Comanches referred to it as the Goo-al-pa. The name "Canadian," however, refers to the fur trappers who frequented the lower reaches of the river. Some scholars have speculated as to whether the name was actually "Cañada" or "Cañadiano," Spanish-derived terms alluding to its steep-sided banks. This stream is often, and mistakenly, referred to as the South Canadian.

The source of the Cimarron River is located in Union County, New Mexico. The confluence with the Arkansas is in Pawnee County and helps form Keystone Lake. The word "Cimarron" means "wild" or "rough" in Spanish. The Cimarron has gone by several names in the past. Explorers Zebulon Pike and Thomas Nuttall referred to it as the Grand Saline because of the high concentration of salts in the water. It was also known as the Red Fork.

Headwaters of the Grand, or Neosho, River are located in Morris County, Kansas. It enters Oklahoma in Craig County. Zebulon Pike labeled it as the Grand, but Stephen Long referred to it as both the Grand and the Neosho River. "Neosho" is an Osage word meaning "clear water." The Verdigris rises in Chase County, Kansas, and enters the state in Nowata County. The name refers to the greenish gray tint of the water. The Grand and Verdigris rivers join the Arkansas in Muskogee County to form the historically significant Three Forks region. Several important early settlements and trading posts, including Fort Gibson, were established in this area.

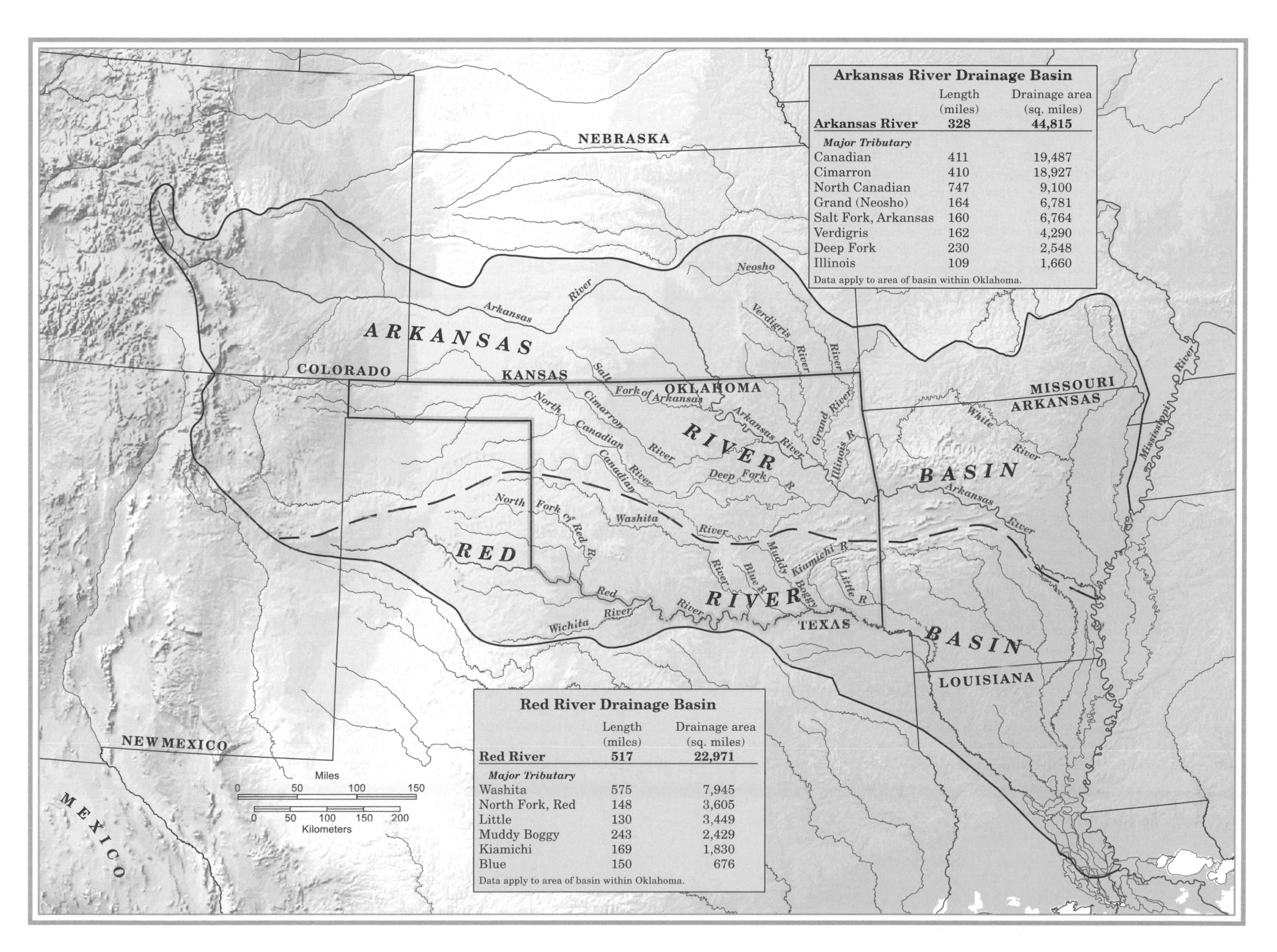

Arkansas River Drainage Basin

	Length (miles)	Drainage area (sq. miles)
Arkansas River	**328**	**44,815**
Major Tributary		
Canadian	411	19,487
Cimarron	410	18,927
North Canadian	747	9,100
Grand (Neosho)	164	6,781
Salt Fork, Arkansas	160	6,764
Verdigris	162	4,290
Deep Fork	230	2,548
Illinois	109	1,660

Data apply to area of basin within Oklahoma.

Red River Drainage Basin

	Length (miles)	Drainage area (sq. miles)
Red River	**517**	**22,971**
Major Tributary		
Washita	575	7,945
North Fork, Red	148	3,605
Little	130	3,449
Muddy Boggy	243	2,429
Kiamichi	169	1,830
Blue	150	676

Data apply to area of basin within Oklahoma.

6. *RIVERS, LAKES, AND RESERVOIRS*

Essay by *Bruce W. Hoagland*

Oklahoma has an abundance of ponds and lakes, both natural and artificial. Oxbow lakes are the product of restless streams meandering to and fro across their floodplains; they can be found along major rivers across the state. Oxbows are concentrated in eastern Oklahoma, with the greatest number in McCurtain County. In western and central Oklahoma, small intermittent ponds occur among the sand dunes of major rivers. These ponds range in size from less than one acre to several acres. In the Panhandle, playa lakes are highly ephemeral water bodies that typically fill in the spring or following heavy storms, although many have been dry for years. They are important migratory stopovers for waterfowl and shorebirds.

Oklahoma residents are probably more familiar with the numerous artificially constructed reservoirs that dot the state. At present, there are an estimated 2,303 public and private lakes in the state, not including the approximately 220,000 ponds constructed for agricultural usage. Reservoir construction resulted in a doubling of the state's water-holding capacity between 1962 and 1984. Eufaula, Texoma, and Grand are the three largest reservoirs in the state. The majority of large reservoirs are operated by the U.S. Army Corps of Engineers (twenty-seven reservoirs), the U.S. Bureau of Reclamation (seven reservoirs), and the state agency, the Grand River Dam Authority (two reservoirs).

Reservoirs serve many purposes, including flood control, water supply, power generation, recreation, navigation, and fish and wildlife conservation. Spavinaw Lake, constructed by the City of Tulsa from 1922 to 1924, was the first major municipal water-supply lake. A fifty-five-mile pipeline was also constructed, to deliver water via a pumping station to a reservoir at Mohawk Park. When completed, Spavinaw was the largest artificial lake in Oklahoma at that time.

Flood-damage abatement has been the impetus for the construction of many reservoirs. Although impoundments constructed by the Corps of Engineers and the Bureau of Reclamation are obvious examples, 2,094 dams in 131 watersheds were constructed as part of the U.S. Department of Agriculture's Upstream Flood Control Project. A series of devastating floods in the 1920s and 1930s (including the disastrous Hammon flood of 1934) led to congressional authorization of a multiagency flood-control survey of the Washita River basin. World War II postponed additional federal action; however, local landowners and business owners organized the Washita Valley Improvement Association on February 29, 1940, to promote flood control and soil conservation in that basin.

The Flood Control Act of December 22, 1944, authorized the U.S. secretary of agriculture, in cooperation with local sponsors, to construct flood-control dams in eleven states. The Soil Conservation Service, in conjunction with the Upper Washita Conservation District, selected Sandstone Creek (located in Roger Mills and Beckham counties) as the first project in Oklahoma. In 1953, Cloud Creek Site One in Washita County became the first flood-control dam completed in the nation. The Watershed and Flood Control Act of 1953 expanded the program, and numerous lakes have been built since that time. Several of these lakes serve as municipal water supplies.

The projected life span of these dams was fifty years. A national pilot project to rehabilitate dams built by the Flood Control Act was announced at the fiftieth-anniversary celebration of Cloud Creek Site One on July 3, 1998. Sergeant Major Creek in Roger Mills County was selected to be the lead watershed project.

Oklahoma municipalities have utilized hydroelectric power since the early twentieth century. Prior to the construction of large-scale hydroelectric projects, some municipalities developed small power-generating stations on water-supply lakes. Presently, there are nine major hydroelectric operations in the state. The first to come online was Pensacola Dam on Grand Lake O' the Cherokees. Pensacola Dam, at 6,100 feet long, is the world's longest multiple-arch dam. Interest in the construction of a dam on the Grand River for flood control and irrigation first developed in the late nineteenth century. In the 1930s, the emphasis was placed on hydroelectric power generation, but Oklahoma utility companies opposed the establishment of a state-run utility. However, Representative Wesley E. Disney (namesake of the town) moved the project through the U.S. Congress in the 1930s. Disney and other project supporters documented the substantial difference in the cost of electricity between Oklahoma and other states and argued that such a project would stimulate economic development. The Grand River Dam Authority was created by the Oklahoma Legislature on January 10, 1935, and President Franklin D. Roosevelt approved a $20 million allocation for construction of Pensacola Dam. Power generated at Pensacola Dam is transmitted to a seventeen-county area. Chief engineer for the project was W. R. Holway, who had earlier engineered the Spavinaw Dam.

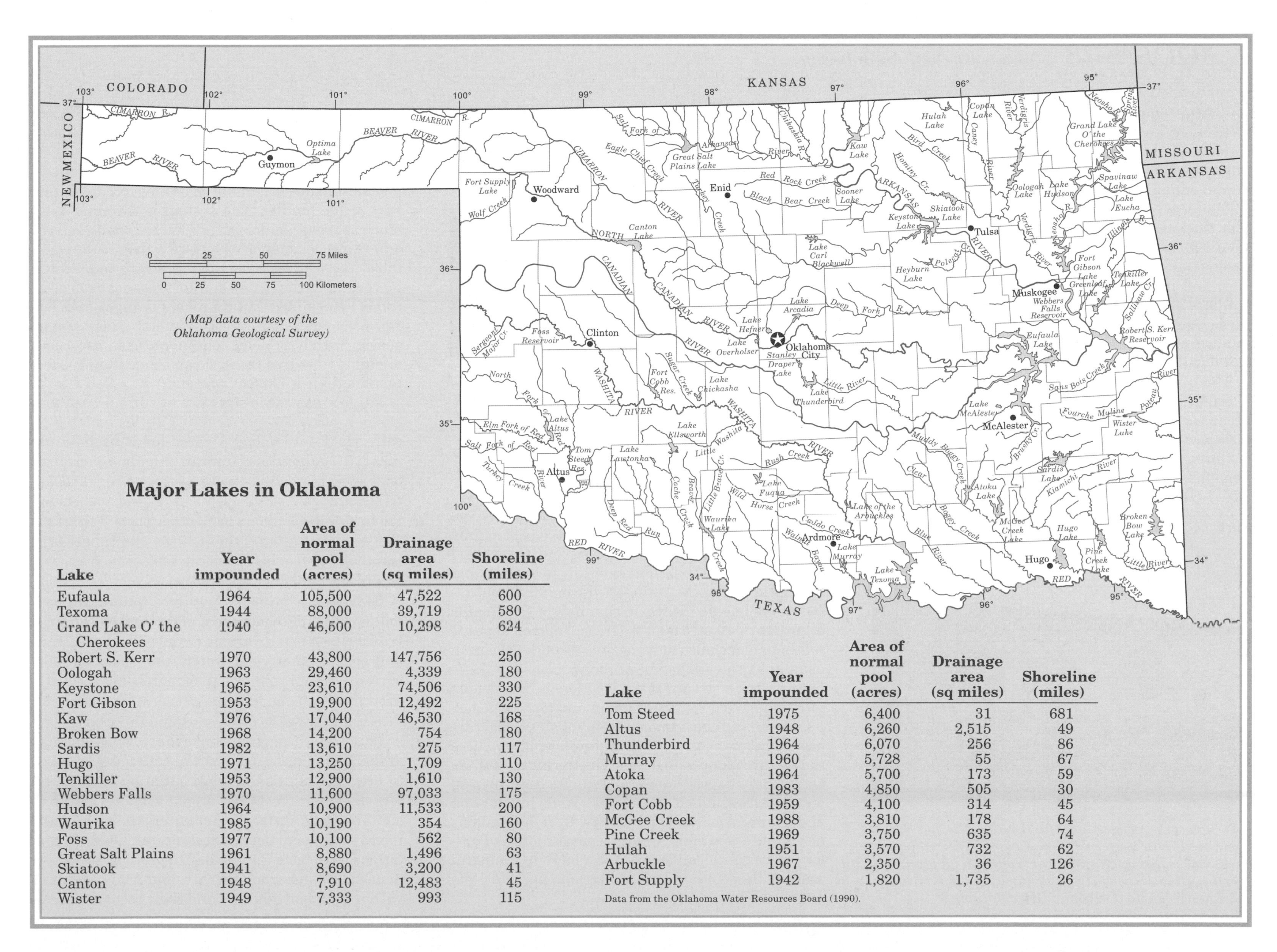

Major Lakes in Oklahoma

Lake	Year impounded	Area of normal pool (acres)	Drainage area (sq miles)	Shoreline (miles)
Eufaula	1964	105,500	47,522	600
Texoma	1944	88,000	39,719	580
Grand Lake O' the Cherokees	1940	46,500	10,298	624
Robert S. Kerr	1970	43,800	147,756	250
Oologah	1963	29,460	4,339	180
Keystone	1965	23,610	74,506	330
Fort Gibson	1953	19,900	12,492	225
Kaw	1976	17,040	46,530	168
Broken Bow	1968	14,200	754	180
Sardis	1982	13,610	275	117
Hugo	1971	13,250	1,709	110
Tenkiller	1953	12,900	1,610	130
Webbers Falls	1970	11,600	97,033	175
Hudson	1964	10,900	11,533	200
Waurika	1985	10,190	354	160
Foss	1977	10,100	562	80
Great Salt Plains	1961	8,880	1,496	63
Skiatook	1941	8,690	3,200	41
Canton	1948	7,910	12,483	45
Wister	1949	7,333	993	115

Lake	Year impounded	Area of normal pool (acres)	Drainage area (sq miles)	Shoreline (miles)
Tom Steed	1975	6,400	31	681
Altus	1948	6,260	2,515	49
Thunderbird	1964	6,070	256	86
Murray	1960	5,728	55	67
Atoka	1964	5,700	173	59
Copan	1983	4,850	505	30
Fort Cobb	1959	4,100	314	45
McGee Creek	1988	3,810	178	64
Pine Creek	1969	3,750	635	74
Hulah	1951	3,570	732	62
Arbuckle	1967	2,350	36	126
Fort Supply	1942	1,820	1,735	26

Data from the Oklahoma Water Resources Board (1990).

7. AQUIFERS

Essay by *Kenneth S. Johnson*

The term "aquifer" refers to those rocks and sediments that are saturated with good- to fair-quality water and are sufficiently permeable to yield significant volumes of water. Bedrock aquifers in Oklahoma consist of sandstone, sand, limestone, dolomite, gypsum, or fractured novaculite and chert. The thickness of these aquifers generally ranges from 100 feet to several thousand feet. The depth to freshwater ranges from a few feet to more than 1,000 feet, and most wells producing water from these aquifers are 100–400 feet deep. Wells drilled into these aquifers generally yield 25–300 gallons per minute, although some wells yield as much as 600–2,500 gallons per minute.

The quality of water in an aquifer commonly is affected by the nature and mineral content of the rock, because all groundwater contains various minerals dissolved from the rocks that the water moves over or through. Water in most bedrock aquifers of Oklahoma has a low-to-moderate mineral content, about 300–1,500 milligrams per liter dissolved solids.

A portion of the recharge area for the Rush Springs Sandstone aquifer in western Blaine County. The red-brown sandstone is porous and permeable and allows precipitation to percolate down to the water table and thus recharge the aquifer. (Photo courtesy of Ken Johnson)

Irrigation is critical to the success of agriculture in the more arid lands of western Oklahoma. Groundwater from the Rush Springs aquifer here is pumped from a depth of several hundred feet and is applied to crops through a center-pivot sprinkler irrigation system. (Photo courtesy of Ken Johnson)

Groundwater is also present in Quaternary-age alluvium and terrace deposits, which consist mainly of unconsolidated sand, silt, clay, and gravel laid down by streams that flow generally to the east and southeast across the state. The term "alluvium" refers to sediments in stream channels or floodplains of present-day streams, whereas "terrace deposit" refers to older alluvium that has been left behind, usually at elevations above the present-day floodplains after a stream shifts position or cuts deeply into underlying rocks. Alluvium and terrace deposits are the youngest (most recent) of all geologic deposits; therefore, they overlie bedrock aquifers where the two are mapped together. The thickness of these Quaternary deposits generally ranges from 10 to 50 feet (locally as much as 100 feet). Wells in alluvium and terrace deposits generally yield 10–500 gallons per minute of water (locally, several thousand gallons per minute), and most water has a low mineral content (less than 1,000 milligrams per liter dissolved solids).

Freshwater is stored in Oklahoma's aquifers as a result of the downward movement of precipitation and surface waters that enter each aquifer at its recharge area. Therefore, freshwater displaces saline water that originally may have occupied that part of the aquifer. The system is dynamic, inasmuch as these aquifers are recharged continually by downward percolation of surface waters to the water table. The vertical or horizontal rate of groundwater movement in the state's aquifers has not been accurately determined, but it probably ranges from 5 to 100 feet per year in most aquifers; under certain geologic and hydrologic conditions, as in cavernous or highly fractured rocks, it can range from 100 feet to more than 1,000 feet per year.

Large areas of the state are underlain mostly by shale or other low-permeability rocks, which typically yield only enough water for household use (about 15 gallons per minute). Highly mineralized (saline) water, unfit for most uses, is present beneath freshwater zones in these rocks, as well as beneath the freshwater aquifers in all other parts of the state. The depth to the top of this saline water ranges from less than 100 feet in some locales to as much as 3,000 feet in the Arbuckle Mountains.

Oklahoma's principal aquifers contain an estimated 320 million acre-feet of freshwater, perhaps half of which is recoverable for beneficial use. Wells and springs that yield water from these aquifers currently supply more than 60 percent of the water used in Oklahoma, chiefly in the west, where surface-water supplies are less abundant.

Because of the great importance of Oklahoma's groundwater resources, special care must be taken to prevent pollution or contamination of the aquifers and their "recharge areas" (areas where precipitation and surface water enters the ground and migrates down to the aquifer). State rules and regulations have been established to prohibit storage or disposal of hazardous-waste materials above or within principal aquifers and their recharge areas.

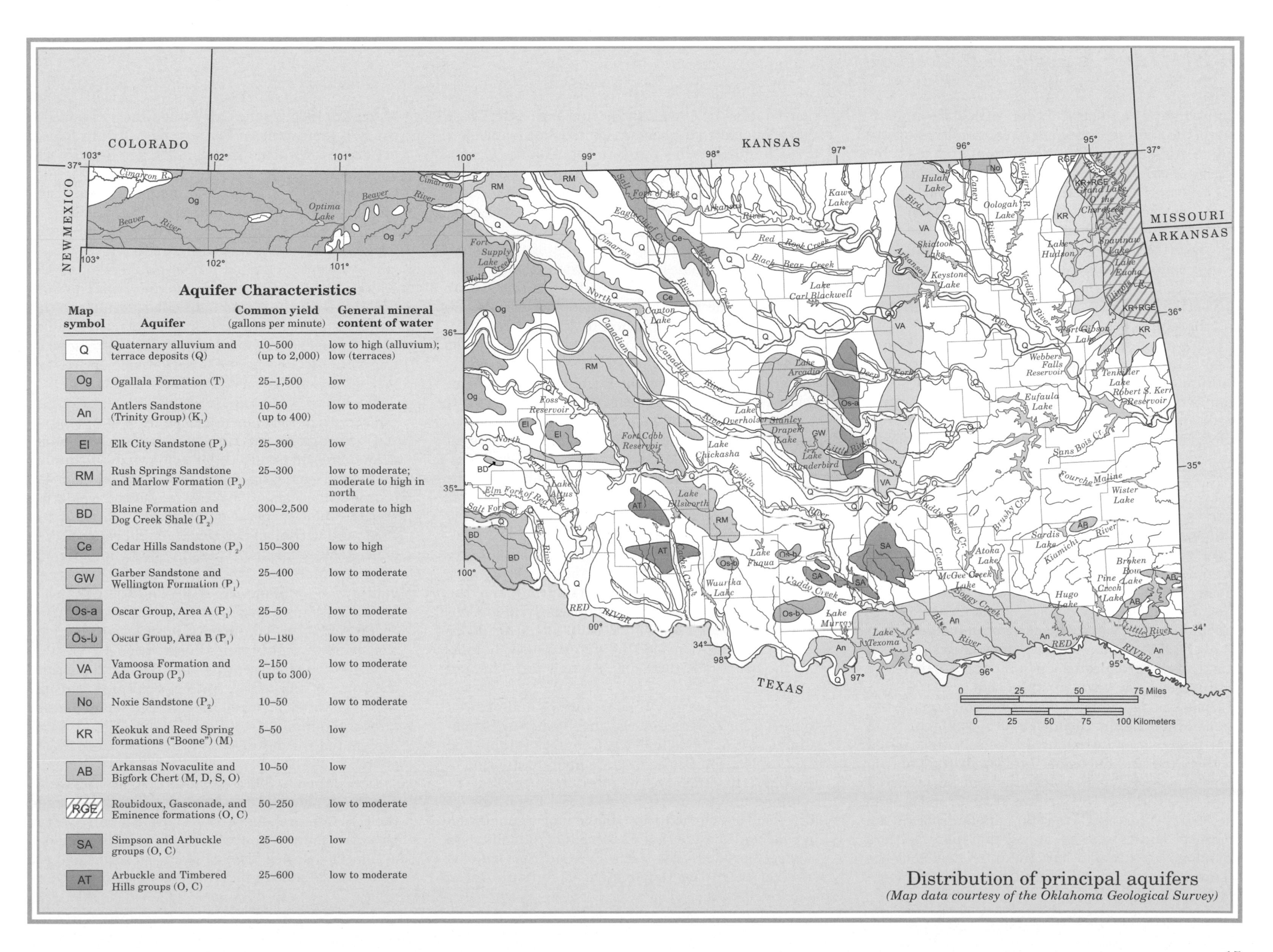

Aquifer Characteristics

Map symbol	Aquifer	Common yield (gallons per minute)	General mineral content of water
Q	Quaternary alluvium and terrace deposits (Q)	10–500 (up to 2,000)	low to high (alluvium); low (terraces)
Og	Ogallala Formation (T)	25–1,500	low
An	Antlers Sandstone (Trinity Group) (K_1)	10–50 (up to 400)	low to moderate
El	Elk City Sandstone (P_4)	25–300	low
RM	Rush Springs Sandstone and Marlow Formation (P_3)	25–300	low to moderate; moderate to high in north
BD	Blaine Formation and Dog Creek Shale (P_2)	300–2,500	moderate to high
Ce	Cedar Hills Sandstone (P_2)	150–300	low to high
GW	Garber Sandstone and Wellington Formation (P_1)	25–400	low to moderate
Os-a	Oscar Group, Area A (P_1)	25–50	low to moderate
Os-b	Oscar Group, Area B (P_1)	50–180	low to moderate
VA	Vamoosa Formation and Ada Group (P_3)	2–150 (up to 300)	low to moderate
No	Noxie Sandstone (P_2)	10–50	low to moderate
KR	Keokuk and Reed Spring formations ("Boone") (M)	5–50	low
AB	Arkansas Novaculite and Bigfork Chert (M, D, S, O)	10–50	low
RGE	Roubidoux, Gasconade, and Eminence formations (O, C)	50–250	low to moderate
SA	Simpson and Arbuckle groups (O, C)	25–600	low
AT	Arbuckle and Timbered Hills groups (O, C)	25–600	low to moderate

Distribution of principal aquifers

(Map data courtesy of the Oklahoma Geological Survey)

8. SOILS

Essay by *Bruce W. Hoagland*

Approximately a thousand years ago, early inhabitants of the state settled along rivers to cultivate corn, beans, and squash in fertile bottomland soils. Intensity of cultivation was low and soil loss limited. The arrival of the Five Tribes during the early nineteenth century led to somewhat increased land-use intensity. However, the situation changed dramatically with the land openings beginning in 1889. This change was catalyzed by the Homestead Act, signed by President Abraham Lincoln in 1862, which promised settlers 160 acres of land to improve, cultivate, and thereupon achieve self-sufficiency.

Homesteaders worked the soil hard and in ways often not conducive to its preservation. Before they could plant crops, the prairie sod had to be "broken," which was no simple task. Prairie sod was a dense mat of interwoven grass roots and soil—so dense, in fact, that settlers on the prairies cut blocks to use as building material for their early homes. Once exposed, the soil became susceptible to wind and water erosion, and the pride that farmers took in their ability to plow straight furrows (regardless of topography) further exacerbated erosion.

As tons of productive farm topsoils were washed down streams, farmers were faced with a difficult choice—allow the land to rest and rejuvenate, or plow. They chose to plow. Soil erosion was greatest on tenant farms, where the need for immediate profits overcame sound long-term agricultural production. Erosion produced deep gullies across the state within just a few years of statehood.

Dust storms, which began to become more frequent, were the manifestation of a combination of poor land use and drought. Loose soil was carried on the wind and deposited in deep drifts, burying crops and equipment. Major dust storms occurred from 1890 through 1896, again in 1909, and during the "Dirty Thirties." In 1893, sandstorms in the Cherokee Outlet were so intense that many settlers abandoned the region, but the dust storms of the 1930s were what finally captured national attention. On May 11, 1934, dust originating on the Great Plains blanketed the eastern United States and blew three hundred miles out into the Atlantic Ocean. New York residents were forced to turn on their lights because dust darkened the skies. Another dust storm—on April 14, 1935—likewise covered eastern cities in dust.

Prior to the extreme conditions of the 1930s, heightened awareness of soil erosion as a national crisis had been developing. The situation was starkly outlined in the pamphlet entitled "Soil Erosion, A National Menace," published in 1928 by Hugh H. Bennett and W. R. Chapline of the U.S. Department of Agriculture. The first major piece of soil and water conservation legislation, the Buchanan Amendment, was passed by Congress on February 16, 1929. It appropriated $160,000 for the establishment of ten regional soil experiment stations to measure rates of soil loss and to develop soil conservation techniques.

One of the stations, the Red Plains Experiment Station, was established in Guthrie in 1929. The first director was N. E. Winters, who helped work the family farm in Kingfisher County during his childhood and had been deeply affected by dramatic erosion of the land. Winters, an ardent conservationist, oversaw demonstration projects throughout the state and directed the several dozen Civilian Conservation Corps camps that were engaged in soil conservation. He traveled the state extensively, touting the benefits of terracing, contour farming, and strip farming.

The work of the experiment stations underscored the need for greater federal involvement in stemming soil loss. Thus, in 1933 Congress established the Soil Erosion Service as a temporary division of the U.S. Department of the Interior, responsible for mapping and documenting soil loss. From this effort, a soil erosion map for Oklahoma was published in 1938 and showed that 52 percent of the soils were severely eroded. The Soils Erosion Service was transferred to the Department of Agriculture on March 25, 1935. Public Law 74-36, which established the Soil Conservation Service, passed both houses of Congress without dissent, and Hugh Bennett was appointed director.

Classifying soil types and mapping their distribution began in Oklahoma prior to statehood. In 1905, the first Oklahoma soil surveys were prepared for Oklahoma County, and from 1914 to 1918, soil surveys were published for Bryan, Muskogee, Canadian, Roger Mills, and Payne counties. The work of soil classification and mapping continues to this day, and many of the state's residents are familiar with the soil survey maps and booklets provided by the National Resource Conservation Service, formerly the Soil Conservation Service.

On June 6, 1935, the National Committee on Soil Conservation recommended the formation of state soil conservation districts to provide conservation demonstration programs for landowners. To qualify for federal funds, states were required to adopt soil conservation legislation. The Oklahoma Legislature adopted the Conservation District Enabling Act in 1937, and within a year, twenty-eight conservation districts were formed. The first Oklahoma districts were the McIntosh Soil Conservation District, organized on January 28, 1938, and the Arkansas-Verdigris District, organized on February 23, 1938. At present, the Oklahoma Conservation Commission oversees eighty-nine conservation districts.

In 1987, almost a century after the first "land run," the value of soil to the state agricultural economy was acknowledged when the Port Silt Loam (named after the community of Port, Washita County) was designated the state soil, much like a state flower or tree.

In Oklahoma, there are seven soil orders, which are the broadest level of the soil classifications in the U.S. Comprehensive Soil Classification System. However, county soils surveys are typically mapped at a more detailed level called a soil series and are usually available in individual county soil surveys.

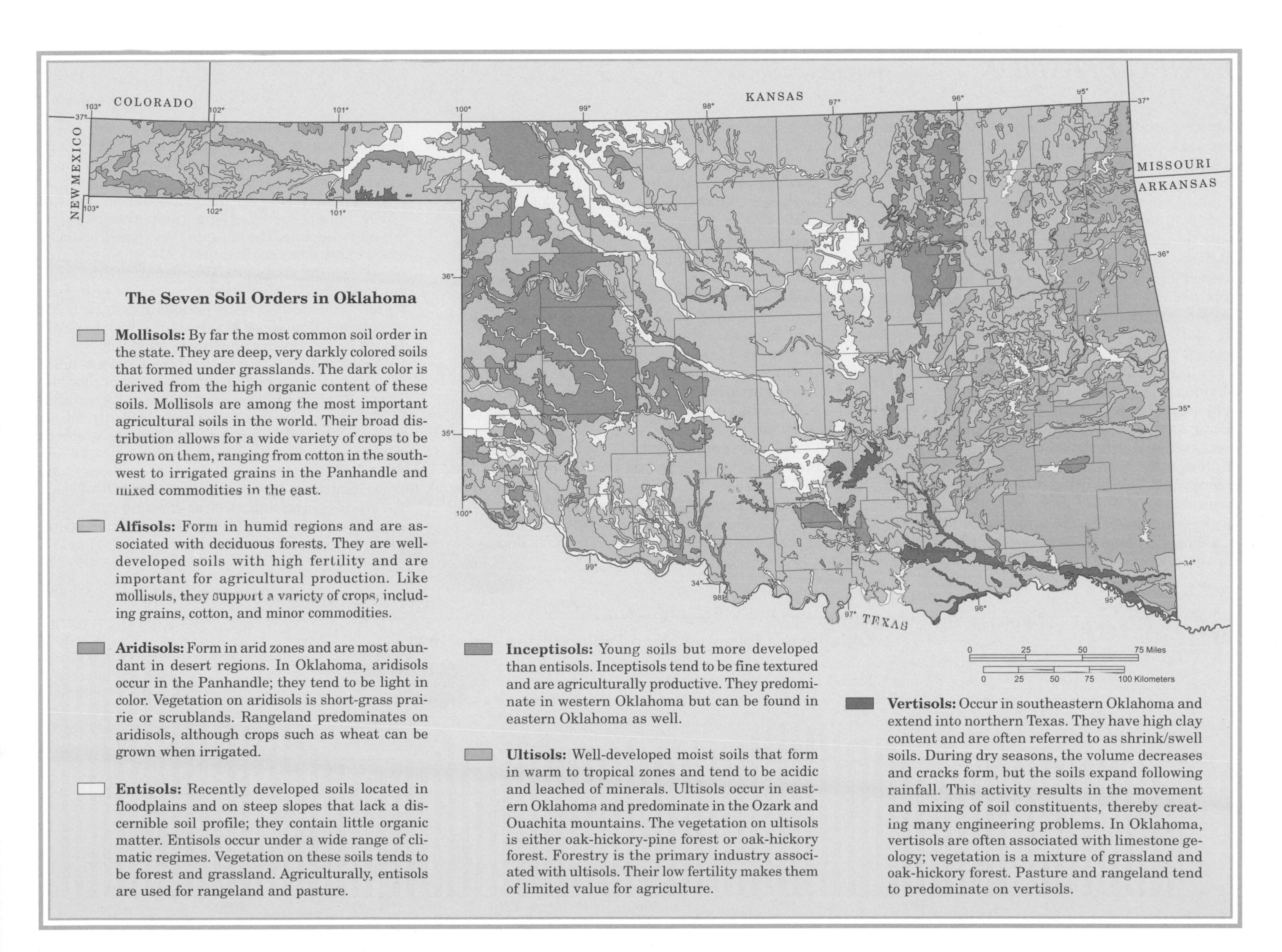

The Seven Soil Orders in Oklahoma

Mollisols: By far the most common soil order in the state. They are deep, very darkly colored soils that formed under grasslands. The dark color is derived from the high organic content of these soils. Mollisols are among the most important agricultural soils in the world. Their broad distribution allows for a wide variety of crops to be grown on them, ranging from cotton in the southwest to irrigated grains in the Panhandle and mixed commodities in the east.

Alfisols: Form in humid regions and are associated with deciduous forests. They are well-developed soils with high fertility and are important for agricultural production. Like mollisols, they support a variety of crops, including grains, cotton, and minor commodities.

Aridisols: Form in arid zones and are most abundant in desert regions. In Oklahoma, aridisols occur in the Panhandle; they tend to be light in color. Vegetation on aridisols is short-grass prairie or scrublands. Rangeland predominates on aridisols, although crops such as wheat can be grown when irrigated.

Entisols: Recently developed soils located in floodplains and on steep slopes that lack a discernible soil profile; they contain little organic matter. Entisols occur under a wide range of climatic regimes. Vegetation on these soils tends to be forest and grassland. Agriculturally, entisols are used for rangeland and pasture.

Inceptisols: Young soils but more developed than entisols. Inceptisols tend to be fine textured and are agriculturally productive. They predominate in western Oklahoma but can be found in eastern Oklahoma as well.

Ultisols: Well-developed moist soils that form in warm to tropical zones and tend to be acidic and leached of minerals. Ultisols occur in eastern Oklahoma and predominate in the Ozark and Ouachita mountains. The vegetation on ultisols is either oak-hickory-pine forest or oak-hickory forest. Forestry is the primary industry associated with ultisols. Their low fertility makes them of limited value for agriculture.

Vertisols: Occur in southeastern Oklahoma and extend into northern Texas. They have high clay content and are often referred to as shrink/swell soils. During dry seasons, the volume decreases and cracks form, but the soils expand following rainfall. This activity results in the movement and mixing of soil constituents, thereby creating many engineering problems. In Oklahoma, vertisols are often associated with limestone geology; vegetation is a mixture of grassland and oak-hickory forest. Pasture and rangeland tend to predominate on vertisols.

9. PRECIPITATION

Essay by *Howard L. Johnson*

Average annual precipitation across Oklahoma varies from more than 55 inches in the extreme southeast to around 16 inches in the western Panhandle. The decrease in precipitation to the west is fairly regular, producing a statewide average of approximately 36 inches a year. That number also represents the average annual precipitation along a line that bisects the state, extending from the Kansas line north of near Blackwell to the Red River just west of Marietta. The Ouachita Mountains in northern McCurtain County, by forcing moisture-laden air aloft, increase precipitation frequency and amount in that area. The Ozark Plateau provides a similar (though lesser) effect in northeastern Oklahoma.

Moisture borne from the Gulf of Mexico by the prevailing south-to-southeasterly winds provides fuel for precipitation within the state. The actual occurrence of precipitation, however, requires the presence of appropriate transient—and usually interrelated—atmospheric features, such as developing areas of low air pressure, disturbances in the upper atmosphere, or areas of uneven surface heating, which, in turn, force moist surface air to rise and cool, forming clouds and thus starting the precipitation process.

Conditions suitable for significant precipitation development are usually, but not exclusively, found in close proximity to the various bands of strong winds four to six miles above the Earth's surface in the prevailing westerlies, known collectively as the jet stream. Seasonal migrations of the strongest and most persistent band—which hovers mainly around the U.S./Canadian border in summer and across the southern United States during midwinter—act to provide most of Oklahoma with two relatively wet seasons (spring and autumn), separated by the drier summer and winter seasons. Winter is the driest of seasons in all but the extreme southeast, where normal summer-month precipitation falls below that of winter.

The state's arid Panhandle, with its proximity to the Rocky Mountains and the dry plateau of the southwestern United States (the source of that region's prevailing warm-season winds), enjoys its only "wet season" during the warm-weather months of June, July, and August. Normal rainfall during the relatively wet Panhandle summer, however, is still less than that of the southeast's relatively dry summer. Normal springtime precipitation, mainly provided by massive thunderstorm systems that frequently develop over the plains during that turbulent season, exceeds the autumn average everywhere in the state. The autumn rains, which are more given to extreme events, appear less reliably than do those of spring, frequently associated with the moisture and circulation of former hurricanes or tropical storms. The autumn rainy periods appear with less consistency than those of springtime, with some autumns being very dry and others quite wet.

Winter precipitation in the form of snow is much more common in the higher elevations of the Panhandle than elsewhere. Seasonal average snowfall is as high as 30 inches in Cimarron County, falling to around 15 inches farther east along the northern border of the Panhandle. Snowfall averages less than 5 inches per year in most of southern Oklahoma, and many years are essentially without snow. Ice storms (involving sleet or freezing rain) are a much-too-frequent and unwelcome form of winter precipitation over much of the state.

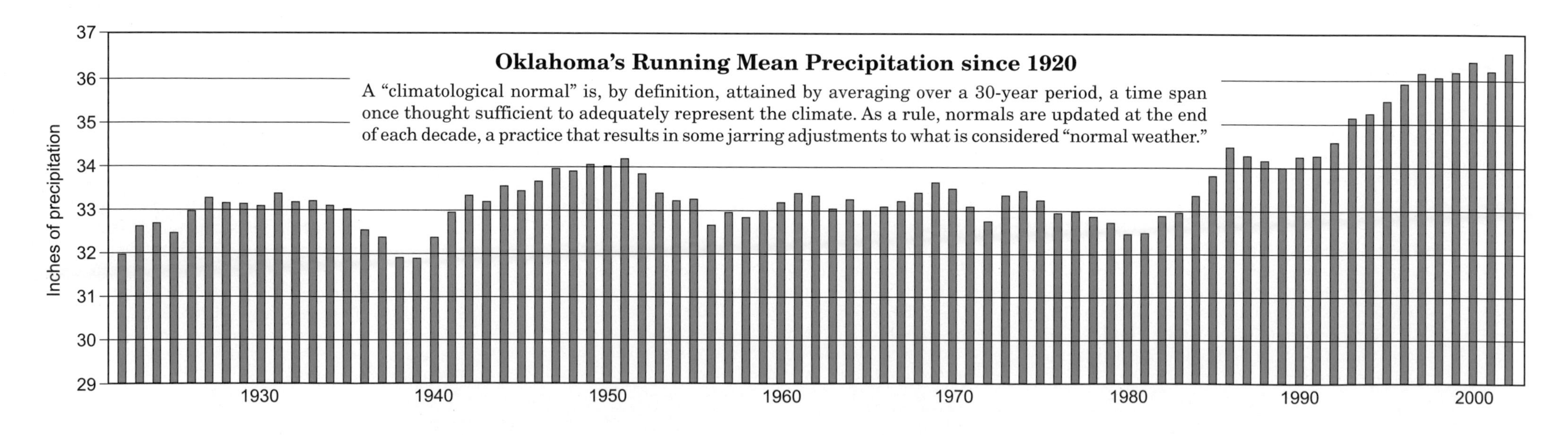

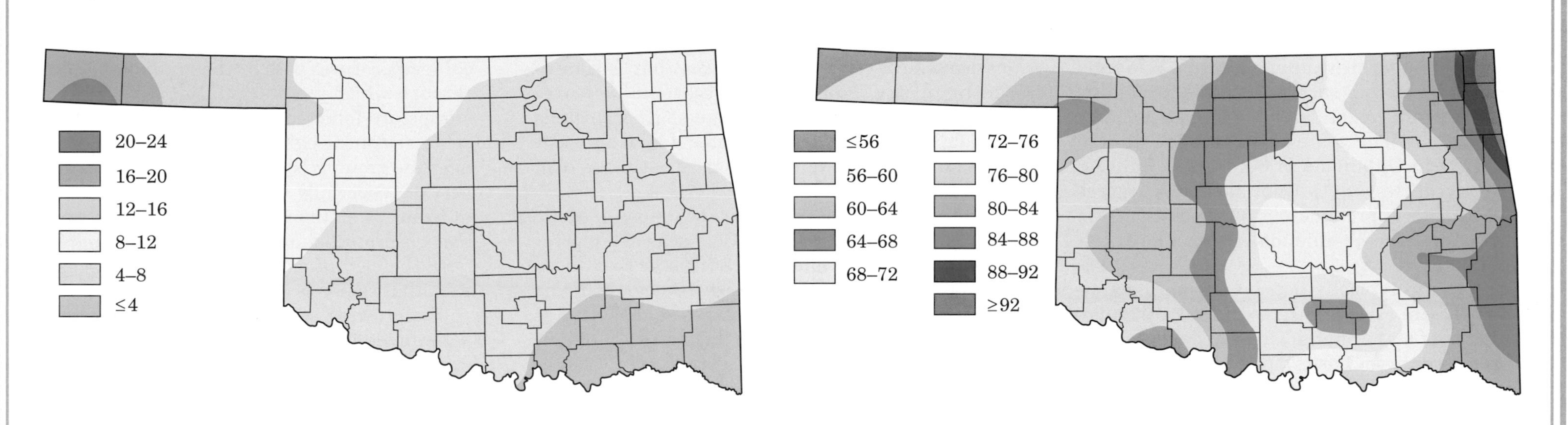

Mean annual snowfall in inches

Mean annual number of days with measurable precipitation

Oklahoma Mesonet

During the early 1990s, agricultural researchers at Oklahoma State University joined with meteorologists from the University of Oklahoma to establish an environmental observing network that would serve the purposes of both groups. The Oklahoma Mesonetwork, commonly known as the "Mesonet," was thus born. The Mesonet consists of more than 110 observing platforms dispersed across the state. Each is instrumented automatically to measure moisture, temperature, humidity, wind, air pressure, rainfall, sunshine, and soil temperature and to transmit those measurements to a central data-collection computer in Norman. Data are collected from each station every 15 minutes through a combination of radio transmissions and a dedicated telephone-line network operated by the Oklahoma Department of Public Safety. The data are processed immediately, checked for quality, and made available to cooperating agencies within 15 minutes. The resulting network, which has been operational since early 1993, is the largest network of its kind and has gained an international reputation for providing high-quality data.

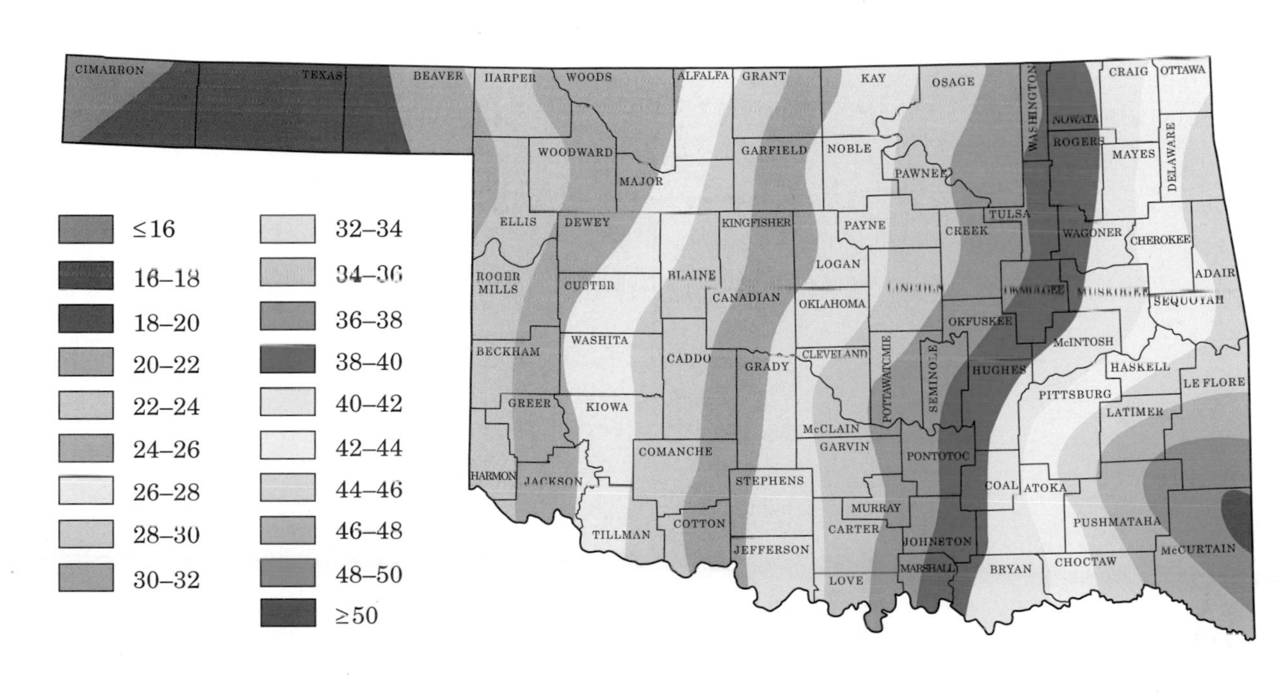

Mean annual precipitation in inches
(includes moisture from snow)

10. TEMPERATURE AND GROWING SEASON

Essay by *Howard L. Johnson*

The average temperature at any location is largely determined by factors such as latitude, humidity, elevation, terrain, vegetative cover, and frequency of precipitation. The statewide-averaged annual temperature in Oklahoma is 60 degrees Fahrenheit. Temperature ranges from about 63 degrees in the south to approximately 55 degrees at the western end of the Panhandle, where elevations exceed 4,000 feet.

Summers are typically hot, by anyone's definition, everywhere except in the western Panhandle. The benefits of higher humidity keep daytime temperatures lower in the eastern part of the state than in the west, but the same factors lead to less cooling at night, so that average summer temperatures vary little from east to west across the state. Southwestern Oklahoma, with few trees and sparse vegetation, is most often victimized by temperature excursions into triple digits. Typically, the weeks immediately following the wheat harvest in western, central, and north-central Oklahoma witness a substantial increase in daytime temperatures that is significantly greater than the usual seasonal increases elsewhere in the state. Persistent southerly winds provide some relief from summer's heat in western and central Oklahoma that is not present in the less windy east.

Winter is marked by regular incursions of Arctic air from the northern plains. Cold-season temperatures, however, are much more variable than those of summer. Temperatures below 10 degrees Fahrenheit are rare, and temperatures seldom stay at those levels for more than a day or two. Cold-air intrusions are typically led by a broad area of southerly winds bringing relatively warm air from the Gulf of Mexico, followed soon thereafter by the cold air. The transition zones (commonly known as "cold fronts") between the two types of air are narrow, and temperature changes can be abrupt. Rain, freezing rain, sleet, or snow frequently accompany such storms, with different types of precipitation falling in various parts of the system, depending on the local temperatures both at the ground and in the air through which the precipitation falls. Most winter storms are followed by a few days of chilly quiescence, featuring light winds and clear skies. The air near the ground cools quickly at night during these periods (especially if there is snow cover), leading to even lower temperatures. Southeastern Oklahoma is protected somewhat by terrain and latitude from the cold of most extreme winter events, but even that region is not immune to winter chill.

The growing season for spring-planted crops is determined by the last arrival of freezing weather in spring and its first arrival in autumn. There is typically about a month's difference between the beginning of the growing season across the state (defined as no temperatures as low as 28 degrees Fahrenheit) and its end. The frost-free period in the western Panhandle typically extends from mid-April through the middle of October. The similar period along the Red River in the southeast extends from late March through early November.

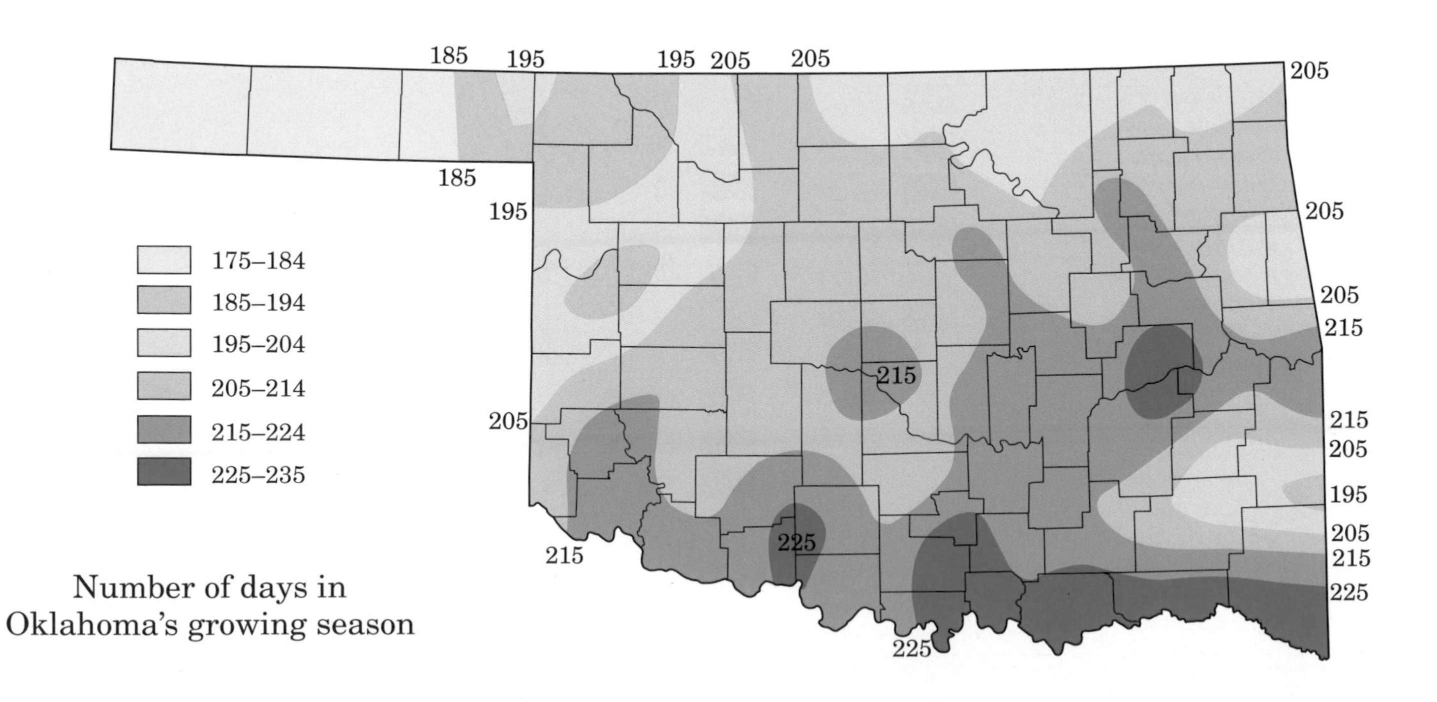

Number of days in Oklahoma's growing season

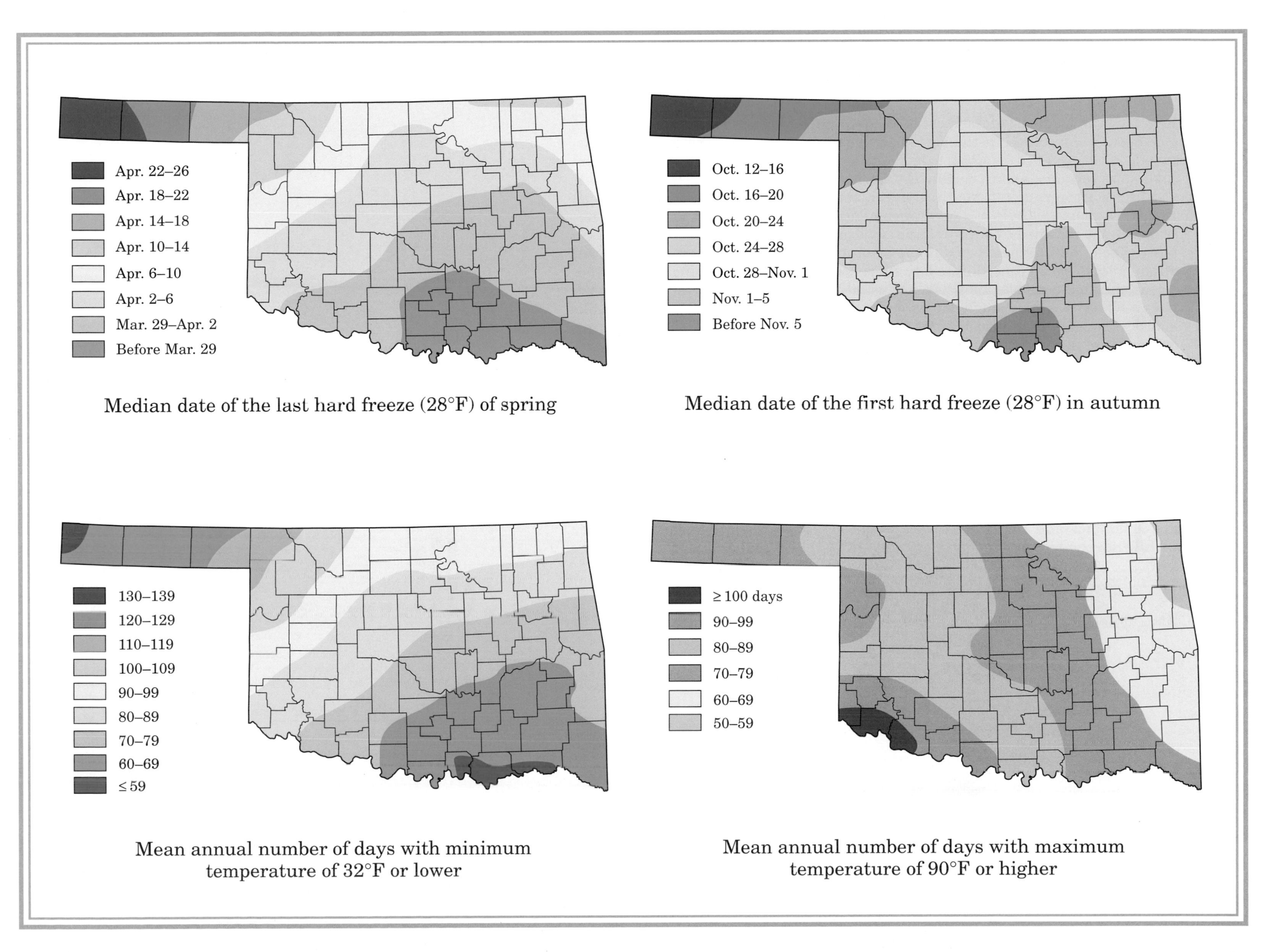

Median date of the last hard freeze (28°F) of spring

Median date of the first hard freeze (28°F) in autumn

Mean annual number of days with minimum temperature of 32°F or lower

Mean annual number of days with maximum temperature of 90°F or higher

11. TORNADOES AND OTHER EXTREME WEATHER EVENTS

Essay by *Howard L. Johnson*

Oklahoma lies at the heart of the most tornado-prone region in the world. On average, 60 tornadoes are observed in the state each year. Annual totals are quite variable, ranging from as few as 17 (in 1988) to as many as 145 (in 1999). Nearly three-quarters of Oklahoma's tornadoes occur during the April–June "storm season," with the single month of May accounting for one-third of the annual total. Most tornadoes are weak and do little damage. Others strike in unpopulated areas and are not much noticed.

Tornadoes are spawned by severe thunderstorms that can develop during any season or at any time of day, although conditions favorable for their development are present most frequently in springtime, during late afternoon through early evening. Severe thunderstorms and the tornadoes they produce usually move from southwest to northeast. Tornadoes sometimes form singly but at other times will be part of a larger ensemble. Tornado development is often associated with isolated, large "supercell" thunderstorms, but complexes of thunderstorms can also produce significant tornadoes.

Woodward was struck by a large tornado (or tornadoes) on April 9, 1947, leaving 107 people dead. Woodward was the most populated location on a path of death and destruction—probably resulting from multiple tornadoes—from White Deer, Texas, to St. Leo, Kansas. An extremely violent tornado, part of one of the largest concentrations of tornadoes ever recorded (75 tornadoes in twenty-one hours across much of central Oklahoma), ripped across the southern end of the Oklahoma City metropolitan area on May 3, 1999. Despite the population density of the affected area, timely warnings combined with effective citizen response held fatalities to an amazingly low, though still tragic, 40. Tornado forecasting, detection, and warning systems—many of them developed in Oklahoma (and all of them developed after 1947)—provided a margin of safety that, while not completely preventing tragedy, was able to reduce it significantly.

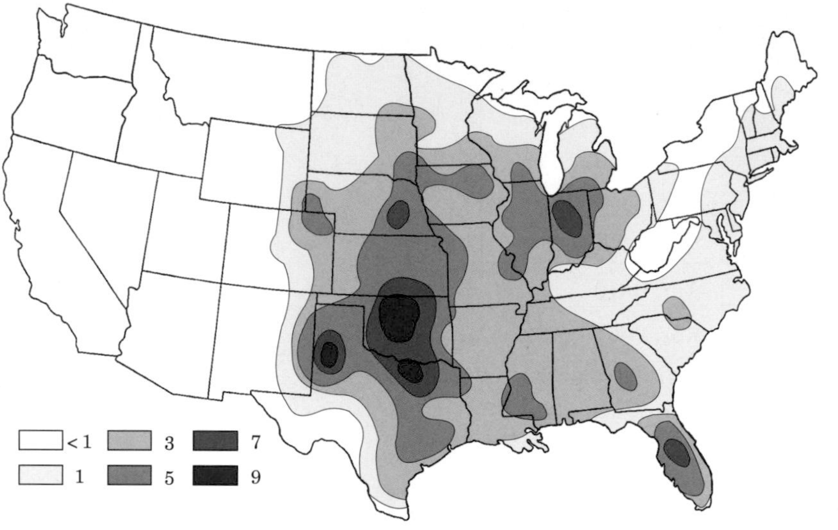

Average number of tornadoes per year per 10,000 square miles

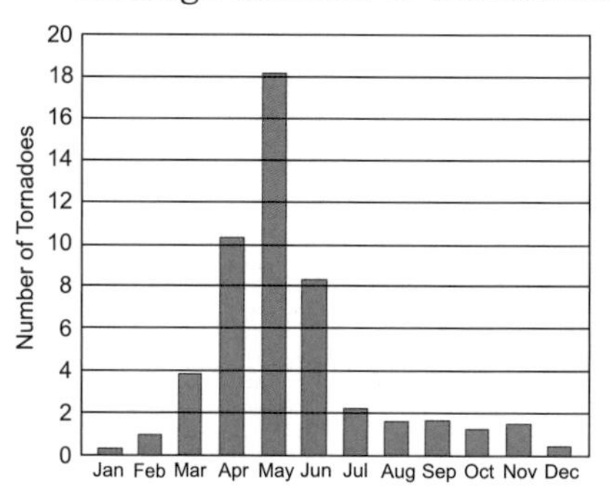

Average number of tornadoes reported in Oklahoma by month, 1950–1991. (Modified from Johnson and Duchon, *Atlas*)

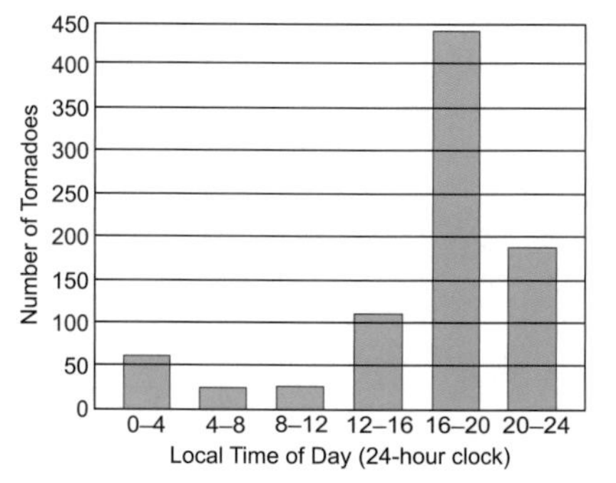

Number of F2 or greater tornadoes reported in Oklahoma by time of day, 1950–1991. (Modified from Johnson and Duchon, *Atlas*)

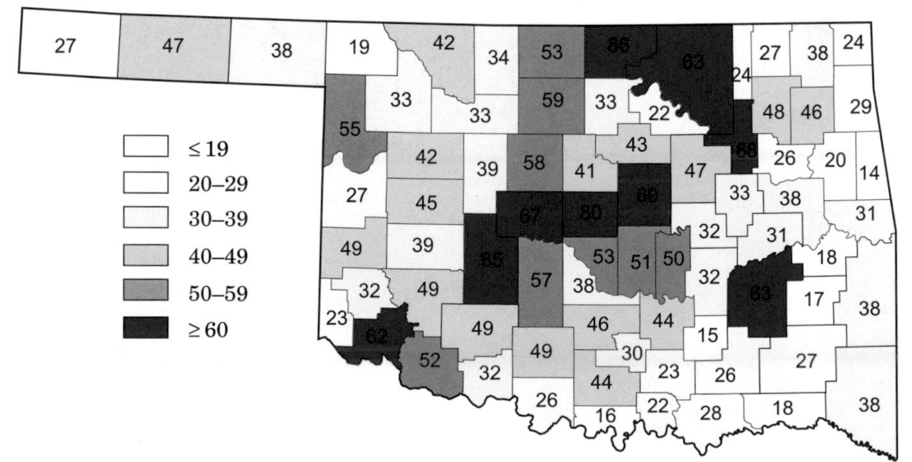

(Map data courtesy of the Oklahoma Geological Survey)

Number of tornadoes reported in each county, 1950–2000

Data provided by Doug Speheger, National Weather Service, Norman, Oklahoma.

Fujita F Scale of Tornado Intensity

Classification	Approximate severity	Estimated wind speed (mph)
F0	weak tornado	40–72
F1	moderate tornado	73–112
F2	significant tornado	113–157
F3	severe tornado	158–206
F4	devastating tornado	207–260
F5	incredible tornado	261–318

The F scale, named for its designer (Tetsuya Fujita), classifies a tornado according to wind speed, in miles per hour (mph), as determined from an analysis of the destruction path. For example, F0 and F1 tornadoes do not cause major damage, while F4 and F5 tornadoes commonly leave wide paths of total destruction.

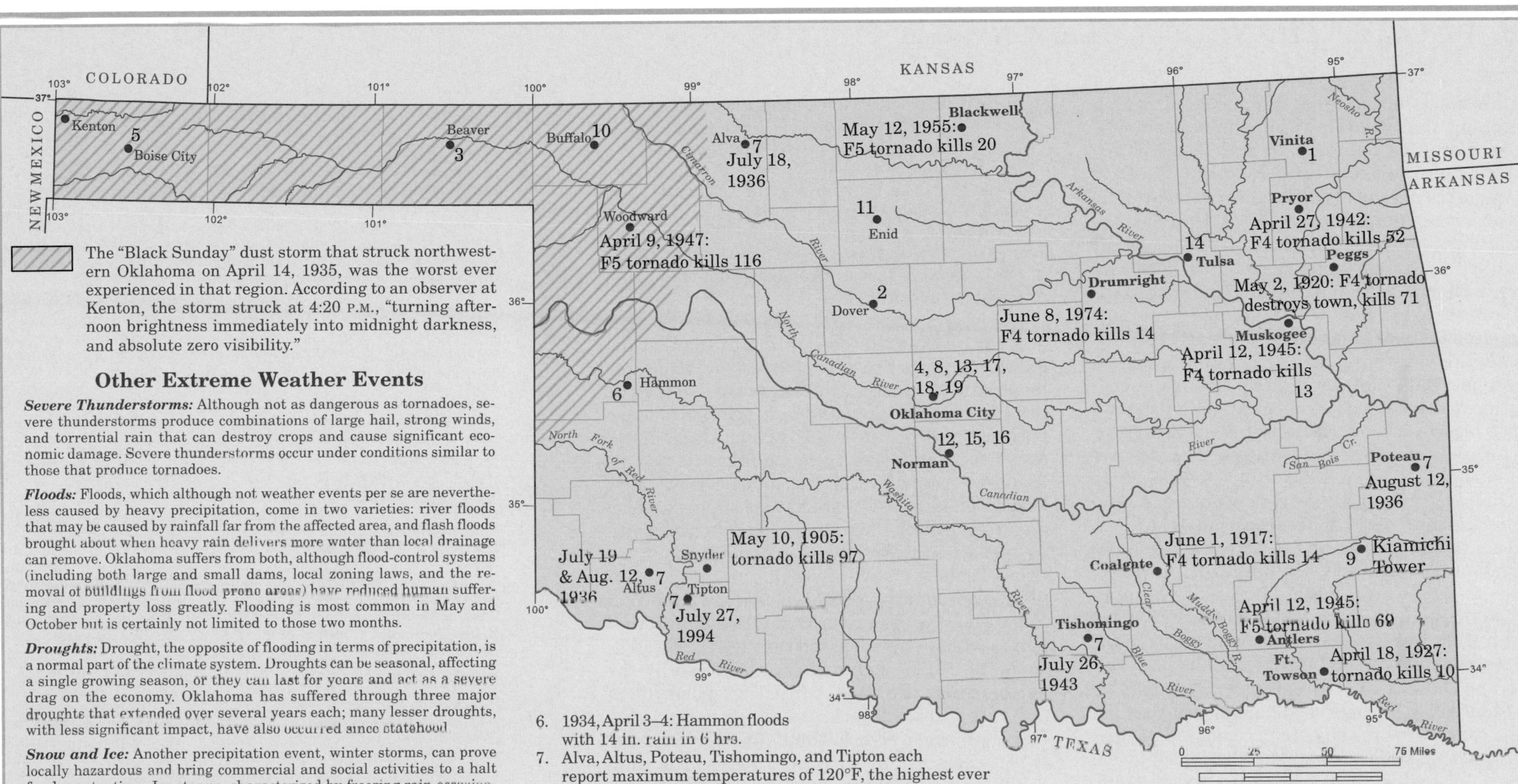

The "Black Sunday" dust storm that struck northwestern Oklahoma on April 14, 1935, was the worst ever experienced in that region. According to an observer at Kenton, the storm struck at 4:20 P.M., "turning afternoon brightness immediately into midnight darkness, and absolute zero visibility."

Other Extreme Weather Events

Severe Thunderstorms: Although not as dangerous as tornadoes, severe thunderstorms produce combinations of large hail, strong winds, and torrential rain that can destroy crops and cause significant economic damage. Severe thunderstorms occur under conditions similar to those that produce tornadoes.

Floods: Floods, which although not weather events per se are nevertheless caused by heavy precipitation, come in two varieties: river floods that may be caused by rainfall far from the affected area, and flash floods brought about when heavy rain delivers more water than local drainage can remove. Oklahoma suffers from both, although flood-control systems (including both large and small dams, local zoning laws, and the removal of buildings from flood prone areas) have reduced human suffering and property loss greatly. Flooding is most common in May and October but is certainly not limited to those two months.

Droughts: Drought, the opposite of flooding in terms of precipitation, is a normal part of the climate system. Droughts can be seasonal, affecting a single growing season, or they can last for years and act as a severe drag on the economy. Oklahoma has suffered through three major droughts that extended over several years each; many lesser droughts, with less significant impact, have also occurred since statehood.

Snow and Ice: Another precipitation event, winter storms, can prove locally hazardous and bring commercial and social activities to a halt for days at a time. Ice storms, characterized by freezing rain occasionally mixed with sleet, are especially troublesome because of damage done by ice buildup to transportation systems, trees, and utility lines. Because most of Oklahoma's winter temperatures are not far from freezing and atmospheric moisture is usually near at hand, the state is especially susceptible to such storms.

Selected Weather-Related Events

1. 1905, February 13: Vinita has all-time state record lowest temperature of –27°F.
2. 1906, September 16: Sudden flooding along the Cimarron River south of Dover washes out the railroad bridge, causing a devastating train wreck.
3. 1911–1912: Heavy winter snowfall gives Beaver a state record for seasonal snowfall of 87.3 in.
4. 1923, October 13–16: Flooding causes a break in Lake Overholser Dam, forcing the evacuation of 15,000 residents in Oklahoma City.
5. 1926, March 30: Boise City has 16 in. of snow.
6. 1934, April 3–4: Hammon floods with 14 in. rain in 6 hrs.
7. Alva, Altus, Poteau, Tishomingo, and Tipton each report maximum temperatures of 120°F, the highest ever recorded in Oklahoma.
8. 1948, March 25: U.S. Air Force forecasters Capt. Robert C. Miller and Maj. Ernest J. Fawbush issue the first scientifically based tornado forecast from Tinker Air Force Base. In 1952 meteorologist Harry Volkman broadcasts the first tornado warning by television on WKY-TV in Oklahoma City.
9. 1957: Annual precipitation at Kiamichi Tower, 84.47 in., is greatest ever observed at any reporting state station.
10. 1971, February 21–22: Blizzard in northwest Oklahoma. Buffalo receives 36 in. of snow—a state record for storm-total snowfall.
11. 1973, October 11: Greatest state daily precipitation at Enid with 15.68 in.
12. 1980: Oklahoma Climatological Survey established at the University of Oklahoma, Norman.
13. 1980: Summer heat wave: Oklahoma City records daily maximum temperature exceeding 100°F 50 times during the season.
14. 1984, May 26–27: Tulsa Memorial Day flood with more than 12 in. of rain overnight. Flooding left 14 dead and destroyed or damaged 5,500 homes and over 7,000 vehicles.
15. 1991, April 26: Severe thunderstorm outbreak; the first time the National Weather Service made operational use of the WSR-88D (Doppler) radar, commonly known as NEXRAD (established in Norman in 1988).
16. 1994, March 1: Oklahoma Mesonet commissioned, the first statewide network of its kind.
17. 1930, November 19: F4 tornado at Bethany kills 23.
18. 1942, June 12: F4 tornado in Oklahoma City kills 35.
19. 1999, May 3: F5 tornado outbreak in central Oklahoma; 75 tornadoes in 21 hours kill 40, injure over 700, and cause damage totaling $1 billion.

12. VEGETATION
Essay by *Bruce W. Hoagland*

Oklahoma is often characterized as a prairie state, but the situation is much more complex. More than fifty years ago, a map based on extensive fieldwork conducted following the Dust Bowl portrayed the distribution of vegetation in the absence of human intervention. However, the natural vegetation of Oklahoma has been heavily modified by human agency over the past century. Ecologists, land managers, and historians are interested in how the Oklahoma landscape appeared to American Indians and early settlers. Fortunately, several early visitors to the region wrote journals containing accounts of the vegetation and wildlife they encountered. Although these records often lack the detail necessary for restoration of native ecosystems, they do provide insight.

One vegetation type written about by several visitors is the Cross Timbers (post oak–blackjack forest), the most common forest type in the state. Josiah Gregg, an early entrepreneur in the region, wrote, "The celebrated cross timbers, of which frequent mention has been made, vary in width from five to thirty miles, and entirely cut off the communication betwixt the interior prairies and those of the Great Plains. They may be considered as a 'fringe' of the great prairies, being a continuous brushy strip, composed of various kinds of undergrowth; such as black-jacks, post-oaks, and in some places hickory, elm, etc. intermixed with a very diminutive dwarf oak."

Washington Irving, during his travels with the Ellsworth expedition, entered the Cross Timbers in October 1832. He was not impressed:

> The whole tract may present a pleasant aspect in the fresh time of the year, when the ground is covered with herbage; when the trees are in their green leaf, and the glens are enlivened by running streams. Unfortunately, we entered it too late in the season. The herbage was parched; the foliage of the scrubby forests was withered; the whole woodland prospect, as far as the eye could reach, had a brown and arid hue. The fires made on the prairies by the Indian hunters, had frequently penetrated these forests, sweeping in light transient flames along the dry grass, scorching and calcining the lower twigs and branches of the trees, and leaving them black and hard, so as to tear the flesh of man and horse that had to scramble through them. I shall not easily forget the mortal toil, and the vexations of flesh and spirit, that we underwent occasionally, in our wanderings through the Cross Timber. It was like struggling through forests of cast iron.

Henry Ellsworth left a different impression, stating that the Cross Timbers region "contains much mast for hogs and wild game—even the little bushes not 10 inches high, are loaded down with acorns—and although travelers have & will decry this land, yet, I am confident it will be found tolerable pasturage, for sheep & cattle besides yielding an inexhaustible supply of wood and timber when the prairies shall not be burnt."

Captain R. B. Marcy, who passed through the Cross Timbers on two occasions, presented a different aspect of the forest type during his search of the source of the Red River: "At six different points where I have passed through it (the cross timbers), I have found it characterized by the peculiarities; the trees, consisting primarily of post-oak and black-jack, standing at such intervals that wagons can without difficulty pass between them in any direction. The soil is thin, sandy, and poorly watered."

Regardless of human influence, the distribution of vegetation is the result of complex interactions with the physical environment. The east-to-west distribution of forest and grassland vegetation mirrors annual precipitation. Also, the local occurrence of plants is often the product of geology and soils. Limestone produces tight clay soil, which tends to be alkaline. In the Arbuckle Mountains, where limestone is abundant, plants tolerant of these conditions (such as black dalea, short lobe oak, and Ashe juniper) flourish. Fire is another factor that influences the distribution of vegetation. In the absence of fire, woody plants such as red cedar quickly colonize prairie habitats, converting them to woodlands and forests.

VEGETATION TYPES

GRASSLANDS

1 **Shortgrass High Plains:** This vegetation type reaches its greatest extent in the Panhandle and far northwestern Oklahoma. In some areas, much of the shortgrass prairie has been converted to wheat and milo production, but large areas of native vegetation persist on shallow soil underlain by sandstone or caliche. Blue grama and buffalo grass are the predominant species in the shortgrass prairie. Other common species include plains blackfoot, plains zinnia, ring muhly grass, sand dropseed, tansy aster, vine mesquite grass, and yellow-spine prairie thistle.

2 **Mixedgrass Eroded Plains:** This vegetation type occupies much of western Oklahoma, and much of it has been converted to wheat or cotton production. The best examples of mixedgrass prairie can be found on shallow soils overlying red sandstone and shale or granite in the Wichita Mountains. Predominant species of this vegetation type include dropseeds, little bluestem, and sideoats grama. Other common grasses include hairy grama and Indiangrass. Associated species include biscuitroot, crowpoison, Engelmann's daisy, hedgehog cactus, old plainsman, prairie clover, skunkbrush, spider milkweed, plains pricklypear, and threadleaf daisy.

3 **Tallgrass Prairie:** This type has declined in acreage, but large expanses still occur in Osage and adjacent counties. Smaller remnants occur throughout eastern Oklahoma as native hay meadows. It intergrades with the post oak–hickory forests in central Oklahoma and the mixedgrass prairie to the west. Forest and woodland vegetation will readily replace tallgrass prairie following land abandonment and fire suppression. The predominant grasses are little bluestem, big bluestem, Indiangrass, and switchgrass. Associated species include lead plant, Indian plantain, prairie clover, heath aster, small panic grass, pallid coneflower, ashy sunflower, and Missouri goldenrod.

WOODLANDS

4 **Piñon Pine–Juniper Mesa:** This vegetation type is found in the northwest corner of the Panhandle. The vegetation and plant species in this region are typical of the Rocky Mountain Front Range in Colorado and New Mexico. Although oneseed juniper and piñon pine are predominant, oneseed juniper often occurs without piñon pine. Common grass species include buffalograss, gramas (blue, black, hairy, and sideoats), and silver bluestem. Associated woody plants include cholla, Gambel oak, mesquite, mountain mahogany, skunkbrush, and soapweed. A stand of ponderosa pine occurs in this region as well.

5 **Sandsage Grasslands:** This vegetation type is common on deep sand deposits and dunes in western Oklahoma. Sandsage is a low-growing shrub with narrow, gray-green leaves; it is often cleared to increase the productivity of pasture grasses for cattle grazing. Predominant grasses include giant sand reed, little bluestem, sand bluestem, and sand dropseed. Mapleleaf grape, netleaf hackberry, sand plum, silky prairie clover, skunkbrush, soapweed, and spectacle pod are also common. Most of the species occurring in sandsage grasslands can also be found in the stabilized dunes and shinnery-oak vegetation types. In fact, these three vegetation types so thoroughly intergrade that they are indistinguishable in parts of western Oklahoma.

Stabilized Dunes: Such dunes occur along the north side of major rivers in western Oklahoma. Excellent examples can be found at Little Sahara State Park in Woods County and at Beaver Dunes State Park in Beaver County. Vegetation cover ranges from sparse to a dense cover of shrubs. In some cases, vegetation is absent.

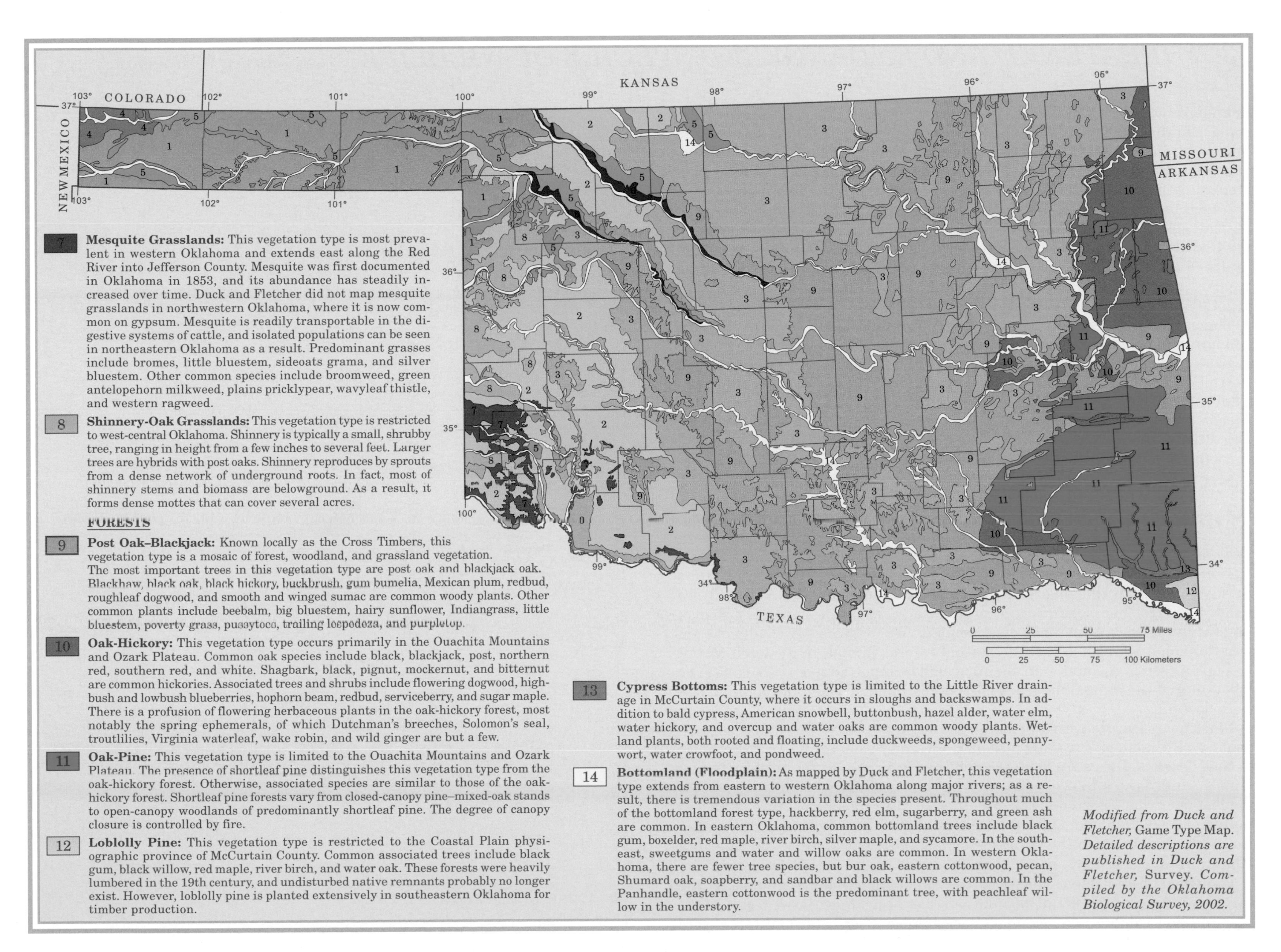

7 **Mesquite Grasslands:** This vegetation type is most prevalent in western Oklahoma and extends east along the Red River into Jefferson County. Mesquite was first documented in Oklahoma in 1853, and its abundance has steadily increased over time. Duck and Fletcher did not map mesquite grasslands in northwestern Oklahoma, where it is now common on gypsum. Mesquite is readily transportable in the digestive systems of cattle, and isolated populations can be seen in northeastern Oklahoma as a result. Predominant grasses include bromes, little bluestem, sideoats grama, and silver bluestem. Other common species include broomweed, green antelopehorn milkweed, plains pricklypear, wavyleaf thistle, and western ragweed.

8 **Shinnery-Oak Grasslands:** This vegetation type is restricted to west-central Oklahoma. Shinnery is typically a small, shrubby tree, ranging in height from a few inches to several feet. Larger trees are hybrids with post oaks. Shinnery reproduces by sprouts from a dense network of underground roots. In fact, most of shinnery stems and biomass are belowground. As a result, it forms dense mottes that can cover several acres.

FORESTS

9 **Post Oak–Blackjack:** Known locally as the Cross Timbers, this vegetation type is a mosaic of forest, woodland, and grassland vegetation. The most important trees in this vegetation type are post oak and blackjack oak. Blackhaw, black oak, black hickory, buckbrush, gum bumelia, Mexican plum, redbud, roughleaf dogwood, and smooth and winged sumac are common woody plants. Other common plants include beebalm, big bluestem, hairy sunflower, Indiangrass, little bluestem, poverty grass, pussytoes, trailing lespedeza, and purpletop.

10 **Oak-Hickory:** This vegetation type occurs primarily in the Ouachita Mountains and Ozark Plateau. Common oak species include black, blackjack, post, northern red, southern red, and white. Shagbark, black, pignut, mockernut, and bitternut are common hickories. Associated trees and shrubs include flowering dogwood, highbush and lowbush blueberries, hophorn beam, redbud, serviceberry, and sugar maple. There is a profusion of flowering herbaceous plants in the oak-hickory forest, most notably the spring ephemerals, of which Dutchman's breeches, Solomon's seal, troutlilies, Virginia waterleaf, wake robin, and wild ginger are but a few.

11 **Oak-Pine:** This vegetation type is limited to the Ouachita Mountains and Ozark Plateau. The presence of shortleaf pine distinguishes this vegetation type from the oak-hickory forest. Otherwise, associated species are similar to those of the oak-hickory forest. Shortleaf pine forests vary from closed-canopy pine–mixed-oak stands to open-canopy woodlands of predominantly shortleaf pine. The degree of canopy closure is controlled by fire.

12 **Loblolly Pine:** This vegetation type is restricted to the Coastal Plain physiographic province of McCurtain County. Common associated trees include black gum, black willow, red maple, river birch, and water oak. These forests were heavily lumbered in the 19th century, and undisturbed native remnants probably no longer exist. However, loblolly pine is planted extensively in southeastern Oklahoma for timber production.

13 **Cypress Bottoms:** This vegetation type is limited to the Little River drainage in McCurtain County, where it occurs in sloughs and backswamps. In addition to bald cypress, American snowbell, buttonbush, hazel alder, water elm, water hickory, and overcup and water oaks are common woody plants. Wetland plants, both rooted and floating, include duckweeds, spongeweed, pennywort, water crowfoot, and pondweed.

14 **Bottomland (Floodplain):** As mapped by Duck and Fletcher, this vegetation type extends from eastern to western Oklahoma along major rivers; as a result, there is tremendous variation in the species present. Throughout much of the bottomland forest type, hackberry, red elm, sugarberry, and green ash are common. In eastern Oklahoma, common bottomland trees include black gum, boxelder, red maple, river birch, silver maple, and sycamore. In the southeast, sweetgums and water and willow oaks are common. In western Oklahoma, there are fewer tree species, but bur oak, eastern cottonwood, pecan, Shumard oak, soapberry, and sandbar and black willows are common. In the Panhandle, eastern cottonwood is the predominant tree, with peachleaf willow in the understory.

Modified from Duck and Fletcher, Game Type Map. *Detailed descriptions are published in Duck and Fletcher,* Survey. *Compiled by the Oklahoma Biological Survey, 2002.*

13. THREATENED AND ENDANGERED SPECIES OF WILDLIFE

Essay by *Bruce W. Hoagland*

Abundant wildlife has drawn many people to the area that has become Oklahoma. But through this contact, the type and abundance of wildlife species have changed dramatically. Although the early story was often one of wanton destruction, Oklahomans in the twentieth century expended tremendous resources in protecting the state's wildlife, as in restoring bison herds to the prairie.

American Indian tribes, both local and distant, relied on the wildlife occupying the region. Chief Pushmataha led several Choctaw hunting expeditions up the Red River from their homelands in the southeastern United States. He returned not only with ample game but also with extensive knowledge of the regional geography—knowledge that would serve him well during his later negotiations with the U.S. government.

The earliest Europeans to visit the area were French and Spanish trappers and hunters in search of furs and hides. French trappers were eager to trap the beavers that plied the rivers of the region. While exploring the Verdigris and North Canadian rivers during his 1819 expedition, Thomas Nuttall employed a trapper named Mr. Lee as guide. Beavers were prized not only for their pelts as a trade commodity but also for their meat as an important source of protein for expeditions. As the century wore on, trapping pressure increased; by the opening of the twentieth century, beaver numbers were drastically reduced. Attempts to reintroduce the beaver in Oklahoma in the mid-twentieth century met with limited success. However, recent efforts have been so successful that many rural and suburban citizens regard these animals as a nuisance!

The best records of early Oklahoma wildlife were left by U.S. Army expeditions and civilian adventurers. All wrote at length of the abundant wildlife. Many came to the territory specifically in hope of good hunting. Early visitors were so successful that many of the large game mammals they sought are either no longer common or occupy a drastically reduced range in Oklahoma. Later hunters were sometimes disappointed. In the 1840s, for example, Captain Randolph Marcy had success hunting several animals in the territory but was quite keen to encounter an elk. Although he reported seeing elk tracks, he failed to find the animal; he learned from his Indian guide that elk numbers were declining.

Black bears featured prominently in the accounts of travelers and early residents. A. P. Chouteau's trading post on the Verdigris shipped many bear hides to New Orleans. Delaware guides caught two bear cubs in the Wichita Mountains during Marcy's 1852 expedition. Less than a hundred years later, in 1934, the last bear was reported in the Wichitas. In 1915 the last bear was killed in southeastern Oklahoma. During the 1960s, Arkansas wildlife managers reintroduced black bears to the Ozarks. Some of these crossed into the Ouachita Mountains and are slowly reestablishing an Oklahoma population.

Hunting substantially reduced populations of many game animals by the early twentieth century. But populations have rebounded as a result of restocking and wildlife management. For example, deer meat and hides were

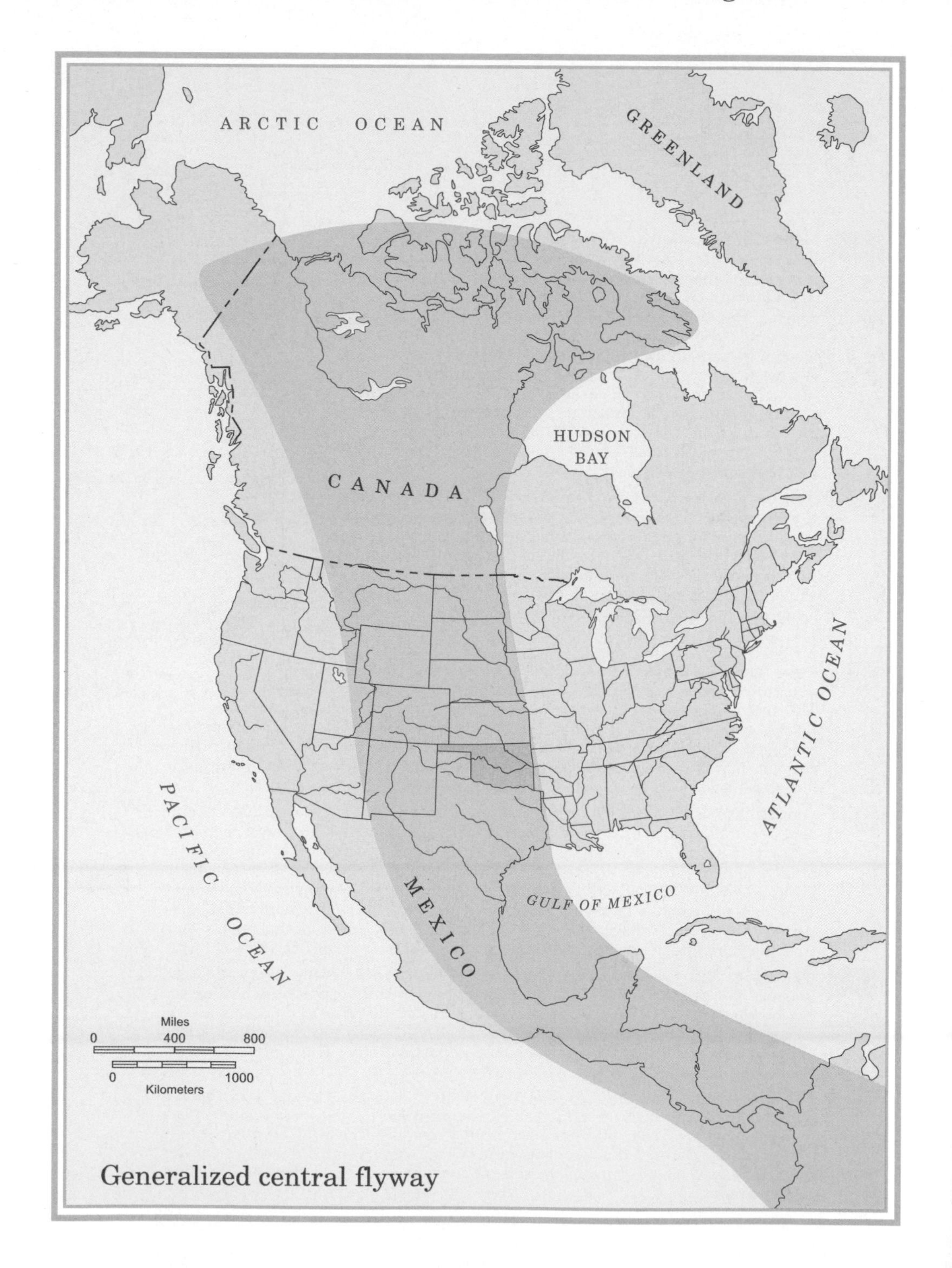

Generalized central flyway

important both for sustenance and for trade in early Oklahoma. Two deer species occur in the state: the whitetail deer, found throughout a large portion of the state; and the mule deer, presently found only in the Panhandle. Whitetail populations declined noticeably in the late nineteenth century. By 1940, viable deer populations were restricted to southeastern Oklahoma. Beginning in 1942, however, deer were relocated from southeastern to northeastern Oklahoma. Deer were also released in parts of western Oklahoma. Presently, Oklahoma has a large deer herd.

Wild turkey is the game bird most commonly reported by early visitors. According to these observers' accounts, turkeys were once found in forests throughout the state. Turkey populations had radically declined by 1920. A 1940 survey found that viable populations existed only in Latimer, Le Flore, McCurtain, and Pushmataha counties. In 1934, the Oklahoma Game and Fish Commission established a turkey farm at Tahlequah; the farm was later moved to Darlington, in Canadian County. A turkey release program was initiated in Carter, Cherokee, Comanche, Delaware, Grady, Latimer, Le Flore, McCurtain, Nowata, Oklahoma, Pushmataha, and Sequoyah counties. These programs proved to be very successful, and as a result, Oklahomans can easily catch a glimpse of these fabulous birds.

The passenger pigeon and Carolina parakeet were not as fortunate as the turkey. As in other parts of the nation, both birds were a common sight for nineteenth-century explorers of the region. Passenger pigeons ranged as far west as Pottawatomie and Garvin counties. The last record for this bird in Oklahoma dates to 1900. Carolina parakeets were found as far west as Osage and Bryan counties. They were first reported from the Shawnee Hills in 1819 and were last seen in the 1880s. Like passenger pigeons, Carolina parakeets lived in huge flocks. Carolina parakeets were destroyed both because they damaged crops and for their colorful feathers. The ivory-billed woodpecker, believed until recently to be extinct, was last reported from Oklahoma in 1884.

Current conservation efforts focus on the lesser prairie chicken and neotropical migrants. Neotropical migrants are birds that spend the winter months in South and Central America and summers in North America. (Many of these birds eat insects, which are in short supply in Oklahoma during winter months.) The scissor-tailed flycatcher, the Oklahoma state bird, is a neotropical migrant.

The federal Endangered Species Act was enacted in 1973 in an attempt to curb the loss of plant and animal species. There are currently nineteen federally listed species in Oklahoma: one plant and eighteen animals. The only plant—the western prairie fringed orchid—is listed as threatened. This plant occurred in northeastern Oklahoma but has not been seen since the late 1970s. Among the animals, eleven are endangered and seven threatened. Seven of the listed animal species are birds. Among these is the bald eagle, our national bird (now recovered from endangered to threatened status, following intensive recovery efforts, notably conducted at Sutton Avian Research Center in Bartlesville).

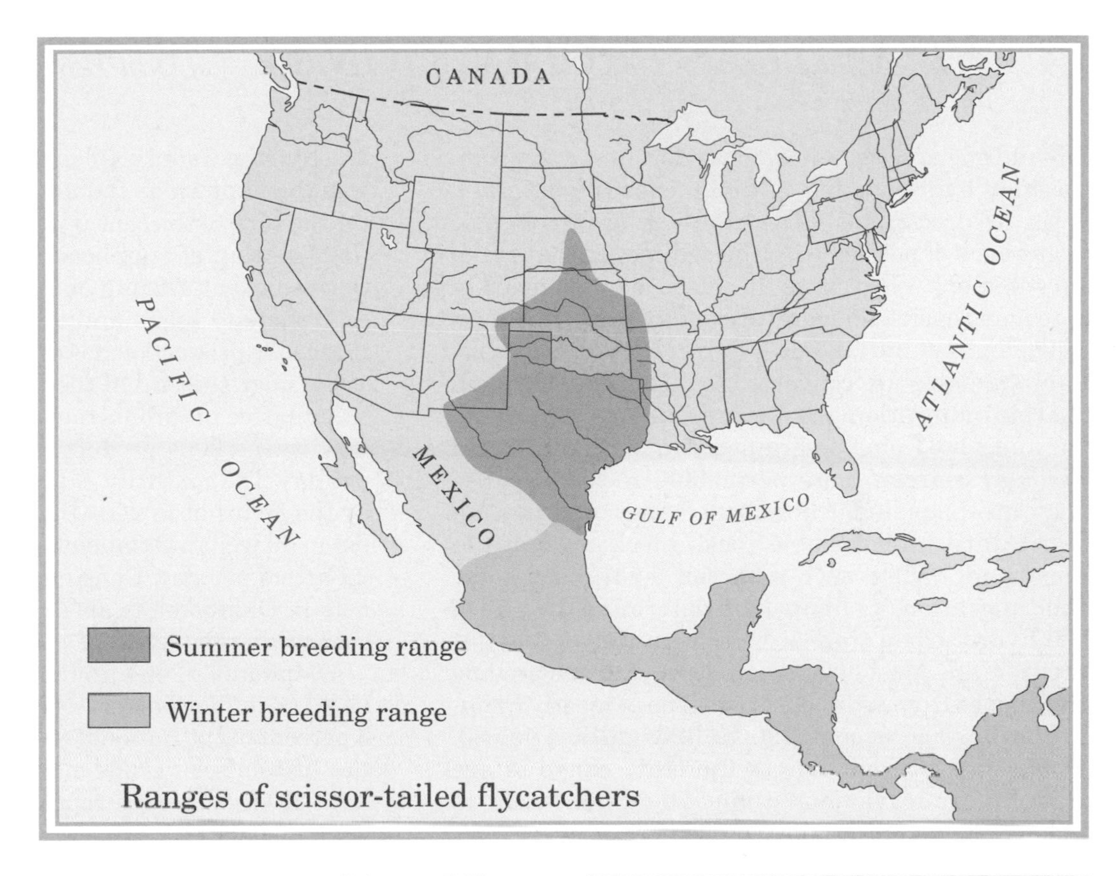

Ranges of scissor-tailed flycatchers

Scissortail Flycatcher, *by George Sutton. (Courtesy Sam Noble Oklahoma Museum of Natural History, University of Oklahoma)*

14. OIL AND GAS PRODUCTION

Essay by *Dan Boyd*

Oil and gas are organic compounds dominantly composed of hydrogen and carbon, hence the umbrella term "hydrocarbons." They form from microscopic organisms deposited with the sediments that make up sedimentary rocks as these are deeply buried in a geologic basin. Temperature and pressure increase with depth of burial, and over geologic time the organic remains are converted to oil and gas through thermal alteration. As oil and gas are generated, they migrate from fine-grained source rocks into and through coarser, more permeable rocks. Because they are buoyant, if unimpeded they migrate upward until impermeable rocks block the path of movement. When such a barrier (seal) blocks further migration, its limits help determine the size of the hydrocarbon trap within which the oil and gas accumulate. Most of Oklahoma's oil and gas production comes from sedimentary basins of mostly Pennsylvanian age (about 290 to 323 million years). However, reservoirs across the state range in age from Precambrian (more than 570 million years) to Cretaceous (65 to 146 million years).

Oil seeps were known in Oklahoma long before the arrival of settlers. However, the first commercial (profitable) well was not drilled until 1896; it was sunk near the city of Bartlesville, in present-day Washington County. Oil production throughout what was then known as Indian Territory rose rapidly after the turn of the century, providing the impetus for the granting of statehood in 1907. Annual production peaked at 278 million barrels in 1927, with many intermediate highs and lows seen since that time. Statewide production has declined continuously since 1984, near the end of the last major drilling boom. Cumulative oil production is about 14.7 billion barrels, with a 2004 production rate of 175,000 barrels per day. The maturity of the industry is highlighted by the fact that in 2004 the average production rate for an oil well in Oklahoma is only slightly more than 2 barrels per day. Consumption of petroleum products in Oklahoma is about 50 percent greater than the state's production of crude oil.

Oklahoma's 2004 annual crude-oil production of about 64 million barrels represents slightly more than 3 percent of the national output and makes the state the fifth-largest crude-oil producer in the country. This production rate represents one-quarter of the peak reached in 1927. Using an average price of $50 per barrel, annual production has a value of more than $3.2 billion. At the end of 2000, the U.S. Department of Energy placed Oklahoma's proven oil reserves at 610 million barrels.

Natural gas is almost always associated with oil, but in the early days, gas was usually looked upon more as a nuisance or drilling hazard. In Oklahoma, exploration did not target natural gas widely until the second half of the twentieth century. Cumulative gas production through 2004 is 94.0 trillion cubic feet, with annual production peaking in 1990 at a rate of about 6.2 billion cubic feet per day. Production in 2004 averaged about 4.5 billion cubic feet per day. In contrast to the maturity of oil industry, the natural gas industry in Oklahoma is relatively young. Drilling in the state, especially exploratory drilling, is dominated by wells with gas objectives. For this reason, gas production in the state is likely to remain strong well into the twenty-first century.

Oklahoma's 2004 annual natural gas production of about 1.65 trillion cubic feet represents about 8 percent of total U.S. production and makes the state the third-largest gas producer in the country. This production rate is about two-thirds of the peak rate reached in 1990. This volume, at a market price of about $6 per thousand cubic feet, has a value of nearly $9.9 billion. At the end of 2000, the U.S. Department of Energy placed Oklahoma's proven gas reserves at 13.7 trillion cubic feet. Statewide gas production is about three times consumption.

Petroleum Industry Milestones in Oklahoma

Pre-1850	Oil seeps or "medicine springs" identified in Indian Territory.
1889	A well on Spencer Creek, near Chelsea, produces minor amounts of oil.
1897	The first commerical well, the Nellie Johnstone #1, is completed near Bartlesville. This field will become the largest and eventually produce 1.5 billion barrels of oil.
1900	Oklahoma Territory Department of Geology and Natural History begins operation with Dr. A. H. Van Vleet as director and Dr. Charles N. Gould as geologist.
1900	University of Oklahoma School of Geology founded by Dr. Charles N. Gould.
1901	First oil discovery of the new century at Red Fork, just southwest of Tulsa.
1903	First natural gas piped into Tulsa for use at a brick plant.
1906	Oklahoma Natural Gas Company is formed to bring natural gas to Oklahoma City.
1908	The state constitution's mandate for the establishment of the Oklahoma Geological Survey, by Senate Bill No. 75. Dr. Charles N. Gould becomes the first director.
1910	E. W. Marland founds Marland Oil Company.
1916	Garber field is discovered, Garfield County. This field is the first investment in the petroleum industry by Herbert H. Champlin, founder of Champlin Refining Company.
1917	Phillips Petroleum Company is established by Frank and L. E. Phillips.
1920	Halliburton Oil Well Cementing Company is founded in Duncan by Erle Halliburton.
1930	"Wild Mary Sudik" well in Oklahoma City field remains out of control for eleven days.
1935	Oklahoma passes the first well-spacing law, with the Corporation Commission to decide size of spacing units.
1946	Kerr-McGee Oil Industries, Inc., founded by Robert S. Kerr and Dean A. McGee.
1982	Oklahoma crude oil reaches high point of $37.60 per barrel.
1986	Oklahoma crude oil reaches modern low of $11.15 per barrel.

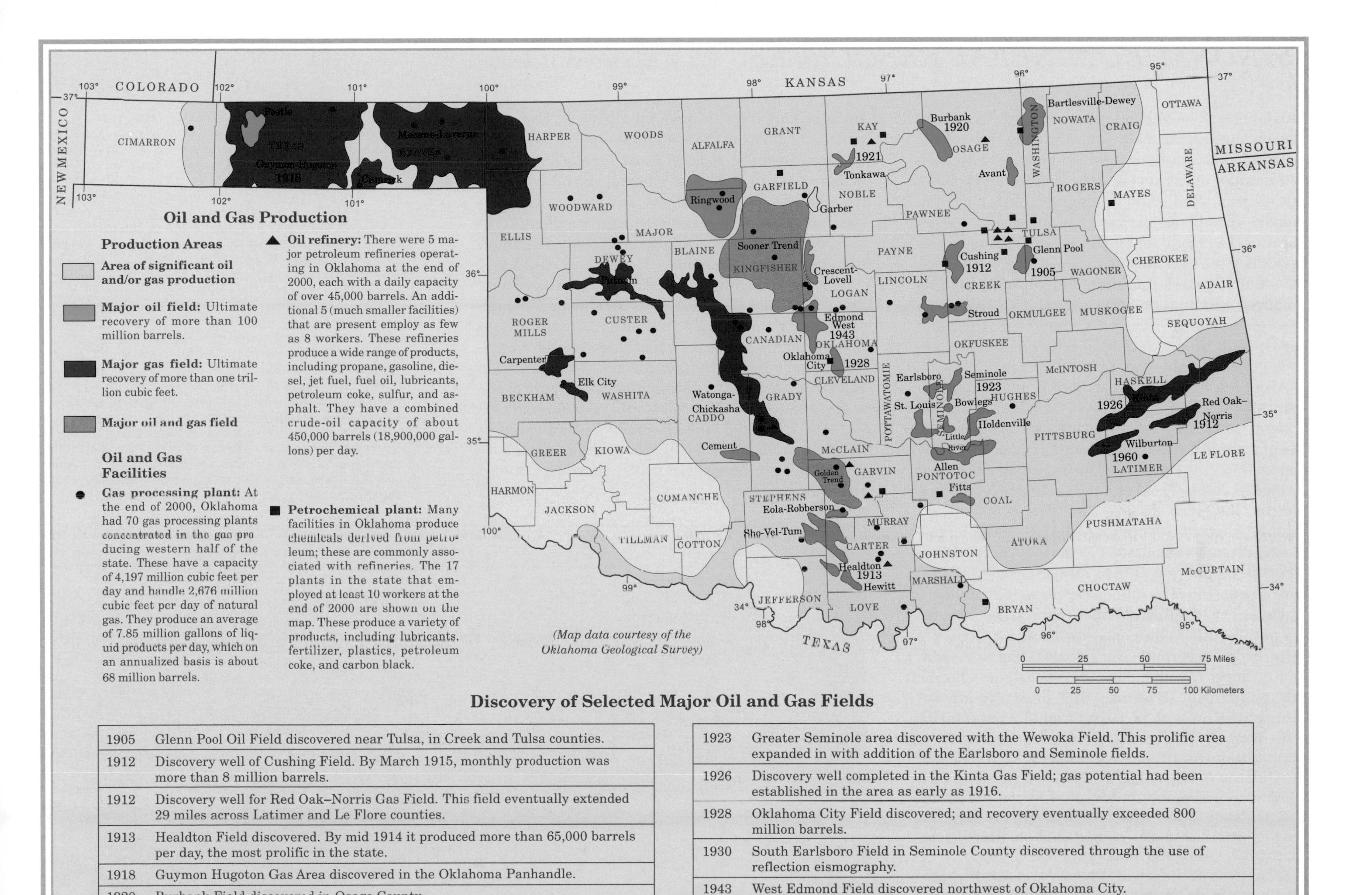

Discovery of Selected Major Oil and Gas Fields

1905	Glenn Pool Oil Field discovered near Tulsa, in Creek and Tulsa counties.
1912	Discovery well of Cushing Field. By March 1915, monthly production was more than 8 million barrels.
1912	Discovery well for Red Oak–Norris Gas Field. This field eventually extended 29 miles across Latimer and Le Flore counties.
1913	Healdton Field discovered. By mid 1914 it produced more than 65,000 barrels per day, the most prolific in the state.
1918	Guymon Hugoton Gas Area discovered in the Oklahoma Panhandle.
1920	Burbank Field discovered in Osage County.
1921	Tonkawa Field discovered in Kay County.

1923	Greater Seminole area discovered with the Wewoka Field. This prolific area expanded in with addition of the Earlsboro and Seminole fields.
1926	Discovery well completed in the Kinta Gas Field; gas potential had been established in the area as early as 1916.
1928	Oklahoma City Field discovered; and recovery eventually exceeded 800 million barrels.
1930	South Earlsboro Field in Seminole County discovered through the use of reflection eismography.
1943	West Edmond Field discovered northwest of Oklahoma City.
1960	Discovery well for the Wilburton "Deep" Gas Field. The Greater Wilburton Field has an estimated ultimate recovery of over 2 trillion cubic feet of natural gas.

15. NONFUEL MINERAL RESOURCES

Essay by *Kenneth S. Johnson*

Oklahoma's tremendous mineral wealth is distributed throughout the state. These mineral resources—including petroleum (crude oil and natural gas), coal, and nonfuel minerals (such as limestone, gypsum, salt, clays, iodine, sand and gravel, lead, zinc, and copper)—are being produced in all seventy-seven counties. In recent years, the mineral industry has been the state's greatest source of revenue. In 2002, the value of petroleum, coal, and nonfuel minerals produced in Oklahoma was about $6.7 billion (it reached a high of nearly $11 billion in 1982 and 1984). Total production of all minerals since statehood (1907) is valued at $172 billion.

Although Oklahoma petroleum production accounts for about 93 percent of Oklahoma's annual mineral output, nonpetroleum mineral resources represent a significant part of the state's current economy and an important reserve of future wealth. The total estimated value of coal and nonfuel-mineral production in Oklahoma during 2002 was $499 million. Leading commodities produced during 2002 comprise crushed stone (valued at $179 million), portland cement, sand and gravel ($43 million), coal ($37 million), glass sand ($28 million), gypsum ($20 million), and iodine ($18 million). Other commodities now being produced in Oklahoma—or for which there are current mining permits—include clays and shale, salt, lime, granite, rhyolite, dolomite, sandstone, volcanic ash, and tripoli. Resources that presently are not being mined (or with no current mining permits) include asphalt, lead, zinc, copper, iron, manganese, titanium, and uranium. Oklahoma ranks first among the states in production of gypsum and iodine; in fact, Oklahoma is the only producer of iodine in the nation. Oklahoma also ranks high among the states in the production of tripoli (second), helium (third), feldspar (fifth), and glass sand (seventh).

Oklahoma has important reserves of certain high-purity minerals suitable as raw materials for various chemical industries. There are major deposits of high-purity limestone, dolomite, and glass sand in the south-central and eastern parts of the state; gypsum and salt are widespread in the west. The abundance and purity of these minerals enable the manufacture of caustic soda, soda ash, chlorine, sulfur, sulfuric acid, lime, sodium silicate, and other chemical products. Oil, natural gas, and water (needed in the manufacture of these products) are plentiful in most parts of the state, and bituminous coal is abundant in eastern Oklahoma.

Historically, lead, zinc, and copper have been very important to local economies in Oklahoma, although no metals are now being produced in the state. Copper and lead were intermittently produced from underground mines in the Ouachita Mountains during the Civil War. And in the southwestern part of the state, near Altus (Jackson County), a surface copper mine produced approximately 1.88 million tons of ore between 1964 and 1975. A decline in copper prices and an increase in production costs caused the mine to close.

The Tri-State Mining District

Large quantities of lead and zinc were produced in the Miami-Picher area of the world-famous Tri-State Mining District of northeastern Oklahoma, southeastern Kansas, and southwestern Missouri. Underground mines in Ottawa County, Oklahoma, produced approximately 1.3 million tons of lead and 5.2 million tons of zinc between 1891 and 1970, when the last mine in the district was closed. Most of the mines were 100–300 feet below the land surface. Oklahoma led the United States in zinc production almost every year from 1918 through 1945. The highest level of production for both metals occurred in 1925.

Closure of the mines resulted from depletion of the higher-grade ores, a decline in the price paid for lead and zinc, and the increasing cost of pumping water from the mines to keep them open. With mine closures, several significant problems were left over from the mining activities, including the large, barren waste dumps that mar the landscape; the presence of abandoned, open mine shafts; the potential for collapse of the land surface into underground spaces; and the seepage of contaminated water from the mines into local drinking water supplies and streams (the cause for U.S. Environmental Protection Agency classification of the area as the "Tar Creek Superfund Site").

Waste materials, or tailings, from the numerous lead and zinc mines in Picher, 1931. (Courtesy Western History Collections, University of Oklahoma Libraries)

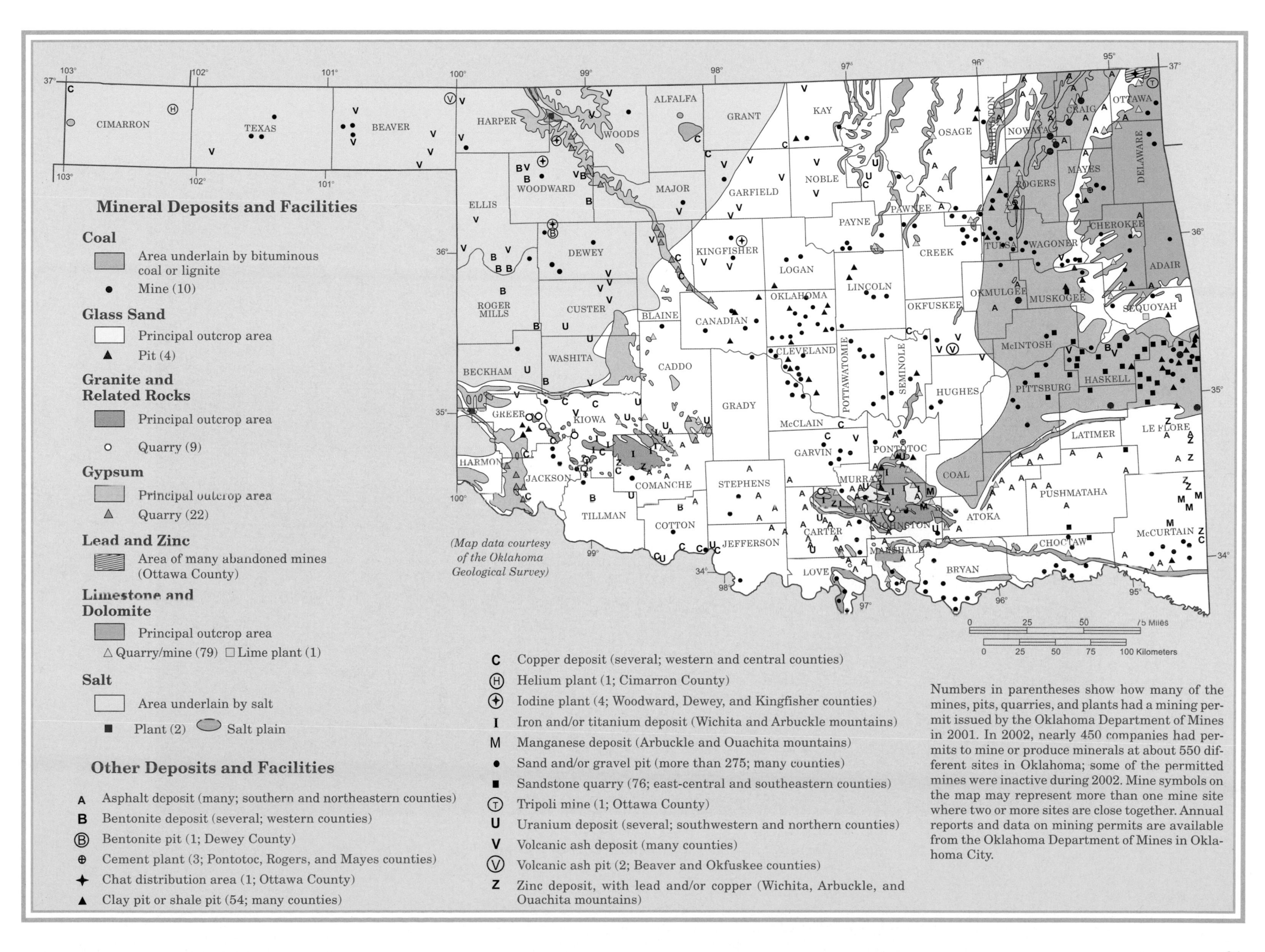
Mineral Deposits and Facilities
Coal
Area underlain by bituminous coal or lignite
Mine (10)
Glass Sand
Principal outcrop area
Pit (4)
Granite and Related Rocks
Principal outcrop area
Quarry (9)
Gypsum
Principal outcrop area
Quarry (22)
Lead and Zinc
Area of many abandoned mines (Ottawa County)
Limestone and Dolomite
Principal outcrop area
Quarry/mine (79)
Lime plant (1)
Salt
Area underlain by salt
Plant (2)
Salt plain
Other Deposits and Facilities
A Asphalt deposit (many; southern and northeastern counties)
B Bentonite deposit (several; western counties)
Bentonite pit (1; Dewey County)
Cement plant (3; Pontotoc, Rogers, and Mayes counties)
Chat distribution area (1; Ottawa County)
Clay pit or shale pit (54; many counties)
C Copper deposit (several; western and central counties)
Helium plant (1; Cimarron County)
Iodine plant (4; Woodward, Dewey, and Kingfisher counties)
I Iron and/or titanium deposit (Wichita and Arbuckle mountains)
M Manganese deposit (Arbuckle and Ouachita mountains)
Sand and/or gravel pit (more than 275; many counties)
Sandstone quarry (76; east-central and southeastern counties)
Tripoli mine (1; Ottawa County)
U Uranium deposit (several; southwestern and northern counties)
V Volcanic ash deposit (many counties)
Volcanic ash pit (2; Beaver and Okfuskee counties)
Z Zinc deposit, with lead and/or copper (Wichita, Arbuckle, and Ouachita mountains)
Numbers in parentheses show how many of the mines, pits, quarries, and plants had a mining permit issued by the Oklahoma Department of Mines in 2001. In 2002, nearly 450 companies had permits to mine or produce minerals at about 550 different sites in Oklahoma; some of the permitted mines were inactive during 2002. Mine symbols on the map may represent more than one mine site where two or more sites are close together. Annual reports and data on mining permits are available from the Oklahoma Department of Mines in Oklahoma City.
(Map data courtesy of the Oklahoma Geological Survey)
CIMARRON
TEXAS
BEAVER
HARPER
WOODS
ALFALFA
GRANT
KAY
OSAGE
WASHINGTON
NOWATA
CRAIG
OTTAWA
DELAWARE
MAYES
ROGERS
ELLIS
WOODWARD
MAJOR
GARFIELD
NOBLE
PAWNEE
PAYNE
TULSA
WAGONER
CHEROKEE
ADAIR
DEWEY
KINGFISHER
LOGAN
CREEK
LINCOLN
OKMULGEE
MUSKOGEE
SEQUOYAH
ROGER MILLS
CUSTER
BLAINE
CANADIAN
OKLAHOMA
OKFUSKEE
McINTOSH
BECKHAM
WASHITA
CADDO
CLEVELAND
POTTAWATOMIE
SEMINOLE
HASKELL
PITTSBURG
HUGHES
GRADY
GREER
KIOWA
McCLAIN
LATIMER
LE FLORE
HARMON
GARVIN
PONTOTOC
JACKSON
COMANCHE
STEPHENS
MURRAY
COAL
PUSHMATAHA
TILLMAN
COTTON
CARTER
JOHNSTON
ATOKA
JEFFERSON
MARSHALL
CHOCTAW
McCURTAIN
LOVE
BRYAN
103°
102°
101°
100°
99°
98°
97°
96°
95°
37°
36°
35°
34°
0 25 50 75 Miles
0 25 50 75 100 Kilometers

Wichita Mountains National Wildlife Refuge, Comanche County. (Photograph by John Elk III, courtesy of Elk Photography)

Part II

Humans on the Landscape

William S. Soule photographed this winter encampment of Comanche Indians, c. 1869. (Courtesy Western History Collections, University of Oklahoma Libraries)

16. EARLY ARRIVALS, 40,000–12,000 B.P.

Essay by *Robert L. Brooks*

Prior to the 1990s, it was commonly accepted that settlement of the New World came about by a rapid migration of people of the Clovis culture across the frozen-over Bering Strait and through North America some 12,000 years ago. Clovis culture was characterized by the presence of mammoth kills and short-term habitation sites in the United States. This widespread acceptance, however, changed markedly after the discovery of the Monte Verde site in Chile in the 1980s. Monte Verde demonstrated evidence of mammoth hunting about 11,000 years ago—without the use of the familiar fluted Clovis spear point. With this new information, archaeologists became more responsive to arguments for an earlier settlement of the New World (ca. 25,000 to 40,000 years ago). While many archaeologists still favor a theory of migration to the New World across the Bering Strait and thence through the intermountain region, several novel approaches have been suggested. One has early settlement originating by people moving around the edge of the Atlantic and coming into North America from the east. Another theory is that groups traveled along the West Coast before moving inland. Multiple entries into the New World from different origin points also remain a distinct possibility.

Oklahoma has two locations that figure prominently in the revised scenario for new arrivals. The Burnham site in Woods County holds evidence for various Pleistocene species (e.g., giant bison, mammoth, three species of horse, and short-faced bear), some seventy-five pieces of chipped stone debris attributed to human manufacture, and a central suite of radiocarbon assays from 28,000 to 32,000 years ago. The second place is the Cooperton mammoth locality in Kiowa County, where mammoth bones with green bone fractures and large nonlocal hammer stones have yielded radiocarbon dates of 17,000–21,000 years B.P. Such evidence has been found not only in Oklahoma but also in many other states, and there is increasing support for the possibility that these early arrivals may have traveled diverse paths in their journeys to the New World.

Probable migration routes

17. *EARLY BIG-GAME HUNTERS, 12,000–8,000* B.P.

Essay by *Robert L. Brooks*

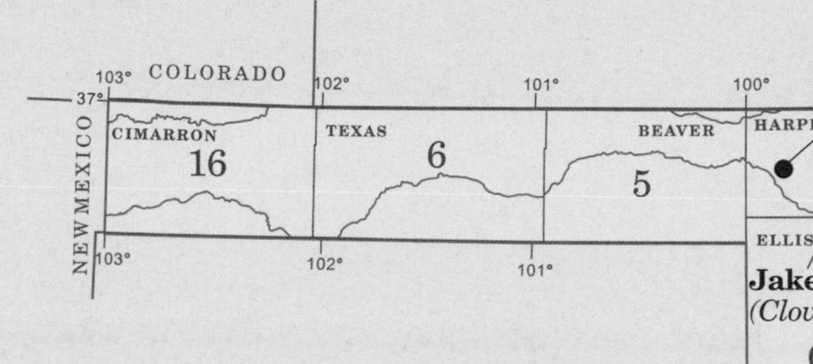

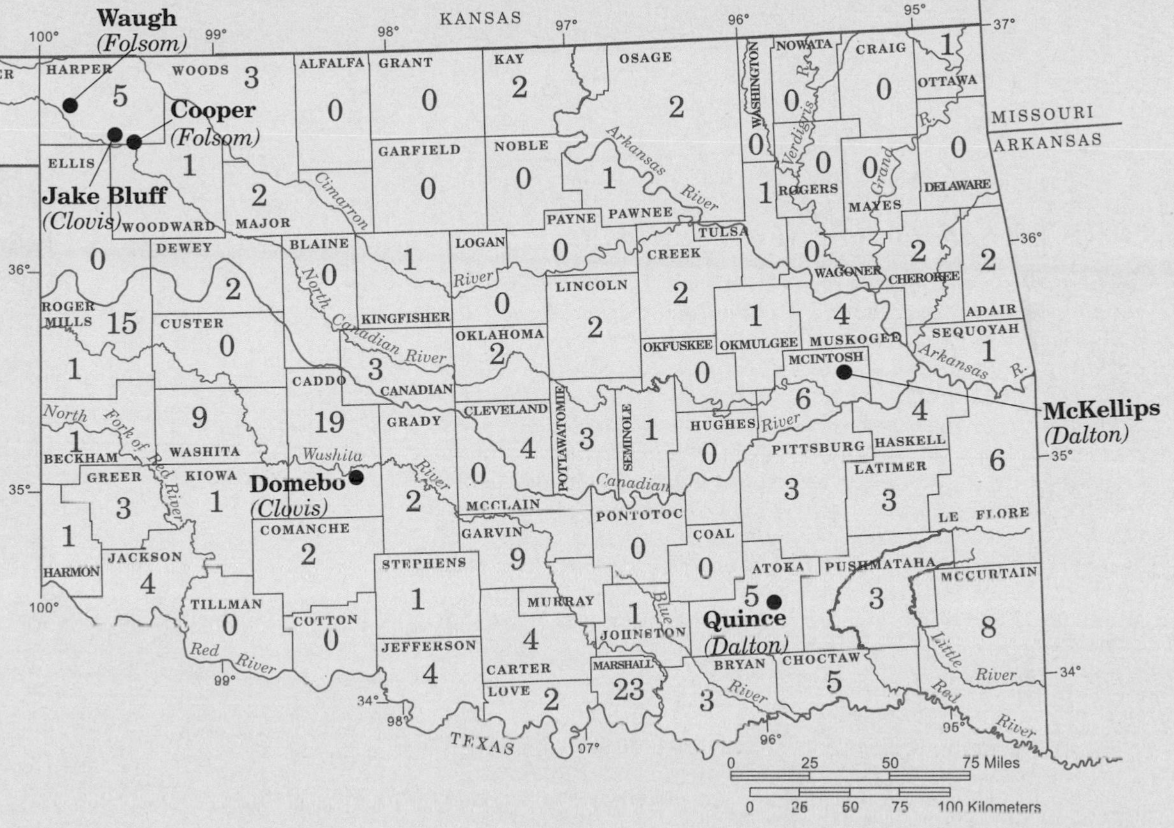

● Paleo-Indian site. Numbers indicate documented early big-game-hunting sites by county as of 2002. In parentheses are the cultural traditions suggested by the archaeological records at these sites.

Cooper Site

Around ten thousand years ago, a group of people we call Folsom drove an extinct form of bison along the Beaver River floodplain and into a deep, narrow gully, thus trapping the animals. This same strategy took place on three separate occasions, probably only a few years apart. The Folsom people left behind evidence of their butchering practices on the skeletal remains of the bison, as well as approximately thirty of their distinctive Folsom spear points and a few other tools. More significantly, after the first event of driving the bison into this gully, they took one of the skulls and painted a thunderbolt on it before placing it, nose-first, into the gully. This is the earliest known artwork found in North America.

Campsites and kill localities of early big-game hunters in Oklahoma are much more evident than those for the earlier arrivals discussed in the previous essay. Also referred to as Paleo-Indians, small bands of these highly nomadic hunters emphasized the hunting of large mammals. Many of the animals present at this time became extinct by 10,000 years ago (e.g., mammoth, giant bison, horse, sloth, and short-faced bear). Campsites and kill localities of early big-game hunters in what became Oklahoma indicate that the surviving larger game animals (bison, deer, elk, and antelope) continued to be hunted. While distinctive spear points associated with these hunters are found throughout Oklahoma, most are surface finds that yield only limited information on the ways of life of these Native groups because of their highly nomadic existence and small group size. The thousands of years that have passed since the early big-game hunters' time on the landscape have largely obliterated evidence of their presence. However, in a few locations, the presence of mammoth and bison kills has provided insights into the Paleo-Indian groups' behavior.

A few sites that have been studied shed light on the lifeways of the early big-game hunters. The Jake Bluff bison kill in Harper County and the Domebo mammoth kill in Caddo County, to name two examples, are associated with Clovis hunters of some 11,000–12,000 years ago. Traces of the Clovis culture have been found throughout Oklahoma. Other early traditions have also been identified within the state's boundaries. Folsom culture bison hunters dating to roughly 10,200–10,800 years ago in western Oklahoma are represented by the Cooper and Waugh sites in Harper County. In eastern Oklahoma, from some 8,000–10,000 years ago, are found sites of the Dalton culture: two of the better-documented sites are Quince in Atoka County and McKellips in McIntosh County. Dalton culture is more adapted to the woodlands and exhibits numerous tools related to woodworking. Dalton peoples' settlements also appear to be slightly larger than those of the western groups and display evidence of a less nomadic existence.

18. HUNTERS AND GATHERERS, 8,000–1,500 B.P.

Essay by Robert L. Brooks

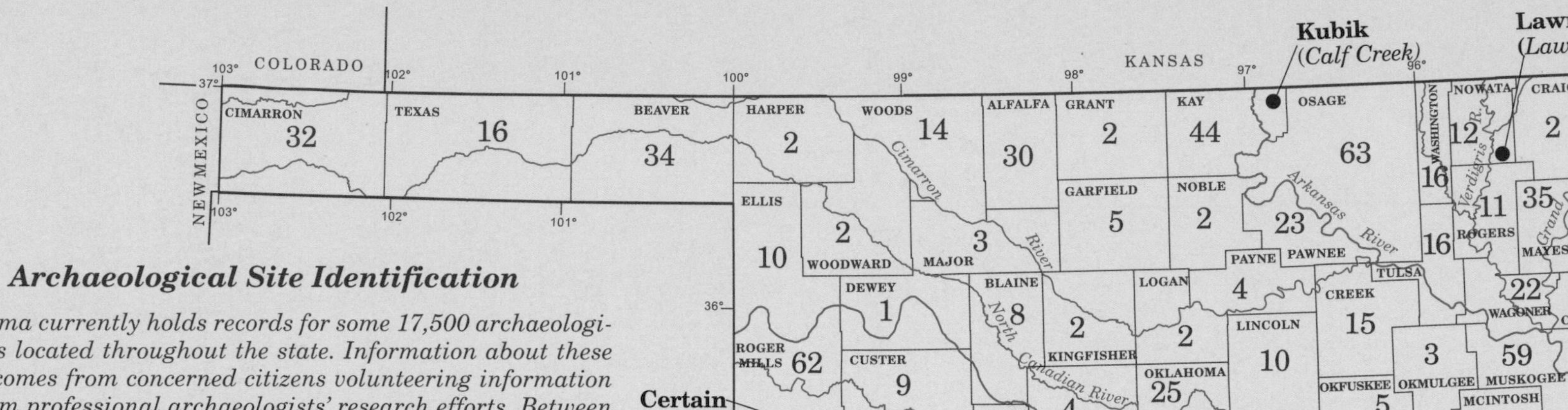

Archaeological Site Identification

Oklahoma currently holds records for some 17,500 archaeological sites located throughout the state. Information about these places comes from concerned citizens volunteering information and from professional archaeologists' research efforts. Between 1936 and 1942, archaeologists working for the Works Progress Administration documented hundreds of archaeological sites. Somewhat later, in the 1950s–1970s, archaeologists with the Oklahoma River Basin Survey found thousands of sites and excavated a number of these prior to the construction of the many Oklahoma lakes (e.g., Tenkiller, Broken Bow, Kaw, Altus, and Texoma). Many thousands of archaeological sites have also been recorded under the requirements of federal laws passed since the 1960s. The Oklahoma Archeological Survey, established in 1970, has spent the past thirty years recording and investigating archaeological sites in Oklahoma.

● Hunter-and-gatherer site. Numbers indicate reported hunter-and-gatherer sites by county, 2002. In parentheses are the cultural traditions suggested by the archaeological records at these sites.

The time period of hunters and gatherers reflects a steadily increasing population, an increasingly sedentary lifestyle, and an expanded repertoire of tools. Dramatic changes in environmental conditions over this 6,500-year span of time resulted in hunting-and-gathering cultures' developing successful coping mechanisms when faced with climatic adversity (e.g., a hot, dry period between 7000 and 4000 B.P.). Despite the adverse conditions, the plant and animal communities from this early day are common to those found in today's world. Decreasing mobility in these peoples' movements led to greater duration in settlements and consequently more evidence of their presence on the landscape. Whereas there are roughly 200 early big-game hunter sites in Oklahoma, there are about 2,500 sites that can be attributed to the hunters-and-gatherers era in the state.

Numerous prehistoric cultures have been identified for this long time period. Calf Creek culture, found throughout Oklahoma, dates to approximately 5,000 years ago. Living during a period of exceptionally hot, dry weather, Calf Creek people made distinctive large spear points, lived in highly mobile small groups, and frequently selected settlement locations with prominent vistas. Between roughly 3,500 and 1,500 years ago, markedly different cultural patterns were found in eastern and western Oklahoma. In the east, groups of the Lawrence and Wister cultures were less nomadic, living in more permanent camps or hamlets while hunting a variety of game and harvesting edible wild plants. Western Oklahoma at this time is characterized by bison-hunting groups who may have practiced logistical hunting of bison from seasonal camps, in contrast to the earlier, highly nomadic early big-game hunters. The bison hunters of some 3,500–1,500 years ago continued to use well-made spear points in their hunting endeavors.

19. BEGINNING AGRICULTURALISTS / VILLAGE FARMERS, CIRCA 1500–500 B.P.

Essay by *Robert L. Brooks*

Beginning approximately 1,500 years ago, intensive harvesting of edible wild plants gradually evolved into the planned harvesting of select cultivated plants. This was the beginning of agricultural practices that by roughly 800 years ago resulted in the existence of village farming communities (growing corn, beans, and squash) throughout Oklahoma. The establishment of agriculture as the principal means of subsistence also corresponded with geometric increases in population and an increasingly sedentary lifestyle. Technological breakthroughs occurred as well: use of the bow and arrow, ceramic production, and improved architecture in the construction of dwellings and—in eastern Oklahoma—ceremonial mound centers. Settled village life, increasingly fixed territorial boundaries, and high agricultural productivity brought about an increased need for greater complexity in social and political organization. This time also was characterized by increasing consolidation in religious/ceremonial complexity in eastern Oklahoma. This appearance of early agriculture marks the first occasion on which we can securely connect prehistoric groups to identified historically documented Native societies.

Because of the aggregation of people in villages (and also greater total population), this period contains the greatest number of documented sites in Oklahoma (over 3,500). These same factors have also permitted identification of numerous distinct groups or cultures throughout Oklahoma. In eastern Oklahoma, sites of the Fourche Maline and Delaware cultures (dating to between 1,000 and 1,500 years ago) have been found. In western Oklahoma, there is a continuation of the bison-hunting tradition of the preceding hunters and gatherers. However, western Oklahoma also contained other groups that had developed a more diversified economy, including farming.

The most profound distinctions occurred between 900 and 500 years ago. Along the Arkansas and Red River valleys in eastern Oklahoma, cultures belonging to a Caddoan tradition lived in hamlets and villages while also constructing large ceremonial centers. Foremost among these visible manifestations of a highly organized mound-building culture are the Spiro center in Le Flore County and the Grobin Davis mound group in McCurtain County. In western Oklahoma, there was another cultural pattern—more adapted to a Plains way of life—termed the Red Bed Plains tradition. The agricultural economy in the west during this period appears to have been even more intensive than that of this Plains culture's Caddoan neighbors. However, the various cultural groups in western Oklahoma did not construct the large ceremonial centers found in the east. This does not mean that their way of life was less religious; their ceremonialism may have been expressed in other ways. Sites prominent in western Oklahoma include the Arthur site in Garvin County, the Heerwald site in Custer County, and Roy Smith in Beaver County.

● Farming site. Numbers indicate reported farming sites as of 2002. In parentheses are the cultural traditions suggested by the archaeological records at these sites.

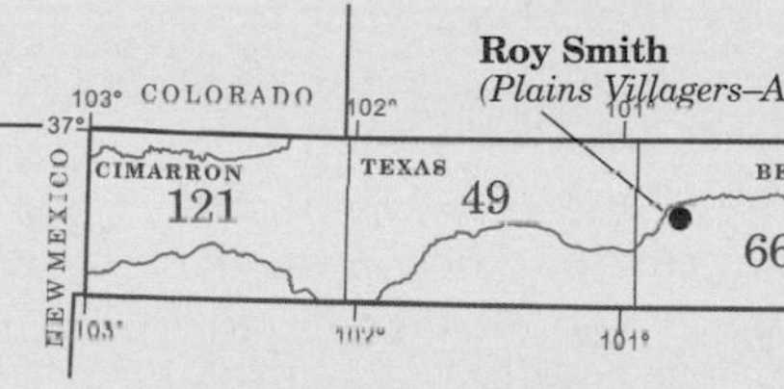

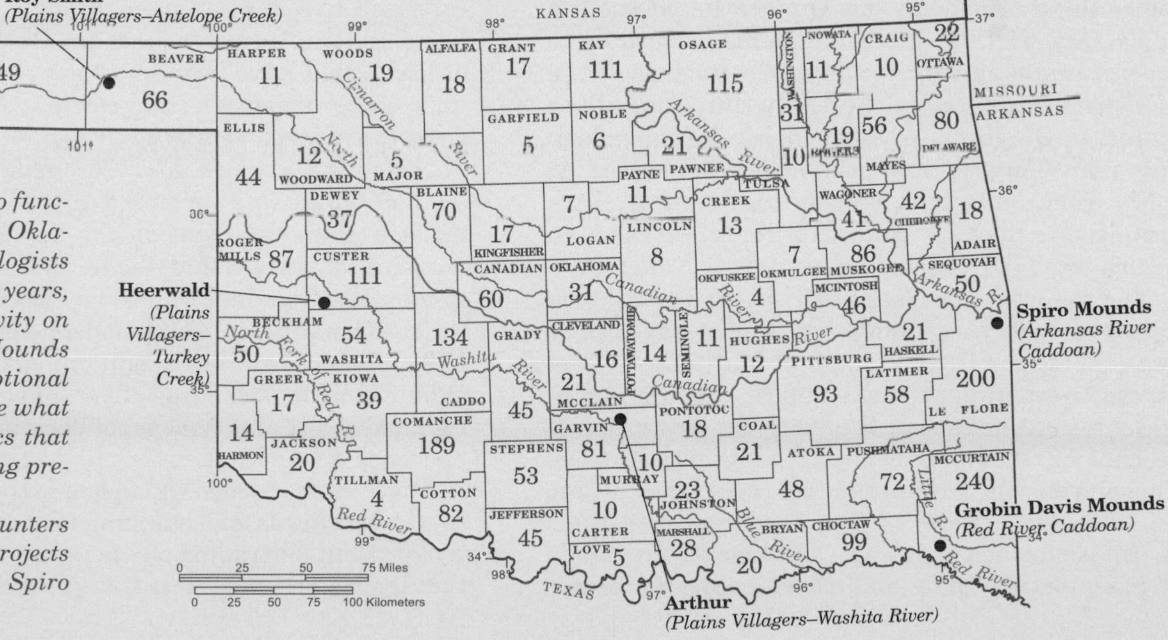

Spiro Mounds

Beginning around 900 years ago, a location on the Arkansas River began to function as an important ceremonial center for prehistoric societies in eastern Oklahoma. We have no way of knowing what they called this place, but archaeologists refer to it as Spiro Mounds, named after the nearby town. For roughly 350 years, this ceremonial center was the focal point for religious and political activity on the western frontier of Mississippian (mound-building) society. Spiro Mounds contains eleven mounds covering an area of eighty acres. While the exceptional funerary offerings to the deceased religious or political leaders of Spiro are what attract the most attention, this ceremonial place has other characteristics that are perhaps even more noteworthy: the mounds were built with engineering precision that also incorporated astronomical information.

The Spiro Mounds remained hidden until 1933, when a group of relic hunters leased the site and began excavating the largest mound. In 1936, the Works Projects Administration assisted the state in protecting the site. Today it is the Spiro Mounds Archaeological State Park.

20. SPANISH AND FRENCH EXPLORERS

Essay by *Danney Goble*

At one time or another—mostly at the same time—maps of both the Spanish and the French empire marked both empires' claim to the vast region within which Oklahoma lies. It has been said that Spain's empire arose because the Spaniards who came in the name of God stayed in the hope of gold. In the case of Oklahoma and its environs, however, they came for gold alone. Not finding it, they did not stay at all.

Their purpose was to find Cíbola—the seven fabled cities said to be so rich that every home had walls of solid gold and doors of pure turquoise. In 1541, Francisco Vasquez de Coronado, governor of New Spain's then most northern province, left Mexico to locate (and to loot) the cities. Behind him stretched a column of 240 mounted men, 60 foot soldiers, more than 800 Indians (valued primarily for their strong backs), at least 1,000 horses, and entire herds of cattle, sheep, and hogs.

Raping and plundering across present-day Arizona and New Mexico, they found little of value beyond a single slave. Called "the Turk" (because "he looked like one"), the poor captive confessed to knowing nothing of Cíbola—but Quivira he claimed to know very well, for it was his home. According to this miserable captive, in Quivira, commoners lived like princes and even the lowly dined off silver plates. In Quivira, every person drank from golden bowls. In Quivira, tiny bells of pure gold tinkled softly from the boughs of every tree. And the Turk promised to take his captors there. All he asked in return was his freedom.

The route that Coronado and his small army took has never been ascertained, but it must have begun near the upper Rio Grande and had to head east across the plains of Texas before turning north, which would have sent it across the westernmost reaches of Oklahoma before crossing into Kansas. There, along the Arkansas River, near present-day Wichita, the exhausted Spaniards reached their destination, such as it was—a village of huts made of grass rather than gold, these being the dome-shaped homes for some understandably bewildered Wichita Indians. Furious, Coronado ordered the Turk's death, before demanding that people he could not understand (the Wichita) use a language they could not comprehend (Spanish) to swear allegiance to what they could not conceive of (the King of Spain). With nothing more accomplished, Coronado and his men made their way home, perhaps crossing Oklahoma's Panhandle en route. Having spent two years wandering, Coronado filed an official report, stunning for what it did not say about what he had not found. "What I am sure of," he solemnly told his prince, "is that there is not any gold nor any other metal in all that country."

Shortly thereafter, Juan de Padilla, a friar who had accompanied Coronado's expedition, returned to that unpromising area. With him were two native converts and a Portugese-born soldier, Andres do Campo. They opened a mission to the Wichitas, but it proved to be as short-lived as the friar, whom Kaw Indians killed, while they chose to enslave his other companions. The survivors took a year to escape and five more to pass through central Oklahoma and southward to reach the Gulf Coast. Their ordeal would have been quicker but for their self-imposed act of penance: they carried a heavy wooden cross every step of the way.

Nearly sixty years after Coronado's expedition, Juan de Oñate was appointed in 1598 to establish a mission and settlement on the upper Rio Grande near present-day Santa Fe. In 1601 he undertook to complete Coronado's quest for riches. After crossing the Canadian into Oklahoma near the Antelope Hills, he marched his expedition north and east to Quivira on the Arkansas River, only to find what Coronado had found: villages of Wichita Indians with no riches of any kind.

The French reached Oklahoma in the 1700s, more than a century later, searching for neither gold nor converts but for trading partners, namely, the tribes that lived along the rivers that ran eastward before emptying into the Mississippi. The Arkansas, the Canadian, and the Red all flowed through Oklahoma: a Frenchman, Jean-Baptiste Bernard, sieur de la Harpe, led the first Europeans to make their way along all three. Other Frenchmen followed, most notably Fabry de la Bruyere and the brothers Pierre and Paul Mallet—the three who became masters of the Canadian and its tributaries.

Thereafter, both France and Spain claimed exclusive sovereignty over all the lands that drained into the lower Mississippi, but only the French backed their claim with their presence. The Spanish came and went; the French came and stayed. Especially among the Wichitas and the Osages, the French entrepreneurs made their own homes, added Native languages to their own, and intermarried freely with the people who surrounded them. Generally young and free-spirited, these so-called *coureurs de bois* brought with them everything from guns to beads for trade, bartering for everything from animal skins to human beings.

All of that happened long ago, but at least one effect is visible even now. The Illinois, the Verdigris, and the Fourche Maline; the Sans Bois, the Kiamichi, and the Ouachita; Sallisaw, Choteau, Salina, and Poteau—Oklahoma's rivers, mountain ranges, and communities still bear names that were first heard with the accents of these French-speaking coureurs de bois.

More important and more immediate was the unconscious but momentous remaking of Native cultures. In exactly the measure that tribes grew to depend on what the French brought them, they were driven to take—primarily from other Indians—what the French demanded. In that way, American Indians became more than merely the Europeans' trading partners. They became commercial hunters, commercial trappers, even commercial warriors—every bit of their new commercial nature in service to an empire that may have begun in Oklahoma but reached around the globe.

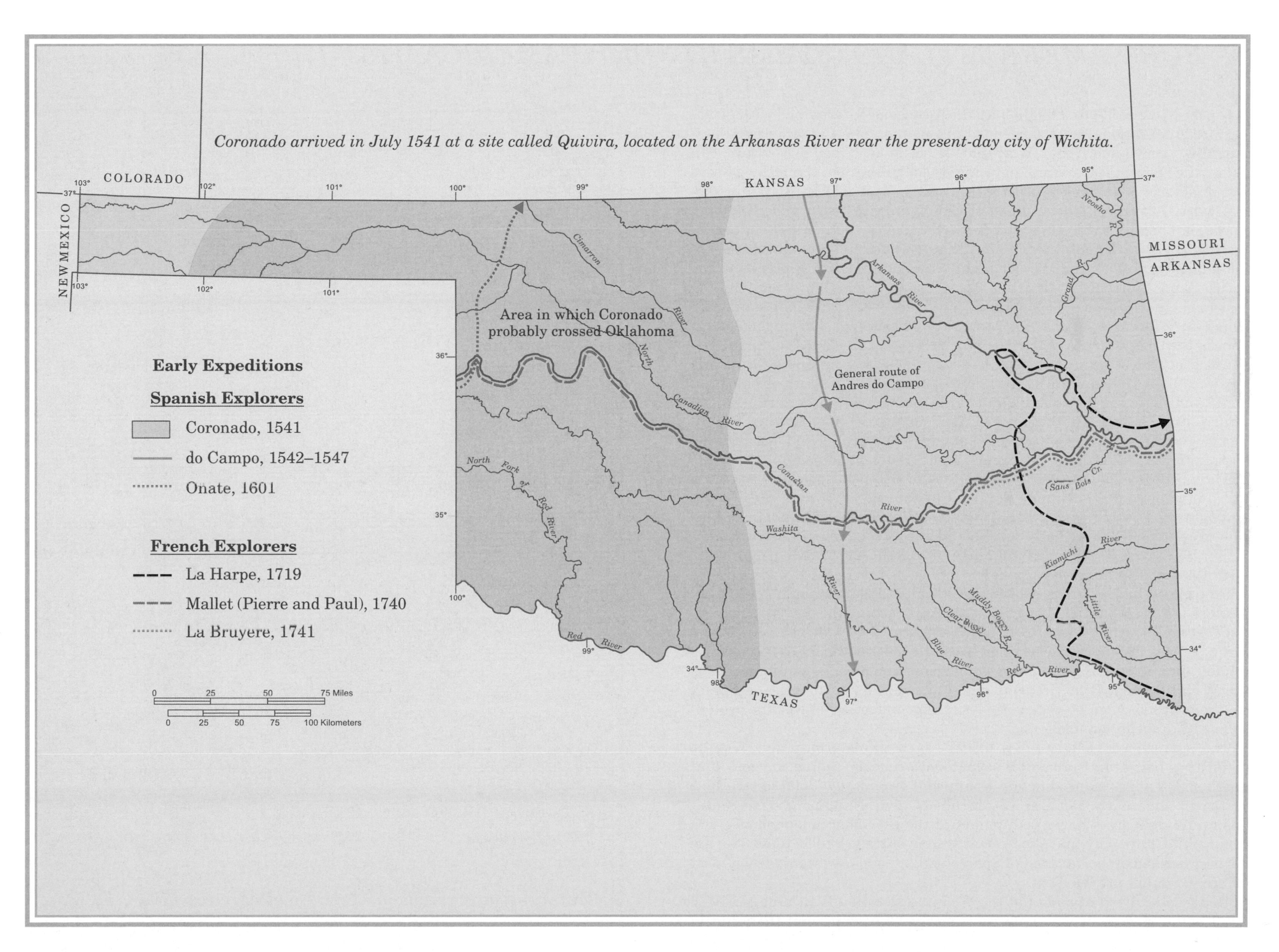
Coronado arrived in July 1541 at a site called Quivira, located on the Arkansas River near the present-day city of Wichita.
COLORADO
NEW MEXICO
KANSAS
MISSOURI
ARKANSAS
TEXAS
Area in which Coronado probably crossed Oklahoma
General route of Andres do Campo
Cimarron River
North Canadian River
Canadian River
Arkansas River
Neosho R.
Grand R.
North Fork of Red River
Washita River
Red River
Sans Bois Cr.
Kiamichi River
Little River
Muddy Boggy R.
Clear Boggy
Blue River
Early Expeditions
Spanish Explorers
Coronado, 1541
do Campo, 1542–1547
Oñate, 1601
French Explorers
La Harpe, 1719
Mallet (Pierre and Paul), 1740
La Bruyere, 1741
0 25 50 75 Miles
0 25 50 75 100 Kilometers

21. *EURO-AMERICAN LAND CLAIMS IN NORTH AMERICA, 1763–1787*

Essay by *Danney Goble*

In the mid- to late 1700s, Oklahoma's future became intertwined with global warfare, international relations, and family politics. The war called by Americans the "French and Indian War" may be better described by its European name, the "Seven Years' War." Defining its long duration, the latter phrase also underscores its importance, for this was the last of four great intercolonial wars that had occupied much of the eighteenth century, as England, France, and Spain battled over the destiny of the North American continent. Ending in 1763 and confirmed by the Treaty of Paris in that year, the last of those bloody conflicts ended in English victory and English supremacy. The entire Saint Lawrence Valley, the Great Lakes region, and every trading post to the north passed from French hands to British. Farther south, the Union Jack flew over everything east of the Mississippi. This included portions of the Gulf Coast as well as the Florida peninsula—lands that had been Spanish provinces until then. The loss was the price Spain paid for having honored the so-called Family Compact that had allied the ruling houses of Spain and France in the recent war, but the loss was not without substantial return. France lived up to its end of the compact by indemnifying Spain's sacrifice in the southeast with the gift of huge (if poorly defined) lands to the north and west, lands that the French had christened Louisiana.

The northern- and westernmost reaches of Spanish Louisiana were uncertain (where did French-now-English Canada end and where did French-now-Spanish Louisiana begin?), but Oklahoma's inclusion in the vast Spanish New World empire was finally certain and totally complete. It also was altogether disastrous for the most prominent of Oklahoma's Native peoples: the Wichitas and affiliated tribes.

French rule had been very good for the Wichitas and their neighbors, mostly because it had amounted to no rule at all. Approaching the natives as potential customers rather than as conquered subjects, the French had cultivated these peoples in particular, for they were the most powerful of the region's inhabitants. In exchange for everything from animal pelts to human slaves, the Wichitas reaped the firearms, ammunition, iron weapons, and horses that made them more powerful still—supreme in fact, whatever the pretensions of European mapmakers.

The Spanish were of no mind to tolerate such self-determination. True, so dispiriting had been Coronado's seventeenth-century search for gold that another 250 years elapsed before Spain sent two more official expeditions across the apparently trackless wastes called Quivira, but Spanish mercantilists and bureaucrats never countenanced the economic independence and commercial autonomy that the French system of trade had fostered. No, the natives would feel the hard fist of Spanish might, and they would feel it most where it would hurt the most.

Geographically, that meant at the Wichitas' so-called Twin Villages. With one located in present-day Jefferson County, Oklahoma, and the other in

European land claims in North America, circa 1750

modern Montague County, Texas, these Twin Villages were both center and symbol of Wichita power. The two constantly oversaw a brisk trade in weapons and manufactured goods and not infrequently served to outfit raids of as many as two thousand warriors, who spread terror to as far away as distant San Antonio.

Imposition of Spanish trade constraints signaled the end of Wichita might. Permitting trade only through licensed agents, the Spanish were able to limit access to horses and guns and other weapons. Spain's abolition of Indian slavery also wiped out that lucrative source of Wichita wealth. In a short time, the Twin Villages were reduced to hollow sepulchers, forgotten monuments to a once proud, then impoverished people. After not much longer, the Wichitas' tombs became real—the final symbols of doom for a defeated, displaced people.

Their fate owed little, however, to the famous events that began on North America's Atlantic coast. The American Revolution gave the world a new republic and cartographers new assignments. Much of what England had won through the Treaty of Paris in 1763 it lost in a second Treaty of Paris twenty years later. Its old colonies became a new nation, one that included nearly everything east of the Mississippi as part of the independent United States. The principal exceptions were the Florida peninsula and the Gulf Coast, which took a less direct route in becoming part of the new nation. England turned over these lands (everything south of the 31st parallel, between the Atlantic Ocean and the St. Croix River) to Spain. Spain thereby regained what its earlier alliance had cost and also, for a time, retained the principal prize that the original alliance had won: Louisiana.

In Oklahoma, though, the alliance that had a more immediate effect was not Spain's Family Compact but the Crown's commercial dealings with the Osages. Fiercely independent patrons of the Spanish merchants out of St. Louis, the Osages already had pushed beyond their Kansas and Missouri homelands and had driven the Wichitas from their villages along the Grand River and its tributaries. The relocation of a sizable band under the Osage chief Claremont to the Verdigris Valley (in present-day Rogers County) was merely one sign that most of northeastern Oklahoma was subject to Osage power. As the eighteenth century ended, Wichita influence ended, too—victim not of European rivalry or international war but of Osage raiding parties that swept over the Twin Villages, completed the devastation of the Wichitas, and struck terror deep into the Texas.

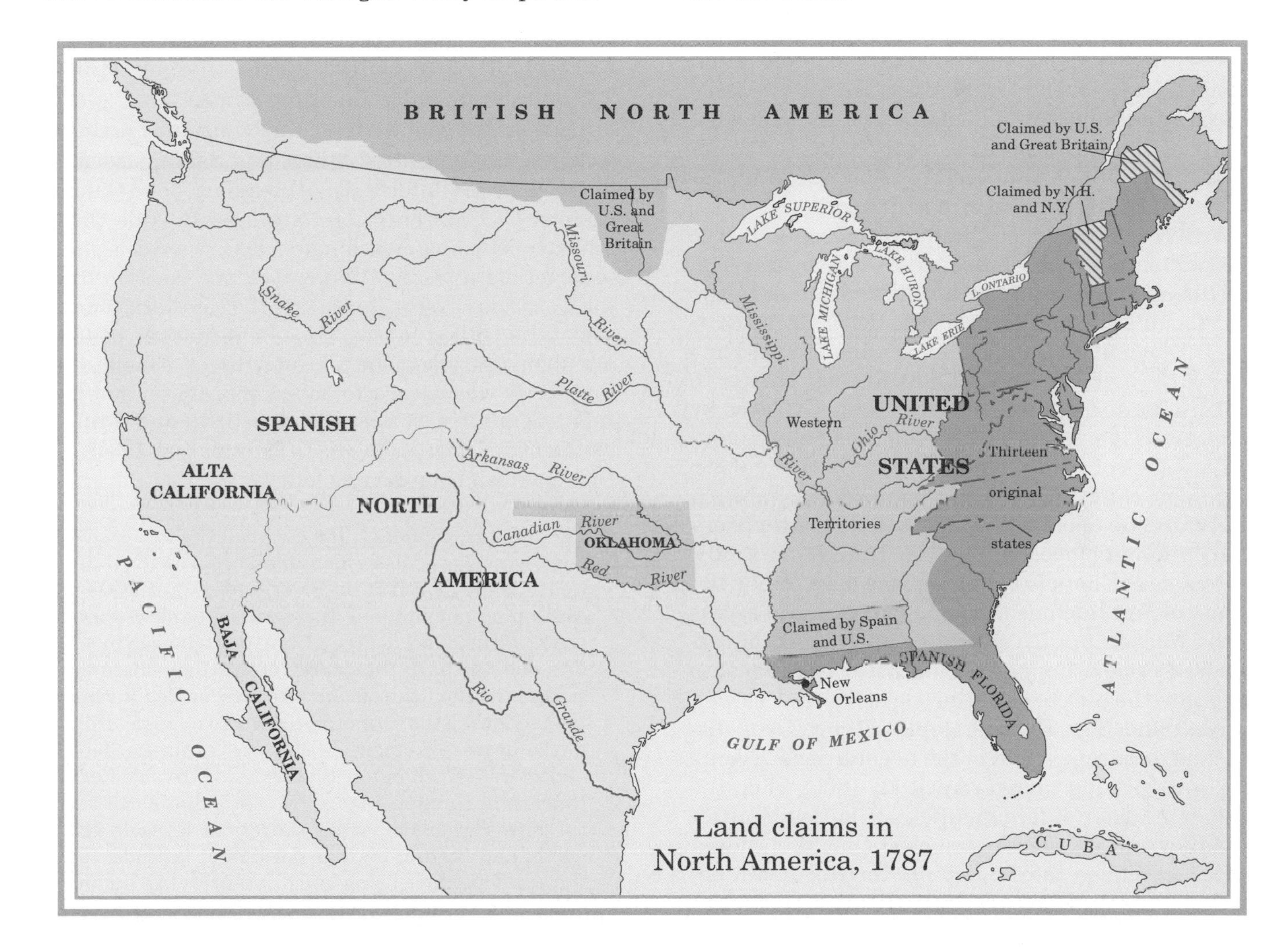

Land claims in North America, 1787

22. *THE LOUISIANA PURCHASE* Essay by *Bruce W. Hoagland*

Present-day Oklahoma's path to becoming part of the United States and ultimately to statehood began with the Louisiana Purchase, itself a product of the United States' desire for free access to the Mississippi River and the port of New Orleans. Such rights were ensured in 1795 when the United States and Spain signed the Treaty of San Lorenzo. The situation changed on October 1, 1800, when King Charles IV of Spain and Napoleon Bonaparte secretly signed the Treaty of San Ildefonso. This treaty ceded the Spanish territory of Louisiana to France in exchange for the northern Italian province of Etruria.

With this exchange of lands, Napoleon hoped to reestablish a French presence in North America, but his plan was foiled by a military defeat in the Caribbean and the threat of war with Great Britain. In November 1801, Napoleon dispatched Marshal V. E. Leclerc and 10,000 French troops to capture Santo Domingo, but they were defeated by Toussaint L'Ouverture's army of freed slaves and the ravishes of yellow fever. In light of this defeat, Napoleon came to view Louisiana as a liability. Therefore, he decided that the sale of the territory was a prudent move, both militarily and financially.

President Thomas Jefferson was alarmed by the Treaty of San Ildefonso. Anxious to maintain access to the Mississippi River and New Orleans, he authorized Robert Livingston, minister to France, to negotiate the purchase of the isle of Orleans as well as West and East Florida. James Monroe was dispatched to Europe to aid in the negotiations. Events took a surprising turn on April 11, 1803, when the French minister of foreign affairs, Charles-Maurice de Talleyrand-Périgord, proposed that the United States purchase the Louisiana Territory; two obstacles had to be overcome before the transaction was completed. First, in the Treaty of San de Ildefonso, France had agreed not to sell the territory of Louisiana, and second, whether President Jefferson had the constitutional authority to make the purchase was unclear. Regardless, France ceded its lands west of the Mississippi River to the United States for $15,000,000 on April 30, 1803. When loans and bonds were paid, the total expense reached $23,213,567. The United States thereby gained 830,000 square miles, doubling in size.

Because the boundaries of the Louisiana Purchase were vague, the United States and Spain needed to define their new international boundary. John Quincy Adams, U.S. secretary of state, and Luis de Onís, minister of Spain in Washington, D.C., were delegated to negotiate a treaty. Adams took the position that the Colorado River in Texas was the southern boundary of the United States. Onís held that the boundary should be along the Missouri River. Finally, the Red River was agreed to as a compromise, and the Adams-Onís Treaty was signed in 1819 and ratified by the U.S. Congress in 1821. The treaty defined the U.S.-Spanish boundary as follows:

> The western boundary line between the two countries, west of the Mississippi, shall begin on the Gulf Coast at the mouth of the river Sabine, in the sea, continuing north, along the western bank of that river, to the 32nd degree of latitude; thence, by a line due north, to the degree of latitude where it strikes the Rio Roxo of Natchitoches, or Red River; then following the course of the Rio Roxo westward, to the degree of longitude 100 west from London and 23 from Washington; then crossing the said Red River, and running thence by a line due north to the river Arkansas, to its source, in latitude 42 north; and thence, by that parallel of latitude, to the sea. The whole being laid down in Melish's map of the U.S. . . . all the islands of the Sabine, and the said Red and Arkansas rivers, throughout the course thus described, to belong to the U.S.; but the use of the waters, and the navigation of the Sabine to the sea, and of the said rivers Roxo and Arkansas, throughout the extent of said boundary, on their respective banks, shall be common to the respective inhabitants of both nations.

It might seem that the southern and western boundaries of Oklahoma were thus firmly delineated eighty-six years prior to statehood, but this was not the case. Although the Treaty of Adams-Onís called for the establishment of a joint boundary commission, a survey was never conducted. Nor were there surveys following Mexico's independence from Spain in 1821 or Texas independence in 1836, even though Congress ratified treaties recognizing the Adams-Onís line. When Texas was admitted to statehood in 1845, the Adams-Onís line was accepted but left unmarked, thus setting the scene for future boundary disputes between Oklahoma and Texas. The location of the 100th meridian would also be disputed by Oklahoma and Texas. Adams and Onís relied upon Philadelphia cartographer John Melish's map, published in 1818, which inaccurately located the 100th meridian.

Once established as part of the United States, the lands within the Louisiana Purchase underwent several jurisdictional changes. First, on March 3, 1804, the Louisiana Purchase was divided into the Territory of Orleans and the District of Louisiana, which included Oklahoma. Then, on March 3, 1805, the District of Louisiana became the Territory of Louisiana, with St. Louis as the territorial capital. On June 27, 1806, the District of Arkansas was subdivided from Louisiana Territory. Louisiana Territory became Missouri Territory on June 4, 1812. Finally, on March 2, 1819, Arkansas Territory was formed, including all of Oklahoma south of 36°30′ and east of the 100th meridian.

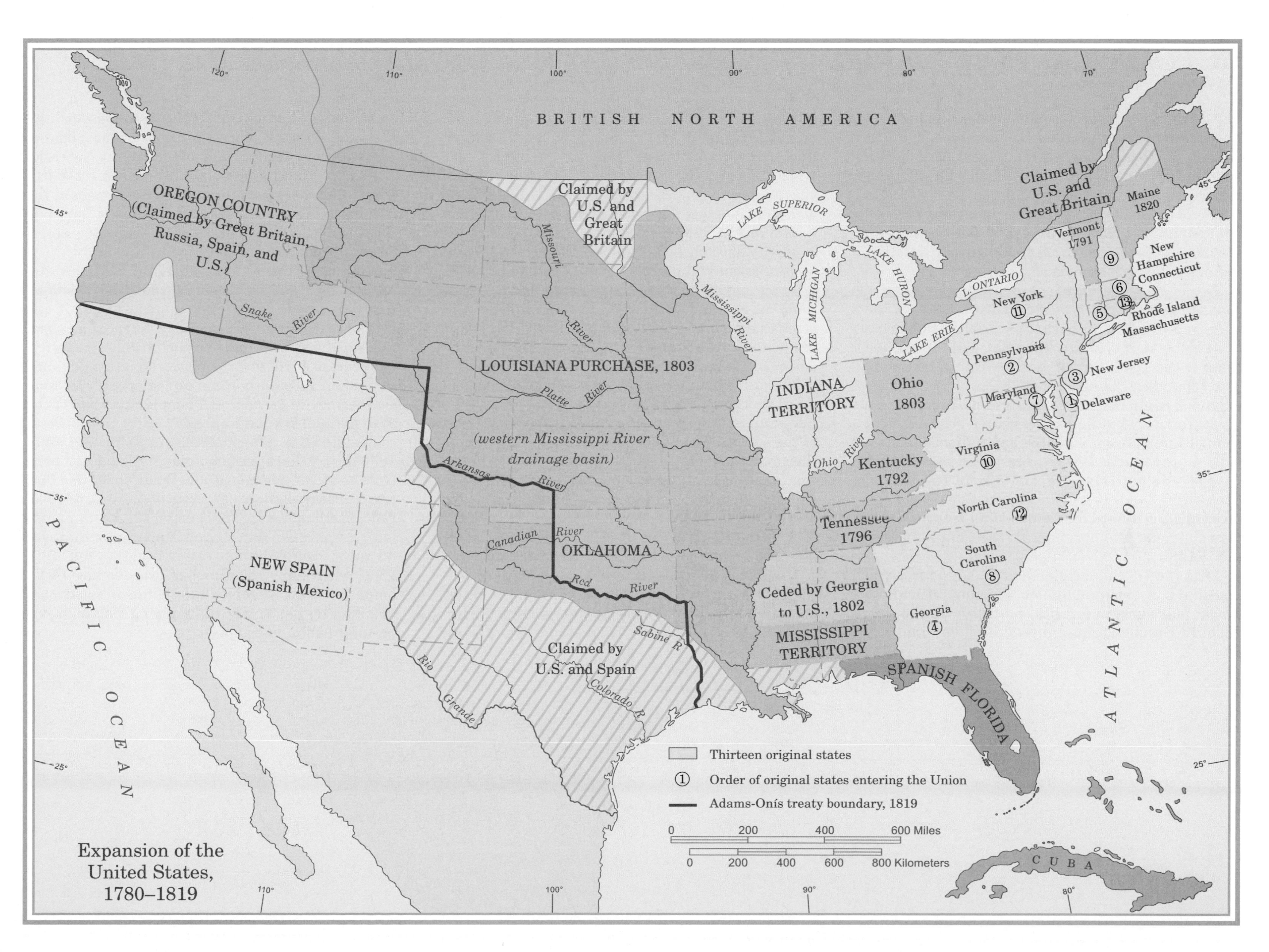

Expansion of the United States, 1780–1819

23. *POLITICAL BOUNDARIES OF PRESENT-DAY OKLAHOMA*

Essay by *Danney Goble*

The delineation of political boundaries involves two closely related but quite distinct processes. The first is high diplomacy: the negotiation of agreements whereby two or more political entities formally set the boundaries that separate them. The second is much more mundane: the physical marking of those boundaries by teams of surveyors. Both have been involved at every corner and along every line that defines today's Oklahoma.

Two of these borders long ago were boundaries separating some of the westernmost reaches of the vast French and Spanish empires. One, the Red River, is now the state's southern border with Texas; the other is the 100th meridian, the western boundary that separates Oklahoma from the Lone Star State's extended panhandle. The purchase of France's Louisiana Territory by the United States brought more than 531 million acres into the new nation, at a price of 22 cents per acre. It was quite a deal—except that no one was entirely sure just where the United States' new lands began and where Spain's old empire ended. Not until the Adams-Onís Treaty of 1819 was a serious attempt made to determine this minor detail.

That the 100th meridian should be the western boundary is easy enough to say but difficult to mark: four surveys put it at four different places. Richard Gannett required two full years and any number of astronomical triangulations and light beacons (Gannett surveyed only at night, rather than risk heat distortions from the daylight) to get it right. Then the U.S. Supreme Court took another year to decree, in 1930, that Gannett's placement was official, fixed, and permanent.

Similarly, the precise meaning of that Red River boundary has long been disputed. The river has done a lot of tossing and turning in its bed since 1819. When it moves, do some Oklahomans suddenly become Texans and vice versa? In fact, where is the river's bed, since the river forks about fifty miles east of the Texas panhandle? Which fork—the north one or the south one—is the main one?

These are neither hypothetical nor irrelevant questions. On the contrary, disputes over these questions have twice brought the two states before the bench of the U.S. Supreme Court and once even brought their respective forces of the National Guard to the edge of armed confrontation. After three years of negotiations, Texas and Oklahoma finally reached a settlement, their governors signing a formal compact of agreement. That was in 1999, a mere 180 years after the secretary and the minister had settled up.

Oklahoma's meandering eastern boundary is a product of several treaties between the United States and the Five Tribes, as well as being the by-product of several acts of Congress (particularly the statutes that brought Arkansas and Missouri into the union). Its straight-as-a-ruler northern boundary is also a by-product, first of the Kansas-Nebraska Act, then of the law making Kansas the thirty-fourth state. Both set the southern border of Kansas at the 37th parallel, which automatically made the same line the northern boundary of any state thereafter created beneath Kansas.

However, when Congress granted Kansas statehood in 1861 and set its southern border, Texas already had been a state for sixteen years. If one overlooks its declaration of independence as a separate republic, Texas had been in the union for thirty-one years in 1876, when Congress admitted Colorado as the thirty-eighth state and placed Colorado's southern boundary along a simple extension of the 37th parallel beyond Kansas.

Despite all that lawmaking and politicking, since 1850 the northernmost boundary of Texas had been fixed at 36°30′ north latitude. What, then, was that one-half degree of latitude south of Kansas and Colorado, north of Texas, and west of the 100th meridian? It was a No Man's Land. Apparently that was all anyone could think to call it. And they did, until 1890, when Congress attached it to the new Oklahoma Territory, thereby finally filling in some long-standing blanks and thereby giving Oklahoma its peculiar panhandle as well.

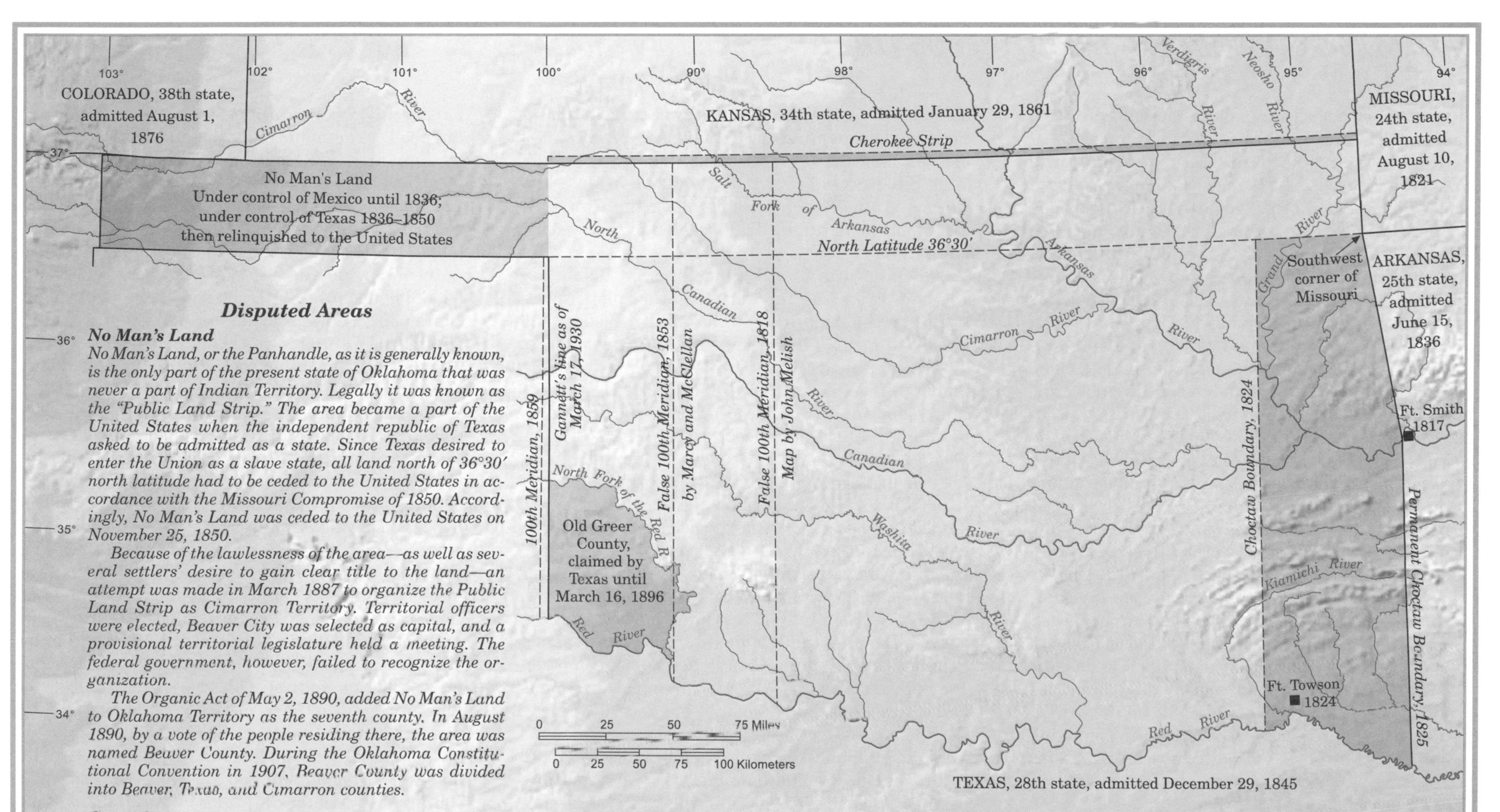

Disputed Areas

No Man's Land

No Man's Land, or the Panhandle, as it is generally known, is the only part of the present state of Oklahoma that was never a part of Indian Territory. Legally it was known as the "Public Land Strip." The area became a part of the United States when the independent republic of Texas asked to be admitted as a state. Since Texas desired to enter the Union as a slave state, all land north of 36°30′ north latitude had to be ceded to the United States in accordance with the Missouri Compromise of 1850. Accordingly, No Man's Land was ceded to the United States on November 25, 1850.

Because of the lawlessness of the area—as well as several settlers' desire to gain clear title to the land—an attempt was made in March 1887 to organize the Public Land Strip as Cimarron Territory. Territorial officers were elected, Beaver City was selected as capital, and a provisional territorial legislature held a meeting. The federal government, however, failed to recognize the organization.

The Organic Act of May 2, 1890, added No Man's Land to Oklahoma Territory as the seventh county. In August 1890, by a vote of the people residing there, the area was named Beaver County. During the Oklahoma Constitutional Convention in 1907, Beaver County was divided into Beaver, Texas, and Cimarron counties.

Greer County

This area was claimed by both Texas and the United States. On February 8, 1860, the Texas legislature created Greer County, Texas. Only a few families moved into the area, and it remained sparsely settled. No post office was established in Greer County until 1886. On March 16, 1896, the Supreme Court of the United States adjudged this area to be part of Indian Territory, and soon it was attached to Oklahoma Territory, organized as a county, and opened for settlement. Those who had previously settled in the area were permitted to retain their land.

During the Oklahoma Constitutional Convention in 1907, the area was subdivided into Beckham, Greer, and Jackson counties. After statehood, the part that had been designated Greer County was further divided to form Harmon County.

Choctaw-Arkansas Boundary

In 1824 an act of Congress fixed the western boundary of Arkansas Territory on a line forty miles west of the southwestern corner of Missouri and then due south to the Red River. The act was a clear violation of the Treaty of Doak's Stand of October 18, 1820. By the 1825 Treaty of Washington, the Choctaw Nation ceded to the United States all of its western land "lying east of a line beginning on the Arkansas, one hundred paces east of Fort Smith, and running thence due south to the Red River." President John Quincy Adams appointed James S. Conway to survey the new line. On November 8, 1825, the survey work began at Fort Smith; it was completed on December 7. The Conway line was inaccurate, as later surveys proved.

After many years of disagreement between the Choctaws and the State of Arkansas, Peter P. Pitchlynn of the Choctaw Nation obtained passage of an act of Congress authorizing a new survey in April and May 1877—not for the purpose of recovering land for the Choctaws but as a basis for payment of damages. According to the survey of 1877, the boundary established in 1825 crossed the Red River west of the treaty line by over four miles and deprived the Choctaws of 136,204 acres. The tribe was paid $68,102 for land given to Arkansas in error. However, of the sum awarded to the Choctaws, 30 percent was taken for attorney fees and 20 percent to pay the expenses of the Pitchlynn delegation.

24. AMERICAN EXPLORERS, 1806–1821

Essay by *Bruce W. Hoagland*

In the aftermath of the Louisiana Purchase in 1803, President Thomas Jefferson commissioned Meriwether Lewis and William Clark to explore the northwestern areas of this new land. After their return, he dispatched other government expeditions into the southwestern areas of the Louisiana Purchase. Other explorers also traveled through this southern region. Some were lured by prospective markets in the Spanish lands to the southwest, particularly Santa Fe in northern New Spain, even though Americans could not legally trade in the region until after Mexican independence in 1821. One of the most unusual and valuable expeditions of this time was a privately supported scientific exploration by the English botanist Thomas Nuttall. The maps, journals, and scientific specimens compiled by all of these explorers provide a valuable glimpse of early Oklahoma.

In June 1806, First Lieutenant Zebulon M. Pike, accompanied by First Lieutenant James B. Wilkinson, was commanded to find the headwaters of the Arkansas River. After proceeding up the Missouri River to the Osage Villages, the party marched westward to the Great Bend of the Arkansas River in Kansas; then the command was split. Pike led one group westward upstream, while Wilkinson led the second in a southeasterly direction down the Arkansas River to the Mississippi. Wilkinson's command was immediately beset with difficulties. He and his men struggled through harsh winter conditions, arriving at the camp of Big Track, an Osage chief, near present-day Muskogee, on December 23. Wilkinson cultivated friendly relations with the chief, who offered the government a tract of land between the Verdigris and Grand rivers for construction of a fur-trading post.

On May 11, 1811, Colonel George C. Sibley and his traveling party left Fort Osage on the Missouri River in search of a rumored mountain of salt. In late June they reached the Grand Saline or Great Salt Plains; from there, they proceeded to explore the Gypsum Hills. Collecting many geological specimens in the region, the men of Sibley's party, which included several Osage guides, were continuously concerned about attack by Comanches, and after two months in the field they returned to Fort Osage. Years later, Sibley would return to Oklahoma in 1825 as a survey commissioner, passing along the Cimarron Cut-off of the Santa Fe Trail, located in the western Panhandle.

Thomas Nuttall left Philadelphia on October 2, 1818, for Arkansas Territory to gather plant specimens for the American Philosophical Society; he arrived at Fort Smith on April 24, 1819. From there, he accompanied Major William Bradford of Fort Smith to the Kiamichi and Red rivers. Nuttall became separated from Bradford but continued his mission to collect botanical specimens. He eventually fell in with some new traveling companions and returned safely to Fort Smith in late June.

On July 6, Nuttall left Fort Smith with a trapper named Lee. His intent was to reach the Rocky Mountains, but illness, insects, and the threat of hostile Indians led Nuttall to abbreviate his plans. After baggage and provisions were lost in an Osage raid, Nuttall returned to Bogy's trading post on September 14. Despite another bout of fever, he reached Fort Smith on September 25, then departed on November 9 for New Orleans. His botanical specimens and notes have left a compelling record of early Oklahoma.

Major Stephen Harriman Long made two visits to present-day Oklahoma. In 1817, he was dispatched to intervene in a conflict between the Osages and Cherokees and to search for a suitable location for a fort on the Arkansas River. From a point on the Red River, he followed the Kiamichi and Poteau rivers to the confluence of the Poteau and Arkansas rivers, which he named Belle Point and where he chose a site for a fort that he named Fort Smith after his commander, General Thomas A. Smith.

In 1820, Long was ordered to find the source of the Platte, Arkansas, and Red rivers. He was accompanied by Edwin James, a botanist; Thomas Say, a zoologist; and Samuel Seymour, an artist. The expedition failed to discover the source of the Arkansas River, so on July 24, in frustration, Long divided his command, sending one contingent—led by Captain John R. Bell—down the Arkansas, while he struck out for the Red River, to the south. Bell's Arkansas River contingent entered Oklahoma on August 19 and was soon beset by privation and exhaustion. Three deserters took valuable scientific notebooks and the party's best horses. After a friendly encounter with the son of the Osage chief Claremont, Bell proceeded to Hugh Glenn's trading post on the Verdigris River and reached Fort Smith a few days later, after spending a night at Bean's saltworks.

Meanwhile, Long's command was following the Canadian River, which he mistook for the Red River. They crossed into Oklahoma on August 18; by the time the men entered central Oklahoma, they were running low of food and water and found themselves bedeviled by ticks and other insects. When Long reached the Arkansas on September 10, he realized that he was not on the Red River, and by the time he arrived at Fort Smith on September 13, he had come to consider the expedition a failure. However, his group did succeed in producing accurate maps of the region and gathering many scientific specimens. The expedition would be remembered for Long's use of the phrase "Great American Desert" to describe the climate of the Great Plains.

Thomas James and his partner, John McKnight, led a civilian expedition up the Arkansas and Cimarron rivers for Santa Fe in May 1821, taking trade goods. They traveled across the Great Salt Plains and through the "shining mountains," or gypsum hills. The party became embroiled in a rivalry between two Comanche chiefs but was rescued by Spanish military scouts and escorted to Santa Fe. On his return, James followed the Arkansas River, joining the Fowler-Glenn party for safety. After the two groups separated, several of James's best horses and mules were stolen by Osage warriors, resulting in the expedition's returning home in July 1822 as a financial failure. Undaunted by their lack of success, James and McKnight set out in 1823 to trade

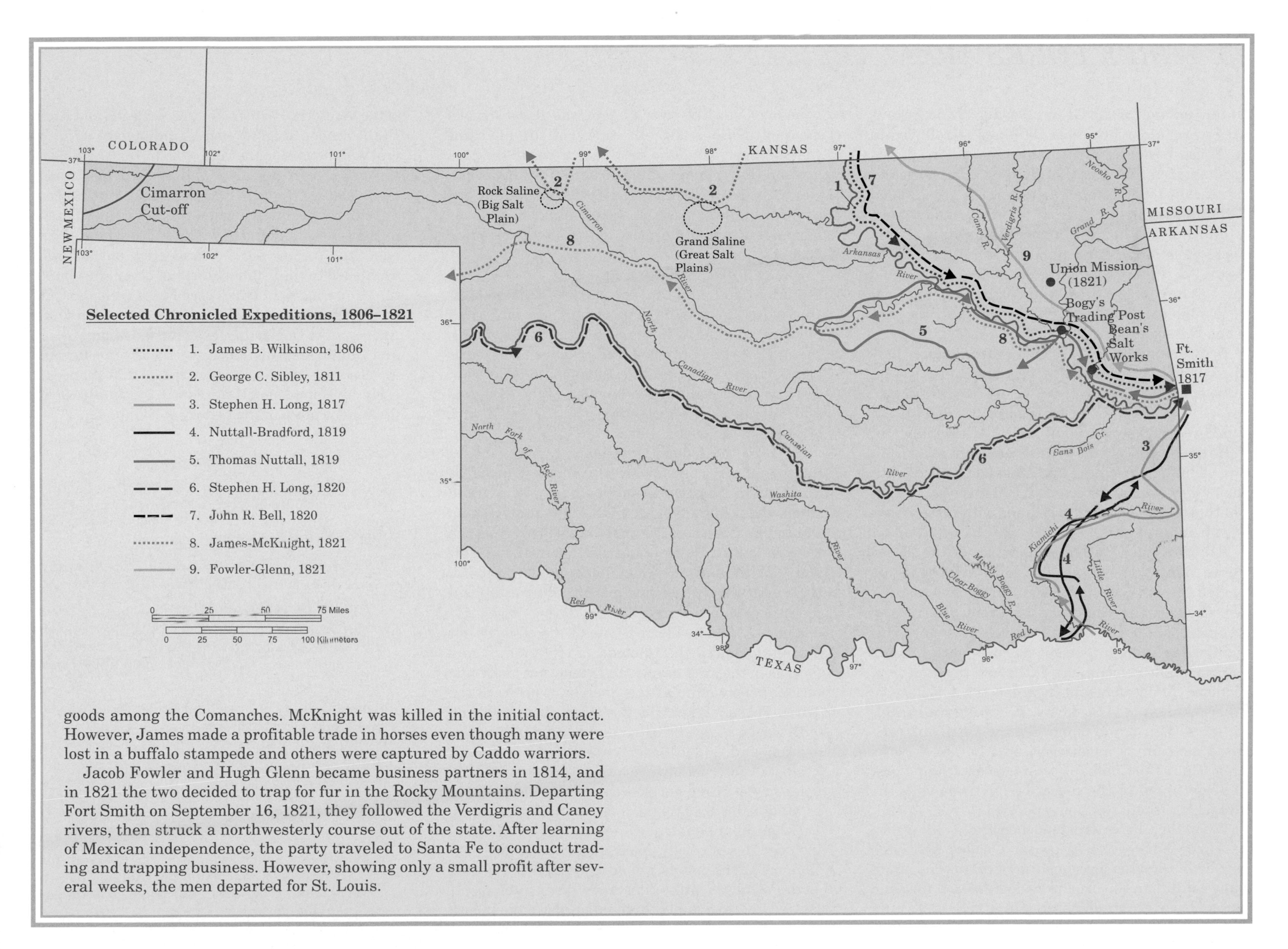

goods among the Comanches. McKnight was killed in the initial contact. However, James made a profitable trade in horses even though many were lost in a buffalo stampede and others were captured by Caddo warriors.

Jacob Fowler and Hugh Glenn became business partners in 1814, and in 1821 the two decided to trap for fur in the Rocky Mountains. Departing Fort Smith on September 16, 1821, they followed the Verdigris and Caney rivers, then struck a northwesterly course out of the state. After learning of Mexican independence, the party traveled to Santa Fe to conduct trading and trapping business. However, showing only a small profit after several weeks, the men departed for St. Louis.

25. THREE FORKS AREA

Essay by *John R. Lovett*

At the junction of the Grand, Verdigris and Arkansas rivers in northeastern Oklahoma—referred to as Three Forks by most historians—there developed an area that was distinctive and historically significant to Oklahoma history. This area played a prominent role in the early fur-trade industry. In later days, within a few miles' radius of the Three Forks junction, a concentration of military posts as well as Indian agencies, missions, and schools came to have a significant impact on the historical development of not only Oklahoma but also the trans-Mississippi West.

In late summer of 1719, the French explorer Bernard de la Harpe set out with a small group from his post on the Red River to explore northward into present-day Oklahoma. On September 3, 1719, in the Three Forks area, south of the Arkansas River, la Harpe held a council with several thousand Indians, including Wichitas and Tawakonis along with their allies. La Harpe recorded in his expedition journal that he presented the Indians with fifteen hundred pounds of gifts.

Following la Harpe's exploration of the Three Forks country, French traders and fur trappers exploited the area as they sought furs and skins. For two decades the Chouteau brothers, Pierre and Auguste, of St. Louis held a fur-trade monopoly with the Osages living in present-day Missouri. In 1802 the Spanish government withdrew the brothers' monopoly, however, and awarded the privilege to other merchants of St. Louis. Following the cancellation of their trade monopoly, the Choteaus relocated their fur-trade enterprise to the Three Forks area. There the Choteaus established a trading post and continued in the lucrative fur trade with the Osages—without Spanish approval.

When the Choteaus established their trading post at Three Forks, the Arkansas Osages had been settled in the area for some thirty years. The abundant wildlife in the area provided the rich furs and skins that were in demand within U.S. and European markets. The river system was also a key element of the Choteaus' fur trade. The fur and skins were shipped down the Arkansas River to the Mississippi River, then to the markets of St. Louis and New Orleans. In addition, the river systems provided a water highway from St. Louis and New Orleans for the return of trade goods to the Choteau trading post at Three Forks.

Following the Louisiana Purchase, Americans in the fur trade found the Three Forks region an attractive locale, with its large Indian population and plentiful wildlife. As in the case of the Choteau post, the river system provided water routes to the eastern markets. Fort Smith, established in the fall of 1817 on Belle Point at the junction of the Arkansas and Poteau rivers, supported the fur trade with goods from the post sutler.

In 1824 the federal government established a nearby military presence with the construction of Fort Gibson. Located on the east bank of the Grand River, the post had as its mission the protection of the Indian tribes that were to be removed from the eastern United States and resettled in Indian Territory. With military protection from Fort Gibson, the Three Forks area saw more trading establishments locate to the area.

Colonel Auguste Pierre Choteau, son of the trader Pierre, advanced the Choteau family interest and fortune in the area to such an extent that many historians refer to him as the "merchant prince of the Three Forks." Fluent in the Osage language and with Osage wives, he expanded the fur-trading operation and added other enterprises, including keelboat construction. With the decrease in the fur trade in the Three Forks area, he was successful in expanding his trading business to the Plains tribes.

Other prominent traders in the Three Forks area included Joseph Bogy, Nathaniel Pryor, and Hugh Glenn. The trading post of Joseph Bogy was located on the Verdigris, with Glenn and Pryor's trading post located approximately three miles above the mouth of the Verdigris. Partners George W. Brand and Henry Barbour opened an extensive trading post with several warehouses on the Verdigris. In 1829 Sam Houston arrived in the area and opened his trading post—called "Wigwam Neosho"—near Fort Gibson.

With the decline in availability of fur (attributable to the general decline of wildlife throughout the region), the trading posts disappeared, but historical events led to the establishment of other sites important to the history of the Three Forks area and Oklahoma. These include the Creek Agency, the Osage Agency, Fort Davis, the Texas Road, Union Mission, and Tullahassee Mission. Nevertheless, the fur-trading posts and the adventurer-traders that shaped the early development of the area will continue to hold a prominent place in the history of Oklahoma.

Localities

1. La Harpe's council: French explorer Jean-Baptiste Bernard, sieur de la Harpe, arrived in the Three Forks area in September 1719. He established a post and held a peace council with Wichitas and Tawakonis.

2. French Point: Location where French traders from Arkansas Post traded with the Tawakonis.

3. Chouteau Trading Post: Established ca. 1802 by the Chouteau brothers. The post was operational until 1807–1808. Auguste Pierre Chouteau reestablished the Chouteau family interest in the Three Forks area in 1817.

4. Joseph Bogy, a French fur trader, established a river landing and trading post on the Verdigris River in 1807 and traded extensively with the Osages.

5. Auguste Pierre Chouteau's farm.

6. Glenn and Pryor Trading Post: Established 1819, operated for 3 years. Pryor was a member of the Lewis and Clark expedition.

7. Ft. Gibson: Established April 20, 1824, with the primary mission of controlling the Osages. The sutler at Ft. Gibson provided some supplies to the fur traders in the Three Forks area.

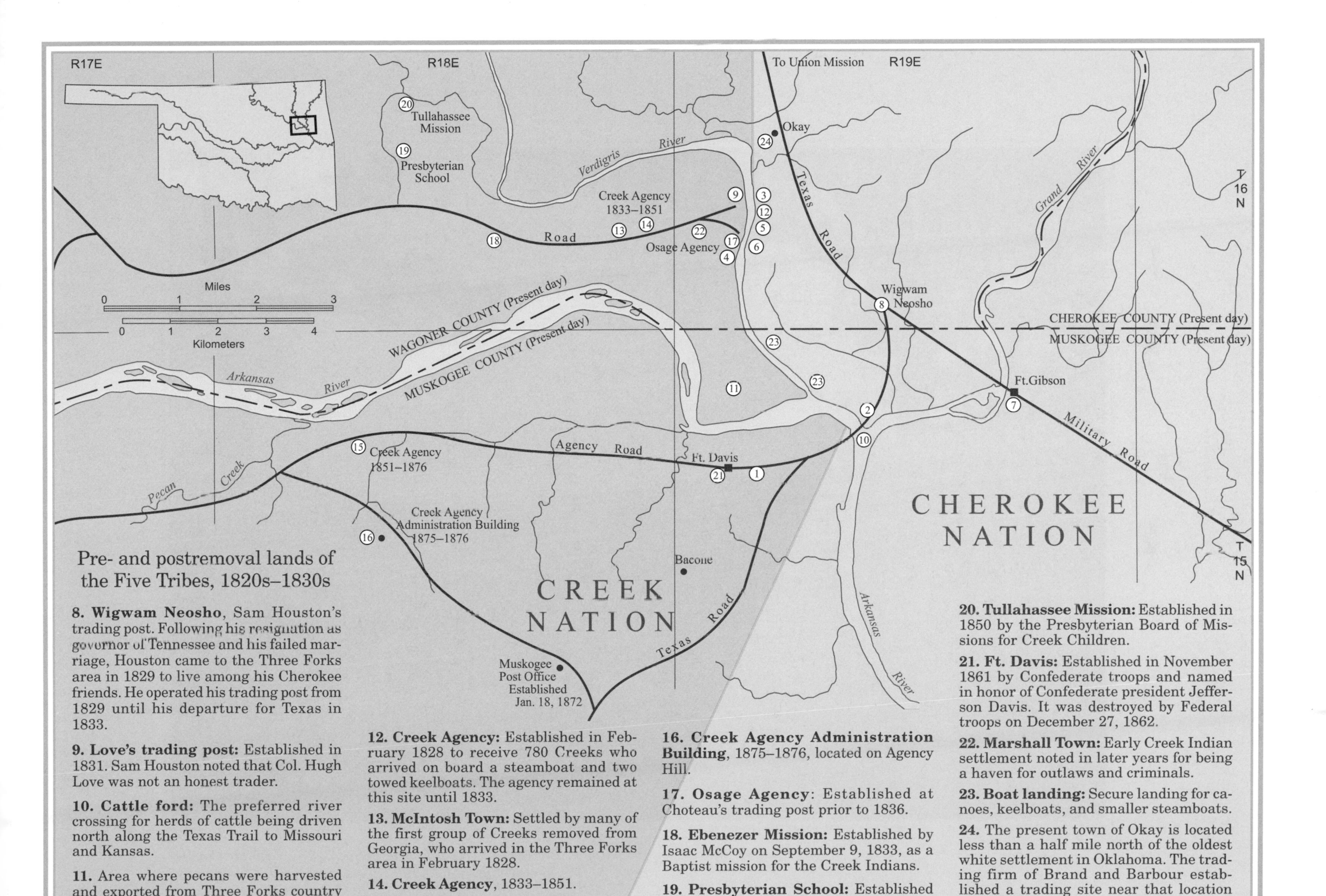

R17E
R18E
R19E
To Union Mission
Tullahassee Mission
Presbyterian School
Verdigris River
Okay
Texas Road
Creek Agency 1833–1851
Road
Osage Agency
Miles
Kilometers
Wigwam Neosho
CHEROKEE COUNTY (Present day)
MUSKOGEE COUNTY (Present day)
WAGONER COUNTY (Present day)
MUSKOGEE COUNTY (Present day)
Arkansas River
Grand River
T 16 N
T 15 N
Ft.Gibson
Military Road
Agency Road
Ft. Davis
Creek Agency 1851–1876
Pecan Creek
Creek Agency Administration Building 1875–1876
Bacone
CREEK NATION
CHEROKEE NATION
Muskogee Post Office Established Jan. 18, 1872
Texas Road
Arkansas River
Pre- and postremoval lands of the Five Tribes, 1820s–1830s
8. Wigwam Neosho, Sam Houston's trading post. Following his resignation as governor of Tennessee and his failed marriage, Houston came to the Three Forks area in 1829 to live among his Cherokee friends. He operated his trading post from 1829 until his departure for Texas in 1833.
9. Love's trading post: Established in 1831. Sam Houston noted that Col. Hugh Love was not an honest trader.
10. Cattle ford: The preferred river crossing for herds of cattle being driven north along the Texas Trail to Missouri and Kansas.
11. Area where pecans were harvested and exported from Three Forks country by the local traders.
12. Creek Agency: Established in February 1828 to receive 780 Creeks who arrived on board a steamboat and two towed keelboats. The agency remained at this site until 1833.
13. McIntosh Town: Settled by many of the first group of Creeks removed from Georgia, who arrived in the Three Forks area in February 1828.
14. Creek Agency, 1833–1851.
15. Creek Agency, 1851–1876.
16. Creek Agency Administration Building, 1875–1876, located on Agency Hill.
17. Osage Agency: Established at Choteau's trading post prior to 1836.
18. Ebenezer Mission: Established by Isaac McCoy on September 9, 1833, as a Baptist mission for the Creek Indians.
19. Presbyterian School: Established in 1831.
20. Tullahassee Mission: Established in 1850 by the Presbyterian Board of Missions for Creek Children.
21. Ft. Davis: Established in November 1861 by Confederate troops and named in honor of Confederate president Jefferson Davis. It was destroyed by Federal troops on December 27, 1862.
22. Marshall Town: Early Creek Indian settlement noted in later years for being a haven for outlaws and criminals.
23. Boat landing: Secure landing for canoes, keelboats, and smaller steamboats.
24. The present town of Okay is located less than a half mile north of the oldest white settlement in Oklahoma. The trading firm of Brand and Barbour established a trading site near that location before 1819.

Winding Stair Mountain National Recreation Area, Talimena Scenic Byway, Le Flore County.
(Photograph by John Elk III, courtesy of Elk Photography)

Part III

Oklahoma as Native America

Choctaw lighthorsemen at Antlers, Choctaw Nation, Indian Territory, 1893. (Courtesy Western History Collections, University of Oklahoma Libraries)

26. THE FIVE TRIBES OF THE SOUTHEASTERN UNITED STATES

Essay by *Michael D. Green*

The concept of the "Five Civilized Tribes" has been an important interpretive tool for students of the history of Indian Territory and Oklahoma. But it is an ethnocentric idea that is no longer meaningful. When the Europeans first began to explore and occupy North America, they were impressed by their discoveries that American Indians looked and lived much differently than did the European newcomers. As they tried to describe and categorize Native people, they used terms and ideas that reflected these obvious differences, but the standard by which they measured the differences was their own appearance and manner of living. It was easy, perhaps natural, for the Europeans to conclude that the differences were actually failures and that Native cultures were thus inferior to their own. From these conclusions came terms such as "savage" and "civilized": Europeans defined themselves as civilized and Indians as uncivilized or savage.

However, many Europeans and Anglo-Americans believed that the Indians could be guided from their savage condition to civilization. Some emphasized education and training, others believed that the goal could be achieved only through God's grace, and most thought that some combination of the two would be necessary, but—by whatever means—these would-be civilizers agreed that American Indians were not intellectually inferior and thus not doomed by race to remain forever uncivilized. Beginning in the early seventeenth century, for example, English colonists in Virginia developed a plan for the education of Native youths. Other plans followed, and by the end of the eighteenth century, some religious groups had established organized systems for missionary outreach. The U.S. government supported these efforts and encouraged the formation of additional civilizing agencies; beginning in 1819, Congress appropriated a $10,000 annual subsidy for Indian missions.

Missionaries and other Americans differed on the definition of civilization, at least in detail, but certain broad attributes seemed clear. Civilized Indian societies should be patterned after Anglo-American rural society in which the men were farmers and stock raisers and the women cooked, cleaned the house, wove cloth, and made clothes. They should live in houses as families, work their own land, attend a Christian church, and send their children to school. They should, in other words, be as much like Anglo-Americans in their appearance, way of life, and manner of belief as possible.

When the Indian nations of the U.S. Southeast were removed to the West in the 1820s and 1830s, they had been closely exposed to Anglo-American culture for a century and a half, and their cultures had changed dramatically. Already agriculturalists, they had become important in an international market economy by virtue of their trade in deerskins and slaves in exchange for manufactured goods. Prolonged contact with traders, including widespread intermarriage, introduced European culture in the most personal and intimate ways into Indian communities. Missionaries with schools and churches simply made decades of intercultural contact more formal and systematic. The immigrants to Indian Territory had by no means ceased to be Indians, but they were very different from what their ancestors had been, and the changes had made them more like Anglo-Americans. According to nineteenth-century thinking, they were becoming civilized. They were also very different from the nomadic, buffalo-hunting, teepee-dwelling Indians encountered on the plains. Anglo-Americans, still measuring Indian cultures by the standard of their own, continued to believe that the Southeastern refugees needed civilizing, but to distinguish them from the Plains Indians, the government began to refer to them as civilized. Thus, after removal, the Cherokees, Creeks, Choctaws, Chickasaws, and Seminoles became the "Five Civilized Tribes" of Indian Territory.

The problem with using such ethnocentric terminology is that it perpetuates the idea that there is only one civilization—that of Anglo-America—and those societies that do not embrace Anglo-American culture are therefore not civilized. Scholars now realize that concepts such as "civilized" and "savage" are relative, not absolute. They cannot describe the people to whom they are applied; they can only describe the attitudes and biases of the people who use them.

The Trail of Tears, *by Jerome Tiger. (Oklahoma Indian Art Gallery, courtesy of Peggy Tiger)*

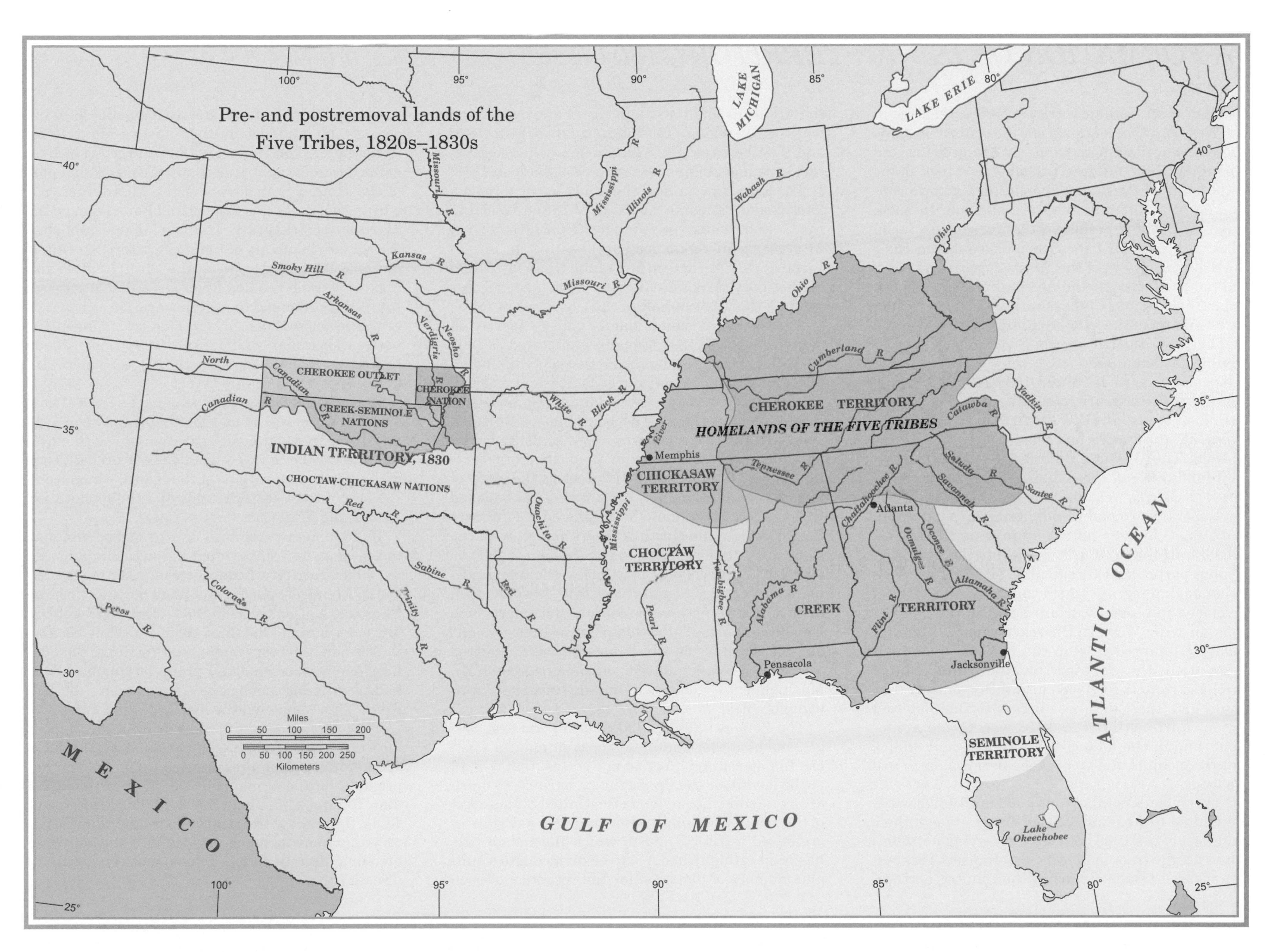

Pre- and postremoval lands of the
Five Tribes, 1820s–1830s
LAKE MICHIGAN
LAKE ERIE
CHEROKEE OUTLET
CHEROKEE NATION
CREEK-SEMINOLE NATIONS
INDIAN TERRITORY, 1830
CHOCTAW-CHICKASAW NATIONS
CHEROKEE TERRITORY
HOMELANDS OF THE FIVE TRIBES
Memphis
CHICKASAW TERRITORY
CHOCTAW TERRITORY
CREEK
TERRITORY
Atlanta
Pensacola
Jacksonville
SEMINOLE TERRITORY
Lake Okeechobee
ATLANTIC OCEAN
GULF OF MEXICO
MEXICO
Missouri R
Mississippi R
Illinois R
Wabash R
Ohio R
Kansas R
Smoky Hill R
Arkansas R
Verdigris R
Neosho R
North Canadian R
Canadian R
Cumberland R
White R
Black R
River
Tennessee R
Catawba R
Yadkin R
Saluda R
Savannah R
Santee R
Chattahoochee R
Ocmulgee R
Oconee R
Altamaha R
Flint R
Alabama R
Tombigbee R
Pearl R
Ouachita R
Red R
Sabine R
Trinity R
Colorado R
Pecos R
Miles
0 50 100 150 200
0 50 100 150 200 250
Kilometers
100°
95°
90°
85°
80°
40°
35°
30°
25°

27. *FORMATION OF INDIAN TERRITORY, 1804–1855* Essay by *Michael D. Green*

The idea of an "Indian Territory," a special place in the West for the colonization of eastern Indians evicted from their homelands by the growing and expanding United States, probably first took shape in the mind of President Thomas Jefferson in conjunction with the purchase of Louisiana. In 1804, Congress granted Jefferson the authority to open talks with eastern tribes about exchanging their lands for tracts west of the Mississippi. Already several bands of eastern Indians had made the move. Some Choctaw and Chickasaw groups lived west of the river, and in the 1790s a group of Cherokees led by The Bowl settled on the St. Francis River in present-day Arkansas.

Negotiations in 1808 and 1817 resulted in further Cherokee migrations to Arkansas. There they settled on lands between the Arkansas and White rivers that the Osages had sold to the United States in 1808. The Western Cherokees secured title to their lands in 1817. The Cherokees' western neighbors, the Osages, resented the expansionism of the newcomers' large and rapidly growing population. The Osages found Cherokee forays up the Arkansas, Grand, and Verdigris rivers into their hunting grounds particularly threatening, and their warriors defended that territory. Attacks and counterattacks developed into open warfare between the two nations. In 1816, Western Cherokee agent William L. Lovely attempted to stop the hostilities through negotiation. He proposed that the United States purchase from the Osages a "hunting outlet" that would give the Cherokees access to the disputed region. Further talks in 1818 won Osage agreement, and in the following year, President James Monroe granted the Cherokees permission to use the tract.

Nevertheless, conflict continued until 1825, when the United States induced the Osages to sell their land west of the 1808 boundary, reserving for themselves a large tract in present-day Kansas. This cession cleared Osage claims to the country north of the Arkansas and Canadian rivers and opened the way for the region's cession to the Creeks in 1826 and the Cherokees in 1828. The new Cherokee Nation encompassed the Osage cession made in 1818.

The Quapaws claimed the lands south of the Arkansas and Canadian rivers. In 1818 they sold it to the United States, reserving for themselves a tract in present-day Arkansas southeast of the site of Little Rock. The eastern half of the Quapaw cession became part of Arkansas Territory; the United States granted the western half to the Choctaws in 1820.

No systematic federal plan or policy underlay all of this activity. In 1817, Congress reiterated its 1808 authorization of presidential discussions with Indian tribes on the subjects of land exchange and removal, but neither Secretary of War John C. Calhoun nor President James Monroe declared himself satisfied. They sought finite congressional legislation not only for removal but also for the formal organization of an "Indian Territory" west of the state of Missouri and territory of Arkansas. They believed that the territory should be organized according to the formula of the Northwest Ordinance, with the same institutions of law and government that characterized other federal territories, including ultimate entry into the union as a state. Despite much favorable interest, Congress did not enact such legislation. In 1827, President John Quincy Adams and his secretary of war, James Barbour, repeated Monroe's recommendation, again unsuccessfully. Meanwhile, the creation of Indian Territory continued piecemeal.

The Removal Act of 1830 contains the first congressional authorization for the creation of a western Indian country. Section one states "that it shall . . . be lawful for the President . . . to cause so much of any territory belonging to the United States, west of the river Mississippi, not included in any state or organized territory, and to which the Indian title has been extinguished, . . . to be divided into a suitable number of districts, for the reception of such tribes or nations of Indians as may choose to exchange the lands where they now reside, and remove there." The Trade and Intercourse Act of 1834 defined Indian country more specifically as that part of the United States west of the Mississippi "not within the states of Missouri and Louisiana, or the Territory of Arkansas." This language established the eastern boundary of Indian Territory. The international boundary between the United States and Mexico marked the Red River as Indian Territory's southern border and the 100th meridian as its western. The 1854 Kansas-Nebraska Act changed the northern boundary of Indian Territory from Canada to Kansas. Thus, little by little, piece by piece, Indian Territory came into being.

In the same drawn-out fashion, the federal government's removal policy took shape. Between 1830 and 1835, under the authorization of the Removal Act, the United States concluded treaties with each of the five Indian nations of the South, which led to the loss of their eastern lands and their relocation west of the Arkansas.

In 1833, as the removal crisis reached a climax in the East, two other refugee groups found homes in Indian Territory. Federal commissioners located a mixed band of Senecas and Shawnees north of the Cherokee Nation between the Grand River and the Missouri border. North of them, in what became the far northeast corner of Indian Territory, the commissioners placed a small group of Quapaws who had been living among the Caddos along the Red River. This completed the map of Indian Territory.

The plan for some form of centralized government for the territory remained alive. In 1834, the Jackson administration presented to Congress another proposal for the formal political organization of Indian Territory, but again the lawmakers rejected it. Thus, throughout the removal period, Indian Territory remained as much an idea as a formally created and discrete place—indeed, more an idea than a reality.

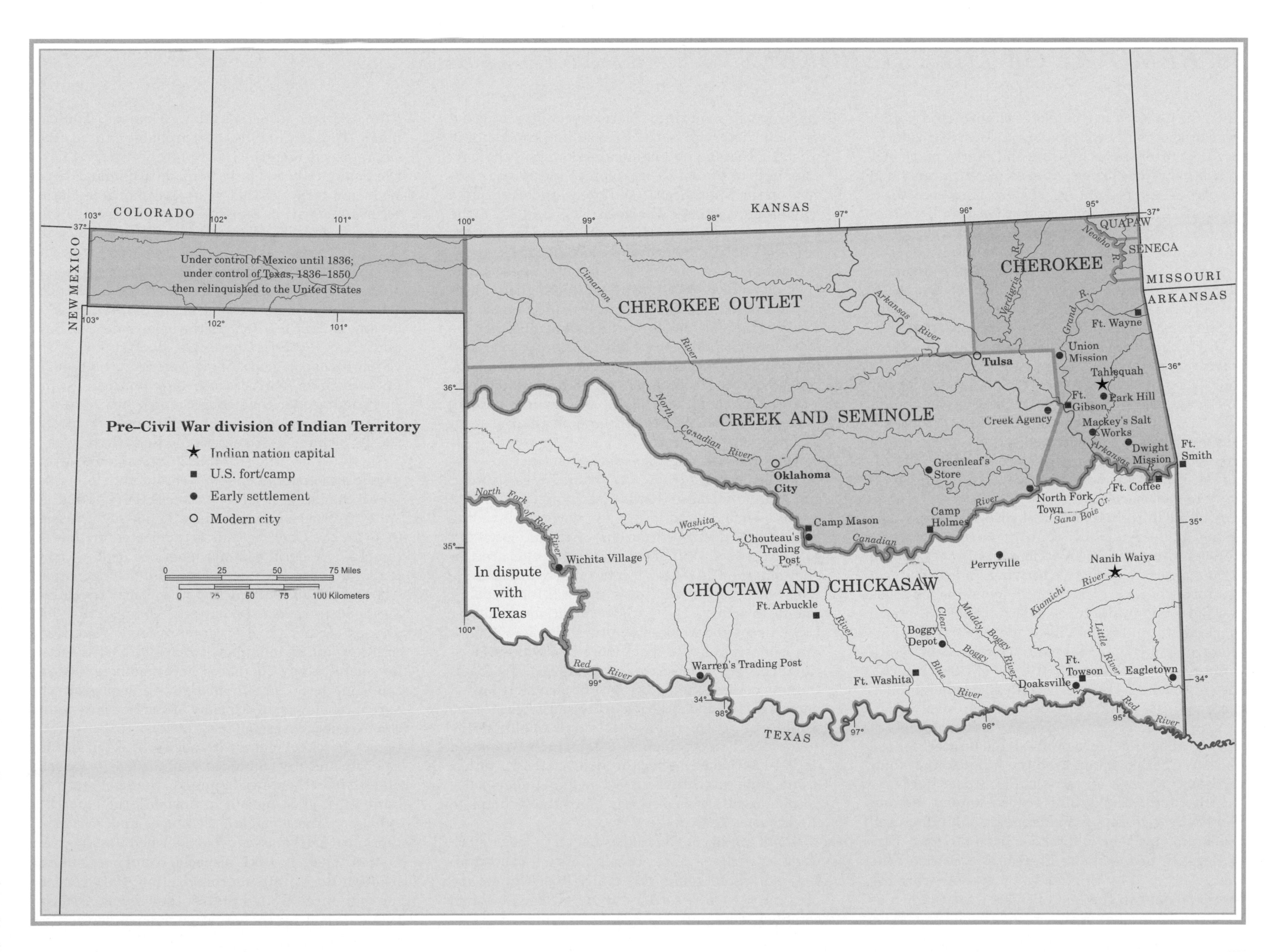

COLORADO
KANSAS
NEW MEXICO
MISSOURI
ARKANSAS
TEXAS
QUAPAW
SENECA
CHEROKEE
CHEROKEE OUTLET
CREEK AND SEMINOLE
CHOCTAW AND CHICKASAW
Under control of Mexico until 1836; under control of Texas, 1836–1850 then relinquished to the United States
In dispute with Texas
Pre–Civil War division of Indian Territory
Indian nation capital
U.S. fort/camp
Early settlement
Modern city
0 25 50 75 Miles
0 25 50 75 100 Kilometers
Tulsa
Oklahoma City
Ft. Wayne
Union Mission
Tahlequah
Park Hill
Ft. Gibson
Creek Agency
Mackey's Salt Works
Dwight Mission
Ft. Smith
Ft. Coffee
Greenleaf's Store
North Fork Town
Camp Mason
Camp Holmes
Chouteau's Trading Post
Wichita Village
Perryville
Nanih Waiya
Ft. Arbuckle
Boggy Depot
Warren's Trading Post
Ft. Washita
Ft. Towson
Doaksville
Eagletown
Cimarron River
Arkansas River
North Canadian River
Canadian River
Washita River
North Fork of Red River
Red River
Verdigris R.
Neosho R.
Grand R.
Sans Bois Cr.
Kiamichi River
Little River
Clear Boggy
Muddy Boggy River
Blue River

28. REMOVAL OF THE CHEROKEES

Essay by *Michael D. Green & Danney Goble*

Until the 1830s, the Cherokees claimed and used a large area of southern Appalachia. Most of this territory they reserved for hunting and shared much of it with other tribes. Their villages were concentrated in a core area in present-day eastern Tennessee, western North Carolina, and northern Georgia. This rugged mountainous country with its lush river valleys was beautiful and secure but difficult to traverse, a factor that encouraged the development of regional clusters of towns in the eastern, central, and western portions of the core.

The Cherokee population may have been as high as thirty thousand in the sixteenth century, but exposure to contagious European diseases such as smallpox and measles led to terrible rates of illness and death and a steady decline in Cherokee numbers. The Cherokees were agriculturalists, hunters, and gatherers who depended largely on corn and deer for their food. They therefore selected their village sites with an eye on both soil fertility and proximity to deer herds.

After an initial exploration by English Virginians in the mid-seventeenth century, ongoing contacts were mainly motivated by economics. By the middle of the eighteenth century, a thriving trade had grown in which Cherokees exchanged deerskins for goods of English manufacture, especially cloth, metal implements, and guns. This trade, along with a parallel trade in Indian war captives sold in the South Carolina slave markets, left little of Cherokee culture untouched. Desire for trade goods heightened the emphasis on hunting deer, which involved increasing numbers of hunters for longer periods of time. Transformed into professional hunters for the market, Cherokee men used the full extent of their territory in search of ever-shrinking deer herds.

This rapidly expanding trade economy, accompanied by growing dependence on manufactured goods, involved the Cherokees in the "Great Wars of Empire" between the French and British. The rush westward by English colonists following the French defeat in the last of these wars (known as the French and Indian War or the Seven Years' War) made deep inroads into Cherokee country. Flushed by their victory over the French and condemning western Indians as enemies and worse, the governments of the southern colonies put heavy pressure on the Cherokees to sell their lands and make way for settlements. Between 1755 and 1777, the Cherokees gave up nearly seventy thousand square miles of their northern and eastern lands, about three-fourths of their total holdings. These sales, engineered by representatives of the English Crown or the colonial legislatures, were made under duress by Cherokee leaders who had been either defeated in battle or convinced by threats that they could not preserve their national domain intact. Cherokee attacks on their aggressively expansionist Carolina neighbors during the American Revolution cost them additional land on their eastern and northern borders.

The 1790s was a critical decade in Cherokee history. The deerskin trade was virtually dead (the result of decimated deer herds and changing markets), and economic hardship was everywhere. Invading armies had destroyed dozens of towns, forcing a southwestward shift of the core population area. In addition, the Cherokees began to have formal relations with the United States. Federal Indian policy sought to achieve two goals: acquisition of land for U.S. citizens and wholesale cultural change of American Indians to make them more like white Americans. The last purpose was rooted in the idea that if Indians became family farmers on privately owned parcels of land and attached to the marketplace, they would fit into American society and would readily surrender the vast amounts of land held in common as national domains by the many tribes. Neither assumption was correct; in fact, federal Indian policy became committed to simply banishing Indians to lands somewhere in the West.

Small groups of Cherokees began to move westward as early as 1782. Better hunting opportunities motivated some, but many hoped to escape proximity to white settlers. By 1794, The Bowl had established a small Cherokee community on the St. Francis River in present-day Arkansas. The economic crisis of the 1790s also probably caused other Cherokees to migrate. By 1817, the Western Cherokee population was large enough to demand attention. In a treaty of that year, the Cherokee Nation received, in part as compensation for cessions in the East, a tract for the Western Cherokees between the White and Arkansas rivers. This grant conflicted with the aspirations of Arkansas Territory, organized in 1819, and led to a treaty in 1828 that exchanged the land in Arkansas for a tract to the west in what became Indian Territory. In the meantime, The Bowl and many Western Cherokees, disgusted that the westward expansion of Anglo-Americans had caught up with them, moved south into Texas to escape. But Anglo-Americans caught them again, and in 1839 an army of the Republic of Texas drove most of the Texas band north across the Red River.

In the East, the unremitting demands of the people and governments of Georgia and Tennessee for all the lands of the Cherokees created an atmosphere of tension and anxiety. Following a cession in 1819, the Cherokees utterly rejected further attempts by federal commissioners to acquire more land. Furthermore, a segment of publicity-conscious Cherokee leaders launched a political revolution designed to reflect the cultural changes that had already occurred and to convince Anglo-Americans that it would be inhumane to expel them from their homeland. Many Cherokees were members of Christian churches. Large numbers were involved in the agricultural market economy of the Southeast, and some owned slaves and grew cotton on their plantations. Cherokee children attended school and learned English, and large numbers of adults learned to read and write in their own language, thanks to the brilliant work of Sequoyah in devising the Cherokee syllabary. These and other changes had, in a quarter century, dramatically transformed the Cherokee Nation. Then, in 1827, a special committee chaired by John Ross drafted a constitution. Patterned after that of the United States, the Cherokee constitution formalized the sovereign independence of the

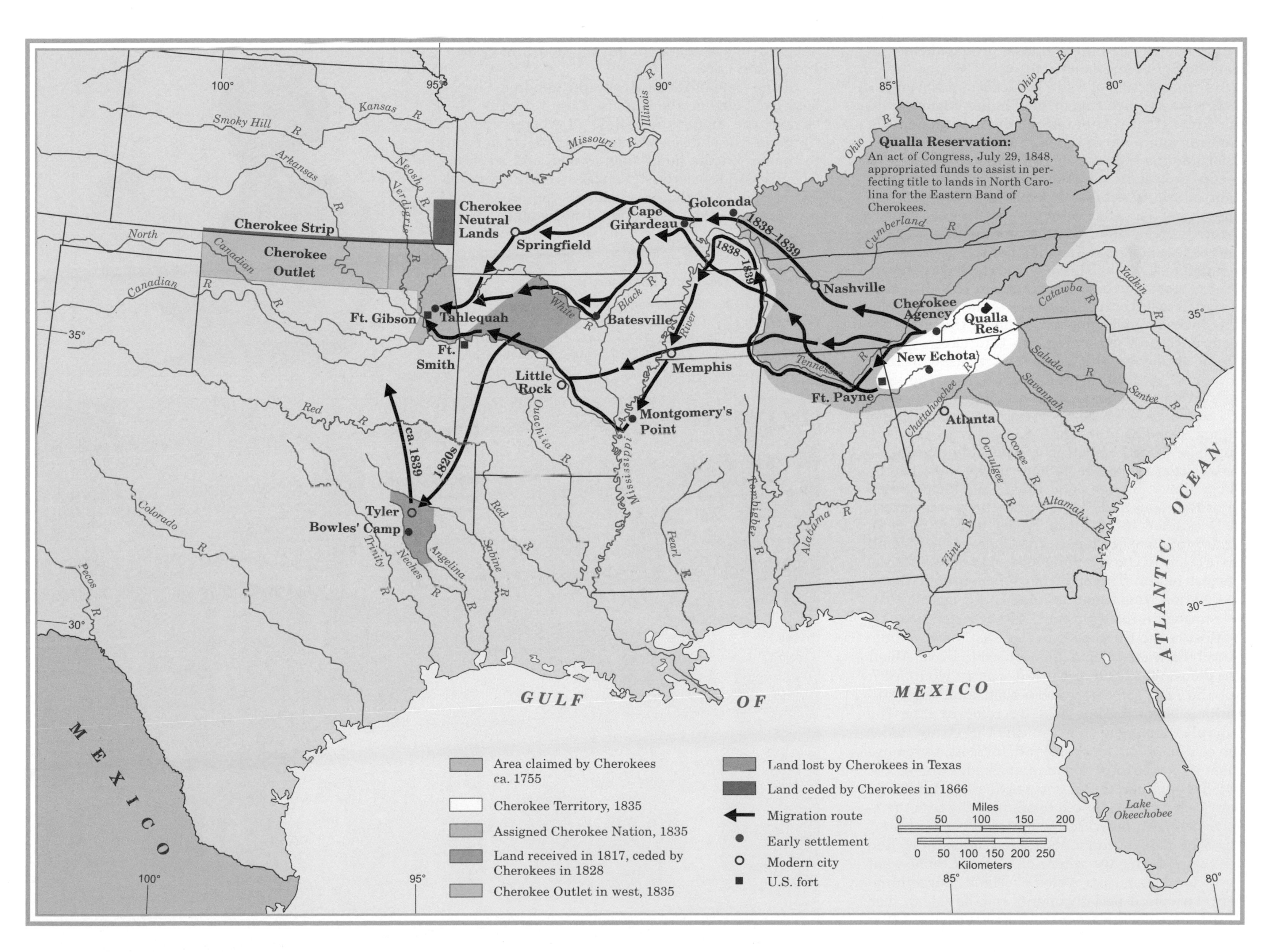

Qualla Reservation:
An act of Congress, July 29, 1848, appropriated funds to assist in perfecting title to lands in North Carolina for the Eastern Band of Cherokees.
Cherokee Strip
Cherokee Outlet
Cherokee Neutral Lands
Springfield
Cape Girardeau
Golconda
1838–1839
1838–1839
Nashville
Cherokee Agency
Qualla Res.
New Echota
Ft. Payne
Atlanta
Batesville
Memphis
Little Rock
Montgomery's Point
Ft. Gibson
Tahlequah
Ft. Smith
ca. 1839
1820s
Tyler
Bowles' Camp
GULF OF MEXICO
ATLANTIC OCEAN
MEXICO
Area claimed by Cherokees ca. 1755
Cherokee Territory, 1835
Assigned Cherokee Nation, 1835
Land received in 1817, ceded by Cherokees in 1828
Cherokee Outlet in west, 1835
Land lost by Cherokees in Texas
Land ceded by Cherokees in 1866
Migration route
Early settlement
Modern city
U.S. fort
Miles
0 50 100 150 200
0 50 100 150 200 250
Kilometers

nation and enabled Ross, elected principal chief, to lead the fight for its survival.

But the election of Andrew Jackson in November 1828 put a staunch supporter of Indian removal into the White House. After bitter debate, proponents of removal won a narrow victory in Congress in May 1830, and the Indian Removal Bill became law. Under its provisions, federal commissioners renewed their efforts to achieve a removal treaty with the Cherokees. The Georgia state government sought to hurry the matter by extending its laws over the Cherokees and forbidding the Cherokee government to function. This legislation—and the harassing actions of state courts and government officials—was designed to force the Cherokees to the treaty table. The Jackson government welcomed this state interference and presented the Cherokees with a simple option: go west to the land set aside in 1828 or submit to continued victimization by the legal institutions of Georgia. Ross and the vast majority of Cherokees opposed removal and, among other things, brought suit against Georgia in the U.S. Supreme Court. However, a small group came to believe that there was no hope in the East. Led by Major Ridge, his son John Ridge, and his nephews Elias Boudinot and Stand Watie, this group agreed in December 1835 to the Treaty of New Echota. Under this treaty's terms, the Cherokees ceded all their lands in the East and agreed to move into the western nation. There, the newly constituted Cherokee Nation would hold its land in fee simple title, free to govern itself without state interference.

Most of the Cherokees in the East, however, declared the treaty illegal and refused to leave. About two thousand, including the Ridge party, left in 1837, but the rest, some seventeen thousand, were still on their farms in May 1838, the removal date. The federal government then sent the U.S. Army, under the command of General Winfield Scott, to remove them by force. Imprisoned in stockades during the hot, dry summer, the Cherokees finally agreed to go west if they were allowed to manage the trek themselves without federal supervision. President Martin Van Buren consented, and most marched westward during the winter of 1838–39. Some went by water, but most traveled overland. Large numbers of people, especially infants and the elderly, died in the camps before their trek, along one or another of the "Trails of Tears," or during their first year in Indian Territory.

At the time of removal, several hundred Cherokees lived outside the bounds of the Cherokee Nation in the mountain valleys of western North Carolina. The state legislature recognized their right to remain on the lands they owned, and so these Cherokees did not go west. Refugees from the removal joined them, and their descendants continue to live in the area as the Eastern Band of Cherokees.

Right: *Sequoyah. (Courtesy Western History Collections, University of Oklahoma Libraries)*

Below: *Cherokee students pose for a photograph in front of the Cherokee Female Seminary, May 1851. The seminary was located at Tahlequah, Cherokee Nation. (Courtesy Western History Collections, University of Oklahoma Libraries)*

A Price to Pay

Formal treaties, including most that the new United States executed with the land's original peoples, typically defined precise boundaries that thereafter can be neatly shown as lines on maps. What happened within those lines—very often, because of those lines—does not appear at all. Not infrequently, the results transpired in ways unimaginable to those whose agreements had set those lines in the first place.

Under such treaties, as many as five thousand Cherokees had crossed the Mississippi and established self-governing communities in Indian Territory by the mid-1830s. The "Cherokee West" some called them; "Old Settlers," they liked to think of themselves. The vast majority of Cherokees—possibly seventeen thousand—remained in the east, and most stubbornly insisted that there they would stay, under the leadership of John Ross (overwhelmingly elected under the formal constitution of 1827). Thus, the treaty that the United States pretended to have negotiated with the Cherokee Nation at the end of 1835 was reached not with a unified nation or even with those officials who represented the majority of a divided nation, but with the so-called Treaty Party, led by the Ridges and their kin. Elected by no one and representing the views of very few, they put their names to the Treaty of New Echota in late 1835—and thereby signed what amounted to their death warrants.

At horrific costs, the contrived treaty at least reassembled what remained of one nation in a single area. The question was who would govern it and how they could establish their authority. Leaders of three bitterly divided factions met at Tukattokah, about ten miles north of Fort Gibson, in June of 1839. "We will govern," announced the Old Settlers. "With our help," added the Treaty Party. Chief John Ross and other elected leaders of the Eastern Cherokee majority said nothing.

Instead, at council's end, their followers acted. Three days later, on the evening of June 22, in different parts of the new nation, unmasked bands of assassins coldly executed both Ridges, father and son, as well as Elias Boudinot, whom they stabbed and hacked to pieces. Boudinot's brother, Stand Watie, escaped death only because he happened not to have been home at the hour scheduled for his execution. It was he who discovered his brother's dismembered body parts strewn across blood-soaked ground—ground that lay not two miles from where John Ross had peacefully and quietly spent the night before.

Top: *The Delaware-Cherokee Indian delegation to Washington, 1866. (Courtesy Western History Collections, University of Oklahoma Libraries)*

Bottom Left: *Major Ridge was a war chief of the Cherokees. Under his leadership of a minority faction, the Cherokees exchanged their land in the eastern United States for land in Indian Territory. (Courtesy Western History Collections, University of Oklahoma Libraries)*

Bottom Right: *John Ross was the leader of one of the rival factions in the Cherokee Nation and was principal chief of the nation from 1827 to 1866. (Courtesy Western History Collections, University of Oklahoma Libraries)*

29. CHEROKEE LANDS IN THE WEST

Essay by *Michael D. Green*

To provide a home for the growing number of Cherokees who had begun to move west in the late eighteenth century, the Cherokee Nation and the United States concluded a treaty in 1817 that located a tract for them between the Arkansas and White rivers. In return, the Cherokee Nation ceded a tract of equal size in the East. The settlers in Arkansas Territory, organized in 1819, resented the Cherokees in their midst and encroached upon the Indians' lands, especially along the Arkansas River. To escape these pressures, the Western Cherokees, numbering perhaps five thousand, agreed in 1828 to exchange the lands for a tract of seven million acres farther west, in the valleys of the Verdigris, Grand, and Arkansas rivers. Though vaguely described, the new domain clearly included a rich tract of bottomland on the lower Verdigris and between the Verdigris and the Arkansas.

But because of faulty information in Washington, the federal government did not realize that the tract granted to the Cherokees in 1828 included a dense settlement of Creeks established under the terms of a treaty concluded with the latter tribe in 1826. This group, numbering perhaps two thousand by 1830 and growing rapidly, occupied both banks of the Verdigris north from its mouth as well as the north bank of the Arkansas. The neck of land between the Verdigris and Arkansas rivers was especially heavily occupied. When the Cherokees began to move west from the Arkansas cession, they found these Creeks and demanded that the occupants withdraw, which the Creeks refused to do. The resulting controversy was not cleared up until early 1833, when a federal commission, chaired by Montfort Stokes, negotiated with both nations a change in the boundary. The new line gave the Creeks title to their Verdigris and Arkansas valley settlements.

The December 29, 1835, Treaty of New Echota provided for the removal of all the remaining members of the Cherokee Nation to the land west of Arkansas and Missouri that had been assigned to the Western Cherokees. The treaty also conveyed an 800,000-acre tract in Kansas, known later as the "Neutral Lands," at a cost to the Cherokees of $500,000. The Cherokee Outlet, as provided in Article 2 of the New Echota treaty, assured the Cherokee Nation of a "perpetual outlet west, and a free and unmolested use of all the country west of [the Outlet]."

By the terms of the 1866 Reconstruction treaty, the United States agreed to sell the Neutral Lands for the benefit of the Cherokee Nation. The government also sold the Cherokee Strip, a tract about two and one-half miles wide and lying along the 37th parallel in Kansas. For many years the Cherokee Nation had been trying, unsuccessfully, to sell this land, on which no Cherokees lived. In return, the treaty required the nation to permit the United States to settle friendly tribes in the Cherokee Outlet. The government located the Osages and Kaws (or Kansas) between the Arkansas River and the 96th meridian. It put the Pawnees, Poncas, Nez Perces, and Oto-Missouris west of the Arkansas. In 1885 the Nez Perces were moved back to their original homelands in Idaho, and their lands were assigned to a remnant of the Tonkawas from Texas.

During the 1880s, the Cherokee National Council leased the rest of the Cherokee Outlet, over six million acres, to cattle companies as grazing land. The lease income, subject to periodic renegotiation, was substantial. The opening of the Unassigned Lands in 1889 and the organization of that region as Oklahoma Territory in 1890—coupled with the allotment of the western reservations and their inclusion in Oklahoma Territory—led to heavy pressure on the Cherokees to sell what remained of the Cherokee Outlet. Congress ordered the Jerome Commission to arrange the purchase. In 1892, the Cherokee National Council agreed to accept the United States' offer of over $8.5 million for the tract, which led to the opening by run of the Cherokee Outlet on September 16, 1893.

Spring roundup in the Cherokee Outlet leases, 1882.
(Courtesy Western History Collections, University of Oklahoma Libraries)

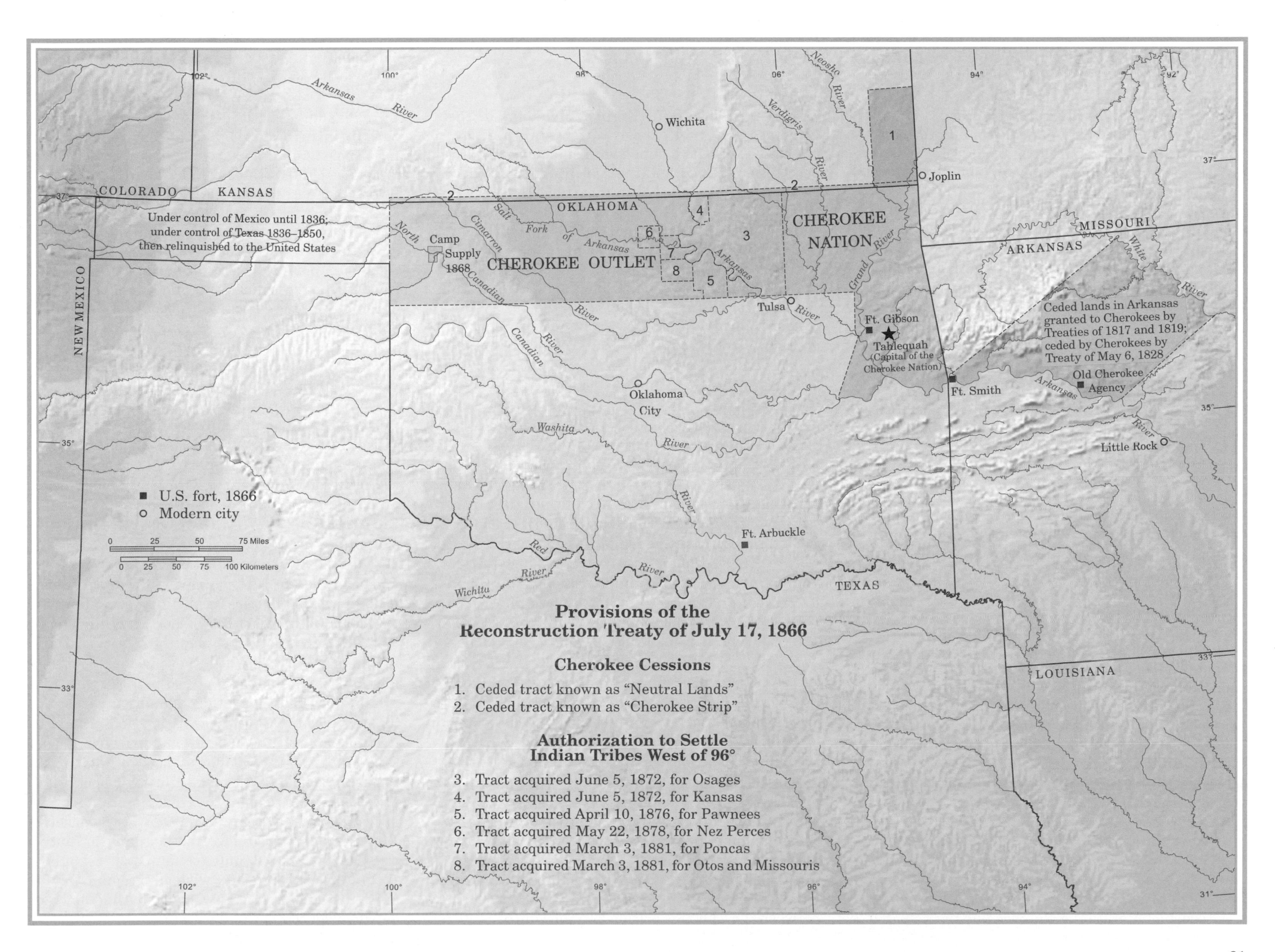
Provisions of the
Reconstruction Treaty of July 17, 1866
Cherokee Cessions
1. Ceded tract known as "Neutral Lands"
2. Ceded tract known as "Cherokee Strip"
Authorization to Settle
Indian Tribes West of 96°
3. Tract acquired June 5, 1872, for Osages
4. Tract acquired June 5, 1872, for Kansas
5. Tract acquired April 10, 1876, for Pawnees
6. Tract acquired May 22, 1878, for Nez Perces
7. Tract acquired March 3, 1881, for Poncas
8. Tract acquired March 3, 1881, for Otos and Missouris
U.S. fort, 1866
Modern city
0 25 50 75 Miles
0 25 50 75 100 Kilometers
COLORADO
KANSAS
OKLAHOMA
NEW MEXICO
MISSOURI
ARKANSAS
TEXAS
LOUISIANA
CHEROKEE OUTLET
CHEROKEE NATION
Under control of Mexico until 1836;
under control of Texas 1836–1850,
then relinquished to the United States
Ceded lands in Arkansas
granted to Cherokees by
Treaties of 1817 and 1819;
ceded by Cherokees by
Treaty of May 6, 1828
Camp Supply 1868
Wichita
Joplin
Tulsa
Ft. Gibson
Tahlequah
(Capital of the
Cherokee Nation)
Ft. Smith
Old Cherokee
Agency
Oklahoma
City
Little Rock
Ft. Arbuckle
Arkansas River
Neosho River
Verdigris River
Salt Fork of Arkansas
Cimarron
North Canadian River
Canadian River
Grand River
Washita River
Red River
Wichita River
White River
102°
100°
98°
96°
94°
92°
37°
35°
33°
31°

30. REMOVAL OF THE CHOCTAWS Essay by *Michael D. Green*

Except for a brief but traumatic experience with the brutal expedition of Hernando de Soto in the early 1540s, the Choctaws had little or no contact with Europeans until the French established Louisiana in 1699. The pragmatic French plan was to gain control of the Mississippi Valley and block the westward economic expansion of the English. The Choctaws—a large, rich, and strategically located nation—were an important part of the French imperial design.

The estimated thirty thousand Choctaws owned some of the richest land in North America: the western end of the Black Belt and the Mississippi Delta. A flat, well-watered coastal plain with warm weather and thick fertile soil, the country enabled the Choctaws to become productive farmers. They could raise three crops of corn a year and several varieties of beans and squash, but unlike many Native groups, they also became keepers of domesticated animals. Hogs thrived, and by the middle of the eighteenth century, the small, strong Choctaw pony had become famous throughout the Southeast for its stamina. Mushulatubbee, chief of the Northeastern District in the early nineteenth century, once remarked that the Choctaws were herdsmen, not farmers.

The French introduced manufactured goods early in the eighteenth century, and the Choctaws—like other southern tribes—responded by increasing their deer hunting to acquire these trade goods. But the French were not particularly interested in whitetail deer skins. Unlike the English, who used the growing economic dependence of their Native trade partners to increase profits, the French preferred Choctaw armies to form an alliance against their mutual European and Indian enemies. The Choctaws were receptive because they needed French guns to defend themselves from the slave raids of the Creeks and Chickasaws.

During the first half of the eighteenth century, the Choctaws were engaged in almost continuous warfare. In addition to defending themselves and making punitive attacks on the Creeks, they helped the French obliterate the Natchez and participated in three unsuccessful French invasions of the Chickasaw Nation. These wars debilitated the Choctaws, cost them (along with epidemics of European diseases) over half their people, and left them exhausted. French defeat in the French and Indian War (1756–1763) put the Choctaws, in this weakened state, at the mercies of the English. In 1765, John Stuart, the British superintendent of the Southern Indian Department, required the Choctaws to give up their claim to the lands from Mobile Bay west to the Mississippi River and north to the Yazoo. This cession lopped off the Choctaws' southern hunting grounds plus the southwestern corner of the nation, which became known as the Natchez District. Beginning in the 1770s, the settler population of the Natchez District grew rapidly. By the end of the eighteenth century, it was quickly becoming one of the richest cotton-producing areas in the South.

With the winning of independence, the United States opened relations with the Choctaws. The first two treaties—1786 and 1801—reaffirmed the earlier cession to the British. The Natchez District had become the western portion of Mississippi Territory, it was the American point of entry into Spanish Florida and New Orleans along the Mississippi River, and its present and future economic importance to the United States was incalculable. Treaties in 1803 and 1805 joined the eastern settlements above Mobile to Natchez, and a cession in 1816 took a large tract off the Choctaws' eastern boundary.

But the Choctaws still held two-thirds of their original homeland, including several hundred miles of Mississippi River frontage, the Black Belt, and the delta. The explosive increase in the population of Mississippi—from about seven thousand in 1800 to thirty-one thousand in 1810 to seventy-five thousand in 1820—brought wholesale encroachments on Choctaw land and intense pressure on the federal government for another cession. Mississippi's entry into the union as a state in 1817 amplified the clamor for more land. The Treaty of Doak's Stand, concluded between the Choctaw Nation and the United States in 1820, addressed the demands of Mississippi citizens by introducing the idea of removal. In return for a massive tract, nearly a third of the Choctaw lands, the United States granted a parcel in the West between the Arkansas and Red rivers and offered inducements for Choctaws who wished to migrate. Few Choctaws made the move, which was fortunate, since the eastern part of the western grant was already occupied by several hundred white settlers. In 1825 the government rectified its error by purchasing from the Choctaws that part of their country in Arkansas.

Political sentiment for a policy to remove all eastern Indians to the West intensified during the 1820s, especially in the booming southern cotton states. Mississippi voters supported Andrew Jackson for president in 1828 almost unanimously, in part because they knew he favored such a policy. The removal bill that Congress enacted in 1830 authorized the president to negotiate with Native nations for an exchange of their lands in the East for comparable tracts in the West. The Choctaws—partly because they already had such a western tract, partly because they still held much Black Belt cotton land, and partly because they seemed ready to accept such a deal—were the first tribe the president approached. In the fall of 1830, Choctaw headmen and federal commissioners signed the Treaty of Dancing Rabbit Creek, in which the Choctaws sold their lands in Mississippi and agreed to move west. The Mississippi state legislature had already extended its laws into the Choctaw territory and prohibited the functioning of the Choctaw national government, thus preparing the way for all sorts of judicial harassment designed to make life for Choctaws in Mississippi unbearable. The treaty guaranteed that in the West, the Choctaws would govern themselves without state interference. Another provision authorized any Choctaw family to claim a parcel of land within the cession if they wished to remain in Mississippi. These Choctaws would then become detribalized citizens of the state.

The Choctaws were the first of the Five Tribes to be removed. In three waves—one each year, beginning in 1831—most of the Choctaws went west. This was a massive undertaking for which the federal government was ill prepared. Disorganization, confusion, poor planning by inept officials, and fraud, along with bitterly cold winter weather, caused intense hardship and suffering and led to the deaths of many hundreds of people. Of the eighteen thousand to twenty thousand Choctaws in Mississippi in 1830, some six thousand remained after the last official companies left in 1833. A few of these were highly acculturated planters, such as Greenwood LeFlore, who chose to retain their cotton plantations. Many, however, were among the poorest Choctaws, some of whom were caught in Mississippi by a state law that prohibited the removal of any indebted Indians. In small groups over the next fifteen years, several hundred per year joined the Choctaw Nation in Indian Territory, but several hundred never left Mississippi. Their descendants remain there today, recognized by the government as the Choctaw Tribe of Mississippi.

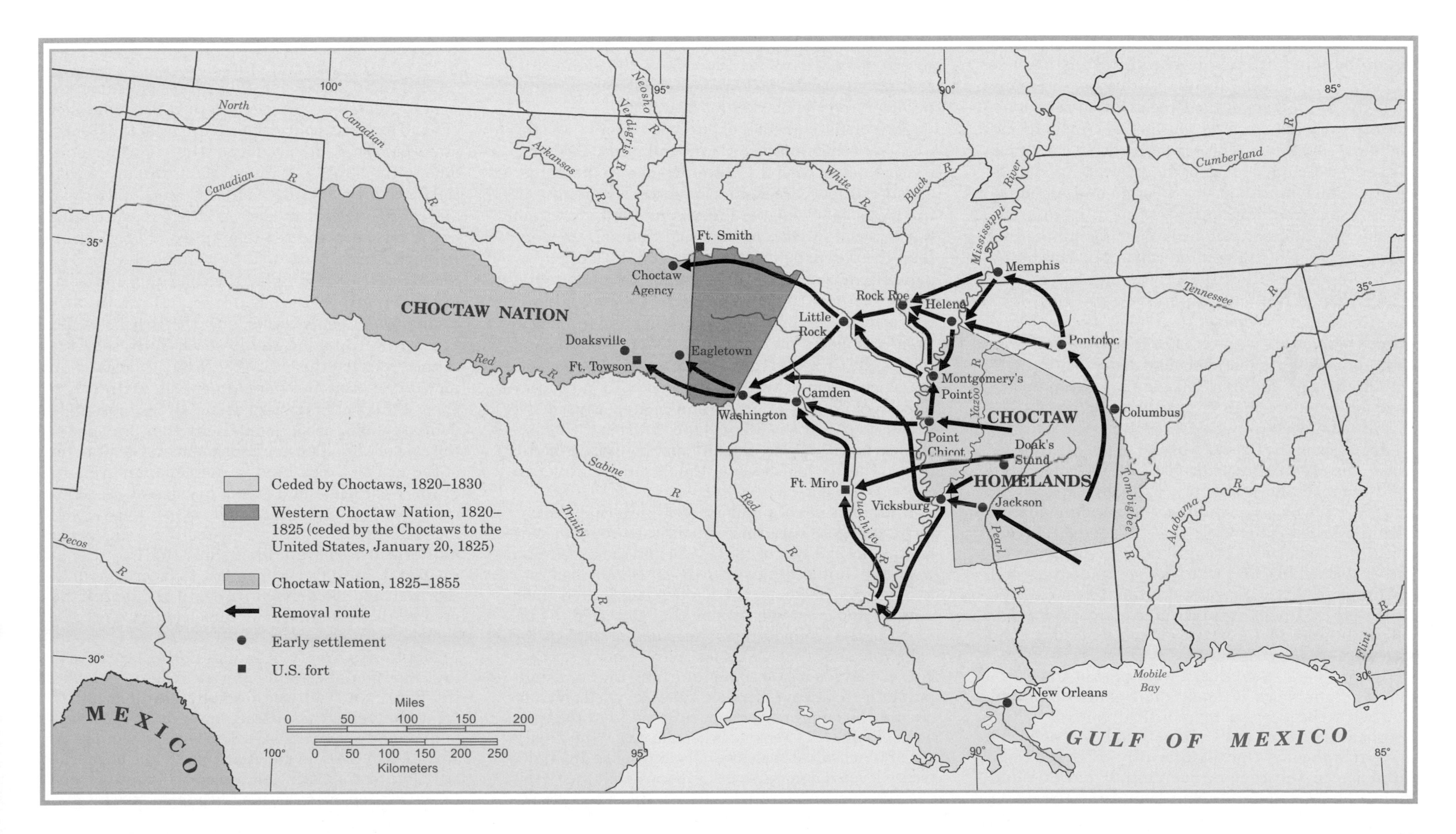

31. REMOVAL OF THE CREEKS

Essay by *Michael D. Green & Danney Goble*

In the eighteenth and early nineteenth centuries, the English and Americans called the Creeks a "confederacy," but it would be more accurate to think of them as an alliance system that bound together into a loose association many different groups of southern Indians. The origins of this alliance system can be traced to the collapse of the Mississippian chiefdoms in the late sixteenth century, but there is no evidence of nation building or organized political institutions until well into the eighteenth century, and in many ways the unification of the Creek Nation remains a work in progress. Located south of the Appalachian highlands, east of the Choctaws, and north of Florida, the Creeks occupied much of the tidewater and piedmont regions of present-day Georgia and Alabama. There they grew large crops of corn, beans, and squash and hunted, primarily deer. Dominated by Muskogee speakers and often called Muskogees, by the eighteenth century the Creeks had become the most powerful Native group in the Southeast. Like the other Native people of the region, they suffered serious population loss from European epidemic diseases, but their numbers rebounded during the eighteenth century, and by 1790 they are estimated to have totaled more than fifteen thousand people.

Until the early nineteenth century, the political organization of the Creek Confederacy was extremely loose. The organizing principles of the Confederacy were alliance and autonomy, with the constituent tribes or towns maintaining their independence within a broad framework that preserved internal peace and sometimes brought various members together for defense and war. The permanent arrival of Europeans in the Southeast ultimately forced the Creeks to begin to organize a systematic foreign policy, but prior to the early eighteenth century, little structure was necessary.

By the 1680s, the Creeks were part of the Carolina trade network. French and Spanish competition with the British for political control of the Southeast enabled the Creeks to follow a policy of play-off diplomacy that significantly enhanced their influence in the region, but neither power could break the economic ties that bound the Creeks to the English. Neither could the Creeks avoid the consequences of economic dependence on the manufactured goods purveyed by Anglo-American traders. Creek men became professional hunters, ranging farther afield in search of deer for skins to trade. Prior to about 1715 and the devastating Yamassee War, a slave trade supplemented the commerce in skins, but after the collapse of the trade in captives, the Creek economy for the rest of the eighteenth century was controlled by the availability of white-tail deer and the market for deerskins.

The population center of the Creek country was the Chattahoochee and the Coosa-Tallapoosa-Alabama river systems, with the Lower Creeks on the former and the Upper Creeks on the latter. Beginning in the 1760s, following the French and Indian War and the removal of both French and Spanish competitors, the English settler population of Georgia began to soar, and with it the demand for additional lands. Increasing pressures on the Creek frontier—characterized by aggressive hunting and grazing—rapidly depleted the remaining deer population and robbed the Creeks of much of the value of their country. These encroachments, coupled with entreaties to sell and offers of goods and money, caused the Creeks to part with slices of land cut from their eastern border. By 1805 the eastern boundary of the Creek Nation had become the Ocmulgee River in central Georgia.

A complex set of problems, both internal and external and both cultural and political, brought about the Creek Civil War of 1811–1814 and the Creek War with the United States in 1813–1814. Divided into two warring factions, the Creeks devastated their country and created a turmoil that attracted the interest of the United States. Responding to pleas for help from one of the Creek factions, General Andrew Jackson and federalized militias from the surrounding states, aided by Cherokee allies, invaded and conquered the opposing faction, referred to at the time as the Red Stick Creeks. Jackson dictated the Treaty of Fort Jackson at the close of hostilities in 1814; the treaty leveled a massive price in land that the Creek Confederacy was forced to pay. The tract the Creeks surrendered, some twenty million acres, included their holdings in central Alabama and southern Georgia. Surrounded by a rapidly growing population of cotton planters eager to exploit the rich Black Belt, the Creeks felt pressure unlike anything in their experience. Cessions in 1818, 1821, 1826, and 1827 took all their lands in Georgia, leaving them only a half-circle tract in eastern Alabama between the Coosa River and the Georgia border.

This rapid succession of land cessions, accompanied by heated negotiations with U.S. commissioners and extreme political pressure from the Georgia state government, produced a crisis atmosphere among the Creeks. William McIntosh, an influential Lower Creek headman from Coweta and a cousin of Georgia's governor, George M. Troup, succumbed to the pressure and the temptation of large bribes. In partnership with a U.S. commission, in 1823 McIntosh tried and failed to achieve through bribery the removal of the Cherokees. In 1824, the same commission opened talks with the Creeks at Broken Arrow. Watching McIntosh carefully, the Creek council rejected the U.S. offer to buy their land and move west. But the more amenable McIntosh reopened talks at his tavern at Indian Springs, and in January 1825, he signed a treaty that provided for the sale of all the Lower Creek land in Georgia, half of the Upper Creek land in Alabama, and removal to the West. He and a few of his closest associates received several thousand dollars as bribes for signing. The Creek council protested the treaty as unauthorized and fraudulent, but the U.S. Senate ratified it anyway. Citing a law that forbade unauthorized land sales on pain of death, the council then ordered the execution of McIntosh and several other signers of the treaty.

McIntosh's Treaty of Indian Springs carried the first mention of establishing a Creek homeland in the West. No land was formally granted, but the treaty provided that a tract between the Arkansas and Canadian rivers equal in size to the cession agreed to in Georgia and Alabama should be marked off. McIntosh's execution forced the United States to reconsider. Negotiations began in Washington,

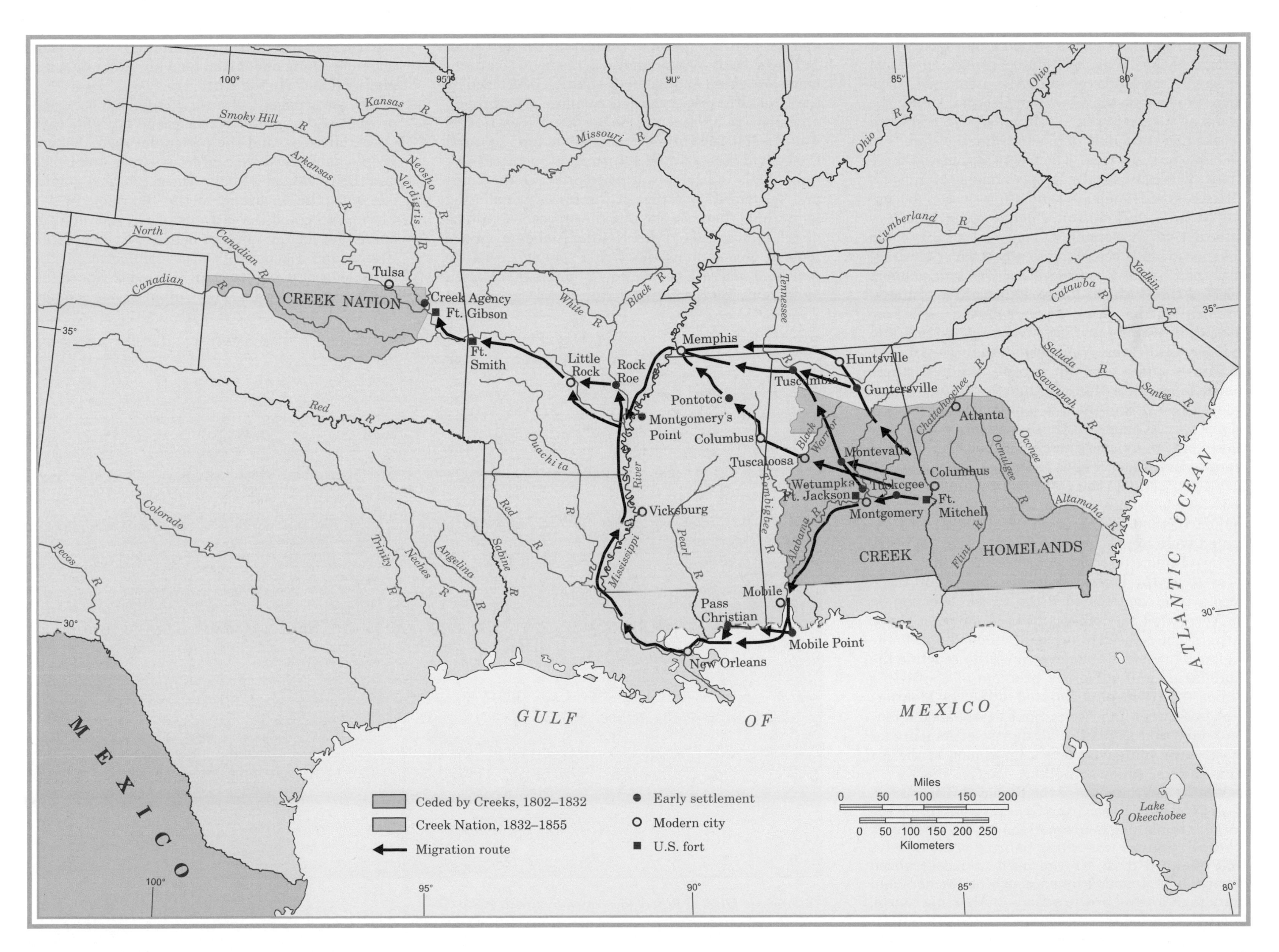
CREEK NATION
Tulsa
Creek Agency
Ft. Gibson
Ft. Smith
Little Rock
Rock Roe
Montgomery's Point
Memphis
Huntsville
Tuscumbia
Guntersville
Pontotoc
Columbus
Tuscaloosa
Montevallo
Atlanta
Columbus
Wetumpka
Tuskegee
Ft. Jackson
Montgomery
Ft. Mitchell
Vicksburg
CREEK HOMELANDS
Mobile
Pass Christian
Mobile Point
New Orleans
GULF OF MEXICO
MEXICO
ATLANTIC OCEAN
Lake Okeechobee
Ceded by Creeks, 1802–1832
Creek Nation, 1832–1855
Migration route
Early settlement
Modern city
U.S. fort
Miles
Kilometers

and in 1826, Creek chiefs signed a new treaty that abrogated the Treaty of Indian Springs. In return for saving the lands ceded in Alabama, the Creeks agreed to give up their lands in Georgia. Under the terms of the Treaty of Washington, the displaced Creeks had the option of moving onto their lands in Alabama or going west. The treaty authorized those Creeks who chose to migrate (presumably McIntosh's relatives and friends) to send a five-person delegation west to select land on which to settle. Members of the delegation were limited only in that they could not choose lands belonging to any state or territory or to the Choctaws or Cherokees. The land rangers selected the Verdigris and Arkansas River valleys, later called the Three Forks country, near Fort Gibson. Beginning in 1828, Creek migrants began to move to the area. As expected, they were mostly McIntosh supporters, but several hundred others joined them. Many figured that the United States would never permit them to remain for long in their country in Alabama so there was no use to tarry there, but many chose to go because they did not want to live under a new, centralist Creek government that claimed the right to execute Creek citizens for violating its laws. During the late 1820s and early 1830s, some three thousand Creeks migrated west to the lower Verdigris River region of eastern Indian Territory near Fort Gibson.

In 1828, the United States granted the Cherokees a tract that included the Creek selection on the Verdigris. Cherokee migrants encountered Creek settlers who refused to surrender their claims to the region. This forced the government to redefine the boundaries and solve the problem of conflicting claims. A settlement negotiated in 1833 by Montfort Stokes between the two nations established a new boundary that saved the Verdigris settlements for the Creeks and gave them a large part of the Arkansas River valley as well.

When Congress passed the Removal Bill in 1830, Lower Creek refugees from Georgia were filling the nation's remaining lands in Alabama, and the Creek National Council was trying to bring order in ways that offended those Creeks used to decentralized government. Invaded by encroaching farmers and herders, harassed by the actions of Alabama courts, and beleaguered by unceasing demands to sell out and get out, the national council finally agreed in 1832 to a treaty. Not a removal agreement, this document presented an ingenious solution developed by the Creeks to preserve their communities through an elaborate allotment scheme. The Creek Nation would sell to the United States all its territory, and the United States would in turn allot tracts to Creek individuals in such a way as to preserve the lands and settlement patterns of the towns. Unallotted land would then be sold, and the proceeds would be distributed to the Creeks. Neither Alabama nor the federal government liked this scheme, because detribalized Creek people would remain in Alabama as citizens, but Secretary of War Lewis Cass signed the treaty, expecting that the allotted Creeks would not enjoy living under Alabama law and would ultimately remove to the West.

The government refused to enforce those treaty provisions that protected the property rights of the Creek allottees, and the period between 1832 and 1836 was marked by conflict between the Creeks and their white neighbors. These conflicts, coinciding with the outbreak of the Seminole War in Florida, terrified the citizens of Georgia and Alabama. Fearing an alliance between Seminoles and Creeks and a general frontier conflagration, they appealed to the government to send troops to forcibly expel the Creeks. The United States complied

Tullahassee Mission School (destroyed by fire in 1880).
(Courtesy Western History Collections, University of Oklahoma Libraries)

in 1836, and by early 1837, over fourteen thousand Creeks had been moved to Indian Territory by the army, their suffering on the trails compounded by the loss of most of their possessions.

These refugees were greeted, warily, by the three thousand Creeks who had moved west over the previous decade. Led by Roley McIntosh and Chilly McIntosh, respectively the half brother and son of William McIntosh, these western Creeks were not happy to be inundated by the people who had executed their kinsman and, in effect, run them out of their eastern homes. After uneasy negotiations at Fort Gibson, however, the McIntosh group and the refugee national council under the leadership of Opothleyahola agreed to divide the land. The original settlers would remain on the Arkansas River and its tributaries; the newcomers would settle on the branches of the Canadian. Separated by a no-man's-land, they would govern themselves according to their respective wishes and not interfere in one another's affairs. Circa 1840, headmen from the two groups began to meet in a national council and revived, at least on the level of relations with the United States, a unified government.

Council Oak

No one knows when the acorn first fell or when the seedling sprouted, so its age is anyone's guess, but the oak is surely around two hundred years old now. We do know that as early as 1836 it towered above the willows, sycamores, and birches huddling shade. That had to be what first drew the people of Lochapocha to it.

There had been 565 of them just a few months earlier, when the army had gathered them up, counted each one, and turned them over to private contractors who had bargained to get them and every other Creek that could be found down out of Alabama for a price. The price the people of Lochapocha paid was high, for not even half of them reached Fort Gibson alive. It was no better for those from Coweta, from Broken Arrow, or from the other towns considered sisters under one mother they all called Tallasi.

From Fort Gibson, the tiny remnant painfully made its way up the Arkansas River, passing through another forty miles of wild country. Then, just as the river was about to make its great bend westward, their leader, Achee Yahola, ordered that their boats be run aground. Ascending a gentle incline and starting with the tree as a southeastern corner, the survivors solemnly laid out an exact replica of the communal square of their old village in Alabama. That done, they laid out in the century-old tradition four logs, all joined at a common point. Amid much prayer, they then lit the fire that declared that they had endured the unendurable and that they intended to resume their old ways in this, their new land, for this, their new life.

The square is long since gone. But the tree is still there, bigger and statelier than ever. The "Council Oak," Tulsans call it, just as they call their town "Tulsa" after the mother community the founders left behind.

Top: *The Creek Council House, now standing in the town square in Okmulgee, was the capitol for the Creek Nation from 1878 to 1907. The legislative branch, comprising the House of Warriors and the House of Kings, used the second floor for their meetings. Administrative and judicial offices were on the first floor. (Courtesy Western History Collections, University of Oklahoma Libraries)*

Left: Going to the Trading Post, *by Fred Beaver. (Oklahoma Indian Art Gallery, courtesy of Vyta Beaver)*

32. REMOVAL OF THE CHICKASAWS

Essay by *Michael D. Green*

The Chickasaws are closely related to the Choctaws in culture and language. When they first came into contact with Europeans—in the early 1540s, when the Spanish under Hernando de Soto entered their lands—the Chickasaws lived in what is now northern Mississippi, northwestern Alabama, and western Tennessee. Their main population center was in the basin of the Tombigbee River. Like the other Southeastern nations, they lived in villages; raised corn, beans, and other field crops; and hunted. They used their own country, and they hunted and traded west of the Mississippi River as well. Accurate population counts do not go back as far as De Soto's invasion, but evidence suggests that the Chickasaws suffered severely from their contact with the Spanish. Late-seventeenth-century estimates, coinciding with the beginning of contact with the French, suggest a population range of 7,000 to 14,000, followed by a drastic decline caused by disease and warfare that bottomed out at 1,600 in 1760. At the time of removal to the West in the late 1830s, the population of the Chickasaw Nation was over 6,000.

The history of the Chickasaws in the eighteenth century is characterized by their close alliance with the English, forged by the Charleston traders and based on a rich trade in which Chickasaws exchanged deerskins (and, until about 1715, war captives to be enslaved) for manufactured goods. This alliance, plus their strategically important command of the east bank of the Mississippi River—the lifeline that linked French Louisiana with French Canada—made them the enemies of the French and France's most loyal Native ally, the Choctaws. With English support, the Chickasaws repulsed three attempts orchestrated by the French in 1736, 1739, and 1752 to exterminate them, but the price of survival was high, as the population estimates from the mid-eighteenth century imply.

Chickasaw participation in the English trade network, vitally important to the Chickasaw Nation's survival, required important cultural changes. Chickasaw men became professional hunters and traders and greatly increased their production of deerskins. This output purchased the guns, powder, and lead necessary for defense as well as the array of manufactured goods that they and their families desired. Over time, the Chickasaws became dependent on these goods. Their needs came to influence national policy, just as similar dependency influenced the policies of the other Southeastern nations. Thus, when the French were removed from the scene following their defeat in the French and Indian War and Chickasaw survival was no longer threatened by French and Choctaw armies, the Chickasaws continued their close trade relations with the English. Traders flooded the Chickasaw Nation, established relations with influential leaders through marriage, and vied for economic control of the nation. One of these traders, James Logan Colbert, established a dynasty that set the social and economic tone and dominated the public affairs of the nation well into the nineteenth century.

The Chickasaws were active allies of the British during the American Revolution. England's Indian allies did not participate in the Treaty of Paris, signed in 1783 by the United States and Great Britain, meaning that they remained in a state of war with the United States. During the winter of 1785–

Bloomfield Academy for Chickasaw Girls, 1853. *(Courtesy Western History Collections, University of Oklahoma Libraries)*

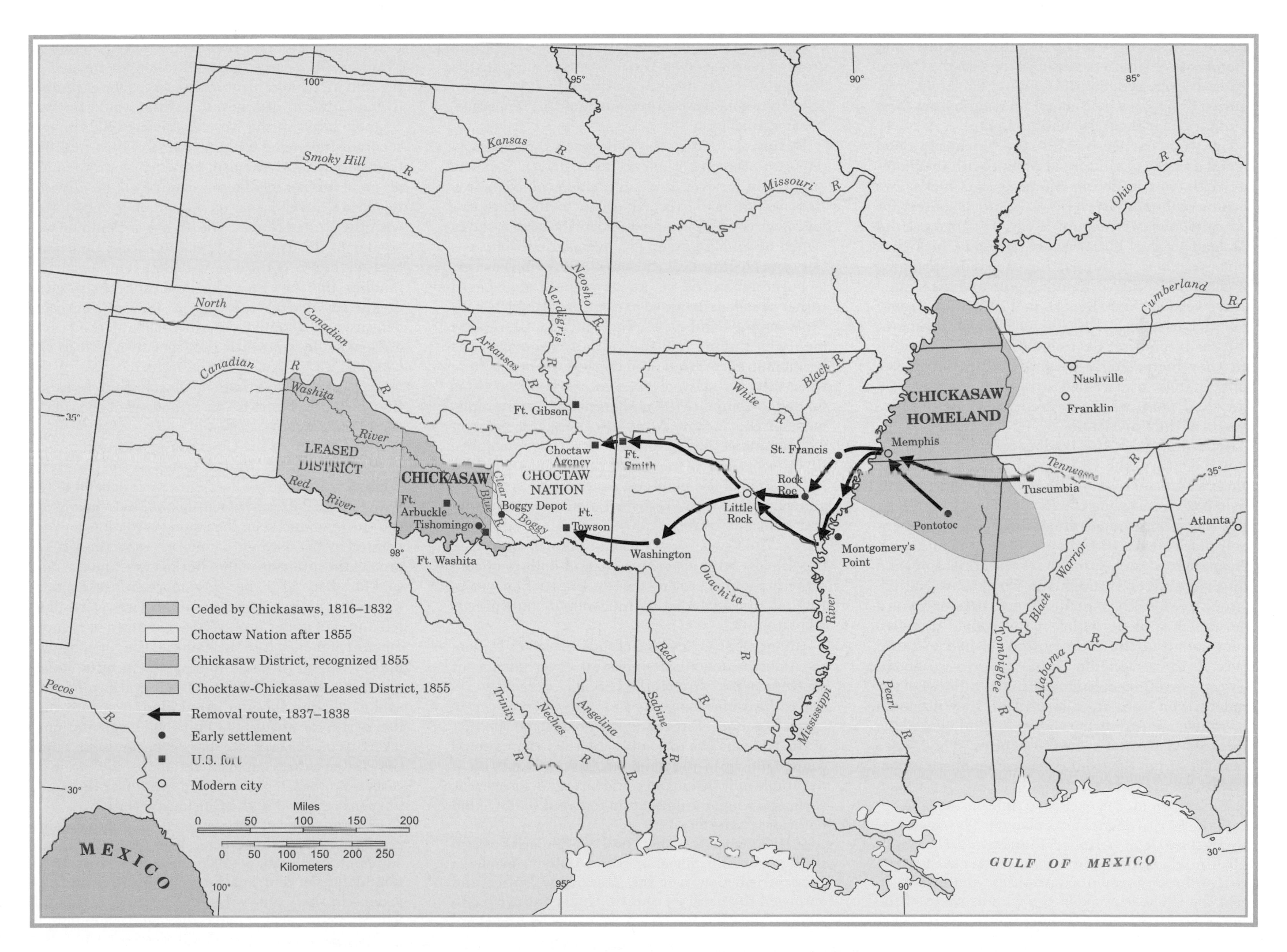

Kansas
R
Smoky Hill
R
Missouri
R
Ohio
R
Neosho
R
Verdigris
R
North
Canadian
R
Arkansas
R
Canadian
R
Washita
River
Cumberland
R
White
R
Black R
CHICKASAW
HOMELAND
Nashville
Franklin
Ft. Gibson
Memphis
LEASED
DISTRICT
Choctaw
Agency
Ft.
Smith
St. Francis
Tennessee
R
CHICKASAW
CHOCTAW
NATION
Rock
Roe
Tuscumbia
Red
River
Clear
Blue
Boggy
Ft.
Arbuckle
Boggy Depot
Ft.
Towson
Little
Rock
Pontotoc
Atlanta
Tishomingo
Washington
Montgomery's
Point
Ft. Washita
Ouachita
River
Black Warrior
Ceded by Chickasaws, 1816–1832
Choctaw Nation after 1855
Chickasaw District, recognized 1855
Chocktaw-Chickasaw Leased District, 1855
Removal route, 1837–1838
Early settlement
U.S. fort
Modern city
Red
R
R
Tombigbee
R
Alabama
R
Pecos
R
Trinity
R
Neches
R
Angelina
R
Sabine
R
Mississippi
Pearl
R
Miles
0 50 100 150 200
0 50 100 150 200 250
Kilometers
MEXICO
GULF OF MEXICO
100°
95°
90°
85°
35°
30°
98°

86, the Chickasaws—along with the Choctaws and Cherokees—signed a treaty of peace with the United States at Hopewell, South Carolina. This treaty recognized Chickasaw land claims and marked out their boundaries for the first time on a map.

Two years earlier, in 1784, the Chickasaws had signed a treaty of alliance at Mobile with the Spanish. With two conflicting alliances, the Chickasaws became embroiled in the U.S.-Spanish contest for control of the Mississippi River. This contest did not lead to war, but it badly divided Chickasaw politics as factions supporting each side struggled for control of the government. Spain and the United States settled their dispute in 1797 in the Treaty of San Lorenzo, but harmony did not return to Chickasaw politics. Factional divisions continued, but they increasingly became cultural struggles between those who wished to continue in traditional ways and those who embraced the values and interests of the Americans.

Beginning with the traders in the early eighteenth century, the Chickasaw Nation became a place where increasing numbers of non-Indians wished to live. During the Revolutionary War, Loyalist Americans found refuge there. Many brought their black slaves with them and built plantations. The main road connecting the lower Mississippi and Ohio valleys cut through the Chickasaw Nation. Later known as the Natchez Trace, this road was a thoroughfare along which many people traveled. Some admired the country and wished to settle there. As the non-Indian population grew, so did the newcomers influence. Along with the children of the traders, who were often bicultural, they formed a powerful clique of entrepreneurs that influenced the Chickasaw Nation's public affairs. They were pleased to grant the federal government permission, in 1801, to upgrade the Natchez Trace to a wagon road in return for the exclusive right to own and operate the ferries and taverns along it. They also supported the sale of peripheral lands, which brought substantial amounts of money into the nation in the form of direct payments, annuities, and bribes. In 1805 the Chickasaws sold their lands north of the Tennessee River, in 1816 they ceded the tract between the Tombigbee and Tennessee rivers and granted permission for U.S. citizens to navigate the Tombigbee to its head at Cotton Gin Port, and in 1818 they sold the country north of the Tennessee-Mississippi border.

During the 1820s, the Chickasaws experienced important changes. Their economy, driven by export production for over a century, made the transition from deerskins to livestock products and baled cotton, much of which was produced by the labor of slaves owned by an elite group of intermarried white settlers and bicultural Chickasaws. Many Chickasaws, however, embraced the new system of male-based rather than female-based agriculture, complete with draft animals and plows. But whereas Chickasaw men who hunted had individually controlled the production of deerskins and enjoyed the profits from their sale, the slave-owning entrepreneurial elites tended to dominate the new economy. For example, most of the income from the thousand bales of Chickasaw cotton shipped down the Tombigbee River from Cotton Gin Port to the gulf in 1830 lined the pockets of the planters. At the same time, new values arrived with Presbyterian missionaries, who had built one church and five schools by the mid-1820s. The Chickasaw National Council supported the schools with several thousand dollars of construction and operating money. Instruction was in English and included both academic and "practical" subjects.

Hungry for the rich land of the Chickasaw Nation, the Alabama and Mississippi state governments put continuous pressure on the U.S. government to remove the Chickasaws and on the Chickasaws to agree to get out. But there was no wish on the part of the Chickasaws to comply. In 1828 the national council did agree to send a delegation west to see if a suitable new homeland could be found; no one was surprised when the delegation reported that it found nothing satisfactory.

In 1830, shortly before the U.S. Congress passed the Removal Bill, Mississippi and Alabama extended state jurisdiction over the Chickasaw Nation and outlawed the national council. Under these circumstances, the Chickasaws agreed to meet with federal commissioners. The resulting treaty (signed at Franklin, Tennessee, in 1830) called for the sale of the nation, its allotment into reserves for each family, and removal if a new delegation could find acceptable lands in the West. Again the land rangers reported that none could be found, which nullified the treaty. In 1832, rampant intrusion by white squatters and further legal harassment by state authorities drove the Chickasaws into another negotiation with the United States. The Treaty of Pontotoc was similar to the Treaty of Franklin except that it increased the size of the reserves allotted to Chickasaw families. But the Chickasaw land rangers still could find no suitable place. Finally, in 1837, a Chickasaw delegation negotiated with the Choctaws the Treaty of Doaksville, by which the Choctaws sold to the Chickasaws for $530,000 the right to settle in the western part of their nation, henceforth to be called the Chickasaw District. This arrangement opened the way for Chickasaw removal.

The removal of the Chickasaws was unlike that of any other tribe. By the terms of the Treaty of Pontotoc, the family allotments were deeded to the individual allottees, which meant that they could sell the land and keep the money. A commission appointed by the national council oversaw the sales to protect the interests of the Chickasaws, and the land sold for about $1.50 per acre, more or less, depending on its quality. Over two million acres were allotted and sold under this system, putting a very large amount of money into the hands of the Chickasaws. Many of them invested this money in farm equipment, livestock, and slaves. The federal government sold at auction the unallotted land, over four million acres, for about $3.3 million. The government used this money to create the Chickasaw fund. While the United States supervised removal and drew all costs from the Chickasaw fund, whatever remained unspent reverted to the Chickasaw Nation.

Federal removal agents began to organize emigration parties immediately. The first left Mississippi in the summer of 1837; the last, early in 1838. Conductors let contracts for transportation and provisions in the usual ways, but because it was not federal money they ignored the usual oversights to prevent fraud and corruption. Through a combination of incompetence and dishonesty, the Chickasaws were robbed blind.

Compared with the removal experiences of the Choctaws, Creeks, and Cherokees, however, Chickasaw suffering was relatively light. But bad food and water took their toll, as did exposure to smallpox on the road through Arkansas. The most serious suffering occurred in Indian Territory. The Kiowas, Comanches, and other southern Plains tribes controlled the area earmarked for the Chickasaws, and the Chickasaw refugees were afraid to occupy their new home. Instead they erected five large temporary camps near the Choctaw settlements on the Red River and north into the Blue and Boggy River basins. Boggy Depot, one of these camps, became Chickasaw headquarters. Federal agents under treaty obligation to feed the immigrants after their arrival delivered provisions, but the meat, flour, and corn were rotten, rancid, and spoiled, and people often sickened and died when they ate the ruined food that was supplied for them.

While the Treaty of Doaksville stipulated that the Chickasaws could settle anywhere in the Choctaw Nation, the Choctaws preferred that they move into the Chickasaw District. Most Chickasaws were eager to do so, if they could live safely there. In response to Chickasaw security needs and Choctaw complaints, in 1841 the U.S. Army established Fort Washita on the Washita River in the southeastern corner of the Chickasaw District. In 1851 the army built a second post, Fort Arbuckle, northwest of Fort Washita. These steps encouraged almost one-fourth of the over four thousand Chickasaws to relocate immediately, and in the mid-1850s, over 90 percent of them lived in their own district.

But the Chickasaw District was part of the Choctaw Nation, and although the Chickasaws could send delegates to the Choctaw National Council, they could never be more than an alien minority within the Choctaw Nation and thus subject to Choctaw law. Growing Chickasaw nationalism, showing the Chickasaws' resentment of this subordinate status, led to various political actions. In 1846 a council at Boiling Springs drafted a statement asserting self-government for the Chickasaw District. Two years later, a similar council drew up a district constitution. This 1848 document, amended in 1849, established a Chickasaw District Council and provided for the popular election of a district chief. These separatist steps soon led to an agreement in 1854 that defined the boundary between the Choctaw Nation and the Chickasaw District. A treaty signed in Washington in 1855 recognized the sovereign Chickasaw Nation, with its capital at Tishomingo. The treaty also affirmed the boundary between the two nations, proclaimed the remaining boundaries as the Red and Canadian rivers and the 98th meridian, and established the country between the 98th and 100th meridians as a Choctaw-Chickasaw joint-use area that would be leased to the United States for $800,000.

Chickasaw Capitol at Tishomingo. (Courtesy W. David Baird)

33. REMOVAL OF THE SEMINOLES

Essay by *Michael D. Green*

During the early eighteenth century, troops from South Carolina and allied Indians, mainly Creeks, repeatedly invaded Spanish Florida. More than a dozen Spanish mission stations extending from the Atlantic to Pensacola housed most of the more than twelve thousand Indians native to northern Florida. Poorly armed, they were easy targets for the Carolina and Creek slave raiders. By 1715 northern Florida and the panhandle had become virtually depopulated.

A host of factors—including factional conflict within the Creek Confederacy, Spanish invitation, and a search for hunting grounds and deer herds—coalesced in the middle decades of the eighteenth century to draw communities out of the Lower Creek country of present-day Georgia and Alabama into Florida. They moved into the country from the Alachua Prairie (present-day Gainesville) west to Tallahassee and beyond. Culturally Creeks, these people came to be known as Seminoles, a term derived from a Muskogee word meaning something like "frontiersman" or "break-away-group."

Another group of "break-aways" found sanctuary in Florida. Spanish policy as early as the 1730s encouraged the black slaves of the English colonies to flee to Florida. In return for their help in defending the colony, Spain recognized them as free. Even during the period between 1763 and 1783, when England held Florida, small groups of slaves sought freedom there. The friendly Seminoles and the impenetrable swamps welcomed them. By 1790, with Spain back in Florida, the Seminoles numbered perhaps two thousand and the blacks associated with them perhaps five hundred.

Georgia planters feared Florida as enemy country—a Spanish colony inhabited by Indians and escaped slaves. During the early nineteenth century, the Georgians frequently raided Florida to capture these blacks. When the Creek refugees arrived in 1814 and more than doubled the Seminole population, the fears of Georgia slave owners intensified. In 1817, a combined force of U.S. and Creek troops invaded to smash the Seminole towns and kidnap the blacks for enslavement. This conflict, known as the First Seminole War, forced many Seminoles and their black associates southward into the peninsula of Florida. In 1819, the United States purchased Florida from Spain and brought it under U.S. jurisdiction as Florida Territory.

U.S. policy toward the Seminoles was influenced, in part, by the desire to encourage the cotton culture of Georgia and Alabama to expand south. To that end, Seminole claims to northern Florida and the panhandle had to be severed. The government also wanted to isolate the blacks allied with the Seminoles and minimize the danger that their presence posed to the security of plantation slavery. The Treaty of Moultrie Creek, concluded in 1823, sought to achieve these goals by setting aside a reservation for the Seminoles in the central peninsula just north of Lake Okeechobee. This was swampland generally considered useless for cotton agriculture.

This solution of isolating the Seminoles in the south had never satisfied the planter interests, who still feared the combined threat of nearby Indians and blacks. They therefore welcomed the Removal Act of 1830 and began immediately to lobby President Andrew Jackson to evict the Seminoles from Florida. This pressure resulted in the negotiation of the Treaty of Payne's Landing. Signed by a group of Seminole leaders in 1832, this treaty called for the sale of all Seminole lands in Florida and the removal of the people, at government expense, to Indian Territory, where they would move in with the Creeks. But the plan depended on an exploration of their new homeland by a party of Seminole headmen. A group of seven spent the winter and spring of 1832–33 in Indian Territory and signed, in March, a document at Fort Gibson that expressed their approval of the arrangement. Mystery and confusion surrounds this treaty, which the Seminole people denounced and rejected, but the U.S. Senate ratified it, and the United States bound the Seminoles to its terms.

The Second Seminole War, which broke out in 1835 and lasted until 1842, was the legacy of the treaties of Payne's Landing and Fort Gibson and the policies they reflected. Most Seminoles were unwilling to leave Florida, move west, and live in the Creek Nation, where they would lose their national identity. Only in 1841 and 1842, after several years of bitter fighting, did the removal of significant numbers of Seminoles occur. By 1844, over 3,800 had been relocated in the Creek Nation. Removal contractors shipped the Seminole emigrants on steamboats from Tampa, Charlotte Harbor, and other western Florida ports to New Orleans and then up the Mississippi and Arkansas rivers on riverboats to Fort Smith and Fort Gibson. Among the emigrant groups were the several hundred blacks who had been associated with the Seminoles for a century. Excluded were perhaps five hundred Seminoles who remained in the swamps of southern Florida.

In early 1849, a handful of Seminole men killed a white man on Florida's Indian River. Despite the fact that this was an isolated incident for which the Seminoles atoned by surrendering the killers to the army, this began the so-called Third Seminole War.

While federal troops and state militia prepared to invade the swamps of southern Florida, Seminole agent Marcellus DuVal received orders from Washington, D.C., to lead a delegation of headmen from Indian Territory to persuade their old friends and relatives to return west with them. Between 1858 and 1859, five such delegations made the journey to Florida and back. Together they removed an additional 314 Seminoles. A few remained in Florida, however, where their numerous descendants continue to live.

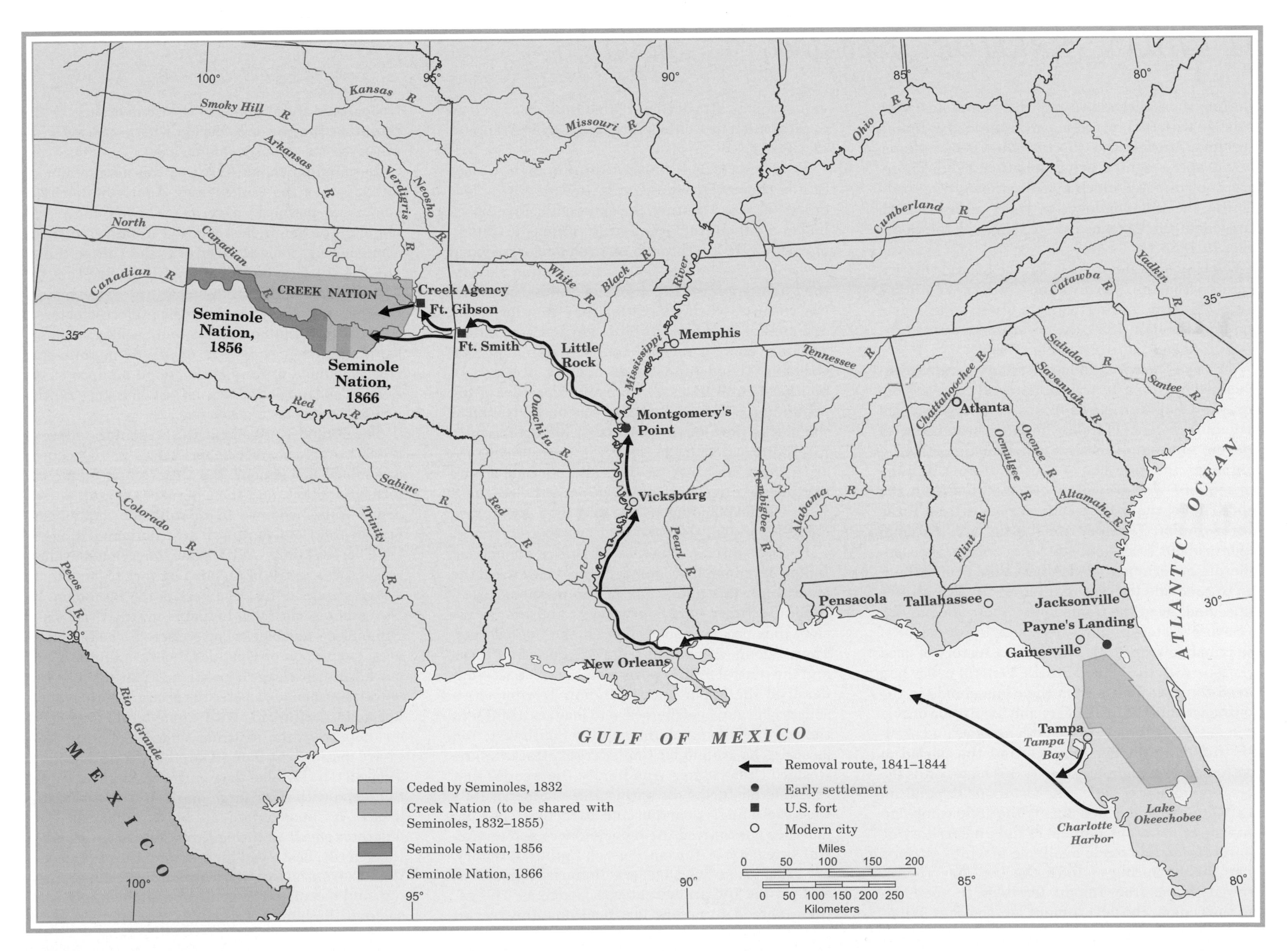

CREEK NATION
Creek Agency
Ft. Gibson
Ft. Smith
Seminole Nation, 1856
Seminole Nation, 1866
Little Rock
Memphis
Montgomery's Point
Vicksburg
New Orleans
Pensacola
Tallahassee
Jacksonville
Payne's Landing
Gainesville
Atlanta
Tampa
Tampa Bay
Charlotte Harbor
Lake Okeechobee
GULF OF MEXICO
ATLANTIC OCEAN
MEXICO
Kansas R
Smoky Hill R
Missouri R
Ohio R
Arkansas R
Verdigris R
Neosho R
Cumberland R
North Canadian R
Canadian R
White R
Black R
Mississippi River
Catawba R
Yadkin R
Tennessee R
Saluda R
Savannah R
Santee R
Chattahoochee R
Red R
Ouachita R
Ocmulgee R
Oconee R
Altamaha R
Sabine R
Colorado R
Trinity R
Red R
Pearl R
Tombigbee R
Alabama R
Flint R
Pecos R
Rio Grande
Ceded by Seminoles, 1832
Creek Nation (to be shared with Seminoles, 1832–1855)
Seminole Nation, 1856
Seminole Nation, 1866
Removal route, 1841–1844
Early settlement
U.S. fort
Modern city
Miles
0 50 100 150 200
0 50 100 150 200 250
Kilometers
100°
95°
90°
85°
80°
35°
30°

34. INDIAN TERRITORY, 1855–1866

Essay by *Michael D. Green*

Neither the Chickasaws nor the Seminoles were satisfied with their postremoval situations in Indian Territory. Stuck in the Choctaw and Creek nations, they deeply resented being denationalized. Therefore, they directed much attention toward reestablishing the independence of their nations. Both succeeded: the Chickasaws in 1855 and the Seminoles in 1856.

The United States quickly put the Leased District, acquired from the Choctaws and Chickasaws in 1855, to use. The army erected two forts, Camp Radziminski and Fort Cobb. In 1859, the government opened the Wichita Agency adjacent to Fort Cobb.

Very soon, however, Indian Territory became overwhelmed by the eastern sectional conflict, secession, and the Civil War. News from the states traveled fast, and residents of Indian Territory watched with interest Abraham Lincoln's victorious presidential campaign, the secession of South Carolina, and the subsequent withdrawal of other states from the union. In February 1861, commissioners from Texas toured Indian Territory, consulting with national leaders about secession; later that spring, the Confederate government sent Albert Pike from Arkansas to conclude treaties of alliance. By fall all five tribes had given the Confederacy their allegiance.

Several factors combine to explain the decisions of the tribal governments. None had a history of good relations with the United States. Federal policy had forced the Five Tribes from their homelands in the Southeast, and the dishonesty and ineptitude of government officials had caused both massive and needless suffering during removal and the period of postremoval rebuilding. Added to this history was the threat of further trouble. The victorious Republican Party had recommended during the 1860 campaign that the lands of the nations of Indian Territory be appropriated and made available to white settlers. Then, in the spring of 1861, the U.S. Army withdrew its forces from Indian Territory. In abandoning the region, the government left the Five Tribes vulnerable to attack from Plains Indians as well as to occupation by Confederate troops from Arkansas and Texas.

In addition to these "pushes" away from the United States, there were many "pulls" toward the Confederacy. For over a century, the elites of the Five Tribes had found their Anglo-American role models (many of whom were kin through an even longer period of intermarriage) in the South. In adopting slavery, they had embraced much of the Southern plantation culture as well. The cotton they grew for export and most of their imports flowed to and from Indian Territory along a river system dominated by New Orleans. Tribal funds were heavily invested in Southern enterprises. And about 15 percent of the population of Indian Territory was black. Not all of the blacks were slaves, slavery in Indian Territory rarely duplicated the most horrible aspects of Southern slavery, and Indians often did not hold strong attitudes of racial prejudice, but nevertheless these were all slaveholding tribes, and the Confederacy meant to protect slavery.

Furthermore, as the United States abandoned Indian Territory, the Confederacy courted it. All the federal officials and many of the missionaries in Indian Territory were Southerners, and after secession, they became spokesmen for the Confederacy. They—along with neighboring Arkansas and Texas and the central military command in the East—understood the importance of Indian Territory as a source of grain, beef, horses, and lead; as a buffer in the way of Union ambitions in the Southwest; and as a staging ground for Confederate attacks on the western Union states. And finally, the treaties that Pike offered during the spring and summer of 1861 were exceedingly generous and attractive. The Confederacy guaranteed the independence and territorial integrity of the nations of Indian Territory, promised to assume all federal financial obligations, and invited Indian delegates to Congress. The nations agreed to accept fortifications and recruit troops (paid and supplied by the Confederacy), while retaining the power to decide where and for what purposes the troops would be used.

Despite this, Indian Territory was not unanimous in support of the Confederacy. A large minority of Cherokees, perhaps a majority of Creeks, and a large majority of Seminoles opposed alliance with the Confederacy. Some were loyal to the United States and the treaties, but all strongly believed that the wisest course for their nations was neutrality. Since the early eighteenth century, the preferred policy of the southern Indian nations had been to avoid entanglement in the wars of white people, and Opothleyahola of the Creeks, John Chupco of the Seminoles, and John Ross of the Cherokees continued to counsel such a course.

The Confederates and neutrals spent the summer of 1861 organizing. The Chickasaws and Choctaws assembled a regiment, the Creeks and Seminoles formed another, and the Cherokees recruited two. Stand Watie, who rose to the rank of brigadier general in the Confederate Army, commanded one of the Cherokee units. At the same time, Opothleyahola called the neutrals of Indian Territory to join him in a large camp on the Deep Fork of the Canadian. By November, some 7,000 Indians—mostly Creeks and Seminoles—and blacks had gathered. The Confederates, suspicious of Opothleyahola's intentions and fearful of such a large opposition gathering, marched with 1,400 men to disperse the group. Opothleyahola led them northward. With Confederate troops hot on their trail, the neutrals staged elaborate rearguard actions at Round Mountain and Chusto Talasah that enabled the women, children, and aged to escape with their large herds and supply trains intact. At Chustenalah, late in December, the Confederates smashed the neutrals' defenses, dispersed their herds, destroyed their supply trains, and sent the survivors on foot into a blizzard. Freezing, starving, and bleeding, the neutrals stumbled into Kansas and the hands of woefully unprepared federal

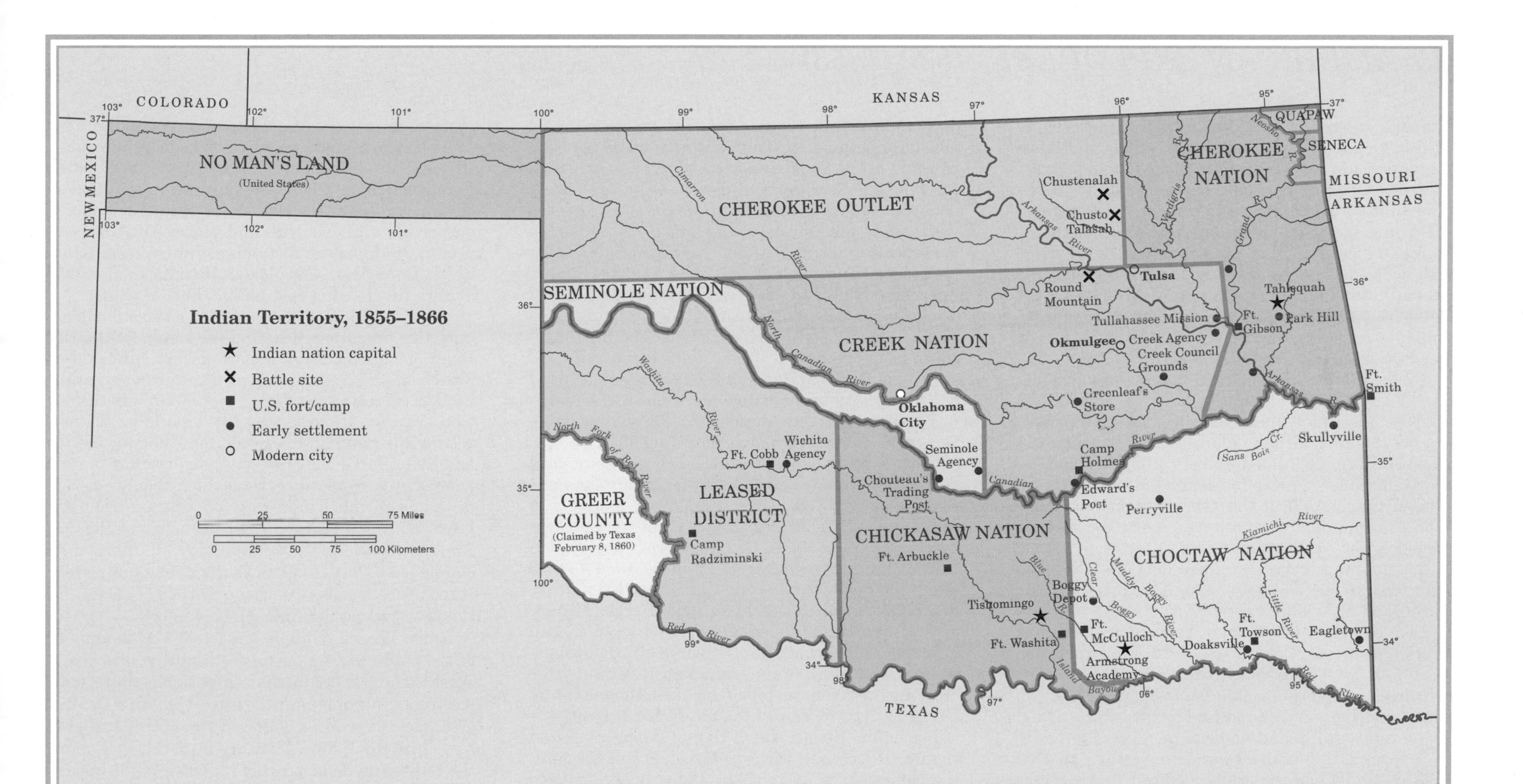

officials. A federal census counted 5,600 Creeks, 1,000 Seminoles, 140 Chickasaws, 315 Quapaws, 197 Delawares, and 300 members of other tribes in the refugee camps. The experience converted many neutrals to Unionists, and the camps in Kansas recruited two brigades of Indian troops committed to fight to retake their homes.

A Union army invaded Indian Territory in the spring of 1862 but quickly withdrew, only to return during the winter of 1862–63 to occupy the Cherokee Nation. This encouraged Unionist Cherokees to form a government that repudiated the Confederate treaty, declared Confederate Cherokees outlaws, and authorized the confiscation of their property. The Union army retook Fort Gibson and drove the Confederate troops south of the Canadian. From this point on, the Canadian River was the line of demarcation in Indian Territory.

When the war ended in mid-1865, the Cherokee Nation (scene of many battles) and the Creek Nation (overrun by guerrillas) were devastated. Along with the Cherokees and Creeks, Seminole men fought on both sides. And the Choctaws and Chickasaws, in addition to putting men in Confederate uniform, were burdened by the need to feed and house thousands of Creek refugees. The end of the war found no nation untouched.

35. AMERICAN EXPLORERS, 1832–1853 Essay by *Bruce W. Hoagland*

Starting in the 1830s, both civilian explorers and military expeditions crossed the largely unknown (to whites, anyway) Indian Territory. Hopes for commercial gain explained most of the private ventures. The military had other purposes, the most immediate being to establish friendly relations with the Plains tribes that roamed the area. Already there had been violent clashes between those tribes and other Indians whom officials in Washington were determined to remove there. The government also intended to secure unmolested passage for the newly permitted trade with Santa Fe.

Henry Ellsworth, appointed Indian commissioner in 1832 by President Andrew Jackson, headed the first and ultimately the best-known attempt to make friendly contact with the Plains tribes. The ultimate fame of this expedition, however, owed little to Ellsworth and even less to his command but is almost entirely attributable to the writings of three civilians who accompanied the military escort: the already famed writer Washington Irving; a nineteen-year-old Swiss count, Albert-Alexandre de Pourtales; and Charles Latrobe, the count's English-born tutor and a talented naturalist as well.

Leaving the army's then westernmost outpost (Fort Gibson) on October 10, 1832, the expedition took four weeks to reach the vicinity of today's Guthrie and Norman. One near-disaster had followed another—not one caused by the Plains tribes. In fact, the group had not seen a single Plains Indian when Ellsworth ordered the return to Fort Gibson. Badly battered, the expedition reached Fort Gibson defeated, the victim not of hostile forces but of mile after mile of what Washington Irving described as "forests of cast iron": the Cross Timbers. However total was the immediate military failure, the expedition's lasting fame was sealed by the civilian tag-alongs. Their published, detailed accounts—the best known was Irving's 1835 *Tour of the Prairies*—gave Americans a first, tantalizing glimpse of this new and difficult land.

Two years later, a force of dragoons (unusually well-appointed, mounted soldiers) made a second attempt to contact the Plains tribes. Brigadier General Henry Leavenworth was in command. Among the junior officers was First Lieutenant Jefferson Davis, who later became president of the Confederacy. The painter George Catlin was something of an artist-in-residence. Foul water and disease—the two surely not unrelated—plagued them from the start. Leavenworth was badly injured after being thrown from his horse while chasing buffalo. Command fell to Colonel Henry Dodge; on July 14, 1934, Dodge, with his impressively attired force, ran across some suitably awed Comanches. With their aid, he was able to arrange a meeting with several chiefs. The first negotiations between the Plains tribes and the U.S. government took place on July 22. Dodge departed on July 25 with twenty tribal representatives, reaching Fort Gibson on August 15. Unbeknownst to Dodge, Leavenworth had died on July 22.

Josiah Gregg—merchant, entrepreneur, and visionary—already had crossed the Great Plains several times by 1839, when the French blockade of Mexican ports sent him in search of the quickest overland route to Santa Fe. Gregg's caravan left Van Buren, Arkansas, on April 21 and followed a route along the north bank of the Canadian River. Forty dragoons joined the caravan near Purcell, where established trails ended. Gregg reentered Indian Territory on February 25, 1840, initially following a route to the south of the Canadian River but later crossing the river and following his outbound route. Gregg arrived in Van Buren on April 22, 1840.

Nathaniel Boone, son of Daniel Boone, operated the Boone Lick saltworks in Missouri before rejoining the military in 1832. In 1843, Boone and his rangers were ordered to investigate salt deposits near the 100th meridian, an international boundary at the time. They departed Fort Gibson on March 14 and passed near Tulsa before entering the open plains near Tonkawa. Boone reconnoitered the Great Salt Plains in early June and thereupon escorted immigrants along the Santa Fe Trail. He reentered the state on June 28 and proceeded to explore the gypsum hills, near Freedom. Following the Canadian River eastward, Boone returned to Fort Gibson on July 31.

Randolph Marcy and his Fifth Infantry crossed into Indian Territory from Fort Smith in May 1849 under orders to escort gold prospectors to Santa Fe. The caravan of gold seekers stretched for miles when the expedition left Fort Smith. The route they followed, which paralleled the Canadian's south bank, became known as the California Road. The trip was surprisingly uneventful, and Marcy left the prospectors to their own fortunes to return from Santa Fe via Doña Ana, New Mexico, then north along the Trinity River to his destination, Fort Washita.

Marcy was less successful with a second expedition, this one ordered to find the source of the Red River. This expedition departed Fort Arbuckle on March 5, 1852, with Brevet Captain George McClellan second in command. McClellan was the one who, on May 29, marked the 100th meridian, thereby setting the boundary between the Choctaw Nation and Texas. McClellan's measurement, unfortunately, was off by several miles. He made a second—and in the long run, much more consequential—error a day later. When he reached the confluence of the Red River with its North Fork, on May 30, Marcy proclaimed the North Fork to be the river's main stem. It took decades and a decision by the U.S. Supreme Court to correct that one mistake.

Amiel Weeks Whipple led across Oklahoma one of the three survey parties sent out by officials in Washington, D.C., to chart a possible route for a future transcontinental railway to the Pacific. Whipple's expedition followed the 35th parallel to cross into the Indian Territory from the east, along the California Road, on July 15, 1853. While in eastern Indian Territory, Whipple noted an abundance of coal, which would become a resource for railroad development by the close of the century. Slowed by capricious weather and illness, the expedition had traveled only as far as Purcell by August. Still moving westward, Whipple left Indian Territory behind on September 4. He finally reached the Pacific (near Los Angeles) on March 21, 1854.

The expedition was a success. Its outcome, though, was nothing. Despite Whipple's hard work and carefully documented observations, a transcontinental railroad route along the 35th parallel was never built to the Pacific Ocean.

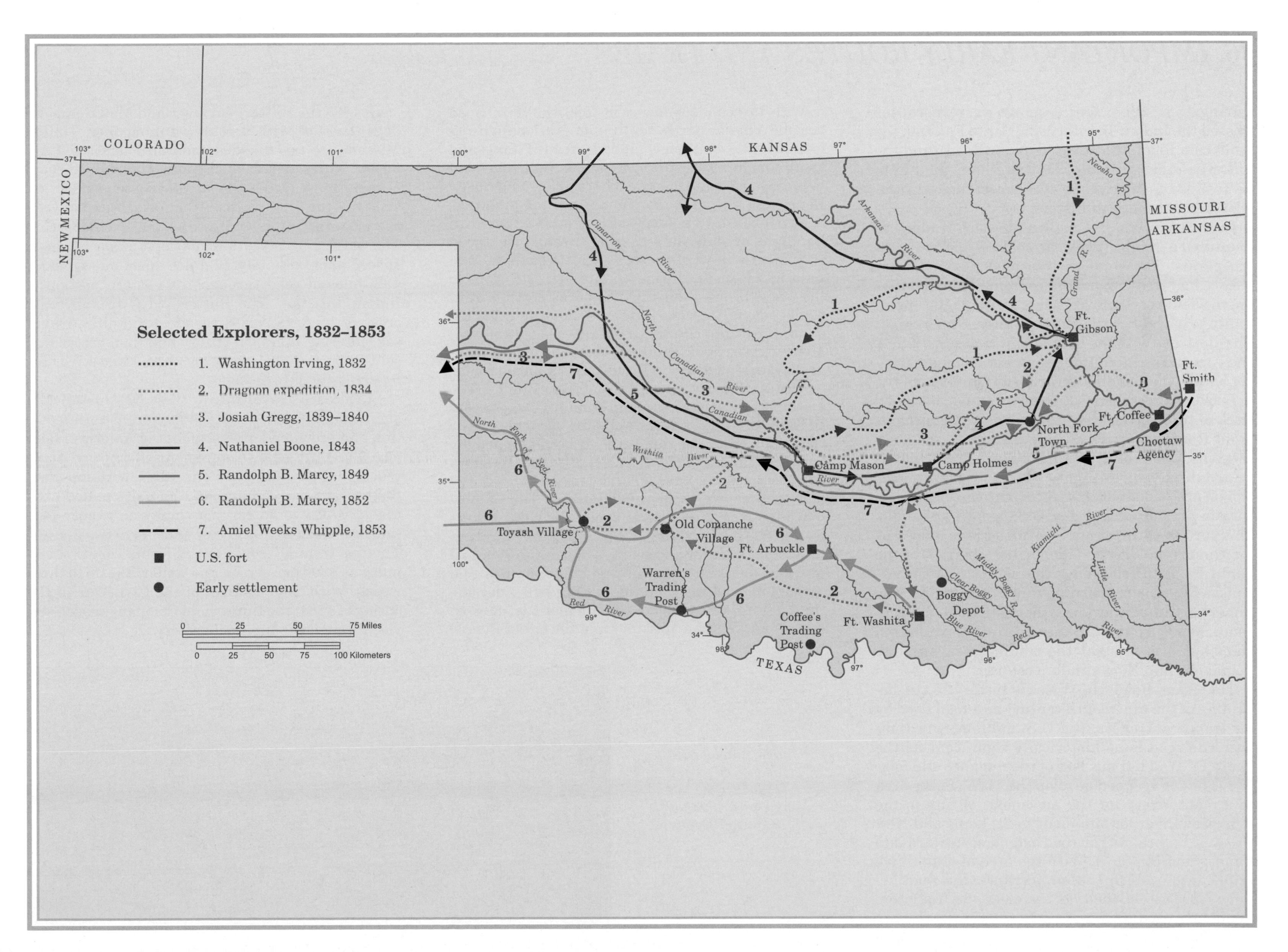

Selected Explorers, 1832–1853
1. Washington Irving, 1832
2. Dragoon expedition, 1834
3. Josiah Gregg, 1839–1840
4. Nathaniel Boone, 1843
5. Randolph B. Marcy, 1849
6. Randolph B. Marcy, 1852
7. Amiel Weeks Whipple, 1853
U.S. fort
Early settlement
0 25 50 75 Miles
0 25 50 75 100 Kilometers
COLORADO
KANSAS
NEW MEXICO
MISSOURI
ARKANSAS
TEXAS
Cimarron River
North Canadian River
Canadian River
Arkansas River
Neosho R.
Grand R.
Washita River
North Fork of Red River
Red River
Kiamichi River
Little River
Muddy Boggy R.
Clear Boggy
Blue River
Ft. Gibson
Ft. Smith
Ft. Coffee
North Fork Town
Choctaw Agency
Camp Mason
Camp Holmes
Toyash Village
Old Comanche Village
Ft. Arbuckle
Warren's Trading Post
Boggy Depot
Coffee's Trading Post
Ft. Washita

36. IMPORTANT EARLY ROUTES AND TRAILS

Essay by *John R. Lovett*

During the 1800s, four famous western routes crossed the Indian Territory: the Santa Fe Trail, the California Road, the Texas Trail (or Road), and the Butterfield Stage Route. Of these four, the Santa Fe Trail is considered one of the most famous trading trails in American history.

In 1821 William Becknell, a Missouri trader, encountered a group of Mexican soldiers on the southern plains. The soldiers informed Becknell that Mexico had won independence from Spain and that the residents of Santa Fe would welcome the opportunity to trade with the United States. Under Spanish rule, trade with the United States was restricted, and Americans faced imprisonment if caught trading within the Spanish-controlled frontier areas.

Becknell proceeded to Santa Fe and sold his small stock of trade goods there. He earned an enormous profit from this activity, being paid in Mexican silver coins. Upon returning to Missouri, Becknell purchased three wagons that he filled with trade goods, and he proceeded southwest to Santa Fe, crossing a portion of the present-day Oklahoma Panhandle. This portion of the Santa Fe Trail became known as the Cimarron Cut-off. The northern portion of the Santa Fe Trail followed a course north of the Arkansas River before turning south to Santa Fe. The Cimarron Cut-off shortened the route from Independence, Missouri, to the Santa Fe Trail by a hundred miles but also brought the trading caravans into Comanche and Kiowa Indian country.

The Texas Road can trace its history to the beginning of the nineteenth century as a trail used by fur trappers, traders, the U.S. military, and Indians. The road is as historically significant as the Santa Fe Trail but has less of the romance and folklore. The road helped develop the Three Forks area as a main artery for the movement of furs to the Arkansas River for shipment to St. Louis and New Orleans. Laterals of the road extend northward into Kansas and Missouri. With the arrival of the Five Tribes into eastern Indian Territory, the road became more established, as travelers and freighters frequently used it.

With Texas independence in 1836, the Texas Road became a major north–south immigration highway for settlers seeking new lands in Texas. Stores and small communities sprang up along the Texas Road to provide food and lodging for travelers. Old Boggy Depot was one of the more important communities; it developed into a flourishing trade center, with hundreds of emigrants passing through the town. In the early days of the Texas cattle trade to Missouri and Kansas, the merchants sold provisions to the Texas drovers pushing the herds north toward rail heads in Kansas. A later merchant to establish a business on the Texas Road was James J. McAlester. In 1870 McAlester established his store at the crossroads of the Texas and California roads.

With the discovery of gold in California in 1848, an important east–west migration highway across Indian Territory was established. Known as the California Road, the route quickly became a heavily traveled thoroughfare. It entered Indian Territory at Fort Smith, Arkansas, and ran west to what is now the western border of Oklahoma. The California Road was the route of choice for gold seekers living in the southern United States. Captain Randolph B. Marcy and soldiers under his command provided a military escort for the first group of gold seekers headed west. For more than half a decade, the California Road served as a major east-to-west route across Indian Territory and the Great Plains.

In 1858 the Butterfield Overland Mail Company began service with a route running from Tipton, Missouri, to Los Angeles and San Francisco, California. With congressional approval, the Butterfield Company provided both mail and passenger service. This was the first transcontinental service between the eastern United States and the Pacific Ocean. The stage line maintained twelve stage stations spaced approximately 15 miles apart along nearly 192 miles of road through the eastern portion of Indian Territory. The Butterfield Overland route crossed the Arkansas River at Fort Smith, Arkansas, entering Indian Territory and then proceeding southwest to Colbert's Ferry on the Red River before crossing into Texas.

Stagecoach travel in the West was historically significant because it served as a transcontinental link and provided a rich segment in American folklore. The Butterfield Company used a heavy stagecoach, manufactured in Concord, New Hampshire. Six to eight horses harnessed in pairs pulled each coach, which could carry as many as twenty passengers, along with a driver and one to two guards. The trip from Missouri to California could cost as much as $200 per person and would take up to three weeks. With the outbreak of the Civil War in the spring of 1861, the Butterfield Company ceased service through the Indian Territory.

The Antelope Hills as viewed from a route across western Oklahoma. (Goins collection)

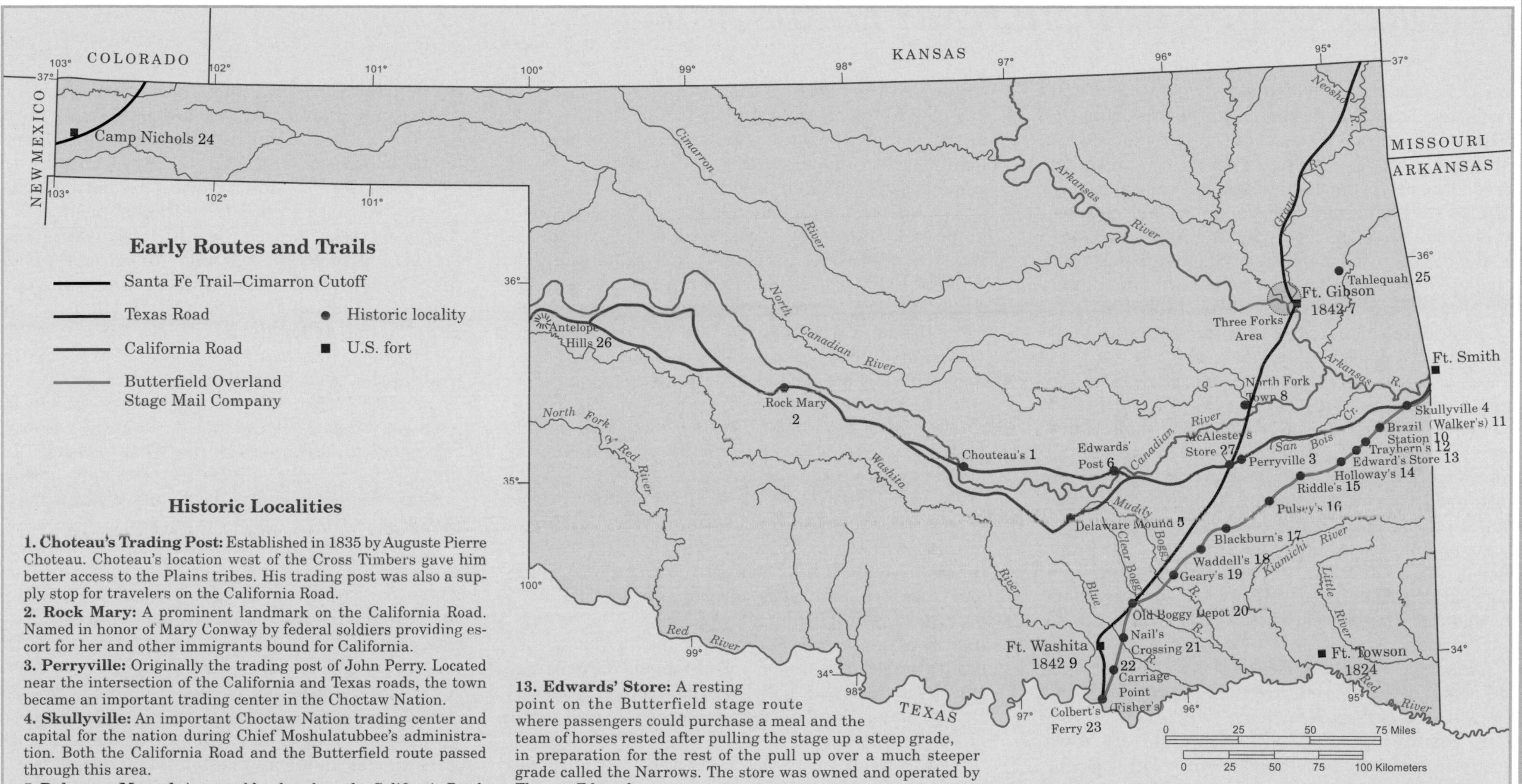

Historic Localities

1. Choteau's Trading Post: Established in 1835 by Auguste Pierre Choteau. Choteau's location west of the Cross Timbers gave him better access to the Plains tribes. His trading post was also a supply stop for travelers on the California Road.

2. Rock Mary: A prominent landmark on the California Road. Named in honor of Mary Conway by federal soldiers providing escort for her and other immigrants bound for California.

3. Perryville: Originally the trading post of John Perry. Located near the intersection of the California and Texas roads, the town became an important trading center in the Choctaw Nation.

4. Skullyville: An important Choctaw Nation trading center and capital for the nation during Chief Moshulatubbee's administration. Both the California Road and the Butterfield route passed through this area.

5. Delaware Mound: A natural landmark on the California Road.

6. Edwards' Post: Established by John Edwards on the Canadian River. Edwards was a licensed Indian trader; his establishment was an important supply point on the California Road and also served as an exchange location for Indian captives.

7. Fort Gibson: Located near the Texas Road, the fort was established in 1824 and served as a supply point for many travelers using the Texas Road.

8. North Fork Town: Early Creek settlement that provided supplies for travelers using the Texas Road.

9. Fort Washita: Established in 1842 on the Texas Road.

10. Brazil Station: Although not an official station for the Butterfield Overland Mail, the station was a supply point for travelers.

11. Walker's: Butterfield Overland Mail station located at Skullyville, Choctaw Nation. Named for the Choctaw chief Tandy Walker.

12. Trayhern's: Butterfield Overland Mail station named for James N. Trayhern, stage station agent and local merchant.

13. Edwards' Store: A resting point on the Butterfield stage route where passengers could purchase a meal and the team of horses rested after pulling the stage up a steep grade, in preparation for the rest of the pull up over a much steeper grade called the Narrows. The store was owned and operated by Thomas Edwards.

14. Holloway's: Butterfield Overland Mail station thought to have been named for William Holloway, the original owner of the station.

15. Riddle's: Butterfield Overland Mail station named for local merchant and toll-bridge concession holder John Riddle.

16. Pulsey's: Butterfield Overland Mail station named for local merchant and farmer Silas Pulsey.

17. Blackburn's: Butterfield Overland Mail station named for local merchant Casper B. Blackburn.

18. Waddell's: Butterfield Overland Mail station. The first name of Waddell remains unknown.

19. Geary's: Butterfield Overland Mail station named for A. W. Geary, a local toll-bridge operator.

20. Old Boggy Depot: An important trade center in the Choctaw Nation and the largest settlement on the stage route between Fort Smith, Arkansas, and Sherman, Texas. Like Walker's station, Boggy Depot included a station and post office.

21. Nail's Crossing: Butterfield Overland Mail station named for Jonathan Nail, a prominent Choctaw who established a store, sawmill, and toll bridge on the Blue River.

22. Fisher's: Butterfield Overland Mail station known locally as Carriage Point. The first name of Fisher remains unknown.

23. Colbert's Ferry: An important crossing site on the Red River. The ferry was owned and operated by B. F. Colbert, a prominent Chickasaw.

24. Camp Nichols: Established in 1865 to protect the traders on the Santa Fe Trail from the Plains tribes.

25. Tahlequah, Cherokee Nation: An important rendezvous and supply point for emigrants moving south to the California Road.

26. Antelope Hills: The Antelope Hills, also known as the Boundary Mounds, was a landform guide for the emigrants on the California Road and during the opening of the high plains.

27. McAlester's Store: In 1870, James J. McAlester established his store at the crossroads of the Texas and California roads.

37. *FORTS, CAMPS, AND MILITARY ROADS, 1816–1865*

Essay by *John R. Lovett*

The U.S. Army established forts in the area now known as Oklahoma for many purposes during the 1816 to 1865 period. Several of the early forts were part of a north–south line of reinforcements that served as a protective buffer for frontier settlements against incursions by hostile American Indians. Other forts were charged with the mission of protecting the resettled members of the Five Tribes from attacks by their new western neighbors. During the Civil War, the Confederates also established forts to consolidate their control of the area and to repel Federal intrusions.

Naturally, the establishment of forts necessitated providing supplies to the installations. Military roads were surveyed, constructed, and maintained for this purpose. The military roads connected the frontier forts with the supply depots in the east and were used for the movement of soldiers and military supplies. These routes also became important trade and immigration roads during the frontier period. Pre-1865 military roads included one from Fort Smith, Arkansas, to Fort Gibson and Fort Towson and another from Little Rock, Arkansas, to Fort Towson.

The soldiers who garrisoned the new frontier forts and constructed the military roads in Indian Territory found themselves far from civilization in less-than-hospitable conditions. The soldiers were required to march over rough terrain for weeks or months to reach the location for the construction of the fort. Because they lived in tents or crude shelters while constructing the fort, many died of illness before they could adjust to the climate and unstable diet. For those who served at forts located near hostile Indians, the threat of attack was a continuous aspect of their service.

The first fort established in the area was located at Belle Point on the south bank of the Arkansas River. Brevet Major Stephen H. Long and Captain William Bradford selected the site; construction began in 1817. The post was located on Choctaw land until the land was ceded to the United States in 1825. Fort Smith was primarily established to help restrain the Cherokee-Osage conflict. Although located in Arkansas, Fort Smith played an important role in the history of Indian Territory. Abandoned and reoccupied twice, Fort Smith continued as a military post until 1871.

In April 1824, the U.S. Army established Fort Gibson on the Grand River. Fort Gibson's primary mission was to protect white trappers and traders in the area and to stop conflicts between the Osage and Cherokee. Several members of the pre–Civil War garrison at Fort Gibson later served as officers during the Mexican War and the U.S. Civil War. These distinguished officers included Stephen W. Kearney, Philip St. George Cooke, David Hunter, Braxton Bragg, and Jefferson Davis, who became president of the Confederacy.

Fort Towson, along the Red River, was built one month after the establishment of Fort Gibson. Towson had a dual mission that consisted of protecting the Choctaws and Chickasaws and establishing a U.S. military presence on Mexico's northern Texas border. Along with Fort Smith in Arkansas and Fort Gibson on the Grand River, Fort Towson served as the U.S. military presence on the Indian Territory frontier until the establishment of Fort Coffee on the Arkansas River in 1834. The garrison at Fort Coffee was tasked with protecting the Choctaws and Chickasaws and intercepting white traders attempting to ship whiskey up the Arkansas River into the Indian Territory.

The westernmost army fort located in Indian Territory prior to the Civil War was Fort Cobb. Named in honor of Treasury Secretary Howell Cobb, the fort was established on October 1, 1859, at the point where Pond Creek enters the Washita River. The fort's primary mission was to serve as a military presence for the newly established Wichita Indian Agency.

During the Civil War, the Confederates constructed two forts in Indian Territory. One, Fort Davis, was built on the west bank of the Arkansas River following the reoccupation of Fort Gibson (on the east bank) by Federal troops. The other was Fort McCulloch, which utilized extensive earthworks for defense. Kit Carson, the famed explorer and brigadier general of New Mexico volunteers, established Camp Nichols for the Union in the present-day Oklahoma Panhandle. The garrison at Camp Nichols provided protection for wagon trains on the Santa Fe Trail.

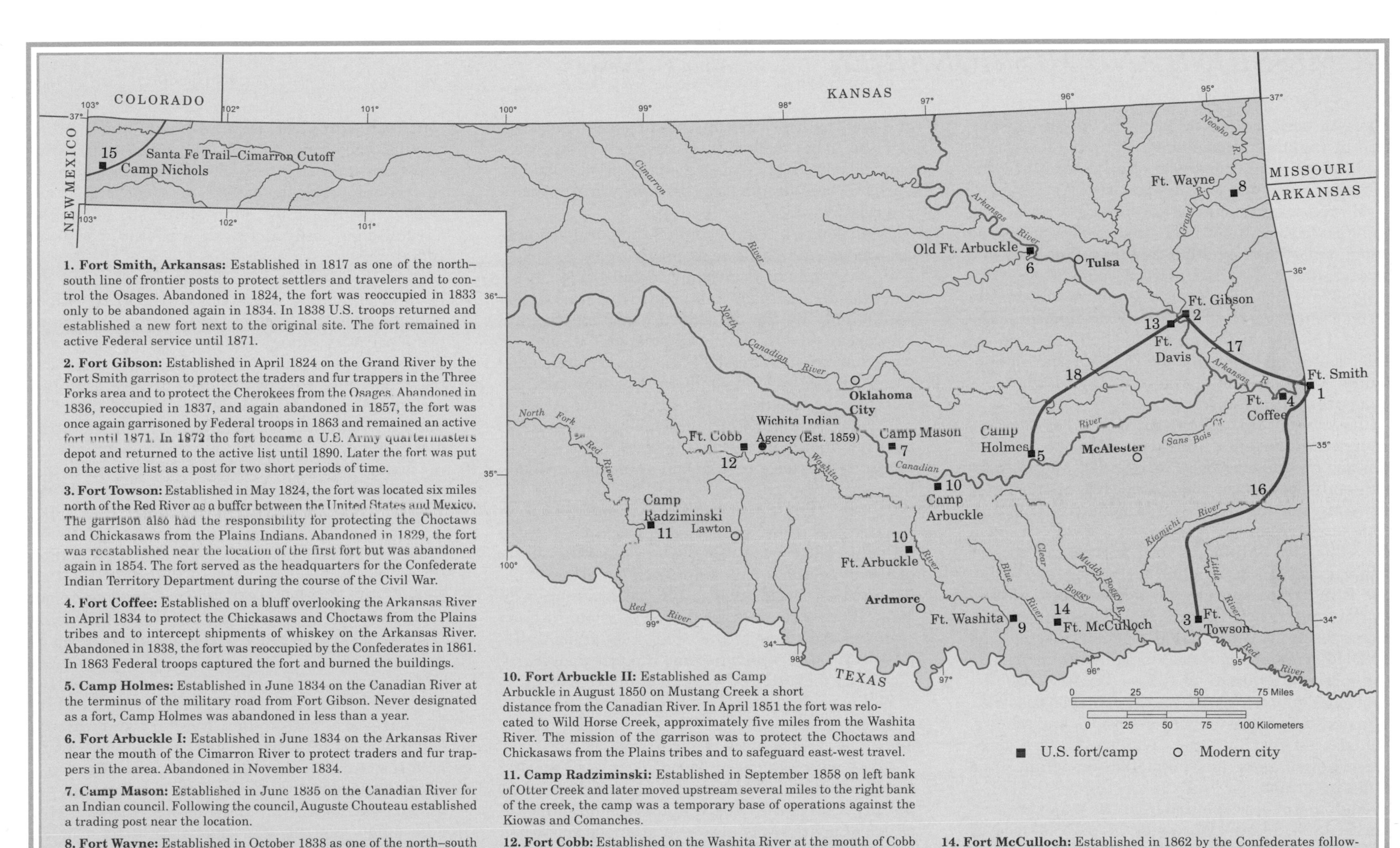

1. Fort Smith, Arkansas: Established in 1817 as one of the north–south line of frontier posts to protect settlers and travelers and to control the Osages. Abandoned in 1824, the fort was reoccupied in 1833 only to be abandoned again in 1834. In 1838 U.S. troops returned and established a new fort next to the original site. The fort remained in active Federal service until 1871.

2. Fort Gibson: Established in April 1824 on the Grand River by the Fort Smith garrison to protect the traders and fur trappers in the Three Forks area and to protect the Cherokees from the Osages. Abandoned in 1836, reoccupied in 1837, and again abandoned in 1857, the fort was once again garrisoned by Federal troops in 1863 and remained an active fort until 1871. In 1872 the fort became a U.S. Army quartermasters depot and returned to the active list until 1890. Later the fort was put on the active list as a post for two short periods of time.

3. Fort Towson: Established in May 1824, the fort was located six miles north of the Red River as a buffer between the United States and Mexico. The garrison also had the responsibility for protecting the Choctaws and Chickasaws from the Plains Indians. Abandoned in 1829, the fort was reestablished near the location of the first fort but was abandoned again in 1854. The fort served as the headquarters for the Confederate Indian Territory Department during the course of the Civil War.

4. Fort Coffee: Established on a bluff overlooking the Arkansas River in April 1834 to protect the Chickasaws and Choctaws from the Plains tribes and to intercept shipments of whiskey on the Arkansas River. Abandoned in 1838, the fort was reoccupied by the Confederates in 1861. In 1863 Federal troops captured the fort and burned the buildings.

5. Camp Holmes: Established in June 1834 on the Canadian River at the terminus of the military road from Fort Gibson. Never designated as a fort, Camp Holmes was abandoned in less than a year.

6. Fort Arbuckle I: Established in June 1834 on the Arkansas River near the mouth of the Cimarron River to protect traders and fur trappers in the area. Abandoned in November 1834.

7. Camp Mason: Established in June 1835 on the Canadian River for an Indian council. Following the council, Auguste Chouteau established a trading post near the location.

8. Fort Wayne: Established in October 1838 as one of the north–south line of frontier forts. The original location south of the Illinois River was abandoned in June 1840 because of the unhealthy location. Fort Wayne was reestablished in July 1840 near Spavinaw Creek but was abandoned in May 1842. During the Civil War, the fort was briefly used by the Confederates.

9. Fort Washita: Established in April 1842 on the Washita River to protect the Chickasaws from the Plains tribes. Fort Washita was abandoned by the Federal garrison in 1861 and reoccupied by Confederate troops from Texas. Following the Civil War, the fort was not reoccupied by a U.S. Army garrison.

10. Fort Arbuckle II: Established as Camp Arbuckle in August 1850 on Mustang Creek a short distance from the Canadian River. In April 1851 the fort was relocated to Wild Horse Creek, approximately five miles from the Washita River. The mission of the garrison was to protect the Choctaws and Chickasaws from the Plains tribes and to safeguard east-west travel.

11. Camp Radziminski: Established in September 1858 on left bank of Otter Creek and later moved upstream several miles to the right bank of the creek, the camp was a temporary base of operations against the Kiowas and Comanches.

12. Fort Cobb: Established on the Washita River at the mouth of Cobb Creek in October 1859 to protect the Indians at the Wichita Agency. The fort was abandoned by the Federal garrison at the outbreak of the Civil War and was reoccupied by Confederate troops. In October 1862, Federal Indians attacked the garrison and burned most of the buildings. The fort saw service again in 1869 but was in operation for less than a year. The fort was abandoned, and the garrison moved to Fort Sill.

13. Fort Davis: Established by the Confederates in November 1861 across the Arkansas River from Fort Gibson to consolidate Confederate control in the northern portion of Indian Territory. In 1862 the fort was destroyed by Federal troops.

14. Fort McCulloch: Established in 1862 by the Confederates following their defeat at Pea Ridge, Arkansas, to consolidate Confederate control in the southern portion of Indian Territory. The fort was primarily a system of earthwork parapets.

15. Camp Nichols: Established in June 1865 by Kit Carson on the Santa Fe Trail (Cimarron branch) to protect travel on the route.

16. Fort Smith to Fort Towson military road.

17. Fort Gibson to Fort Smith military road.

18. Fort Gibson to Camp Holmes military road.

38. *MISSIONS AND MISSIONARIES* Essay by *Alvin O. Turner*

Missions were a powerful factor in the transformation of Indian culture during the nineteenth century. Mission locations also often determined the routes of roads and location of towns.

Moravian missionaries initiated efforts among the Five Tribes in 1801. Their successes triggered expanded efforts by other denominations as well as organization of the United Foreign Mission Society (UFMS), a joint Presbyterian and Dutch Reformed initiative in 1817. The UFMS sponsored the work of Epaphras Chapman and Job Vinal among the Osages in Oklahoma and the establishment of Union Mission—the first mission in Oklahoma—near present-day Mazie in 1821.

That same year, the American Board of Commissioners for Foreign Missions (ABCFM), a joint missionary endeavor for Presbyterian and Congregationalist churches, established Dwight Mission in Arkansas, among the Western Cherokees. That mission moved to Indian Territory in 1828. Even stronger Christian influences arrived with successive tribal migrations into Indian Territory. Many within the Five Tribes had already adopted Christianity by the time of their Trails of Tears. Frequently, missionaries from the ABCFM or their Baptist and Methodist counterparts accompanied the tribes on the forced migrations to Indian Territory and became major forces in tribal cultural and political life. The missionaries established missions and schools, translated tribal languages, published Bibles, sponsored newspapers, and promoted temperance and other programs.

The Cherokees benefited from two major endeavors. In 1835, Samuel Worcester (of ABCFM) located at Dwight Mission, where he established a printing press and produced the first materials printed in Oklahoma. In 1837, he moved to Park Hill, near Tahlequah, where he built the Cherokee seminary and eventually printed millions of pages of missionary and tribal materials. Worcester's efforts were particularly effective among mixed-blood elements. Park Hill became known as the Athens of the American Southwest.

Evan Jones, a Baptist, built a comparable ministry among full-bloods near present-day Westville; his establishment eventually included the Cherokee Female Seminary and printing operations exceeded only by Worcester's. Jesse Bushyhead, a Cherokee convert, was a key element in most of Jones's successes. The ABCFM's Cyrus Byington and Cyrus Kingsbury built similar ministries among the Choctaws and Chickasaws. By 1838, the ABCFM had come to maintain ten schools among those tribes. Byington published the first Choctaw grammar in 1843, and Albert Wright's translation of biblical texts followed shortly.

In 1842, Evan Jones initiated Baptist work in the Creek Nation, which had opposed missionary influence before then. Jones's work and the efforts of Joseph Island, a Creek minister, led to the establishment of the Muskogee Baptist Association in 1851. By that time, Presbyterian missionaries had resumed work among the Creeks, founding Tullahassee Mission, which became the principal learning center for the Creek Nation under the direction of William S. and Ann Eliza Robertson. John Bemo, a Seminole convert, spearheaded initial efforts among his people in the same period.

Missionary influences played key roles in shaping tribal responses to the slavery issue and subsequent participation in the Civil War. Missionary influence on tribal politics was also seen after the war when John Jones, son of Evan, played a major role in facilitating the reunification of the Cherokees.

Despite delays caused by tribal divisions and other problems, the resumption of missionary work contributed greatly to stabilization in Indian Territory in other ways as well, and missionary influences continued to grow. John Jumper resigned as chief of the Seminoles in 1877 to devote full attention to his preaching. John McIntosh, son of the Creek leader Chilly McIntosh, was welcomed as an Indian missionary among the tribes of the Southwest in the same decade. The decade also saw expanded missionary efforts among the Plains tribes with the introduction of President Ulysses S. Grant's peace policy, encouraging Mennonites, Quakers, and other pacifists to work as Indian agents among these tribes. Notable work by members of these groups—including John J. Methvin, Frank Hall Wright, and numerous others—did not reach its full potential, however, because of limited resources and changing federal policies and problems faced by the tribes. As a result, missions were comparatively limited in western Oklahoma, with most formed after 1890. Among the most important were Sacred Heart (Catholic: Pottawatomie), Seger Colony (Mennonite: Cheyenne and Arapaho), Rainy Mountain (Baptist: Kiowa), and Whirlwind (Episcopal: Cheyenne). Converts from Plains tribes—such as David Pendleton Oakerhater (Episcopal: Cheyenne)—also served as missionaries.

The most important factor shaping missionary responses after 1890 was the rapid influx of white populations in both Indian Territory and western Oklahoma. This flood of people overwhelmed available resources in the mainstream denominations, which often shifted their focus to ministries in the growing settlements. Indian missions soon declined accordingly, but this loss was partly offset by state and local religious organizations establishing churches among tribal communities across the state. Baptists and Methodists were particularly successful in this regard.

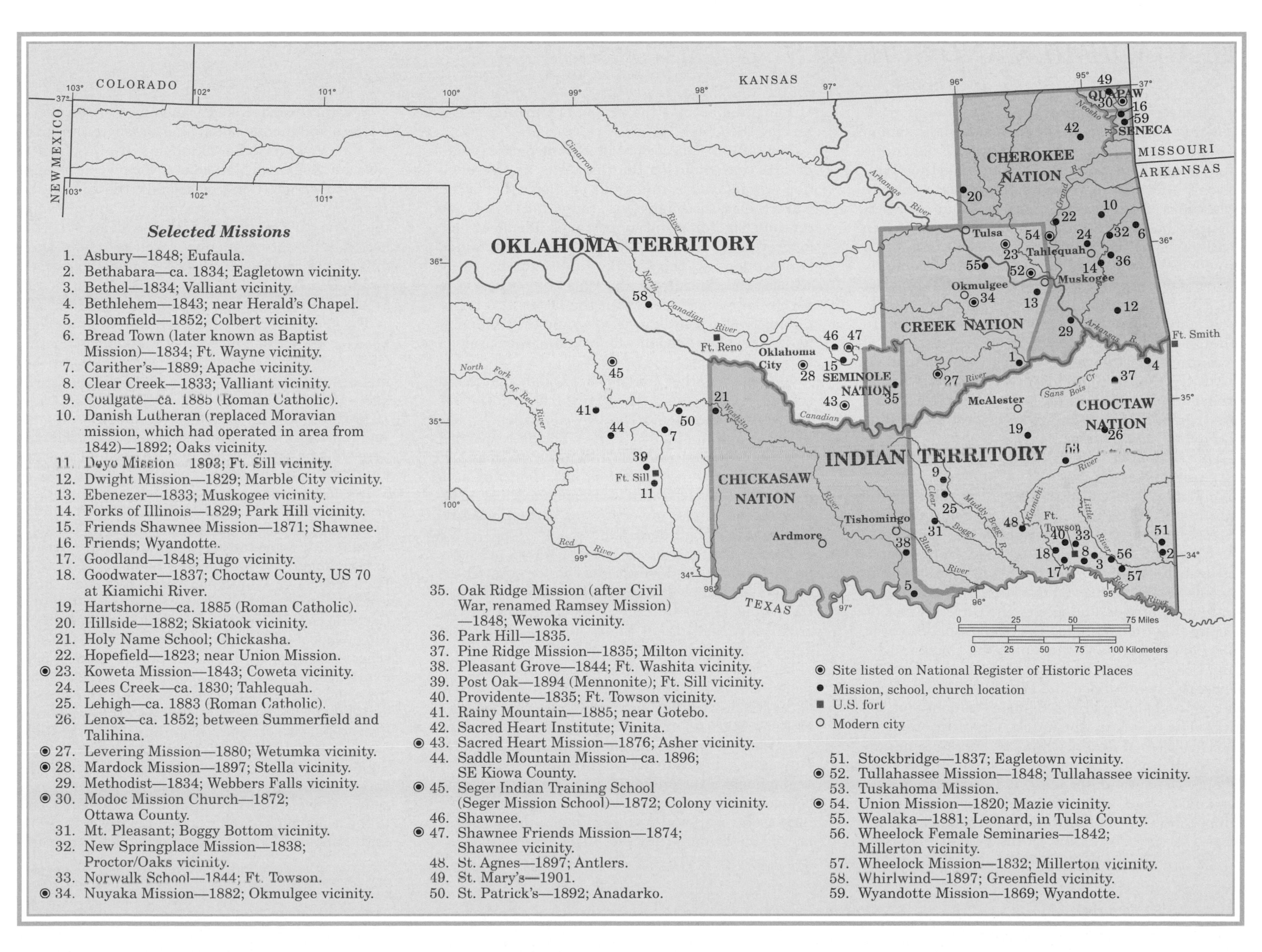

COLORADO
KANSAS
NEW MEXICO
MISSOURI
ARKANSAS
TEXAS
OKLAHOMA TERRITORY
INDIAN TERRITORY
CHEROKEE NATION
CREEK NATION
SEMINOLE NATION
CHICKASAW NATION
CHOCTAW NATION
QUAPAW
SENECA
Tulsa
Tahlequah
Muskogee
Okmulgee
Oklahoma City
McAlester
Tishomingo
Ardmore
Ft. Reno
Ft. Sill
Ft. Towson
Ft. Smith
Cimarron
Arkansas River
North Canadian River
Canadian River
North Fork of Red River
Washita
Red River
Grand R.
Neosho
Sans Bois Cr
Kiamichi
Little River
Muddy Boggy R.
Clear Boggy
Blue River
0 25 50 75 Miles
0 25 50 75 100 Kilometers
Selected Missions
1. Asbury—1848; Eufaula.
2. Bethabara—ca. 1834; Eagletown vicinity.
3. Bethel—1834; Valliant vicinity.
4. Bethlehem—1843; near Herald's Chapel.
5. Bloomfield—1852; Colbert vicinity.
6. Bread Town (later known as Baptist Mission)—1834; Ft. Wayne vicinity.
7. Carither's—1889; Apache vicinity.
8. Clear Creek—1833; Valliant vicinity.
9. Coalgate—ca. 1885 (Roman Catholic).
10. Danish Lutheran (replaced Moravian mission, which had operated in area from 1842)—1892; Oaks vicinity.
11. Deyo Mission—1893; Ft. Sill vicinity.
12. Dwight Mission—1829; Marble City vicinity.
13. Ebenezer—1833; Muskogee vicinity.
14. Forks of Illinois—1829; Park Hill vicinity.
15. Friends Shawnee Mission—1871; Shawnee.
16. Friends; Wyandotte.
17. Goodland—1848; Hugo vicinity.
18. Goodwater—1837; Choctaw County, US 70 at Kiamichi River.
19. Hartshorne—ca. 1885 (Roman Catholic).
20. Hillside—1882; Skiatook vicinity.
21. Holy Name School; Chickasha.
22. Hopefield—1823; near Union Mission.
23. Koweta Mission—1843; Coweta vicinity.
24. Lees Creek—ca. 1830; Tahlequah.
25. Lehigh—ca. 1883 (Roman Catholic).
26. Lenox—ca. 1852; between Summerfield and Talihina.
27. Levering Mission—1880; Wetumka vicinity.
28. Mardock Mission—1897; Stella vicinity.
29. Methodist—1834; Webbers Falls vicinity.
30. Modoc Mission Church—1872; Ottawa County.
31. Mt. Pleasant; Boggy Bottom vicinity.
32. New Springplace Mission—1838; Proctor/Oaks vicinity.
33. Norwalk School—1844; Ft. Towson.
34. Nuyaka Mission—1882; Okmulgee vicinity.
35. Oak Ridge Mission (after Civil War, renamed Ramsey Mission) —1848; Wewoka vicinity.
36. Park Hill—1835.
37. Pine Ridge Mission—1835; Milton vicinity.
38. Pleasant Grove—1844; Ft. Washita vicinity.
39. Post Oak—1894 (Mennonite); Ft. Sill vicinity.
40. Providente—1835; Ft. Towson vicinity.
41. Rainy Mountain—1885; near Gotebo.
42. Sacred Heart Institute; Vinita.
43. Sacred Heart Mission—1876; Asher vicinity.
44. Saddle Mountain Mission—ca. 1896; SE Kiowa County.
45. Seger Indian Training School (Seger Mission School)—1872; Colony vicinity.
46. Shawnee.
47. Shawnee Friends Mission—1874; Shawnee vicinity.
48. St. Agnes—1897; Antlers.
49. St. Mary's—1901.
50. St. Patrick's—1892; Anadarko.
51. Stockbridge—1837; Eagletown vicinity.
52. Tullahassee Mission—1848; Tullahassee vicinity.
53. Tuskahoma Mission.
54. Union Mission—1820; Mazie vicinity.
55. Wealaka—1881; Leonard, in Tulsa County.
56. Wheelock Female Seminaries—1842; Millerton vicinity.
57. Wheelock Mission—1832; Millerton vicinity.
58. Whirlwind—1897; Greenfield vicinity.
59. Wyandotte Mission—1869; Wyandotte.
Site listed on National Register of Historic Places
Mission, school, church location
U.S. fort
Modern city

39. ACADEMIES AND SCHOOLS

Essay by *Alvin O. Turner*

Academies were the principal providers of post-elementary education in Oklahoma until the spread of public high schools after statehood. Even thereafter, many of the academies maintained their educational efforts until well into the twentieth century. Academies usually are defined as "nonpublic secondary schools," but this was not always the case in Oklahoma, where many of the schools also often provided elementary education and were frequently a part of public educational systems maintained by the Five Tribes. The term was also often applied to vocational schools, especially after the Civil War. In other instances, comparable schools were designated as seminaries rather than academies or equivalent institutions. As a result, there has never been a comprehensive list of the state's academies. Nevertheless, a great many are known, as is the broad outline of their collective history.

The first academies developed in conjunction with mission-based educational efforts among the Five Tribes. These efforts were augmented by the creation of public school systems among the Five Tribes, beginning with the Cherokees in 1841 and the Choctaws the next year. By 1848, Indian Territory was home to at least sixteen manual training schools and eighty-seven boarding schools. Important academies established in the Choctaw Nation during this time included the Armstrong, Spencer, and Fort Coffee academies plus the Goodland Indian School for the boys and New Hope School for Girls, the Iyannubbee and Wheelock female seminaries, and the Koonsha Female Academy for the girls. The best-known Cherokee institutions were the Cherokee Male and Cherokee Female seminaries (located near Tahlequah and Park Hill, respectively). Bloomfield Academy and Burney Institute for Girls, the Chickasaw and Wapanucka academies, and Colbert Institute were the principal facilities serving Chickasaw youths, while Tullahassee Mission had become the principal learning center serving the Creek Nation.

Virtually all educational efforts among the Indian nations ceased during the Civil War, and resumption was delayed by numerous problems thereafter. Nevertheless, both religious groups and the nations continued building and supporting academies, some for freedmen. By 1900, the Cherokees maintained two academies, the Creeks had eight boarding schools, the Chickasaw and Choctaw nations supported four academies (with the latter also maintaining twelve boarding schools), and the Seminoles had Mekasukey Academy for boys and the Sasakwa Female Academy.

A number of other academies in Oklahoma offered education to freedmen, the Plains tribes, and growing white populations. The Dawes Academy (near Berwyn) and another at Fort Arbuckle responded to the educational goals of Chickasaw freedmen. At least six academies, including one identified as a high school, served Cherokee freedmen. Elliot Academy offered similar opportunities to the Choctaws' ex-slaves and their descendants.

Roman Catholics sponsored St. Mary's Academy for girls and Sacred Heart Mission for boys. Those academies received students from most tribes in Oklahoma. Other Catholic schools such as the Sacred Heart Institute at Vinita also offered an academic curriculum.

The beginnings of federal educational efforts directed toward the Indian nations led to the creation of the Riverside school near Anadarko, Concho near El Reno, a school at Fort Sill, the St. Louis Industrial School at Pawhuska, and Chilocco near Newkirk. However, the federal government generally deemphasized the preparatory curriculum that had been characteristic of earlier academies and urged increased vocational training among those schools as well as the ones they established.

Several church-linked academies were formed in western Oklahoma: Oklahoma Presbyterian Academy at Newkirk, the Oklahoma High School at Norman (Southern Methodist), Northwestern Academy at Carrier (Congregational), the Corn Bible Academy (Mennonite Brethren), two sponsored by the Society of Friends, the Stella Academy at Cherokee, and the Gate Academy, as well as at least three different Cordell academies sponsored successively by the Dutch Reformed denomination and then by groups affiliated with the Churches of Christ.

The spread of public high schools eliminated the need for most academies. The first public schools in Oklahoma were established as county high schools, in Logan, 1907–1911; Alfalfa, 1905–1909; Creek, 1909–1913; Okfuskee, 1909–1935; and Cimarron, 1919–1932. Despite such developments and the rapid spread of district high schools, some academies persisted. Others developed in subsequent years as alternatives to the public schools. Holland Hall at Tulsa and Casady were established by Episcopal groups in 1922 and 1947, respectively. Other church-linked high schools, particularly Roman Catholic, remain an important part of educational offerings in Oklahoma. Many—such as Bishop McGuinness High School in Oklahoma City—persisted, often drawing much of their student body from the non-Catholic population. The only self-identified preparatory school in Oklahoma is Cascia Hall, a Catholic school in Tulsa. By 1970, however, Roman Catholics had largely abandoned the separate schools that they had maintained across the state. In contrast, Oklahoma, as elsewhere, saw a proliferation of church-based schools responding to white-flight pressures and varied religion-based concerns about public schools. Public concerns about quality of education and other issues in the recent past have spawned even more educational efforts comparable to the academies of the past, and many of these institutions use that term to describe their mission.

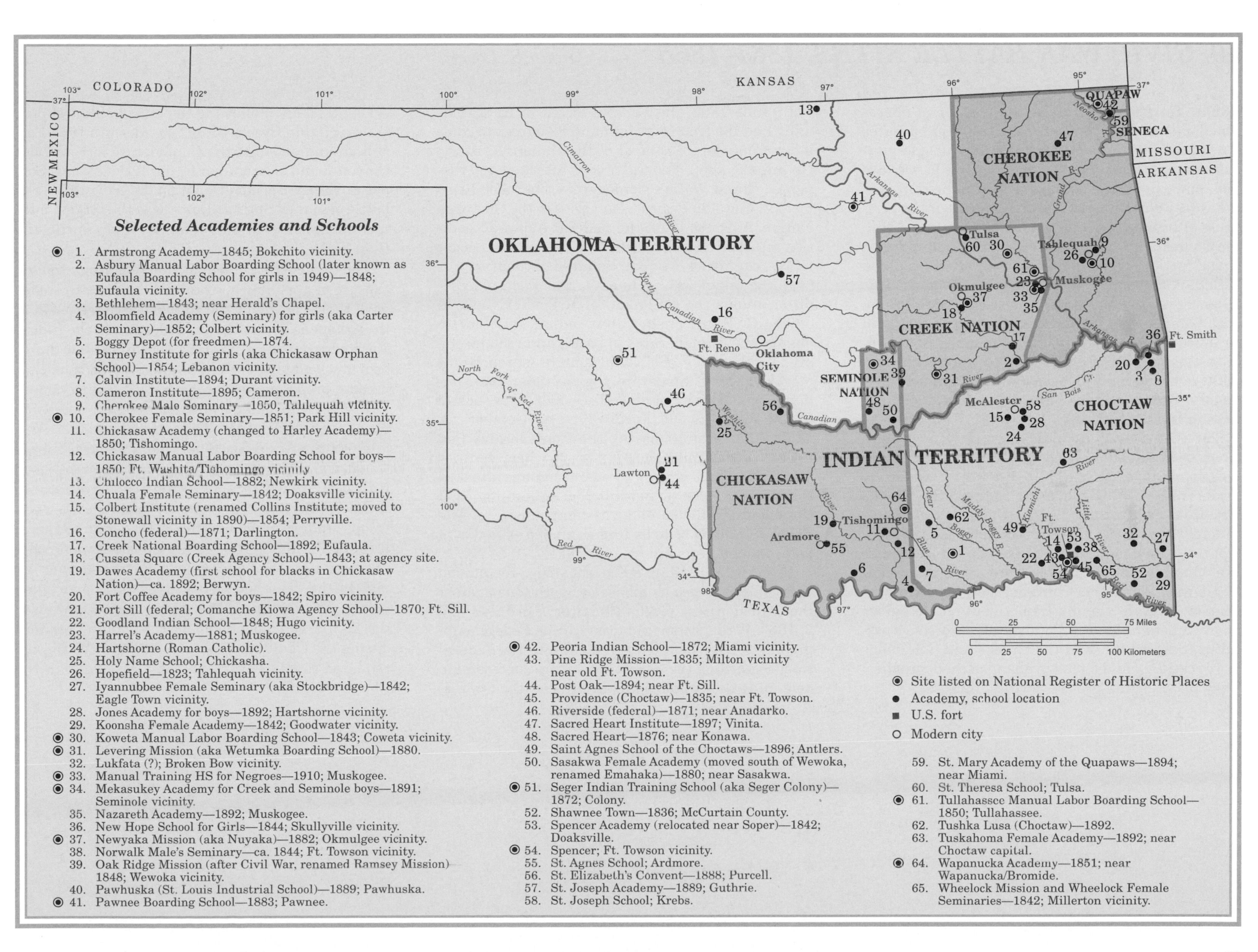
Selected Academies and Schools
1. Armstrong Academy—1845; Bokchito vicinity.
2. Asbury Manual Labor Boarding School (later known as Eufaula Boarding School for girls in 1949)—1848; Eufaula vicinity.
3. Bethlehem—1843; near Herald's Chapel.
4. Bloomfield Academy (Seminary) for girls (aka Carter Seminary)—1852; Colbert vicinity.
5. Boggy Depot (for freedmen)—1874.
6. Burney Institute for girls (aka Chickasaw Orphan School)—1854; Lebanon vicinity.
7. Calvin Institute—1894; Durant vicinity.
8. Cameron Institute—1895; Cameron.
9. Cherokee Male Seminary—1850, Tahlequah vicinity.
10. Cherokee Female Seminary—1851; Park Hill vicinity.
11. Chickasaw Academy (changed to Harley Academy)—1850; Tishomingo.
12. Chickasaw Manual Labor Boarding School for boys—1850; Ft. Washita/Tishomingo vicinity.
13. Chilocco Indian School—1882; Newkirk vicinity.
14. Chuala Female Seminary—1842; Doaksville vicinity.
15. Colbert Institute (renamed Collins Institute; moved to Stonewall vicinity in 1890)—1854; Perryville.
16. Concho (federal)—1871; Darlington.
17. Creek National Boarding School—1892; Eufaula.
18. Cusseta Square (Creek Agency School)—1843; at agency site.
19. Dawes Academy (first school for blacks in Chickasaw Nation)—ca. 1892; Berwyn.
20. Fort Coffee Academy for boys—1842; Spiro vicinity.
21. Fort Sill (federal; Comanche Kiowa Agency School)—1870; Ft. Sill.
22. Goodland Indian School—1848; Hugo vicinity.
23. Harrel's Academy—1881; Muskogee.
24. Hartshorne (Roman Catholic).
25. Holy Name School; Chickasha.
26. Hopefield—1823; Tahlequah vicinity.
27. Iyannubbee Female Seminary (aka Stockbridge)—1842; Eagle Town vicinity.
28. Jones Academy for boys—1892; Hartshorne vicinity.
29. Koonsha Female Academy—1842; Goodwater vicinity.
30. Koweta Manual Labor Boarding School—1843; Coweta vicinity.
31. Levering Mission (aka Wetumka Boarding School)—1880.
32. Lukfata (?); Broken Bow vicinity.
33. Manual Training HS for Negroes—1910; Muskogee.
34. Mekasukey Academy for Creek and Seminole boys—1891; Seminole vicinity.
35. Nazareth Academy—1892; Muskogee.
36. New Hope School for Girls—1844; Skullyville vicinity.
37. Newyaka Mission (aka Nuyaka)—1882; Okmulgee vicinity.
38. Norwalk Male's Seminary—ca. 1844; Ft. Towson vicinity.
39. Oak Ridge Mission (after Civil War, renamed Ramsey Mission) 1848; Wewoka vicinity.
40. Pawhuska (St. Louis Industrial School)—1889; Pawhuska.
41. Pawnee Boarding School—1883; Pawnee.
42. Peoria Indian School—1872; Miami vicinity.
43. Pine Ridge Mission—1835; Milton vicinity near old Ft. Towson.
44. Post Oak—1894; near Ft. Sill.
45. Providence (Choctaw)—1835; near Ft. Towson.
46. Riverside (federal)—1871; near Anadarko.
47. Sacred Heart Institute—1897; Vinita.
48. Sacred Heart—1876; near Konawa.
49. Saint Agnes School of the Choctaws—1896; Antlers.
50. Sasakwa Female Academy (moved south of Wewoka, renamed Emahaka)—1880; near Sasakwa.
51. Seger Indian Training School (aka Seger Colony)—1872; Colony.
52. Shawnee Town—1836; McCurtain County.
53. Spencer Academy (relocated near Soper)—1842; Doaksville.
54. Spencer; Ft. Towson vicinity.
55. St. Agnes School; Ardmore.
56. St. Elizabeth's Convent—1888; Purcell.
57. St. Joseph Academy—1889; Guthrie.
58. St. Joseph School; Krebs.
59. St. Mary Academy of the Quapaws—1894; near Miami.
60. St. Theresa School; Tulsa.
61. Tullahassee Manual Labor Boarding School—1850; Tullahassee.
62. Tushka Lusa (Choctaw)—1892.
63. Tuskahoma Female Academy—1892; near Choctaw capital.
64. Wapanucka Academy—1851; near Wapanucka/Bromide.
65. Wheelock Mission and Wheelock Female Seminaries—1842; Millerton vicinity.
Site listed on National Register of Historic Places
Academy, school location
U.S. fort
Modern city
OKLAHOMA TERRITORY
INDIAN TERRITORY
CHEROKEE NATION
CREEK NATION
SEMINOLE NATION
CHICKASAW NATION
CHOCTAW NATION
QUAPAW
SENECA
KANSAS
COLORADO
NEW MEXICO
MISSOURI
ARKANSAS
TEXAS
Tulsa
Tahlequah
Muskogee
Okmulgee
Oklahoma City
Ft. Reno
Ft. Smith
McAlester
Lawton
Tishomingo
Ardmore
Ft. Towson
0 25 50 75 Miles
0 25 50 75 100 Kilometers

40. *CIVIL WAR BATTLE SITES, 1861–1865*

Essay by *John R. Lovett*

Indian Territory was an active theater of operation for both the Federals and the Confederates during the Civil War. Several small battles, numerous skirmishes, and devastating guerrilla warfare took place in Indian Territory during the course of the war. Even though a large majority of the residents of Indian Territory wished to remain neutral, the Cherokees, Choctaws, Chickasaws, Seminoles, a Creek faction, and some Osages and Caddos allied with the Confederate government in Richmond. This alliance is partly attributable to geographic location, with Confederate Texas located to the south and Arkansas on the east. In addition, many of the Indian agents were sympathetic to the South, and many of the Indians held slaves. To compound these factors, Federal troops had earlier abandoned the forts in Indian Territory.

The first battles in Indian Territory took place when Opothleyahola tried to lead Creek and Seminole neutralists to safety in Kansas. Pursued by Texas troops and Confederate Indians, the Creeks and allies fought their first battle at Round Mountain on November 19, 1861; they repulsed the Confederate attack and continued north. On December 9th, Opothleyahola's people were again successful in turning back the Confederates, this time at Chusto Talasah (Caving Banks), but on December 26 at Chustenalah, the Confederates were successful in their attack, and the Creeks and Seminoles were scattered and forced to abandon their supplies. They fled in small groups north to Kansas.

In June 1862, the Federal forces in Kansas finally had the troop strength and resources to challenge Confederate control of the Indian Territory. On June 6, 1862, Federal troops attacked and dispersed Stand Watie's Confederate Cherokee Regiment at Cowskin Prairie near Grove in the Cherokee Nation. A month later, the Federal Indian Expedition attacked three hundred Confederates at Locust Grove, capturing over one hundred of them.

In the fall of 1862, a much larger Federal expedition under the command of Brigadier General James G. Blunt pushed into Indian Territory to engage the Confederates in battle and reclaim the area for the Union. Following a night march, Blunt attacked the Confederate troops under the command of Colonel Douglas H. Cooper and Colonel Stand Watie at Old Fort Wayne on October 22, 1862. After a short battle, the Confederates fled toward Fort Smith, leaving an artillery battery behind. The following day, Federal Indians attacked the Wichita Agency and killed a large number of Confederate-allied Tonkawas camped nearby. The Federal Indians killed a large number of Tonkawa men, women, and children.

In April 1863, Blunt's Federal troops reoccupied Fort Gibson to use as a base of operations against the Confederates in Indian Territory. On July 1 and 2, 1863, Watie attempted to capture a Federal supply wagon train bound for Fort Gibson. The Federal troops guarding the supply train were successful in defending the supplies and driving off the Confederate attackers. Following the attack on the supply train at Cabin Creek, Blunt moved south from Fort Gibson and defeated the Confederate forces under the command of Brigadier General Douglas H. Cooper at Honey Springs Depot on July 17, 1863. The battle of Honey Springs Depot was the largest military engagement in the Indian Territory during the Civil War.

The Confederate defeat at Honey Springs and the capture of Fort Smith, Arkansas, by Federal troops gave them control of the Indian Territory north of the Arkansas River. The Confederates in the Indian Territory continued military operations but did so on a much smaller scale. The guerrilla warfare that became predominant devastated the countryside.

In 1864 the Confederates achieved two small victories with the capture of the steamboat *J. R. Williams* on the Arkansas River and a Federal supply wagon train. The steamer was bound for Fort Gibson with supplies when Stand Watie's cavalry captured it. Their other success came at Cabin Creek when troops under the command of Brigadier General Richard M. Gano and Brigadier General Stand Watie captured a Federal supply wagon train at approximately the same location where Watie had failed before. The capture of the supply wagon train was the last large engagement in the Indian Territory during the Civil War. On June 23, 1865, Watie surrendered to Federal troops near Doaksville in the Choctaw Nation.

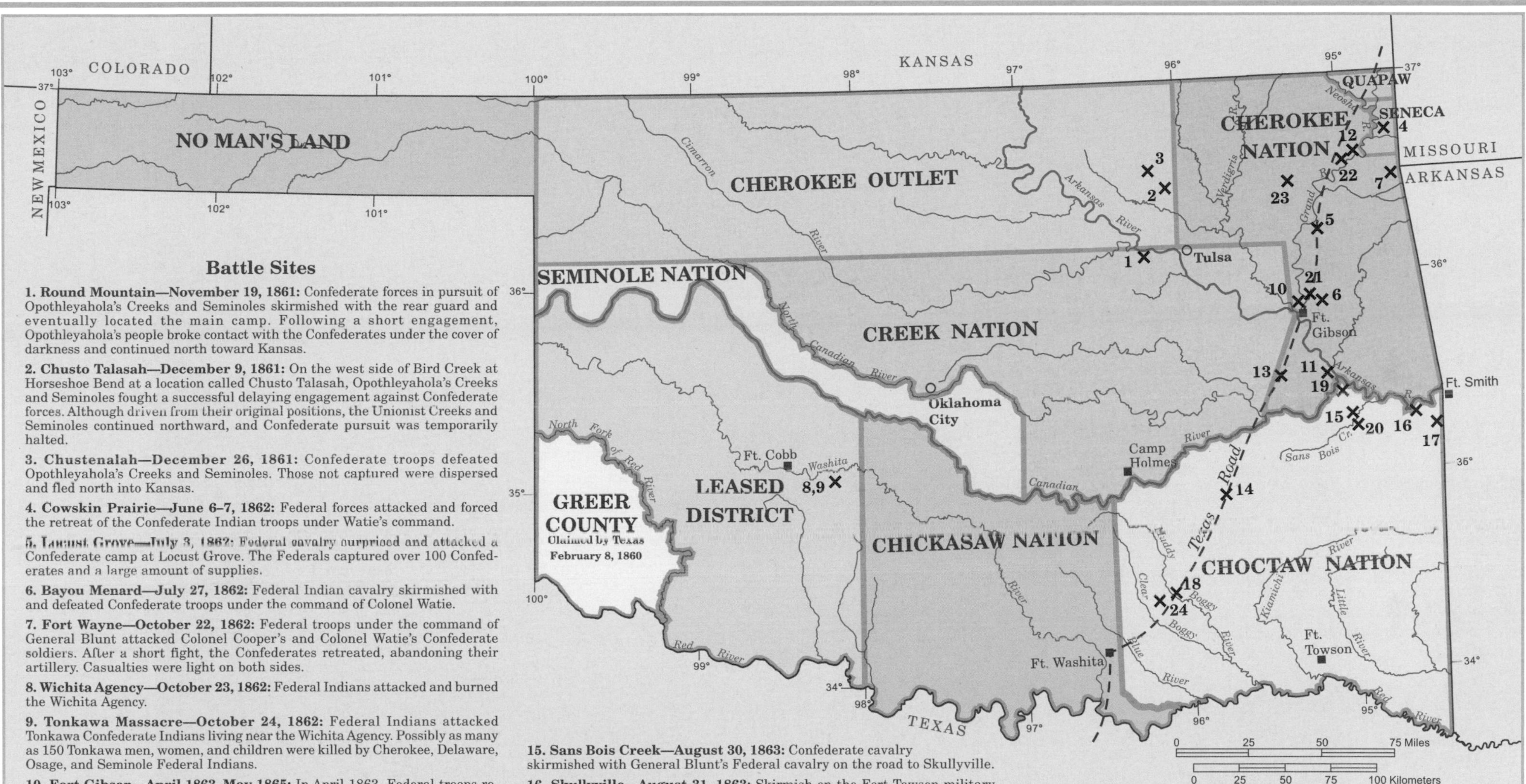

Battle Sites

1. Round Mountain—November 19, 1861: Confederate forces in pursuit of Opothleyahola's Creeks and Seminoles skirmished with the rear guard and eventually located the main camp. Following a short engagement, Opothleyahola's people broke contact with the Confederates under the cover of darkness and continued north toward Kansas.

2. Chusto Talasah—December 9, 1861: On the west side of Bird Creek at Horseshoe Bend at a location called Chusto Talasah, Opothleyahola's Creeks and Seminoles fought a successful delaying engagement against Confederate forces. Although driven from their original positions, the Unionist Creeks and Seminoles continued northward, and Confederate pursuit was temporarily halted.

3. Chustenalah—December 26, 1861: Confederate troops defeated Opothleyahola's Creeks and Seminoles. Those not captured were dispersed and fled north into Kansas.

4. Cowskin Prairie—June 6–7, 1862: Federal forces attacked and forced the retreat of the Confederate Indian troops under Watie's command.

5. Locust Grove—July 3, 1862: Federal cavalry surprised and attacked a Confederate camp at Locust Grove. The Federals captured over 100 Confederates and a large amount of supplies.

6. Bayou Menard—July 27, 1862: Federal Indian cavalry skirmished with and defeated Confederate troops under the command of Colonel Watie.

7. Fort Wayne—October 22, 1862: Federal troops under the command of General Blunt attacked Colonel Cooper's and Colonel Watie's Confederate soldiers. After a short fight, the Confederates retreated, abandoning their artillery. Casualties were light on both sides.

8. Wichita Agency—October 23, 1862: Federal Indians attacked and burned the Wichita Agency.

9. Tonkawa Massacre—October 24, 1862: Federal Indians attacked Tonkawa Confederate Indians living near the Wichita Agency. Possibly as many as 150 Tonkawa men, women, and children were killed by Cherokee, Delaware, Osage, and Seminole Federal Indians.

10. Fort Gibson—April 1863–May 1865: In April 1863, Federal troops reoccupied the fort, and it became the center of operations for the Federals in the Indian Territory. Numerous skirmishes took place in the vicinity of Fort Gibson as a result of the activities of Confederate scouting parties in their attempts to gain information on Federal activities.

11. Webbers Falls—April 25, 1863: Federal troops under the command of Colonel William A. Phillips attacked Colonel Watie's Confederates, who were there to provide guard for a meeting of the Confederate Cherokee National Council. Phillips's cavalry surprised and routed the Confederates.

12. First Cabin Creek—1–2 July, 1863: Confederate troops under the command of Colonel Watie attacked and attempted to capture a Federal supply wagon train bound for Fort Gibson. The Federal troops guarding the supply train broke through the Confederate line, and the Confederates fled the area.

13. Battle of Honey Springs Depot—July 17, 1863: Federal forces including white, Indian, and black troops under the command of General Blunt defeated and dispersed the white and Indian Confederate troops of General Cooper.

14. Perryville—August 25, 1863: Federal troops under the command of Major General James G. Blunt skirmished with and forced the retreat of Brigadier General William E. Steele from Perryville. The Federals burned Perryville, destroying abandoned Confederate supplies.

15. Sans Bois Creek—August 30, 1863: Confederate cavalry skirmished with General Blunt's Federal cavalry on the road to Skullyville.

16. Skullyville—August 31, 1863: Skirmish on the Fort Towson military road south of Skullyville between General Blunt's Federal cavalry and Confederate cavalry under the command of Brigadier General William L. Cabell. With assistance from Federal infantry and artillery forces, Cabell's troops were driven across the Poteau River into Arkansas.

17. Devil's Backbone (or Backbone Mountain)—September 1, 1863: Federal cavalry and artillery under the command of Colonel William F. Smith attacked and forced the retreat of Confederate troops under the command of General Cabell at a gap in Devil's Backbone on the Fort Towson military road. Casualties were less than 20 for both Federals and Confederates.

18. Muddy (or Middle) Boggy—February 13, 1864: Seminole, Chickasaw, and Choctaw Confederate cavalry along with troops from Texas were ambushed by the 14th Kansas cavalry. Confederate killed and wounded were less than 50. Federal troops withdrew when word of Confederate reinforcements reached them.

19. Pleasant Bluff on the Arkansas River—June 15, 1864: Colonel Stand Watie's Confederates captured the Federal steamboat *J. R. Williams*, bound for Fort Gibson with supplies.

20. Iron bridge on Sans Bois—June 16, 1864: Skirmish between Confederate Chickasaws and Federal cavalry. Federal forces withdrew, leaving the Confederates in control of the bridge.

21. Hay station near Fort Gibson—September 16, 1864: The Confederate troops under the command of Brigadier General Stand Watie and Brigadier General Richard M. Gano surprised and attacked Federal soldiers cutting hay on the military road north of Fort Gibson. Federal casualties included approximately 40 black soldiers, many of whom continued to fight until their ammunition was exhausted; few were given an opportunity by the Confederates to surrender.

22. Second Cabin Creek—September 18–19, 1864: The combined Confederate commands of General Watie and General Gano captured a Federal supply wagon train bound for Fort Gibson. Following a brisk engagement, most of the Federal troops guarding the train and the teamsters escaped to Fort Smith, Arkansas.

23. Pryor Creek—September 19, 1864: Federal reinforcements from Fort Gibson skirmished with General Watie's and General Gano's Confederate troops as they withdrew with the captured Federal supply wagon train.

24. Old Boggy Depot—April 24, 1865: Federal cavalry ambushed a small Confederate detachment, inflicting light casualties.

The Nature Conservancy's Tallgrass Prairie Preserve, Osage County. (Photograph by John Elk III, courtesy of Elk Photography)

Part IV

Where the Frontier Ends

Oklahoma City shortly after the Land Run of April 22, 1889. (Courtesy Western History Collections, University of Oklahoma Libraries)

41. BUFFALO COUNTRY

Essay by *Bruce W. Hoagland*

The American bison (*Bison bison L.*) is one of the continent's most enigmatic animals. Bison once ranged from the East Coast to the Rocky Mountains and limited points west. In Oklahoma, they were most abundant in the western three-quarters of the state, with sporadic occurrences in the rugged Ouachita and Ozark Mountain ranges.

The bison is the largest land mammal in North America, weighing 1,350 pounds on average. Bison live for approximately fifty years and reach sexual maturity at age three. Bison develop a thick winter coat in the early fall and shed it in the spring. Loss of the winter coat causes skin irritation, which bison attempt to relieve by "wallowing." Bulls are known to wallow more frequently than cows, particularly when other bulls are present.

The number of bison prior to European contact has been the subject of much debate. In 1910, naturalist Ernest Thompson Seton estimated that 75 million bison inhabited the Great Plains in 1800. He based this estimate on cattle productivity data in the 1900 agricultural census. He did not, however, account for drought and differences in the feeding preferences of bison and cattle. When later researchers consider these factors, the estimate decreases to about 28–30 million animals.

In 1540, Coronado and his companions were the first Europeans to encounter bison in Oklahoma. Over 270 years later, Thomas Nuttall reported bison in the vicinity of the Potato Hills in present-day Latimer County. Henry Ellsworth wrote in 1832 that "the large close eaten prairies spread with buffalo dung, showed, we were near the great herd." Captain Randolph Marcy, in 1847, wrote that "the second day after crossing the Canadian we came upon one of the grandest sights to be seen on this continent. From a bluff rising out of the prairie we could see in westerly direction, probably 4,000 buffaloes, covering the plain as far as the eye could reach to the southwest and north."

Few Americans could have imagined that completion of the transcontinental railroad—the Union Pacific, in 1862—would hasten the demise of the bison, but the railroads brought hunters west and sent robes and meat east. In addition, the railroad cut the herds in half. In 1872, completion of the Atchison, Topeka, and Santa Fe railroad to Dodge City brought buffalo hunters to the southern plains. Bison-hunting camps appeared along the Arkansas, Cimarron, Red, and Canadian rivers throughout the 1870s. Each camp typically was manned by a shooter, a cook, and three or four skinners. Hunts typically began in late fall, when bison developed their winter coat. The hunt would begin before sunrise, when the shooter would take a position downwind and lay prone. At sunrise, he would shoot the lead cow and as many additional animals as possible.

The Santa Fe railroad shipped approximately 460,000 bison hides between 1872 and 1874. But waste from the hunts was staggering: an estimated three bison died from wounds for each hide shipped, and many hides were lost to spoilage because of improper preparation. A market also existed for bison

A small herd of buffalo near the Wichita Mountains.
(Courtesy Western History Collections, University of Oklahoma Libraries)

meat, with a preference for the young and females. And many animals were killed for only their tongue, which was considered a delicacy.

At the close of the nineteenth century, only a few thousand bison existed, primarily in private herds or zoological parks. The federal government maintained one herd at Yellowstone National Park. In 1905, the New York Zoological Society offered several bison to the U.S. government to establish a second publicly protected herd. The offer was accepted, and the Wichita Forest Reserve was proclaimed a game preserve in June of that year. The New York Zoological Society was invited to select an appropriate site for release of the animals in the Wichita Game Preserve. Their choice was Winter Valley, located appoximately in the center of the preserve.

There were concerns about wildfire, coyotes and wolves, and Texas fever at the Wichita Game Preserve, but Superintendent E. F. Morrissey dealt with predators by initiating an eradication program to remove the few wolves and coyotes at the facility. Texas fever, a tick-borne protozoan that destroys red blood cells, had ravaged the cattle industry. To destroy ticks, the bison would be sprayed with crude oil upon their arrival.

Frank Rush was placed in charge of the relocation and was to manage the bison once they arrived. He traveled to New York and selected the fifteen bison from those at the New York Zoological Society. The initial plan called for transporting the bison in cattle cars, but Rush recommended shipping them in individual crates for safer handling. Once crated, the animals were loaded onto two specially designed railcars that left New York on October 11, 1907. The event had received national attention, and wherever the train stopped, large crowds gathered.

The route had been planned so that the animals would be in transit for as brief a time as possible, but in St. Louis the two cars were separated. Thus, the first car arrived in Cache on October 16, the second on October 17, 1907. The crates were then loaded onto wagons and transported to the Wichita Game Preserve. The crowds that witnessed the bison release included a large group of American Indians led by Quanah Parker.

The bison arrived in excellent health. The first calf was born on October 30, 1907, and was named Hornaday (after William T. Hornaday, director of the New York Zoological Society). A second calf was born on November 16, 1907, when Oklahoma attained statehood, and was promptly named Oklahoma. Today, the Wichita Mountains National Wildlife Refuge maintains a herd of approximately six hundred animals. The bison are an integral component of a management plan that attempts to restore natural processes, including fire, to the mixed-grass prairie landscape. To prevent the bison from overpopulating the refuge, animals are sold at auction every October.

Since the animal's return to the Wichitas, the bison has been designated as the state mammal. Numerous bison herds now graze upon ranches and private preserves throughout the state. The Nature Conservancy's Tallgrass Prairie Preserve, near Pawhuska in Osage County, maintains a bison herd of approximately twelve hundred animals. Three hundred bison were released at the preserve in 1993 in an effort to return fire and grazing to this tallgrass prairie landscape. Although we will not see herds the size of those reported by Marcy and others, bison will continue to thrive in the prairies and pastures for years to come.

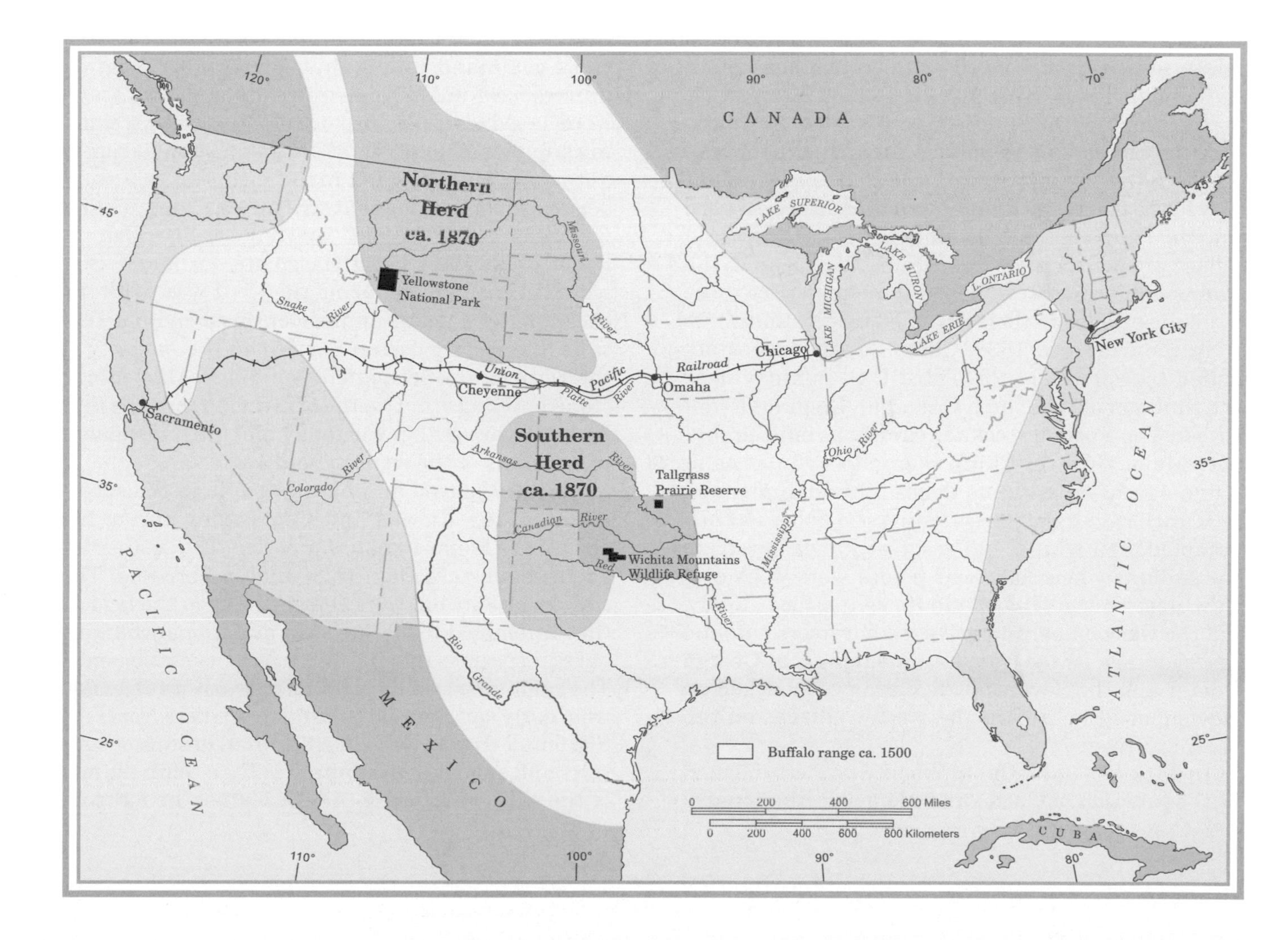

42. *FORTS, CAMPS, AND MILITARY ROADS, 1865–1907*

Essay by *John R. Lovett*

At the end of the Civil War in April 1865, the U.S. government initiated measures to restrict the Plains tribes to more clearly defined reservations. In October 1867, at Medicine Lodge Creek in Kansas, more than seven thousand Plains Indians met with government officials in a peace council to discuss the matter. The meeting concluded with reservations being assigned to the Comanches, Kiowas, Cheyennes, and Arapahos. However, many of the tribal members did not truly recognize the reservations. They continued living life according to their traditional customs, which included following the great buffalo herds throughout the Plains and raiding white settlements (as well as those of other Indian nations) in Texas, Kansas, and Indian Territory.

To campaign more effectively against the fast-moving warriors of the plains and force them onto the assigned reservations, the U.S. government moved the north–south line of frontier forts westward into the Plains Indians' domain. These forts provided a base of operation for the U.S. cavalry against the Plains tribes and were hoped to help restrict these nomadic peoples to their assigned reservations.

In the winter of 1868, Camp Supply was established by soldiers of the Third U.S. Infantry near the junction of the North Canadian River and Wolf Creek. The wooden stockade camp was built to support Major General Philip Sheridan's winter campaign against the Plains tribes. Sheridan planned to launch cavalry strikes against the tribes as they occupied their winter villages. He intended to strike the Indians when their war ponies were weak and thin, destroy the village and its winter food supply, kill the war ponies, and drive the survivors onto the reservations. It was from Camp Supply that George Custer and the Seventh U.S. Cavalry embarked on November 23 to attack the winter villages on the Washita River.

In January 1869, Camp Wichita was established at the junction of Cache and Medicine Bluff creeks to replace Fort Cobb as a base of operations against the Kiowas, Comanches, and Cheyennes. The garrison consisted of four companies of the Tenth U.S. Cavalry and two companies of the Sixth U.S. Infantry, under the overall command of Colonel Benjamin Grierson. Grierson was a Civil War hero and served as the commanding officer of the Tenth U.S. Cavalry. This cavalry, one of two African American cavalry regiments, was formed in 1866, and its members would become famous throughout the West as the "Buffalo Soldiers."

Like their counterparts who built the forts in pre–Civil War Indian Territory, the soldiers under Grierson's command found themselves at a location hundreds of miles from railroads and towns and were forced to rely on the surrounding area for building supplies. Camp Wichita began as a collection of temporary buildings, but in the spring of 1869, work began on more-permanent structures. Camp Wichita was renamed "Fort Sill" by General Sheridan, in honor of his West Point classmate Joshua W. Sill, who had been killed during the Civil War. With the exception of a small number of hired civilian artisans, the fort's garrison performed the majority of the work on the permanent buildings. Many of the stone buildings that were constructed in those first few years are still in use today and are a testament to the skills of the frontier soldiers.

Fort Sill played an important role in the subjugation of the Kiowas and Comanches during the 1871–1875 Plains Indian war period. The post served as Headquarters District of Indian Territory. The cavalry at Fort Sill were continuously in the field as they attempted to block Kiowa and Comanche war-party incursions into the Texas frontier settlements. The raiding season for the Indian warriors extended from early spring to early fall. The soldiers from Fort Sill found themselves chasing small groups of warriors and engaging in running battles. With the end of the warfare in the southern plains, the fort continued to accept new missions: in 1894, Apache prisoners (including the famed warrior Geronimo) were transferred to Fort Sill to live under the control of military authority.

Fort Reno was established in July 1874 on the North Canadian River to protect the Darlington Agency. The Darlington Agency was headquarters for the Cheyenne-Arapaho reservation, and the garrison was tasked with providing an armed presence to maintain order and keep the Indians on the reservation, especially following the 1874 uprisings.

Cantonment was established in 1879 by federal troops on the North Canadian River after a group of Northern Cheyennes led by Dull Knife escaped from the Cheyenne-Arapaho reservation in an attempt to reach their former northern homeland. The government and people of Kansas demanded that a federal presence be established at the reservation to help contain the Cheyennes and prevent any additional outbreaks.

New military roads were established to connect the frontier forts with supply bases in Kansas and Arkansas. During the dynamic plains wars, the military roads were essential in quickly moving supplies to provide the cavalry with food, ammunition, clothing, and fresh horses. Three military roads connected Fort Sill with Arkansas and Kansas. Fort Reno's main supply artery was through Fort Supply, which in turn was connected with Fort Dodge, Kansas. From Fort Supply, one military road led to Fort Sill, while another continued south to Texas. The Fort Supply military road to Texas was a vital supply link for the cavalry campaigning against the Comanches in the Texas panhandle.

Of those forts still active at the conclusion of the Indian wars in Indian Territory and Texas, only Fort Sill continues in service today. Fort Reno was abandoned but later reactivated as a remount station; still later, it served as a prisoner-of-war camp during World War II.

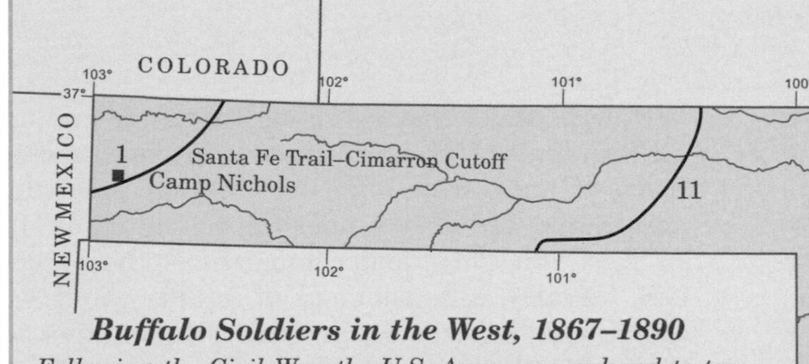

Buffalo Soldiers in the West, 1867–1890

Following the Civil War, the U.S. Army was reduced to ten cavalry and twenty-five infantry regiments, primarily for service against the hostile Indians of the West. Two cavalry regiments (the 9th and 10th) and two infantry regiments (the 24th and 25th) were composed of African American privates and noncommissioned officers, under white commissioned officers. For a quarter of a century, these regiments, known as the Buffalo Soldiers, fought against hostile Cheyennes, Comanches, Kiowas, Apaches, Utes, and Sioux and against Mexican outlaws and border desperadoes in nearly 200 engagements. For months and even years at a time, the garrisons of many frontier posts consisted of detachments from these regiments. The campaigns against the Apache chiefs Victorio and Nana were conducted almost entirely by the Buffalo Soldiers. The quality of their long service in the West is indicated by the fact that between 1870 and 1890, fourteen African American soldiers were awarded the Congressional Medal of Honor.

U.S. Military Facilities

1. Camp Nichols: Established June 1865 by famed scout and trailblazer Brigadier General Kit Carson on the Santa Fe Trail (Cimarron branch) to protect travel on that important trail.

2. Camp/Fort Supply: Established in November 1868 to support Major General Philip Sheridan's winter campaign against the Plains tribes. The fort, which was first designated a camp, was a vital supply link with Fort Dodge, Kansas, and supported the cavalry operating in that theater of operation. Fort Supply was abandoned by the U.S. Army in November 1894.

3. Fort Sill: Established in January 1869 to serve as a base of operations against the Kiowas and Comanches and as a buffer along the northern Texas frontier. The fort was originally called Camp Wichita but was renamed in honor of General Joshua Sill, who was killed in the Civil War. Fort Sill played an important role during the 1870–1874 operations against the Plains tribes.

4. Fort Reno: Established on the North Canadian River in July 1874 to protect the Darlington Indian Agency, on the opposite bank of the river. Abandoned in 1908, the fort was reactivated as a remount station and continued in active service during World War II as a prisoner-of-war camp for German and Italian soldiers.

5. Camp Beach: Established on Otter Creek in August 1874 as a forward supply base for cavalry operating out of Fort Sill.

6. Cantonment: Established in March 1879 on the North Canadian River to serve as a buffer between the Cheyenne-Arapaho Reservation and Kansas. After the departure of the Northern Cheyennes to their homeland, the post was abandoned in 1882.

7. Camp Guthrie: Established in April 1889 to help maintain order in the 1889 land opening. Camp Guthrie was abandoned in June 1890.

8. Fort Gibson: Established in April 1824 on the Grand River by the Fort Smith garrison to protect the traders and fur trappers in the Three Forks area and to protect the Cherokees from the Osages. Abandoned in 1836, reoccupied in 1837, and again abandoned in 1857, the fort was once more garrisoned (by Federal troops) in 1863 and remained an active fort until 1871. In 1872 the fort became a U.S. Army quartermaster's depot and returned to the active list until 1890. Later the fort was put on the active list as a post for two short periods of time.

9. Fort Cobb: Established on the Washita River at the mouth of Cobb Creek in October 1859 to protect the Indians at the Wichita Agency. Abandoned by the Federal garrison at the outbreak of the Civil War, the fort was reoccupied by Confederate troops. In 1862, Federal Indians attacked the garrison and burned most of the buildings. The fort saw service again in 1869 but was in operation for less than a year when the fort was abandoned and the garrison moved to Fort Sill.

○ Modern city ● Indian agency ■ U.S. fort/camp

10. Fort Arbuckle II: Reoccupied by Federal troops in November 1866, the fort continued in service until it was abandoned in June 1874. Fort Arbuckle had a limited role in the Plains wars but did provide support to Fort Sill.

11. Military road: Fort Bascom, New Mexico, to Fort Dodge, Kansas.

12. Military road: North–south road through Fort Supply.

13. Military road: Fort Supply to Fort Sill.

14. Military road: Fort Supply to Fort Reno.

15. Military road: Fort Sill to Fort Smith.

16. Military road: Fort Sill to Fort Towson.

17. Military road: Fort Smith to Fort Towson.

18. Military road: Fort Gibson to Fort Smith.

43. BATTLES DURING THE INDIAN WARS

Essay by *John R. Lovett*

From the battle on Grand River Prairie near the Arkansas River in 1847 to the last battle near Turkey Springs in 1878, Indian Territory was the site of numerous skirmishes and battles between the U.S. Army and the Plains tribes. While the majority of these armed encounters were relatively small, some involved several hundred soldiers and Indians as combatants.

Prior to the Civil War, a line of frontier posts was established in Indian Territory as part of a larger line of forts that stretched from Texas to Minnesota, designed to protect white settlements from incursions by Plains tribes. For three decades following the Louisiana Purchase, the area between the line of forts and the Rocky Mountains was viewed as the "Great American Desert," unsuitable for settlement. Following the war with Mexico of the 1840s, which resulted in the acquisition of new territory in present-day New Mexico and Arizona in 1848 and 1854, armed encounters became more common between the Plains tribes and the U.S. Army as commerce and Anglo-American settlement in the Southwest intensified.

The role of the military in Indian Territory was primarily to provide protection from the Plains tribes for the newly resettled Five Nations, Anglo-American settlements in Texas and Kansas, and emigrant routes to California and Oregon. The areas directly around the posts were relatively secure, but the vastness of the overall area and the limited number of troops available required aggressive patrols into the heartland of the southern plains. The U.S. Army employed the tactics of containment, interdiction, and punishment to achieve its mission. The containment element involved using military force to restrict the movement of the Plains villages. Interdiction meant intercepting and blocking Indian raiding parties. Punishment typically was administered against the home villages of raiding parties.

Warfare between the U.S. Army and the Plains tribes meant not only the death, wounding, or capture of combatants through battle, however. Campaigning against the nomadic Plains peoples also involved decimating the great herds of bison on which they depended for sustenance and, in the same vein, attacking winter camps to kill the war ponies and destroy food supplies. The strategy was expected to have the effect of restricting these independent Indians to their assigned reservations, where they were promised food and other necessary provisions. In actuality, the U.S. soldiers often turned the attacks into massacres; mercy was not expected from the Plains Indians, and none was extended.

In this conflict, the cavalry (developed from the earlier mounted dragoons) proved to be the most effective force against the raids of the mounted Plains warriors. While the infantry helped garrison the frontier posts and marched as escort for military supply trains, the mobility of the cavalry was what provided some degree of success in locating and engaging Plains tribes in battle. However, the Indian warriors' mobility also provided them with an advantage in battles and skirmishes against the U.S. Army; the warriors were skilled in ambush and would not hesitate to disengage and scatter if the fight appeared to be going in favor of the cavalry.

On June 26, 1847, Company B of the First Dragoons fought a skirmish with Comanche warriors at the Grand River Prairie near the Arkansas River. This encounter between the U.S. Army and the Comanches left five soldiers killed and six wounded (numbers of Comanches killed and wounded were not listed in the regimental returns, a common oversight in official records). This type of small-unit action was common throughout the Indian barrier. Casualties were usually low, and many actions were casualty-free, at least on the part of the army.

In 1858 Major General David Twiggs, commanding the regular U.S. Army troops in Texas, launched the first large-scale offensive military operation into Indian Territory. Under the command of Major Earl Van Dorn, four companies of the Second U.S. Cavalry, a detachment of infantry, and 135 Indian auxiliaries from the Brazos Reservation departed from Fort Belknap, Texas. They moved north across the Red River to strike the Comanches. On October 1, Van Dorn's column located and attacked the Comanche village of Buffalo Hump. Unknown to Van Dorn, on the morning of the attack, Buffalo Hump was speaking with the commander of Fort Arbuckle in an effort to secure peace between the Comanches and the soldiers. Van Dorn's attack was successful, and the village was destroyed. Nearly sixty Comanches were killed in the initial attack, and a dozen more were pursued into the hills and killed; numerous women were among the casualties, as many of the men were out hunting. Van Dorn lost a mere three men.

With the outbreak of the Civil War and the withdrawal of Federal troops from the Indian Territory forts, the supremacy of the tribes of the southern plains for the most part went unchallenged in the region. The decade following the Civil War was a period of almost continuous warfare between the U.S. Army and the Arapahos, Kiowas, Cheyennes, and Comanches.

The largest battle of General Philip Sheridan's 1868–69 winter campaign took place when Lieutenant Colonel George Armstrong Custer led the Seventh U.S. Cavalry against Black Kettle's camp on the Washita River. The determined campaigns of 1874 and 1875 in the Indian Territory and Texas finally saw the collapse of the resistance of the Native peoples of the southern plains. As is the case across the plains, it was the sword and not the olive branch that transformed the nomadic life of the great horse culture into the restricted agency life.

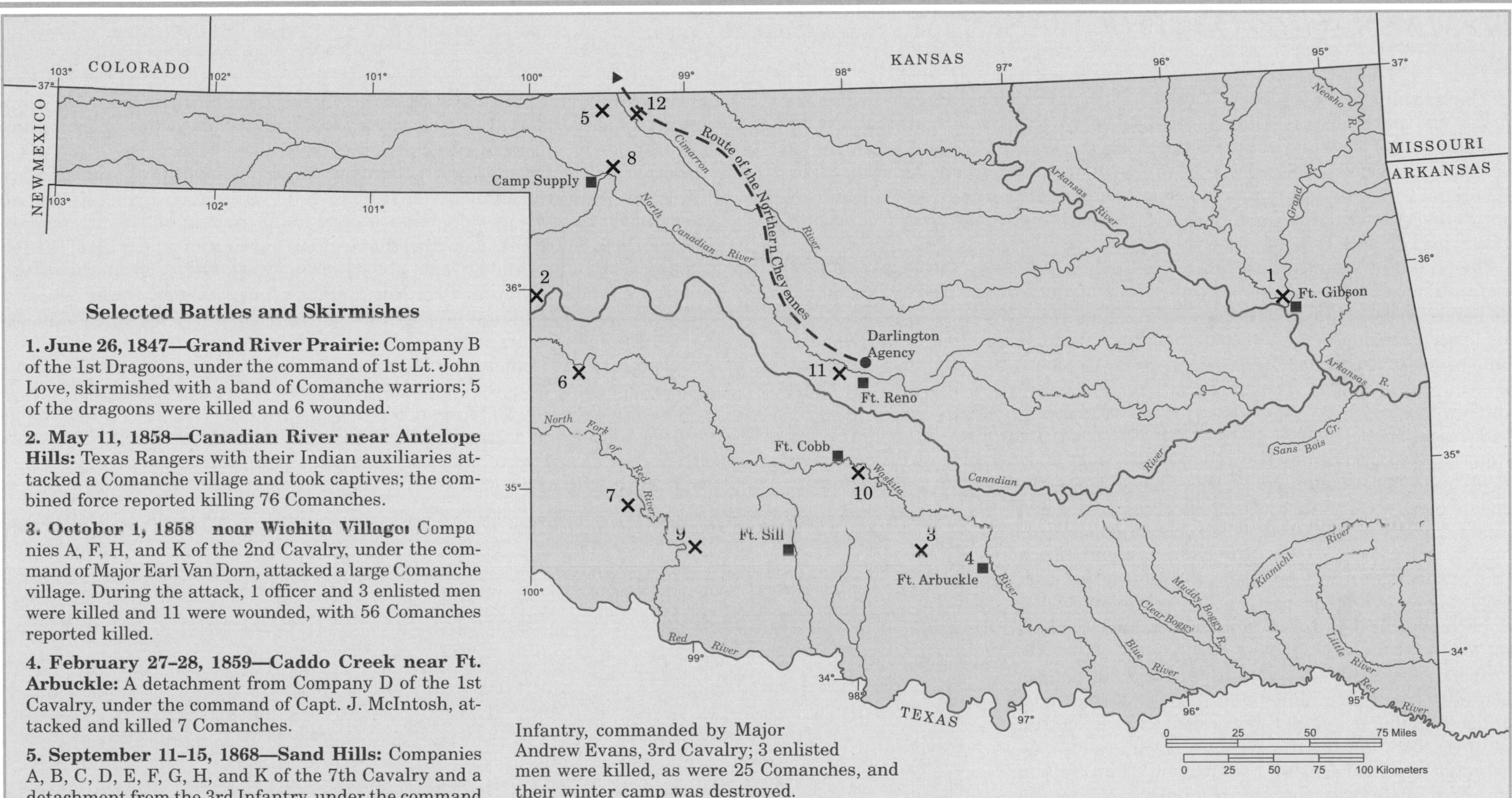

Selected Battles and Skirmishes

1. June 26, 1847—Grand River Prairie: Company B of the 1st Dragoons, under the command of 1st Lt. John Love, skirmished with a band of Comanche warriors; 5 of the dragoons were killed and 6 wounded.

2. May 11, 1858—Canadian River near Antelope Hills: Texas Rangers with their Indian auxiliaries attacked a Comanche village and took captives; the combined force reported killing 76 Comanches.

3. October 1, 1858—near Wichita Village: Companies A, F, H, and K of the 2nd Cavalry, under the command of Major Earl Van Dorn, attacked a large Comanche village. During the attack, 1 officer and 3 enlisted men were killed and 11 were wounded, with 56 Comanches reported killed.

4. February 27–28, 1859—Caddo Creek near Ft. Arbuckle: A detachment from Company D of the 1st Cavalry, under the command of Capt. J. McIntosh, attacked and killed 7 Comanches.

5. September 11–15, 1868—Sand Hills: Companies A, B, C, D, E, F, G, H, and K of the 7th Cavalry and a detachment from the 3rd Infantry, under the command of Lt. Col. Alfred Sully, engaged Cheyenne and Kiowa warriors. During this series of skirmishes, 3 enlisted men were killed and 5 wounded, with 22 Indians reported killed.

6. November 27, 1868—Black Kettle's camp: The 7th Cavalry, under the command of Lt. Col. George A. Custer, attacked the winter camp. Casualties included 2 officers and 19 enlisted men killed and 3 officers and 13 enlisted men wounded; 103 Cheyennes were reported killed, with 53 captured and the village and pony herd destroyed.

7. December 25, 1868—North Fork of the Red River (Soldier Springs): Companies A, C, D, F, G, and I of the 3rd Cavalry and Companies F and I of the 37th Infantry, commanded by Major Andrew Evans, 3rd Cavalry; 3 enlisted men were killed, as were 25 Comanches, and their winter camp was destroyed.

8. June 11, 1870—near Camp Supply: Companies A, F, H, I, and K of the 10th Cavalry and Companies B, E, and F of the 3rd Infantry reported killing 10 Indians in a running battle.

9. September 19, 1871—Foster Springs: A detachment from Company B of the 10th Cavalry was attacked by Kiowas; 1 enlisted man was killed.

10. August 22–23, 1874—Wichita Agency: Companies E, H, I, and L of the 25th Infantry, under the command of Lt. Col. John Davidson. During this fight with the Kiowas and Comanches, 4 enlisted men were wounded and 1 Comanche killed.

11. April 6, 1875—near the Cheyenne Agency: Company M of the 6th Cavalry, Companies D and M of the 10th Cavalry, and a detachment from Company H of the 5th Infantry, under the command of Lt. Col. Thomas Neill, 6th Cavalry. Casualties included 19 enlisted men wounded and 11 Cheyennes killed.

12. September 13, 1878—Turkey Springs: Companies G and H of the 4th Cavalry, under the command of Capt. Joseph Rendlebrock, went in pursuit of the Northern Cheyennes; 2 enlisted men were killed and 1 wounded.

44. MASSACRE ON THE WASHITA

Essay by *John R. Lovett*

On the morning of November 27, 1868, Lieutenant Colonel George Armstrong Custer and eleven troops of the Seventh Cavalry (some eight hundred men) attacked a quiet Cheyenne winter camp along the Washita River. The entire village was destroyed. Black Kettle, a Cheyenne peace chief and survivor of the 1864 Sand Creek massacre, and his wife Magpie were among those killed. How many others died remains uncertain but the deaths may have exceeded one hundred, with fifty others taken captive.

The preceding summer had flared with Indian raids along the Texas and Kansas frontiers, and those states' governors had demanded that Washington punish the bands involved, forcibly return all the Indians to their assigned reservations, and put a permanent end to such depredations. It fell to General Philip Sheridan, commander of the army's Department of the Missouri, to accomplish those purposes; he settled upon a rare, winter campaign, designed to strike the Plains bands when they least expected and were least able to resist.

The campaign opened as Custer led his Seventh Cavalry, several infantry companies, and a large supply train out of Fort Dodge on November 12. Several days' travel brought the column to the site Sheridan had designated for a forward supply depot. Established as Camp Supply, it was the place from which Custer led his forces southward a few days later, closely following an Indian trail toward the Antelope Hills. In freezing weather, across snow-covered ground, each soldier bore a Spencer carbine, a Colt ball-and-cap revolver, and rations to last for thirty days.

Upon reaching the Canadian River, Custer dispatched a small force under Major Joel Elliott upstream, to search for Indian villages. Elliott ran across a fresh trail, leading south, toward the Washita River, and his detachment rejoined Custer's column on Thanksgiving Day. Without pause, the entire force set out for the Washita that evening.

Soon, Custer's Osage scouts reported the smell of smoke, next the signs of a sizable horse remuda, and finally the faint sounds of camp activities—all evidence that an encampment lay ahead, nestled in a loop of the Washita. Custer thereupon drew his battle plan: four columns would strike the village without warning.

At dawn on November 27, the assault columns moved on the village, undetected by the sleeping Indians until the soldiers were almost upon them. At the sound of a rifle shot, Custer ordered his bugler to sound the charge, while his accompanying regimental band struck up a Custer favorite: "Garry Owen." Amid the cacophony of music, gunfire, and screams, most of the villagers ran for their lives. A few warriors established themselves in nearby wooded gullies, but cavalry troopers, many fighting on foot, wiped out every pocket of resistance.

Away from the main attack, Elliott set off with a small force, pursuing the Cheyennes fleeing along the river. It was a fatal mistake. Arapaho, Kiowa, and other Cheyenne warriors from larger camps to the east cut off Elliott's men and then cut them down. Nineteen died that way, accounting for nearly all of Custer's casualties: two officers and twenty enlisted men were killed, with another twenty troopers wounded. Cheyenne sources maintain that between eleven and fourteen warriors died and that nineteen women and children were killed alongside them, but some scholars set the count much higher.

Unable to locate Elliott and his troops but aware that many more warriors were approaching from the east, Custer ordered the village destroyed, immediately and utterly. Dutiful troopers hurried to burn every teepee, slaughter eight hundred ponies, and destroy anything that could not be carried off. They left—with 247 saddles, 573 buffalo robes, and more than 50 women and children.

An artist's imaginative rendering of the Seventh Cavalry charging into Black Kettle's village at daylight, November 27, 1868. (Engraving from Harper's Weekly, *December 26, 1868, courtesy Western History Collections, University of Oklahoma Libraries)*

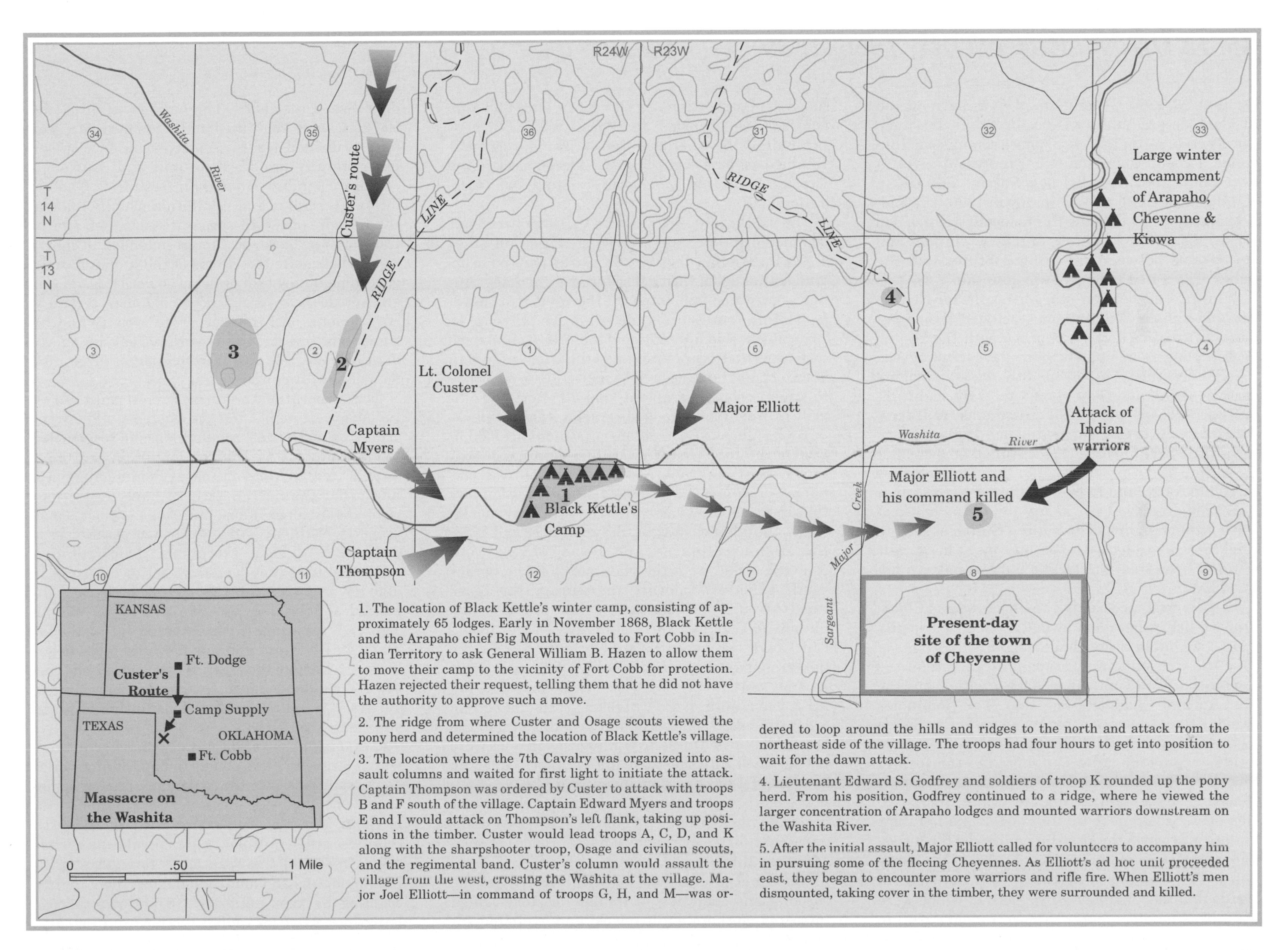

1. The location of Black Kettle's winter camp, consisting of approximately 65 lodges. Early in November 1868, Black Kettle and the Arapaho chief Big Mouth traveled to Fort Cobb in Indian Territory to ask General William B. Hazen to allow them to move their camp to the vicinity of Fort Cobb for protection. Hazen rejected their request, telling them that he did not have the authority to approve such a move.

2. The ridge from where Custer and Osage scouts viewed the pony herd and determined the location of Black Kettle's village.

3. The location where the 7th Cavalry was organized into assault columns and waited for first light to initiate the attack. Captain Thompson was ordered by Custer to attack with troops B and F south of the village. Captain Edward Myers and troops E and I would attack on Thompson's left flank, taking up positions in the timber. Custer would lead troops A, C, D, and K along with the sharpshooter troop, Osage and civilian scouts, and the regimental band. Custer's column would assault the village from the west, crossing the Washita at the village. Major Joel Elliott—in command of troops G, H, and M—was ordered to loop around the hills and ridges to the north and attack from the northeast side of the village. The troops had four hours to get into position to wait for the dawn attack.

4. Lieutenant Edward S. Godfrey and soldiers of troop K rounded up the pony herd. From his position, Godfrey continued to a ridge, where he viewed the larger concentration of Arapaho lodges and mounted warriors downstream on the Washita River.

5. After the initial assault, Major Elliott called for volunteers to accompany him in pursuing some of the fleeing Cheyennes. As Elliott's ad hoc unit proceeded east, they began to encounter more warriors and rifle fire. When Elliott's men dismounted, taking cover in the timber, they were surrounded and killed.

45. INDIAN TERRITORY, 1866–1889

Essay by *Michael D. Green*

On June 23, 1865, General Stand Watie surrendered all Confederate military forces in Indian Territory. Shortly thereafter a Federal peace commission convened a grand council of tribal representatives at Fort Smith, but the final negotiations and treaty signings took place in Washington in 1866. The Federal position was that the Confederate treaties had erased more than a century of treaty relations and obligations between the United States and the tribes. There had to be a new beginning.

While the effects were staggering, the terms were few and simple. The nations rescinded their Confederate treaties and made peace with the United States, they emancipated their slaves and agreed to extend to the freedpersons full and equal rights of citizenship, and they agreed to grant rights-of-way to railroads, accept the jurisdiction of federal district courts in cases involving non-Indians, work toward the establishment of a unified government for Indian Territory, and sell to the United States large blocks of land to be distributed to the tribes previously removed to Kansas and to the tribes of the southern plains. The United States agreed to reinstate relations with the nations. The details differed from treaty to treaty, but the pattern applied to all.

In their combined treaty, the Choctaws and Chickasaws ceded their jointly owned Leased District. By 1870 the United States had designated portions of it as the Cheyenne and Arapaho Reservation; the Comanche, Kiowa, and Apache Reservation; and the Wichita and Caddo Reservation. The Seminoles ceded their entire nation, part of which was included in the Cheyenne and Arapaho Reservation, while another part became the Pottawatomie and Shawnee Reservation. The Seminoles then purchased a new nation carved out of the Creek cession. The Creeks gave up the western half of their nation, into which the government moved the Iowas, Sacs and Foxes, and Kickapoos, as well as the Seminoles. The Cherokees agreed to sell the Neutral Lands and the Cherokee Strip, both of which were in Kansas, and accepted the government's plan to move the Osages, Tonkawas, Poncas, Otos and Missouris, Kaws (Kansas), and Pawnees into the eastern half of the Cherokee Outlet. The government retained as "Unassigned Lands" a large block in the Creek cession that was never designated as reservation land.

During the late 1860s and 1870s, the government completed the process of moving these and other tribes into Indian Territory. It also attempted to organize the region with a territorial government under a governor appointed by the president and a legislature representing the tribes. The Creeks periodically hosted international councils at Okmulgee to discuss matters of interest to the tribes of Indian Territory, but none desired to subject its sovereignty to a territorial government, and all efforts by officials in Washington to achieve such a thing failed.

By far the most portentous provision included in each of the 1866 treaties was the requirement that the Five Nations grant right-of-ways to railroad companies. The U.S. government assumed originally that there should be two lines, one running north–south, the other east–west. Between 1870 and 1873, the Missouri, Kansas, and Texas (MK&T) constructed a line from the Kansas-Cherokee border south, generally following the route of the Texas Road, through the Cherokee, Creek, and Choctaw nations to Colbert's Ferry on the Red River in the Chickasaw Nation. In 1871 the Atlantic and Pacific (later renamed the St. Louis and San Francisco) built its line westward from Missouri and crossed the MK&T at Vinita in the Cherokee Nation; a decade later, it pressed southwest and in 1882 entered the Creek Nation at Tulsa. But railroad companies were not satisfied with these two lines authorized by the treaties of 1866 and demanded that Congress approve more, regardless of the wishes of the Indian governments. Without consulting the tribes, Congress chartered eleven additional railroads between 1882 and 1888.

The tribal governments had little control over the corporations operating in Indian Territory, which imported workers, built towns, and exploited Indian-owned resources. The nations (after the initial agreement contained in the 1866 treaties) were bitterly divided over further economic development but generally preferred to limit and restrict the corporate penetration of their territories. Their efforts at restraint and regulation usually failed in the face of concerted corporate economic and political power, however. Congress tended to charter railroads despite the efforts of the Indian national governments to block or delay them. Thus did Congress erode the sovereign power of Indian Territory's governments. All this corporate activity had two significant effects: the move to break up the Indian nations, and the introduction of large numbers of non-Indian workers.

The corporations were more powerful than the Indian governments, but the existence of those governments (with laws, regulations, and responsibilities for protecting the commonly owned lands) complicated and in some cases hindered business. Except for the narrow strip of land needed for a right-of-way, for example, railroads could not acquire property. Neither could any other corporation or individual. With some exceptions, the corporations concluded that they would be better off if the Indian governments were dissolved, the nations disbanded, and the land made available to non-Indians. This view was widely disseminated during the late nineteenth century and won powerful allies in government. Despite the treaties that guaranteed their sovereign independence, the Five Nations of Indian Territory found themselves constantly fighting to survive.

Corporate penetration of Indian Territory brought with it large numbers of non-Indians. Many worked on the railroads or in the coal mines, lumber camps, or oil fields. Business and professional people settled in Vinita, Muskogee, McAlester, Bartlesville, and the countless other railroad, coal, and oil towns. These people resented their status as foreigners in the Indian nations and loudly demanded their "rights," claiming that their numbers (110,000 in a total population of 180,000 for Indian Territory in 1890) justi-

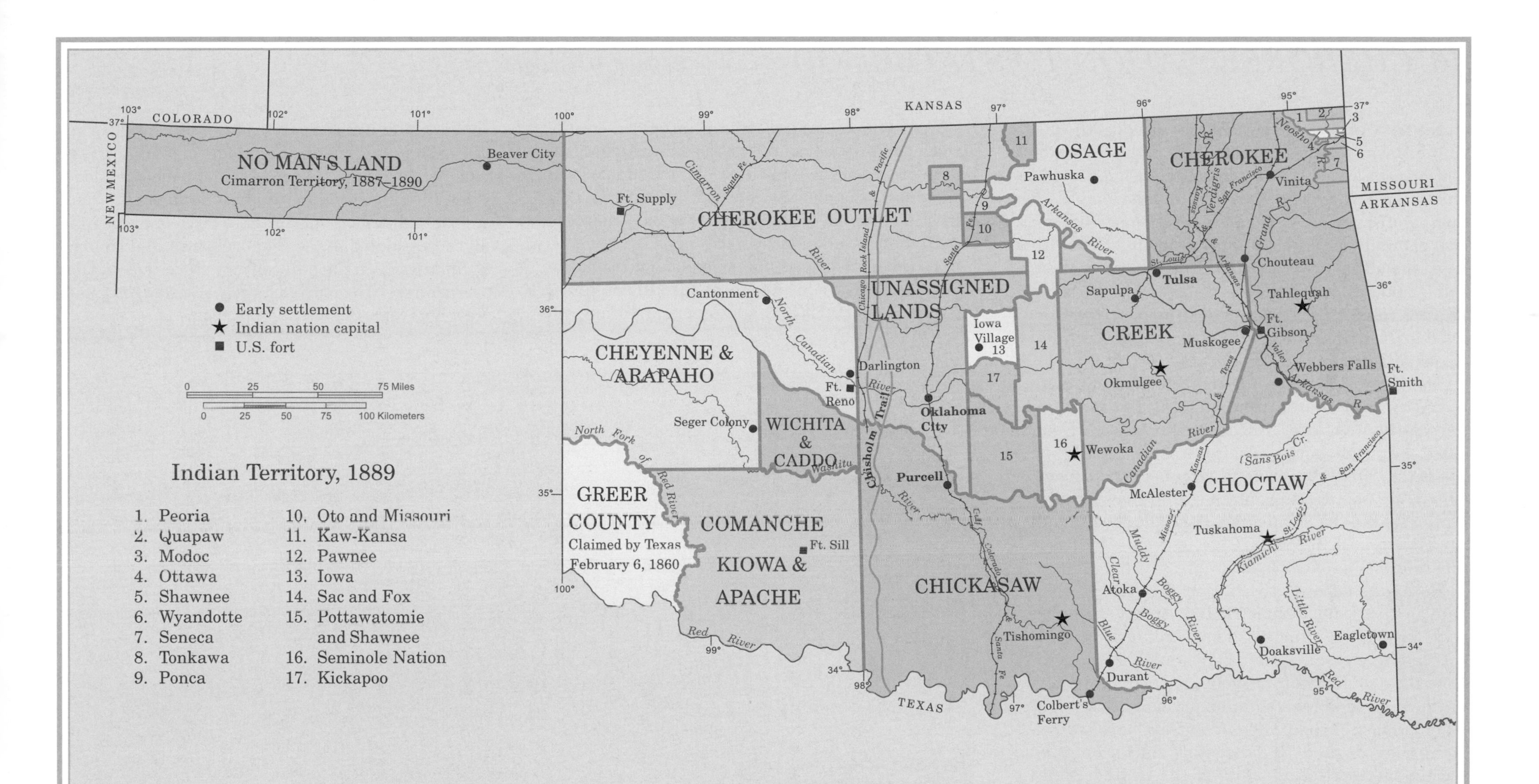

fied their demands. While sometimes at odds with the corporations, they agreed that the nations should be disbanded.

For most tribes in the United States, the Dawes General Allotment Act of 1887 made such sentiments policy. The Dawes Act called for breaking up tribal social and political organizations, distributing reservation lands to individual members of the tribes, and selling the rest of the lands for homesteading. The law specifically exempted the Five Nations of eastern Indian Territory but applied to the rest. Legislation in 1893 and 1895 extended the provisions of the Dawes Act to the Cherokees, Choctaws, Chickasaws, Creeks, and Seminoles.

Events began to move very rapidly after 1887. The U.S. government opened the Unassigned Lands for settlement in 1889. The next year, federal officials organized that region, plus "No Man's Land" (the Panhandle), as Oklahoma Territory. Then, in the early 1890s, the United States added to Oklahoma Territory the newly allotted reservations. Oklahoma Territory joined the corporations and white residents of Indian Territory in the call to break up the nations, disband their governments, allot their lands, and unite the two territories into a new state of Oklahoma.

46. CHEROKEE NATION TO STATEHOOD

Essay by *Michael D. Green*

In the forty-six years between the arrival of the victims of Jacksonian removal and 1885, the Cherokee Nation was wracked by political upheaval, social chaos, the devastating Civil War, and the long, slow, and painful process of achieving economic recovery. The population of the nation was about 22,000 citizens, including over 2,000 free blacks. In addition, some 2,000 more former black slaves who were not citizens (plus a rapidly growing number of whites) lived in the nation, enough that noncitizens outnumbered citizens.

The Cherokees were mainly farmers and ranchers. With more than a hundred thousand acres under cultivation, they raised cotton, corn, wheat, cattle, hogs, and horses. Their towns were small and scattered, many built along streams or railroads. The major population centers within the Cherokee Nation, except for Tahlequah, the capital, were railroad towns such as Vinita, Claremore, and Sallisaw, where few Cherokees lived.

Railroads entered the nation through a provision in the 1866 Reconstruction treaty, bringing with them large numbers of non-Indians who grew increasingly resentful of their status. As noncitizens they could not own lands, participate in government, or send their children to Cherokee schools. Aliens (most of them illegal) in the Cherokee Nation, they argued that because they remained within the territorial limits of the United States they should be permitted all the rights of U.S. citizens. Unwilling to conform to Cherokee law, they created a massive legal problem for the Cherokee Nation.

The Cherokees governed themselves under a constitution adopted in 1839 but patterned on that of 1827. They had an elected principal chief, a supreme court and district courts, and a two-house legislature. Each of the nine electoral districts elected two senators, while citizens elected members of the council on the basis of proportional representation.

Twenty-three-hundred children attended seventy-five elementary schools. Those seeking higher education attended the male and female seminaries in Tahlequah or one of the mission boarding schools. Christian Cherokees supported over sixty churches, mostly Baptist and Methodist.

The political and economic leaders of the nation tended to be well-educated men—usually literate in English, comfortable in Anglo-American society, and generally divorced from traditional Cherokee culture. The rapidly growing middle class of artisans, business owners, and professional people tended to be of the same group. But large numbers of Cherokees remained outside of these circles, living quiet lives in isolated areas. Their culture had changed dramatically in the half century since removal, but the changes had occurred largely according to Cherokee, not Anglo-American, patterns.

Cherokee Male Seminary near Tahlequah, Cherokee Nation, Indian Territory, 1890. (Courtesy Western History Collections, University of Oklahoma Libraries)

Cherokee Nation, 1889

Through all the changes in the Cherokee Nation, some places endured. Many of the towns in the nation were of historic interest. Tahlonteeskee (the old capital of the Western Cherokees) no longer flourished, but Tahlequah (the capital of the united tribe on the Illinois River) and nearby Park Hill held many remembrances for the older Indians. The Three Forks area, where the Verdigris and the Grand empty into the Arkansas, was a region of long-continued exchange of goods. White settlers were moving to locations near Jacob Bartle's store on Caney River, and Bartlesville was marked for growth and increasing trade. Settlers at Coodys Bluff crossed the Verdigris to trade in the stores at Nowata, which also had "spring-wagon customers" from Lenapah and Talala. Webbers Falls on the Arkansas, Locust Grove and Salina north of Fort Gibson on the Grand, and Briartown on the Canadian were old and well-established trade centers. Briartown, the southernmost Cherokee settlement, was Stand Watie's place of refuge during the Civil War when his daring raids north of the Arkansas River caused him to be sought by overwhelming military forces.

Population of the Cherokee Nation, Indian Territory

Census	Population
1890	56,309
1900	101,754
1907	140,415

Includes all Indians, whites, and blacks.

Larger Towns of the Cherokee Nation, 1907

Town	Population	Post office established
Bartlesville	4,215	May 6, 1879
Vinita	3,157	—[a]
Claremore	2,064	June 25, 1874
Tahlequah	1,916	May 6, 1847
Sallisaw	1,698	December 8, 1888[b]

[a] Date unknown.

[b] Formerly Childer's Station, post office established June 26, 1878; name changed to Sallisaw, December 8, 1888.

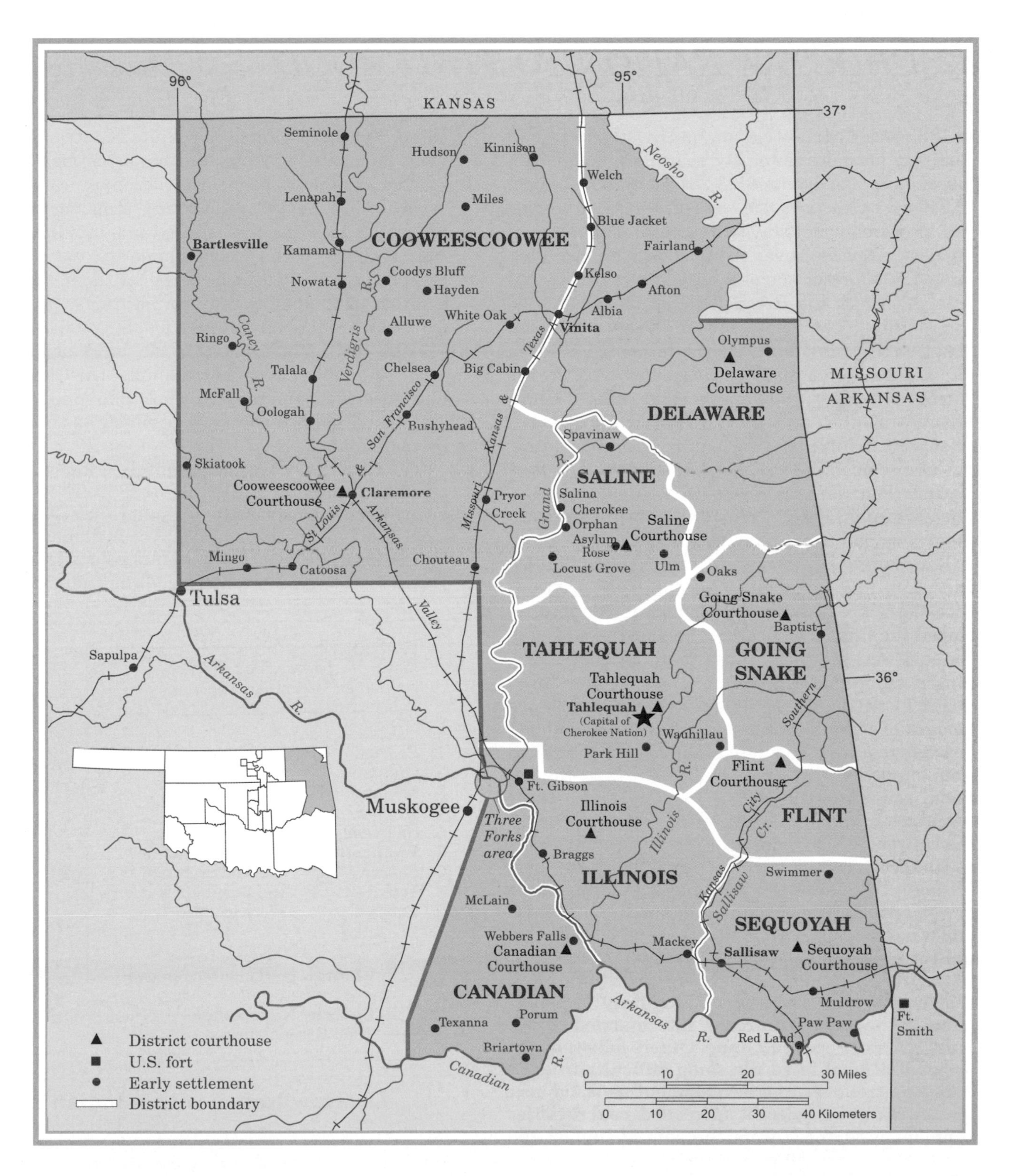

47. CHOCTAW NATION TO STATEHOOD

Essay by *Michael D. Green*

In 1885, the Choctaw Nation had existed in Indian Territory for more than fifty years. An official census of that year counted 13,281 citizens, of whom 12,816 were Choctaws, 427 were intermarried whites, and 38 were former slaves. The total population of the nation was well over 40,000, however, including some 4,500 former slaves whose status was in dispute. Although the Reconstruction treaty of 1866 had required the Choctaws to admit their freedmen to national citizenship, the national council delayed compliance. Some 30,000 whites also lived in the nation, and their numbers were growing quickly. Choctaw planters and ranchers employed some, but most were involved in railroading and coal mining, the two main industrial activities in the Choctaw Nation. The western towns of McAlester, Krebs, Coalgate, and Lehigh were mining towns. Between them they had about 8,000 people in 1885.

Railroading and coal mining were related industries. The 1866 treaty that reestablished relations with the United States included an article that required the Choctaws to admit one north-south and one east-west railroad through their nation. In 1872, construction of the Missouri, Kansas, and Texas (MK&T) railroad was completed. An enormous amount of wood and stone for ties, bridges, and ballast was required, and individual Choctaws profited from supplying these materials. Efforts by the national council to control the exploitation of these resources were slow to take effect, largely because the railroad preferred to contract with individuals on its terms, but ultimately the council succeeded. Through the efforts of a national agent, appointed by the council, lumber and stone production came under national authority, which produced a substantial royalty for the nation's treasury.

Railroads made coal mining profitable, and shortly after the construction of the "Katy" (the nickname of the MK&T railroad), intermarried citizen J. J. McAlester opened a mine. Others followed. The national council faced the same difficulty in exercising control over coal development as it did over the railroads, but when it succeeded, coal royalties supplemented those from the sale of timber and stone. Annuities paid by the United States for previous land sales and interest from investments provided a significant part of the national income, but royalties became the main source of money for the nation: in 1885 the coal royalty amounted to more than $50,000. While the vast majority of the Choctaw people derived little direct benefit from the penetration of their nation by corporations, royalties from coal production (estimated at 500,000 tons per year by 1885) paid for most of the national government's public services. For example, the Choctaws had the largest and reputedly best public education system in Indian Territory, all of which was financed by coal royalties.

The Choctaws governed themselves under a constitution drafted at Doaksville in 1860. They had a national government with a popularly elected principal chief, a two-house national council, and a system of local, district, and national courts based on three districts and seventeen counties. Members of the senate were elected on the district level, while representatives served the counties. In 1882 the council moved its capital to the new town of Tuskahoma.

While industrial development kept the Choctaw Nation in a state of social confusion, the vast majority of Choctaws continued to live on smallholdings where they grew corn and raised a few cattle, hogs, and horses. They sent their children to school in large numbers, however, and by 1885 the number of Choctaws monolingual in their own language was rapidly declining. Agricultural produce remained commercially important as well; cotton and cattle were by far the most important sources of income for the Choctaw people.

Methodists and Presbyterians, along with the Baptists who entered the Choctaw mission field in 1858, accounted for the overwhelming majority of Choctaw Christians. According to the 1890 census, these and several small denominations claimed over 8,500 Choctaw members.

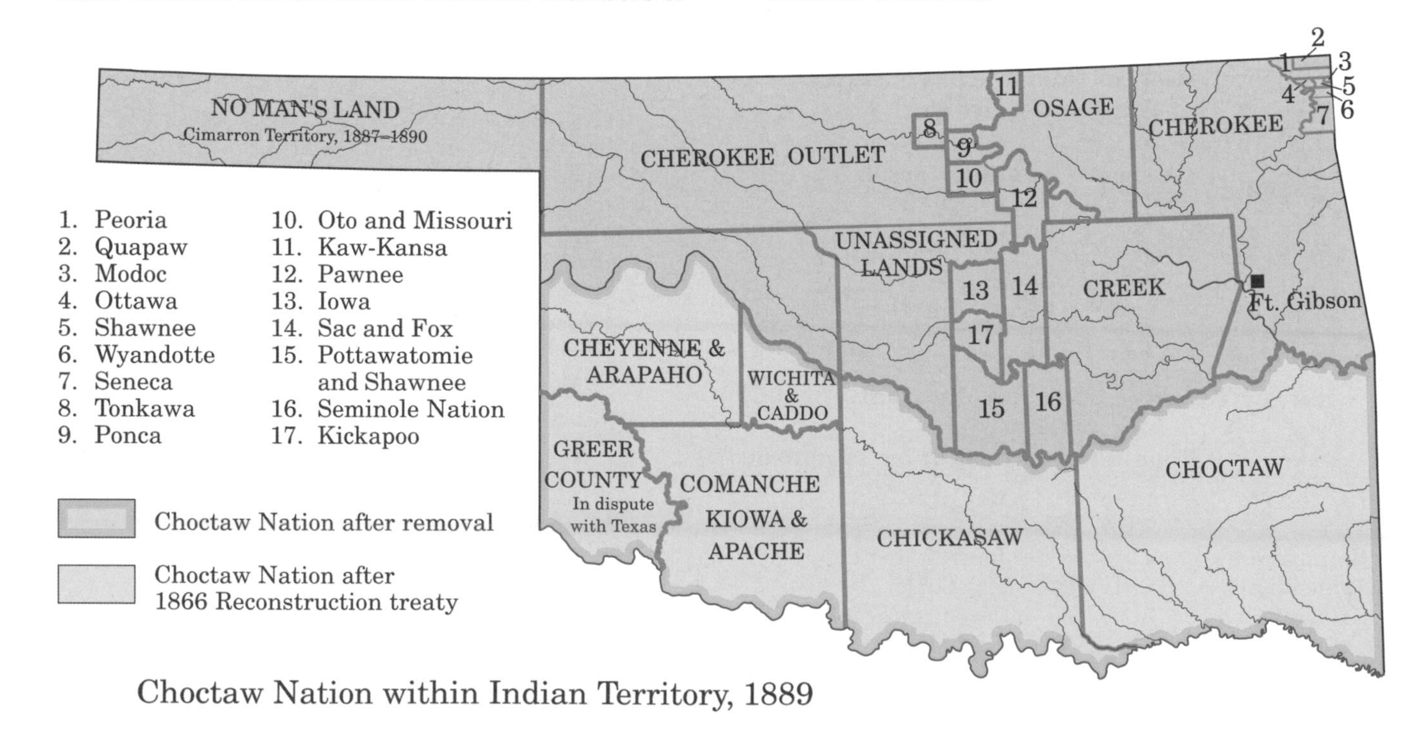

Choctaw Nation within Indian Territory, 1889

Choctaw society had continued to develop in the pattern begun in the East. The operators of the big ranches and farms tended to come from a relatively small number of elite bicultural families, while most Choctaws farmed at a subsistence level. The distinction reflected the cultural experiences of those who had been raised to value property and its accumulation, as opposed to those with more traditional, less acquisitive values. But education—especially in the highly successful Spencer (boys) and New Hope (girls) academies—tended to blur these cultural differences.

Principal Chiefs of the Choctaw Nation, 1864–1907

Dates of service	Name
1864–1866	Peter P. Pitchlynn
1866–1870	Allen Wright
1870–1874	William Bryant
1874–1878	Coleman Cole
1878–1880	Isaac Garvin
1880–1884	Jackson McCurtain
1884–1886	Edmund McCurtain
1886–1888	Thompson McKinney
1888–1890	Ben F. Smallwood
1890–1894	Wilson N. Jones
1894–1896	Jefferson Gardner
1896–1900	Green McCurtain
1900–1902	Gilbert Dukes
1902–1907	Green McCurtain

Population of the Choctaw Nation, Indian Territory

Census	Population
1890	43,808
1900	99,781
1907	182,066

Includes all Indians, whites, and blacks.

Larger Towns of the Choctaw Nation, 1907

Town	Population	Post office established
McAlester	8,144	March 31, 1873
Durant	4,510	March 8, 1882
Coalgate[a]	2,921	January 23, 1890
Hugo	2,676	November 1, 1901
Hartshorne	2,435	March 5, 1890
Lehigh	2,188	April 4, 1882

[a] Formerly Liddle, post office established September 18, 1889; name changed to Coalgate on January 23, 1890.

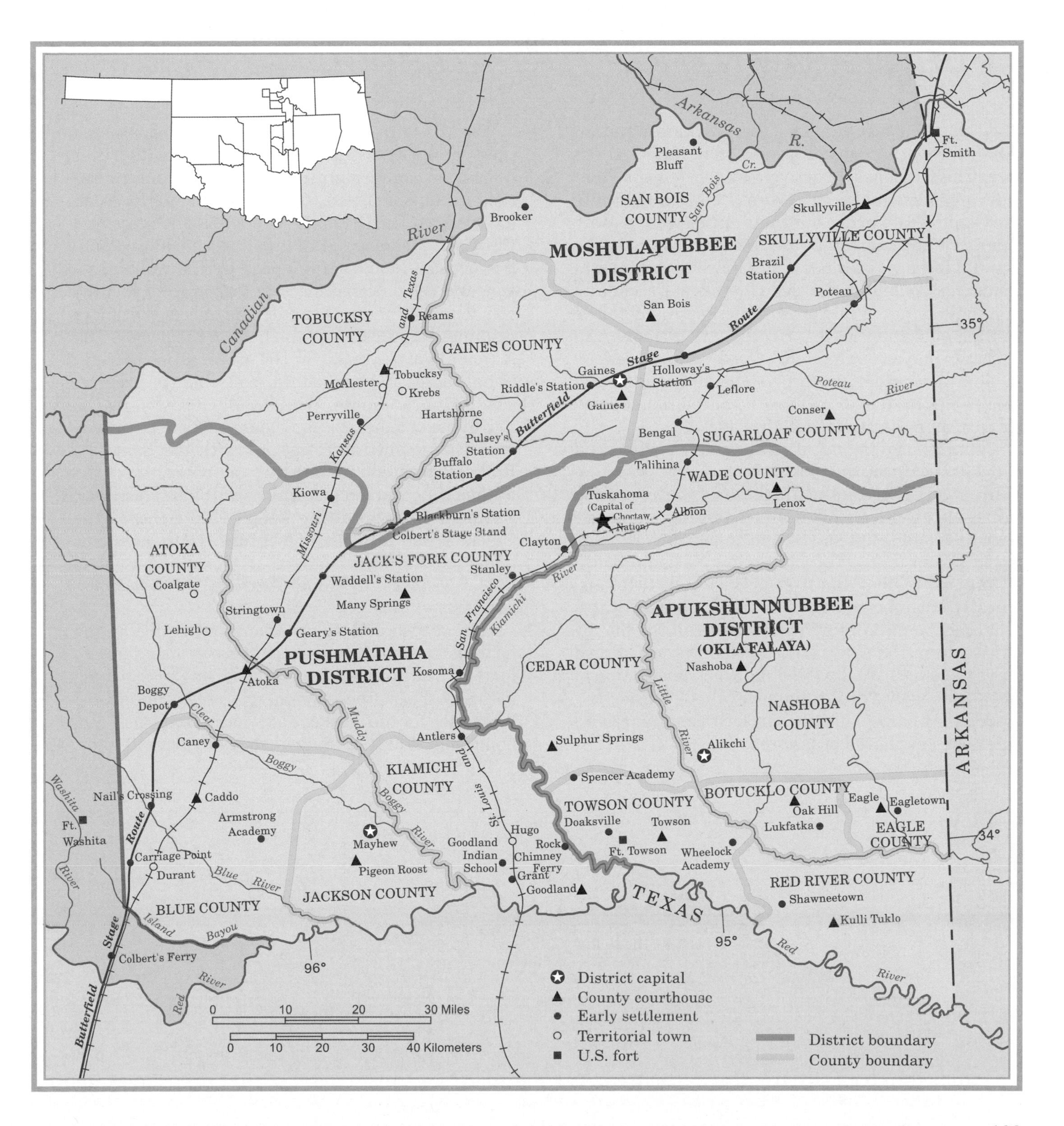

48. CHICKASAW NATION TO STATEHOOD Essay by *Michael D. Green*

The U.S. Civil War damaged the Chickasaw Nation less severely than any other nation in Indian Territory. The Chickasaws actively supported the Confederate cause and sent several hundred men into the Confederate army, but their duties were mainly defensive and their nation was never invaded. The war did disrupt the home front, however, as several thousand Confederate-allied Cherokee, Creek, and Seminole refugees fled toward the Red River before advancing Union forces. Chickasaw farmers and ranchers played a large role in feeding these people. In addition, under the provisions of the 1866 Reconstruction treaty, the two hundred Chickasaw slave owners had to free their slaves.

Certain provisions of that treaty influenced Chickasaw life for the rest of the century. According to the treaty's terms, the Chickasaws were required to extend full citizenship rights to the approximately one thousand freed slaves and to permit railroads to cross their lands. The Chickasaw National Council refused to obey the first provision, which periodically strained relations with the United States and cost the nation its $75,000 share of the money earned from the sale of the Leased District. Freed slaves fleeing Texas swelled the black population of the Chickasaw Nation by several thousand. Excluded from citizenship, the blacks became an underclass to be exploited or ignored.

The Missouri, Kansas, and Texas Railroad crossed the southeastern tip of the nation in 1872. Other lines tried to gain right-of-ways as well, but the national council refused to authorize them. Railroad lobbyists worked the halls of Congress and pressured Chickasaw leaders to fall into line. Chickasaw politics became heavily influenced by the railroad issue, and the national election for governor in 1886 was fought in large part over the effects that more rail lines would have on the lives of the people. The National Party argued for the preservation of traditional values and against railroads, but the Progressive Party candidate, William M. Guy, won by the narrowest of margins. Immediately following his victory, Guy opened negotiations with the Santa Fe Railway to extend its line through the center of the nation. As occurred elsewhere in Indian Territory, railroads brought white people and cities to the Chickasaws. Ardmore, one of these railroad towns, had a population of 5,700 in 1890, making it one of the largest cities in Indian Territory. But few Chickasaws lived in these towns.

Agriculture and stock raising remained at the heart of the Chickasaw economy. Large operators ran huge farms with black and white labor. Concentrated in the southeast, these commercial outfits raised corn and cotton for the market and welcomed the new economic opportunities made possible by the railroads. Farther west, Chickasaw ranchers raised thousands of head of cattle and horses. But most Chickasaws did not have large operations. Blessed with good soil, they could live well on their small farms.

The Chickasaw national government rested on the 1856 constitution, amended in 1867. With a large annual income from its national fund, the council in 1867 reopened eleven neighborhood elementary schools that had been closed during the war. In 1876 the council increased this number to twenty-three. Administered and taught largely by Chickasaws, this far-flung school system was supplemented by four secondary schools (Chickasaw Male Academy, Bloomfield Female Seminary, Wapanuka Institute, and the Lebanon Orphan School) and a scholarship program large enough to send 60 to 100 of the most promising youths to the states to college each year. Of some 6,000 Chickasaws in 1880, an estimated 3,600 could read and write English. No other nation in Indian Territory could boast such a high literacy rate.

The Chickasaw policy of running their own schools denied the mission boards the customary educational role of mission schools; despite that, the Methodists, Baptists, and Cumberland Presbyterians were active. In the mid-1880s, these denominations had dozens of churches and a combined membership estimated at between five hundred and one thousand people.

Principal Chiefs of the Chickasaw Nation, 1866–1907

Dates of service	Name
1866–1870	Cyrus Harris
1870–1871	W. P. Brown
1871–1872	Thomas J. Parker
1872–1874	Cyrus Harris
1874–1878	B. F. Overton
1878–1880	B. C. Burney
1880–1884	B. F. Overton
1884–1886	Jonas Wolf
1886–1888	William M. Guy
1888–1892	William L. Byrd
1892–1894	Jonas Wolf
1894–1896	Palmer S. Mosley
1896–1898	Robert M. Harris
1898–1902	Douglas H. Johnston
1902–1904	Palmer S. Mosley
1904–1907	Douglas H. Johnston

Population of the Chickasaw Nation, Indian Territory

Census	Population
1890	57,329
1900	139,260
1907	191,655

Includes all Indians, whites, and blacks.

Larger Towns of the Chickasaw Nation, 1907

Town	Population	Post office established
Ardmore	8,759	October 27, 1887
Chickasha[a]	7,862	June 20, 1892
Ada	3,257	July 10, 1891
Sulphur	2,939	October 2, 1895
Purcell	2,553	April 21, 1887
Duncan	2,451	April 7, 1884
Pauls Valley	2,157	August 21, 1871
Madill	1,587	April 29, 1901

[a] Formerly Waco, then changed to Pensee on September 11, 1891; name changed to Chickasha on June 20, 1892.

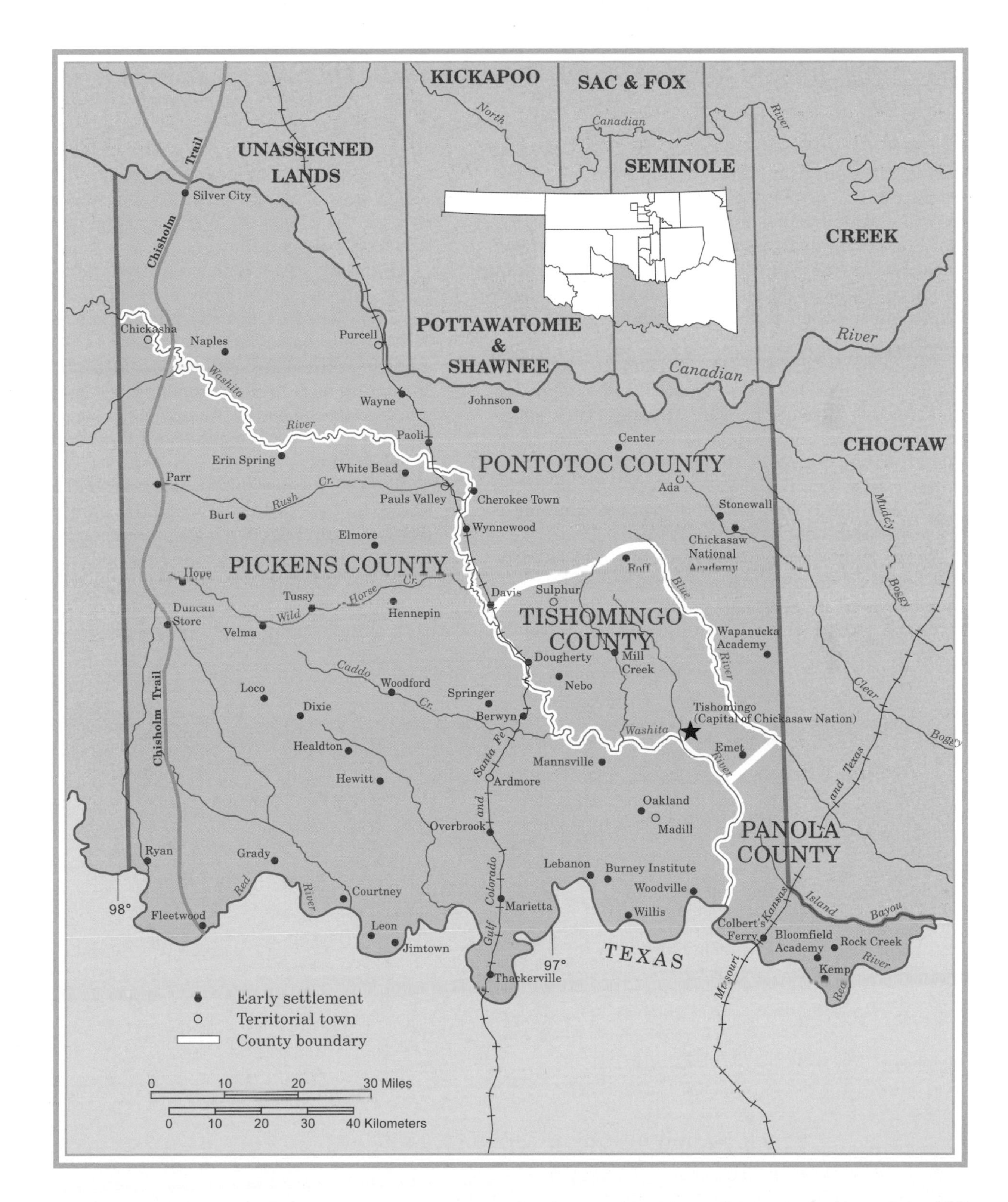

49. CREEK NATION TO STATEHOOD

Essay by *Michael D. Green*

The U.S. Civil War devastated the Creek Nation through factionalism and reprisals from both Confederate and Union forces. In 1861, neutralist Creeks led by Opothleyahola—pushed into the Union camp after several battles with Confederate-allied Creeks—became refugees in Kansas. Throughout the war, Union and Confederate Creek soldiers fought one another, and together they ravaged their nation.

The Reconstruction treaty of 1866, conducted to reopen relations with the United States, required the Creeks to give up the western half of their country, free their approximately 1,500 slaves, and grant full citizenship rights to the freedpersons. Pro-Confederates dominated the Creek delegation at the negotiations and won for their group a commanding position in Creek public affairs.

At the same time, a task force of Creek leaders was drafting a constitution. Promulgated in 1867, the document provided for popularly elected principal and second chiefs, a two-house national council, and a judicial system with six district courts and a supreme court. Members of the House of Kings were elected by the towns, while membership in the House of Warriors was proportional, based on town population.

The treaty of 1866 also required that the Creeks allow railroads into their country. During 1871–1872, the Missouri, Kansas, and Texas Railroad built south along the eastern border of the Creek Nation, following the old Texas Road. Muskogee and Eufaula sprang up as railroad towns and became centers of white economic power that, by 1885, was an increasing threat to the integrity and sovereignty of the Creek Nation.

By 1885, Protestant missionaries had been in the nation for over forty years, and the country was dotted with churches. The missionaries had also founded several boarding schools. Five operated in 1885, funded by the nation but generally operated by white teachers under Creek superintendence. These, along with twenty-eight neighborhood schools, educated some 1,100 Creek children. Instruction was in English. Non-English-speaking children were taught English, but not very well, and the English-speaking children of bicultural families had a clear educational advantage.

Indeed, the increasing dominance of Creek life by bicultural people—with their English language, school education, church membership, business activities, and interest in profits and possessions—caused deep strains to develop in Creek society. Often these strains assumed political dimensions, and sometimes they became so heated as to resemble civil war. Four times between 1867 and 1901, opponents of the constitutional government (to many, the most obvious and obnoxious example of the American cultural invasion) attempted to overthrow it. In 1885 the nation was still recovering from the Green Peach War, which had pitted culturally conservative opponents of constitutionalism and political centralization against those who functioned comfortably with American cultural values.

Creek Nation in Indian Territory, 1889

Population of the Creek Nation, Indian Territory

Census	Population
1890	17,912
1900	40,674
1907	144,457

Includes all Indians, whites, and blacks.

Larger Towns of the Creek Nation, 1907

Town	Population	Post office established
Muskogee	14,418	January 18, 1872
Tulsa	7,298	March 25, 1879
Sapulpa	4,259	July 1, 1889
Okmulgee	2,322	April 29, 1869
Holdenville[a]	1,868	November 15, 1895
Checotah	1,524	June 17, 1886
Bristow	1,134	April 25, 1898
Eufaula	974	February 6, 1874

[a] Formerly Fentress Post Office; name changed to Holdenville on November 15, 1895.

Creek Governance

On October 12, 1867, a brief written constitution was adopted by a vote of the Creek people. The national council, composed of the House of Kings and the House of Warriors, was given the power to formulate and pass laws. The principal chief, with his appointed private secretary, was given the function of law enforcement. The erudite messages of semiliterate chiefs are to be explained only by their skill in the selection of secretaries.

The constitution of 1867 divided the Creek Nation into six districts. The national council elected a judge for each district, the principal chief appointed six district attorneys with the approval of the council, and the voters of each district elected a captain and four privates to serve as a light-horse police force. District officers were chosen for a term of two years. The principal chief, a second chief to succeed him in the event of his death in office, and members of the national council were elected, each to serve for four years in his office.

Trial by jury was provided for civil and criminal cases. All suits at law in which the amount in dispute was more than $100 were tried by the supreme court, composed of five justices named by the national council for terms of four years.

Perhaps the most distinctive feature of the Creek government was its use of the town as the unit of elections and administration. After the Creeks removed to the West, the people no longer restricted their residence to the town, but the older system of governmental units was preserved.

Principal Chiefs of the Creek Nation, 1867–1907

Dates of service	Name
1867–1875	Samuel Chocote
1875–1876	Locher Harjo
1876–1879	Ward Coachman
1879–1883	Samuel Chocote
1883–1887	Joseph M. Perryman
1887–1895	Legus Perryman
1895–1895	Edward Bullette
1895–1899	Isparhecher
1899–1907	Pleasant Porter

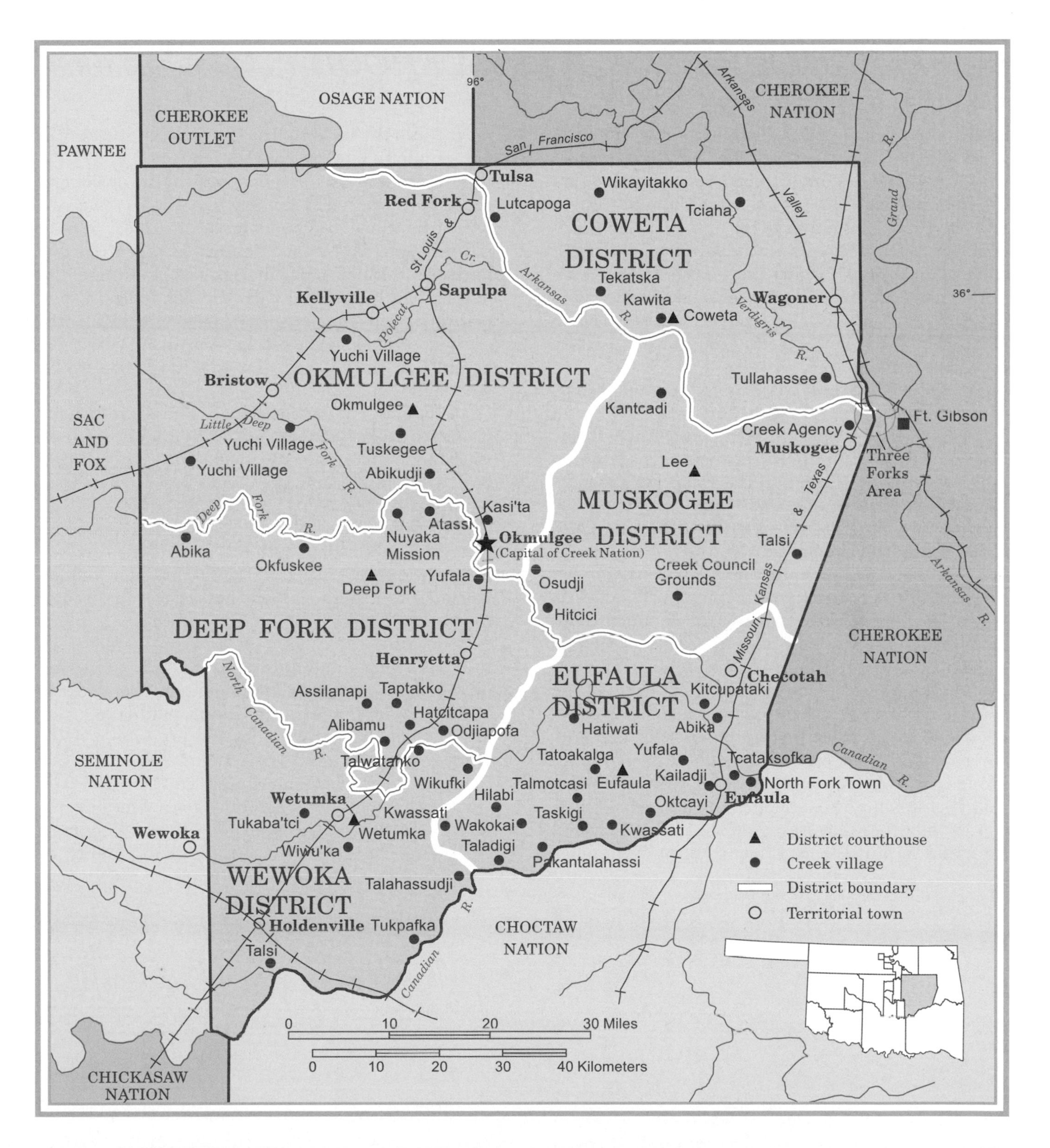

50. SEMINOLE NATION TO STATEHOOD

Essay by *Michael D. Green*

Under the terms of the two treaties negotiated in 1833 at Fort Gibson between the United States and the Creeks and Seminoles, the Creeks set aside for the Seminoles a tract between the Canadian River and the North Canadian River in the southeastern portion of their nation. But Creek removal occurred from 1835 through 1836, and many of those emigrants moved into the country set aside for the Seminoles. By the time the Seminoles began to arrive in 1841, the lands they were to occupy were already heavily populated by Creeks.

For the next several years, most Seminoles lived in camps in the general vicinity of Fort Gibson, with some on the Creek side of the line and others in the Cherokee Nation. One group of about eight hundred led by Micanopy settled on the Deep Fork, southwest of the fort. No one was happy with these arrangements. The Cherokees wanted the Seminoles to move out, the Creeks wanted the Seminoles under their control, and the Seminoles wanted to begin making permanent settlements. Thomas L. Judge, the Seminole agent, joined the Seminole council in urging the United States to assist in reaching some satisfactory conclusion to the problem. The outcome was an arrangement agreed to at Fort Gibson in January 1845, which wiped out the Seminole District and authorized the Seminoles to settle anywhere in the Creek Nation, as individuals, in small groups, or in large concentrations. The Seminoles could establish towns and govern themselves, subject to the general oversight of the Creek National Council. Within the next year, many Seminoles moved into the valley of the Little River and carved out an unofficial Seminole Nation.

This scheme did not meet many of the objections consistently raised by the Seminoles, who remained without a homeland and were still subject, if only indirectly, to Creek law. Conflict between the two nations continued, particularly over the status of the blacks, long associated with the Seminoles. Creek planters tried a variety of means—some legal, others not—to enslave the blacks, who (along with their Seminole friends) lived in fear that the Creeks would succeed.

In 1856, the Seminoles finally won. In return for promises to help convince the Seminoles still in Florida to surrender and move west, the United States purchased from the Creeks and deeded to the Seminole Nation a strip of land lying between the Canadian and North Canadian rivers that extended from the 97th to the 100th meridian. This tract included the settlements on the Little River and attracted those Seminoles who had scattered through the Creek Nation.

Soon after the Seminoles took up residence in their new homeland, however, the U.S. Civil War intruded. Even though an estimated three-fourths of them favored neutrality in this conflict, a small group of leaders—including the prominent John Jumper—signed a treaty in August 1861 with the Confederate States. John Chupco and Billy Bowlegs led many Seminoles, including most black Seminoles, into the neutralist camp of Creek headman Opotheyahola, and when the Creeks fled north to Kansas ahead of Confederate Indian forces, these Seminoles went, too. During the war, Seminole men fought in either army, while their families sought refuge in Kansas or the Chickasaw Nation.

The 1866 Reconstruction treaty required that the Seminoles cede to the United States their entire country, a tract of 2,170,000 acres, for fifteen cents per acre ($325,500). This was their punishment for having sided with the Confederacy. To replace this land, the United States agreed to sell the Seminole Nation, for fifty cents an acre, a 200,000-acre tract cut from the southeastern corner of the cession wrung from the Creeks in their Reconstruction treaty. But the Seminole agent moved the people onto the tract before it was surveyed and inadvertently put them east of the line, on Creek lands. After years of argument over jurisdiction and despite prolonged opposition from a substantial settlement of Creeks, in 1882 Congress purchased an additional 175,000 acres from the Creeks, at one dollar an acre, and deeded it to the Seminoles, thus nearly doubling the size of their nation. The Seminoles quickly established their capital at Wewoka.

The Seminole Nation contained good, well-watered land capable of producing bumper crops. In addition to cultivating corn and other grains for food, the Seminoles grew cotton for export and ran a significant number of cattle. No railroad entered their nation until 1895, which meant that they (unlike the other nations) were not overrun by non-Indian intruders. They were also spared much of the rapid and massive economic and cultural change that corporate, urban America imposed on the other nations.

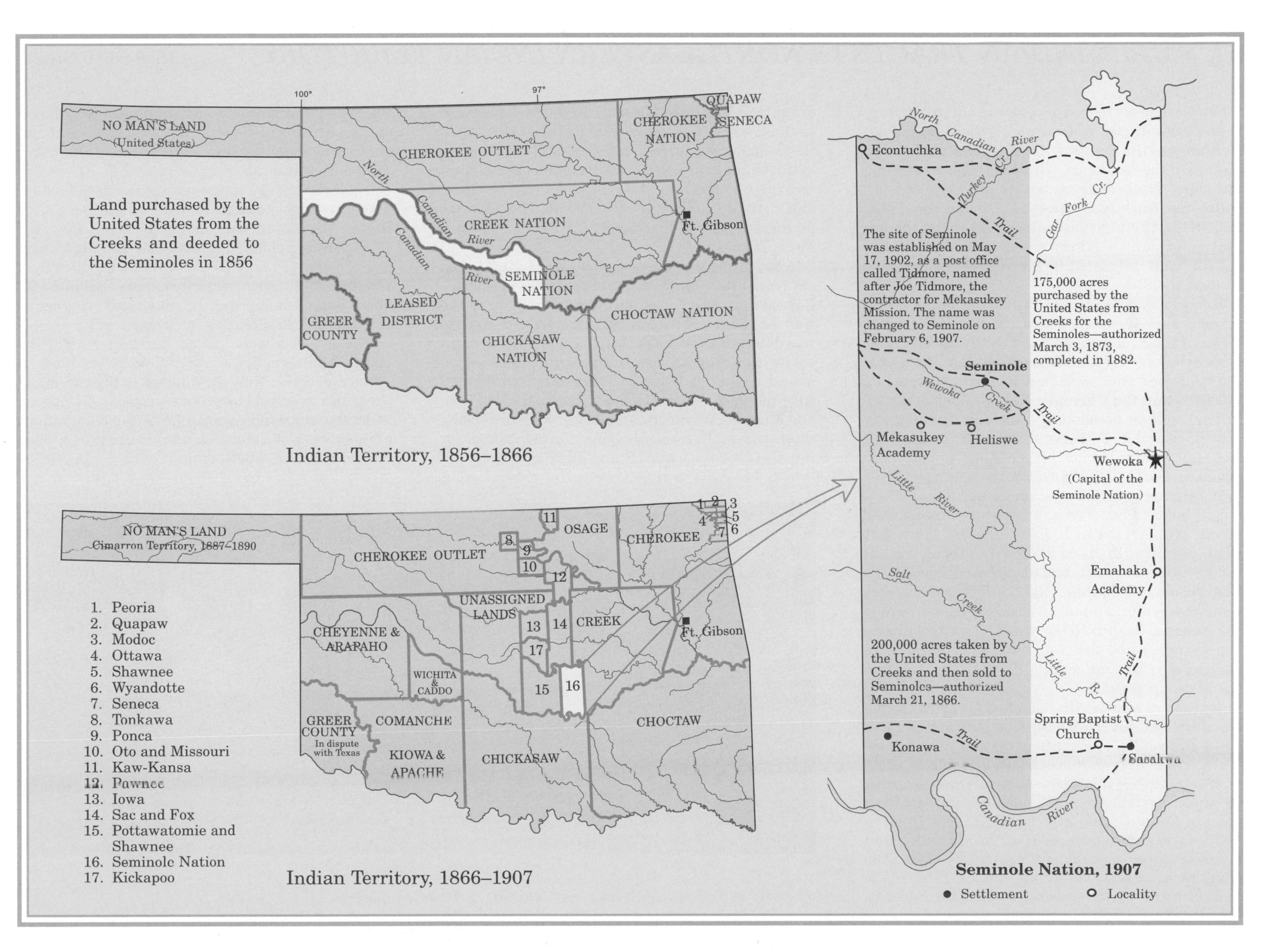
NO MAN'S LAND
(United States)
CHEROKEE OUTLET
CHEROKEE NATION
QUAPAW
SENECA
North Canadian River
Canadian
CREEK NATION
Ft. Gibson
SEMINOLE NATION
GREER COUNTY
LEASED DISTRICT
CHICKASAW NATION
CHOCTAW NATION
Land purchased by the United States from the Creeks and deeded to the Seminoles in 1856
Indian Territory, 1856–1866
NO MAN'S LAND
Cimarron Territory, 1887–1890
CHEROKEE OUTLET
OSAGE
CHEROKEE
UNASSIGNED LANDS
CREEK
CHEYENNE & ARAPAHO
WICHITA & CADDO
GREER COUNTY
In dispute with Texas
COMANCHE
KIOWA & APACHE
CHICKASAW
CHOCTAW
1. Peoria
2. Quapaw
3. Modoc
4. Ottawa
5. Shawnee
6. Wyandotte
7. Seneca
8. Tonkawa
9. Ponca
10. Oto and Missouri
11. Kaw-Kansa
12. Pawnee
13. Iowa
14. Sac and Fox
15. Pottawatomie and Shawnee
16. Seminole Nation
17. Kickapoo
Indian Territory, 1866–1907
Econtuchka
North Canadian River
Turkey Cr.
Trail
Gar Fork Cr.
The site of Seminole was established on May 17, 1902, as a post office called Tidmore, named after Joe Tidmore, the contractor for Mekasukey Mission. The name was changed to Seminole on February 6, 1907.
175,000 acres purchased by the United States from Creeks for the Seminoles—authorized March 3, 1873, completed in 1882.
Seminole
Wewoka Creek
Mekasukey Academy
Heliswe
Wewoka
(Capital of the Seminole Nation)
Little River
Salt Creek
Emahaka Academy
200,000 acres taken by the United States from Creeks and then sold to Seminoles—authorized March 21, 1866.
Little R.
Spring Baptist Church
Konawa
Sasakwa
Canadian River
Seminole Nation, 1907
Settlement
Locality

51. SMALL INDIAN TRACTS IN NORTHEASTERN INDIAN TERRITORY

Essay by *Michael D. Green*

When Congress created a western Indian territory in the early 1830s, it drew no northern boundary. Neither was the Removal Act of 1830 limited to the nations of the Southeast, whose marches west along the many Trails of Tears have since come to symbolize the tragedy of removal. During the 1830s and 1840s, the U.S. government arranged the migration of many northern tribes as well. Most, but not all, were relocated in the region that became Kansas in 1854.

Early in 1831, leaders of a small community composed of survivors from a half-dozen Iroquois tribes signed a removal treaty. Called the Senecas of Sandusky, they agreed to exchange their lands in northern Ohio for a tract in Indian Territory bounded by Missouri and the Cherokee Nation. Farmers, they carried all their possessions—including a full array of agricultural machinery—on an eight-month-long trek characterized by delays, privation, and mismanagement. Some 350 arrived on the Cowskin River in the summer of 1832. A second group from Ohio, a mixed band of Senecas and Shawnees numbering about 250, arrived in Indian Territory later that same year. But the land assigned to them, west of the first Seneca grant, had also been deeded to the Cherokees. In December 1832, a federal/Cherokee commission worked out an arrangement whereby the Neosho (Grand) River would mark the Cherokee boundary and the two groups of refugees from Ohio would share the country between the river and the Missouri state line.

In 1833, a treaty with homeless Quapaws living along the Red River with the Caddos granted them 150 square miles near the joint Seneca-Shawnee reserve. These Indians, once the inhabitants of a vast territory south of the Arkansas River in present-day Arkansas, Oklahoma, and Louisiana, had sold their domain to the United States in 1818 and 1824. In 1838, surveyors discovered that the Quapaw grant encroached on the Seneca reserve. Most of the Quapaw squatters moved out, but by 1852, many had returned to a new reserve north of the Senecas. Their lands bounded Missouri on the east and Kansas on the north. Several Quapaw chiefs allied with the Confederacy in 1861, but most of the men fought in the Union army. Neither arrangement could protect their homes from the ravages of war, however, and virtually all Quapaw civilians fled into Kansas for the duration, settling among the Ottawas on their reservation.

A key element in the post–Civil War Indian policy of Congress was the removal of the tribes in Kansas. Carved out of the original Indian Territory by the Kansas-Nebraska Act of 1854, the state of Kansas was determined to make room for white homesteaders by expelling the eastern tribes that had been removed west in the 1840s. The Peorias (a confederated tribe that included Kaskaskias, Piankashaws, Weas, and Miamis), Wyandottes, and Ottawas were among these tribes. To form permanent reservations for them, in 1867 the United States purchased land from the Senecas, Shawnees, and Quapaws. The end result separated the Senecas and Shawnees into two reservations and located in their midst the tribes ousted from Kansas.

The final change in the map of northeastern Indian Territory occurred in 1874 when the United States purchased four thousand acres from the Shawnees on which to locate some 150 Modocs recently defeated in the Modoc War and expelled from Oregon. These northwestern Indians accounted for about half of their tribe; the other half returned to the Klamath Reservation in Oregon.

These tribes were subject to the terms of the Dawes Allotment Act of 1887 whereby the lands of each reservation were distributed to the citizens of the tribes to be held as private property. Beginning in 1889 and extending until 1902, the reservations of this corner of Indian Territory were thus broken up and the lands allotted.

Seneca Indian School, Wyandotte, Indian Territory, 1902.
(Courtesy Western History Collections, University of Oklahoma Libraries)

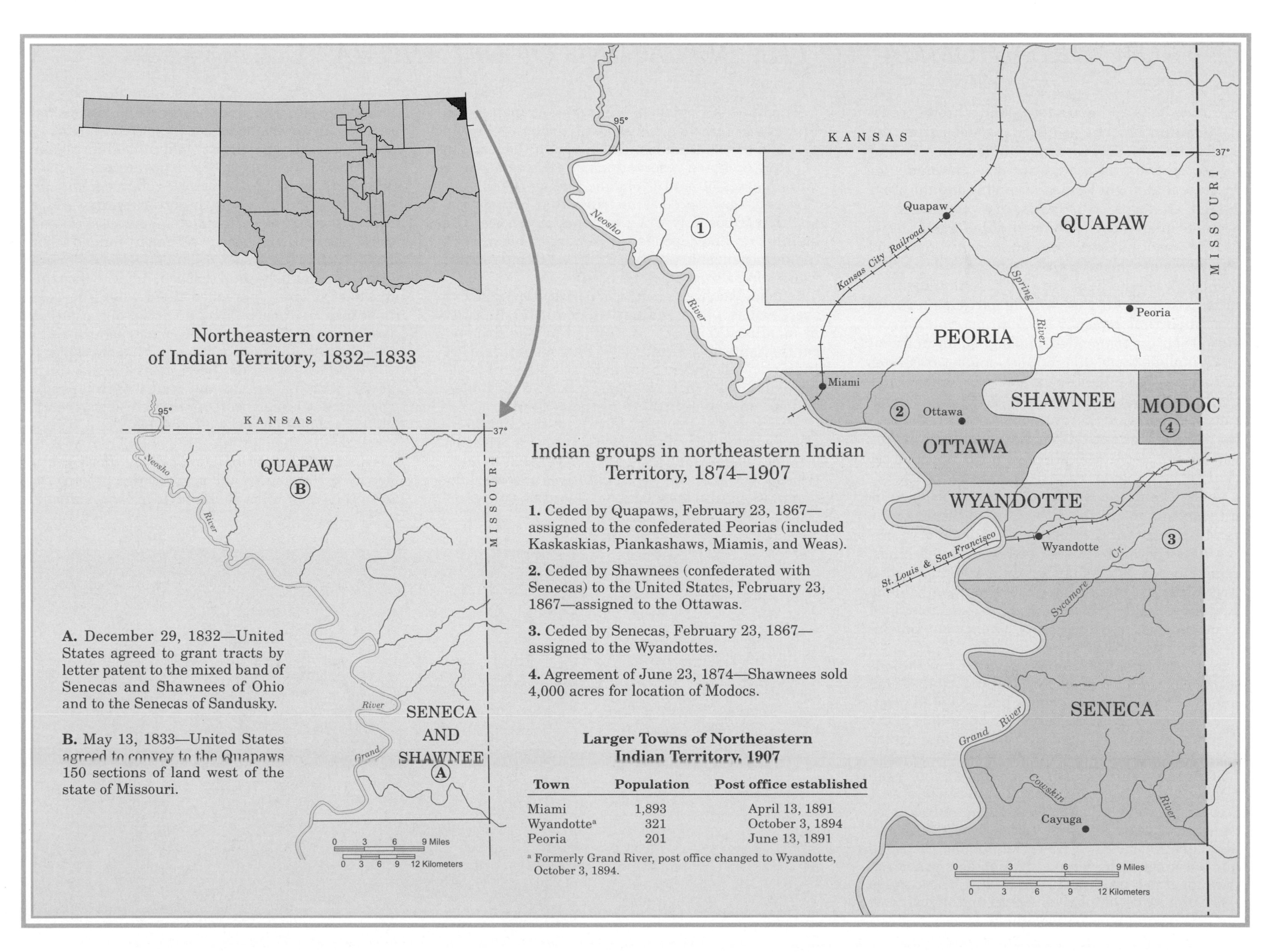

Northeastern corner of Indian Territory, 1832–1833

A. December 29, 1832—United States agreed to grant tracts by letter patent to the mixed band of Senecas and Shawnees of Ohio and to the Senecas of Sandusky.

B. May 13, 1833—United States agreed to convey to the Quapaws 150 sections of land west of the state of Missouri.

Indian groups in northeastern Indian Territory, 1874–1907

1. Ceded by Quapaws, February 23, 1867—assigned to the confederated Peorias (included Kaskaskias, Piankashaws, Miamis, and Weas).

2. Ceded by Shawnees (confederated with Senecas) to the United States, February 23, 1867—assigned to the Ottawas.

3. Ceded by Senecas, February 23, 1867—assigned to the Wyandottes.

4. Agreement of June 23, 1874—Shawnees sold 4,000 acres for location of Modocs.

Larger Towns of Northeastern Indian Territory, 1907

Town	Population	Post office established
Miami	1,893	April 13, 1891
Wyandotte[a]	321	October 3, 1894
Peoria	201	June 13, 1891

[a] Formerly Grand River, post office changed to Wyandotte, October 3, 1894.

52. FROM "OKLA-HOMMA" TO THE BEGINNING OF OKLAHOMA

Essay by *Danney Goble*

Okla-homma is an Indian term, and a literal translation would be "red people." It comes from the Choctaw language; a Choctaw named Allen Wright is said to have first thought of it as the name for any state that might be made from his and the other nations. That was in the 1870s. In a very few years, the name might have been inevitable. There was no state as of yet, but there was an identity. Place and term were one: this was Okla-homma.

Choctaws and others were party to that identity, but in no sense were they willing participants in its most important phase. The Indians—more accurately, their governments—had signed formal treaties that made them allies of the Confederate States of America. The alliances gained the Confederates very little, but they cost the Indians quite a lot, beginning with half of their nations' lands, as the penalty that the United States imposed for their having been the Confederates' allies (a penalty never exacted of the Confederates themselves).

In any event, the federal government's demands on these Indians enabled the United States to demand further that they accept confinement on reservations carved from the newly acquired lands. Some tribes resisted stoutly, while others accepted (most of them sullenly). Neither course made any difference. Eighty thousand Indians, still imagined as "red people," were to occupy twenty-one adjoining reservations.

By far the greatest number of American Indians lived in what was left of the Five Nations' lands. Small bands of Senecas and Quapaws had accepted reservations in the 1830s. After the war, remnants of the Wyandottes, Peorias, Ottawas, and Miamis agreed to leave Kansas for reservations near the Senecas and Quapaws. By far the most populous tribe to join them were the Osages, fifteen hundred of whom gave up what little was still theirs in Kansas and accepted a new reservation on lands taken from the Cherokees. Their kinsmen, the Kaws, later joined them and were assigned their own reservation along the eastern bank of the Arkansas River. Four tribes occupied reservations west of the river. South and slightly east were the reservations of five others.

The Kiowas, Comanches, Apaches, Arapahos, and Cheyennes—by then, not so much tribes as bits and pieces of tribes—numbered about eight thousand in all; they occupied reservations stretching across 8 million acres of land. Nomadic and warlike to the very end, they were Plains tribes that became reservation tribes only when they had no choice. The buffalo they had depended upon were all but extinct; the immeasurable prairies they had freely roamed were being surveyed and fenced.

Official Washington attached little importance to these tribes' pasts and anticipated little difficulty in molding their futures. Guided by the firm yet gentle hands of peaceful folk (only one of the U.S. Indian agents was not a Quaker), Indians were going to put down their weapons, pick up their Bibles, and become white in all things important.

The Bibles might as well have been weapons themselves, so central were they to this crusade. The government made sure that every person sent to these tribes was Christian. Representatives of several denominations also invaded the reservations under orders to preach, tend, and convert. Their lessons were repeated in government schools as well, since Christianity was very much part of the official curriculum.

Federal officials saw these government schools as something like little factories engineered to process Indian children into miniature whites. Associated with every one of the eight agencies overseeing these reservations was a government-funded school. In addition to the gospel, its students learned to read and write English—had to learn, in fact, since their teachers severely punished them when they used their own languages. The remainder of the curriculum was generally given over to instruction in other useful skills, such as farming and housekeeping.

The effects were not necessarily long-lasting or decisive. Plains Indians may have had to depend on government-issued beef, but they chose to receive it alive so that they might hunt, slay, and butcher cattle as they had buffalo. Many agreed to walk the "Jesus road"; but quite a few, even of these, continued their sun dances and peyote cults, proving that even the reservation could nurture *okla-homma.*

Young Indian women at the Anadarko Agency, ca. 1895. (Photo by Annette Ross Hume, courtesy Western History Collections, University of Oklahoma Libraries)

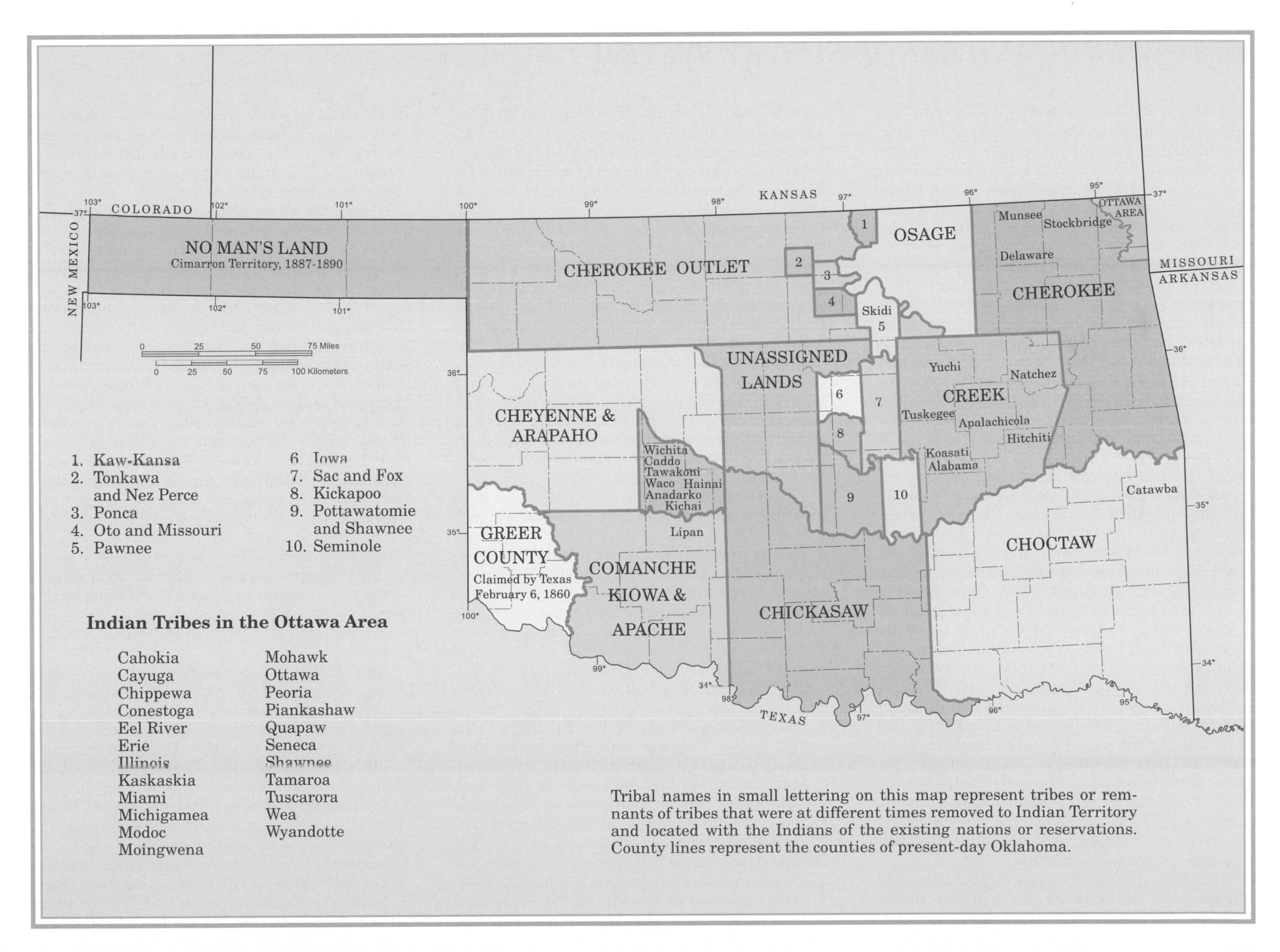

KANSAS
COLORADO
NEW MEXICO
MISSOURI
ARKANSAS
TEXAS
NO MAN'S LAND
Cimarron Territory, 1887-1890
CHEROKEE OUTLET
OSAGE
OTTAWA AREA
Munsee
Stockbridge
Delaware
CHEROKEE
Skidi
UNASSIGNED LANDS
Yuchi
Natchez
CREEK
Tuskegee
Apalachicola
Hitchiti
Koasati
Alabama
CHEYENNE & ARAPAHO
Wichita
Caddo
Tawakoni
Waco Hainai
Anadarko
Kichai
Lipan
GREER COUNTY
Claimed by Texas February 6, 1860
COMANCHE KIOWA & APACHE
CHICKASAW
CHOCTAW
Catawba
0 25 50 75 Miles
0 25 50 75 100 Kilometers
1. Kaw-Kansa
2. Tonkawa and Nez Perce
3. Ponca
4. Oto and Missouri
5. Pawnee
6. Iowa
7. Sac and Fox
8. Kickapoo
9. Pottawatomie and Shawnee
10. Seminole
Indian Tribes in the Ottawa Area
Cahokia
Cayuga
Chippewa
Conestoga
Eel River
Erie
Illinois
Kaskaskia
Miami
Michigamea
Modoc
Moingwena
Mohawk
Ottawa
Peoria
Piankashaw
Quapaw
Seneca
Shawnee
Tamaroa
Tuscarora
Wea
Wyandotte
Tribal names in small lettering on this map represent tribes or remnants of tribes that were at different times removed to Indian Territory and located with the Indians of the existing nations or reservations. County lines represent the counties of present-day Oklahoma.

53. TOWNSHIP AND RANGE SURVEY SYSTEM

Essay by *Bruce W. Hoagland*

The settlement of Oklahoma was facilitated by land surveys conducted in the latter part of the nineteenth century. Land in Oklahoma was surveyed using the township-and-range system. Land surveys in the colonial United States followed the metes-and-bounds system, which described land parcels often of unequal size and lacking uniformity and often created voids between adjacent parcels. Following independence, the United States came into possession of vast western territories, and the government desired that these lands be settled in an orderly fashion. Espousing the notion of "survey before settlement," the Continental Congress passed the Land Ordinance in 1785. The resulting public land surveys applied a survey unit of uniform shape and size, thus rectifying the deficiencies of the metes-and-bounds system. The primary subdivision in the public land survey was the thirty-six-square-mile congressional townships (not to be confused with civil townships), which were further subdivided into one-square-mile sections. The General Land Office, established on April 25, 1812, conducted surveys throughout the United States except for nineteen eastern and southern states, which had been surveyed using the metes-and-bounds system. The General Land Office was merged with the Grazing Service in 1946 to form the Bureau of Land Management.

The public land survey starts with the establishment of an initial point. The location of an initial point is not predetermined by any political entity, and some states have multiple initial points. There are two initial points in Oklahoma: one in south-central Oklahoma, established in 1879 by surveyor Ehud Darling; the other in the southwest corner of the Panhandle, established in 1881. The significance of the initial point cannot be overstated, since the location and legal description of all land in the state is made in reference to that point. If the initial point were to be moved in any direction, all land ownership descriptions would change.

From the initial point, an east-west baseline and a north-south meridian are surveyed. The Indian Meridian was established in 1870 and is the reference for most of the state. The Cimarron Meridian was established in 1881 for surveys in the Panhandle. Additional east-west lines are established at six-mile intervals to the north and south of the baseline. The resulting grid comprises the congressional townships.

Each township is further subdivided into 36 one-square-mile sections. The total area of a section is approximately 640 acres. Sections are further subdivided into quarter-sections, which are one-half mile on a side and contain approximately 160 acres of land. Irregularities were commonplace in surveys. Because of the curvature of the Earth, townships often measure less than six miles on the north line. In addition, irregularities were also produced when a township or section line crossed a river. The result is incomplete sections of less than 640 acres in land. To correct for these deficiencies, incomplete sections are divided into lots. Correction lots are usually 40 acres, but those along rivers may be smaller.

When Oklahoma Territory was organized in 1890, the Organic Act stipulated that four sections in each township be set aside to fund public institutions. Similar arrangements were not made in Indian Territory. Sections 16 and 36 in Oklahoma Territory were reserved for public schools, section 13 for higher education, and section 33 for public buildings. These lands were leased and the money held in trust. Funds from section 13 were divided, with one-third going to the University of Oklahoma and the University Preparatory School, one-third to the Agricultural and Mechanical University and the Colored Agricultural Normal University, and one-third to the normal schools. The Oklahoma School Lands Office manages these public lands at present.

In the 1870s, only the future Oklahoma Territory, the Chickasaw Nation, and Quapaw, Seneca, and Peoria lands in the northeast were surveyed. The Choctaw and Chickasaw nations had agreed to allow their lands west of the 98th meridian to be surveyed in accordance with a treaty signed on June 22, 1866. The Chickasaw Nation agreed to land surveys within its boundaries to maximize the amount of land allotted to tribal members rather than to nontribal members and the railroads. Indian Territory was surveyed in the 1890s as the dissolution of tribal government began. The Panhandle was also surveyed then, and Oklahoma Territory was resurveyed.

During the surveys, monuments were constructed to designate the intersection of survey lines. At times, to specify the location of monuments, surveyors recorded distances and directions to nearby natural features. This recording process has provided a great deal of information on historic vegetation. Surveyors also described the physical environment and human habitations encountered along survey lines. For example, surveyors documented the suitability of soils for agricultural production, classifying these as first, second, or third rate. Vegetation was recorded as prairie, brush prairie, mesquite brush prairie, wetland, and forest. The maps produced by the surveyors also indicated land use, settlements, agricultural fields, American Indian villages, and black settlements. Sawmills, coal mines, quarries, limekilns, roads, cattle trails, and other features of economic interest were mapped as well. Finally, the surveys have left an indelible stamp on the Oklahoma landscape. Thousands of miles of section-line roads crisscross the state along section lines. The width of these roads and rights-of-way varies with statutes between the tribes and state government.

The width requirements of the rights-of-way differed between Indian Territory and Oklahoma Territory. In Indian Territory, the width of dedicated right-of-ways for public roads along section lines varied from nation to nation. This variance was a result of the individual treaties signed by each nation and the U.S. government following the Civil War. Because of this, the rights-of-way in Indian Territory vary from a maximum of 49.5 feet in the Creek Nation to no required rights-of-way in the Quapaw area. In Oklahoma Territory, the width of dedicated rights-of-way for public roads was established by the Oklahoma Organic Act of 1890, which provided for a total of 66 feet along each section line.

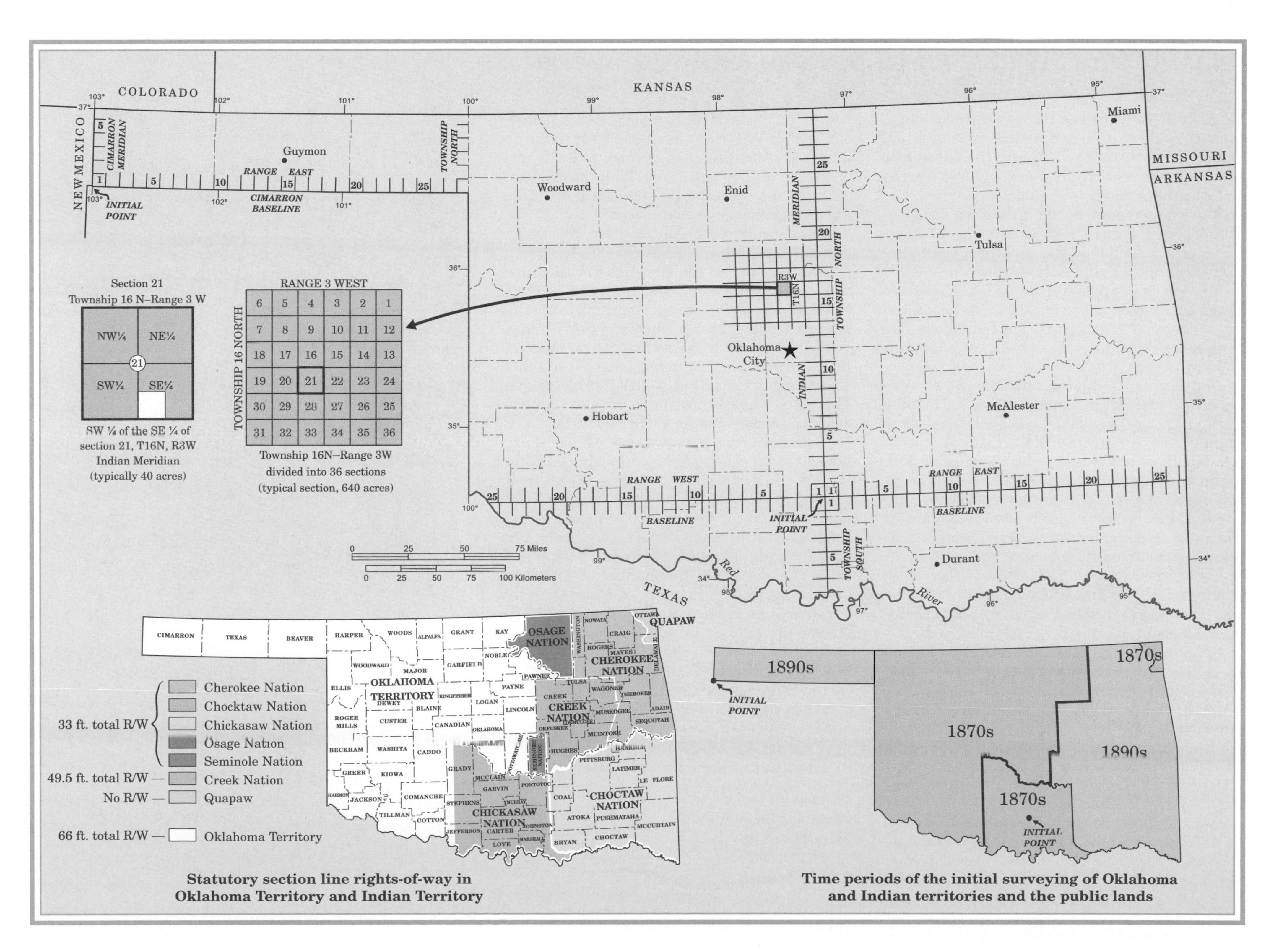

Statutory section line rights-of-way in Oklahoma Territory and Indian Territory

Time periods of the initial surveying of Oklahoma and Indian territories and the public lands

54. *MAJOR CATTLE TRAILS, 1866–1889*

Essay by *John R. Lovett*

From the Civil War's end through the mid-1880s, more than seven million Texas cattle crossed the Indian Territory on their way to the famed cow towns of wild-and-woolly Kansas. Most started their journeys along any number of feeder trails that originated deep in the interior of Texas before converging into three main trails, all crossing central Oklahoma: the Shawnee, Chisholm, and Western (or Dodge City) trails.

The first closely followed the old Texas Road into eastern Indian Territory, but those who pioneered it, in 1866, quickly experienced its limitations. The timbered and mountainous landscape of eastern Indian Territory was anything but ideal for moving large herds of semiwild cattle. In addition, resident American Indians usually demanded that the Texans pay to cross their lands. If refused, they often scattered herds and took cattle. Bands of white outlaws pretty much stuck to stealing both cattle and horses, without any pretense of negotiations. Cattle and cowboys that reached the Kansas and Missouri borders were often met by armed groups of farmers, fearful of Texas fever, a tick-borne illness that afflicted cattle. Not a few herds simply turned around and retraced their path southward. Hardly any cattlemen profited from the 1866 drives, and most had no taste whatsoever for trying it again.

In 1867, Illinois cattleman and farmer Joseph G. McCoy realized that markets in the East held undeveloped potential for sales of Texas cattle. To exploit that market, McCoy purchased an entire township on the new Kansas Pacific Railroad. Abilene, he called it, and there he built shipping pens, barns, stables, and a hotel, then sent representatives to Texas to urge cattlemen to drive their herds to this Abilene.

Probably because the only established portion of the route they blazed followed the wagon road that Jesse Chisholm had already opened, the entire length of the trail was known to Texas cattle ranchers as the Chisholm Trail. Far enough west to bypass the heavily wooded eastern Indian Territory, the route offered ample grazing along its entire way. Water was available from rivers and numerous streams, most of them fordable most of the year. The Chisholm Trail was also far enough west in Kansas that it avoided both farming areas and hostile Jayhawkers.

In the spring of 1871, the Atchison, Topeka, and Santa Fe railroad reached Newton, Kansas, sixty-five miles south of Abilene. Newton thereupon usurped Abilene's place, and Texas herds coming up the Chisholm Trail began ending up in the shipping pens first of Newton and later of Wichita.

In 1872, Dodge City was founded on the Santa Fe railroad, some fifty miles north of the Indian Territory border and near the 100th meridian. Thereafter, the Western (or Dodge City) Trail became the route favored by Texas cattlemen. By 1876, Dodge City rightfully became known as the "queen" of the Kansas cow towns—although other titles associated with the female gender were occasionally attached to it. In the Western Trail's peak year (1881), over 300,000 head of Texas cattle used it to cross western Oklahoma, typically in herds of around 2,500 each.

By the mid-1880s, the number of Texas trail herds using the Chisholm and Western trails saw a dramatic drop. Factors that led to this decline include the 1884 act by which Kansas imposed a quarantine on entering herds, the rapid growth of ranching on the northern plains, and the expansion of railroads into Texas. By 1890, use of the great cattle highways across Oklahoma had ended, and the era of cattle drives passed into history.

Diagram of herd on trail (afternoon)

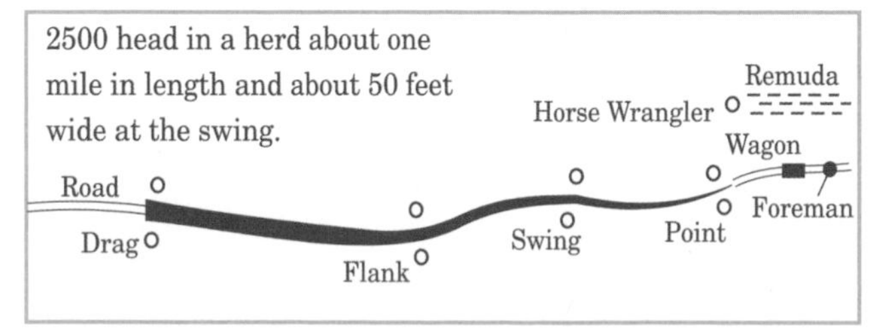

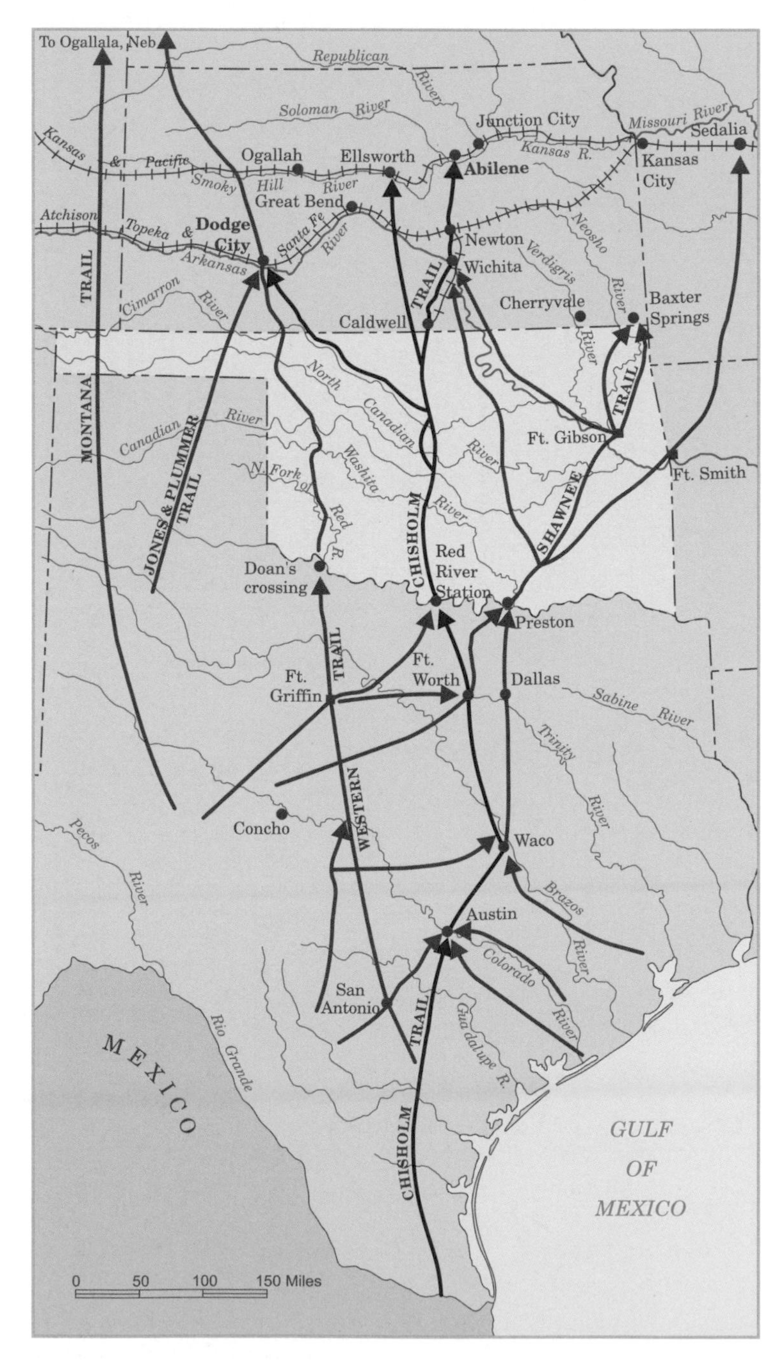

Cattle trails leading to railheads

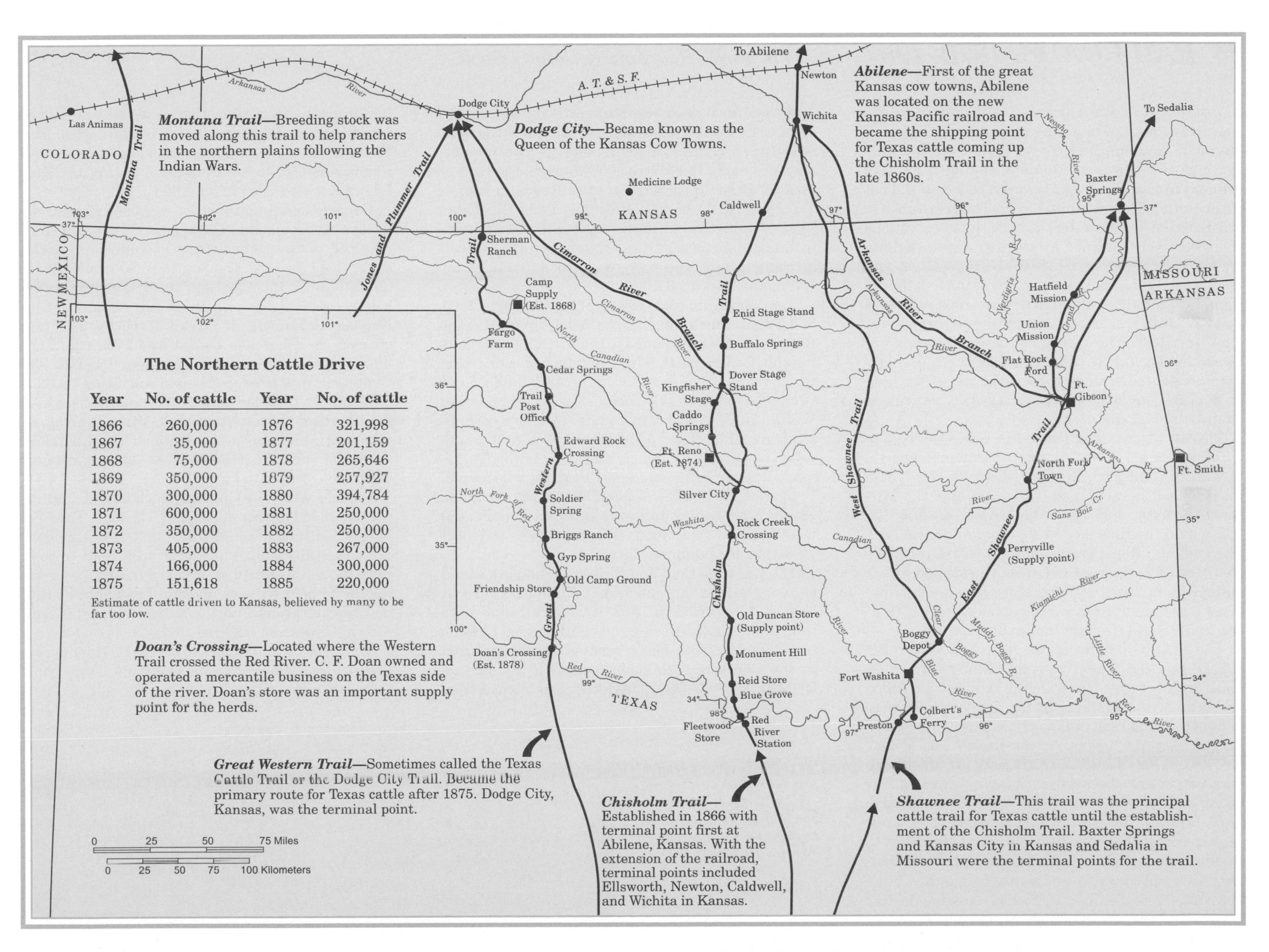

The Northern Cattle Drive

Year	No. of cattle	Year	No. of cattle
1866	260,000	1876	321,998
1867	35,000	1877	201,159
1868	75,000	1878	265,646
1869	350,000	1879	257,927
1870	300,000	1880	394,784
1871	600,000	1881	250,000
1872	350,000	1882	250,000
1873	405,000	1883	267,000
1874	166,000	1884	300,000
1875	151,618	1885	220,000

Estimate of cattle driven to Kansas, believed by many to be far too low.

55. RAILROADS, 1870–1907

Essay by *Bruce W. Hoagland & Danney Goble*

Railroads were the engine of settlement in the American West. The Army Appropriation Act of March 3, 1853, funded a survey for a possible transcontinental railway route along the 35th parallel through Indian Territory. However, railroads did not enter Indian Territory until 1870. The resistance to construction in Indian Territory by the Five Nations was effectively nullified by treaties negotiated following the Civil War. In 1866, the federal government negotiated treaties with each of the five Indian republics, requiring them to permit construction of a north-south and an east-west railroad through Indian Territory. The U.S. government intended to award land grants to the railroads if the Indian nations consented or when the lands entered the public domain, but the nations successfully petitioned against land grants.

Three railroads applied to the U.S. Congress to build through Indian Territory: the Leavenworth, Lawrence, and Fort Gibson (LL&FG); the Union Pacific's southern branch (which became the Missouri, Kansas, and Texas, or MK&T, on May 23, 1870); and the Kansas and Neosho Valley (K&NV). The Indian nations protested that according to the treaty of 1866, only one north-south railroad was to enter Indian Territory. Therefore, Congress stipulated that the first railroad to reach Chetopa, Kansas, could build through Indian Territory.

The LL&FG fell out of the race early. When the K&NV reached Baxter Springs, Kansas, the race appeared to be over. However, the railroad line ended opposite Quapaw lands, not Cherokee, which were not open for railroad construction. Thus, the K&NV turned toward Chetopa. As the K&NV and MK&T (or "Katy") line drew closer, tensions mounted, culminating in a row between track-laying crews on May 28, 1870. The race was won by the Katy on June 6, 1870. Robert S. Stevens, general manager of the Katy, drove a spike into the last tie in Kansas, and Elias C. Boudinot then drove the first spike in Indian Territory. Katy rail crews pressed south though the Cherokee Nation into the Choctaw Nation, crossing the Red River into Texas on December 24, 1872.

Agricultural goods were the primary commodity shipped by the railroads. With the recent settlement of southern Kansas, farmers and railroad promoters were eager to construct rail lines to the Gulf of Mexico. Prior to the arrival of railroads in Indian Territory, cattle had been driven along the Texas Road to railheads in Kansas; one of the primary commodities transported by the Katy was cattle, as well as coal. In fact, the Katy was the only outlet for Oklahoma coal until 1889.

Completing an east–west rail line through Oklahoma took much longer. The Atlantic and Pacific Railroad (A&P) petitioned to construct a line following the 35th parallel, with the intent of connecting St. Louis and San Francisco. The A&P entered the Cherokee Nation at Seneca, Missouri, reaching Vinita (and the Katy) in Indian Territory on September 1, 1871. The A&P assumed that land grants would be awarded, but none was forthcoming. Therefore, all construction in Indian Territory was halted. Bankrupt, the A&P was acquired by the St. Louis and San Francisco Railway (known as the Frisco) in 1876. The Frisco reached Tulsa in 1885 and built westward to Oklahoma City.

The Choctaw Coal and Railway Company would become the first railroad to span the state from east to west. Organized in 1888, it constructed a route from Wister to McAlester and another from El Reno to Oklahoma City. The company was reorganized as the Choctaw, Oklahoma, and Gulf (CO&G) on October 3, 1894. The CO&G line, established from McAlester to Oklahoma City, was the route along which Indian Territory coal was shipped to Fort Reno. In 1902, the CO&G completed its east-west line across Oklahoma. It became part of the Rock Island line on December 1, 1903.

Congressional approval of rights-of-way for additional railroads into Oklahoma Territory in 1885 resulted in the construction of additional north-south lines. In 1887, the Southern Kansas Railway (an affiliate of the Atchison, Topeka, and Santa Fe) began construction of a line from Arkansas City, Kansas, to Purcell, in Indian Territory. The rails crossed the Cherokee Outlet and Ponca and Oto lands before entering the Unassigned Lands. The Cherokees protested, but it was ruled that the U.S. government held the power of eminent domain in the Cherokee Outlet. Meanwhile, through an agreement with the Chickasaw Nation, the Gulf, Colorado, and Santa Fe (GC&SF) was laying track from Galveston, Texas, to Purcell.

Farther west, the Chicago, Rock Island, and Pacific reached Pond Creek on July 15, 1888. The Rock Island continued laying track along the Chisholm Trail, reaching Minco on February 14, 1890. In 1892, construction resumed, and the railroad crossed the Red River before the year's end. The Santa Fe then laid tracks through northwestern Oklahoma from Kiowa, Kansas, to Higgins, Texas.

The location and names of several Oklahoma cities are directly linked to the railroads. Throughout the boom years of construction, railroads and land

When the Cherokee Outlet was opened on September 16, 1893, this train was one of the first to arrive from Kansas. (Courtesy Western History Collections, University of Oklahoma Libraries)

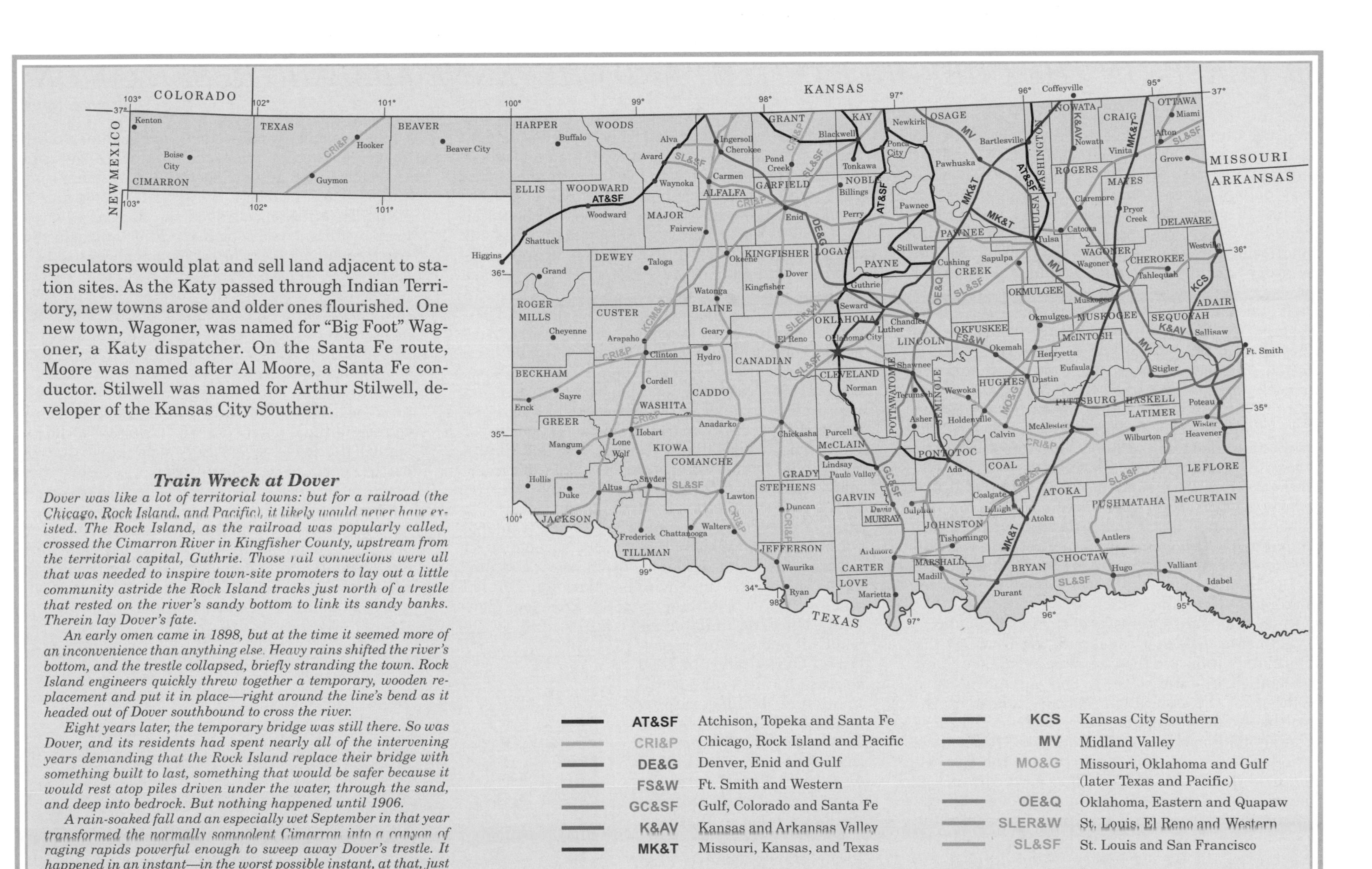

speculators would plat and sell land adjacent to station sites. As the Katy passed through Indian Territory, new towns arose and older ones flourished. One new town, Wagoner, was named for "Big Foot" Wagoner, a Katy dispatcher. On the Santa Fe route, Moore was named after Al Moore, a Santa Fe conductor. Stilwell was named for Arthur Stilwell, developer of the Kansas City Southern.

Train Wreck at Dover

Dover was like a lot of territorial towns: but for a railroad (the Chicago, Rock Island, and Pacific), it likely would never have existed. The Rock Island, as the railroad was popularly called, crossed the Cimarron River in Kingfisher County, upstream from the territorial capital, Guthrie. Those rail connections were all that was needed to inspire town-site promoters to lay out a little community astride the Rock Island tracks just north of a trestle that rested on the river's sandy bottom to link its sandy banks. Therein lay Dover's fate.

An early omen came in 1898, but at the time it seemed more of an inconvenience than anything else. Heavy rains shifted the river's bottom, and the trestle collapsed, briefly stranding the town. Rock Island engineers quickly threw together a temporary, wooden replacement and put it in place—right around the line's bend as it headed out of Dover southbound to cross the river.

Eight years later, the temporary bridge was still there. So was Dover, and its residents had spent nearly all of the intervening years demanding that the Rock Island replace their bridge with something built to last, something that would be safer because it would rest atop piles driven under the water, through the sand, and deep into bedrock. But nothing happened until 1906.

A rain-soaked fall and an especially wet September in that year transformed the normally somnolent Cimarron into a canyon of raging rapids powerful enough to sweep away Dover's trestle. It happened in an instant—in the worst possible instant, at that, just as a fully loaded Rock Island passenger train roared around the bend south of town, on its way to . . . death.

Nobody knows just how many died that day; the companies kept no records of who had bought tickets to ride the rails to their doom. The victims probably numbered more than a hundred, though, for bodies were still washing up, twenty or more miles downstream, for several days.

56. LEASES IN THE CHEROKEE OUTLET AND CHEYENNE-ARAPAHO RESERVATION

Essay by *Josh Clough*

After the Civil War, cattle prices in the East soared as demand for beef exceeded supply. Cows sold at auction there often brought between thirty-five and forty dollars a head, more than seven times the amount they realized when sold in Texas. In 1866, Texas cattlemen, seeking to maximize profits, began driving large herds northward through Indian Territory to railheads in Kansas and Missouri. The routes they traveled soon developed into major cattle trails, such as the Chisholm Trail and the Great Western Trail, which bisected lands owned by the Cheyenne and Arapaho tribes and the Cherokee Nation. To derive some income from the thousands of cattle streaming across their borders, Indians charged cattlemen a small fee for each cow passing through and also collected grazing taxes from ranchers who fattened their herds on Native pasturelands. Stockmen grazing cattle illegally on tribal lands, however, were a constant problem. In an effort to reduce the number of intruders and therefore increase revenue, the Cherokees and the Cheyenne-Arapahos began leasing large tracts of land to cattle ranchers willing to pay for grazing rights in the early 1880s. In aggregate, the leases signed in 1883 totaled more than nine million acres.

By far the more successful of the two tribal lease experiments was that consummated between the Cherokee Nation and the Cherokee Strip Live Stock Association in June of 1883. The agreement gave members of the association (mainly Kansas ranchers) the exclusive right to graze cattle on the more than six million acres of the Cherokee Outlet for a period of five years. For this privilege, the association paid the Cherokees $100,000 per year; at less than two cents an acre, it was more than double the amount that grazing taxes had brought the tribe the previous year. Once both parties had signed the lease, directors of the livestock association divided the Cherokee Outlet lands into more than one hundred grazing tracts that were then subleased to individuals and corporations. Stockmen were permitted to construct fences, corrals, and other improvements on their parcels but had to leave them behind when the lease expired. Both the Chisholm Trail and the Great Western Trail remained open.

The lease worked out well for both parties. Ranchers, by formally leasing the land, gained some security that they would not be evicted from the Outlet along with intruders by either the federal government or the Cherokee Nation. Because any agitation by outsiders jeopardized their business interests, the association also worked with the tribe to prevent illegal homesteading in the Outlet by Kansans known as "Boomers." Led by David L. Payne, Boomers attempted to establish colonies on Cherokee land several times during the 1880s, only to be escorted back across the border by federal troops who had been notified by Outlet stockmen. The Cherokees, in turn, earned significant revenue from a tract of land that had previously been of limited value to them. The Outlet was too far from the Cherokee Nation proper for tribal farmers to use it profitably, and Cherokee ranchers did not own enough livestock to occupy more than a fraction of its available pasture. Income generated from the Outlet lease was put to good use by tribal leaders, who divided it among the nation's more than 150 schools, seven district governments, and numerous orphanages and hospitals. Although the Cherokee National Council voted to renew the lease in 1888, President Benjamin Harrison unilaterally voided it and ordered ranchers off Outlet lands in 1890 because the federal government had decided to purchase the Outlet and open it to settlement. Stripped of their lease income and bullied by federal negotiators, the Cherokees ceded the Outlet to the government in 1891.

The Cheyenne-Arapaho Reservation may have sat in close geographic proximity to the Outlet, but the outcome of the two lease experiments could not have been more different had they been located on separate continents. In May of 1883, twenty-five Cheyenne and Arapaho chiefs and headmen (at the suggestion of their agent, John D. Miles) agreed to lease 3,177,880 acres of their 4,294,412-acre reservation to stockmen for ten years at two cents an acre. Although Miles encouraged the deal as a way of keeping intruders off the reservation and of feeding tribal members (part of the payment was to be in cattle, part in cash), he clearly had other reasons for bringing the two sides together. Of the seven individuals who signed leases, six were personal acquaintances of the agent's. Miles undoubtedly received kickbacks from the ranchers, who also more than likely paid Cheyenne and Arapaho leaders to sign the agreements. Many tribal members repudiated the leases by refusing to accept their portion of the semiannual payments, and even those who had signed the leases eventually demanded that the cattle ranchers be evicted from the reservation. Stock raisers had apparently made themselves unwelcome by enclosing more territory than had been agreed to and by pushing Cheyennes and Arapahos off legally held land and disturbing the Indian farmers' livestock. In response to complaints from the tribes, the government ordered the lessees off the reservation in the summer of 1885.

A Cheyenne-Arapaho camp, near Fort Reno and the Darlington Agency, in 1890. (Courtesy Western History Collections, University of Oklahoma Libraries)

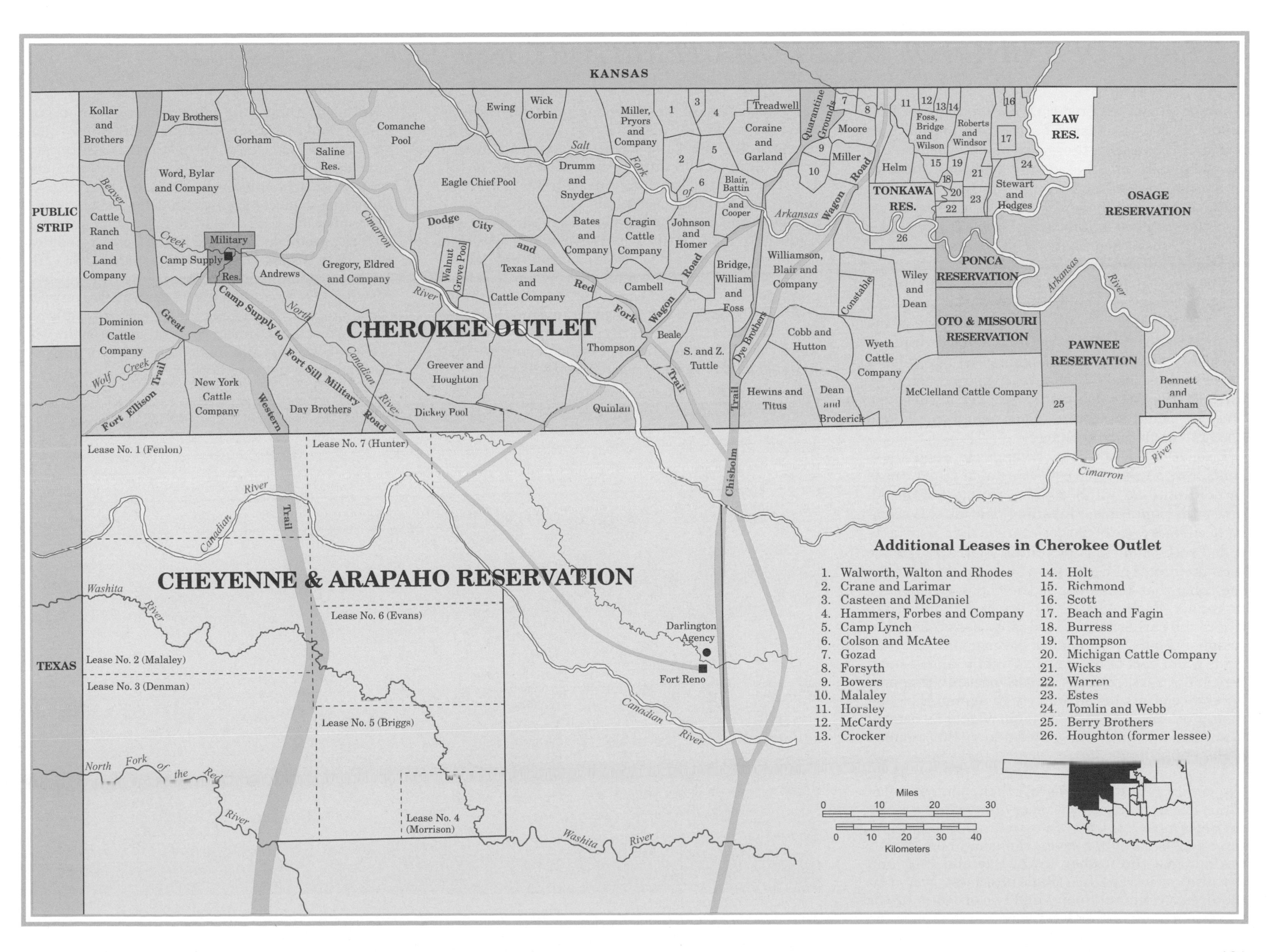
KANSAS
PUBLIC STRIP
TEXAS
CHEROKEE OUTLET
CHEYENNE & ARAPAHO RESERVATION
KAW RES.
OSAGE RESERVATION
TONKAWA RES.
PONCA RESERVATION
OTO & MISSOURI RESERVATION
PAWNEE RESERVATION
Kollar and Brothers
Day Brothers
Gorham
Saline Res.
Comanche Pool
Ewing
Wick Corbin
Miller, Pryors and Company
Treadwell
Coraine and Garland
Moore
Miller
Foss, Bridge and Wilson
Roberts and Windsor
Helm
Stewart and Hodges
Word, Bylar and Company
Eagle Chief Pool
Drumm and Snyder
Blair, Battin and Cooper
Cattle Ranch and Land Company
Military Res.
Camp Supply
Andrews
Gregory, Eldred and Company
Walnut Grove Pool
Texas Land and Cattle Company
Bates and Company
Cragin Cattle Company
Johnson and Homer
Bridge, William and Foss
Williamson, Blair and Company
Constable
Wiley and Dean
Cambell
Dominion Cattle Company
Thompson
Beale
S. and Z. Tuttle
Cobb and Hutton
Wyeth Cattle Company
Greever and Houghton
New York Cattle Company
Day Brothers
Dickey Pool
Quinlan
Hewins and Titus
Dean and Broderick
McClelland Cattle Company
Bennett and Dunham
Dodge City and Red Fork Wagon Road
Arkansas Wagon Road
Quarantine Grounds
Camp Supply to Fort Sill Military Road
Great Western Trail
Fort Ellison Trail
Dye Brothers Trail
Chisholm Trail
Salt Fork of Arkansas
Arkansas River
Beaver Creek
Wolf Creek
Cimarron River
North Canadian River
Canadian River
Washita River
North Fork of the Red River
Lease No. 1 (Fenlon)
Lease No. 7 (Hunter)
Lease No. 6 (Evans)
Lease No. 2 (Malaley)
Lease No. 3 (Denman)
Lease No. 5 (Briggs)
Lease No. 4 (Morrison)
Darlington Agency
Fort Reno
Additional Leases in Cherokee Outlet
1. Walworth, Walton and Rhodes
2. Crane and Larimar
3. Casteen and McDaniel
4. Hammers, Forbes and Company
5. Camp Lynch
6. Colson and McAtee
7. Gozad
8. Forsyth
9. Bowers
10. Malaley
11. Horsley
12. McCardy
13. Crocker
14. Holt
15. Richmond
16. Scott
17. Beach and Fagin
18. Burress
19. Thompson
20. Michigan Cattle Company
21. Wicks
22. Warren
23. Estes
24. Tomlin and Webb
25. Berry Brothers
26. Houghton (former lessee)
Miles
0 10 20 30
0 10 20 30 40
Kilometers

57. LAND OPENINGS OF OKLAHOMA TERRITORY, 1889–1906

Essay by *Danney Goble*

When the historian Frederick Jackson Turner first pondered the significance of free land to America's history, in the 1880s, there was much to ponder but little land left—and that usually had gone unclaimed because no one had wanted it. Just below the nation's midpoint, however, lay a heart-shaped region of nearly two million acres. Maps designated it as the "Unassigned Lands." Thousands—tens of thousands—wanted it.

The term "unassigned" is best understood if taken literally. These were lands that had belonged to the Creek and Seminole nations until 1866, when the Reconstruction treaties gave the federal government the right to relocate other Indians and newly freed slaves on these lands. That never happened, of course, which is why these rich lands remained unassigned. They were neither unwanted nor unknown, though; Boomers made sure of that.

Known for their booming demands to "open" these lands, Boomers started collecting along the Kansas border in the early 1880s and spent most of the decade either agitating or invading. The latter, a seemingly endless cycle of pathetic forays that invariably ended with expulsions by military force, may have been their most effective form of agitation, since the one thing that ended it was the U.S. government's surrender. Paying off the Creeks and Seminoles to ignore the earlier, unrealized purposes of these unassigned lands, the federal government in effect made them part of the nation's public lands—not a very large part, perhaps, but a most inviting one. Three weeks into his presidency, Benjamin Harrison then proclaimed that these lands would be opened to settlement under the general laws that applied to the public lands.

The greatly publicized event of April 22, 1889, triggered a rapid-fire series of other openings, all of which began to transform reservations into a state. On September 22, 1891, an estimated twenty thousand people raced for seven thousand homesteads available in the former Iowa, Sac and Fox, and Pottawatomie lands. In a single afternoon, every plot acquired a claimant; many had two or more. It was a different story farther west, however. Although the eastern portions of the Cheyenne and Arapaho lands filled rather quickly upon the reservation's opening, on April 19, 1892, the western sections—isolated from rail lines and much drier—took years to fill. Until then, cattle ranchers ran their herds over the unclaimed and unfenced lands.

The grandest of the land openings came on September 16, 1893. One hundred thousand people lined the borders of the old Cherokee Outlet that day. At the appointed hour, the mad dash began. The first claim is said to have been taken by a hard-riding cowboy who staked out a town lot in Enid. If so, the cowhand did not necessarily hang up his spurs to don a clerk's shirt and tie—not uncommonly, the first arrivals let the slower ones bid for their rights.

Although these (and later) openings conjure images of would-be farmers dashing for their own quarter-sections of free land, the fact is that a surprising number of expectant claimants went to town: more accurately, to an intended town site. This was especially true in places such as Enid. On the morning of September 16, Enid was little more than an imaginary city pretending to straddle the Chicago and Rock Island railroad tracks. Nonetheless, it—like Tecumseh and Chandler before it—had already been designated the seat of a future county. The prospect of claiming any lot in any county seat, especially one already blessed with rail connections, brought with it enough obvious and immediate value to draw everything from cowboys to bankers.

Mattie Beal Payne House in Lawton, ca 1905. (Courtesy Museum of the Great Plains, Lawton)

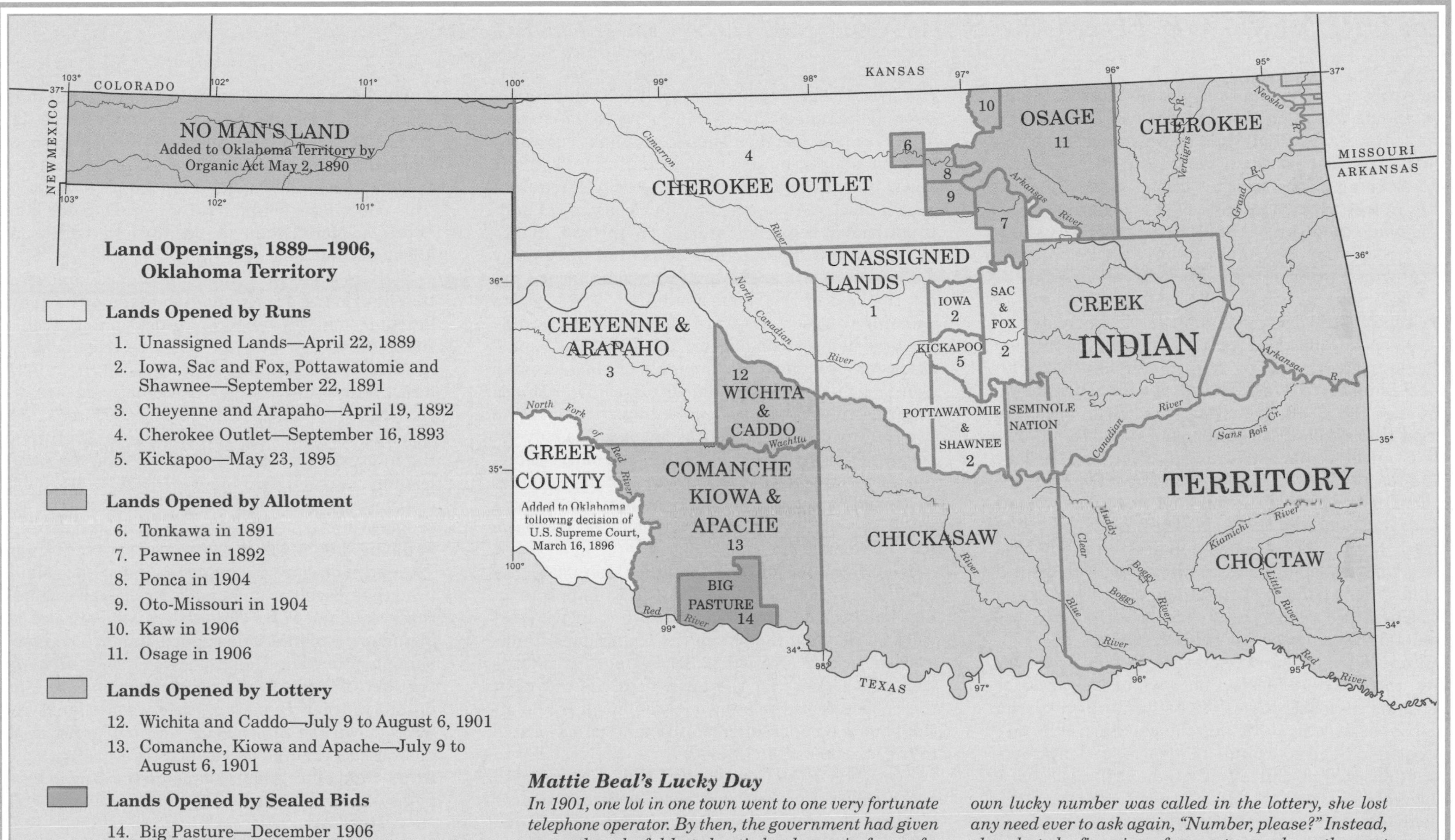

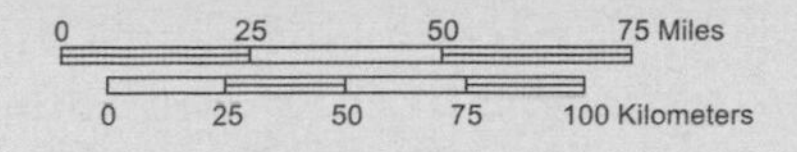

Mattie Beal's Lucky Day

In 1901, one lot in one town went to one very fortunate telephone operator. By then, the government had given up on the colorful but chaotic land runs in favor of a more orderly lottery system. Would-be claimants registered with land officials, then waited to make their choices as names were drawn in order. In the case of the sprawling Comanche, Kiowa, and Apache lands, among the very first names drawn was that of Mattie Beal. Until then, Mattie Beal had worked as an operator for the Wichita, Kansas, phone company. Once her own lucky number was called in the lottery, she lost any need ever to ask again, "Number, please?" Instead, she selected a fine piece of property—perhaps the most valuable in the whole region: a full quarter-section, 160 acres, that sat right on the edge of the Lawton town site. A year later, Mattie Beal and her newly acquired husband—Charles W. Payne, manager of Lawton's first lumberyard—built the city's first mansion, a fourteen-room structure that is today on the National Register of Historic Sites.

58. *OPENING OF THE UNASSIGNED LANDS* Essay by *John R. Lovett*

On April 22, 1889, the first portion of present-day Oklahoma was opened to settlement in "Harrison's Horse Race." This land run forever changed the historical landscape of the area, as the settlers gained access to unsettled frontier lands. While no accurate numbers are available of the hopeful settlers who made the "Run of 1889," in excess of fifty thousand people are estimated to have participated in this historic event.

The first area that was opened for settlement had been part of the original Indian Territory created by federal policy in earlier years. The area was first assigned to the Creeks by treaty in 1832–1833, with the Seminoles to be added if they were amenable to the idea. By 1856, the Creeks and Seminoles had decided to divide their lands, and the area fell into the Seminole region. Following the Civil War, the Five Nations were required to sign new treaties with the federal government. The Seminoles ceded all of their lands and relocated east to lands relinquished by the Creek Nation. The area surrendered to the federal government then became known as the "Unassigned Lands." This portion of Indian Territory was slated to be used as a settlement area for other Indian tribes as determined by the federal government.

For the Unassigned Lands, the next two decades saw the 1872–1873 land surveys of the area for settlement, construction of the Santa Fe railroad across the area in 1887, and the purchase of former Creek and Seminole lands to remove settlement restrictions that permitted only Indians in the area. A movement to open the Unassigned Lands to settlement began as early as the late 1860s and gained momentum in the early 1880s under the leadership of David L. Payne. Payne and his followers, known as "Boomers," invaded the land on several occasions and established illegal settlements. When intercepted by U.S. cavalry, Payne and his followers were escorted to Kansas and Texas under guard.

Potential homesteaders and land-grant railroads supported the opening of the Unassigned Lands. However, the governments of the five Indian republics and the range-cattle barons opposed the change. The "Boomers" and their supporters finally succeeded in their efforts, however, and on March 23, 1889, newly inaugurated President Benjamin Harrison issued a proclamation opening the Unassigned Lands to settlement beginning at noon on April 22, 1889.

The Unassigned Lands consisted of roughly 2,950 square miles. The area was to be opened under the laws of the Homestead Act of 1862, with a warning that settlers were not to enter or occupy the land before noon on April 22, 1889. The Homestead Act provided that any male or single woman over twenty-one could claim 160 acres. The act also required that the settler make improvements and live on the land for six months out of the year over a period of five years. At the completion of five years, the land would become the property of the settler at no cost. The settler also had the option of paying $1.25 an acre for the land after living on the claim for twelve months.

No provision had been made for the platting of town sites prior to the opening. Town-site companies had been chartered in Kansas but did not start work on platting the lots in the Unassigned Lands until after noon on April 22, 1889. Upon arrival, the would-be settlers for the town sites claimed what they hoped would be a town lot. Following the platting, many businessmen found their claims located in the street or in an alley.

Two acres in the Unassigned Lands were reserved specifically for government use. The first was near Guthrie Station, and the second was at the Kingfisher Stagecoach Station. Guthrie and Kingfisher were assigned as general land offices. Four town sites were also designated: Guthrie, Kingfisher, Norman, and Oklahoma Station. Federal troops were ordered to the area to patrol and remove any people found in the settlement area prior to the opening, as well as to maintain order and peace following the opening.

The homesteaders were allowed to travel to the border area of the Unassigned Lands three days before the run. Tens of thousands of them gathered along the borders of the run area as they awaited the official signal to stake their claims. Cavalry patrols policed the boundary and apprehended many of the "Sooners" who had illegally entered the area ahead of time.

Settlers who entered the Unassigned Lands from the south crossed the Canadian River at the known fords to avoid the dangerous quicksand. Purcell, in Indian Territory, was a major access point for the southern boundary, largely because of the railroad north from Texas. Larger crowds also gathered at Buffalo Springs and the Fort Reno–Darlington area. The Santa Fe railroad ran north to south through the approximate center of the Unassigned Lands, leading many settlers to choose this route and means of transportation to make the land run. The passenger trains left Arkansas City, Kansas, beginning at daylight on April 22.

At noon on April 22, bugles sounded and soldiers fired their carbines and pistols to signal the start of the great land run. The settlers who crossed the boundary into the Unassigned Lands sought the boundary markers left by government surveyors that were inscribed with specific location data. Upon finding the marker, each prospective new landowner wrote down the information and proceeded to the nearest federal land office at Guthrie or Kingfisher. At the land office, they completed the official forms and swore to their eligibility to the claim under the Homestead Act.

By the end of that day, many thousands of people had crossed the boundary into the Unassigned Lands in search of a land claim. A great number of them settled in Guthrie and Oklahoma City. By wagon, cart, train, horseback, and even on foot, these homesteaders had participated in a unique experiment in U.S. history that would eventually lead to the full settlement of Oklahoma.

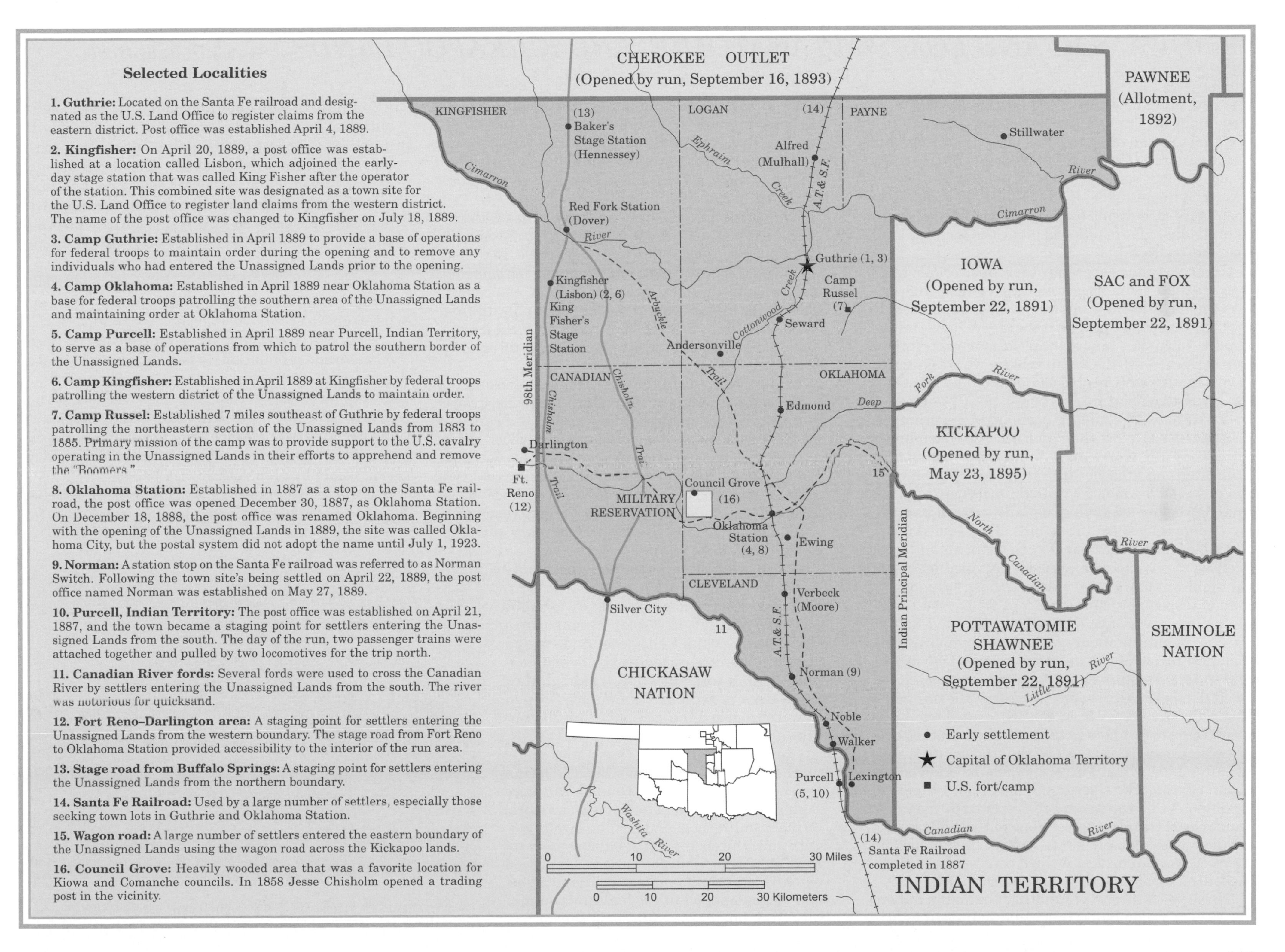

Selected Localities
1. Guthrie: Located on the Santa Fe railroad and designated as the U.S. Land Office to register claims from the eastern district. Post office was established April 4, 1889.
2. Kingfisher: On April 20, 1889, a post office was established at a location called Lisbon, which adjoined the early-day stage station that was called King Fisher after the operator of the station. This combined site was designated as a town site for the U.S. Land Office to register land claims from the western district. The name of the post office was changed to Kingfisher on July 18, 1889.
3. Camp Guthrie: Established in April 1889 to provide a base of operations for federal troops to maintain order during the opening and to remove any individuals who had entered the Unassigned Lands prior to the opening.
4. Camp Oklahoma: Established in April 1889 near Oklahoma Station as a base for federal troops patrolling the southern area of the Unassigned Lands and maintaining order at Oklahoma Station.
5. Camp Purcell: Established in April 1889 near Purcell, Indian Territory, to serve as a base of operations from which to patrol the southern border of the Unassigned Lands.
6. Camp Kingfisher: Established in April 1889 at Kingfisher by federal troops patrolling the western district of the Unassigned Lands to maintain order.
7. Camp Russel: Established 7 miles southeast of Guthrie by federal troops patrolling the northeastern section of the Unassigned Lands from 1883 to 1885. Primary mission of the camp was to provide support to the U.S. cavalry operating in the Unassigned Lands in their efforts to apprehend and remove the "Boomers."
8. Oklahoma Station: Established in 1887 as a stop on the Santa Fe railroad, the post office was opened December 30, 1887, as Oklahoma Station. On December 18, 1888, the post office was renamed Oklahoma. Beginning with the opening of the Unassigned Lands in 1889, the site was called Oklahoma City, but the postal system did not adopt the name until July 1, 1923.
9. Norman: A station stop on the Santa Fe railroad was referred to as Norman Switch. Following the town site's being settled on April 22, 1889, the post office named Norman was established on May 27, 1889.
10. Purcell, Indian Territory: The post office was established on April 21, 1887, and the town became a staging point for settlers entering the Unassigned Lands from the south. The day of the run, two passenger trains were attached together and pulled by two locomotives for the trip north.
11. Canadian River fords: Several fords were used to cross the Canadian River by settlers entering the Unassigned Lands from the south. The river was notorious for quicksand.
12. Fort Reno–Darlington area: A staging point for settlers entering the Unassigned Lands from the western boundary. The stage road from Fort Reno to Oklahoma Station provided accessibility to the interior of the run area.
13. Stage road from Buffalo Springs: A staging point for settlers entering the Unassigned Lands from the northern boundary.
14. Santa Fe Railroad: Used by a large number of settlers, especially those seeking town lots in Guthrie and Oklahoma Station.
15. Wagon road: A large number of settlers entered the eastern boundary of the Unassigned Lands using the wagon road across the Kickapoo lands.
16. Council Grove: Heavily wooded area that was a favorite location for Kiowa and Comanche councils. In 1858 Jesse Chisholm opened a trading post in the vicinity.
CHEROKEE OUTLET
(Opened by run, September 16, 1893)
PAWNEE
(Allotment, 1892)
KINGFISHER
LOGAN
PAYNE
(13)
Baker's Stage Station (Hennessey)
(14)
Alfred (Mulhall)
Stillwater
Ephraim Creek
A.T.& S.F.
Cimarron
River
Cimarron
Red Fork Station (Dover)
River
Guthrie (1, 3)
Camp Russel (7)
IOWA
(Opened by run, September 22, 1891)
SAC and FOX
(Opened by run, September 22, 1891)
Kingfisher (Lisbon) (2, 6)
King Fisher's Stage Station
Arbuckle Trail
Cottonwood Creek
Seward
Andersonville
98th Meridian
CANADIAN
OKLAHOMA
Chisholm Trail
Fork River
Edmond
Deep
KICKAPOO
(Opened by run, May 23, 1895)
Darlington
Ft. Reno (12)
Council Grove
(16)
15
MILITARY RESERVATION
Oklahoma Station (4, 8)
Ewing
North Canadian
River
CLEVELAND
Verbeck (Moore)
Silver City
11
Indian Principal Meridian
POTTAWATOMIE SHAWNEE
(Opened by run, September 22, 1891)
SEMINOLE NATION
CHICKASAW NATION
Norman (9)
Little River
Noble
Walker
Purcell (5, 10)
Lexington
Early settlement
Capital of Oklahoma Territory
U.S. fort/camp
Washita River
Canadian
River
(14)
Santa Fe Railroad completed in 1887
0 10 20 30 Miles
0 10 20 30 Kilometers
INDIAN TERRITORY

59. IOWA, SAC AND FOX, POTTAWATOMIE, AND KICKAPOO LANDS

Essay by *Danney Goble*

The first lands attached to the new Oklahoma Territory under the Organic Act came from the small reservations assigned to the Iowa, Sac and Fox, and Pottawatomie tribes: in September 1891, twenty thousand home seekers gathered for chances on seven thousand homesteads. It was 1895 before the Kickapoos agreed to divide roughly a tenth of their lands as individual allotments and make the rest available to homesteaders.

Chronology and geography thereupon collaborated to make these some of the roughest, rawest, and wildest regions in the new territory. No longer subject to the strict antiliquor laws that the federal government applied to Indian lands, these former reservations were governed—to the extent that they were governed at all—under statutes hastily adopted by the territory's First Legislature.

Obsessed with claiming permanent government-subsidized booty for their hometowns (including a university for Norman, a land grant college for Stillwater, and a teacher-training school for Edmond), the untested lawmakers waited until their session's final day before approving (usually without as much as reading) any substantive bills. They ended up directing county commissioners to grant retail liquor licenses to anyone who applied, provided only that the applicant pay a $200 annual license fee and be "a man of respectable character."

Lexington was almost perfectly situated for the purpose of entrepreneurs eager to sell liquor within a stone's throw of Indian reservations. One of several so-called instant cities, Lexington was no city at all. It did, however, rest on the bank of the Canadian River directly across from Purcell, and Purcell was second only to Ardmore as the largest city in the bone-dry Chickasaw Nation. More than bones were wetted after 1891, when Purcell's residents and visitors began crossing the river to imbibe at one or more of Lexington's thirteen saloons that opened by the year's end. At least two more saloons opened on a midstream sandbar, both accessible by a rickety though heavily traveled wooden bridge. A third consisted of a floating saloon moored to the river's north bank.

Three years after its founding, Lexington did not yet have a single bank, but it did maintain nearly a dozen saloons (not counting the ones in the riverbed). In 1902, eight saloons occupied the single block of Broadway between Main and First Street. A card room was behind one, a billiard parlor behind a second, and so-called sleeping rooms were attached to a third.

Even more notorious among the so-called whiskey towns were those towns in the new Pottawatomie County. Again, geography was responsible. Bordered on the east by the Creek and Seminole nations and on the south by the Chickasaw Nation, the county opened its first saloon at Keokuk Falls in its first year of existence, in 1891. Nine years later, the county had an estimated sixty-two saloons plus three commercial distilleries.

Some towns, including Earlsboro and Wanette, built mixed economies that offered both hardware and the like for homesteaders and liquidware for all. The greatest notoriety was reserved for those with singular (some said sinister) purposes: Keokuk Falls, Corner (so called because it sat in the county's extreme southeast corner), and Violet Springs (most favorably situated of all), whose Main Street was a gated fence marking the town's boundary with the Seminole Nation.

Booze was their business—their only business—and a rough business it was. One report claimed that as many as eight men were killed in Violet Springs in a single day. Keokuk Falls never had enough people to be recognized by the census bureau; still, it was known well enough that stage drivers regularly announced, when they approached the station, "Stop 20 minutes and see a man killed."

Corner outdid even those notorious places. The Dalton Gang, the Christian Brothers, and Bill Doolin's bunch—all were regulars to a place that began with no store, no blacksmith shop, and not one dwelling—with nothing at all but a saloon made of rawhide. Although eight more years passed before Corner got a general store, a second saloon opened in the budding community first; business rivalry took the form of a running, bloody duel played out by pathological outlaws, drink-maddened cowboys, and rowdy Indians. Any respectable benefit went entirely to the only physician in the region, Dr. Jesse Mooney. Mooney lived ten miles away—close enough to escape immediate threats but not their consequences: a steady practice in the treatment of knifings, shootings, lacerations, and the gouging of eyeballs. The good doctor also cleaned up what remained of several fingers and at least one ear, all having been bitten off (although presumably not by the same psychopath).

The booze-fed enmity lasted into the first two years of statewide prohibition. It took an outraged crowd's famously photographed and well-distributed hanging of four killers at Ada to end the violence permanently. Officially the killers' fatal victim was publicly identified as U.S. Marshal Angus Bobbitt, but everyone knew him as the owner of Corner's original saloon before he pinned on his tin badge.

Corner never recovered, and it soon became a ghost town—as did Violet Springs and Keokuk Falls. Having lived by the sauce, all died by the sauce, too.

Sac and Fox bark house, ca. 1880. (Courtesy Western History Collections, University of Oklahoma Libraries)

Sac and Fox Reservation: This reservation of 750 square miles was assigned to the tribe by legislative action of the United States on February 18, 1867. The area was part of the land ceded to the United States by the Creek Nation on June 14, 1866. On February 13, 1889, Congress confirmed an agreement by which the nation ceded portions of the reservation back to the United States. These ceded areas were opened for settlement by run on September 22, 1891.

Pottawatomie Reservation: By a treaty of February 27, 1867, delegates from the tribe along with members of a governmental commission visited Indian Territory to select a reservation site of 900 square miles. The delegates returned without making a selection, but in 1870 tribal delegates once again agreed to travel to Indian Territory. This time they accepted a site west of the Seminole lands between the Canadian and North Canadian rivers. This site comprised land ceded by the Seminole Nation on March 21, 1866, and the Creek Nation on June 14, 1866. On March 3, 1891, Congress confirmed agreements with the Citizen Band of Pottawatomie and the Absentee Shawnee by which the two tribes ceded portions of their reservations to the United States. These ceded areas were opened for settlement by run on September 22, 1891.

Iowa Reservation: On August 15, 1883, by executive order, the U.S. president set apart a reservation of approximately 656 square miles for the Iowas. Later, this area was opened for settlement by run on September 22, 1891.

Kickapoo Reservation: In accordance with acts of the U.S. Congress during the 1870s, the Kickapoos were induced to return from Mexico to a reservation in Indian Territory, defined by executive order of the U.S. president on August 15, 1883. This reserve of 322.5 square miles was a portion of the land ceded to the United States on June 14, 1866, by the Creek Nation for the future location of other tribes. On March 3, 1893, an act of Congress confirmed an agreement made on September 9, 1891, whereby the Kickapoos, after allotment, ceded the remainder of their reservation to the United States. This area was then opened for settlement by run on May 23, 1895.

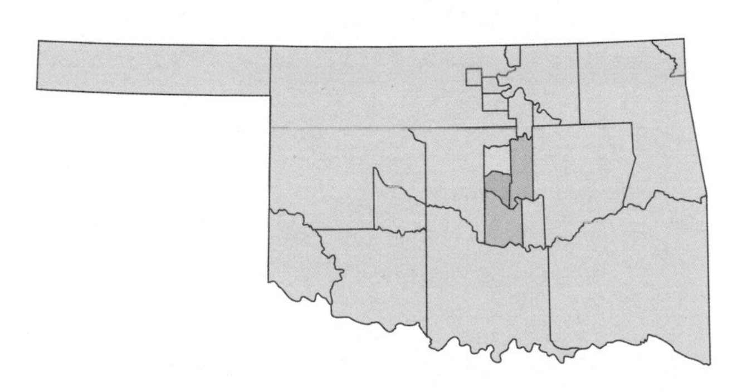

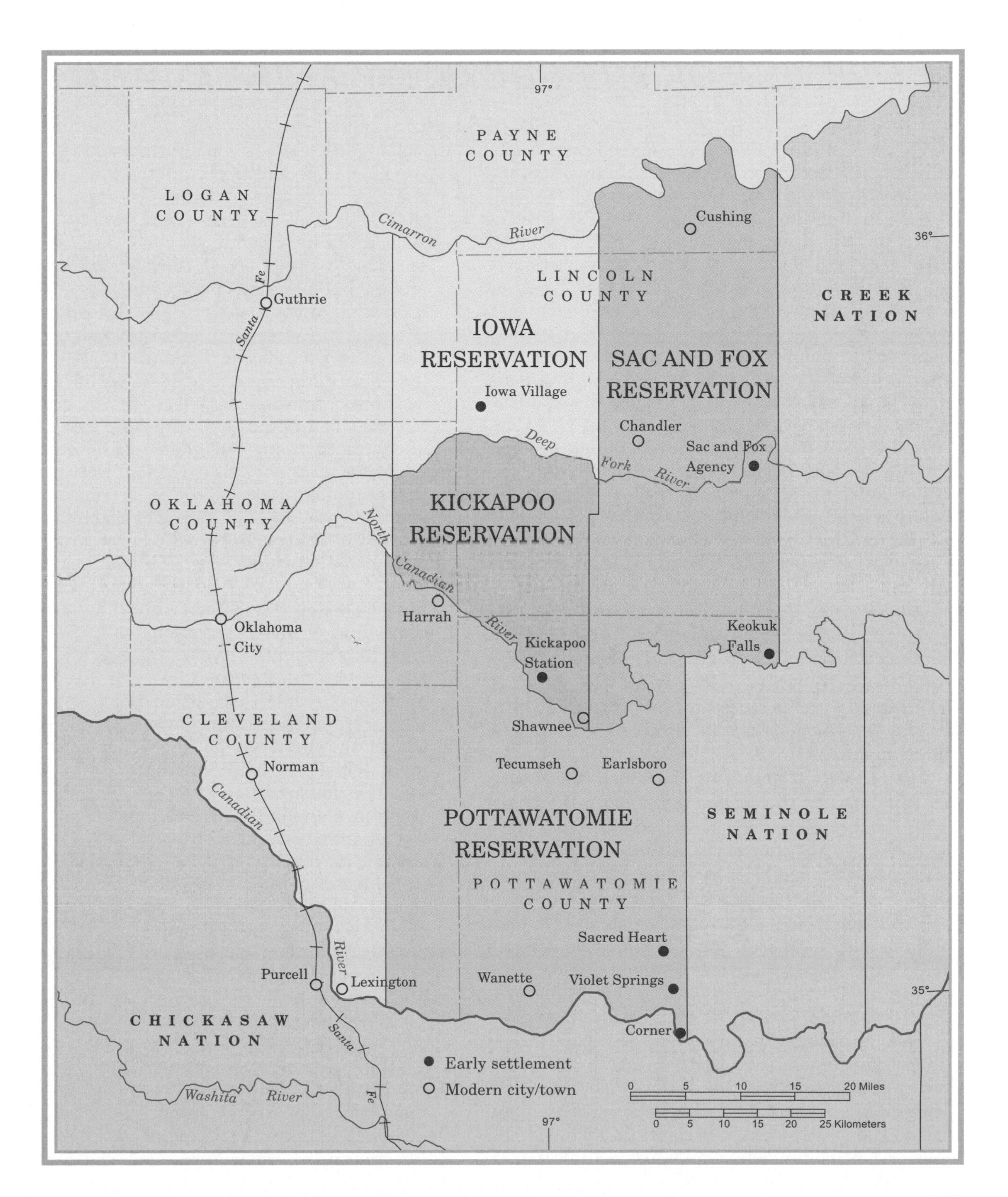

60. OPENING OF THE CHEYENNE AND ARAPAHO RESERVATION

Essay by *Josh Clough*

Barely twenty years after being forced onto a 4.2-million-acre reservation in western Indian Territory, the Cheyennes and Arapahos were compelled to sell all but a half-million acres of it to the U.S. government. For this land cession, the tribes received $1,500,000, or about 35 cents an acre. Of this princely sum, $1,000,000 was deposited in the U.S. Treasury to draw 5 percent interest annually, and each year the $50,000 in interest income was to be dispersed among tribal members in a per capita payment. The remaining $500,000 was to be divided equally among tribal members in two $250,000 payments after the cession agreement had been ratified by the U.S. Congress in 1891. Although the government paid the first installment as promised, it took $67,500 out of the second payment and gave it to lawyers who had allegedly represented the interests of the tribes during negotiations for the reservation but in reality had worked in collusion with federal authorities to obtain its cession. The Cheyenne-Arapaho people, of course, protested this unauthorized withdrawal, but to no avail. Indian Service officials refused to refund the money despite the findings of independent investigators that the attorneys' contract with the tribes was "tainted with misrepresentation, fraud, and bribery" and represented "an outrage upon the Cheyenne and Arapaho Indians."

Given the extralegal means by which the government had gained the cession agreement, the tribes were probably not terribly surprised when they were cheated out of a portion of the subsequent payments for the reservation. The process for taking Cheyenne-Arapaho lands began in 1889. That year, Congress granted the president authority to create a three-man commission, known as the Cherokee or Jerome Commission, to negotiate with Indian tribes in western Indian Territory for the sale of their reservations. This unholy trinity of commissioners arrived on the Cheyenne-Arapaho Reservation in July 1890 and faced the difficult task of convincing three-fourths of the adult male population to part with their land. Most tribal members staunchly opposed ceding any land to the government; the resistors included Old Crow (a Cheyenne), who explained to the commission why their reservation was not for sale: "The land is money to us and that is all the kind of money we want . . . the land and the streams . . . that run through it is all the wealth that I want." Unfazed by such resistance, commissioners threatened tribal members to either accept the offer or face forced allotment of the reservation, in which case they would receive no compensation at all. Although a handful of chiefs and other men eventually signed the cession agreement, nowhere near the three-fourths majority was obtained. Faced with an impossible situation, commissioners used bribery and coercion to secure additional signatures and took the liberty of adding the names of women, children, and even nonexistent individuals to the list. Notwithstanding the fraudulent nature of the cession document, Congress accepted its validity and by doing so sealed the fate of the Cheyenne-Arapaho Reservation.

From July to September of 1891, the 3,295 members of the two tribes chose 160-acre allotments of land on what would soon become their former reservation. Individuals eighteen years of age or older selected their own allotments, while those of minors were chosen by parents. Cheyenne and Arapaho allotments clustered in the fertile and well-timbered valleys of the Washita, Canadian, and North Canadian rivers, and the people settled in small social units called bands as they had traditionally done. By doing so, they subverted one of the main purposes of allotment—to break up the communal living patterns of Native peoples—and gained some protection from the whites surrounding them.

Once allotment had been completed, the federal government opened nearly 3.5 million acres of the Cheyenne-Arapaho Reservation to settlement via a land run. On April 19, 1892, between twenty-five thousand and thirty thousand settlers swarmed across reservation boundaries to stake their claims to homesteads. Overnight the Cheyennes and Arapahos became a minority in their own homeland, making up only 10 percent of the population in the six counties formed from the breakup of the reservation. But they did not disappear, nor did they stop fighting for justice in the loss of their lands. In 1965 the two tribes brought suit against the United States, calling the $1.5 million that they had received for the land ceded "unconscionable." The Indian Claims Commission agreed, ruling in their favor and awarding them a $15 million judgment. While the Cheyenne and Arapaho tribes did not get their lands back, they proved that the sale of their reservation had been a sale in name only. In reality, the cession of their lands had been extortion of the worst variety—that of a guardian against its ward.

On April 19, 1892, settlers await the opening of the Cheyenne-Arapaho surplus land. (Courtesy Western History Collections, University of Oklahoma Libraries)

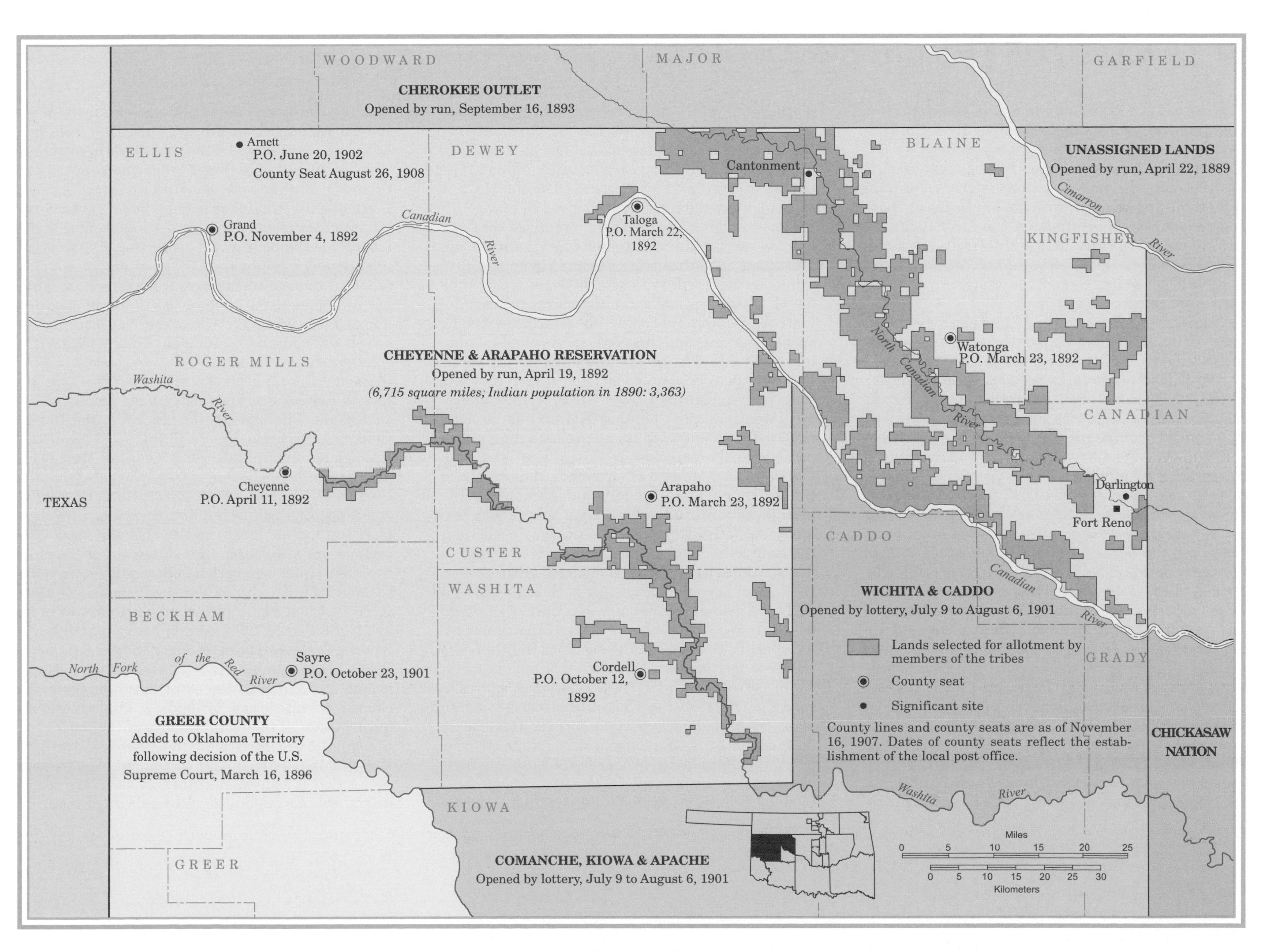
WOODWARD
MAJOR
GARFIELD
CHEROKEE OUTLET
Opened by run, September 16, 1893
ELLIS
Arnett
P.O. June 20, 1902
County Seat August 26, 1908
DEWEY
Cantonment
BLAINE
UNASSIGNED LANDS
Opened by run, April 22, 1889
Cimarron River
Grand
P.O. November 4, 1892
Canadian River
Taloga
P.O. March 22, 1892
KINGFISHER
Watonga
P.O. March 23, 1892
North Canadian River
ROGER MILLS
CHEYENNE & ARAPAHO RESERVATION
Opened by run, April 19, 1892
(6,715 square miles; Indian population in 1890: 3,363)
Washita River
CANADIAN
Cheyenne
P.O. April 11, 1892
TEXAS
Arapaho
P.O. March 23, 1892
Darlington
Fort Reno
CADDO
CUSTER
WASHITA
WICHITA & CADDO
Opened by lottery, July 9 to August 6, 1901
Canadian River
BECKHAM
Lands selected for allotment by members of the tribes
County seat
Significant site
GRADY
North Fork of the Red River
Sayre
P.O. October 23, 1901
Cordell
P.O. October 12, 1892
County lines and county seats are as of November 16, 1907. Dates of county seats reflect the establishment of the local post office.
GREER COUNTY
Added to Oklahoma Territory following decision of the U.S. Supreme Court, March 16, 1896
CHICKASAW NATION
Washita River
KIOWA
GREER
COMANCHE, KIOWA & APACHE
Opened by lottery, July 9 to August 6, 1901
Miles
0 5 10 15 20 25
0 5 10 15 20 25 30
Kilometers

61. OPENING OF THE CHEROKEE OUTLET

Essay by *Josh Clough*

The story of the 1893 land run is well known to most Oklahomans: at noon on September 16, 1893, U.S. cavalrymen stationed along the perimeter of the Cherokee Outlet sounded their bugles, signaling the opening of the territory to settlement. Over one hundred thousand people converged on the Outlet hoping to stake a claim to one of the forty thousand homesteads of 160 acres that were being made available. But before this event could occur, the Cherokee Nation, which owned the Outlet, had to be convinced to part with it.

Negotiations for acquiring the Outlet began in July of 1889, roughly six months after the Cherokee National Council had agreed to lease the Outlet to the Cherokee Strip Live Stock Association for another five years. Representing the government at the bargaining table was the three-man Cherokee or Jerome Commission, the same body responsible for divesting the Cheyennes and Arapahos and a dozen other Oklahoma tribes of their reservations. When commissioners arrived in Tahlequah, the capital of the Cherokee Nation, any hopes they had for a quick deal soon evaporated in the summer heat. Their offer to purchase all Cherokee lands west of the 96th meridian for $1.25 an acre was rebuffed by Principal Chief Joel B. Mayes, who stated that because all tribal land was held in common, it could not be sold without an amendment to the nation's constitution—a prospect he thought highly unlikely. "When it comes to an Indian putting a price on his land," Mayes remarked, "he is at a loss, for he has never considered it a matter of speculation. The ideal of 'Mother Earth' to him is almost a literal expression, and I believe I can safely say to you from what knowledge I have of the Cherokee people that they will not consent to sell those lands for $1.25 an acre." Ideological reasons aside, the Cherokees had little incentive to part with a tract of land that earned them a substantial, steady income. Furthermore, cattle ranchers of the association had agreed to pay $200,000 annually for yearly grazing rights to the Outlet in 1888 and had promised to double this amount when the lease was renewed in 1893.

Government negotiators soon realized that in a bidding war for the Outlet, they could not win. Congress had authorized the Jerome Commission to purchase the territory west of 96 degrees longitude for $1.25 an acre, and commissioners could not deviate too far from this price. The ranchers faced no such constraints and therefore, in the minds of commissioners, had to be eliminated from the equation. President Benjamin Harrison gave negotiators their wish in February 1890. His Proclamation No. 10 stated that the Cherokee Nation had no legal right to lease Outlet lands and declared their agreement with the association to be illegal and void. Harrison also ordered all livestock removed from the Outlet and forbade additional stock from being brought within its borders. With this pronouncement, then, the Cherokees lost not only a substantial source of revenue but also their leverage in negotiations with the government. After seeing their lease agreement summarily cancelled by federal edict, tribal leaders knew that the Outlet would be taken from them with or without their consent. As a result, they decided to sacrifice the Outlet to preserve the Cherokee Nation.

On December 19, 1891, the Cherokees agreed to cede the Outlet to the United States for $1.40 an acre. Tribal members knew it was an unfair price for the land, but being compensated financially was not really the point; they hoped that by selling their lands west of the 96th meridian, they would be able to enjoy "safety, protection, and equality of rights" and a "government the majority are in favor of" in the Cherokee Nation proper. This, they believed, would be possible only if the thousands of intruders (that is, unauthorized non-Indian persons) in the Cherokee Nation were removed by federal troops. Consequently, Cherokee leaders had a clause written into the cession agreement stipulating that the federal government would assist the tribe in evicting intruders. Sadly, the U.S. government not only failed to remove trespassers from Cherokee lands but also gave them preferential rights in choosing homesteads when the Cherokee Nation was dissolved and opened to settlement around the turn of the century.

Eventually the Cherokees received the opportunity to redress grievances stemming from the cession of the Cherokee Outlet. In 1961, the Indian Claims Commission decided in the tribe's favor in a suit against the United States, awarding the Cherokees $14 million. The commission concluded that the Cherokees had had a fee simple title to the Outlet when negotiations began and therefore President Harrison had no legal right to void the lease. The commission also found, in a statement of the obvious, that tribal members had been subjected to duress during talks with the Jerome Commission. More recently, Chad Smith (principal chief of the Cherokee Nation since 1999) offered his own analysis of how the Outlet had been obtained: "Sale of the Cherokee Outlet was acquiescence to Presidential, Congressional, and bureaucratic extortion to appease the clamor of white greed for land . . . [and it] was acquired through the blatant abuse of the trust relationship of Congress with the Cherokee Nation." Knowing the circumstances surrounding the Outlet's acquisition, is it any wonder that the Cherokee people do not feel like celebrating the land run of 1893?

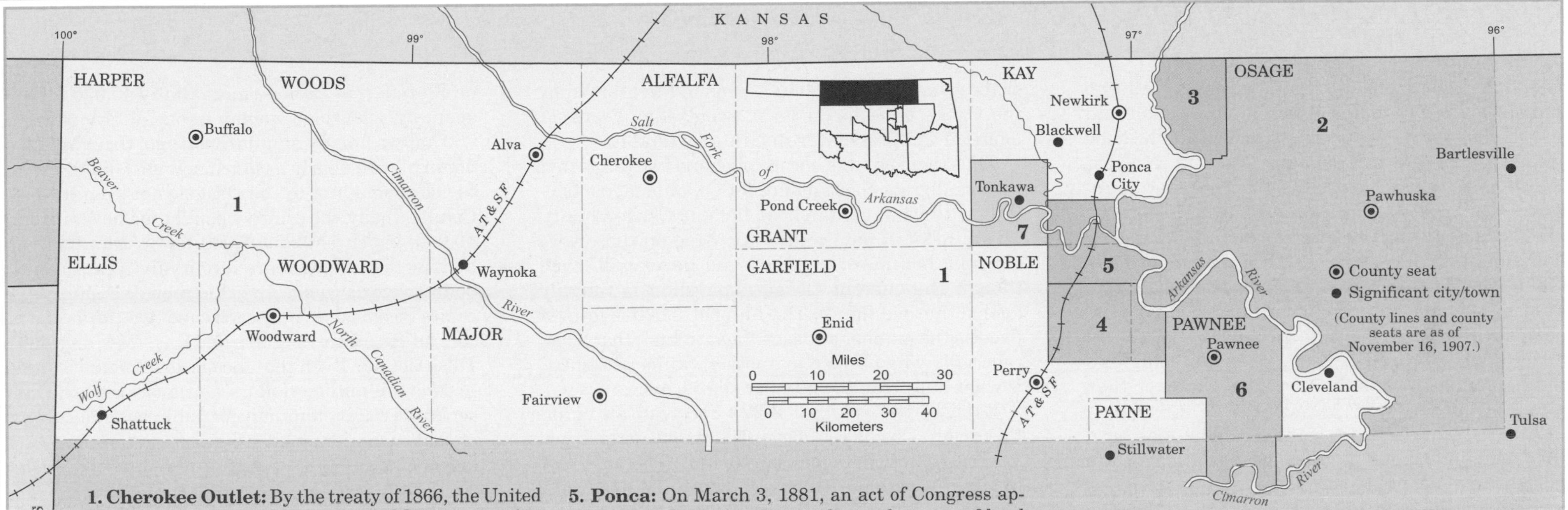

County seat
Significant city/town
(County lines and county seats are as of November 16, 1907.)

1. Cherokee Outlet: By the treaty of 1866, the United States was authorized to settle (with compensation to the Cherokees) friendly Indians on unoccupied lands west of 96° longitude. Under this provision, reservations were provided for the Osages, Kansas (Kaws), Pawnees, Nez Perces (later given to the Tonkawas), Poncas, Otos, and Missouris. The remainder of the Outlet was opened for settlement by run on September 16, 1893.

2. Osage Reservation: On July 15, 1870, Congress made provisions for a reserve in Indian Territory for the Osages, to provide for their removal from Kansas. The boundaries of the tract selected by the Osages, containing 2,297 square miles, were confirmed by Congress on June 5, 1872; as part of this agreement, the Osages consented to allow the Kansa Indians to settle in the northwestern part of the reservation. These lands were opened by allotment in 1906.

3. Kansa Reservation: On June 5, 1872, an act of Congress confirmed a reservation of 156.5 square miles for the Kansa Tribe. These lands were opened by allotment in 1906.

4. Oto and Missouri: This new reserve in Indian Territory was provided by an act of Congress on March 3, 1881. It was purchased from the Cherokee domain west of 96° longitude and contained 201.76 square miles. These lands were opened by allotment in 1904.

5. Ponca: On March 3, 1881, an act of Congress appropriated funds for the purchase of a tract of land from the Cherokees west of 96° longitude. This reserve contained 159.25 square miles and was opened by allotment in 1904.

6. Pawnee: By an act of Congress on April 10, 1876, provisions were made for the sale of the Pawnee reservation in Nebraska and the purchase of a new reservation in Indian Territory. This reserve was selected partly from lands of the Cherokees and partly from lands of the Creeks in accordance with treaties of 1866 with these two nations. This reserve contained 442.25 square miles and was opened by allotment in 1892.

7. Nez Perce: An act of Congress on May 27, 1878, provided for the removal of the Nez Perces (Joseph's band) from Fort Leavenworth to a reserve in Indian Territory. The reserve was purchased for them from Cherokee land west of 96° longitude. The Cherokee Nation issued a deed dated June 14, 1883, for the reserve (containing 141.75 square miles) made to the United States in trust for the Nez Perces. The Nez Perces, determined to return to their homelands in Idaho, deeded their claims to the United States on May 22, 1885. This reserve was then made available to a small group of Tonkawas. It was opened by allotment in 1891.

Population of Selected Towns in the Cherokee Outlet, 1907

Town	Population	Post office established
Alva	2,800	Aug. 25, 1893
Blackwell	2,644	Dec. 1, 1893
Buffalo[a]	—	June 15, 1889
Cherokee	964	Feb. 7, 1894
Cleveland[b]	1,441	April 14, 1894
Enid	10,087	Aug. 25, 1893
Fairview	887	April 18, 1894
Newkirk[c]	1,778	Jan. 18, 1894
Pawhuska	2,408	May 4, 1876
Pawnee	1,943	May 4, 1876
Perry	2,881	Aug. 25, 1893
Ponca City[d]	2,529	Oct. 23, 1913
Pond Creek[e]	1,155	Sept. 29, 1893
Shattuck	1,009	Nov. 17, 1893
Tonkawa	1,238	March 9, 1894
Waynoka[f]	217	April 10, 1889
Woodward	2,018	Feb. 3, 1893

[a] Formerly Brule, changed to Buffalo on June 6, 1907. Population unknown.
[b] Formerly Herbert.
[c] Formerly Lamereux.
[d] Formerly New Ponca; post office changed to Ponca on July 7, 1898, and to Ponca City on October 23, 1913.
[e] Original town was Round Pond. Present-day Pond Creek is 4 miles south of the original town site, now known as Jefferson.
[f] Formerly Keystone.

62. *THE OSAGE NATION, 1872–1906*

Essay by *Danney Goble*

No people have lived in Oklahoma longer and no land has given Oklahoma more than the people and land sharing the name "Osage." Elements of the tribe were here before white men ever knew of this vast prairie land. When Europeans did come, they arrogantly declared the land theirs through dubious rights of so-called discovery or conquest, but only their alliances with the powerful Osage people made it theirs in effect—and even then it was on loan from these proud and independent people. Across Missouri, down western Kansas, then across Oklahoma to the Red River and beyond, Osage hunting and raiding parties had their way with whatever they wanted, whenever they wanted it.

Until the United States wanted it. What had been ruled by the Osages came to be assigned to the Osages, and bit by bit the part that was assigned became smaller and smaller. By 1872, when the United States forced upon the once-mighty Osages a new treaty that pushed them entirely from Kansas, all that remained was about 2,300 square miles. It may not have been much—not compared to what had been the extent of their homelands—but it was enough. Best of all, the Osages could count on it. Whites, tribal leaders are supposed to have said, had never shown much interest in such a treeless land, its undulating hills sealed with an impenetrable mat of grasses and buried beneath worthless wildflowers.

No one much seemed to care what (if anything) might lie beneath all that, which may have been why federal officials gave the Osages what turned out by one measure to be a singular deal. By federal law of 1906, every square inch of Osage land was to be divided equally among the 2,229 individuals that Washington had enrolled as Osage tribal citizens, with each receiving 160 acres as personal "homestead" and some 500 more as separate "surplus." What lay below—all "the oil, gas, coal, or other minerals covered by the lands"—was to be retained by the Osage tribe for at least twenty-five years, or longer if Congress later saw fit to extend it.

Thus there entered one number and two terms that have had great consequence for Oklahoma, particularly with what at statehood became Osage County. The number of names that appeared on those very old rolls has never changed and never will, even though the current Osage population is roughly double that old figure. The number 2,229 is forever fixed as the number of Osage "headrights"; that term, especially when linked to another, "mineral rights," is what has given the number significance.

Each of the original 2,229 received an equal "headright." None could ever sell it, lease it, borrow against it, or otherwise dispose of it. The only way to lose it was to die—at which point, the headright passed to one's heir or heirs (if the latter, as equal fractions). And what was one headright worth? Exactly 1/2,229th of the value of all mineral rights once assigned collectively to 2,229 Osage citizens. As early as 1919, that added up and divided out to about $20,000 (the equivalent of approximately $200,000 in 2000)—the income derived in one year from the mineral rights held by an Osage family of five.

The reason had no more to do with the grasses than with the wildflowers. The reason was oil. Everyone knew, back in 1906, that those mineral rights—particularly the right to punch through that grass, trample the flowers, and drill for oil—had to be worth something. Nobody had any idea how much the value of the mineral rights would be until the 1920s, when the Osage lands were flooded with oil and the Osage people were awash with money. In 1923, the tribe split up $27 million. The headright, with moneys previously received, was enough that someone could spend $12,000 for a fur coat, $3,000 for a diamond ring, $5,000 for a new car, $7,000 for new furniture and $600 to ship it to California, and $12,800 on Florida real estate—more than $40,000 all told, spent by one Osage woman in one afternoon.

That was many an afternoon ago, though, and oil doesn't mean nearly as much now as it did then—not to Oklahoma, not to the Osages, not even to Osage County. Today, the county's population hovers around 40,000, which is about 7,000 fewer than had been making their living there seventy-five years ago. Nor do they live as well as they did then; the county's per capita income does not reach even two-thirds of what can be found in neighboring Kay, Washington, or Tulsa County. Even that income level would be worse but for the million dollars and more that the state sends the county annually for public assistance. Some of that money may even have to go to a few of the Osages, although probably not much, for those headrights still have some worth and the Osages are still a proud and independent people.

That has not changed. Neither has some of the land—still lush with bluestem, Indiangrass, and switchgrass, still undulating in hills aglow with the colors of nearly eight hundred plant species. Like the oil reserves beneath it in Oklahoma, that kind of land is considerably diminished in extent; what remains is not even a tenth of the vast tallgrass prairie that once carpeted 142 million acres in fourteen states. In fact, about all that remains in large, unbroken tracts is to be found nowhere but in the Flint Hills of Oklahoma and Kansas. None of the land is sustainable as a functioning ecosystem. In 1989, the Nature Conservancy purchased 30,000 acres of what had been the sprawling Barnard Ranch, north of Pawhuska. Since expanded by another 9,000 acres and designated the Tallgrass Prairie Preserve, the area today is home to bison and songbirds and wildflowers, serving as a precious reminder of and tribute to what it had been when all it had been was a land and a people sharing the name "Osage."

THE GREAT AND LITTLE OSAGES

On July 15, 1869, Congress made provision for a reserve in Indian Territory for the Great and Little Osages who were living in Kansas. The tract selected by the Osages was later amended and confirmed by an act of Congress on June 5, 1872. As a condition of this act, the Great and Little Osages agreed to allow the Kansas (Kaw) tribe to settle on 156.5 square miles in the northwestern corner of their reserve. In 1881, the Great and Little Osages joined under a written constitution to become the Osage Nation.

Population of Osage and Kaw Reservations, 1890–1907

Ethnic group	Population
Osage Reservation, June 1, 1890	
Osages	1,509
Quapaws	71
Others	197
Total	1,777
Kaw Reservation, June 1, 1890	
Kansas	198
Total in 1890	**1,975**
Total in 1900	**6,717**
Total in 1907	**15,332**

Larger Towns of the Osage Reservation, 1907

Town	Population in 1907	Post office established
Pawhuska[a]	2,408	May 4, 1876
Fairfax	470	February 16, 1903
Hominy	468	February 10, 1891
Foraker	237	February 13, 1903

[a] With the Osage Agency nearby, the town of Pawhuska was named after the Osage chief Paw Hiu Skab ("white hair").

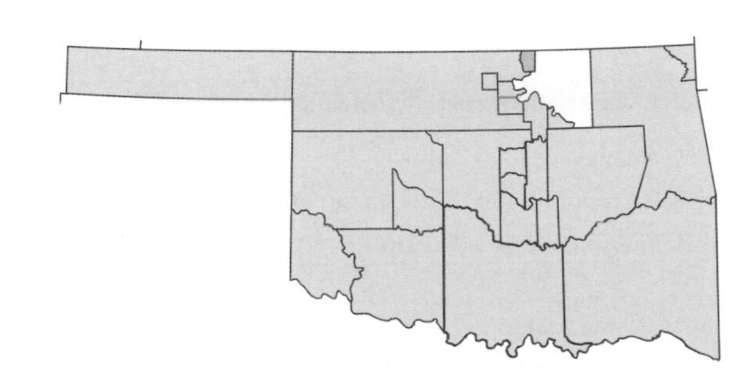

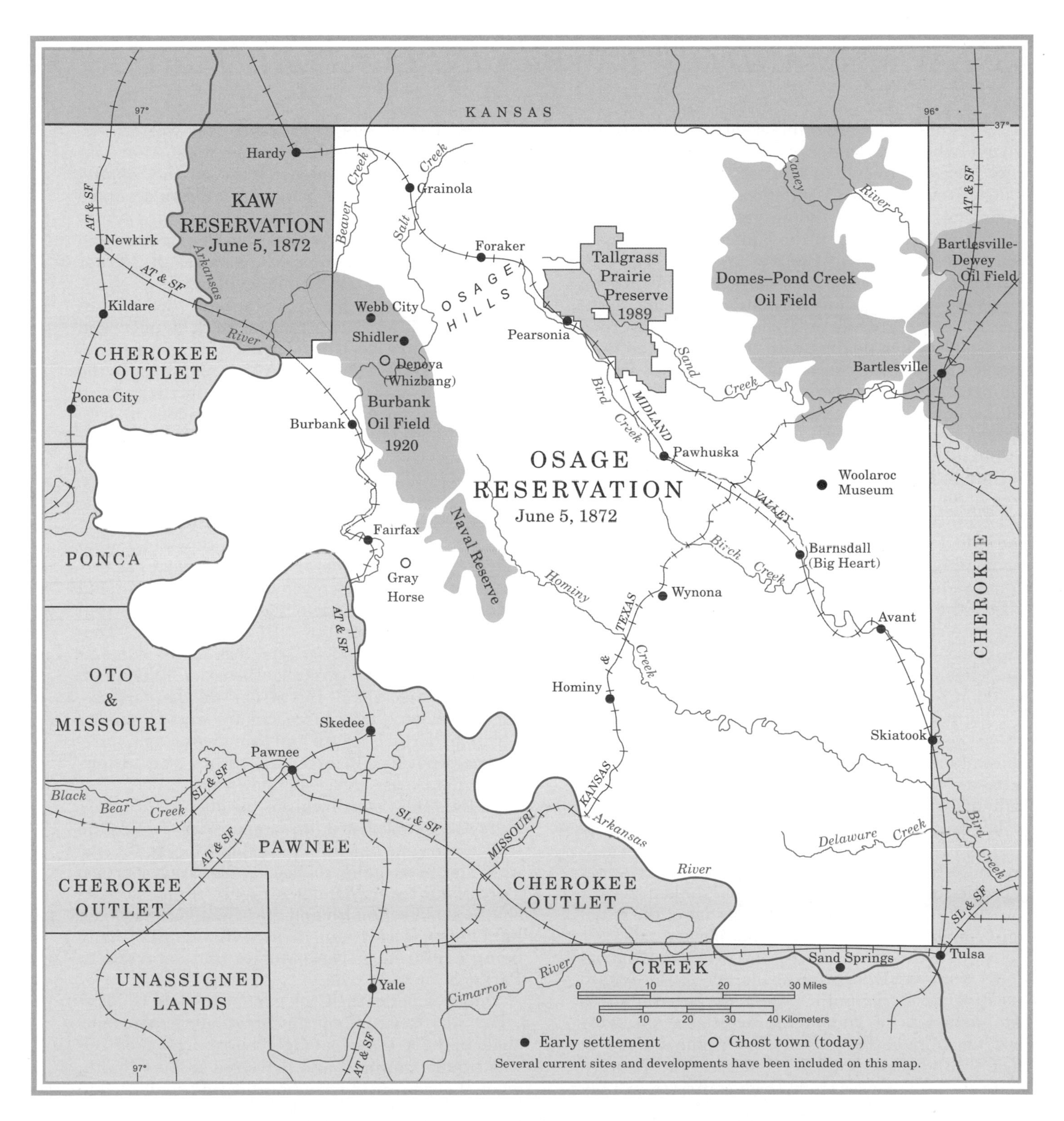

63. LAWMEN AND OUTLAWS IN INDIAN TERRITORY, 1866–1907

Essay by *John R. Lovett*

Strict regulations were established on trade and intercourse between whites and the Indian tribes that were relocated to Indian Territory beginning in the 1830s. To enforce those regulations, the seventy-four-thousand-square-mile Indian Territory was placed under the jurisdiction of the United States District Court, Western District Court of Arkansas. The U.S. marshals and their deputies were given the mission of protecting the Indian population from encroachments by whites, while the Indians usually governed themselves when dealing with crimes between Indians. The federal marshals dealt with crimes by whites against Indians and also enforced the prohibitions of selling liquor to Indians. Not until the 1870s were serious steps taken to rid the Indian Territory of the criminals who had sought haven there.

Indian Territory proved to be a very dangerous area of operations for the U.S. marshals. In 1872 a Cherokee named Zeke Proctor wounded a white man and killed the man's Cherokee wife as the result of an ongoing feud between Proctor and the Cherokee woman's family. Proctor was charged with murder within the Cherokee court system. A federal posse of ten men was ordered to arrest Proctor if the Cherokee court acquitted him. As the posse approached the schoolhouse where the trial was being held, it was met with a volley of rifle fire. The gun battle left eight of the lawmen dead, along with three Cherokees in the schoolhouse. Known as the Going Snake fight, this was a rare occurrence of violence between the federal marshals and the tribes of the Indian Territory.

The relationship between the two was more often one of cooperation. The Indians viewed the federal marshals as their defenders from the criminal activities of whites. The federal marshals in return could ask for and receive the assistance of the tribal light-horse police in their pursuit of criminals.

In 1871 Congress moved the Western District Court from Van Buren, Arkansas, across the Arkansas River to Fort Smith, Arkansas. The court was established in the abandoned facilities of the army fort. On May 2, 1875, Isaac C. Parker arrived at Fort Smith as the new federal judge of the Western District Court; he served in this position from 1875 to 1896. Parker had jurisdiction over western Arkansas and the entire Indian Territory. After taking office, he appointed two hundred U.S. deputy marshals and built an immense gallows designed to hang twelve men at one time. During his twenty-one-year tenure, seventy-nine men were hanged and hundreds were sent to prison. As a result, Parker became known as the "Hanging Judge."

Judge Parker's federal marshals included veteran lawmen such as Heck Thomas, Heck Bruner, and Bill Tilghman as well as a former African American slave named Bass Reeves. Parker's marshals, in the performance of their duties in Indian Territory, faced some of the most dangerous desperadoes in U.S. history—both individual criminals and the more lethal gangs that formed from time to time. Parker's marshals could easily take their place in U.S. history as Homeric heroes of the American West.

Ned Christie, from a prominent Cherokee family, was one of the most dangerous outlaws in Indian Territory whom the federal marshals faced. Christie's outlaw career began when he killed deputy marshal Daniel Maples. Christie eluded capture for several years. In one encounter with Heck Thomas, Thomas wounded Christie in the face. At his home in the Rabbit Trap Canyon, southeast of Tahlequah, Christie built a small but strong wooden fortress. On November 2, 1892, sixteen marshals surrounded Christie's fort. Using a small cannon and dynamite, the marshals finally forced the outlaw from his fortress, and Christie was shot down and killed.

In 1894 Bill Cook (a whiskey peddler in the Creek Nation) organized an outlaw gang. With Cook as the leader, the gang had a very short but successful tenure. The Cook gang robbed banks, stagecoaches, stores, and trains. Under pressure from the marshals out of Fort Smith and the Cherokee and Creek light horse, Cook's gang dispersed, with Bill finally being captured in New Mexico and returned to Parker's court for trial.

One member of the Cook gang, Crawford Goldsby (alias Cherokee Bill), continued to elude federal marshals and the Cherokee light horse. Cherokee Bill was finally captured and delivered to Fort Smith, where he was convicted of murder and sentenced to hang by Judge Parker. On March 17, 1896, Cherokee Bill was hung at the federal gallows at Fort Smith.

The Rufus Buck gang terrorized the citizens of the Creek Nation for a period of two weeks. The five members of the gang were captured by federal marshals and Creek light horse and were taken to Fort Smith to stand trial. All five were hung on July 1, 1896, for the crimes of murder, rape, and robbery.

With the allotment of Indian land, the termination of Indian Territory, the rapid influx of white settlers, and statehood, the former Indian Territory saw a decrease in crime. In addition, as the population increased, local law enforcement became more effective, and the days of the organized outlaw gangs in Indian Territory came to an end.

Selected Localities

1. Going Snake District (schoolhouse)—April 15, 1872: 3 Cherokees and 8 U.S. deputy marshals were killed in a gun battle. This battle had the highest number of U.S. marshals killed at one time, from the establishment of the U.S. marshals to the present.

2. Fort Smith: Location of the Federal Western District Court of Arkansas. The majority of those hanged during Judge Parker's tenure committed their crimes in Indian Territory and were captured and taken to Fort Smith by Parker's U.S. deputy marshals.

3. Robbers Cave: Used by various outlaws as a hideout during the Indian Territory period.

4. Near Younger's Bend—1883: Belle Starr was charged in Judge Parker's court at Fort Smith for stealing horses, and eastern newspapers headlined her as "Queen of Bandits." The ranch of Sam Starr (on a bend of the Canadian River) was named Younger's Bend by his wife, Belle, to honor her former lover Cole Younger, one of the notorious members of the James-Younger gang. Younger's Bend became a haven for outlaws in the Indian Territory. On February 2, 1889, Belle Starr was killed by an unknown assassin.

5. Leliaetta—September 15, 1891: The Dalton gang robbed an MK&T train.

6. Adair—July 15, 1892: The Dalton gang robbed an MK&T train. Even though the train carried an armed guard of 8 Indian police, the Dalton gang escaped unharmed with $17,000 following a gun battle with the guards.

7. Berryhill Farm: Site of Dalton gang hideout.

8. Rabbit Trap Canyon—November 2, 1892: U.S. deputy marshals killed the Cherokee outlaw Ned Christie. Christie held the marshals at bay for several hours before being forced into the open, where he was shot and killed.

9. Nowata—July 1892: The Henry Starr gang robbed the Nowata railroad depot. Henry Starr was Belle Starr's uncle by marriage.

10. Lenapah—December 14, 1892: Henry Starr killed U.S. deputy marshal Floyd Wilson. Wilson had been tracking Starr and was killed while attempting to arrest him.

11. Pryor Creek—May 2, 1893: The Henry Starr gang robbed an MK&T train.

12. Frank Cheney farm, 7 miles north of Wagoner—June 1893: Following the successful robbery of the People's Bank at Bentonville, Arkansas, on June 5, 1893, the Starr gang broke up to avoid pursuit by U.S. marshals. Henry Starr and gang member Kid Wilson were later captured in Colorado Springs, Colorado. Starr returned to Parker's court at Fort Smith, where he had two death sentences overturned but was sent to federal prison. President Theodore Roosevelt commuted his sentence in 1902. In 1921 Starr was fatally wounded during a bank robbery at Harrison, Arkansas.

13. Houston Wallace farm, near Elk—June 8, 1894: Bill Dalton was killed by U.S. deputy marshals and local lawmen. The reward for Dalton was $1,700 at the time of his death.

14. Eagletown—July 13, 1894: Frank Cheney, a former Starr gang member and friend of Henry Starr's, was killed by U.S. marshals and members of a posse.

15. Red Fork—July 16, 1894: Bill Cook's gang robbed a Frisco train.

16. Okmulgee—September 21, 1894: Cook's gang robbed the Parkinson general store.

17. Claremore—October 10, 1894: Cook's gang robbed the depot of the MK&T railroad.

18. Checotah—October 10, 1894: Cook's gang robbed the depot of the MK&T railroad.

19. Coretta—October 20, 1894: Cook's gang wrecked and robbed an MK&T train. Gang members activated a switch and forced the train onto a siding, where the moving train struck empty boxcars. None of the passengers or the train's crew was injured in the wreck, but two passengers were wounded during the robbery.

20. Lenapah—November 9, 1894: Cook's gang robbed the Schufeldt and Son store and the post office. During the robbery, Cherokee Bill killed Ernest Melton, one of Lenapah's leading citizens. Pursued by U.S. marshals and Indian light horse, the Cook gang scattered. Bill Cook was captured in New Mexico and returned to Fort Smith to stand trial.

21. Near Nowata—January 30, 1895: Crawford Goldsby (aka Cherokee Bill), former member of the Cook gang, was captured by U.S. deputy marshal Ike Rogers.

22. Catoosa—February 7, 1895: Jim French, a former member of the Cook gang, was wounded while attempting to rob a store. He died a short distance away.

23. Braggs—March 28, 1895: Sam McWilliams (aka the Verdigris Kid) and George Sanders, former members of the Cook gang, were killed robbing the T. J. Madden store.

24. Near McDermott—August 9, 1895: Rufus Buck's gang robbed the Norberg and Orcutt's stores.

25. South of McDermott—August 10, 1895: Rufus Buck's gang was captured by U.S. marshals and Creek light horse along with over 100 volunteers.

26. Eight miles north of Chickasha—October 1, 1897: The Jennings gang robbed a Rock Island train.

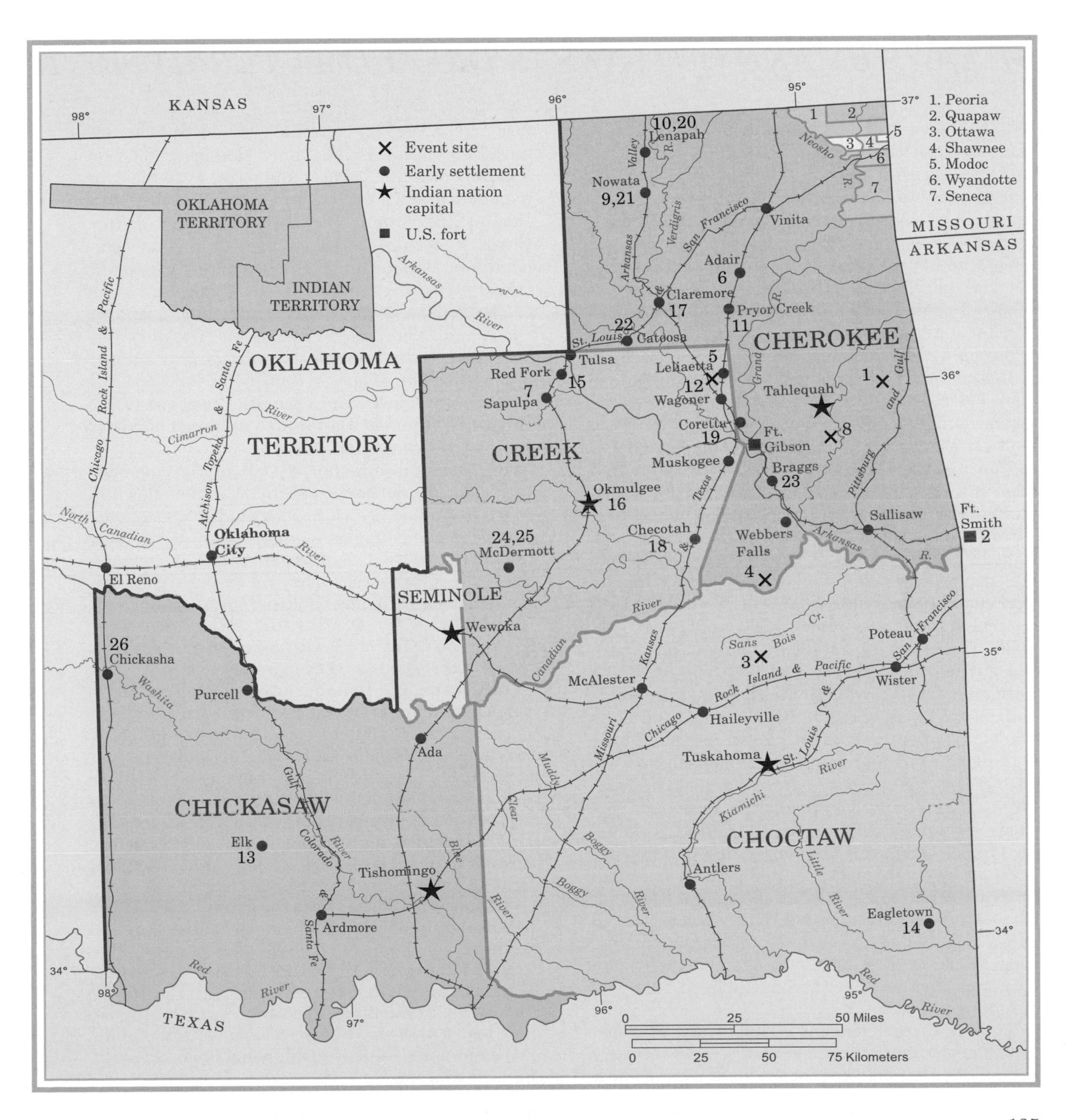

64. LAWMEN AND OUTLAWS IN OKLAHOMA TERRITORY, 1890–1907

Essay by *John R. Lovett*

With the opening of the Unassigned Lands to settlement on April 22, 1889, and the land runs and lottery system that opened the rest of Oklahoma Territory to settlement over the next few years, thousands of settlers converged on the region. Although most of the newcomers were law-abiding citizens, those who had less respect for the law also arrived in Oklahoma Territory. In addition, individual bandits and organized gangs operating from Indian Territory often crossed over into the new settlements to pursue their criminal activities.

Before the establishment of town and county lawmen, federal marshals held the sole responsibility for law enforcement in the new territory. Near the land office at Guthrie, U.S. Marshal Thomas Needles established the headquarters for his three hundred deputies. During this settlement period, the federal marshals were kept busy tracking down criminals within the territory.

In 1892 Henry Andrew "Heck" Thomas became a U.S. deputy marshal in Oklahoma Territory. He had worked for the court of Judge Isaac Parker from 1886 to 1892 and was a seasoned veteran of law enforcement. Thomas is considered by many to have been one of the great lawmen of the Southwest. While working in Oklahoma Territory, Thomas joined forces with fellow deputy marshals Bill Tilghman and Chris Madsen, and they became known as the "Three Guardsmen" of the territory. Thomas selected the most dangerous outlaws to pursue because the largest rewards were paid for them. He was wounded six times in gunfights and headed the posse that killed the famous Oklahoma Territory outlaw Bill Doolin.

As in any part of the United States, although crimes committed by individuals against individuals took place in Oklahoma Territory, the organized gangs were what proved to be especially troublesome. Some of these outlaw gangs and their more infamous members have become an important part of American folklore.

The James-Younger gang is said to have provided the blueprint for the organized Oklahoma Territory gangs. Bob Dalton (leader of the Dalton gang and a former U.S. deputy marshal) is said to have admired the success of the James-Younger gang. Bob and his brothers, Emmett and Grat, were the core members of the gang. Other outlaws—such as Bill Doolin, Bill Powers, Dick Broadwell, and "Bitter Creek" Newcomb—periodically served as gang members. The Daltons' first Oklahoma Territory train robbery took place in May 1891 at Wharton.

The demise of the Dalton gang came about on October 5, 1892, not in Oklahoma Territory but across the line in Kansas, when the gang attempted to rob two banks at once in Coffeyville. Bob and Grat Dalton were killed, along with Bill Powers and Dick Broadwell. Emmett Dalton was wounded and captured by the town's defenders.

Because of a lame horse, Dalton gang member Bill Doolin did not participate in the fatal Coffeyville raid. Doolin had been a cowboy but became an outlaw after a shootout in southern Kansas. He was considered by the U.S. marshals and local lawmen to be a very dangerous man. He was charged with many crimes, including bank and train robbery, selling whiskey to Indians, rustling, and murder. Considered the "King of the Outlaws," he was pursued by several of the best U.S. marshals.

Bill Doolin, Bill Dalton, and other gang members participated in the largest outlaw-lawmen gunfight in Oklahoma Territory history. This famous gunfight took place at Ingalls, Oklahoma Territory, on the morning of September 1, 1893, when a posse led by U.S. deputy marshal John W. Hixon attempted to capture or kill members of the Doolin-Dalton gang. Doolin and his gang escaped, with the exception of Arkansas Tom Jones, who was captured. The gunfight at Ingalls left three deputy marshals dead.

Although Doolin survived the gunfight at Ingalls, he was captured by Bill Tilghman at Eureka Springs, Arkansas, on January 15, 1896. Large crowds of interested viewers gathered in Guthrie, Oklahoma Territory, when Tilghman returned with Doolin. On July 5, 1896, Doolin escaped from jail. On August 25, 1896, a posse led by Heck Thomas killed Doolin as he prepared to leave Oklahoma Territory with his wife and son.

In 1898 an Oklahoma newspaper reported that the "outlaw days" in Oklahoma were coming to an end. With the continued settlement of Oklahoma Territory through the establishment of new towns, the formation of county governments, and statehood in 1907, the days of organized outlaw gangs truly came to an end. Law enforcement became more effective with statehood in establishing control over what had once been vast unpopulated areas ruled by the six-gun.

Heck Thomas, U.S. deputy marshal, Oklahoma Territory, 1892. (Courtesy Western History Collections, University of Oklahoma Libraries)

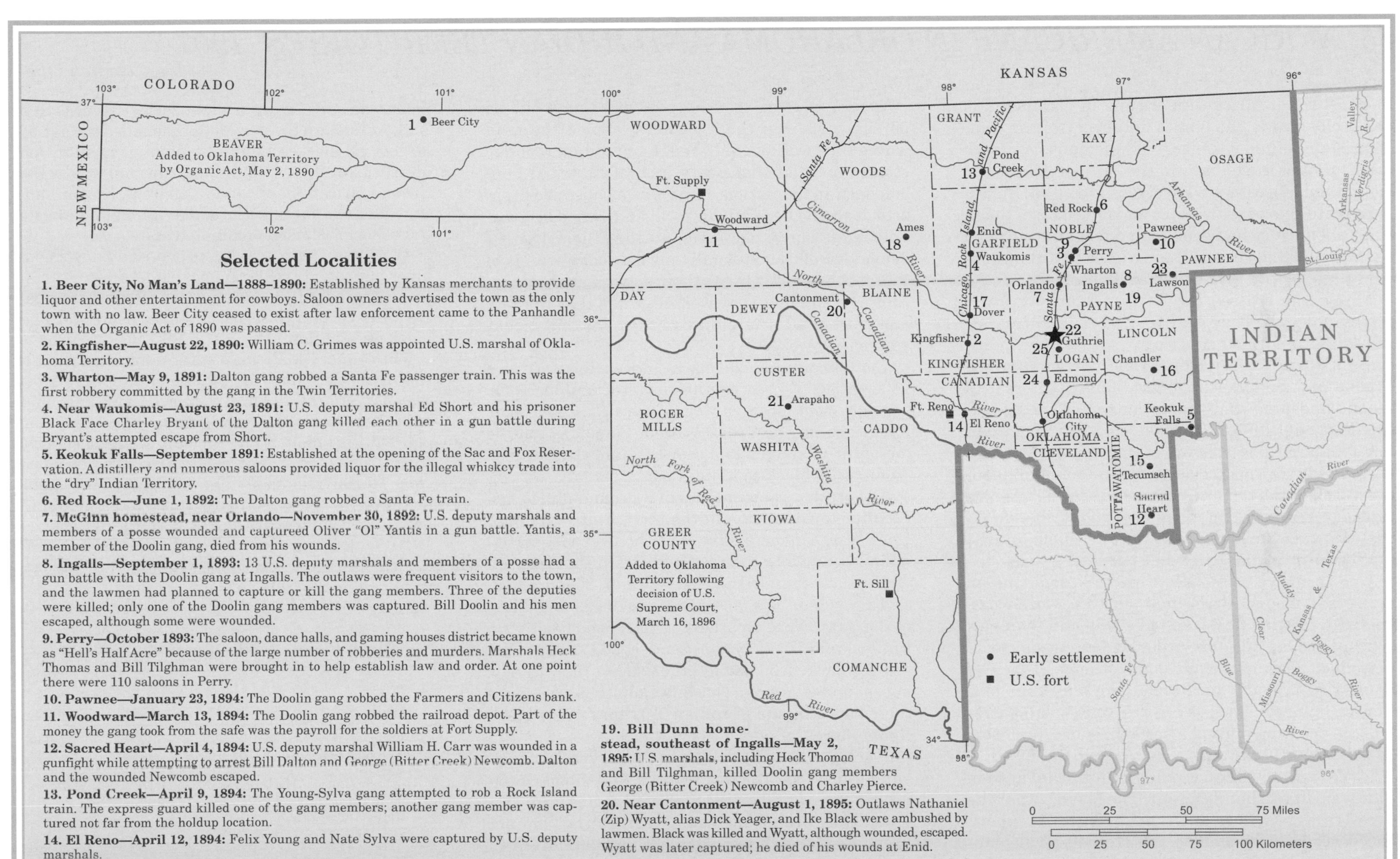

Selected Localities

1. Beer City, No Man's Land—1888–1890: Established by Kansas merchants to provide liquor and other entertainment for cowboys. Saloon owners advertised the town as the only town with no law. Beer City ceased to exist after law enforcement came to the Panhandle when the Organic Act of 1890 was passed.

2. Kingfisher—August 22, 1890: William C. Grimes was appointed U.S. marshal of Oklahoma Territory.

3. Wharton—May 9, 1891: Dalton gang robbed a Santa Fe passenger train. This was the first robbery committed by the gang in the Twin Territories.

4. Near Waukomis—August 23, 1891: U.S. deputy marshal Ed Short and his prisoner Black Face Charley Bryant of the Dalton gang killed each other in a gun battle during Bryant's attempted escape from Short.

5. Keokuk Falls—September 1891: Established at the opening of the Sac and Fox Reservation. A distillery and numerous saloons provided liquor for the illegal whiskey trade into the "dry" Indian Territory.

6. Red Rock—June 1, 1892: The Dalton gang robbed a Santa Fe train.

7. McGinn homestead, near Orlando—November 30, 1892: U.S. deputy marshals and members of a posse wounded and captureed Oliver "Ol" Yantis in a gun battle. Yantis, a member of the Doolin gang, died from his wounds.

8. Ingalls—September 1, 1893: 13 U.S. deputy marshals and members of a posse had a gun battle with the Doolin gang at Ingalls. The outlaws were frequent visitors to the town, and the lawmen had planned to capture or kill the gang members. Three of the deputies were killed; only one of the Doolin gang members was captured. Bill Doolin and his men escaped, although some were wounded.

9. Perry—October 1893: The saloon, dance halls, and gaming houses district became known as "Hell's Half Acre" because of the large number of robberies and murders. Marshals Heck Thomas and Bill Tilghman were brought in to help establish law and order. At one point there were 110 saloons in Perry.

10. Pawnee—January 23, 1894: The Doolin gang robbed the Farmers and Citizens bank.

11. Woodward—March 13, 1894: The Doolin gang robbed the railroad depot. Part of the money the gang took from the safe was the payroll for the soldiers at Fort Supply.

12. Sacred Heart—April 4, 1894: U.S. deputy marshal William H. Carr was wounded in a gunfight while attempting to arrest Bill Dalton and George (Bitter Creek) Newcomb. Dalton and the wounded Newcomb escaped.

13. Pond Creek—April 9, 1894: The Young-Sylva gang attempted to rob a Rock Island train. The express guard killed one of the gang members; another gang member was captured not far from the holdup location.

14. El Reno—April 12, 1894: Felix Young and Nate Sylva were captured by U.S. deputy marshals.

15. Tecumseh—May 1894: U.S. deputy marshals broke up a horse-rustling organization, arresting 17 prominent citizens. The horse thieves operated from Arkansas to Arizona.

16. Chandler—July 31, 1894: The Bill Cook gang robbed the Lincoln County Bank. During the robbery and pursuit, a citizen of Chandler was killed, and Elmer Lucas of the Cook gang was wounded and captured.

17. Dover—April 3, 1895: The Doolin gang robbed a Rock Island train.

18. Near Ames—April 4, 1895: U.S. deputy marshals overtook the Dalton gang, and in a gun battle, Doolin gang member Tulsa Jack Blake was killed. The rest of the Doolin gang escaped.

19. Bill Dunn homestead, southeast of Ingalls—May 2, 1895: U.S. marshals, including Heck Thomas and Bill Tilghman, killed Doolin gang members George (Bitter Creek) Newcomb and Charley Pierce.

20. Near Cantonment—August 1, 1895: Outlaws Nathaniel (Zip) Wyatt, alias Dick Yeager, and Ike Black were ambushed by lawmen. Black was killed and Wyatt, although wounded, escaped. Wyatt was later captured; he died of his wounds at Enid.

21. Near Arapaho—March 5, 1896: U.S. deputy marshal Chris Madsen and a posse of farmers killed Doolin gang member George Waightman, alias Red Buck.

22. Guthrie—July 5, 1896: Bill Doolin (captured by U.S. deputy marshal Bill Tilghman at Eureka Springs, Arkansas, on January 15, 1896) escaped from the federal jail.

23. Near Lawson—August 25, 1896: Doolin was killed by lawmen led by U.S. deputy marshal Heck Thomas. Doolin's body was taken to Guthrie, where several thousand citizens viewed it.

24. Edmond—August 16, 1897: Brothers Al and Frank Jennings, along with former Doolin gang member Richard "Little Dick" West and the O'Malley brothers, robbed a Santa Fe passenger train.

25. Four miles south of Guthrie—April 8, 1897: U.S. deputy marshals Bill Tilghman and Heck Thomas, with the assistance of a posse, killed Richard "Little Dick" West.

65. AFRICAN AMERICANS IN OKLAHOMA AND INDIAN TERRITORIES, 1907

Essay by *Danney Goble*

The history of African Americans in Oklahoma is much older than the state's and every bit as complex. Many of today's black Oklahomans can trace their families' roots back to the Trail of Tears. For most, their ancestors were slaves forced by Indian masters to share what whites had forced upon them. After all, slavery had been high among the cultural adaptations that so impressed whites that they honored these as the Five *Civilized* Tribes.

Many who crossed the Trail of Tears were not slaves, however. They were free, often because they shared both African American and Native American ancestry. Within every tribe, particularly the Creeks and Seminoles, generations of interracial unions had produced generations of offspring neither black nor Indian. They were both, and neither. For official purposes, however (most important was an individual's racial classification on tribal population rolls), they had to be one or the other. Which category—African American or Native American—they were assigned depended pretty much on who did the counting and for what purpose.

Upon completing the westward trek, some Indian masters immediately set their slaves to work clearing land, plowing fields, and planting and then harvesting crops. In short order, a few managed to reproduce territorial equivalents of some of the Old South's greatest plantations. One was that of a Choctaw planter who put nearly five thousand acres into cotton, every stalk of it seeded, tended, and picked by the five hundred black slaves who were his.

More typical was an economic and social system that was altogether different. The slavery that the Five Tribes practiced and that their slaves experienced scarcely resembled the stereotypical plantation slavery of the southern Cotton Kingdom. Granted, slaves were slaves wherever there was slavery, and slaves had no choice but to labor under and produce for their masters. Within those bounds, however, these particular slaves did have choices, and the choices they made resulted in a form of slavery peculiar to—maybe even unique to—Indian Territory.

Indian masters may have owned them, but no person (not even their masters) owned the land where they worked and lived. Each Indian republic stoutly insisted that every inch of its tribal land belonged to the nation. Land was a collective property; it should be available to all and owned by none. So long as slaves delivered all that their masters demanded of them (usually measured in pounds of cotton or bushels of corn), those slaves had their own choices about how they worked, when they worked, and most of all where they worked, for that meant where they would live.

Fundamental to slavery in Indian Territory was what the slaves created: their own semiautonomous, all-black communities. Many were clustered near Muskogee, in the Creek Nation. Some can still be found in Oklahoma, and they have survived as predominantly black communities.

The presence of numerous black communities was peculiar to Oklahoma in the territorial years. The Civil War, Emancipation, and the eventual settlement of outsiders changed nothing in that respect. Older, slave-founded black communities flourished, and altogether new ones sprang to life as well. Most of the latter were creations of those whom both the Indians and their freedpersons called "States Negroes": blacks who had left the Old South, with new hopes for new places. Not infrequently, they placed their hopes in one of Indian Territory's new black communities, of which Boley was one.

Much the same happened in Oklahoma Territory, and for most of the same reasons. Oklahoma Territory appeared just as the Southern states were systematically disenfranchising, segregating, and not infrequently lynching their black populations. Even Kansas, once seen to be a promised land by so-called Exodusters, was turning its back on an honored abolitionist tradition.

Chronology, circumstance, and geography all came together in Oklahoma Territory. Thousands of African American men and women were among the famed "Eighty-niners." They, like later black homesteaders, tended to cluster in well-defined areas. The most famous was near Guthrie, where former Kansas State Auditor Edward Preston McCabe founded the nation's largest all-black community, naming it after John Mercer Langston: a Virginian, Langston was by then the one African American in Congress. Rumor had it that McCabe intended to make all-black Langston the basis for a black-dominated state.

Of course, that never happened—and never could have happened. White homesteaders were certain to outnumber black ones, just as white homesteaders were certain to resist anything even hinting of black domination.

With time, Oklahoma's whites did more than resist. Although many of Oklahoma Territory's first schools were racially mixed, school codes later mandated absolute racial segregation. When Oklahoma entered the union, it had the only state constitution with schoolhouse segregation as a constitutional principle. In 1907, the new state segregated other public facilities by statute. In only three more years, the new state completed the cycle of southern racism: in 1910, Oklahoma systematically and fraudulently denied African Americans their most fundamental right of all—the right to vote.

Black Population by Territory, 1890–1907

Territory	Census 1907	1900	1890
Indian Territory	80,649	36,853	18,636
Oklahoma Territory	31,511	18,831	2,973
Total	112,160	55,684	21,609

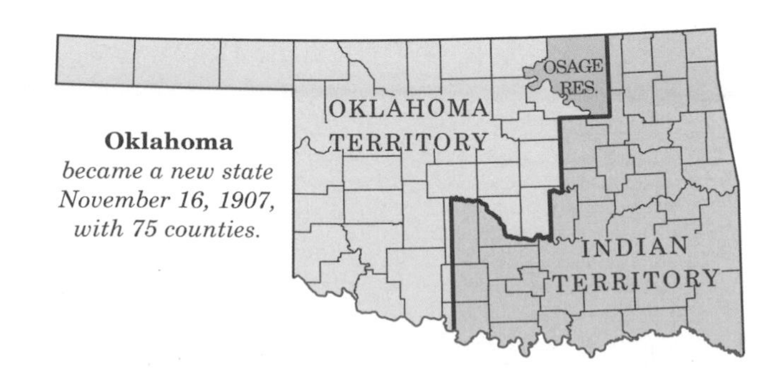

Oklahoma *became a new state November 16, 1907, with 75 counties.*

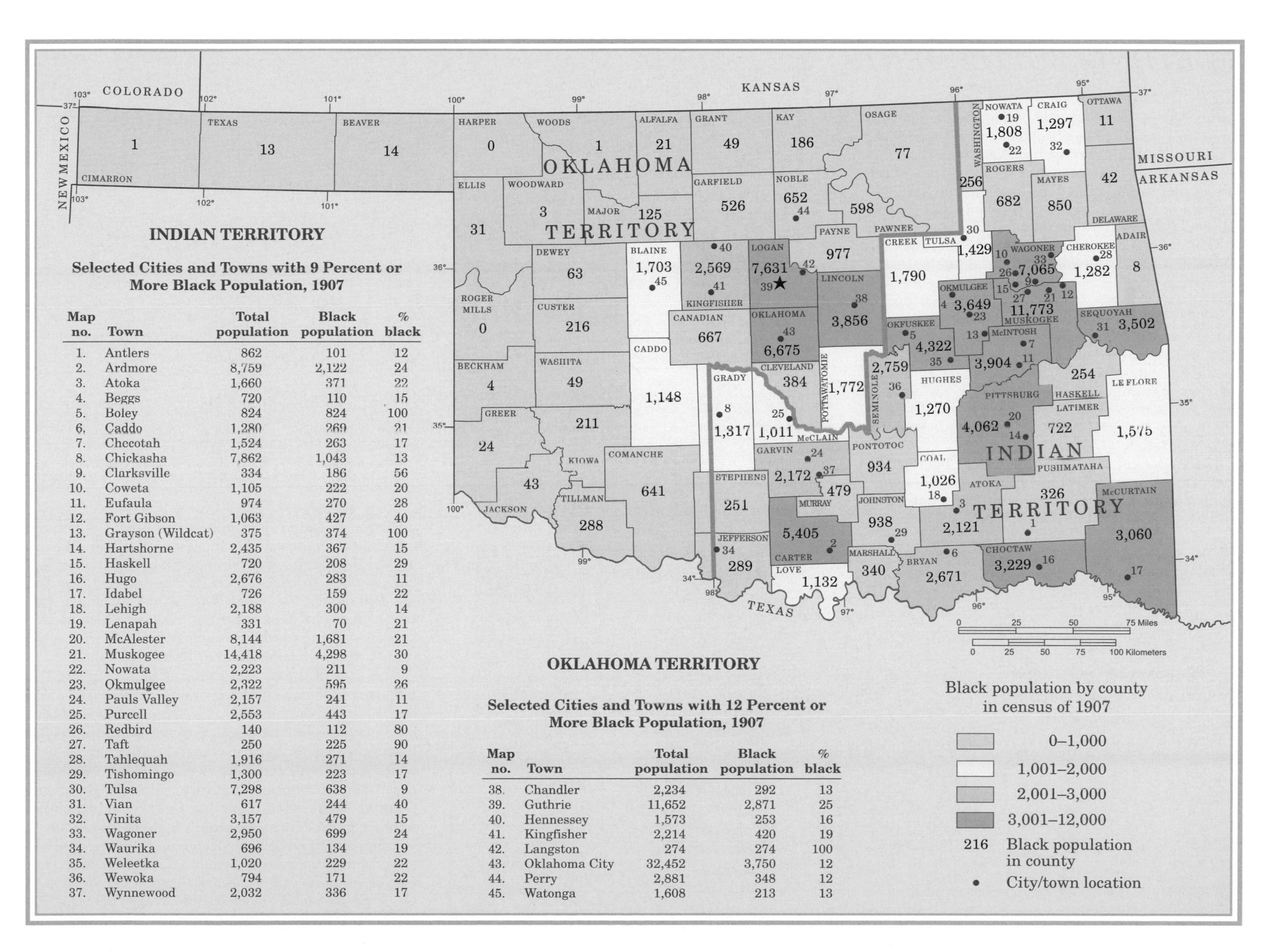

INDIAN TERRITORY

Selected Cities and Towns with 9 Percent or More Black Population, 1907

Map no.	Town	Total population	Black population	% black
1.	Antlers	862	101	12
2.	Ardmore	8,759	2,122	24
3.	Atoka	1,660	371	22
4.	Beggs	720	110	15
5.	Boley	824	824	100
6.	Caddo	1,280	269	21
7.	Checotah	1,524	263	17
8.	Chickasha	7,862	1,043	13
9.	Clarksville	334	186	56
10.	Coweta	1,105	222	20
11.	Eufaula	974	270	28
12.	Fort Gibson	1,063	427	40
13.	Grayson (Wildcat)	375	374	100
14.	Hartshorne	2,435	367	15
15.	Haskell	720	208	29
16.	Hugo	2,676	283	11
17.	Idabel	726	159	22
18.	Lehigh	2,188	300	14
19.	Lenapah	331	70	21
20.	McAlester	8,144	1,681	21
21.	Muskogee	14,418	4,298	30
22.	Nowata	2,223	211	9
23.	Okmulgee	2,322	595	26
24.	Pauls Valley	2,157	241	11
25.	Purcell	2,553	443	17
26.	Redbird	140	112	80
27.	Taft	250	225	90
28.	Tahlequah	1,916	271	14
29.	Tishomingo	1,300	223	17
30.	Tulsa	7,298	638	9
31.	Vian	617	244	40
32.	Vinita	3,157	479	15
33.	Wagoner	2,950	699	24
34.	Waurika	696	134	19
35.	Weleetka	1,020	229	22
36.	Wewoka	794	171	22
37.	Wynnewood	2,032	336	17

OKLAHOMA TERRITORY

Selected Cities and Towns with 12 Percent or More Black Population, 1907

Map no.	Town	Total population	Black population	% black
38.	Chandler	2,234	292	13
39.	Guthrie	11,652	2,871	25
40.	Hennessey	1,573	253	16
41.	Kingfisher	2,214	420	19
42.	Langston	274	274	100
43.	Oklahoma City	32,452	3,750	12
44.	Perry	2,881	348	12
45.	Watonga	1,608	213	13

66. ETHNIC SETTLEMENTS

Essay by *Danney Goble*

Rarely have Oklahomans appreciated the fact that the state's post-Indian settlement coincided with the high tides of immigration into America. The nineteenth century's irregular but steady trickle of the foreign-born swelled to flood stage in the final two decades of that century and reached tidal proportions in the first two decades of the twentieth. It may have been coincidence that 1907 marked both Oklahoma's entry to the union and the one-year record for immigration, but the convergence was anything but irrelevant. After all, roughly one in twelve of the Oklahomans who greeted statehood in 1907 were foreign-born or the children of foreign-born immigrants. That ratio is similar to that of people claiming African American ancestry within the new state's population. Moreover, the total of first- and second-generation immigrants (130,430) was nearly twice that of the state's American Indian population (75,012).

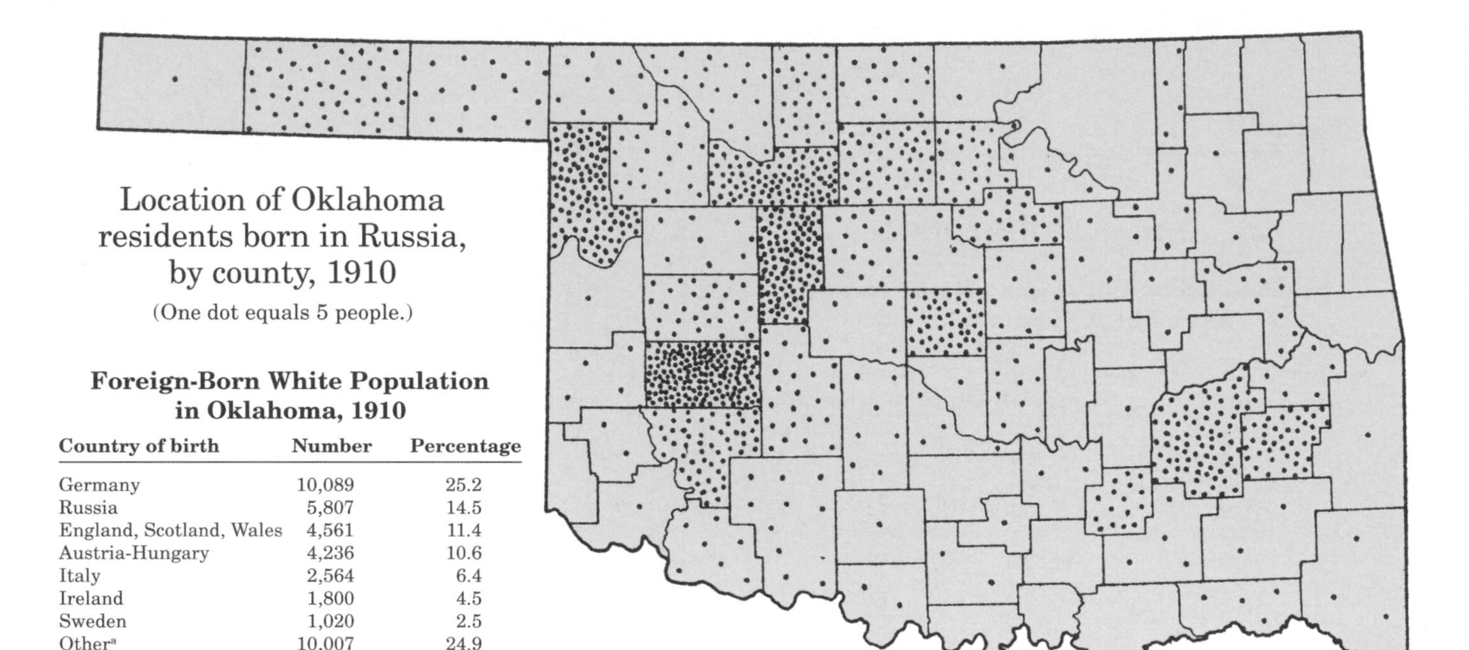

Location of Oklahoma residents born in Russia, by county, 1910

(One dot equals 5 people.)

Foreign-Born White Population in Oklahoma, 1910

Country of birth	Number	Percentage
Germany	10,089	25.2
Russia	5,807	14.5
England, Scotland, Wales	4,561	11.4
Austria-Hungary	4,236	10.6
Italy	2,564	6.4
Ireland	1,800	4.5
Sweden	1,020	2.5
Other[a]	10,007	24.9
Total	40,084	100.0

[a] Most of the non-European immigrants came from Canada (2,831) and Mexico (2,645).

Two historical circumstances multiplied the impact of those numbers. First, only a few nations were disproportionate contributors of their sons and daughters. (The great bulk came from seven nations, all European, and two neighboring countries—each the birthplace of a thousand or more statehood-era Oklahomans.) Second, upon reaching Oklahoma, the foreign-born tended to concentrate in a relatively few and identifiable regions. One effect of this settlement pattern is that the most meaningful way to discuss this subject—and to present it cartographically—is at the county and area levels, rather than statewide.

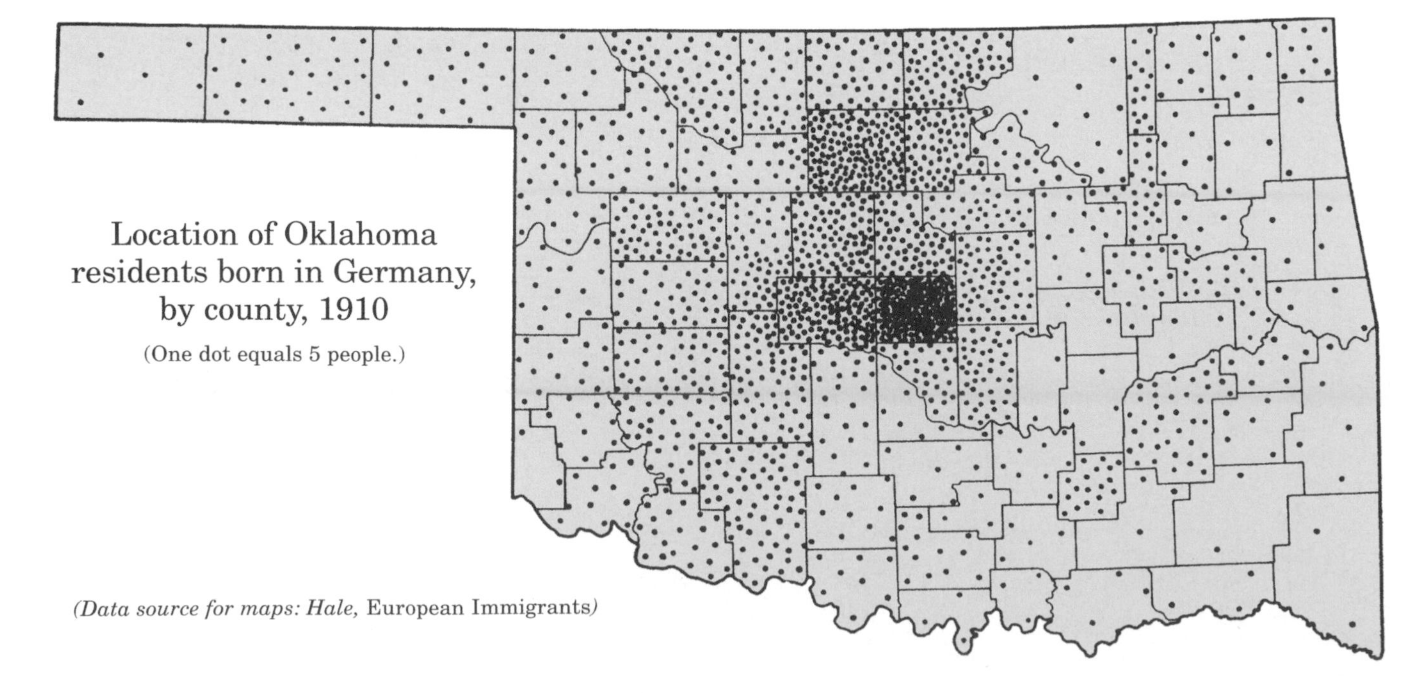

Location of Oklahoma residents born in Germany, by county, 1910

(One dot equals 5 people.)

(Data source for maps: Hale, European Immigrants*)*

The case of the largest group is illustrative of this pattern. Oklahoma's first decennial federal census—that of 1910—enumerated 10,089 Oklahomans who had been born in Germany. The German-born thus accounted for just over a quarter of the new state's entire foreign-born white population, and most were found in a handful of north-central counties. One in ten lived in Oklahoma County. Neighboring Canadian County had a smaller number but did have the state's highest percentage of German birth. Garfield and Kingfisher counties also had significant numbers of Germans. Like most of the foreign-born (and of the American-born, for that matter), Germans scattered anywhere and everywhere that the siren call of fertile soil beckoned, but a surprising number ignored that summons in favor of urban life. Indeed, three cities (Oklahoma City, El Reno, and Enid) provided homes for nearly a tenth—960—of Oklahoma's German-born Oklahomans in 1910.

Much the same was true of another group considered German, if not by the census takers, by everyone else—themselves included. The census designated them as Russian-born, and they did come from at least six nationalities within the vast Russian empire even though they were German in culture and language. For more than a century, their ethnicity scarcely had mattered. Anxious to colonize vast, underused regions, a series of Russian czars had lured them with promises of the autonomy that produced a string of self-contained German-speaking colonies from Bessarabia to the middle Volga. That changed in 1871, when absorption rather than colonization of these German communities became the imperial ukase. Year by year, their oppression increased. Year by year, more of these ethnic Germans fled. Most became farmers on America's Great Plains.

Those who settled Oklahoma's plains fell almost entirely into two roughly equal groups. About half of the 4,300 Germans from Russia were Mennonites. The first arrived with the opening of the Cheyenne-Arapaho Reservation, in 1891. Two years later, others crowded the starting line for the great run into the Cherokee Outlet. As a result, one concentration of Mennonites ran from Gotebo, Bessie, and Corn to Geary; another extended from Fairview to Meno to Enid, past Medford, and beyond.

Almost as many of these immigrant Germans were Lutheran. Religious differences aside, the demographic consequences were similar: concentrations of Lutheran settlements near Okeene as well as in southern Noble and northern Payne counties. Densest was the area around Shattuck, in Ellis County, where, in 1910, one resident in six was Russian born and German speaking.

The coal fields of southeastern Oklahoma were a very special case. Coal mining communities were known alternately for ethnic diversity or for ethnic autonomy, depending upon how and where one looked. Starting in the depressed 1870s, Welsh-, Scots-, Irish-, and English-born miners poured into Indian Territory, more by way of declining Pennsylvania fields than directly from their countries of origin. Similarly, Italians, Lithuanians, Slovaks, Poles, Hungarians, and Russians came to the mines in the 1880s; some were veterans of eastern fields, while others were newcomers recruited by agents. Some mining communities—McAlester, Wilburton, and Alderson among them—became polyglot mixtures. Others amounted to equivalents of a Little Italy (Krebs, most notably) or a Little Russia (one being Hartshorne—which still maintains one of the few, and oldest, Russian Orthodox churches found west of the Mississippi and south of Alaska). Even as late as 1930, 5,116 of Oklahoma's estimated 5,465 coal miners were European immigrants or their children.

By then, the former tide of European immigration was less than a flood—indeed, barely a trickle—for World War I temporarily shut it down. Peace brought both Harding-era "normalcy" as well as the nation's first, and tightly restrictive, quota system, beginning in 1921 and worsening thereafter, with the worst coming in 1924. The Great Depression then nailed the coffin shut on immigration.

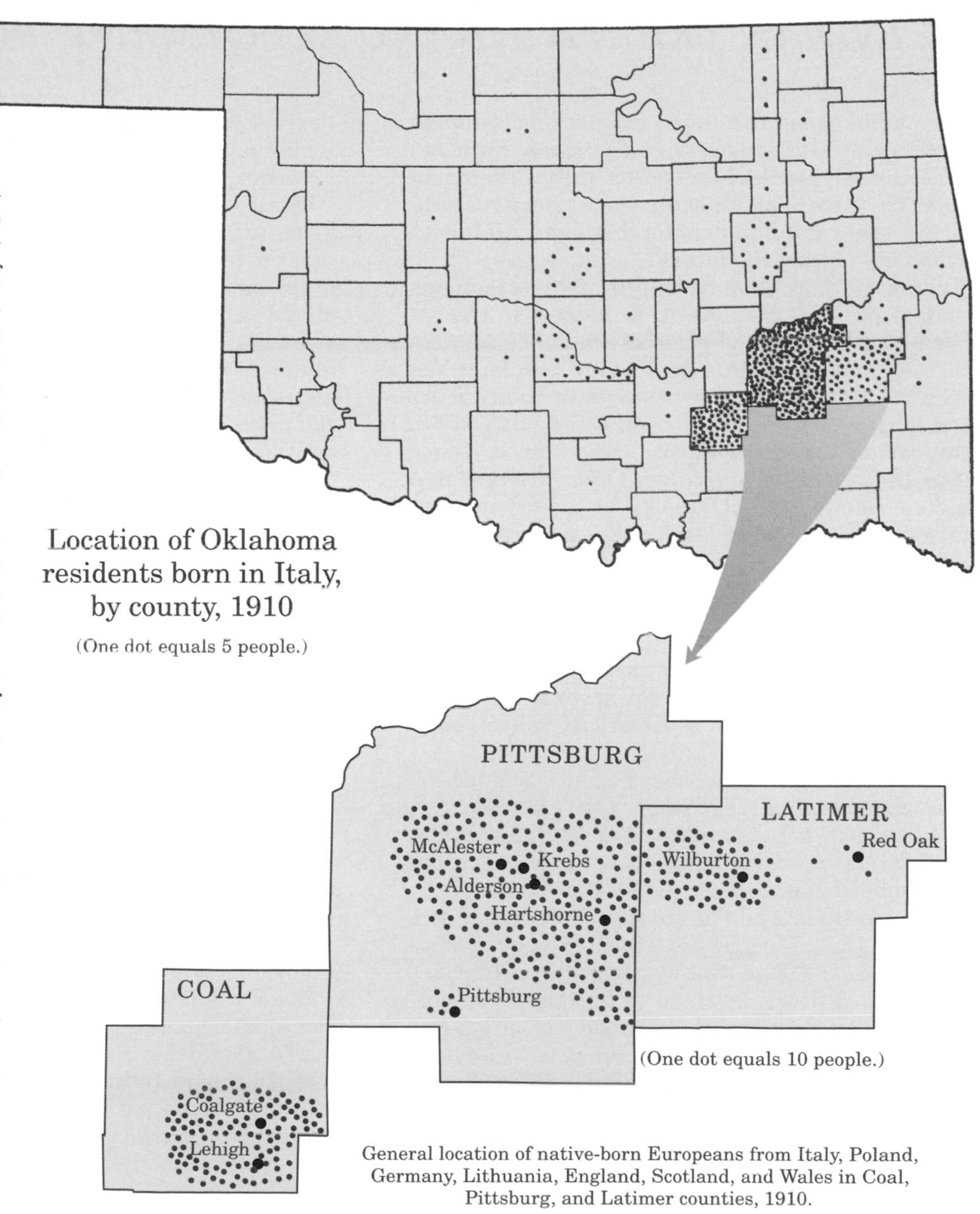

Location of Oklahoma residents born in Italy, by county, 1910

(One dot equals 5 people.)

General location of native-born Europeans from Italy, Poland, Germany, Lithuania, England, Scotland, and Wales in Coal, Pittsburg, and Latimer counties, 1910.

Many of these immigrants, especially Italians (who began arriving in this area as early as 1875), found work in the mining industry. After their arrival, Italians constituted the largest foreign-born workforce in the mines. In 1910, half of the population of the mining town of Krebs was Italian.

67. INDIAN TERRITORY AND ALLOTMENT, 1890–1907

Essay by *Michael D. Green & Danney Goble*

Allotment spelled the end of the nations of Indian Territory as landed sovereign republics. Although the Dawes General Allotment Act of 1887 exempted them, the pace of allotment in the western reservations and the public outcry for dissolving all Indian tribalism forecast the future.

Supporters of allotment used many arguments against the Five Nations. As foreigners in the nations, non-Indians had no access to public services such as schools; neither could they own land, not even the ground on which they built their homes and businesses, and of course they had no voice in government. These disabilities, they claimed, denied them their rights as Americans. Others charged that Indian Territory had become a haven for outlaws. In addition, the railroads and other corporate interests were eager to gain access to tribally owned land, coal, oil, and timber resources. Together these groups formed a powerful lobby designed to convince Congress that the communal ownership of some thirty-one thousand square miles of rich land by five tribes of Indians totaling less than seventy thousand people was antithetical to American values, progress, and prosperity.

The Indian Territory tribes began to feel federal pressure soon after the passage of the Allotment Act. In 1889, the Cherokees refused to sell their Outlet, preferring to lease the land to cattle companies, but President Benjamin Harrison disallowed such leasing arrangements and forced the Cherokees to sell. Then, in 1893, Congress extended the policy of allotment to the Five Nations when it authorized President Grover Cleveland to appoint a commission to open negotiations with the tribal governments. Members of the Dawes Commission—named after its chairman (and author of the 1887 allotment act), retired senator Henry M. Dawes of Massachusetts—traveled to Indian Territory in 1894 to open talks with tribal authorities. They met with such steadfast resistance that they convinced lawmakers to force compliance. In 1895, Congress ordered a thorough land survey and in 1896 authorized the Dawes Commission to make census rolls of the citizens of each nation in preparation for mandated allotment. Seeing no alternative, the governments of the Five Nations opened talks with the commission. If allotment was inevitable, they reasoned, perhaps cooperation could win better terms.

Even while these negotiations were under way, however, Congress enacted the final blow to the sovereignty of the Five Nations through the draconian Curtis Act, passed in 1898, which abolished all tribal laws and courts and brought all residents of Indian Territory—Indian as well as non-Indian—under direct federal authority. The tribal governments continued to meet until allotment was completed, but they could do nothing without presidential approval. The Choctaws and Chickasaws reached agreement with the commission in 1897, the Seminoles in 1898, the Creeks in 1901, and the Cherokees in 1902. A law passed in 1906 finalized the process by subjecting the executive branches of the tribal governments to direct federal control, including the power of appointment.

The basic process involved the simple arithmetic of surveying and evaluating every acre of Indian land, subtracting those tracts to be maintained as cemeteries or set aside as town sites or resource-rich lands to be sold later by auction, and dividing the amount of land that remained by the number of people on each nation's tribal rolls. Complicating factors included the distinction between individual homestead lands and communal "surplus" lands, provisions to prevent the sale of homestead lands for a set period of time, and the difficulty of determining the quotient of Indian blood for each person in an Indian nation.

Even after the allotments were made, many of the Indian citizens of the former nation neither selected allotments nor accepted the allotments selected for them. Rather, they ignored or rebuffed the efforts of the Dawes Commission and the tribal governments to complete the process. While such passive resistance was widespread, more active and assertive opposition also occurred. Some Cherokees reactivated the Keetoowah society, a secret order that in the 1850s had fought against the influence of Anglo-American culture in the nation. Among the Creeks, Chitto Harjo (roughly translated as "Crazy Snake") led a movement that attempted to reestablish preconstitutional forms of government. Committed to upholding the 1832 treaty that granted the Creeks perpetual and absolute title to their Indian Territory lands, the so-called Snake government called a council in 1901 that denied the right of the U.S. Congress to nullify treaties and forbade any Creek citizen to accept an allotment on pain of whipping. This resistance movement stalled the allotment process among the Creeks, terrified both the Dawes commissioners and the allotted Creeks, and caused the federal government to send the U.S. cavalry and U.S. marshals into the nation to restore order. Chitto Harjo's opposition stimulated similar demonstrations among the Choctaws and the Cherokee Keetoowahs. Federal forces quelled them as well.

The insistence of Congress on the allotment of Indian Territory had been caused by many factors. But only the corporations achieved their goal. None of the allotment agreements negotiated with the Dawes Commission produced surplus land for homesteads, and even the most acculturated Indians valued their tribal institutions and wished to preserve these institutions—if not for themselves, for their more traditional fellows. Their solution was to enter Indian Territory into the union as a separate state. Like the decisions to accept allotment, the separate-statehood movement in Indian Territory was a recognition that if some form of statehood was inevitable, the best form was one that the Indians would design and control.

But Congress was committed to the idea that Oklahoma Territory and Indian Territory should be fused into a single state. Like the national governments of the people who had made it their home for nearly a century, there seemed no longer to be a place for an Indian territory in the United States.

Grafting: A Brisk Trade

"Grafting" was the name widely and unabashedly used for what swiftly emerged as the Indian Territory's principal, and most lucrative, industry: the brisk trade in Indian allotments. Not even the best-intended restrictions could stop it. In fact, they may have encouraged it. If for every rule there were many evasions, that meant that there was just that much more confusion among the Indians—and that much more opportunity for the grafters.

Land that could not be sold might be leased, maybe for as long as ninety-nine years, maybe for as little as five dollars. There were ways to persuade the illiterate and the infirm to give others their powers of attorney. Because every citizen, from infants on up, shared in the division, guardians had to be assigned for the young and the incompetent—but rarely was anyone held accountable for taking advantage of the allottees. Then there was the ultimate evasion: all restrictions on the sale of a given allotment ended automatically on the death of the original allotee, no matter how sudden or suspicious that death might be.

In addition, grafting affected entire towns. Occupants of lots were eligible to buy them prior to auction at half their appraised worth. Among the beneficiaries were many "occupants" who did not live in the territory, much less in the towns involved. Tulsa is but one example; there, nearly every occupant exercised this option, and several exercised the option many times over, buying other lots using the names of friends, relatives, employees, and other "dummies." Some invented names to buy cheaply unoccupied lots on which they claimed to have erected invented improvements. So common was this last practice that the total proceeds credited to the Creek Nation for the sale of every unoccupied town lot in the city of Tulsa was exactly $659—a pauper's price for what was already princely property.

Allotment of tribal lands created wealth for some, poverty for others, confusion for most. So confusing was it that in 1906 the U.S. Senate appointed a Select Committee to Investigate Affairs in the Indian Territory. After a series of open hearings in a number of cities, the senators filed their official report. Its two volumes of testimony mostly gathered dust in a few libraries, but the brittle pages still record the cry of those whose confusion grew from their sense of utter betrayal.

68. THE TWIN TERRITORIES, 1900

Essay by *Danney Goble*

Few scenes are more associated with Oklahoma than hard-charging horsemen tearing through clouds of dust toward a future in which nothing was certain and everything was expected. Overlooked are the scenes that opened the moment those riders dismounted, but to understand Oklahoma is to study those scenes and ponder their significance. Look for them in Oklahoma Territory's brand-new towns and cities.

Not that most pioneers lived in towns; the great majority were on farms covering outlying quarter-sections. Moreover, towns owed everything, starting with their presence, to the country. Town folk depended absolutely on there being enough country folk to buy what they sold or want what they did. Ironically, this very dependency gave towns their importance. Because they had to serve the country, the towns built the territory.

That started with the fact that too many towns competed for the trade of too few farmers. Too many had too much ambition for all to succeed—to exist, for that matter. Some won. More lost. Whatever the outcome, competition was always somewhere behind nearly everything that happened. In the beginning, a quirk of timing put it right behind.

So intense had been the need to silence all the commotion over the Unassigned Lands that the federal government had permitted settlement of the region a year before giving it a government. Until then, the settlers were on their own, not that they minded. Self-interest coalesced into common purpose, and the territory's townspeople did what they had to do—everything. They had only themselves, but that was enough. Parents turned out to build their children's schools with lumber donated by merchants, on land given without cost, and with teachers paid by subscription. Lot owners had to take on the original survey, lay out the first streets, and mark off their own lots. All in all, if the people did not do it, it did not happen; that is both how and why so much did happen.

Following the passage of the Organic Act in 1890, Congress set up a territorial government, and public officials began to shoulder such duties. It was hard to tell any difference, though. Governments merely did what citizens had done before; they did anything they had to do to promote their towns.

This was why publicly funded schools sprang up quickly. The better a community's schools, the greater its allure, which was why territorial schools had to be the best. Water mains, sewer lines, sidewalks, paved and lighted streets—a city infrastructure—likewise came as soon as possible. As for moral codes and public righteousness, everyone might know that drink was bad for the soul, that prostitution was deadly to the spirit, and that Satan himself was a gambler; still, that was no reason to let a few fanatics drive off paying customers. Let the church crowd have its laws, but let other people have what they wanted, too.

These were all public acts, performed by public officials. Other acts could not be done as openly. Some involved gifts of public money to private interests, and railroads were the biggest private interests around. They had been for some time, and they had learned to make the most of it. Before they laid a rail or put a nail in a depot, they found out who was willing to pay, and how much. Pay the railroad, get the rail line; it had been as simple as that.

But when Oklahoma Territory came along, it was no longer simple, not even legal, so inventiveness had to enter where the law ended. Take the city that printed its own scrip, exchanged scrip for dollars, handed the dollars to a railroad, then took back the scrip as tax payments—saloon taxes, in fact. This was a case of the race going not to the swift but to the sneaky: Oklahoma City, it was.

The blast of a railroad's whistle first signaled that change was coming to the former Indian Territory as well. Bucklucksey, for example, was nothing more than a village in the Choctaw Nation until J. J. McAlester began mining coal nearby. Once railroads started buying all the coal that they needed and shipped the rest to anywhere that anybody would buy it, Bucklucksey metamorphosed into the industrial city of McAlester. In the Creek Nation, pretty much the same thing happened: when the east–west railway reached the Arkansas River, a Creek village called Lochapocha became a cow town named Tulsa. People poured into the Indian nations, most because riding herd or renting land or working the coal mines offered more than they had elsewhere. Never to be citizens, in no time these non-Indians were a majority in what even they still called Indian Territory.

Frontier photographer William Prettyman had a small tower built on which he positioned cameras so that an associate could capture the beginning of the Run of 1893. Prettyman himself joined the thousands of hopeful settlers in the race for land. (Courtesy Western History Collections, University of Oklahoma Libraries)

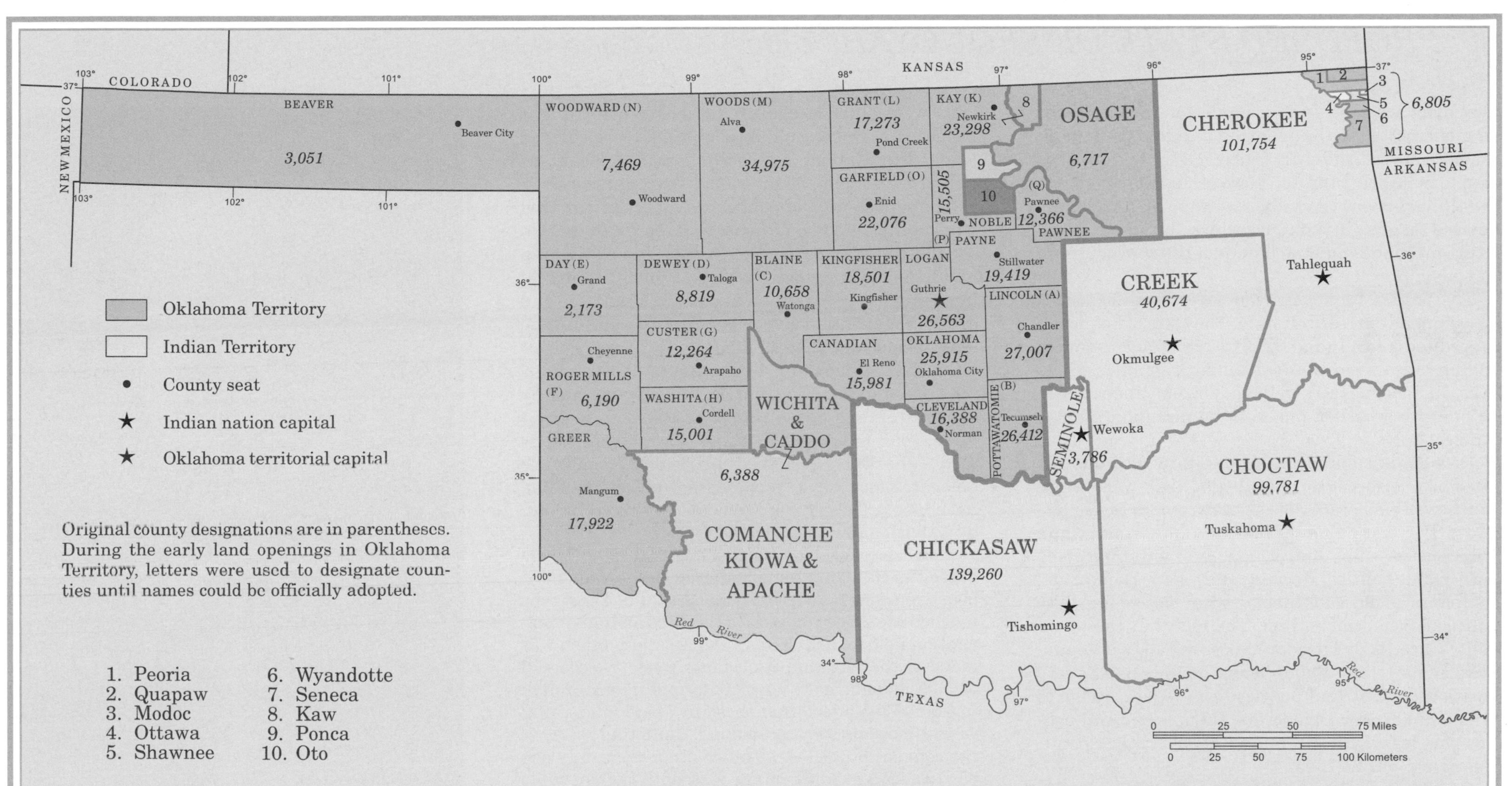

Population of the Twin Territories, 1900

Territory	Population
Oklahoma Territory	398,331
Indian Territory	392,060
Total	790,391

Population figures are taken from U.S. Bureau of the Census for 1900.

Congress gave the territory west of the Five Nations a formal government by means of the Organic Act of May 2, 1890. The direct and immediate application of this law was to the Unassigned Lands and No Man's Land in the northwest. As areas to the east, west, and north of the central district were added by successive land openings, the territorial courts and other agencies of government were expanded.

On March 16, 1896, the U.S. Supreme Court decided that Greer County was not a part of the state of Texas. Since the Organic Act placed the south and west boundaries of Oklahoma Territory at the Texas border, the decision made the area a part of the new territory. In May 1896, Congress passed an act concerning the status of homesteads in Greer County (obtained under the authority of Texas) and declared the area a county of Oklahoma Territory.

By 1896 the number of counties had increased to twenty-three, and by 1900 the population had grown to 400,000. As counties were added, they were designated by letters until names could be officially adopted: A and B counties on the eastern border of the original Oklahoma District (the Unassigned Lands), C through H in the Cheyenne-Arapaho area, and K through Q in the Cherokee Outlet. In 1900, all twenty-three counties of Oklahoma Territories were known by names rather than letters, had organized county governments, had designated county seats, and were continuing to increase in population.

69. PROPOSED STATE OF SEQUOYAH, 1905

Essay by *Danney Goble*

Sequoyah was the Indian name for the Cherokee who is credited with inventing a unique Indian alphabet, one so brilliantly conceived that it made his people instantly literate. However, what looked like an alphabet was actually a syllabary, a carefully devised set of eighty-six characters, the name of each a certain sound. Say the names of the characters on the page; literacy results.

The name "Sequoyah" was later used for a proposed but never-realized state. The state of Sequoyah is credited as an Indian effort to fashion a uniquely Indian state from the five Indian republics. However, like Sequoyah's syllabary, what appeared to be one thing turned out to be something different altogether.

Its would-be founding fathers were not Indian at all. They were white; specifically, they were white southern Democrats, mostly newcomers to the territory. Because no more than a handful could claim tribal citizenship, almost none had anything to do with tribal politics. Because they were Democrats, there was no place for them in what passed for white politics of the time, either. The fact that the president (since 1901, Theodore Roosevelt) was a Republican meant that Republicans monopolized every position in nontribal politics from federal judge to census taker. For Democrats, then, territorial politics was less a cause than a habit, a rather pointless cause—until 1905.

By 1905, anyone able to figure knew that statehood, in one form or another, was imminent for both Indian Territory and its neighbor to the west; each was too populous to be denied any longer. Those able to figure votes in Congress knew that the form would be as one state, not two. Separately, there were too many potential Democratic voters in each territory for a Republican Congress (and a Republican president) to risk two states that would send two sets of Democrats to Washington.

Statehood was therefore certain, and its form was set. In 1905, only its leadership was doubtful. The odds were stacked against the eastern territory's Democrats. None could be counted as a celebrated leader, there having been nothing to lead. None was a famed champion of any cause—except his own.

The opportunity for political advancement arrived when a little-known newspaper announced that an even lesser-known Cherokee named James Norman had somehow convinced two tribal chiefs to join him in calling for a convention to meet in Muskogee and draft a constitution able to join five nations into one state: Sequoyah. The ambitious had no worries about their chances for launching careers at this otherwise meaningless convention. Twenty-six hastily drawn districts chose representatives to meet at Muskogee, but their choosing was sometimes by means charitably described as irregular. Some of the delegates may have "represented" places they had never seen. Others were "elected" by secretly huddling with a few select friends.

However chosen, 305 delegates and alternatives made the cut. Only some bothered to show up, however; from seven districts, none at all did. Those who reached Muskogee publicized theirs as an Indian convention held on behalf of an Indian state. Much was made of the fact that its leaders were five coequal vice presidents, each to speak for a different Indian nation. Few noticed that these five held offices that were almost entirely ceremonial; the actual power at the convention rested with five other men, only one of whom was as much as one-sixteenth Indian, while three had no Indian ancestry whatsoever.

As others orated, these five and other insiders pieced together a constitution by copying whatever they liked from wherever they found it. Sent to Washington, their text failed to win congressional approval.

The list of the convention's five dominant figures—Charles Haskell, Robert Owen, W. W. Hastings, Bill Murray, and John Thomas—is a roster of Oklahoma's political elite during early statehood: its first governor, first U.S. senator, two of its earliest congressmen, and a federal judge. They had invented themselves.

Charles N. Haskell, first governor of the state of Oklahoma. (Courtesy Western History Collections, University of Oklahoma Libraries)

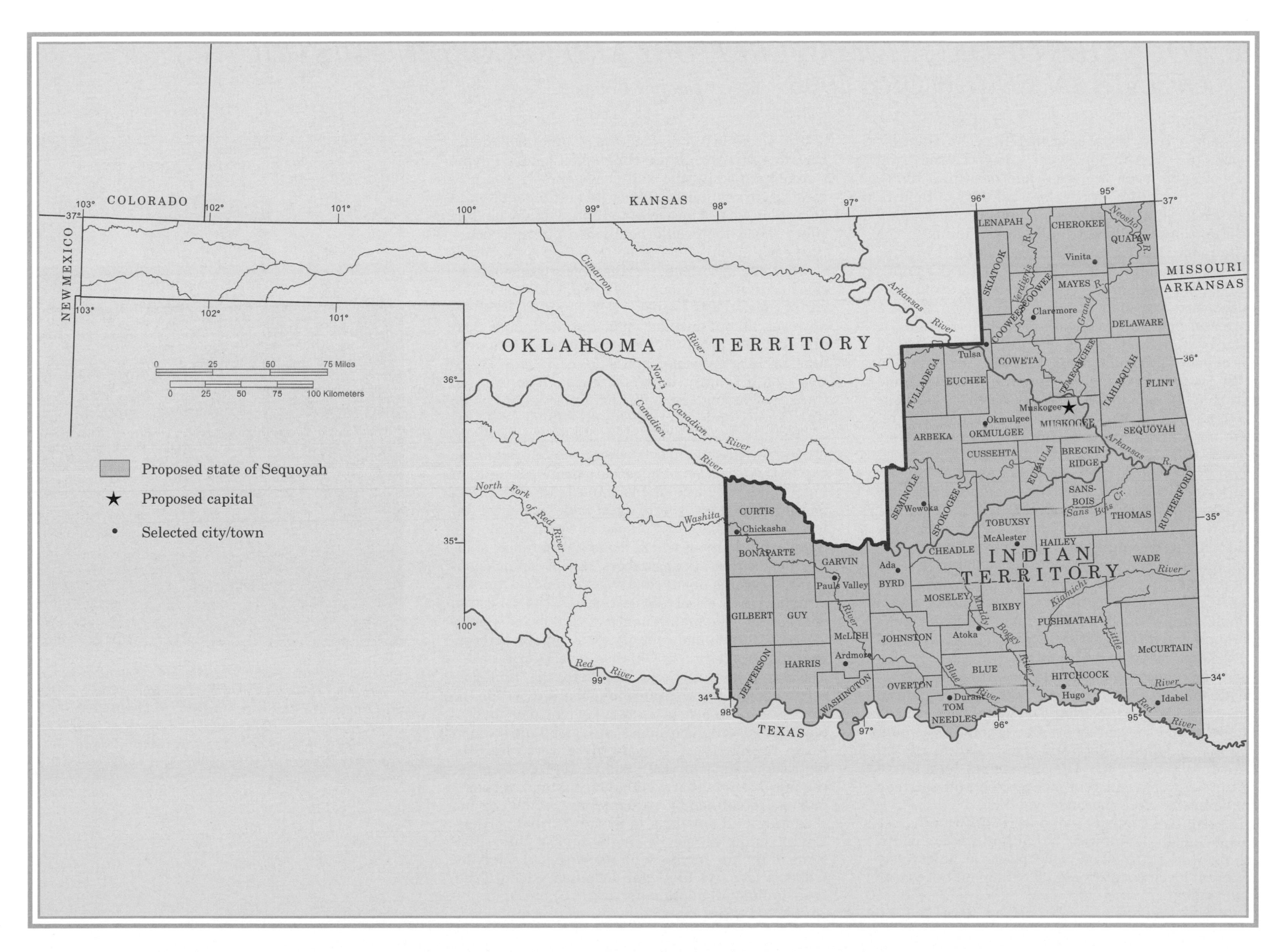
COLORADO
KANSAS
NEW MEXICO
MISSOURI
ARKANSAS
TEXAS
OKLAHOMA TERRITORY
INDIAN TERRITORY
Proposed state of Sequoyah
Proposed capital
Selected city/town
0 25 50 75 Miles
0 25 50 75 100 Kilometers
Cimarron River
Arkansas River
North Canadian River
Canadian River
North Fork of Red River
Washita
Red River
Verdigris R.
Neosho R.
Grand R.
Kiamichi River
Muddy Boggy River
Blue River
Little River
Sans Bois Cr.
LENAPAH
CHEROKEE
QUAPAW
SKIATOOK
COOWEESCOOWEE
MAYES
DELAWARE
TULLADEGA
EUCHEE
COWETA
TEMEHICHEE
TAHLEQUAH
FLINT
ARBEKA
OKMULGEE
MUSKOGEE
SEQUOYAH
CUSSEHTA
EUFAULA
BRECKINRIDGE
SANS-BOIS
THOMAS
RUTHERFORD
SEMINOLE
SPOKOGEE
TOBUXSY
HAILEY
WADE
CURTIS
BONAPARTE
GARVIN
BYRD
CHEADLE
MOSELEY
BIXBY
PUSHMATAHA
McCURTAIN
GILBERT
GUY
McLISH
JOHNSTON
JEFFERSON
HARRIS
WASHINGTON
OVERTON
BLUE
HITCHCOCK
TOM NEEDLES
Vinita
Claremore
Tulsa
Muskogee
Okmulgee
Wewoka
McAlester
Chickasha
Ada
Pauls Valley
Atoka
Ardmore
Durant
Hugo
Idabel

70. COUNTIES OF OKLAHOMA TERRITORY AND RECORDING DISTRICTS OF INDIAN TERRITORY, 1906

Essay by *Danney Goble*

Oklahoma Territory was settled in a rush, literally. Before the most famous race, known as the Land Run of 1889, even Congress had been in a hurry. Only in the final hours of the final days of their final session did lawmakers get around to cleaning up lingering Chickasaw and Creek claims to the Oklahoma District and thereby making it eligible for homesteaders' settlement as part of the public lands. Before adjourning, they formally and officially authorized President Benjamin Harrison to set a date and hour after which homesteaders could file their lawful claims. Harrison promptly announced his choice: 12:00 high noon, April 22, 1889.

So great was the rush to get settlers on Oklahoma soil that no one—not President Harrison, not one member of Congress—paused long enough to remember one small detail: How would these settlers govern themselves? It was a full year after Oklahoma's initial land rush before Congress, in the Organic Act of 1890, provided for even a rudimentary structure of territorial government.

In the interim, settlers got by, using common sense and drawing on long-established political habits. For that matter, when Congress did act, it, too, drew upon practices dating to the Republic's earliest days. Like nearly every territory before it, Oklahoma had a simple, three-branch territorial government. Immediate executive authority was vested in a territorial governor, assisted only by a territorial secretary. Neither was subject to popular election; they were presidential appointees. The same was true for the judicial branch: three presidentially appointed territorial judges would separately oversee each of three judicial districts and collectively comprise a territorial supreme court. Only the bicameral legislative branch—twenty-six representatives and thirteen councilmen—were chosen by voters.

Legislative contests alone were sufficient cause to spark political interest. What ignited real political fireworks turned on government at an entirely different level: not *territorial* government but *county* government.

The Organic Act divided the original Oklahoma District into six counties: Kingfisher, Logan, Payne, Canadian, Oklahoma, and Cleveland. It also provided that new lands opened to settlement would be automatically incorporated into Oklahoma Territory. They, too, would be divided into new counties, each initially identified by letter: A County, B County, etc. In the end, the alphabet would not have reached quite far enough; by 1906, Oklahoma Territory consisted of twenty-seven counties. By then, however, all but one had taken another name, usually that of a prominent geographical feature or of an especially esteemed statesman. The one exception was K County, in which frugal citizens saved the cost of buying new stationery by taking the name Kay County and using up what they had.

County government provided a collective outlet for the territory's political energies. Voters had no say in the selection of governors or judges and not much more influence when it came to territorial legislators. But a few voters could make plenty of difference in filling county offices, of which there were many, and many of which made a difference: sheriffs, prosecutors, tax assessors, school commissioners. Everything about county government from the designation of county seats through the collection of taxes and the maintenance of civil order was up for grabs; that made county government both essential and exciting in Oklahoma Territory.

Not in Indian Territory. Except for the tribal governments and the separate municipalities within the territory, there was no formal structure of government: no governor, no judges, no legislators, no sheriffs or tax assessors. Instead there were recording districts (twenty-nine of them by 1906). Except for the few districts that were divided by major rivers, most were defined by straight lines, drawn by bureaucrats and oblivious to existing tribal borders. Equally simple was the single duty of these divisions of Indian Territory, for each existed solely for tribal citizens to file legal documents identifying their individual allotments.

Choctaw and Chickasaw Indians enrolling at a special government railroad car in the Choctaw Nation. Under the General Allotment Act of 1887, individually enrolled American Indians received a parcel of land. The remaining land was open to settlement and sold. (Courtesy Western History Collections, University of Oklahoma Libraries)

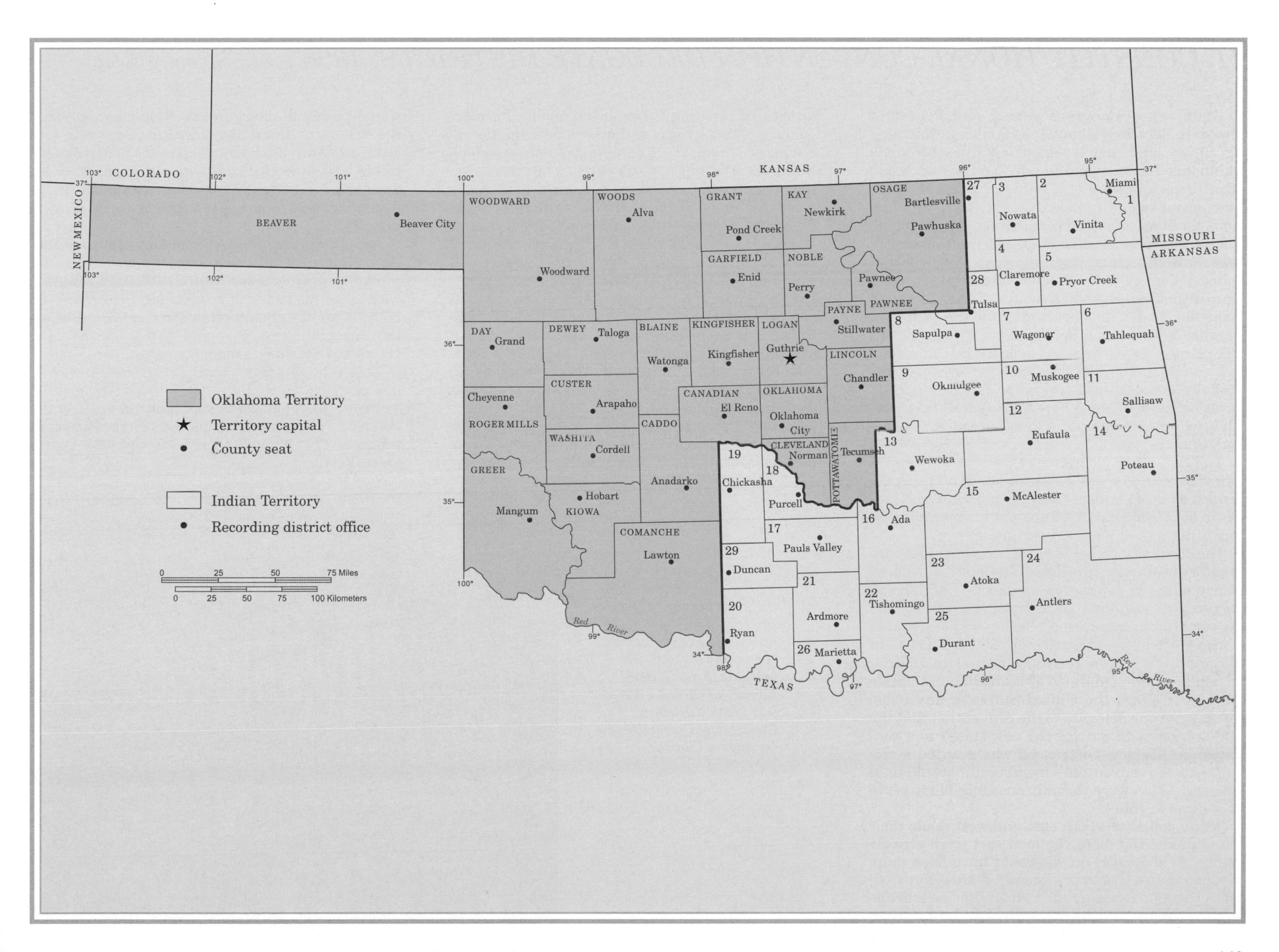

COLORADO
KANSAS
NEW MEXICO
MISSOURI
ARKANSAS
TEXAS
Red River
BEAVER
Beaver City
WOODWARD
Woodward
WOODS
Alva
GRANT
Pond Creek
KAY
Newkirk
OSAGE
Bartlesville
Pawhuska
GARFIELD
Enid
NOBLE
Perry
Pawnee
PAWNEE
PAYNE
Stillwater
DAY
Grand
DEWEY
Taloga
BLAINE
Watonga
KINGFISHER
Kingfisher
LOGAN
Guthrie
LINCOLN
Chandler
CUSTER
Arapaho
Cheyenne
ROGER MILLS
CANADIAN
El Reno
OKLAHOMA
Oklahoma City
CADDO
Anadarko
WASHITA
Cordell
CLEVELAND
Norman
POTTAWATOMIE
Tecumseh
GREER
Mangum
Hobart
KIOWA
COMANCHE
Lawton
Miami
Nowata
Vinita
Claremore
Pryor Creek
Tulsa
Sapulpa
Wagoner
Tahlequah
Okmulgee
Muskogee
Sallisaw
Eufaula
Wewoka
Poteau
Chickasha
Purcell
McAlester
Ada
Pauls Valley
Duncan
Atoka
Antlers
Tishomingo
Ardmore
Durant
Ryan
Marietta
Oklahoma Territory
Territory capital
County seat
Indian Territory
Recording district office
0 25 50 75 Miles
0 25 50 75 100 Kilometers

71. CONSTITUTIONAL CONVENTION DELEGATE DISTRICTS, 1906

Essay by *Danney Goble*

In 1906, when Congress passed and President Theodore Roosevelt signed the Oklahoma Enabling Act, many said that it was about time. After all, Oklahoma Territory and Indian Territory each had about three-quarters of a million residents at the time, about twice as many as had lived in any previous territory admitted to the union.

Veterans of the so-called Sequoyah Convention had been waiting for just such an event. With the Enabling Act, many of these Indian Territory Democrats figured that their time had come, and they set out to make the most of the opportunity. On the west side, Oklahoma Territory's Democrats and Republicans alike girded themselves for battle in their unending partisan wars. The difference, both parties knew, was that this contest was going to be fought for spoils never before possible. A new state meant a new legislature, new judgeships, and new executive posts—not to mention new U.S. senators and representatives as well as new presidential electors. First, though, a new state meant a new constitution. Everything depended on that—which was why leaders of both parties in both territories were anxious to make any new constitution their party's constitution.

The law igniting all this turmoil directed that each territory be divided into fifty-five districts, "each as nearly equal in population as may be." Oklahoma Territory was to supply Districts 1 through 55, and the semiautonomous Osage Nation was designated as the 56th district. Districts 57 through 111 were to come from Indian Territory. Except in District 56, eligible voters (defined as resident, adult, male citizens of either the United States or any tribe) would send one delegate to the convention that the law charged with writing the new state's new constitution. Because District 56 was granted a second seat, the convention's membership would total 112 men. (Men were the only ones eligible to serve as well as to vote.)

While politicians both east and west made their calculations, the more common sort were already acting. At the time, no one could have been more common than a farmer or a worker. Years before Congress thought to merge the two territories into one state, farmers and workers already had united: farmers by creating a single Indiahoma Farmers Union, workers by way of the Twin Territorial Federation of Labor. The Enabling Act's passage took these organizations one step further, forming a coalition that linked farmers and workers behind a common cause and pledged their support to only those candidates who supported that cause. The test came in Shawnee in 1906, when the farmers' union and the workers' federation pledged to press upon every candidate in every district their so-called Twenty-Five Demands. The twenty-five constituted the most advanced notions of the day. Any constitution to embrace them would found not merely a new state but an entirely new kind of state, one that strictly regulated corporations, that vigilantly protected workers and children, that swiftly responded to public needs and opinions.

Some of the candidates were readier than others to heed those demands; ambitious Democrats were most ready of all. Much of what workers and farmers wanted, after all, came directly from provisions that the eastern brethren had placed in Sequoyah's constitution. Much also showed up in the platform written to unite the Democrats of both territories. No wonder nearly every Democratic candidate made nearly identical promises to support nearly identical principles.

Republican candidates did not. Instead, most depended on past loyalties from the Civil War and hinted at prospects for future patronage rewards, which had worked before. After all, those were the tactics that had given Indian Territory Republicans their overriding purpose and had made the GOP Oklahoma Territory's majority party.

This time, however, the results were decidedly different. Of the 112 elected, 99 were Democrats, 112 were Republicans, and 1 had run as an Independent. The rout was complete when that last man renounced his independence in favor of the Democratic Party.

A large crowd gathered for the inauguration of Charles Haskell as governor of the new state of Oklahoma on November 16, 1907. The building is the Carnegie Library at Guthrie. (Courtesy Western History Collections, University of Oklahoma Libraries)

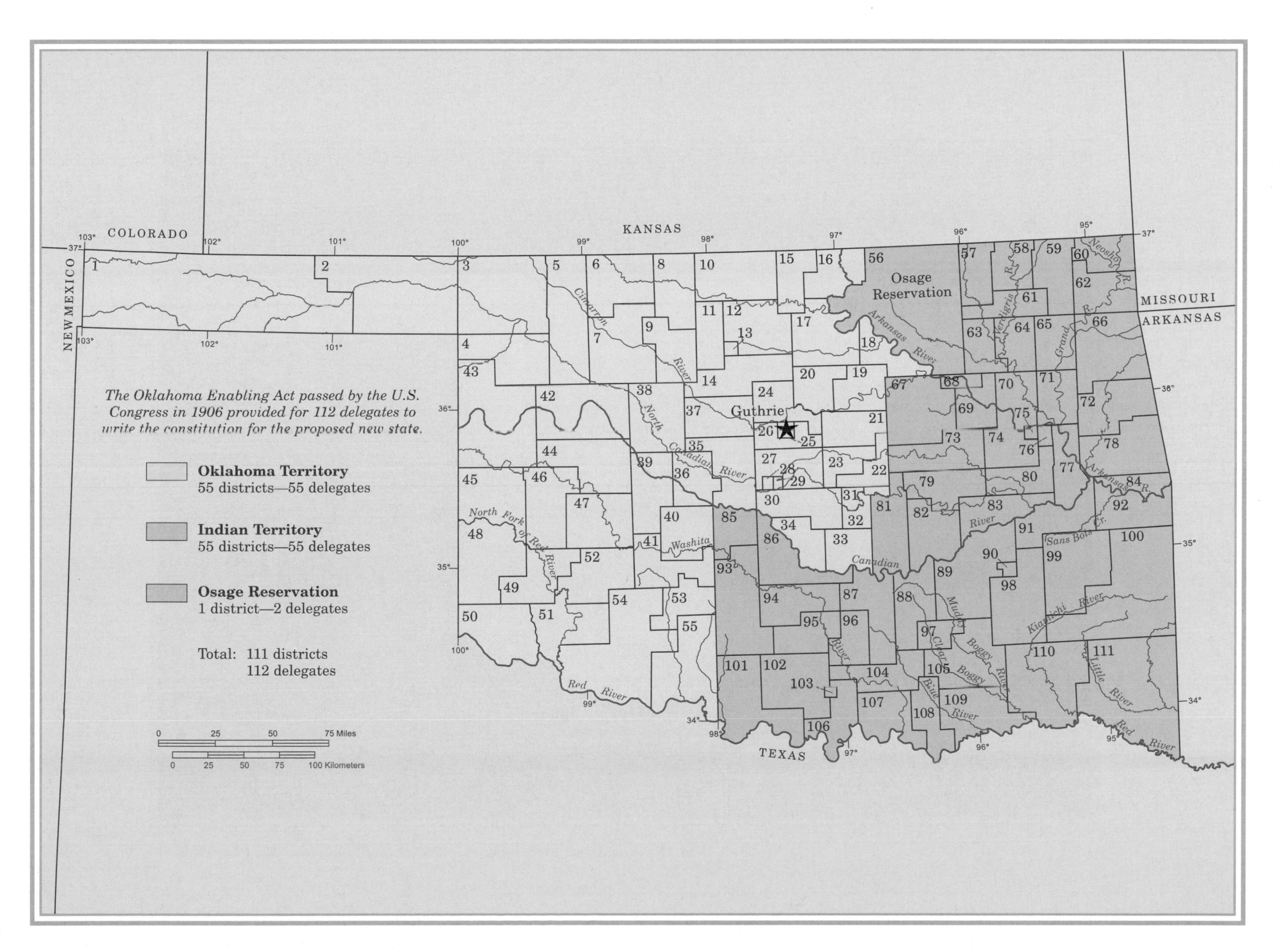

COLORADO
KANSAS
NEW MEXICO
MISSOURI
ARKANSAS
TEXAS
Osage Reservation
Guthrie
The Oklahoma Enabling Act passed by the U.S. Congress in 1906 provided for 112 delegates to write the constitution for the proposed new state.
Oklahoma Territory
55 districts—55 delegates
Indian Territory
55 districts—55 delegates
Osage Reservation
1 district—2 delegates
Total: 111 districts
112 delegates
Cimarron River
North Canadian River
Arkansas River
Verdigris R.
Grand R.
Neosho R.
North Fork of Red River
Washita
Canadian River
Sans Bois Cr.
Kiamichi River
Muddy Boggy River
Clear Boggy
Blue River
Little River
Red River
0 25 50 75 Miles
0 25 50 75 100 Kilometers

Black Mesa, Cimarron County. (Photograph by John Elk III, courtesy of Elk Photography)

Part V

Brand New State . . . Gonna Treat You Great

Emma Coleman photographed this automobile decorated as an Independence Day parade float, Norman, July 4, 1918. (Courtesy Western History Collections, University of Oklahoma Libraries)

72. POPULATION AT STATEHOOD, 1907 *Charles Robert Goins*

The bugles sounding at high noon on April 22, 1889, signaled the beginning of the great land run opening the Unassigned Lands to settlement. As time revealed, they were also announcing the conception of a new state. The birth of Oklahoma as a state took another eighteen years to happen, but from the very beginning of that first run, statehood was clearly only a matter of time.

Oklahoma Territory was established in 1890. That crucial event was followed within a decade by four more land runs, the opening of two Indian reservations by lottery, the settlement of the Big Pasture region by sealed bids, and finally the allotment of remaining Indian lands. All of these events, when pieced together, turned the land once set aside for homelands for Indian tribes into something quite different. That difference would require the Indian peoples of both Indian Territory and Oklahoma Territory to share their lands with arriving settlers wanting to establish farms and town sites, to build homes and railroads, and very soon to become the residents of a new state.

By 1906, the population of both territories had reached the point at which talk of statehood rang across the land of both territories and all the way to Washington, D.C. President Theodore Roosevelt heard the clamor from the west and signed the Oklahoma Enabling Act on June 16, 1906, thus providing authorization for joining the two territories into one new state.

One year later, on June 20, 1907, the president directed the secretary of commerce and labor to take a special census of the population of the two territories as of July 1, 1907. Response to the presidential order was fast and furious, with William C. Hunt, chief statistician for population, placed in charge. The territories were divided into five districts, the boundaries of which were defined as close as possible to those of the five proposed congressional districts apportioned to the future state of Oklahoma. The five districts were then subdivided into 1,461 enumeration districts.

To carry out the assignment, census takers were selected quickly and put to work immediately. They were chosen (as much as possible) without regard to partisan politics, with preference being given to rural and city postal employees, teachers and students, and (where reasonable) agents managing cotton gins—because all were presumed to be thoroughly familiar with their localities. The census data they were assigned to gather consisted of identifying the relationship of each person to the head of family, in addition to all household members' race, sex, and age. Compensation for the enumerators was to be not less than three dollars and not more than five dollars per day, requiring ten hours of fieldwork each day with no allowance made for travel expenses.

On June 30, twenty-five census clerks arrived in Guthrie and established offices in the city hall, which were procured for them by Governor Frank Frantz. District offices were established, and the task of collecting the census began on July 1. Because of the uncertainty of various boundary lines and the unsettled nature of the territories, there were some difficulties and delays in gathering the census; however, after its completion, census director S.N.D. North concluded that this had been the quickest census ever accomplished and probably the most satisfactory. Seventy-two days later, on September 10, the last returns were turned in to the supervisor in charge.

Area of Counties, 2005

County	Square miles	County	Square miles	County	Square miles
Adair	577	Greer	644	Oklahoma	718
Alfalfa	881	Harmon	539	Okmulgee	702
Atoka	990	Harper	1,041	Osage	2,304
Beaver	1,818	Haskell	625	Ottawa	485
Beckham	904	Hughes	815	Pawnee	595
Blaine	939	Jackson	804	Payne	697
Bryan	943	Jefferson	774	Pittsburg	1,378
Caddo	1,290	Johnston	658	Pontotoc	725
Canadian	905	Kay	945	Pottawatomie	793
Carter	834	Kingfisher	906	Pushmataha	1,423
Cherokee	776	Kiowa	1,031	Roger Mills	1,146
Choctaw	801	Latimer	729	Rogers	711
Cimarron	1,841	Le Flore	1,608	Seminole	641
Cleveland	558	Lincoln	966	Sequoyah	715
Coal	521	Logan	749	Stephens	891
Comanche	1,084	Love	532	Texas	2,049
Cotton	642	Major	580	Tillman	879
Craig	763	Marshall	427	Tulsa	587
Creek	970	Mayes	684	Wagoner	591
Custer	1,002	McClain	580	Washington	424
Delaware	792	McCurtain	1,901	Washita	1,009
Dewey	1,008	McIntosh	712	Woods	1,290
Ellis	1,232	Murray	425	Woodward	1,246
Garfield	1,060	Muskogee	839		
Garvin	814	Noble	742		
Grady	1,105	Nowata	581		
Grant	1,004	Okfuskee	629		

Source: Oklahoma Department of Libraries, *Oklahoma Almanac*.

Total area (including land and water) is 69,898 square miles.

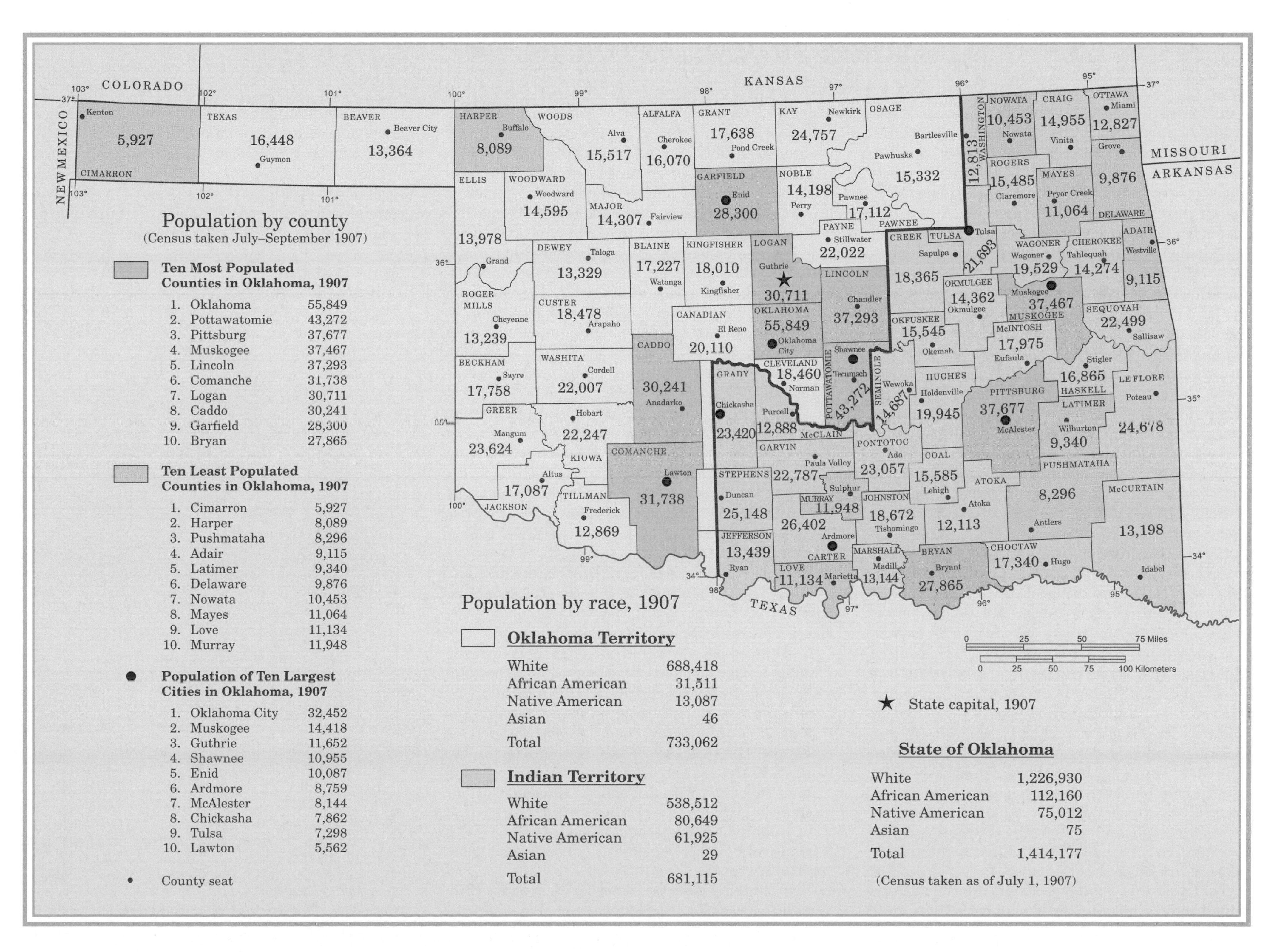
Population by county
(Census taken July–September 1907)
Ten Most Populated Counties in Oklahoma, 1907
1. Oklahoma 55,849
2. Pottawatomie 43,272
3. Pittsburg 37,677
4. Muskogee 37,467
5. Lincoln 37,293
6. Comanche 31,738
7. Logan 30,711
8. Caddo 30,241
9. Garfield 28,300
10. Bryan 27,865
Ten Least Populated Counties in Oklahoma, 1907
1. Cimarron 5,927
2. Harper 8,089
3. Pushmataha 8,296
4. Adair 9,115
5. Latimer 9,340
6. Delaware 9,876
7. Nowata 10,453
8. Mayes 11,064
9. Love 11,134
10. Murray 11,948
Population of Ten Largest Cities in Oklahoma, 1907
1. Oklahoma City 32,452
2. Muskogee 14,418
3. Guthrie 11,652
4. Shawnee 10,955
5. Enid 10,087
6. Ardmore 8,759
7. McAlester 8,144
8. Chickasha 7,862
9. Tulsa 7,298
10. Lawton 5,562
County seat
Population by race, 1907
Oklahoma Territory
White 688,418
African American 31,511
Native American 13,087
Asian 46
Total 733,062
Indian Territory
White 538,512
African American 80,649
Native American 61,925
Asian 29
Total 681,115
State capital, 1907
State of Oklahoma
White 1,226,930
African American 112,160
Native American 75,012
Asian 75
Total 1,414,177
(Census taken as of July 1, 1907)
0 25 50 75 Miles
0 25 50 75 100 Kilometers
COLORADO
KANSAS
NEW MEXICO
TEXAS
MISSOURI
ARKANSAS
CIMARRON 5,927 Kenton
TEXAS 16,448 Guymon
BEAVER 13,364 Beaver City
HARPER 8,089 Buffalo
WOODS 15,517 Alva
ALFALFA 16,070 Cherokee
GRANT 17,638 Pond Creek
KAY 24,757 Newkirk
OSAGE 15,332 Pawhuska
Bartlesville
WASHINGTON 12,813
NOWATA 10,453 Nowata
CRAIG 14,955 Vinita
OTTAWA 12,827 Miami
ELLIS 13,978 Grand
WOODWARD 14,595 Woodward
MAJOR 14,307 Fairview
GARFIELD 28,300 Enid
NOBLE 14,198 Perry
Pawnee 17,112 PAWNEE
ROGERS 15,485 Claremore
MAYES 11,064 Pryor Creek
DELAWARE 9,876 Grove
DEWEY 13,329 Taloga
BLAINE 17,227 Watonga
KINGFISHER 18,010 Kingfisher
LOGAN 30,711 Guthrie
PAYNE 22,022 Stillwater
CREEK 18,365 Sapulpa
TULSA 21,693 Tulsa
WAGONER 19,529 Wagoner
CHEROKEE 14,274 Tahlequah
ADAIR 9,115 Westville
ROGER MILLS 13,239 Cheyenne
CUSTER 18,478 Arapaho
CANADIAN 20,110 El Reno
OKLAHOMA 55,849 Oklahoma City
LINCOLN 37,293 Chandler
OKMULGEE 14,362 Okmulgee
MUSKOGEE 37,467 Muskogee
SEQUOYAH 22,499 Sallisaw
OKFUSKEE 15,545 Okemah
McINTOSH 17,975 Eufaula
BECKHAM 17,758 Sayre
WASHITA 22,007 Cordell
CADDO 30,241 Anadarko
GRADY 23,420 Chickasha
CLEVELAND 18,460 Norman
POTTAWATOMIE 43,272 Shawnee Tecumseh
SEMINOLE 14,687 Wewoka
HUGHES 19,945 Holdenville
PITTSBURG 37,677 McAlester
HASKELL 16,865 Stigler
LE FLORE 24,678 Poteau
LATIMER 9,340 Wilburton
GREER 23,624 Mangum
KIOWA 22,247 Hobart
COMANCHE 31,738 Lawton
McCLAIN 12,888 Purcell
GARVIN 22,787 Pauls Valley
PONTOTOC 23,057 Ada
COAL 15,585 Lehigh
JACKSON 17,087 Altus
TILLMAN 12,869 Frederick
STEPHENS 25,148 Duncan
MURRAY 11,948 Sulphur
JOHNSTON 18,672 Tishomingo
ATOKA 12,113 Atoka
PUSHMATAHA 8,296 Antlers
McCURTAIN 13,198 Idabel
JEFFERSON 13,439 Ryan
CARTER 26,402 Ardmore
LOVE 11,134 Marietta
MARSHALL 13,144 Madill
BRYAN 27,865 Bryant
CHOCTAW 17,340 Hugo

73. COUNTIES AND CONGRESSIONAL DISTRICTS, 1907

Essay by *Danney Goble*

"Small enough for a farmer to reach his county seat in a day's wagon ride"—this is the common explanation for Oklahoma's historic abundance of counties, most of which are now too small for efficient service. There is some truth to that piece of wisdom. More than a third of the constitutional convention's delegates left behind farms or ranches when they went to Guthrie to define Oklahoma's county boundaries and designate their county seats, and not many of the others were more than a few years away from the land themselves. Nonetheless, the multitude of counties owed little to the delegates' current occupations or to their past experiences but much to their future ambitions. The more counties, the more county seats. The more county seats, the more government jobs, contracts, and services. The more of those prizes, the more favor from more voters. It was as simple as that—more counties meant more votes.

Except that it was anything but simple. The delegates empowered convention president William H. Murray, of Tishomingo, to name every member of every committee; Murray knew that assignment to the committee on counties would be most delegates' first choice. (For some, truth be told, it was their only choice.) For that reason, those whom he placed there were entirely beholden to him. Moreover, two of the committee's members were two of the convention's most powerful men: Charles N. Haskell, of Muskogee; and Murray, known as "Alfalfa Bill," the so-called Sage of Tishomingo.

Even then, the committee became ensnared by countless local rivalries and petty jealousies. Weeks of fruitless cajoling, bargaining, and pleading ended only when Murray ordered Haskell to work its members without rest until they reached some resolution. Four full days ended with one exhausted committee member recommending that the convention define seventy-five quite irregular counties and designate seventy-five quite thankful seats.

That this was done directly in the constitution added appreciably to the document's inordinate length. Page after page of Article XVII, Section 8 drones on with detailed legal descriptions better suited to an advanced geography text than to a charter of fundamental governing principles. New counties popped up all over the former Indian Territory, and those inherited from the former Oklahoma Territory were divided into two, three, or even more new ones—enough to put every farmer within a day's journey of a county seat, enough to put seventy-five towns in debt to their deserving sons. Some (such as Haskell) were judged so deserving that counties were named for them. One, in fact, got two: Murray and Alfalfa counties. Tishomingo, county seat for the first of those two counties, thereby became forever indebted to its one-time sage.

The rest of the convention's work turned out to be almost as durable. Between 1907 and 1912, two new counties were defined—Harmon and Cotton counties. The first had been part of the first Greer County, the other the southern portion of Comanche County. In the century that followed, no counties were eliminated and only eight saw their county seats reassigned.

Compared to the wrangling over county lines and county seats, defining the five congressional districts that had been assigned to Oklahoma in the U.S. House of Representatives was simple. The chief external factors that affected their drawing were partisan calculations; since all but a handful of delegates were Democrats, partisan calculations were reduced to squeezing as many Republicans as possible into as few congressional districts as possible. The GOP received the absolute minimum: one. It embraced the broad wheat belt stretching along the border with Republican Kansas. The four remaining districts were drawn so that each of them shared a border—and a habit of voting—with Democratic Texas, Democratic Arkansas, or Democratic Missouri.

No thinking observer, whether Democrat or Republican, was deluded enough to imagine that these geographical differences were simple coincidences. Everyone accepted the situation for what it was. The decisions on congressional districting were purely political—and accurate, too. In Oklahoma's first congressional elections, every district did exactly as intended, with four sending Democrats and only one sending a Republican to Washington.

One of the most colorful politicians of Oklahoma history was William H. "Alfalfa Bill" Murray. A teacher, farmer, journalist, and lawyer, Murray first entered Democratic Party politics with the movement for Oklahoma statehood. After serving as the president of the Oklahoma Constitutional Convention and playing a major role in the drafting of the state's constitution, the "Sage of Tishomingo" became the first speaker of the new state's House of Representatives. (Courtesy Western History Collections, University of Oklahoma Libraries)

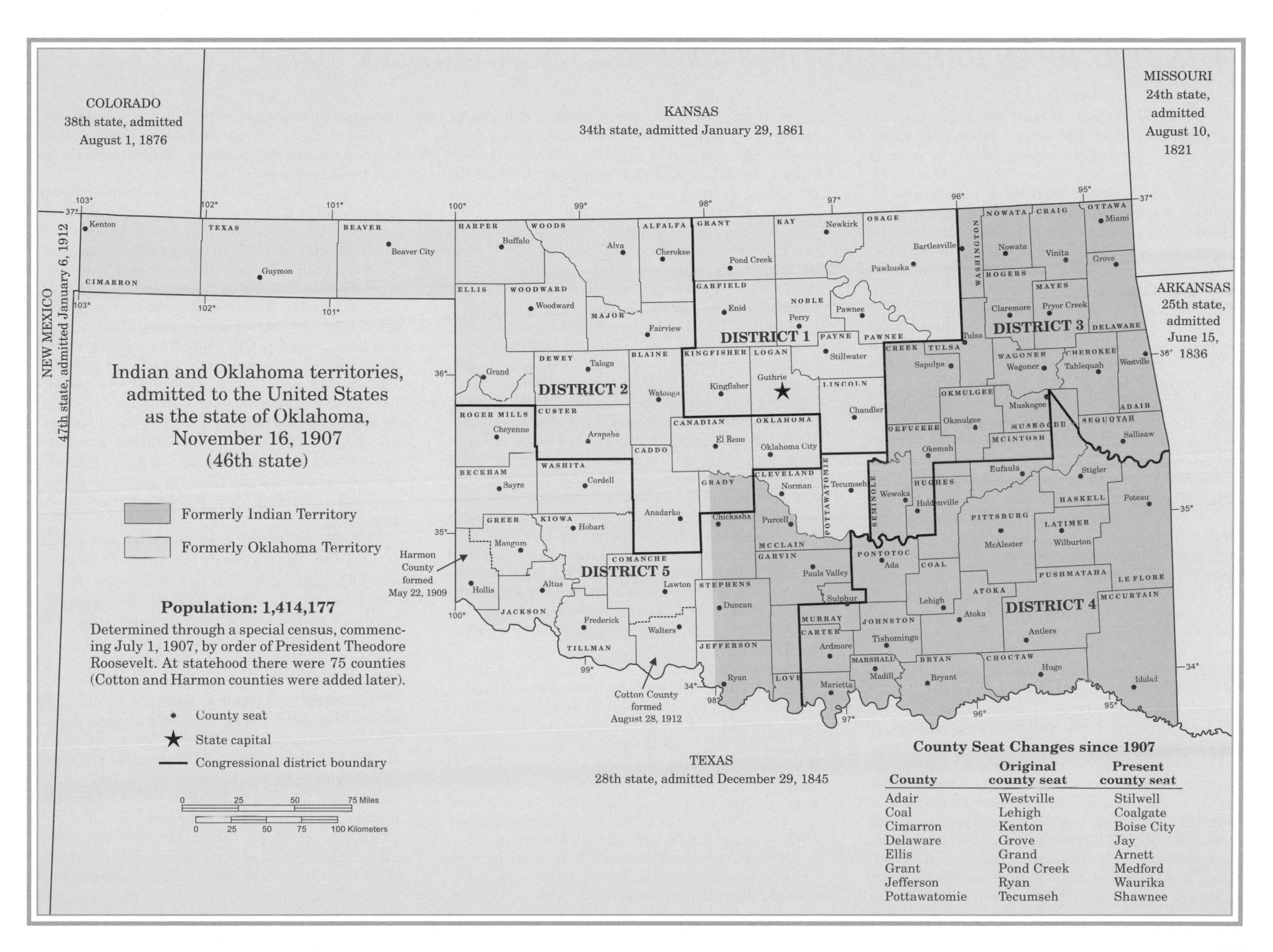

County Seat Changes since 1907

County	Original county seat	Present county seat
Adair	Westville	Stilwell
Coal	Lehigh	Coalgate
Cimarron	Kenton	Boise City
Delaware	Grove	Jay
Ellis	Grand	Arnett
Grant	Pond Creek	Medford
Jefferson	Ryan	Waurika
Pottawatomie	Tecumseh	Shawnee

74. INTERURBAN RAIL LINES, 1903–1950

Essay by *Danney Goble & Bruce W. Hoagland*

At one time or another, at least seventeen interurban lines connected and served more than thirty Oklahoma communities, among them the obvious ones: Oklahoma City, Tulsa, Lawton, Muskogee, Enid, and Ardmore. The majority of the interurbans, however, went to places that were a long way from obvious. Why would anyone build an interurban line to link Miami to Commerce to Cardin to Picher to Century? Why did this one last for more than thirty years and others for more than fifty? Finally, what killed them off, almost all at the same time?

The answer starts with the essential quality that distinguished interurban railways from others. A mix of chronology with geography (equally peculiar and brief) completes it.

No less than the Saint Louis and San Francisco (known as the Frisco) or the Chicago, Rock Island, and Pacific (the Rock Island), interurbans were, of course, rail lines. Except that unwary pedestrians still stumble over their rusting relics (usually because they still run down the exact middle of their towns' very busiest streets), they otherwise have nothing in common with the great Santa Fe or the mighty Rock Island, not even those main lines' long-since-retired stretches.

By definition, interurbans were powered by electricity, not steam or diesel; that difference made all the difference in their existence. For one thing, it meant that relatively little capital was needed to get an interurban rail line up and running. A handful of local business sorts could usually come up with enough money, especially if a banker or two was among them (better yet if oilmen, mine owners, or the like wanted in).

Unlike interstate—not to mention transcontinental—steam-powered railroads, the one real expense for interurban rail lines was to secure a source of electricity. "Securing" usually meant building, which is why many of Oklahoma's first generating plants were built by Oklahoma's first interurban companies. Until the recent demolition of one of these early electricity-generating facilities to clear the way for a new shopping area and to reroute a highway, nearly every resident of Oklahoma City easily could have recognized one of the first and most impressive examples: the Belle Isle power plant, which the Oklahoma Railway Company (ORC) built to power its lines in 1908.

Oklahoma's statehood year, 1907, was something of a high-water mark for its interurbans. Thirteen of Oklahoma's seventeen integrated systems were built either in the four years that preceded or the four that followed 1907. The addition of a forty-sixth star to the U.S. flag had nothing to do with that, however; rather, this boom in construction of interurbans involved the interaction between demography and geography in the forty-sixth state.

Oklahoma entered the union as hardly a metropolitan state but not exactly a rural one either. Much of the population clustered around (even though they did not live within) a surprising number of modest cities.

One was Tulsa, but barely a stone's throw away lay another that considered itself Tulsa's equal—in most respects, its superior. Sapulpa was both older than Tulsa and considerably larger. It also seemed to have greater prospects. After all, Sapulpa was the westernmost terminus of the mighty Frisco and even had the machine shops and roundhouses that serviced the great railroad. Compared to that, what did Tulsa have?

Then there was Oklahoma City. To its north lay Edmond (site of Oklahoma's first teacher-training school), not to mention Guthrie (Oklahoma Territory's capital and, by act of Congress, the state's, too). To the south lay Moore and Norman (home of the territorial university, which became the state university). To the west was El Reno, neighbor to a major Indian agency as well as serving as a vital site on the fabled Rock Island line. Compared to any of those, what did Oklahoma City have?

The answer is that Tulsa and Oklahoma City were hubs of locally financed, locally built, and locally owned interurban systems. Both of these rail systems could carry workers to their jobs and shoppers to their stores, and that meant that both communities had reasons aplenty for newcomers to buy homes and build businesses there.

In 1908, Tulsa's tiny local interurban line began to reorganize and to extend its tracks across the Arkansas River, through Sapulpa, and down to the red-hot Kiefer oil fields. In retrospect, that may have been the moment when Tulsa became Tulsa—and when Sapulpa was fated to remain just Sapulpa.

Even earlier (before statehood, in fact), Oklahoma City had opened the territories' first interurban line. True, the ORC got off to a shaky start in 1903; but it took off in 1908, when that new Belle Isle facility gave the company all the power it needed to keep its cars constantly moving—some to Moore and Norman, some to El Reno, and others through Edmond and into Guthrie. Not coincidently, that was when Oklahoma City took off as well. Within two years, Guthrie may have still had its ORC interurban stop, but Oklahoma City had the capital.

Oklahoma City still has the capital, just as Tulsa is still Tulsa. Neither has an interurban line, though. The ORC shut down and was abandoned in 1947. The Tulsa-Sapulpa Union Railway (the name eventually given the reorganized interurban line) discharged its last passenger in 1933. Like all the others—the last interurban passenger line, the Nowata-Union Electric Railway, closed in 1948—they had been superseded. Workers who once had ridden the interurbans to their jobs were driving their own cars to work instead. (Among them were the lead and zinc miners who once had ridden the interurban between Miami, Commerce, Cardin, Picher, and Century.) Shoppers whom interurbans had carried downtown were not even shopping downtown anymore. Affordable cars; convenient, all-weather roads; ubiquitous shopping centers—these had finished off Oklahoma's once-proud interurbans.

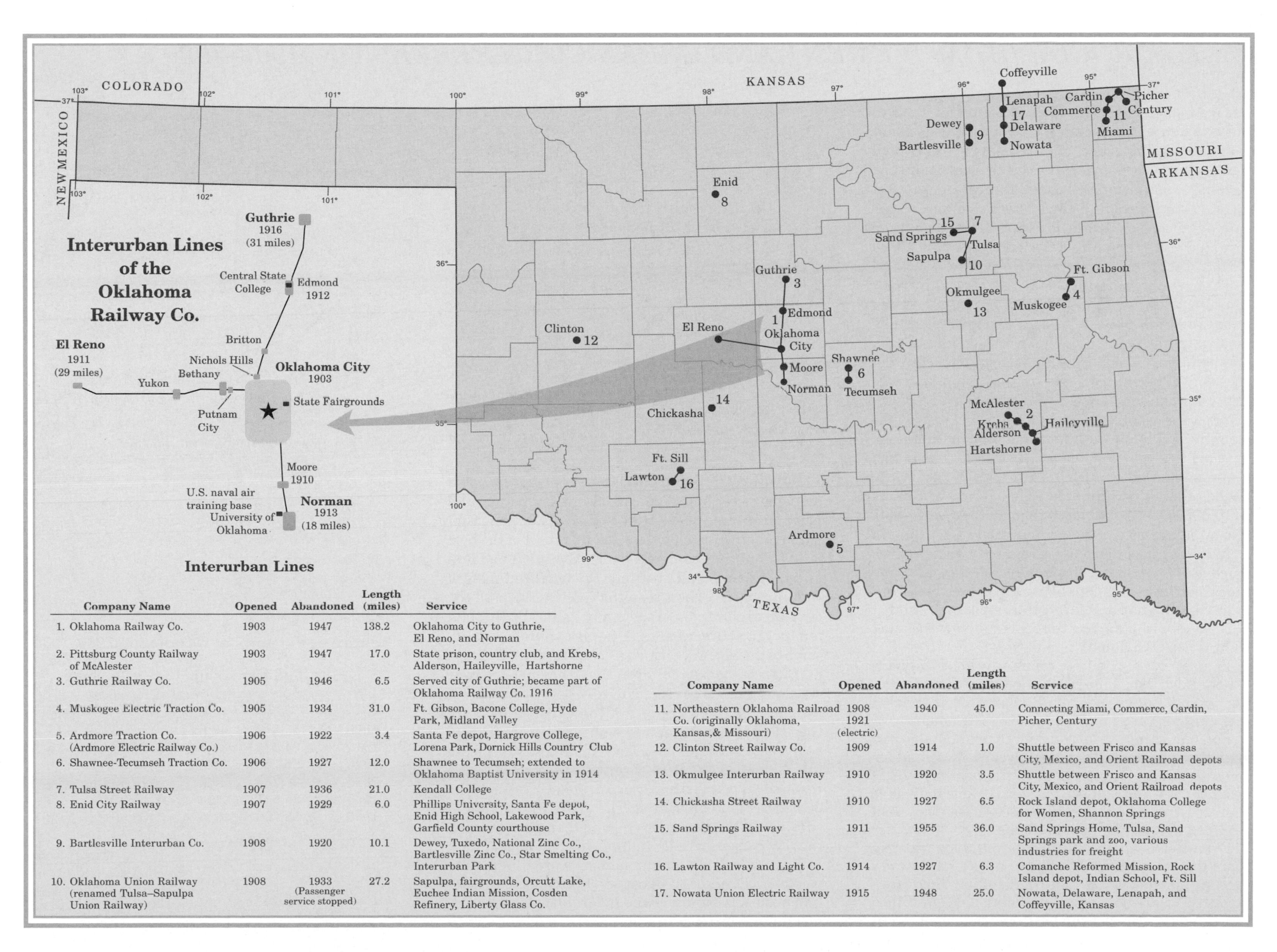

Interurban Lines

Company Name	Opened	Abandoned	Length (miles)	Service
1. Oklahoma Railway Co.	1903	1947	138.2	Oklahoma City to Guthrie, El Reno, and Norman
2. Pittsburg County Railway of McAlester	1903	1947	17.0	State prison, country club, and Krebs, Alderson, Haileyville, Hartshorne
3. Guthrie Railway Co.	1905	1946	6.5	Served city of Guthrie; became part of Oklahoma Railway Co. 1916
4. Muskogee Electric Traction Co.	1905	1934	31.0	Ft. Gibson, Bacone College, Hyde Park, Midland Valley
5. Ardmore Traction Co. (Ardmore Electric Railway Co.)	1906	1922	3.4	Santa Fe depot, Hargrove College, Lorena Park, Dornick Hills Country Club
6. Shawnee-Tecumseh Traction Co.	1906	1927	12.0	Shawnee to Tecumseh; extended to Oklahoma Baptist University in 1914
7. Tulsa Street Railway	1907	1936	21.0	Kendall College
8. Enid City Railway	1907	1929	6.0	Phillips University, Santa Fe depot, Enid High School, Lakewood Park, Garfield County courthouse
9. Bartlesville Interurban Co.	1908	1920	10.1	Dewey, Tuxedo, National Zinc Co., Bartlesville Zinc Co., Star Smelting Co., Interurban Park
10. Oklahoma Union Railway (renamed Tulsa–Sapulpa Union Railway)	1908	1933 (Passenger service stopped)	27.2	Sapulpa, fairgrounds, Orcutt Lake, Euchee Indian Mission, Cosden Refinery, Liberty Glass Co.

Company Name	Opened	Abandoned	Length (miles)	Service
11. Northeastern Oklahoma Railroad Co. (originally Oklahoma, Kansas,& Missouri)	1908 1921 (electric)	1940	45.0	Connecting Miami, Commerce, Cardin, Picher, Century
12. Clinton Street Railway Co.	1909	1914	1.0	Shuttle between Frisco and Kansas City, Mexico, and Orient Railroad depots
13. Okmulgee Interurban Railway	1910	1920	3.5	Shuttle between Frisco and Kansas City, Mexico, and Orient Railroad depots
14. Chickasha Street Railway	1910	1927	6.5	Rock Island depot, Oklahoma College for Women, Shannon Springs
15. Sand Springs Railway	1911	1955	36.0	Sand Springs Home, Tulsa, Sand Springs park and zoo, various industries for freight
16. Lawton Railway and Light Co.	1914	1927	6.3	Comanche Reformed Mission, Rock Island depot, Indian School, Ft. Sill
17. Nowata Union Electric Railway	1915	1948	25.0	Nowata, Delaware, Lenapah, and Coffeyville, Kansas

75. THE SOCIALIST MOVEMENT AND GREEN CORN REBELLION, 1907–1920

Essay by *Danney Goble*

Oscar Ameringer thought he had seen it all. Born in Bavaria and a Marxist since his youth, he had spent years taking the gospel of Socialism to his adopted country's worst slums. But even he could not take seriously his assignment to Oklahoma. Were not farmers capitalist and thus sworn enemies of the employed classes? Had not Karl Marx dismissed rural folk with the unkindest of phrases: "the idiocy of rural life?"

Then Oscar Ameringer visited Harrah. That's where he saw "toothless old women with suckling infants on their breasts" and, cowering beside them, "youngsters emaciated by hookworms, malnutrition, and pellagra." The desperate poverty made an impression: "The things I saw on that trip," he wrote thirty years later, "are the things you never forget."

What he described is what fed a socialist movement in Oklahoma. Socialism had been in Oklahoma as a political party since at least 1890, but it had never amounted to much. As late as 1907, not one of the Socialist Party's candidates had received as many as 10,000 votes. A year later, though, they got 21,000. The number was 41,000 just four years after that, in 1912, when Socialists were regularly receiving as much as 30 percent of the statewide vote and sometimes more. Already, Oklahoma had passed New York in having the nation's largest dues-paying Socialist Party—notwithstanding the fact that New York had eight times Oklahoma's population.

Figures can be cited to explain why all of this happened. Each was a measure of circumstances peculiar to Oklahoma. Nearly all shared their tangled roots in the state's unique mode of settlement.

For one thing, relatively few Oklahomans had been there for more than a few years. Most had arrived as adults. They had left little behind, mostly because they had had little to leave. Hope may have been their one transferable asset. If so, they had gambled everything on Oklahoma.

Even those who had been there the longest had come to possess little but hope. In the new state's eastern portion (what had been Indian Territory), land titles were no longer the Indian nations' collective property. Most of the best land belonged to but a few whites. Publicized as a means of ending tribal monopoly over land that could be put to better (and more profitable) use, tribal dissolution and individual allotments ended up denying most of the best land to most newcomers as well. Allotment had produced grafting, and grafting (the legalized theft of Indian property) had resulted in ownership by the few and exploitation of the many, generally through tenancy or sharecropping. Unable to purchase land, some of the hopeful farmed as cash renters. Because many were too poor for even that, they handed over shares of their crops instead. Nowhere—not even in the most blighted regions of the Old South—were these two forms of economic subsistence as common as in eastern Oklahoma. There, landless rates were at least 70 percent in twenty-five counties and reached 90 percent and more in some. The few who owned the land prospered. The many who worked it survived, if they were lucky—and then only by drawing down their ever-dwindling stock of hope.

The underlying circumstances were different in western Oklahoma. Because Oklahoma Territory had been settled under the federal Homestead Act, most of the farmers in the western counties owned

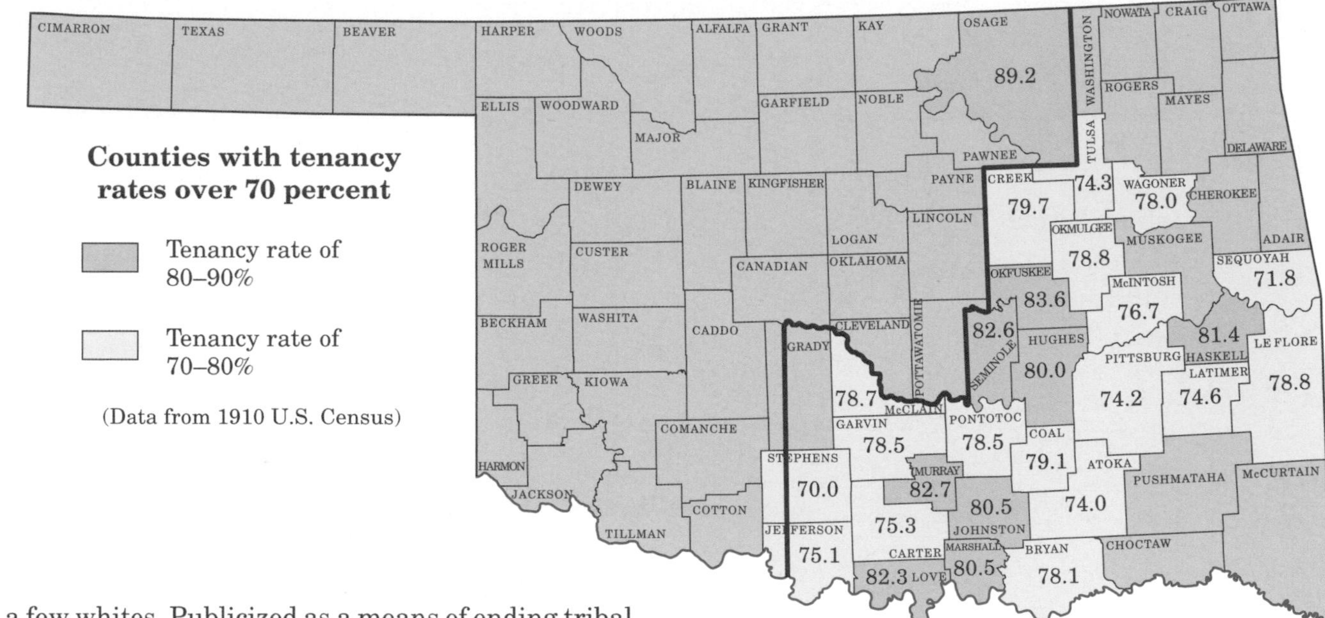

Tenure of Farmers in Oklahoma, 1900–1935

	Full ownership		Tenancy	
Year	**No.**	**%**	**No.**	**%**
1900	53,519	49.6	47,250	43.7
1910	64,884	34.1	104,137	54.8
1920	69,786	36.3	97,836	51.0
1925	60,764	30.8	115,498	58.6
1930	53,647	26.3	125,329	61.5
1935	58,796	27.6	130,661	61.2

Source: Southern, *Farm Tenancy.*

their land outright. Most of them (three-quarters or so), however, owned it under substantial mortgages. Arriving with more hope than capital, they had been compelled to borrow as much as possible as soon as possible. The territory's few lenders—who similarly had more demand than they did capital—were thus free to charge as much as possible to as many as possible. Start with high rates of interest, add high obligations, and throw in low prices—the sum of the equation was more than enough to make borrowers angry. Sometimes, it was enough to make them bitter—and enough to turn voters toward socialism.

By 1914, enough had reached that point that western Oklahomans picked five of their Socialist comrades to represent them in the state legislature. In the eastern regions, 1914 also was the year in which scores of Socialists won local and county races. Statewide that year, Socialists pulled a fifth of Oklahoma's total vote in the governor's race, carrying three counties and placing a close second in another twenty-five (including almost every county along and south of the Canadian River). Down there, Socialists—not Republicans—counted as the so-called loyal opposition.

Within three years, however, few were willing to accord the party anything that smacked of loyalty in any form. What had happened was not altogether surprising; for years, up and down the Canadian River valley, first-generation immigrants of German descent had been settling. For too long too many had been losing too much, including the hope for a better future for their children, but given no choice, they had to accept that. What they could not abide was altogether different: they refused to lose their sons to the war that the United States joined in April 1917. Instead, a thousand or more of them went to war right there at home.

Dismissed as the Green Corn Rebellion (the name came from the rebels' presumed diet for their assault on Washington), it did not amount to much as rebellions go. As a much-welcomed political opportunity, though, it meant everything. Claiming the rebellion to be the work of Socialists, state officials moved swiftly and ruthlessly to silence the Socialist press and jail the Socialist leadership.

One of the papers shut down was Oscar Ameringer's.

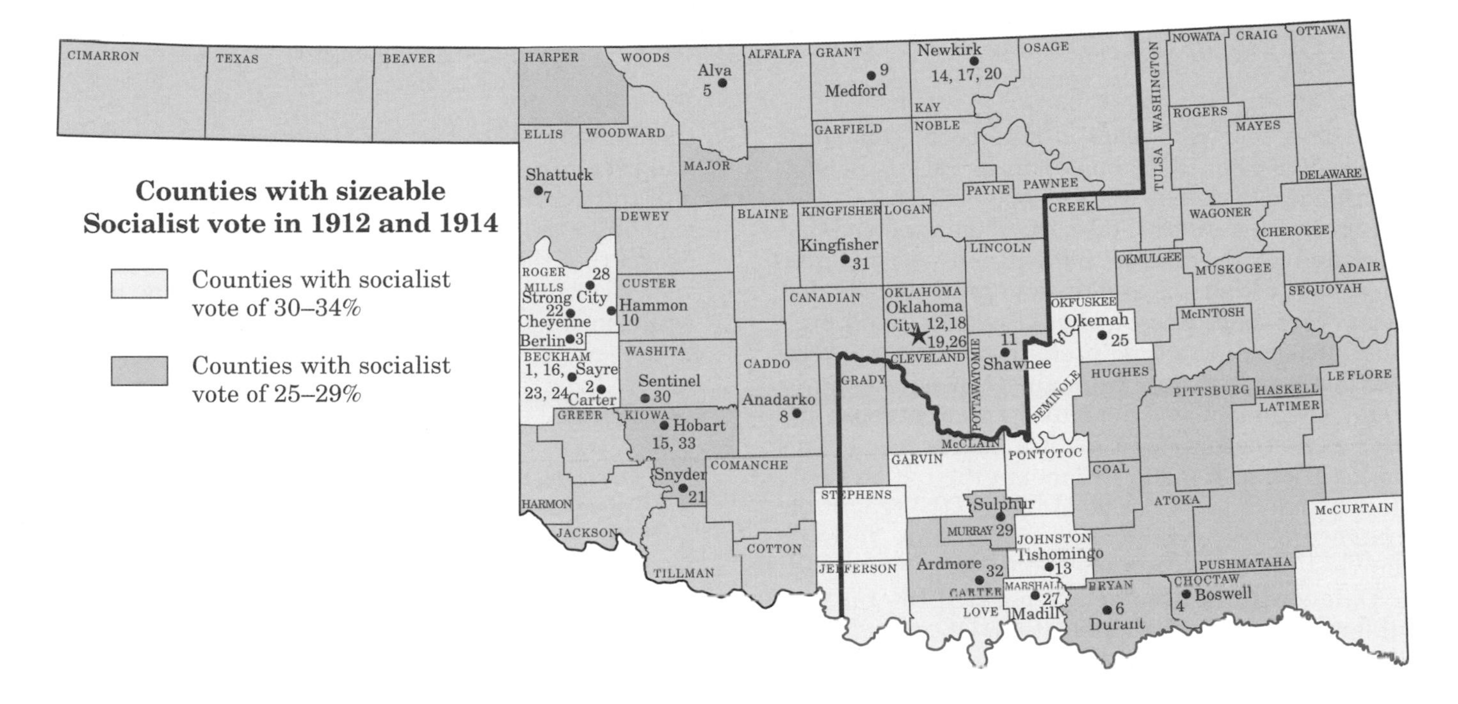

Oklahoma Socialist and Farmers' Union Newspapers

1. *Agitator* (Sayre, Beckham County)
2. *Beckham County Advocate* (Carter, Beckham County)
3. *Berlin Herald* (Berlin, Roger Mills County)
4. *Boswell Submarine* (Boswell, Choctaw County)
5. *Constructive Socialist* (Alva, Woods County)
6. *Durant Independent Farmer* (Durant, Bryan County)
7. *Ellis County Socialist* (Shattuck, Ellis County)
8. *Farmers' Union Advocate* (location unknown)
9. *Grant County Socialist* (Medford, Grant County)
10. *Hammon Advocate* (Hammon, Roger Mills County)
11. *Indiahoma Union Signal* (Shawnee, Pottawatomie County)
12. *Industrial Democrat* (Oklahoma City, Oklahoma County)
13. *Johnston County Socialist* (Tishomingo, Johnston County)
14. *Kay County Populist* (Newkirk, Kay County)
15. *Kiowa Breeze* (Kiowa County)
16. *Musings of the Old Kuss* (Sayre, Beckham County)
17. *Newkirk Populist* (Newkirk, Kay County)
18. *Oklahoma Leader* (Oklahoma City, Oklahoma County)
19. *Oklahoma Pioneer* (Oklahoma City, Oklahoma County)
20. *Oklahoma Socialist* (Newkirk, Oklahoma Territory)
21. *Otter Valley Socialist* (Snyder, Kiowa County)
22. *Roger Mills Sentinel* (Cheyenne, Roger Mills County)
23. *Sayre Citizen* (Sayre, Beckham County)
24. *Sayre Social Democrat* (Sayre, Beckham County)
25. *Sledge Hammer* (Okemah, Okfuskee County)
26. *Social Democrat* (Oklahoma City, Oklahoma County)
27. *Socialist Herald* (Madill, Marshall County)
28. *Strong City Herald* (Strong City, Roger Mills County)
29. *Sulphur New Century* (Sulphur, Murray County)
30. *Sword of Truth* (Sentinel, Washita County)
31. *Tenant Farmer* (Kingfisher, Kingfisher County)
32. *Union Review* (Ardmore, Carter County)
33. *Woodrow's Monthly* (Hobart, Kiowa County)

76. THE TULSA RACE RIOT, 1921

Essay by *Danney Goble*

In its first fourteen years of statehood, Oklahoma followed the South in most things racial. In fact, Oklahoma sometimes went a little further.

Like every southern state, Oklahoma decreed that black and white children must attend separate public schools. Oklahoma and the others all claimed that these were "separate but equal" schools, and even federal courts for a time pretended that they were. The fact was that they were always separate, never equal. Oklahoma was the only state to establish the pretense in the form of a constitutional principle. This constitution also made Oklahoma the nation's only state to mandate that separate schools be separately financed by separate taxes on separate revenue sources—all separate, none equal.

Oklahoma law similarly separated the races in all forms of public transportation. Of course, every southern state had those laws, but Oklahoma was able to claim pride of place even there: only Oklahoma had made its segregation statute the first act to become law.

Again like every southern state, Oklahoma had eliminated the voting rights of a once-sizable black electorate, but Oklahoma did this, too, with unequaled determination and ingenuity. The state disenfranchised blacks not once but twice: once by statute, once by constitutional amendment. The latter's approval by "voters"—at least 23,000 of whom had not voted at all—reeked of unconscionable deception and unconcealed fraud.

Oklahoma shared something else with its southern counterparts, and that was the most awful of all. By 1921, Oklahomans had lynched at least thirty-seven black men and one black woman, a mother left hanging from a bridge, her son dangling beside her. There were those who wanted to make Dick Rowland, a sixteen-year-old Tulsan, number thirty-nine.

On May 30, 1921, in the city of Tulsa, Rowland stepped into an elevator operated by a white girl, Sarah Page. No one knows what happened next. Some speculate that Rowland might have tripped going in. Others suppose that maybe he stumbled when the car jerked upward. Some even suggest that the two were secret lovers about to reopen a continuing quarrel. Page told a different story; she said that he had tried to rape her. Reporting that Rowland had been arrested and was being held in the county jail, the next evening's *Tulsa Tribune* narrated her side of the story. That was when Tulsans started to expect that the boy would be lynched, probably that very night. Some of these expectant Tulsans were white, and many of them gathered at the courthouse that evening. Others were black, and many of them resolved that another lynching must not happen; they, too, collected around the courthouse on the evening of May 31.

Two races, two crowds; one gunshot, then many—the Tulsa race riot had begun.

Firing as they went, blacks first retreated from the courthouse area and crossed the Frisco tracks, where they formed a defensive line. White Tulsans rushed to the scene. Most brought their own weapons; others carried some $43,000 worth of guns and ammunition stolen from pawnshops and sporting-goods stores along the way. More than a thousand of these whites were also appointed "special deputies." No one knew just what a special deputy did, but at least one swore that his orders were to "Go get a Nigger."

Tulsa's riot thus became Tulsa's war, and its battlefield was what Tulsa's whites—even their newspapers—called "Little Africa." Its 11,000 residents (all black, of course) called it "Greenwood," the name of its chief thoroughfare. At sunrise on May 31, Greenwood had maintained countless small businesses, including two newspapers, two theaters, thirteen churches, a hospital, and a library.

At sunset on June 1, only one of the schools (Booker T. Washington High School) remained. Gone were the businesses, the churches, the hospital, and the library. Gone, too, were the homes of 1,115 families. Gone was everything of value from another 563 homes, each one systematically looted.

The calculation of human casualties officially begins at 232, the number who required surgery within twenty-four hours, mostly for gunshot wounds. An additional 531 people received medical attention in the next three days. White officials at the time put the death toll in the mid-30s. Contemporaries (some black, some white) figured 300 or more. That number will never be known and will always be disputed.

What is known is that too much was lost and too many died.

Greenwood Street in Tulsa shows the destruction following the Tulsa Race Riot of 1921. (Courtesy Western History Collections, University of Oklahoma Libraries)

At Riot's End

- *By the time martial law was declared at 11:30 A.M. on June 1, the race riot had nearly run its course. Scattered bands of whites—some of whom had been awake for more than twenty-four hours—continued to loot and burn the homes of African Americans, but many were going home. Along the northern and eastern edges of black Tulsa, where houses were mixed with stretches of farmland, the white rioters had a difficult time distinguishing the homes of blacks from those of neighboring whites.*
- *A final skirmish occurred around 12:30 P.M. on June 1, when remnants of the white mob converged upon a two-story building near where the Santa Fe railroad tracks cut across the section line at Pine Street. For quite some time, defenders inside the building had been able to hold off their attackers, most of whom had gathered along the railroad embankment to the east. But when a new group of whites—armed with high-powered rifles—arrived, the blacks inside were overwhelmed. The building and a nearby store were then set on fire.*
- *Following the martial law declaration, the state troops finally began to head toward what remained of Tulsa's African American neighborhoods, disarming whites and sending them away from the district. While black eyewitnesses later condemned both the Tulsa police and the local National Guard units for their actions during the riot, they largely praised the state troops.*
- *Yet even with an end to the violence, for black Tulsans, a whole new set of ordeals had just begun. Thousands had fled to the country, hiding in the woods, while hundreds more had gathered near Golden Gate Park. Homeless, penniless, and often unsure of the fate of loved ones, those who began to venture back to town soon found themselves placed under armed guard.*
- *Convention Hall having been filled to capacity, black Tulsans were also taken to the fairgrounds and to McNulty Baseball Park. A few blacks also found refuge at First Presbyterian Church and other white churches downtown. Crowds of whites often cheered as the imprisoned African Americans were led away.*
- *White Tulsans as a whole, meanwhile, were sluggish in their response to martial law. While sporadic looting continued along the edges of the targeted community, crowds of whites continued their search for black maids and butlers—though not always with success. Several white families hid blacks inside their homes.*
- *National Guard units from other Oklahoma towns arrived in Tulsa throughout the day, and with their help, the streets were finally cleared. All businesses were ordered to close by 6:00 P.M.; and one hour later, only members of the military or civil authorities—physicians and relief workers—were allowed on the streets. Adjutant General Charles F. Barrett later claimed that by 8:00 P.M., order had been restored. Normalcy, however, was another matter.*
- *For some, it would never return. Upwards of ten thousand black Tulsans were without homes or businesses, their lifetime possessions either consumed by fire or carried away by whites. New struggles—first to get free, then to protect their land, and finally to rebuild their community—loomed ahead.*
- *An untold number of Tulsans—both white and black—had been killed or lay dying. Even before the sun set on June 1, the gravediggers were at work. They would stay busy for days to come.*
- *A couple of other details seem particularly ironic in retrospect. Sheriff William M. McCullough quietly slipped out of town with Dick Rowland. Sarah Page refused to prosecute, and Rowland was later exonerated.*

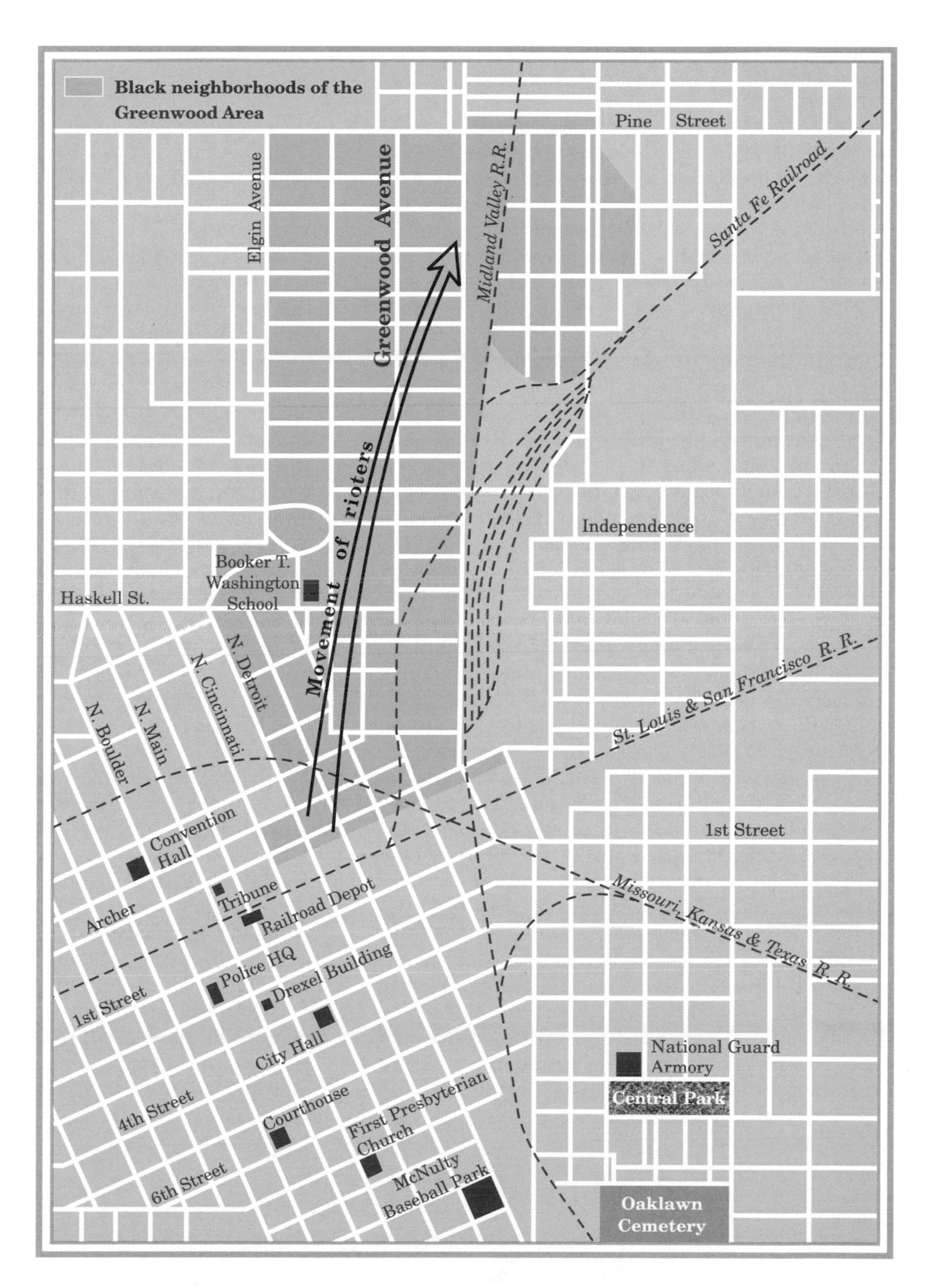

77. THE KU KLUX KLAN IN THE 1920s

Essay by *Danney Goble*

Ku Klux Klan—however odd the name sounds to us now, Oklahomans by the tens of thousands once found that peculiar combination of syllables enchanting and alluring. What is more, they seriously and solemnly considered the organization for which the name stood to be synonymous with dignity and probity. So numerous and so serious were they that an estimated 150,000 Oklahomans loyally paid their Klan membership dues (called klectokens by the faithful) in the early 1920s. For ten dollars a month, they bought what they regarded as the honor of membership in the Knights of the Ku Klux Klan.

They believed not only that it was an honor for them but also that rarely was honor as sorely needed as in their day. Unlike the extinct KKK of the post–Civil War period (or the more recent pretenders to the name), this Ku Klux Klan was a nationwide phenomenon, present in every state, powerful in every region. It openly flaunted racism, nativism, and bigotry—considered virtues by some—but its appeal in Oklahoma was probably more immediate and local than that. After all, Oklahoma had barely enough Jews, Catholics, or foreigners to count, much less fear. As for blacks, they were the ones doing the fearing—just ask the survivors of Tulsa's bloody 1921 race riot. No, the Klansmen were more likely to think that Oklahoma's trouble was that it had too many bootleggers, too many gamblers, too many whoremongers, and too many faithless husbands. They were why Oklahoma needed a Ku Klux Klan.

So persuaded, thousands of attorneys, shopkeepers, merchants, clerics, physicians, store managers, educators, landlords, bankers, and the like rushed down to their local klaverns, put down their initial klectokens, and ordered their official robes and hoods. Respectable men all (of course they were respectable; respectability was why they were there), each was then entitled to greet the others with the somber question "AYAK?" to which another would respond "AKIA!"—"Are you a Klansman?" "A Klansman I am!"

The largest klaverns advertised their presence with stunning temples, at least for the worship of self and status. None was more impressive than Tulsa's Beno Hall. (Klansmen said that the name was a diminutive form of "benevolence"; black Tulsans, on the contrary, said it meant that there "be no" black folks allowed.) Tulsa's 1,500 Klansmen spent $60,000 to buy Centenary Methodist Church, thousands more to raze it, then $200,000 to build a 3,000-seat assembly hall, the largest in the state and one of the largest in the entire Southwest. Tulsa's women also were among the founders of Kamelia, the Klan's women's auxiliary, with its national headquarters in nearby Claremore. No one knows how many good Ku Klux Klansmen and Ku Klux Klanswomen enrolled their children in Tulsa's Junior Ku Klux Klan.

Despite all this, there was nothing funny about this KKK; nor was there any risk of confusing the KKK with Rotary, Kiwanis, or any other lodge or family activity. Beneath the silly robes and goofy hoods were serious men, earnest men who were certain of their moral rectitude. They cloaked themselves in secrecy not to disguise their probity but to display it. Alas, too many used the cloak of their Klan shrouds to mask other reasons for their membership. Clad in KKK regalia, they had all the assurance necessary of a mass anonymity that could turn upstanding moral men into vicious vigilantes.

At the Klan's peak—probably in 1923—scarcely an evening passed without some klavern's burning of a fiery cross somewhere in Oklahoma. Much worse happened, too, and nearly as often: whippings, beatings, floggings, even castrations and other brutal mutilations. These Klan activities were undeniably crimes, not that police departments and local prosecutors were anxious to treat them as such. Only in the end did these acts of moral terror and intimidation become so vicious and so outrageous that officials had to respond.

One conspicuous politician did respond: Governor John Calloway "Jack" Walton declared unofficial but total war on the Ku Klux Klan. Walton devoted every weapon available to him—including the weapons of war—to this historic political struggle. In both the city and the county of Tulsa, soldiers under the governor's personal command ousted elected officials, while uniformed troops patrolled city streets and bayonet-wielding warriors shut down a hostile press. Within days, private citizens were summoned to stand before military tribunals.

Walton's victories (whether in Tulsa or, later, elsewhere) proved to be purely Pyrrhic. Incensed by the governor's heavy-handed tactics and backed by an outraged public, state representatives impeached Jack Walton on multiple charges, almost none of which had anything to do with the KKK. No doubt hastened by the embattled chief executive's threat to empty the state prison under a blanket parole, the senate immediately suspended him from office, then leisurely took its time to convict and remove him. The end came just eight months into his term.

For Walton, the defeat was anything but final. Hanging around politics for years, he eventually won a seat on the corporation commission. For the Klan, however, any expectations of a permanent victory were quickly dispatched: Oklahoma's experiment in terror ended as soon as Walton exposed it. The Ku Klux Klan spent the next few years dying.

Selected Cities Where Klan-Related Events Occurred

Oklahoma City—1921: The original headquarters of Oklahoma's Ku Klux Klan was Room 503 of the downtown Baltimore Building. In time, the organization took over an entire building, but by 1926 the decline in Klan fortunes had again reduced its headquarters to a single room. In between those dates, the city was the site for publication of the Klan's statewide newspaper, *The Fiery Cross.* **March 7, 1922:** Cabdriver Edward S. Merriman was abducted by two men disguised as police officers; he was then taken out of town and whipped by eight carloads of white-robed men for "immorality with a young woman."

Muskogee—July 1921: In this first reported incident of Klan-sponsored violence in Oklahoma, 15–20 Klan members seized Billy Ware at gunpoint, spirited the young dishwasher out of town, and whipped him, on the allegation that Ware had kidnapped a young boy who could have identified him as a burglar. Although the incident was observed by a local newspaperman and related in detail to the Muskogee Police Department, no investigation or charges ensued. **1922:** With both the national denomination and local congregations divided on the Klan issue, Presbyterian minister Stephen B. Williams resigned his pulpit to become an itinerant lecturer on behalf of the Ku Klux Klan.

Tulsa—August 31, 1921: In a public ceremony, some 300 Tulsans were formally initiated as members of Tulsa Klan No. 2. **September 1921:** 20 hooded vigilantes whipped suspected car thief and hijacker J. E. Frazier. Over the four months that followed and with Tulsa county attorney John Seaver's praise of the Klan, other masked bands whipped 12 more individuals in the county. **March 1922:** Masked men abducted and whipped prominent African American John K. Smitherman. They then cut off a portion of his ear and attempted to force him to eat it. **November 1921–July 1923:** According to formal indictments, at least 31 Tulsans (each an admitted Klansman) engaged in at least 12 flogging episodes in the county.

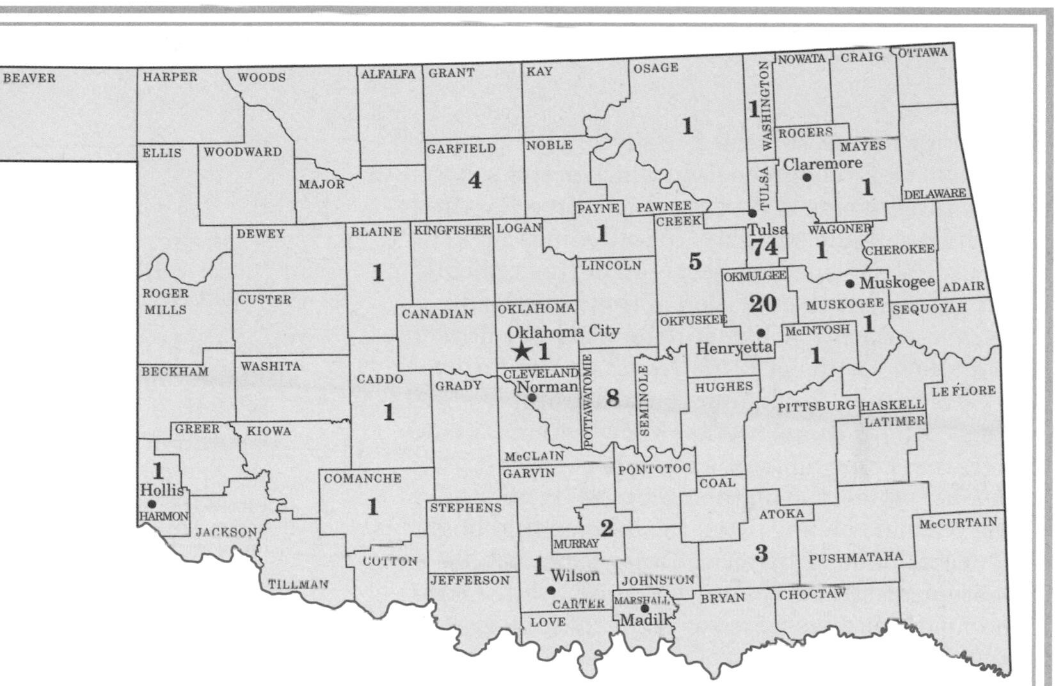

Reported incidents involving the Ku Klux Klan, by county

Governor Jack Walton, Martial Law, and the KKK

Oklahoma City—August 1922: Klan candidates swept primary elections in both parties, ensuring the so-called Invisible Empire's control of county and municipal governments. **September 1923:** After a grand jury's investigation into his misdeeds, Governor Walton declared martial law upon Oklahoma County, where guardsmen took over the police station, city hall, and county courthouse. Later that month, a large group of legislators attempted to gather at the state capitol to explore their options, since the legislature was out of session and not scheduled to reconvene until 1925. Walton declared martial law on the capitol grounds, surrounded it with barbed-wire and machine-gun nests, and stationed troops there to turn the legislators away. **March 1923:** With strong Klan backing, Oklahoma's Ninth Legislature amended the state's first free textbook bill to ban books teaching the theory of evolution.

Harmon County—1923: In an early move against the Klan, Governor Walton ordered state prosecutors to assist the local county attorney's investigation of a Klan whipping near Hollis.

Henryetta—July 12, 1923: After reaching what he called "perfect accord" with Okmulgee County officials, Governor Walton ordered that martial law be lifted.

Tulsa—August 14, 1923: After Klansmen beat and mutilated accused drug peddler Nathan Hantaman, Governor Walton declared martial law in the city and county of Tulsa.

Madill—September 11, 1923: In a speech at the Marshall County fair, Governor Walton boldly (and probably unconstitutionally) proclaimed that Klan parades were to be "banned in Oklahoma from now until the termination of my administration."

Oklahoma City—September 23, 1923: Claiming what he called a Klan conspiracy, Governor Walton placed the entire state under martial law.

Oklahoma City—November 11, 1923: The state senate convened as a court of impeachment and 11 days later found Walton guilty; his short term as governor was over.

Selected Incidents of Violence Involving the KKK, 1921–1924

Type of incident	No.
Floggings	102
Reports of masked action	21
Reports of the Klan	42
Reports of regalia	8
Reports of black hoods	3
Killings	3
Burning of buildings	4
Burning of people	1
Mutilation	3
Beatings	24
Threats	7
Tarring/feathering	3

By all accounts, some of these numbers are considered too low.

Carter County—December 1921: Near the tiny community of Wilson, some 150 robed and hooded Klansmen authorized 9 of their number to raid the home of suspected liquor dealer Joe Carroll. Carroll and 2 of the Klan raiders were shot to death in the ensuing gun battle.

Norman—1922: Holder of a Ph.D. in chemistry from the University of Michigan and a member of the University of Oklahoma's original faculty, Edwin DeBarr added to his existing obligations as an uncommonly popular professor and the university's vice president to assume the mantle of Grand Dragon of the newly created Oklahoma Realm of the Imperial Knights of the Ku Klux Klan. He served until 1923, when university regents forced him to resign that position.

Claremore—March 1923: Based on nearby chapters of the WAP (White American Protestant) study club, national Klan organizer and leader William J. Simmons designated this Oklahoma town as headquarters for the KKK's nationwide ladies auxiliary, the Kamelia. Oklahoma chapters existed in Tulsa, Guthrie, and other cities. Tulsa was headquarters of an internal rival organization called the Women of the Klan.

78. EDUCATION IN THE YOUNG STATE

Essay by *Danney Goble*

Few things are as shrouded in myth as is pioneer education. One-room schools in which pretty schoolmarms taught kids of all ages their three Rs, then sent them outside for playground games or kept them in to enjoy spelling bees—all of this typically comes to mind at the mention of frontier schooling. What was education like in "the good old days"? Watch a few reruns of *Little House on the Prairie,* many Americans think, and you will know.

Know what? Know myths, know fictions, know half truths, know no truths at all.

In most states, the mythologizing of frontier education perhaps means little. In Oklahoma, though, the concealment of historical knowledge behind a stereotypical screen counts for quite a bit. Oklahoma's pioneer days were so recent that the grandparents of this generation of state leaders very well might have attended a one-room schoolhouse. In addition, what happened (and did not happen) in Oklahoma's frontier schools quite visibly impacts today's Oklahoma.

Often what happened was hardly by choice. From a twenty-first-century perspective, one might very well assume that settlers wanted the best for their children. In fact, that desire may have been what brought them to early Oklahoma in the first place; surely for some, their hopes included a better life for their children, and that meant the best education possible.

Yes, it often did, and part of Oklahoma's historical record proves it. The homesteaders who poured into Oklahoma Territory often made building a schoolhouse and hiring a schoolteacher their first items of public business—not infrequently doing so well before there was any organized government to make them or even to tell them how. But in too many cases it came down to the spirit being willing while the flesh was too weak—or the pocketbook too empty, anyway. Homesteaders tended not to have much (else they might not have been homesteaders), and in the beginning, they could not buy adequate school equipment or pay respectable salaries for schoolteachers.

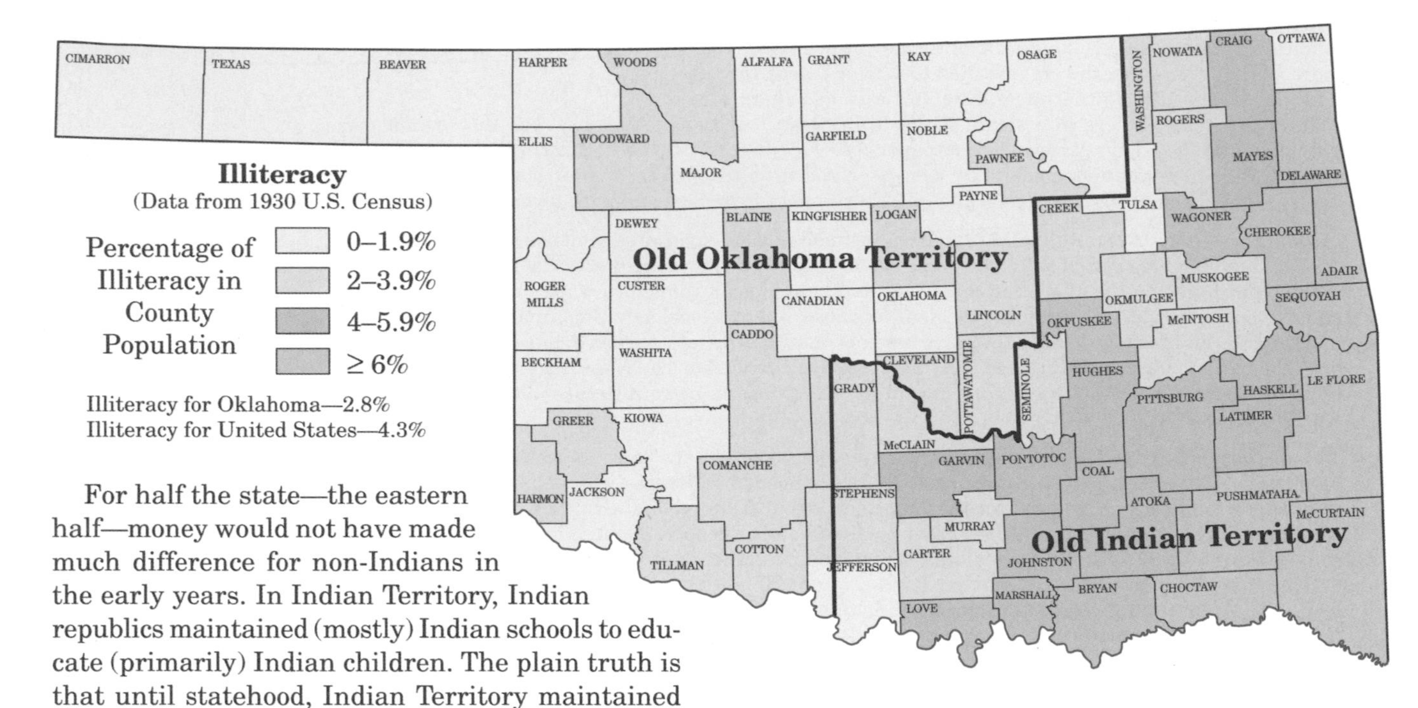

For half the state—the eastern half—money would not have made much difference for non-Indians in the early years. In Indian Territory, Indian republics maintained (mostly) Indian schools to educate (primarily) Indian children. The plain truth is that until statehood, Indian Territory maintained no public education for the vast majority of its white and black residents.

The difference between east and west was glaringly obvious as early as the first decennial census to include Oklahoma. When Oklahoma's seventy-six counties of 1910 are arrayed in order by the percentage of the population ten years of age and older who are illiterate, all but three of the thirty most literate counties had been in Oklahoma Territory; of the thirty-one least literate, all but two had been in Indian Territory. The gap between the two extremes was significant: in Grant County, less than 1 percent of the population were illiterate, while in Adair County, more than 20 percent were illiterate.

Size of Rural Elementary Schools, by County, 1936

Size	No. of schools	Percentage of rural schools in state
One-room	3,306	57.5
Two-room	1,273	22.1
Three-room and larger	1,173	20.4
Total	5,752	100.0

Data from State Board of Education.

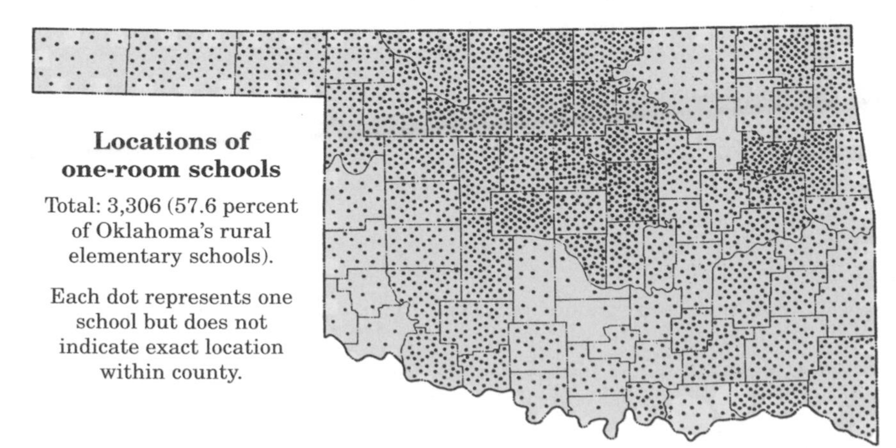

Locations of one-room schools

Total: 3,306 (57.6 percent of Oklahoma's rural elementary schools).

Each dot represents one school but does not indicate exact location within county.

That pattern changed slightly with time, but a generation and more after pioneer settlement, Oklahoma's schools still ran up against great financial difficulties, as their rural setting and relatively small size indicates. As late as 1935, well over half (57.5 percent) of the state's public schools consisted of one room. Barely a fifth (20.4 percent) had as many as three. Just four of Adair County's schools were even that large; only one in neighboring Cherokee County could claim three rooms.

Illiteracy rates for that next generation improved to the point where, by 1930, Oklahomans were more likely to be literate than were their fellow countrymen—statewide. County by county, though, it was a different story, with great clusters of counties (approximately all those that had been in the old Indian Territory) still having illiteracy rates greater than—often double—the national rate.

What difference did that make in the development of the new state of Oklahoma? Keep in mind that when times are good, the poorly educated do not fare as well as those blessed with better schooling, while hard times hit the illiterate much harder.

That may explain why Oklahoma's per capita income was only 85 percent of the nation's in 1919 and dropped to 65 percent a decade later, in 1929, just as the good times were going bad. Three years later, in 1932, Oklahomans earned barely half (54 percent) what other Americans received. In 1932, times were hard all over. In Oklahoma, they would have had to improve considerably just to get that bad.

Early Universities and Colleges, Relocated or Closed

Several early-day colleges and universities have been reorganized under new names, and in some instances they have been moved to new locations. A number of others have entirely disappeared. Kingfisher College, founded in 1894 by the Congregational Church, became a very fine academic institution but fell on hard times in the 1920s and was absorbed by the University of Oklahoma; today it is remembered by the Kingfisher College Chair of Religion and Philosophy at that university. Henry Kendall College, established at Muskogee in 1894, was moved to Tulsa in 1907 and became the University of Tulsa in 1920. Epworth University, founded in Oklahoma City in 1904, was relocated to Guthrie, returning to Oklahoma City in 1911 and evolving into Oklahoma City University in 1924.

Indian University, founded in Tahlequah in 1880, was moved in 1881 to Bacone, near Muskogee, and in 1910 was renamed for its founder, Almon C. Bacone. Church schools that were discontinued include Southwestern Baptist College at Mangum, St. Joseph's at Guthrie, Monte Cassino at Tulsa, Oklahoma Wesleyan at Oklahoma City, Oklahoma Baptist at Blackwell, and Oklahoma Presbyterian College in Durant.

By 1924, Oklahoma had ten public institutions and five private institutions offering four or more years of college. There were also six public and four private junior colleges offering two years of college work and ten public junior colleges offering one year of college work. In 1924, the University of Oklahoma established educational standards to guide local school systems in the establishing of one-year municipal junior colleges. The academic offerings would be approved by the university, and each junior college was to be inspected at least once during the year. By late 1930s, twenty-seven municipal junior colleges existed across the state (with various levels of success), but nearly all have disappeared.

79. WHEAT FARMING, 1907–2000

Essay by *Bruce W. Hoagland*

Until the very late nineteenth century, wheat hardly figured as a major territorial crop. Sod busting took time and work, too much of both to be accomplished in a few years. That aside, much of the (potentially) best wheat lands suffered from a drought that began in 1893, the very year that the so-called Cherokee Strip was thrown open to thousands of would-be wheat growers.

Not until 1896 did these farmers get a decent wheat harvest, but the following year's production was remarkable. In just twelve months, the acreage planted in wheat had doubled. Moreover, nearly every acre was producing record yields. The difference that made such a difference was the introduction of Turkey Red wheat. Unlike the soft, spring forms then familiar to midwestern farmers, Turkey Red was a hard, winter wheat almost perfectly suited for north-central Oklahoma. Mennonites, who had perfected the strain in their Crimean homelands, brought it to the windswept plains in the mid-nineties. By statehood, in 1907, it had proven its worth. Oklahomans harvested 11,431,640 bushels of wheat that year, with a value of $9,545,525. The state's best-producing lands were among its northernmost counties: Grant, Alfalfa, Garfield, and Woods.

As with many sectors of agriculture, mechanization utterly transformed twentieth-century wheat growing. As late as 1900, horses and humans remained the most common sources of power. Even early combines were horse-drawn, and most farmers had as much use for the steam-traction engines that replaced the original horse-power as they would have had for huge, cumbersome, and expensive locomotives—which is what these engines amounted to. Light and affordable gasoline-powered tractors became common only in the 1920s, and it was 1938 before self-propelled combines appeared. Modern combines have become so costly that their ownership and use has become something of an independent industry; nomadic contractors head south out of Canada every spring, pass through Oklahoma later in the year, and leave behind mountains of grain.

Towering grain elevators collect, store, and provide a central location for shipping that golden grain to anywhere that anyone eats bread. Many are impressive enough to be confused with temples to Ceres. If no longer quite what it once was, Enid has long been Oklahoma's leading elevator town. At its peak, Enid had the second-highest grain-storage capacity in the United States and was home to the largest wheat-exporting organization in the world.

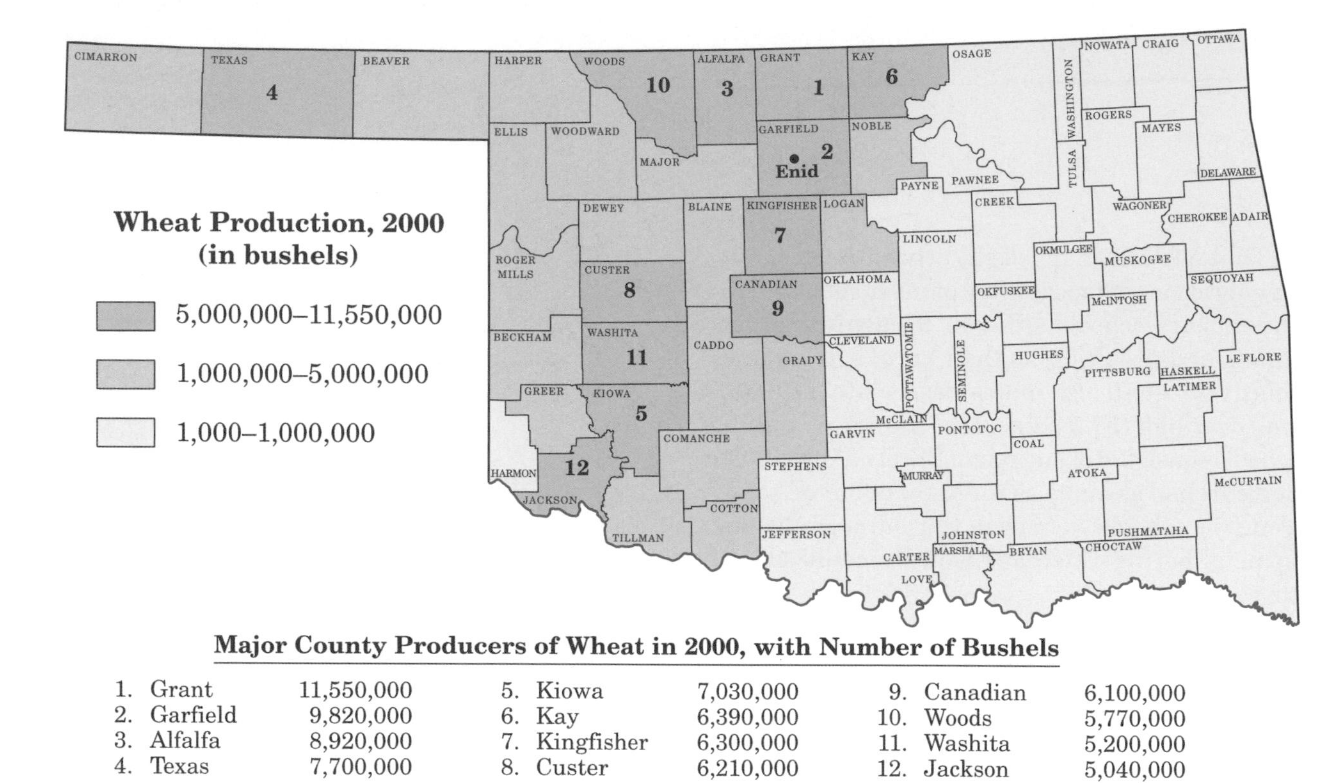

Major County Producers of Wheat in 2000, with Number of Bushels

	County	Bushels		County	Bushels		County	Bushels
1.	Grant	11,550,000	5.	Kiowa	7,030,000	9.	Canadian	6,100,000
2.	Garfield	9,820,000	6.	Kay	6,390,000	10.	Woods	5,770,000
3.	Alfalfa	8,920,000	7.	Kingfisher	6,300,000	11.	Washita	5,200,000
4.	Texas	7,700,000	8.	Custer	6,210,000	12.	Jackson	5,040,000

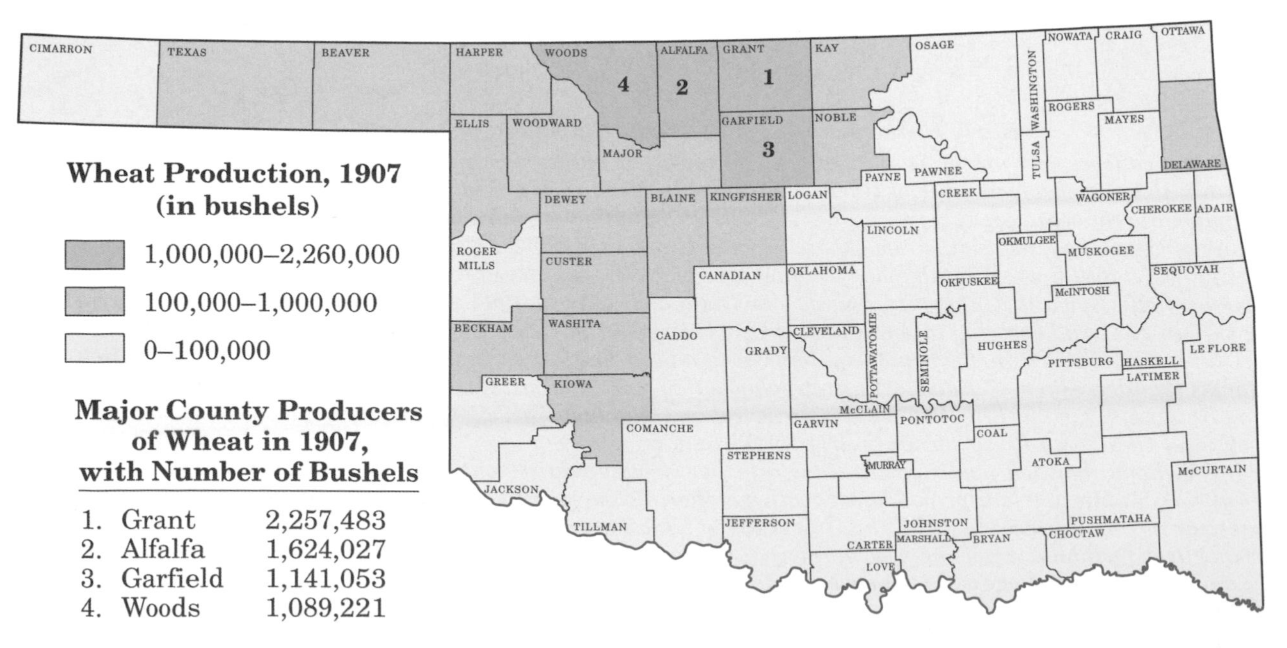

Major County Producers of Wheat in 1907, with Number of Bushels

	County	Bushels
1.	Grant	2,257,483
2.	Alfalfa	1,624,027
3.	Garfield	1,141,053
4.	Woods	1,089,221

80. *COTTON FARMING, 1907–2000*

Essay by *Bruce W. Hoagland*

As with much else in the state's history, cotton growing in Oklahoma is older than Oklahoma itself. The Five Nations began to grow cotton almost immediately upon their arrival. By 1840 twelve cotton gins were processing a thousand bales in the Choctaw Nation alone. By the end of tribal rule, so many citizen-landlords were using noncitizen tenants (meaning whites and blacks coming into the territory) that Indian Territory seemed less an "Indian" territory than the most recent addition to King Cotton's domain. In 1907, seventy-one of Oklahoma's then seventy-five counties produced cotton; more than a fifth of the new state's cultivated land was planted in cotton.

As a sovereign, King Cotton was a miserly despot. Land once in range and virgin prairie turned a quick profit with cotton, but the land paid a high price: erosion and a swift drop in fertility. If anything, the human price was even greater—at least, it was more immediately apparent. J. P. Connors, president of the Oklahoma Board of Agriculture, had it right when he said, in 1908, that "the poorer farmer a man is, the more cotton he grows, [and] the more cotton a man grows the poorer he is." Not that his maxim made any difference: a year later, 46 percent of Oklahoma's farms grew cotton.

Things became even worse thereafter, even as they appeared to be getting better. The 1920s turned out to be Oklahoma's best (or, depending on your perspective, worst) years for cotton. The peak came in 1926, when 5.3 million acres, more than a third of the state's cropland, was given over to that one crop. All that changed, however, in a stunningly short time. First the boll weevil and then the Great Depression freed thousands of Oklahomans from King Cotton's grip, even if it hardly felt liberating at the time.

Oklahomans still grow cotton, but not nearly as much as before 1930. The state's 274,000 bales of 2000 was barely a third of the cotton growers' output in 1907, not even a sixth of the 1926 record. Long ranking only behind Texas and Mississippi, Oklahoma currently stands fourteenth nationally in cotton production.

Finally, it is a different Oklahoma that produces cotton. Greer, Lincoln, and Pottawatomie counties had set the pace in 1907; several southeastern counties surely would have beat them but for the fact that their soil already had lost much fertility to cotton. In 2000, neither any of the original pacesetters nor any southeastern county was at the top: Jackson, Harmon, and Tillman counties dominate in modern production, and all lie in southwestern Oklahoma, where cotton has never been king but where fertilization, mechanization, and irrigation have made cotton pay at last.

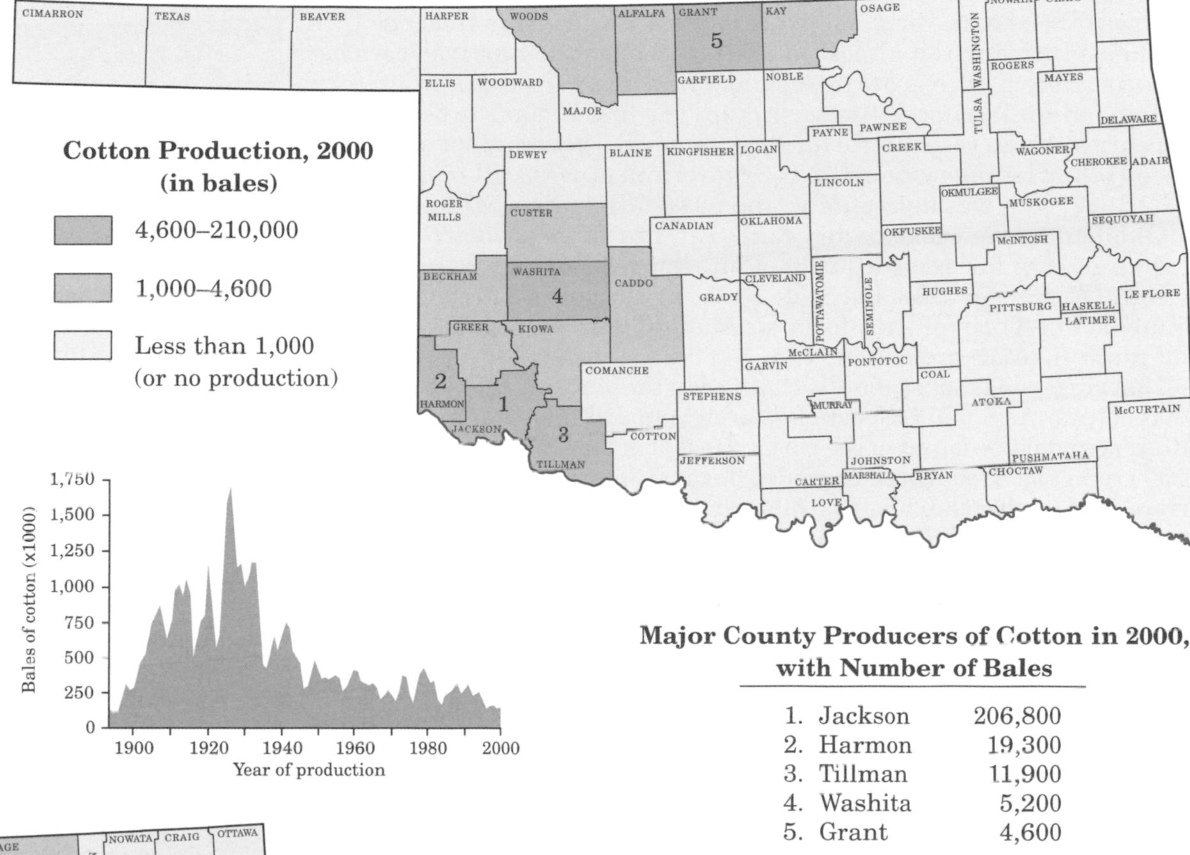

Major County Producers of Cotton in 2000, with Number of Bales

1.	Jackson	206,800
2.	Harmon	19,300
3.	Tillman	11,900
4.	Washita	5,200
5.	Grant	4,600

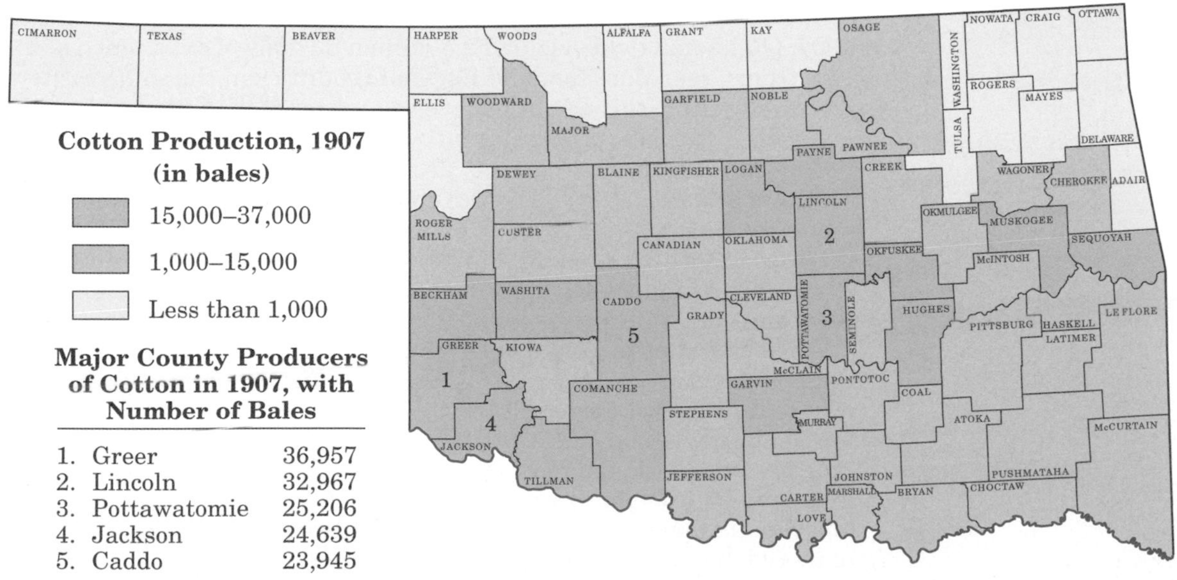

Major County Producers of Cotton in 1907, with Number of Bales

1.	Greer	36,957
2.	Lincoln	32,967
3.	Pottawatomie	25,206
4.	Jackson	24,639
5.	Caddo	23,945

81. CORN AND OTHER GRAIN FARMING, 1907–2000

Essay by *Bruce W. Hoagland*

Corn was Oklahoma's original primary crop. The Indians from the U.S. Southeast introduced it almost immediately upon their arrival, corn being what they had to grow to sustain themselves. In short order, corn became Indian Territory's first cash crop. The first Indians to be removed sold corn to those responsible for their removal—government officials—to feed other Indians whom the U.S. government was still removing.

By 1907, corn was indisputably the new state's principal crop. Grown by Oklahomans in every county that year, the value of their 73 million bushels of corn far exceeded that of either wheat or cotton. In its *First Biennial Report,* in 1908, the State Board of Agriculture proudly ranked Oklahoma seventh (of then forty-six states) in acreage devoted to corn and ninth in total production.

That situation is substantially changed in the mature state: Oklahoma's 2000 output (37.8 million bushels) barely equaled half that in 1907. The difference could be found in the curious fact that two-thirds of Oklahoma's 2000 crop came from three counties: Texas, Cimarron, and Beaver, comprising the Panhandle. Flat as a table and dry as dust, this is land laid out for mechanized agriculture and dependent on irrigation. Both cost money, so much that corn growing has become a luxury few farmers can afford.

Oklahoma and broomcorn—the latter's commercial use inherent in its name—have been together since 1889. As early as 1915, Oklahoma led the nation in broomcorn production. Except for drought-ruined 1937, the state's supremacy lasted through 1942. By then, Lindsay had begun to bill itself as Broomcorn Capital of the World, a title that presumably made Cheyenne, Chickasha, Marlow, and Maysville provincial capitals in the Great Broomcorn Empire.

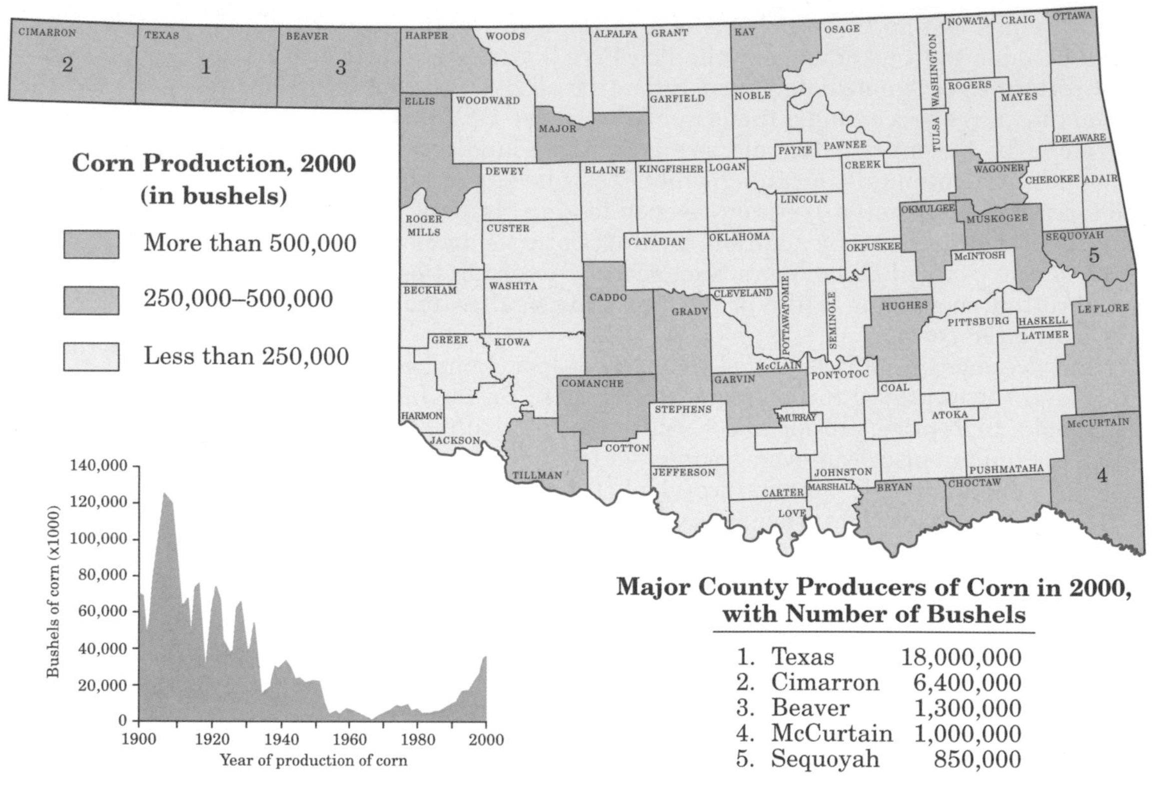

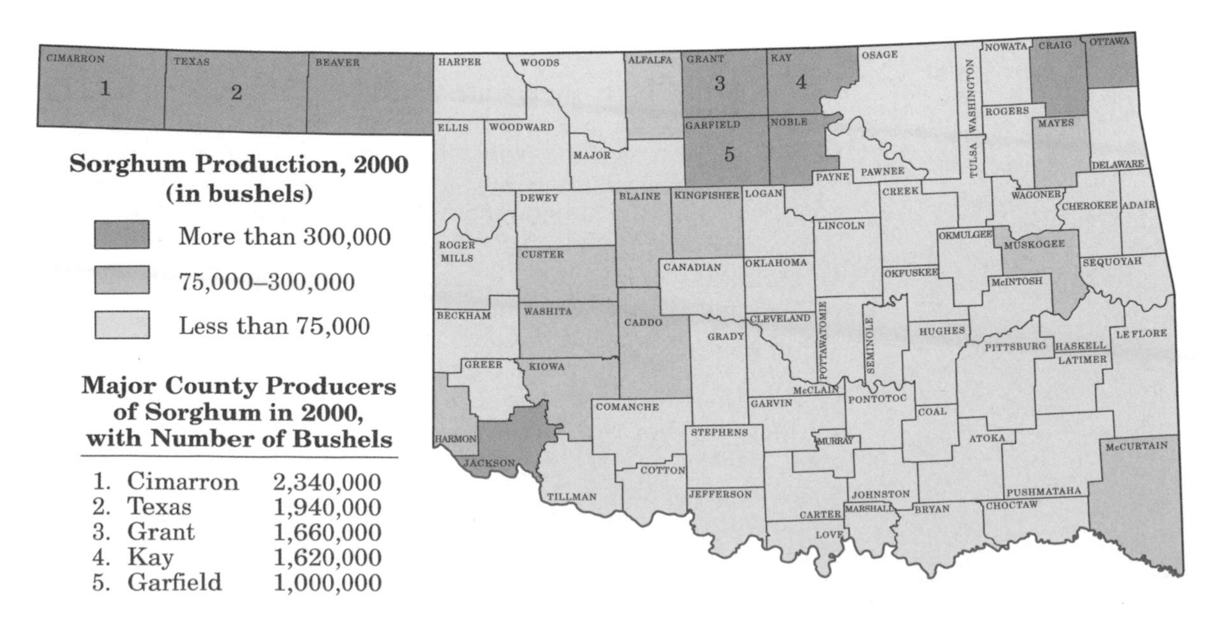

Several of the state's traditional grain crops have gone the way of corn and broomcorn: down. None has diminished more than oats. In 1907, Oklahoma fields yielded 2.8 million bushels of oats, much of the crop from Greer, Jackson, and Beckham counties in the southwestern corner. The state turned out not even a quarter of that amount in 2000, and very little came from the southwest.

Not all grain production has declined, though. Two grain crops—sorghum and rye—have gone the opposite way. Grain sorghum yields increased nearly eight times over between 1907 and 2000. That huge increase is nothing compared to rye yields, however, which multiplied by a factor of eighty. Turnarounds for any crop in that direction have been unusual, with increases of that magnitude almost unheard of.

An explanation is visible in geography. Sorghum production has consistently been associated with Oklahoma's extreme northwest; rye production has moved there. All three Panhandle counties are nearly the top producers of one or both. The addition of Ellis, Harper, and Grant counties fills in the top tier for rye. Usually flat, frequently open, often irrigated, with long growing seasons—this combination of topography and climate makes investments in agriculture pay off. It does. But only to those who can pay for water and machinery.

82. LIVESTOCK PRODUCTION

Essay by *Bruce W. Hoagland & Danney Goble*

The history of stock raising in Oklahoma is the history of agriculture in Oklahoma—for that matter, the history of just about any significant economic activity in Oklahoma. Forever shrouded in myths of sturdy pioneers and hardy individualism, it has moved as far and as fast from those early days as possible. Corporate, commercial, and concentrated, contemporary stock raising is a big business. In fact, it is big business writ large.

Take cattle. In the 1880s, the Cherokee Strip Live Stock Association was a nearly perfect example of corporate stock raising, even if it was anything but typical of the time. Buy a cow then or somewhat later, and the odds were that the animal would be of the small, scrawny variety called scrub cattle. The seller likely would have owned a small subsistence or mixed-production farm, off of which he sold a few cows from time to time.

If we jump ahead more than a century, the picture changes greatly. In the year 2000, Oklahoma was home to more than 5,000,000 cattle, highly concentrated geographically. Particularly impressive in this respect was Osage County, where lush prairie grasses sustained 135,000 head. Admittedly, even that is a small number when contrasted with Texas County's 310,000 cattle, but very few of the latter were going to be there long. Crammed into feedlots, they gorged on quality feed until ready for slaughter, after which their carcasses were shipped to pack grocers' meat sections, where their parts would be sold as expensive, grain-fed, marbleized beef. Texas County's Hitch family established Oklahoma's first feedlot in 1953. In 2000, Oklahoma had twenty-eight feedlots, and the largest six could handle between them no fewer than 192,000 cattle on any given day.

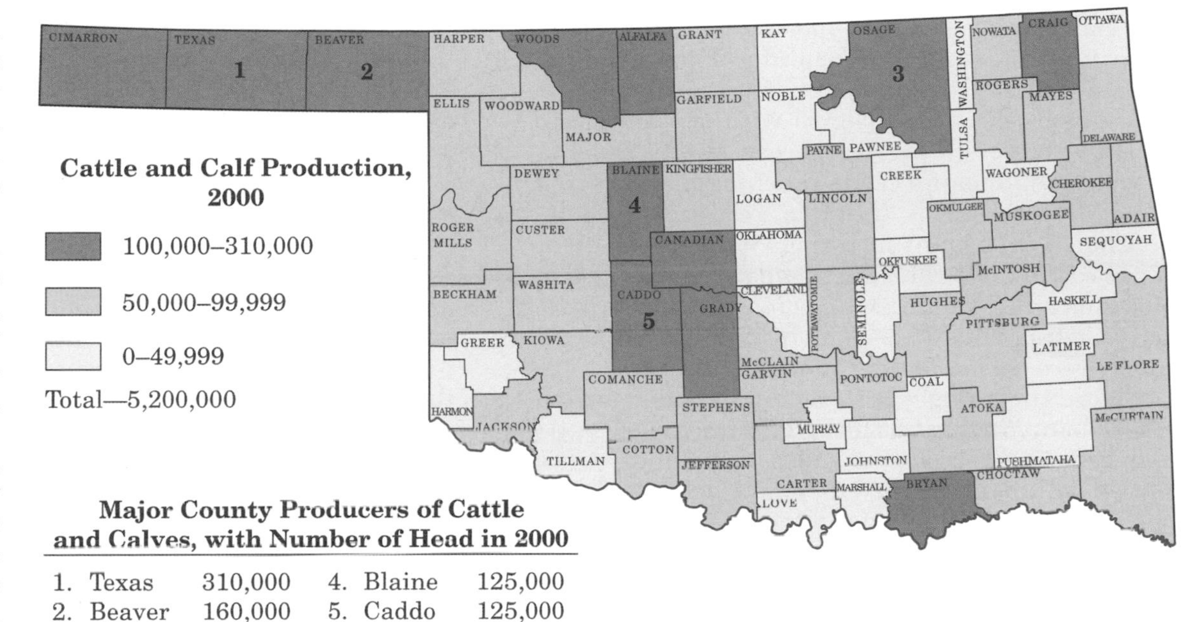

Cattle and Calf Production, 2000

- 100,000–310,000
- 50,000–99,999
- 0–49,999

Total—5,200,000

Major County Producers of Cattle and Calves, with Number of Head in 2000

1. Texas	310,000	4. Blaine	125,000
2. Beaver	160,000	5. Caddo	125,000
3. Osage	135,000		

Prefer pork? There already was plenty of that in 1907—from 1,206,800 animals. In every county, nearly every farmer raised hogs back then. By 2000, only 2,700 farms still produced hogs, but these corporate farms produced a lot more pork. The giant Seaboard Corporation, which came to the Panhandle in the early 1990s, had developed a massive integrated pork-processing industry by then. Throughout 2000, about 4,500,000 hogs were packed into Seaboard pens and stuffed with feed produced by Seaboard mills, until these avid consumers were themselves ready to become food—at Seaboard slaughterhouses, which processed more than 12,000 a day.

Seaboard (like the big cattle feedlots) is an example of CAFOs: Confined Animal Feeding Operations. The pork and beef producers, though, were neither alone nor necessarily the biggest of their kind in terms of the number of animals processed. The top CAFOs could be found in eastern Oklahoma, in the chicken business, but not as the stereotypical farmwives picking up a little egg money on the side. These poultry barns held an estimated 5.32 million chickens, producing 931 million eggs annually. Sales of poultry and eggs accounted for $427 million in 2000.

Chickens (and eggs), pigs, and cows—these have become commodities rather than creatures, and their production and processing are now matters of public controversy. Consider only one of the many environmental effects: if estimates are accurate that the waste produced by 4 million hogs equals that of 8 million humans, then Seaboard's pig pens pour into Texas County 2.6 times as much waste as the entire human population lays upon the entire state of Oklahoma.

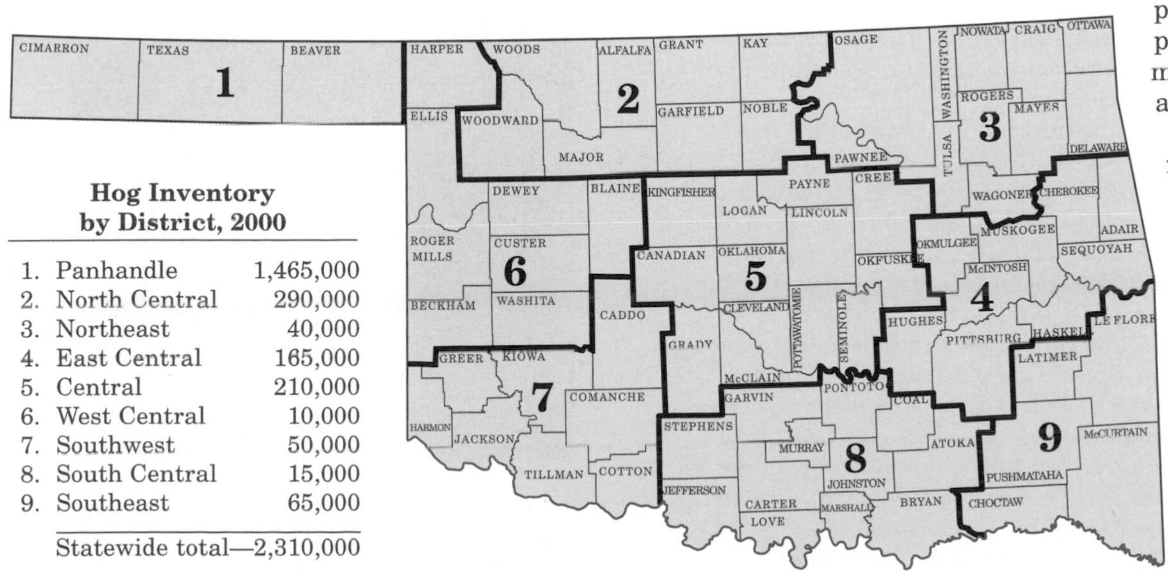

Hog Inventory by District, 2000

District	Hogs
1. Panhandle	1,465,000
2. North Central	290,000
3. Northeast	40,000
4. East Central	165,000
5. Central	210,000
6. West Central	10,000
7. Southwest	50,000
8. South Central	15,000
9. Southeast	65,000

Statewide total—2,310,000

83. PROMINENT CATTLE RANCHES

Essay by *John R. Lovett*

The range cattle industry in Oklahoma played an important role in the economic development of the state and contributed much to the state's folklore and history. From its origins with the arrival of the Five Tribes to the prosperous family ranches of today, Oklahoma's cattle ranching has survived drought, dust storms, inflation, recession, and depression. While many historians focus on the great Texas cattle drives and the range cattle industry in Montana and Wyoming, Oklahoma's cattlemen were active in the industry decades before the first Texas cattle were driven to the railhead in Kansas.

Before their removal to Indian Territory in the 1830s, many Indians of the Five Tribes raised cattle and hogs in their southeastern homelands. Once settled in Indian Territory, they discovered that their new western home provided a relatively fertile landscape that easily supported a pastoral life. The lush river and creek bottomlands and the relatively mild winters increased the herds and provided the tribes with a surplus of cattle well beyond the numbers needed for the local market.

With the discovery of gold in California and the great migration over the California Road through Indian Territory, the Indian cattle rancher found an excellent market for surplus cattle. The Choctaws were particularly impacted by the boom in the cattle industry because of their location on the California Road.

Cattle of the Five Nations were also exported in modest numbers to Missouri, Kansas, and Arkansas prior to 1861. The outbreak of the Civil War proved to be devastating to the range cattle industry in Indian Territory. Both Confederate and Union forces operating in Indian Territory confiscated the cattle as a source of supplies with little thought of compensating owners with payments. Many cattle thieves from Kansas also operated in the area, stealing a large number of Indian cattle. The organized theft of Indian cattle continued past 1865 and became such a problem that the Indian governments requested federal assistance in ending this practice.

By 1884 the Indian herds had recovered and were estimated at 700,000 head of cattle. Several members of the tribes made fortunes in the cattle business from leasing grazing land to Texas ranchers as well as from the large number of cattle they owned. With allotment and the end of tribal communal landownership, open-range grazing in Indian Territory transitioned to enclosed pastures with smaller herds.

Texas stock raisers used large portions of the Indian Territory as grazing pasture for herds on the cattle trails to Kansas, and some used a given area as an extension of their ranches that bordered the area. Texas cattle could be found in large numbers on Indian agency lands. Several Indian agents attempted to claim compensation for their wards from the owners of the offending cattle, while on other occasions they requested federal troops to remove the intruders. Indian leaders also negotiated with Texas stock raisers, receiving money for themselves and their tribe. Quanah Parker was very successful in arranging leasing contracts between the Comanche tribe and the Texas cattle ranchers. As a result of his skills, thousands of dollars became available to the tribe.

In 1882 with the help of their agent, the Cheyennes and Arapahos leased three million acres to Texas stock raisers at two cents an acre for ten years. However, problems developed almost immediately with the arrangement. In 1885 the federal government ordered the Texans to remove their cattle from all Cheyenne and Arapaho lands. This removal affected several cattle ranchers and almost a quarter-million head of cattle.

In 1880 cattlemen succeeded in obtaining a lease from the Cherokee Nation to graze cattle on 6,344,562 acres of unoccupied land known as the Cherokee Outlet. The group of cattlemen formed the Cherokee Strip Live Stock Association. The more than one hundred members of the association were assigned surveyed tracts of grazing land within the lease area. They built corrals and buildings and fenced their assigned areas. The association paid the Cherokee government $100,000 for a five-year lease. Congressional investigations and public demand for the opening of the area to settlement led to the downfall of the association. In 1892 the Cherokee government agreed to sell the Cherokee Outlet to the federal government so that the area could be opened for settlement.

With the opening of Oklahoma Territory and Indian Territory for settlement, the large ranching operations on Indian land ended. Many of the ranches that continue to operate in Oklahoma today were first established on a 160-acre homestead. Numerous other ranches were established and failed. The Miller Brothers' famous 101 Ranch covered 135,000 acres before its demise in the 1930s. Hereford cattle began making their appearance on Oklahoma ranches soon after statehood. Herefords were raised in such numbers that many referred to Oklahoma as "Hereford Heaven." Today, Oklahoma cattle ranchers are proud of their heritage and history, and the cattle industry continues to be one of the state's leading businesses.

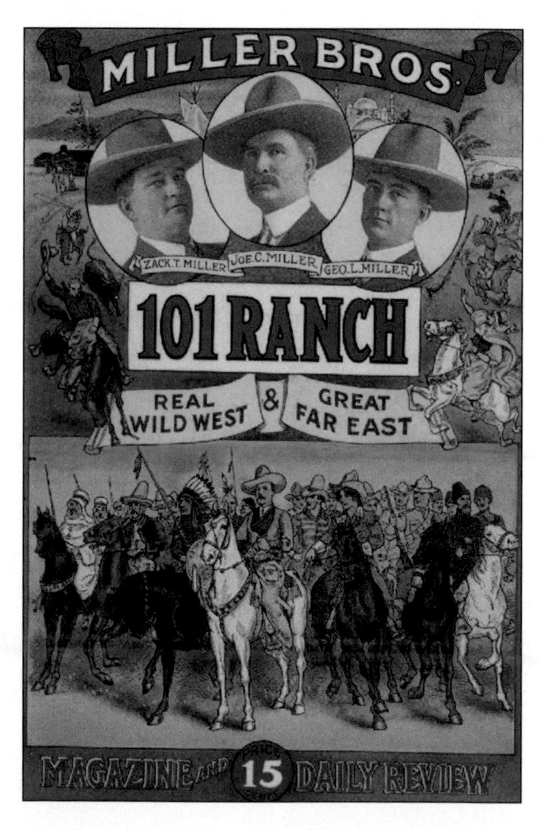

Program cover promoting the Miller Brothers 101 Ranch and Wild West Show, 1927. (Courtesy Western History Collections, University of Oklahoma Libraries)

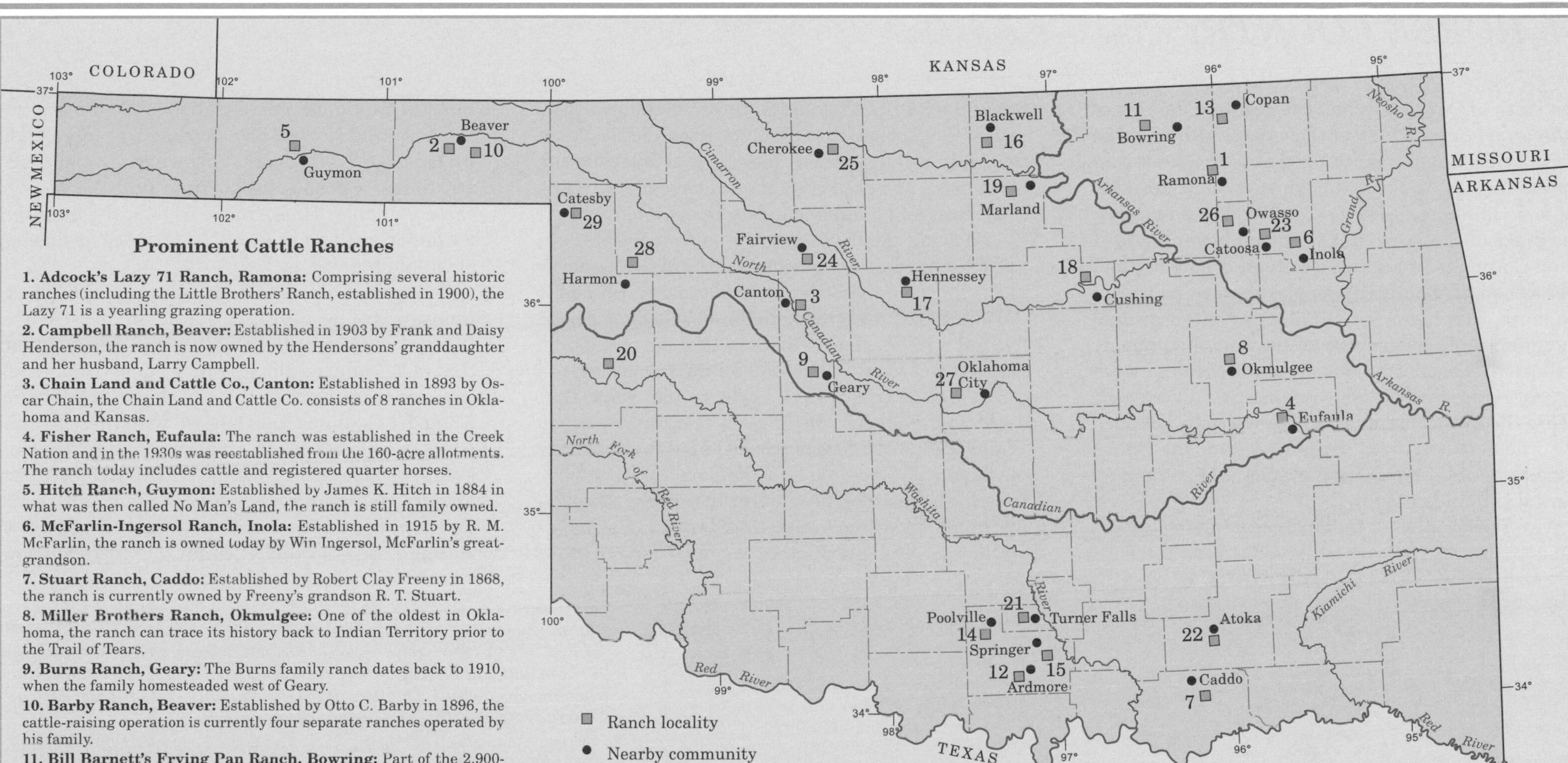

Prominent Cattle Ranches

1. Adcock's Lazy 71 Ranch, Ramona: Comprising several historic ranches (including the Little Brothers' Ranch, established in 1900), the Lazy 71 is a yearling grazing operation.

2. Campbell Ranch, Beaver: Established in 1903 by Frank and Daisy Henderson, the ranch is now owned by the Hendersons' granddaughter and her husband, Larry Campbell.

3. Chain Land and Cattle Co., Canton: Established in 1893 by Oscar Chain, the Chain Land and Cattle Co. consists of 8 ranches in Oklahoma and Kansas.

4. Fisher Ranch, Eufaula: The ranch was established in the Creek Nation and in the 1930s was reestablished from the 160-acre allotments. The ranch today includes cattle and registered quarter horses.

5. Hitch Ranch, Guymon: Established by James K. Hitch in 1884 in what was then called No Man's Land, the ranch is still family owned.

6. McFarlin-Ingersol Ranch, Inola: Established in 1915 by R. M. McFarlin, the ranch is owned today by Win Ingersol, McFarlin's great-grandson.

7. Stuart Ranch, Caddo: Established by Robert Clay Freeny in 1868, the ranch is currently owned by Freeny's grandson R. T. Stuart.

8. Miller Brothers Ranch, Okmulgee: One of the oldest in Oklahoma, the ranch can trace its history back to Indian Territory prior to the Trail of Tears.

9. Burns Ranch, Geary: The Burns family ranch dates back to 1910, when the family homesteaded west of Geary.

10. Barby Ranch, Beaver: Established by Otto C. Barby in 1896, the cattle-raising operation is currently four separate ranches operated by his family.

11. Bill Barnett's Frying Pan Ranch, Bowring: Part of the 2,900-acre ranch includes Bill Barnett's mother's original Osage allotment.

12. Daube Cattle Co., Ardmore: The 6 ranches of the Daube Cattle Co. can trace their origin to Sam Daube, a German immigrant who settled in Ardmore in 1885.

13. Mullendore Cross Bell Ranch, Copan: A ranch with 40,000 acres, originally established by Buck Boren, who made the run into the Cherokee Outlet in 1893.

14. Brady Ranch, Poolville: Established in 1892 by Jim Eaves and later operated by their daughter Mamie and her husband, J. Roy Brady; the original ranch house was restored and is listed as an Oklahoma historical site.

15. Zeller Ranch, Springer: The Zeller Ranch was established by Sherman Jones in 1898.

16. Wooderson Farms, Blackwell: Established by L. E. Wooderson, a Missouri native who came to Oklahoma in the late 1800s and started raising cattle and growing wheat.

17. Baker's Ranch, Hennessey: An important watering and grazing stop on the Chisholm Trail.

18. Turkey Track Ranch, Cushing: Established by James Jerome and Leslie Combs, the ranch was primarily used to fatten Texas trail-drive cattle before they reached the railheads in Kansas.

19. Miller Brothers' 101 Ranch, Marland: The ranch was established in 1893 by George W. Miller. Operated under the direction of his sons—Joe, Zack, and George Jr.—the ranch was best known for the 101 Wild West Show.

20. Cheyenne & Arapahoe Cattle Co., present-day Roger Mills County: Organized by Texas cattlemen in 1878 on leased Cheyenne and Arapaho land. Before it was forced by the federal government to vacate the land in 1885, the cattle company covered more than one million acres.

21. Hook Nine Ranch, near Turner Falls: Formed by F. D. Hendrix and C. E. Royer in 1890, the ranch operated until the late 1890s. Hendrix and Royer experimented with feeding the cattle cottonseed on the pasture.

22. Alinton Telle Ranch, near Atoka: Established by Alinton Telle in the early 1880s, Telle was a nephew of Choctaw governor Allen Wright.

23. Daugherty Ranch, near Catoosa: Established on leased Creek land in 1885 by James Monroe Daugherty, the ranch operated until 1906. At the peak of its operation, the ranch raised over 40,000 cattle.

24. Texas Land & Cattle Co., near Fairview: One of the largest members of the Cherokee Strip Live Stock Association. The company had offices in Caldwell and Kansas City, Kansas.

25. U Ranch, near Cherokee: Established by Major Andrew Drumm in 1874, the ranch included 150,000 acres. Drumm was also the first president of the Cherokee Strip Live Stock Association.

26. Mashed O Ranch, near Owasso: Established in 1880 by W. E. Halsell (an intermarried Cherokee) who used Texas longhorns as his first stock.

27. Council Grove Ranch, Council Grove: Established by Monford Johnson in the early 1870s and abandoned in 1886 when Johnson discovered that his operation was not in the Chickasaw Nation. Council Grove was the name of Jessie Chisholm's trading post, and the area today is now part of Oklahoma City.

28. Southwestern Land and Cattle Co., near Harmon: Successor to the New York Cattle Company, a member of the Cherokee Strip Live Stock Association. The company had offices at 757 Broadway in New York as well as in Chicago.

29. Cattle Ranch and Land Co., near Catesby: A member of the Cherokee Strip Live Stock Association. The business office for the company was located at 110 Dearborn Street in Chicago.

84. HORSE COUNTRY *Charles Robert Goins*

The state of Oklahoma has the greatest density of registered horses of any of the states. Although the officially designated state animal is the American buffalo (bison), the elegant horse is what strongly defines Oklahoma's history and popular imagery. The story of the horse in Oklahoma began in 1541 when Coronado brought his column of soldiers and over a thousand horses through the western part of the state. The horse was unlike any other animal the inhabitants had ever seen. In time the progeny of these first modern horses—either through trading, straying, or raiding—became part of the culture of the Plains Indians and dramatically changed the order of their lives. In later years, the Plains Indians were both admired and feared for their remarkable horsemanship.

With the creation of Indian Territory, the eastern Indian tribes and nations being removed to the West brought with them horses for farming and transportation. Even before that time, the nomadic peoples of the central and southern plains were following the bison herds and protecting their independence using their swift and tough mounts with enviable skill.

Following the Civil War, the movement of thousands of head of cattle from southern Texas north along the several cattle trails leading to railheads in Kansas required men on horseback. This period has left a rich legacy of folklore that surrounds the American cowboy. Within this same time frame, the confrontation (referred to as the Indian wars) that developed between the U.S. cavalry and various Plains Indians tribes also contributed to the history of the role of the horse in Oklahoma.

In the late part of the nineteenth century, the opening of areas within Indian Territory to non-Indian settlement brought another wave of horse history to what would become Oklahoma. Beginning with the first land run in 1889, nothing was more highly prized than a fast horse. Following the claiming of 160 acres, a good solid horse to pull the plow became valuable. Thus, from early on, the horse was an important and essential part of the evolvement of Oklahoma.

Today the horse is still a major part of the lives of thousands of people of the state. The horse culture that so richly identifies Oklahoma is predominantly that of the quarter horse, which equestrian historians can trace back to colonial days. At that time, English bloodlines were crossed with those of Spanish-ancestry horses to produce a mount that had great speed for short distances. These compact and heavily muscular horses usually range in size from fourteen to sixteen hands high at the withers (in equine terms, a hand is equal to four inches) and

(Courtesy Dr. Dan and Nancy Goodwin)

This painting by Augusta Metcalf (1881–1971) is of horses drinking from a large water tank on a ranch near Durham in Roger Mills County. She painted this in 1955 at the request of Dan Goodwin, who had grown up in Durham and had just graduated from Oklahoma A&M Veterinary School. When he was a child, Dan began taking drawing lessons from Metcalf.

In his retrospective on Durham, Dan recalls,

> *I was her student when I was nine years old. I liked to draw pictures, so she told me that if I would furnish her with a drawing book, she would draw a picture on the top of each page and return the book to me with instructions to reproduce the drawing beneath hers. I bought the book for 5 cents and delivered it to her. She drew her pictures. I reproduced them and returned the book to her. She graded my work generously and said my pictures were pretty good.*

Dan's comments on Metcalf's painting are detailed:

> *This is a typical Roger Mills County pasture with buffalo grass, sage brush and bear grass. A band of mares has come to water. The sorrel stallion, who is in charge of this band, is rounding up the stragglers in the background. He has made his mark on the foals around the tank—they too, are all sorrel colored. Cattle are grazing in the distance. The windmill is a Dempster. It is turned off because the tank is full. A tomato can hangs on a peg for anyone who is thirsty. The thirsty person would turn on the windmill and hope that there is enough breeze to pump the water that is waiting about 200 feet below the earth's surface.*

Quotations from Goodwin, *Remembrances of Durham.*

Horses in Oklahoma, 2005

In August of 2005, the American Horse Council released a study on the horse culture and industry in the United States, which accounted for all horses in this country. Oklahoma had the seventh-greatest total number of horses and at 4.75 horses per square mile had the fifth-greatest density of horses. This study also indicates that the horse industry produces an annual economic impact to the state of approximately $1.2 billion dollars.

As part of the strong horse culture in Oklahoma, the state is home to several outstanding world-class and national horse shows. Among these events are

- ***National Appaloosa Horse Show***
- ***Greater Oklahoma Hunter Preview***
- ***Greater Oklahoma Hunter-Jumper Horse Show***
- ***Grand National and World Championship Morgan Horse Show***
- ***American Quarter Horse Association Championship Quarter Horse Show***
- ***World Barrel Racing Futurity***
- ***United States Team Roping Championship***
- ***Palomino World Championship Horse Show***
- ***Pinto World Championship Horse Show***

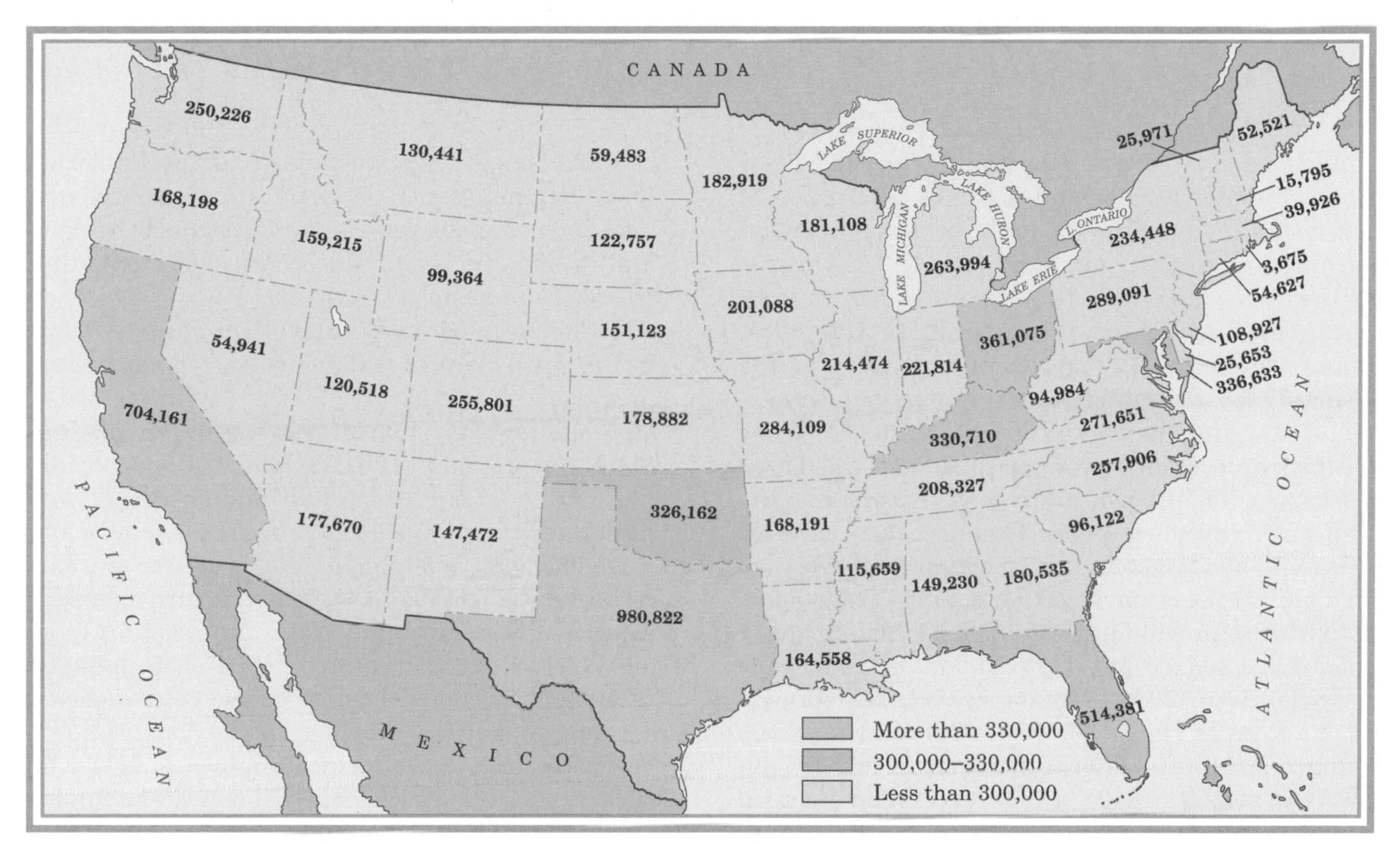

Estimated number of horses by state in the coterminous United States, 2005

Source: American Horse Council, "Economic Impact."

exhibit one or more of thirteen colors. This popular horse has been called "the common man's horse" (although the quarter horse is the preference of many women as well); for three hundred years, quarter horses have been cow horses, race horses, and kid horses.

The importance and value of this breed of horse led to the founding of the American Quarter Horse Association (AQHA) in 1940, with international headquarters located in Amarillo, Texas. In 2004 there were 2,860,362 horses in the United States registered with AQHA. The five states with the greatest registration are Texas, Oklahoma, California, Missouri, and Colorado. Oklahoma thus has the highest density of registered horses of any state. With 51,179 owners of registered horses, the state also has the highest ratio of registered horses to people.

The breeding of quarter horses has a long history in Oklahoma, beginning in western Oklahoma Territory with a stallion named Peter McCue (1895–1923), which many racing aficionados of the time believed to have had more influence on the bloodlines of racing quarter horses than did any other. This incredible horse stood sixteen hands high, weighed 1,430 pounds, was a great sprinter, and could run a quarter mile (440 yards) in twenty-one seconds flat—this distance being the source of the breed's name. He was owned by Milo Burlingan and stood at stud in Cheyenne.

States with Greatest AQHA Registration, 2005

State	No. of horses registered	Land area (sq. miles)	Horses per square mile
1. Texas	478,172	261,914	1.83
2. Oklahoma	199,191	68,679	2.90
3. California	150,922	155,973	0.97
4. Missouri	107,742	68,898	1.56
5. Colorado	99,395	103,729	0.96

Two other great stallions that had Oklahoma connections were discovered and developed by the famous horseman Walter Merrick (b.1911), who grew up in western Oklahoma. He was instrumental in seeing the potential of a chestnut stallion named Three Bars (1940–1968), which he leased and brought to Oklahoma to stand at stud beginning in 1951. Before Three Bars died, an heir to that great stallion was born on January 12, 1967. This chestnut colt, called Easy Jet, began racing as a two-year-old in 1969; after his next racing season, as a three-year-old, he was retired to stud. His amazing two-year record of 38 racing starts included 27 wins as well as 7 second-place and 2 third-place finishes. Over the next twenty-two years, Easy Jet became one of the most sought-after stallions by horse breeders across the nation.

85. STATE HIGHWAYS, 1929, AND U.S. HIGHWAY 66 *Charles Robert Goins*

Noted historian Grant Foreman's *Down the Texas Road* provides a clear and detailed description of pathways and trails forged in the early days of what became Indian Territory, especially by the Osages, as they traveled on hunting expeditions or to trading points such as the French frontier town of St. Louis. This early-day trail became known as the Osage Trace. As hunters and trappers, military expeditions, and (later) settlers continued to move westward, a major route emerged from the Three Forks area following a southwesterly course to the Red River and the plains of Texas. As early as 1822, this route had become a major corridor of traffic from St. Louis to Texas and was known as the Texas Road.

With the unfolding of Oklahoma's history, other roads have had a colorful impact on this land. In the far western tip of the Panhandle, a southern branch of the famous Santa Fe Trail was known as the Cimarron Cut-off. With the discovery of gold in California in the late 1840s, a very active road emerged from Fort Smith, Arkansas, and passed through central Oklahoma; it became known as the California Road. Beginning in 1858, the first transcontinental mail and passenger service, the Butterfield Overland Mail Company, began stagecoach operations that crossed southeastern Oklahoma.

These early pathways played an important role in the settlement of Oklahoma and in some ways provided the framework for the beginning of the state's highway system. At the time of the constitutional convention in 1907, Oklahoma had a population of almost one and a half million people, and most local travel at that time was by horseback or wagon. Traveling or shipment of goods for any long distance was usually by train. Even with extensive railroad lines across the state, the need for more and better roads soon became critical. This need was recognized by the delegates to the constitutional convention, so they provided in the constitution a provision for a department of highways. However, such a department was not established and funded until 1911. Sidney Suggs of Ardmore was appointed

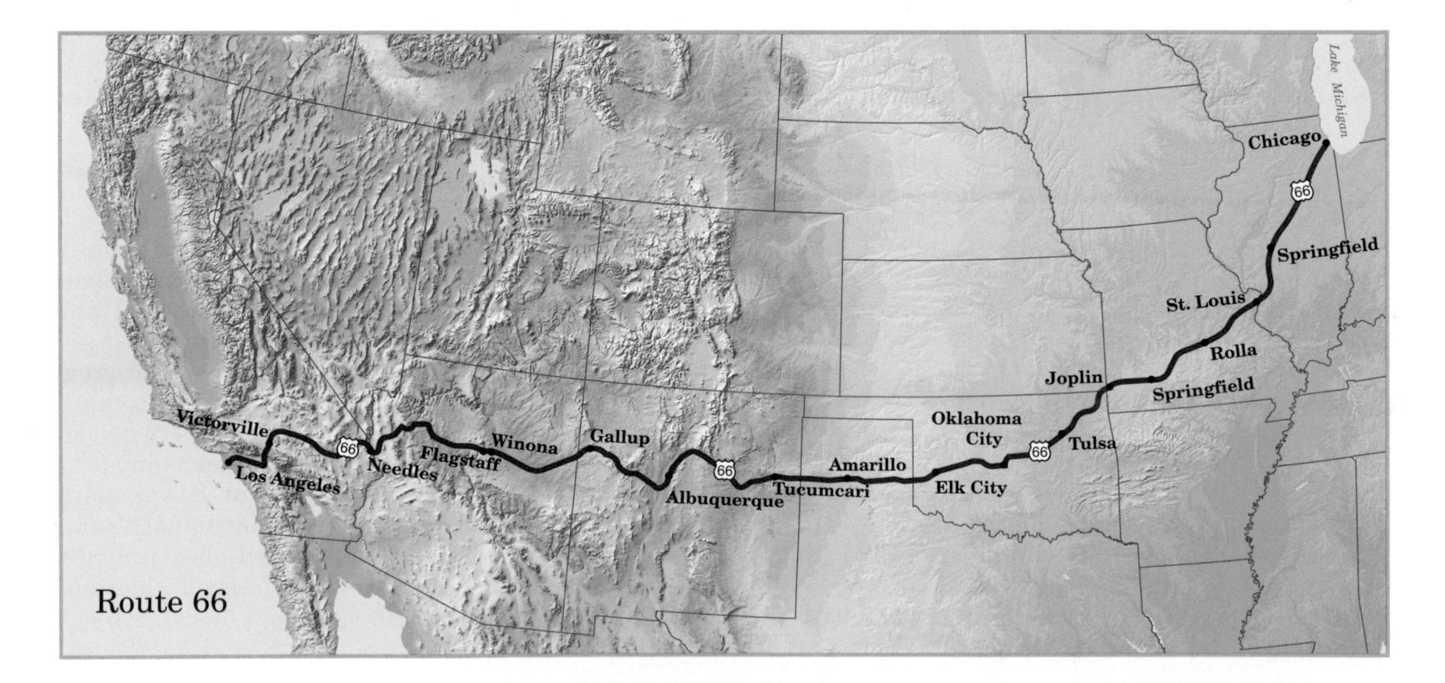

Route 66

Get Your Kicks on Route 66

Life on the road may never have been better, more fun, or more interesting than traveling down Route 66 during the '40s, '50s, or '60s. John Steinbeck, in his memorable novel The Grapes of Wrath, *called it the mother road. If we accept that analogy, then Oklahoma was the nurturing beginning place of this remarkable pathway between Chicago and Los Angeles. The vision and planning behind the route belonged to former state highway commissioner Cyrus S. Avery, who in 1927 became president of the National U.S. Highway 66 Association. Avery's great knowledge and connections with various highway interests placed him in a position to greatly influence the routing and the choice of highway designation for what became U.S. Highway 66.*

On November 11, 1926, the American Association of State Highway Officials (of which Avery was a member) assigned the number 66 to the U.S. highway system. Route 66, beginning in Chicago, runs through eight states, covering approximately 2,000 miles: 400 of those miles are in Oklahoma. Eleven years were required for completion of the piecemeal paving of the entire route, with the last stretch paved in 1937. Frank Phillips, founder of Phillips Petroleum, chose the number "66" to help promote his gasoline. The number had become magical.

In 1946, the highway was made instantly famous when bandleader Bobby Troupe wrote his great song "Get Your Kicks on Route 66." Nat King Cole became one of the first of nearly two hundred performers to record this hit song. This immortalizing through lyrics was followed in 1960 by the television series Route 66, *featuring Martin Milner, George Maharis, and their blue Corvette convertible.*

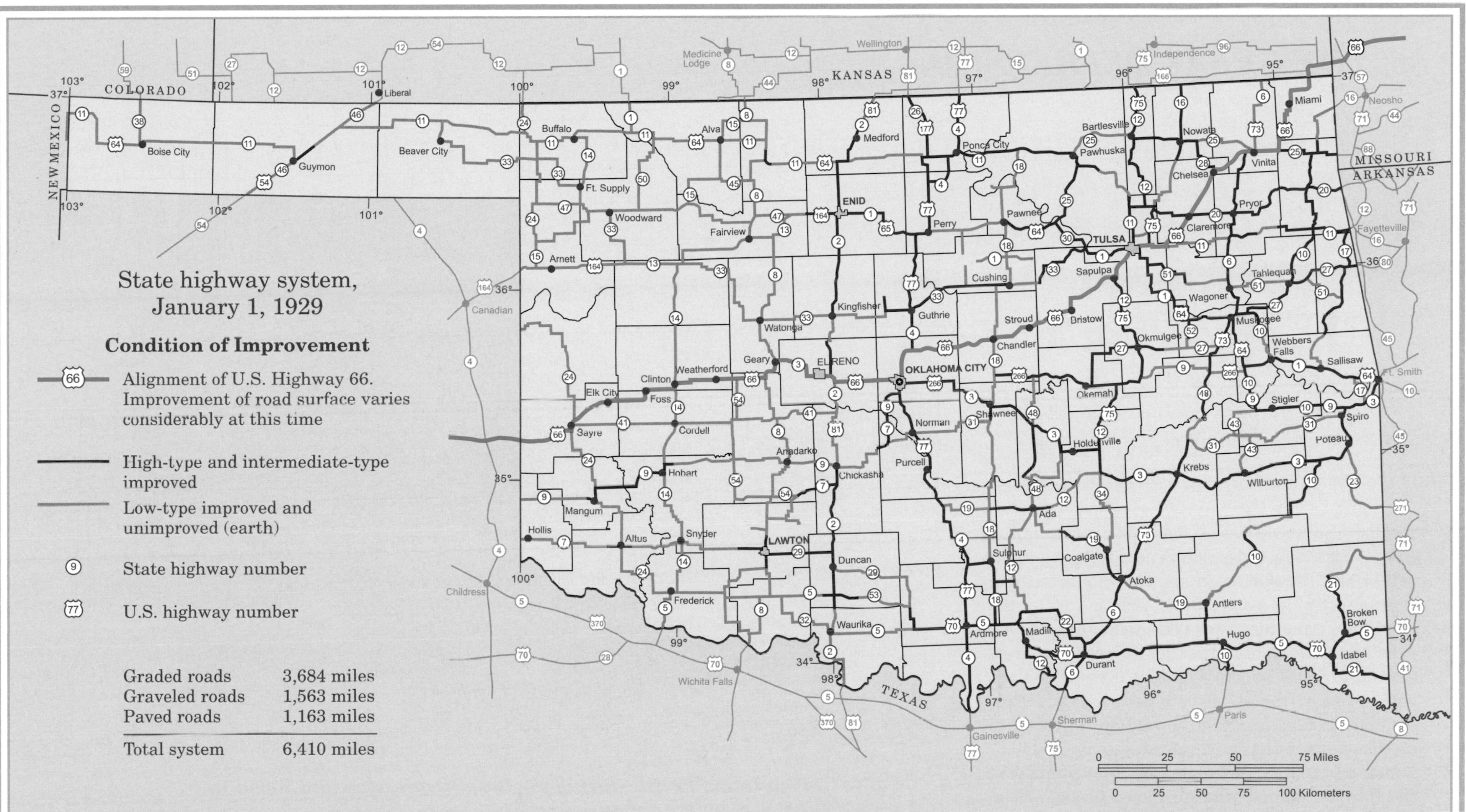

as the first and only highway commissioner; the legislature generously provided him with a two-person staff.

What may seem to have been a lack of interest in roads and highways by the legislature may be better understood when one realizes that the first motorized vehicle had not arrived in Oklahoma until 1905. However, this situation began to change quickly, and by 1911 Commissioner Suggs could report that Oklahoma had 9,000 automobiles. He also reported that the state had a network of 79,883 miles of road but that only 499 miles were improved. As the number of roadways and automobiles increased, the need for substantial bridges became a major concern. In 1917, two large bridges were constructed: one spanned the Canadian River, connecting McIntosh and Pittsburg counties; the other crossed the Red River south of Marietta.

The future role that highways would play in Oklahoma was becoming clear as the numbers of automobiles increased across the country. In 1929 there were 24,494,600 automobiles in the United States (1 for every 4.9 inhabitants). At that date, Oklahoma had 502,503 registered automobiles (4.7 for each inhabitant). Another way to measure the quickly increasing popularity of the automobile is through the fact that in 1919 there were approximately 5,000 filling stations (service stations) in Oklahoma; by 1929, there were four times as many—19,000 (or 1 for each 26.5 automobiles).

86. THE GREAT DEPRESSION

Essay by *Danney Goble*

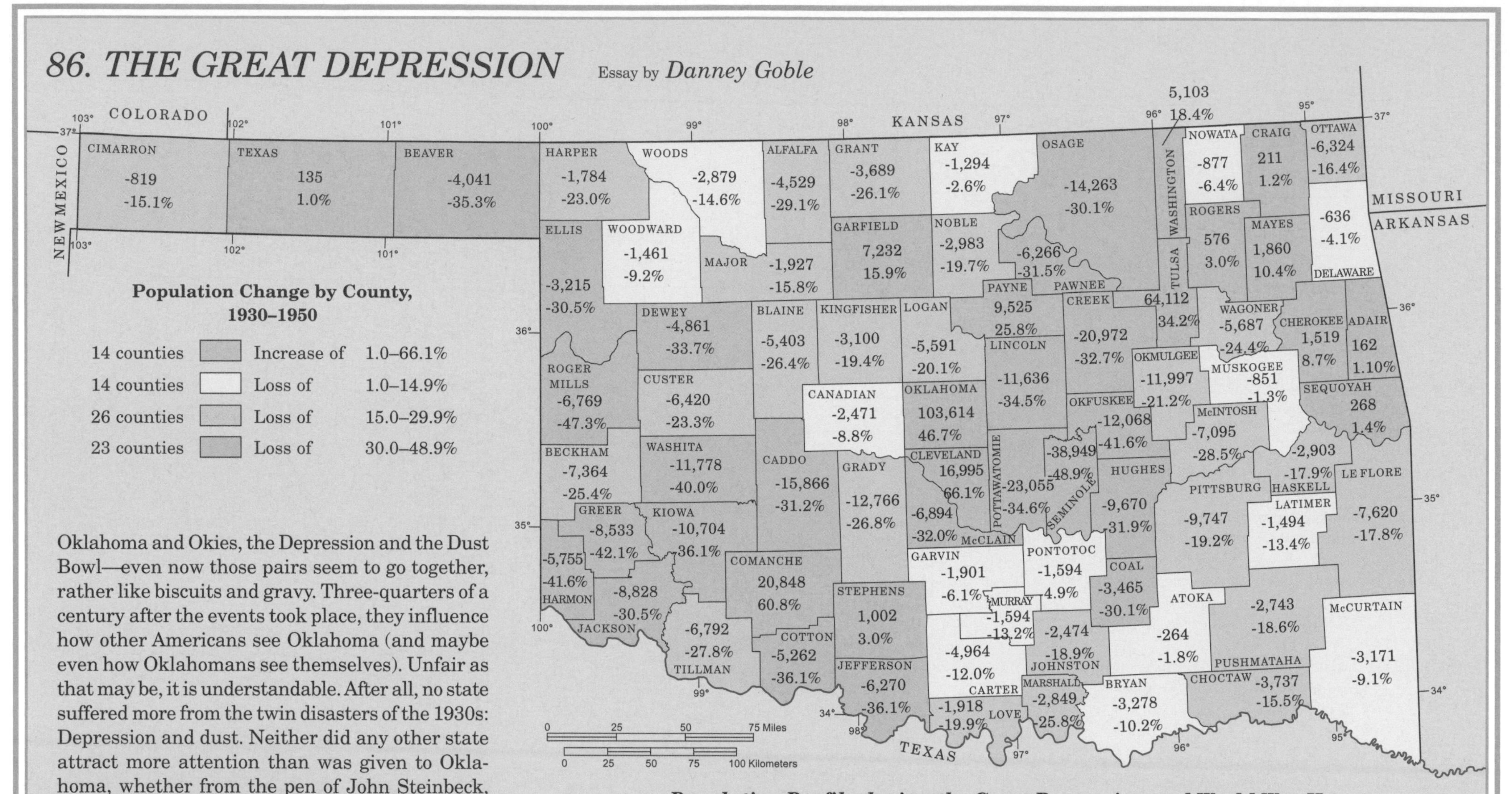

Oklahoma and Okies, the Depression and the Dust Bowl—even now those pairs seem to go together, rather like biscuits and gravy. Three-quarters of a century after the events took place, they influence how other Americans see Oklahoma (and maybe even how Oklahomans see themselves). Unfair as that may be, it is understandable. After all, no state suffered more from the twin disasters of the 1930s: Depression and dust. Neither did any other state attract more attention than was given to Oklahoma, whether from the pen of John Steinbeck, the films of John Ford and Pare Lorenz, or the photographs of Dorothea Lange, Russell Lee, Arthur Rothstein, and others.

Why so much suffering and so much attention? Start with the fact that Oklahomans had to deal with all the misfortunes common to Depression-era Americans, then add circumstances peculiar (perhaps unique) to their state. One of these peculiarities is that the entire economy rested on two pillars: oil and farming. They both failed, utterly and simultaneously.

Population Profile during the Great Depression and World War II

From 1930 to 1950, 62 out of the 77 counties of Oklahoma lost population. Of those counties losing population, 31 lost over a quarter of their population, and of those, 13 lost over one-third of their population. Oklahoma and North Dakota were the only states to lose population during both decades; Oklahoma lost approximately 2.5 times more people than North Dakota lost. It would take Oklahoma until the early 1960s to regain a population equal to that of 1930.

Population change in Oklahoma, 1930–1950

Year	State population	Change in number	Percentage of change
1930	2,396,040		
1940	2,336,434	–59,606	–2.5
1950	2,233,351	–103,083	–4.4
Population loss		–162,689	–6.8

For oil, the disaster's beginnings could be precisely located. The day was October 3, 1930. The place was a farm in Rusk County, Texas, owned by a grieving widow, Daisy Bradford. Columbus M. "Dad" Joiner, a wildcatter theretofore reputed to be more successful at bedding widows than finding oil, hit the discovery well that opened the fabulous East Texas field. Within six months, more than a thousand wells had been drilled among the nearby pine barrens and scrub timber. They pumped a steady 340,000 barrels every twenty-four hours. This underground ocean, stretching out for forty-five miles and covering 140,000 acres, doubled the country's entire oil production soon after its discovery. Fully developed, this one field yielded far more than the nation needed—or wanted.

Prices evaporated. As of mid-1933, posted prices stood at a dime a barrel. Plenty of barrels of Oklahoma oil sold at six cents, and some as low as two. The powerful Sun Oil Company reported a net income of fifty-three cents for the first two quarters of 1933. Nearly every lesser company—and practically every oil company was Sun's lesser—could only marvel at such success. Many oil companies fell into holes metaphorically deeper than any well, and they took their employees with them. In Tulsa alone, oil companies laid off half their production workers, two-fifths of their pipeline hands, and nearly a third of their refining employees.

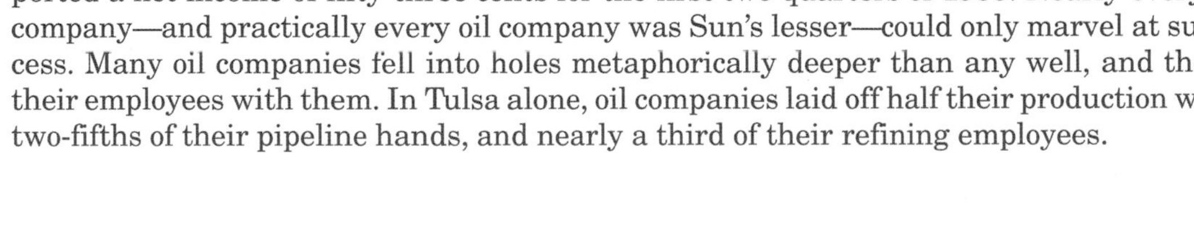

Right: *A family of Oklahoma sharecroppers, stalled on a lonely highway, 1930s. (Courtesy Western History Collections, University of Oklahoma Libraries)*

Residence in 1930 of 19,786 agricultural families moving to California, 1930–1939

(Defined by occupation being reported as farmers or farm laborers prior to migration. One dot represents five families.)

Data from U.S. Department of Agriculture, Bureau of Agricultural Economics, with the cooperation of California State Department of Education.

Residence in 1930 of 69,896 nonagricultural families moving to California, 1930–1939

(Defined by occupation being reported in nonagricultural industries. One dot represents five families.)

Family distribution for eastern states, not available.

tional Joad family, these real-life Oklahomans sold the little they could, loaded anything they could carry, and left everything else behind. Once more they did what they or their forebears had done before. They pulled up, pulled out, and headed west to California, this time not as pioneers but as Okies.

Altogether, some 60,000 people–2.5 percent of Oklahoma's 1930 population—were gone by 1940. More probably would have been lost but for the emergency measures that President Franklin Roosevelt launched in 1933, part of his New Deal. The best of the New Deal's relief efforts put money in the pockets of thousands hired to work on public projects, many of which still stand. School buildings, sidewalks, athletic facilities, guard armories, even painted murals that still adorn a few post offices—all of these remain as visible reminders of the Great Depression in Oklahoma, telling the story of what Oklahomans built and of what Oklahomans endured.

Left: *Dust storm at Boise City during the Dust Bowl of the 1930s. (Courtesy Western History Collections, University of Oklahoma Libraries)*

Below: *A father with his two sons during a dust storm in Cimarron County in the 1930s. (Courtesy Western History Collections, University of Oklahoma Libraries)*

Then there was farming. Commodity prices broke in 1921 and never recovered during the rest of the decade. Of course Depression-era farmers were lucky to get a nickel a pound for their cotton no matter whether it came from Arizona or from Oklahoma. The difference was that Oklahoma's cotton farmers rarely got to keep those nickels. To a far greater extent than in any other state, most were tenants: landless, rent-paying farmers. The most fortunate could afford rent at a fixed cash price. The vast majority, however, had no choice but to pay with shares of their crops.

Farmers in Oklahoma's wheat country had done better in that respect, being more likely to own their land. They also were more likely to have borrowed against it to buy the latest farm machinery. Most were proud that they followed the advice of the Extension Service's county agents, especially when these experts lectured farmers that they needed to kill off the native grasses, plow up anything their tractors could reach, plant as much wheat as possible, and then leave their fields lying open, beneath thin layers of dust—as though dirt were a type of mulch to conserve precious water.

The farmers diligently followed instructions, right up until the rain stopped falling and the wind started howling. In the wheat country, that came in the mid to late 1930s. By then, landless farmers by the tens of thousands and out-of-work oil-field workers had given up. Like the *Grapes of Wrath*'s fic-

Percentage of Farms Operated by Tenants, 1920–1930

30–39% (6 counties)

40–59% (26 counties)

60–80% (45 counties)

(Map data from U.S. Census of Agriculture, 1930)

Farm Tenancy, 1920–1930

"Farm tenancy in Oklahoma increased from 51 to 62 percent between 1920 and 1930. The situation is particularly bad in the eastern part of the State, where much of the land was bought from the Indians at low prices and is being held for oil production or other speculative purposes. The owners are but slightly interested in a year-to-year income from the land and make no worthwhile permanent improvements. Competition for better farms causes poorer tenants to gravitate to the poor grade farms. Each year and half the tenant farmers move from one farm to another, which has resulted in costly neglect of the soil. The present nature and extent of farm tenancy in Oklahoma must be changed if the State is to properly conserve its resources and improve the social and economic position of the farm population."

Quotation from Oklahoma State Planning Board, "Compendium of Maps."

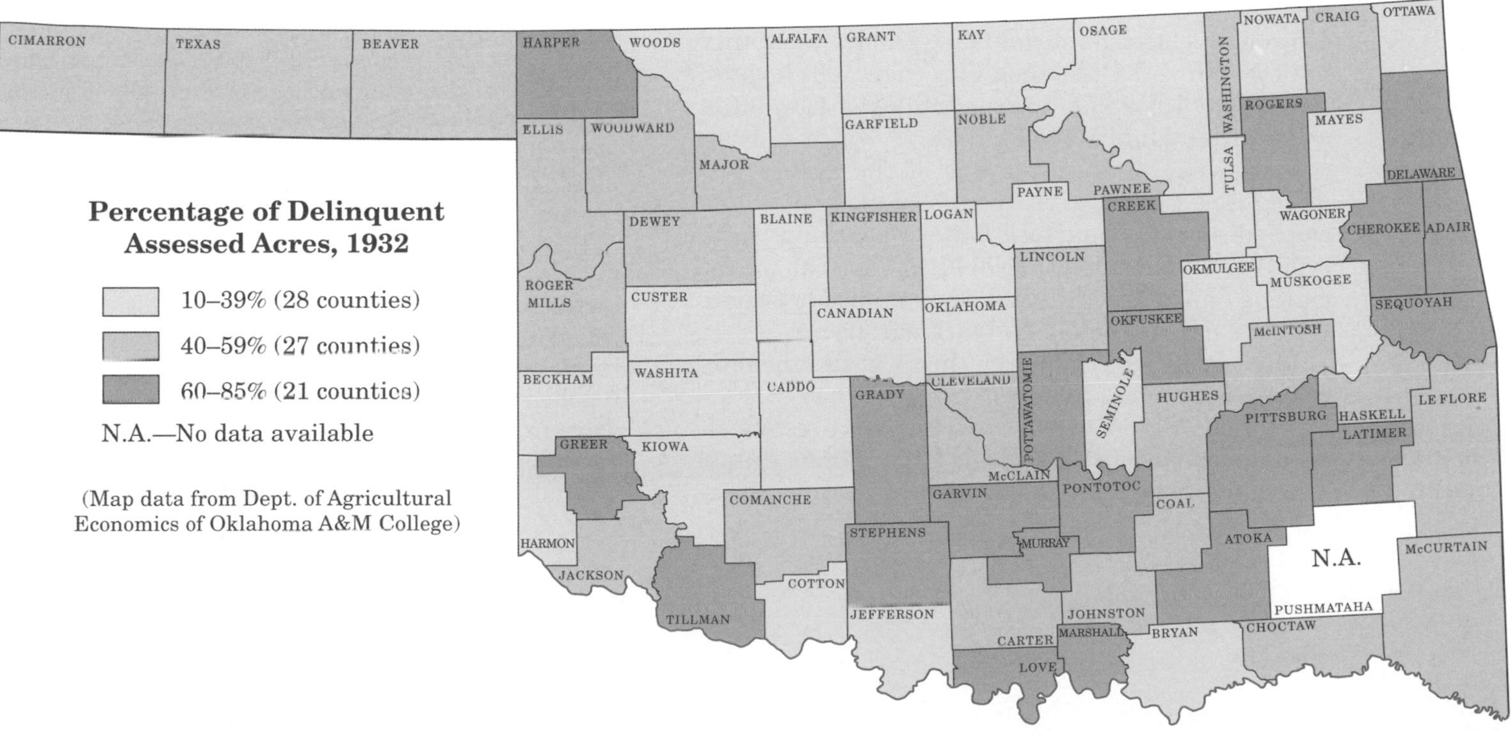

Farmland Tax Delinquency, 1932

"Taxes were delinquent on 46 percent of the assessed farm acreage of Oklahoma in 1932 and even in 1928, a year of agricultural prosperity, 22 percent was delinquent. The farm problem, reflected by this situation, is based on low prices for agricultural products, hazards to crop yield such as droughts and floods, improper use of land, bad farm management, increasing tax levies, lenient penalties for delinquency, and other causes. Under present farm practices the better land is generally able to sustain its taxes, while the poor land, although it carries a low assessment, does not afford earnings sufficient to meet even this obligation."

Quotation from Oklahoma State Planning Board, "Compendium of Maps."

87. CIVILIAN CONSERVATION CORPS CAMPS

Essay by *Bruce W. Hoagland & Danney Goble*

One of the most imaginative elements of President Franklin Roosevelt's New Deal was the Civilian Conservation Corps (CCC). It was what President Roosevelt might have called bold experimentation, not least because it demanded cooperation among four cabinet-level departments. The War Department built and administered its many camps. The Department of Labor enrolled the young men who served in the CCC. Agencies within the Interior Department and Agriculture Department designated what needed to be conserved and how this should be done.

That only males were enrolled was hardly surprising, given the times. The requirements were that a man be unemployed but with dependents to support, physically fit, and between the ages of eighteen and twenty-five. (This last qualification was later stretched in both directions to become seventeen and twenty-eight, respectively.) CCC enrollees in Oklahoma were assigned to one of forty-nine work camps; only Texas and Illinois had more. Pay was modest: $30 per month, $25 of which was sent to dependents.

The real benefits were not found in pay envelopes. Every corpsman received three nutritious meals every day, which was three more than many might otherwise have had. Medical officers were at hand for health care; dentists came regularly. For some, it was their first experience with either. On-the-job training ensured them marketable skills as carpenters, masons, woodworkers, engine repairmen, and the like. CCC camps also ran regular, school-like courses to fill out the basic education that many lacked.

Critics howled that none of this had anything to do with conservation, and they had a point (albeit a narrow one). An estimated 40,000 men learned to read in CCC camps. How much human potential that otherwise might have been lost was thus saved? Whatever the number, it deserves to be called conservation—of human resources, if nothing more.

By 1942, when the CCC became one of the many casualties of World War II, 107,676 men had passed through Oklahoma's camps. They had come from Maine to California and every state in between. What they left behind touched all of Oklahoma. Their success was best seen in what Oklahomans no longer had to see: rolling, black clouds of onrushing dust storms. More visible but no less lasting were their contributions to Oklahoma's state park system. The first seven state parks—Beavers Bend, Boiling Springs, Lake Murray, Osage Hills, Quartz Mountain, Robbers Cave, and Roman Nose—all originated in CCC projects, as did several others later added to the state's park system.

Urban parks in Tulsa and Oklahoma City also owed much to the CCC. Two camps were located in Oklahoma City. One greatly improved the existing zoo and developed its surrounding grounds; the other built Northwest Oklahoma City (now Will Rogers) Park. One Tulsa camp turned miles of raw, often swampy land into Mohawk Park.

Tulsa also maintained one of the state's few mixed-race camps, even though black and whites slept in separate quarters. Otherwise, camps were typically divided along racial lines. Five camps, including one at Fort Sill and a second at Fort Reno, were established solely for black enrollees.

More ambitious than even the CCC was the mission that President Roosevelt assigned the U.S. Forest Service in 1934: to plant enough trees to establish a shelterbelt to run through six Great Plains states. The notion was that strategic and scientific placement of trees could do nothing but good, and plenty of that, by protecting crops and wildlife from wind, sheltering residents from windblown snow and sand, and eventually providing wood for construction and external marketing.

Oklahoma projects were directed from Oklahoma City, with Forest Service district offices in Elk City, El Reno, Mangum, and Enid. Thirteen counties were included in the original project; nine were added in 1939.

Each project was a cooperative venture between a farmer and the federal government. Upon the owner's application, land was evaluated for suitability. If it passed muster, the farmer furnished fence material and prepared the site. CCC crews then planted seedlings, while workers for the New Deal's Works Progress Administration built fences, killed rodents, and planted a few trees, too. Oklahoma's first shelterbelt was planted on the H. E. Curtis farm, near Mangum, on March 18, 1935.

Shelterbelts ranged from 100 to 165 feet wide and varied in length. Trees were planted in rows 10 feet apart, with tall trees in center rows, short ones along the sides, and shrubs on the margins. Black locust, catalpa, Chinese elm, cottonwood, green ash, hackberry, honey locust, mulberry, Osage orange, pecan, plum, Russian olive, red cedar, and walnut varieties were the most commonly planted.

Some shelterbelts fell victim to drought, others to grasshopper infestations, and some to poor maintenance. Even so, on the day the project closed (on June 30, 1942), the shelterbelt experiment left behind 145 million trees. Growing in a zone that reached across 100 miles and more, they ran all the way from the Brazos River in Texas to the U.S.–Canadian border, a distance of 18,600 miles.

That was bold experimentation.

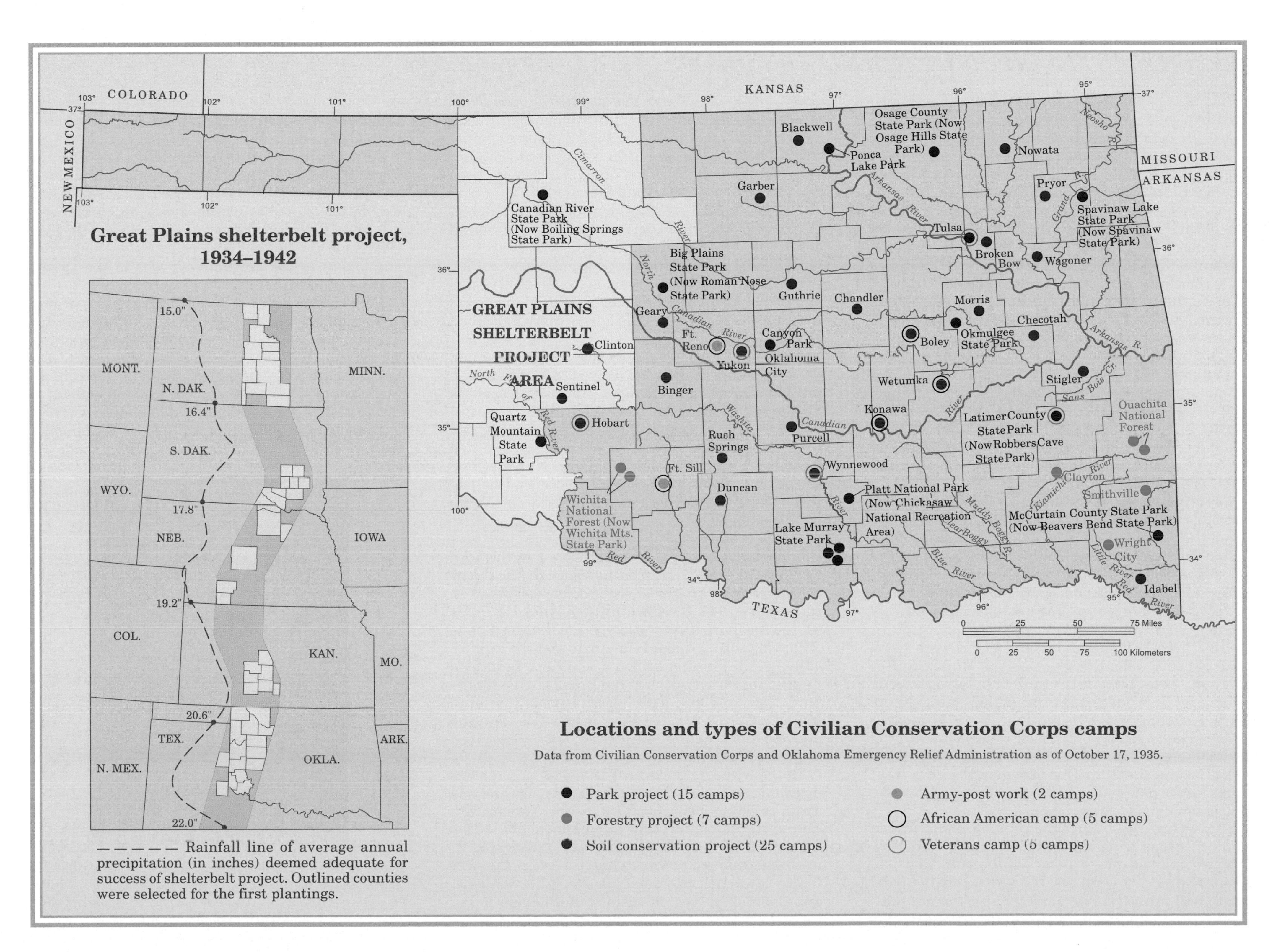
Great Plains shelterbelt project, 1934–1942
MONT.
N. DAK.
MINN.
S. DAK.
WYO.
NEB.
IOWA
COL.
KAN.
MO.
TEX.
OKLA.
ARK.
N. MEX.
15.0"
16.4"
17.8"
19.2"
20.6"
22.0"
Rainfall line of average annual precipitation (in inches) deemed adequate for success of shelterbelt project. Outlined counties were selected for the first plantings.
COLORADO
KANSAS
NEW MEXICO
MISSOURI
ARKANSAS
TEXAS
GREAT PLAINS SHELTERBELT PROJECT AREA
Blackwell
Ponca Lake Park
Osage County State Park (Now Osage Hills State Park)
Nowata
Garber
Pryor
Spavinaw Lake State Park (Now Spavinaw State Park)
Canadian River State Park (Now Boiling Springs State Park)
Tulsa
Broken Bow
Wagoner
Big Plains State Park (Now Roman Nose State Park)
Guthrie
Chandler
Morris
Geary
Checotah
Ft. Reno
Yukon
Canyon Park
Oklahoma City
Boley
Okmulgee State Park
Clinton
Wetumka
Stigler
Sentinel
Binger
Ouachita National Forest
Quartz Mountain State Park
Hobart
Konawa
Latimer County State Park (Now Robbers Cave State Park)
Rush Springs
Purcell
Wynnewood
Ft. Sill
Clayton
Duncan
Platt National Park (Now Chickasaw National Recreation Area)
Smithville
Wichita National Forest (Now Wichita Mts. State Park)
McCurtain County State Park (Now Beavers Bend State Park)
Lake Murray State Park
Wright City
Idabel
Cimarron
North Canadian River
Arkansas River
Grand R.
Neosho R.
Canadian River
Washita
Red River
North Fk. of Red River
Muddy Boggy R.
Clear Boggy
Blue River
Kiamichi River
Little River
Sans Bois Cr.
Arkansas R.
75 Miles
100 Kilometers
Locations and types of Civilian Conservation Corps camps
Data from Civilian Conservation Corps and Oklahoma Emergency Relief Administration as of October 17, 1935.
Park project (15 camps)
Forestry project (7 camps)
Soil conservation project (25 camps)
Army-post work (2 camps)
African American camp (5 camps)
Veterans camp (5 camps)

88. THE 45TH THUNDERBIRD DIVISION

Essay by *John R. Lovett*

In 1895, the territorial legislative assembly authorized the establishment of one volunteer regiment of militia. Recruiting and support for the militia was a community affair in acquiring both recruits and their uniforms and supplies. Many of the officers and senior noncommissioned officers were the leaders of their communities. The militia or citizen-soldiers had already established a long tradition in the history of the United States, and although Oklahoma is a relatively new state when compared to most others, the history and tradition of these soldiers on the battlefield around the world has long been an intense source of pride for Oklahomans.

The militia was subject to the same rules and regulations that applied to the regular army. Oklahoma's governor could call on the militia to protect the citizens of the territory. Members of the Oklahoma Territory militia volunteered to serve with Leonard Wood and Theodore Roosevelt's First Volunteer Cavalry and saw action in Cuba during the Spanish-American War.

With statehood in November 1907, the militia was formed into the Oklahoma National Guard. Funding from the state was inadequate, but officers and enlisted men continued to volunteer. In the spring of 1916, the National Guard was called into federal service to provide troops for a security zone to protect U.S. citizens living along the unstable Mexican-U.S. border.

In March 1917 the Oklahoma troops were again ordered into federal service as the United States drew closer to entering the conflict in Europe. Along with troops from Texas, the Oklahoma soldiers served in the 36th Division. In July 1918 the division sailed from New York for France. On reaching France, some of the men were transferred to other units, while the 36th Division moved to the front lines in late September and fought in two of the closing campaigns of the war.

Following World War I, the Oklahoma guardsmen joined troops from Colorado, Arizona, and New Mexico and became members of the 45th Division. Guard armories were established throughout the state and formed a partnership with communities and surrounding areas. The Oklahoma troops saw service around the state that included natural disaster relief, labor disputes, a show of force against the Ku Klux Klan, the 1921 Tulsa race riot, and Governor William A. ("Alfalfa Bill") Murray's famous "Red River Bridge War" with Texas.

On August 31, 1940, President Franklin D. Roosevelt ordered the 45th Division once again to federal service, and with the Japanese attack on Pearl Harbor, Oklahoma troops prepared to enter the conflict. After training in several states, the 45th Division shipped out for the European theater of operation in June 1943, landing at the Port of Mers El Kaiber, North Africa.

The 45th Division soldiers saw their first action on the beaches of Sicily on July 10, 1943, with elements of the division engaging Hermann Goering's SS Panzer Division. As the Allied advance continued across Sicily, men of the 45th Division perfected their skills as combat troops. With Sicily in Allied hands, the 45th Division landed in Italy on September 10, 1943. At Salerno, the division helped throw back the German counterattack on the Allied beachhead.

On September 22, Second Lieutenant Ernest Childers won the first Medal of Honor in the 45th Division. As the advance continued north, the troops continued to be an extremely effective combat unit. In January 1944, the 45th Division landed at Anzio on the western Italian coast just south of Rome. Following the breakout from Anzio and the capture of Rome, the division landed in southern France on August 15, 1944, and advanced rapidly to the Rhineland. The soldiers of the 45th Division entered Munich, Germany, a few days before V-E Day. The division had spent 511 days in combat and received the praise of General George S. Patton.

In 1946 the Thunderbird Division was reorganized into an exclusively Oklahoma division and was again called to federal service for the Korean War. The 45th entered the battle on December 10, 1952—the first U.S. National Guard unit to do so. Fighting both Chinese and North Korean forces, the 45th troops saw battle at numerous sites that would become part of their unit history: Bethlehem Point, Luke's Castile, the Punchbowl, and Heartbreak Ridge. The division completed 429 days in combat in this war.

Although the 45th Division did not serve in the Vietnam War, a large number of Vietnam War veterans joined the unit following their active-duty service. In 1969 the 45th Division was again reorganized, this time from a division to a brigade. In 1991 an Oklahoma artillery unit was called to federal service and fought in the Persian Gulf War in the Desert Storm campaign.

Following the 9/11 attack in 2001 and the war on terrorism, the role of the Oklahoma National Guard has changed dramatically. Members of the 45th have served and continue to serve in Afghanistan and Iraq. Oklahoma soldiers have also supported operations in Bosnia. The recent service by members of the 45th Brigade in Iraq and Afghanistan will add to the long and patriotic traditions of Oklahoma's citizen-soldiers.

A World War II–era poster admonishing U.S. civilians and military personnel not to talk openly about activities related to the war effort. (Courtesy Western History Collections, University of Oklahoma Libraries)

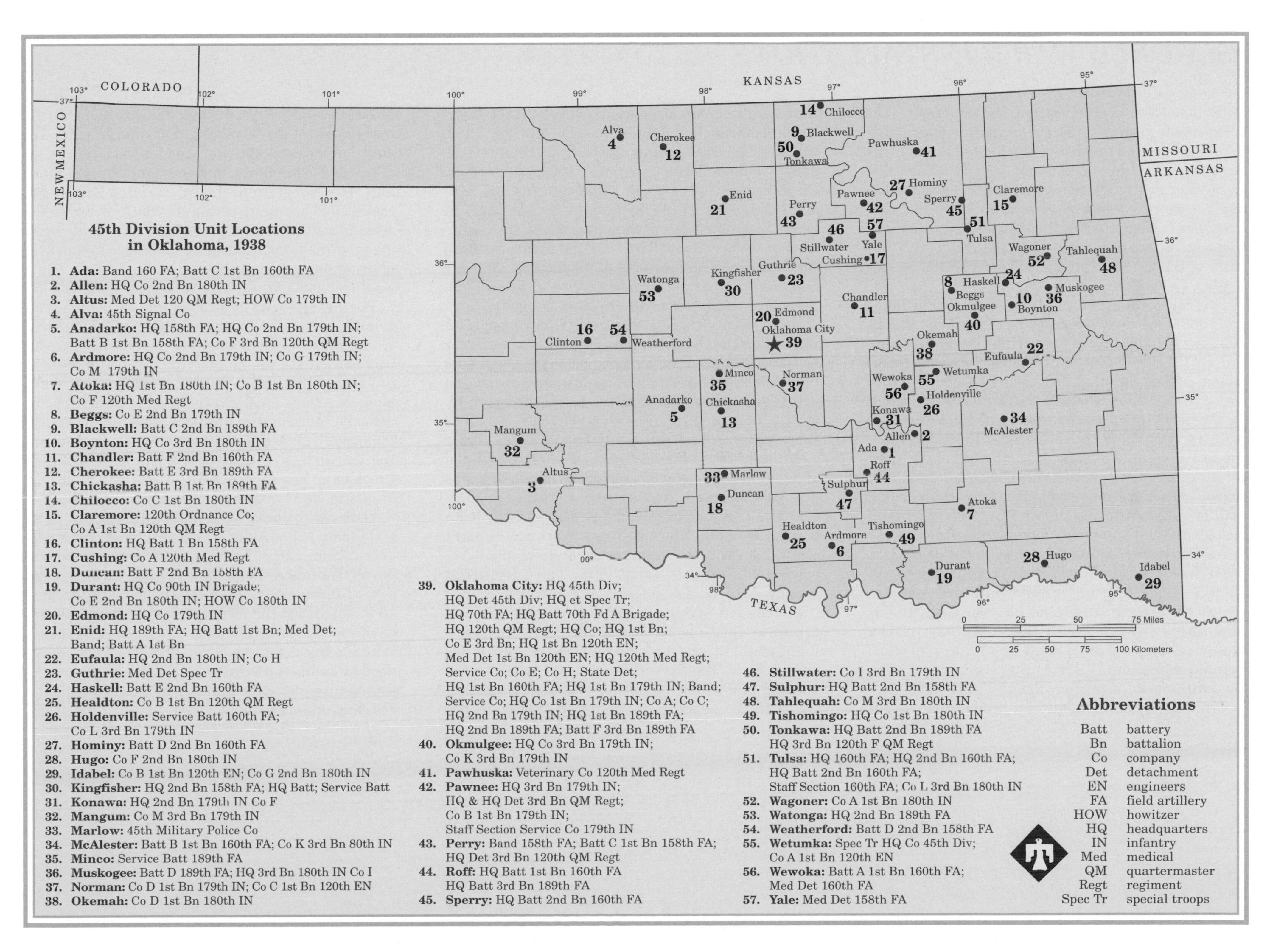
45th Division Unit Locations in Oklahoma, 1938
COLORADO
KANSAS
NEW MEXICO
MISSOURI
ARKANSAS
TEXAS
103°
102°
101°
100°
99°
98°
97°
96°
95°
37°
36°
35°
34°
14 Chilocco
9 Blackwell
50 Tonkawa
Pawhuska 41
Alva 4
Cherokee 12
27 Hominy
Pawnee 42
Sperry 45
Claremore 15
Enid 21
Perry 43
46 Stillwater
57 Yale
51 Tulsa
Cushing 17
Wagoner 52
Tahlequah 48
Watonga 53
Kingfisher 30
Guthrie 23
8 Beggs
Haskell 24
10 Boynton
36 Muskogee
Okmulgee 40
Chandler 11
20 Edmond
Oklahoma City 39
16 Clinton
54 Weatherford
Okemah 38
Eufaula 22
Minco 35
Norman 37
Wewoka 56
55 Wetumka
Holdenville 26
Anadarko 5
Chickasha 13
Konawa 31
Allen 2
34 McAlester
Mangum 32
Ada 1
Roff 44
Altus 3
33 Marlow
Sulphur 47
Duncan 18
Atoka 7
Healdton 25
Ardmore 6
Tishomingo 49
28 Hugo
Durant 19
Idabel 29
0 25 50 75 Miles
0 25 50 75 100 Kilometers
1. Ada: Band 160 FA; Batt C 1st Bn 160th FA
2. Allen: HQ Co 2nd Bn 180th IN
3. Altus: Med Det 120 QM Regt; HOW Co 179th IN
4. Alva: 45th Signal Co
5. Anadarko: HQ 158th FA; HQ Co 2nd Bn 179th IN; Batt B 1st Bn 158th FA; Co F 3rd Bn 120th QM Regt
6. Ardmore: HQ Co 2nd Bn 179th IN; Co G 179th IN; Co M 179th IN
7. Atoka: HQ 1st Bn 180th IN; Co B 1st Bn 180th IN; Co F 120th Med Regt
8. Beggs: Co E 2nd Bn 179th IN
9. Blackwell: Batt C 2nd Bn 189th FA
10. Boynton: HQ Co 3rd Bn 180th IN
11. Chandler: Batt F 2nd Bn 160th FA
12. Cherokee: Batt E 3rd Bn 189th FA
13. Chickasha: Batt B 1st Bn 189th FA
14. Chilocco: Co C 1st Bn 180th IN
15. Claremore: 120th Ordnance Co; Co A 1st Bn 120th QM Regt
16. Clinton: HQ Batt 1 Bn 158th FA
17. Cushing: Co A 120th Med Regt
18. Duncan: Batt F 2nd Bn 158th FA
19. Durant: HQ Co 90th IN Brigade; Co E 2nd Bn 180th IN; HOW Co 180th IN
20. Edmond: HQ Co 179th IN
21. Enid: HQ 189th FA; HQ Batt 1st Bn; Med Det; Band; Batt A 1st Bn
22. Eufaula: HQ 2nd Bn 180th IN; Co H
23. Guthrie: Med Det Spec Tr
24. Haskell: Batt E 2nd Bn 160th FA
25. Healdton: Co B 1st Bn 120th QM Regt
26. Holdenville: Service Batt 160th FA; Co L 3rd Bn 179th IN
27. Hominy: Batt D 2nd Bn 160th FA
28. Hugo: Co F 2nd Bn 180th IN
29. Idabel: Co B 1st Bn 120th EN; Co G 2nd Bn 180th IN
30. Kingfisher: HQ 2nd Bn 158th FA; HQ Batt; Service Batt
31. Konawa: HQ 2nd Bn 179th IN Co F
32. Mangum: Co M 3rd Bn 179th IN
33. Marlow: 45th Military Police Co
34. McAlester: Batt B 1st Bn 160th FA; Co K 3rd Bn 80th IN
35. Minco: Service Batt 189th FA
36. Muskogee: Batt D 189th FA; HQ 3rd Bn 180th IN Co I
37. Norman: Co D 1st Bn 179th IN; Co C 1st Bn 120th EN
38. Okemah: Co D 1st Bn 180th IN
39. Oklahoma City: HQ 45th Div; HQ Det 45th Div; HQ et Spec Tr; HQ 70th FA; HQ Batt 70th Fd A Brigade; HQ 120th QM Regt; HQ Co; HQ 1st Bn; Co E 3rd Bn; HQ 1st Bn 120th EN; Med Det 1st Bn 120th EN; HQ 120th Med Regt; Service Co; Co E; Co H; State Det; HQ 1st Bn 160th FA; HQ 1st Bn 179th IN; Band; Service Co; HQ Co 1st Bn 179th IN; Co A; Co C; HQ 2nd Bn 179th IN; HQ 1st Bn 189th FA; HQ 2nd Bn 189th FA; Batt F 3rd Bn 189th FA
40. Okmulgee: HQ Co 3rd Bn 179th IN; Co K 3rd Bn 179th IN
41. Pawhuska: Veterinary Co 120th Med Regt
42. Pawnee: HQ 3rd Bn 179th IN; HQ & HQ Det 3rd Bn QM Regt; Co B 1st Bn 179th IN; Staff Section Service Co 179th IN
43. Perry: Band 158th FA; Batt C 1st Bn 158th FA; HQ Det 3rd Bn 120th QM Regt
44. Roff: HQ Batt 1st Bn 160th FA; HQ Batt 3rd Bn 189th FA
45. Sperry: HQ Batt 2nd Bn 160th FA
46. Stillwater: Co I 3rd Bn 179th IN
47. Sulphur: HQ Batt 2nd Bn 158th FA
48. Tahlequah: Co M 3rd Bn 180th IN
49. Tishomingo: HQ Co 1st Bn 180th IN
50. Tonkawa: HQ Batt 2nd Bn 189th FA; HQ 3rd Bn 120th F QM Regt
51. Tulsa: HQ 160th FA; HQ 2nd Bn 160th FA; HQ Batt 2nd Bn 160th FA; Staff Section 160th FA; Co L 3rd Bn 180th IN
52. Wagoner: Co A 1st Bn 180th IN
53. Watonga: HQ 2nd Bn 189th FA
54. Weatherford: Batt D 2nd Bn 158th FA
55. Wetumka: Spec Tr HQ Co 45th Div; Co A 1st Bn 120th EN
56. Wewoka: Batt A 1st Bn 160th FA; Med Det 160th FA
57. Yale: Med Det 158th FA
Abbreviations
Batt battery
Bn battalion
Co company
Det detachment
EN engineers
FA field artillery
HOW howitzer
HQ headquarters
IN infantry
Med medical
QM quartermaster
Regt regiment
Spec Tr special troops

89. WORLD WAR II INSTALLATIONS

Essay by *John R. Lovett*

With global war on the horizon, the administration of President Franklin Roosevelt instituted measures to prepare for the defense of the United States. Under the leadership of Oklahoma governor Robert S. Kerr—along with Oklahoma's senators, congressmen, and community leaders—several military installations were established in the state. The military activity in the state increased dramatically with the entry of the United States into World War II on December 7, 1941.

Fort Sill, established as a frontier outpost in January 1869, had survived military reductions, and in 1902 the 29th battery of field artillery moved to Fort Sill. In 1911 the school for field artillery was established, setting the stage for the fort's transition from cavalry to artillery. In 1930 the fort was designated as the permanent location for the U.S. Army field artillery. With the outbreak of war in Europe in 1939, the fort saw rapid expansion, and when the United States entered into World War II, the field artillery school was enlarged and produced more than 30,000 artillery officers during the war. In 1942 an air field was also established for aviation training.

As the United States continued to prepare for possible entry into World War II, Oklahoma City leaders hoped to bring a major military installation to the area. In 1940 the U.S. War Department announced that it would take over part of the municipal airport, to be used for military aircraft. Community leaders such as Stanley Draper, E. K. Gaylord, Fred Jones, Tom Braniff, and others lobbied for the establishment of a proposed air depot that the government planned to locate in the Oklahoma, Kansas, and Texas area. On April 8, 1941, the War Department announced that the air repair depot would be located just east of Oklahoma City. On February 2, 1942, the 1,820-acre site was officially designated the Oklahoma City Air Depot. A Douglas Aircraft plant was also established adjacent to the air depot. The Douglas plant produced the U.S. Army Air Corps' C-47 transport, while air depot employees performed service and modifications on B-17, B-24, and B-29 bombers.

Over twenty-three thousand civilian employees worked for the Douglas aircraft plant, and well over thirteen thousand were employed at the Oklahoma City Air Depot. With the large number of men on active duty, close to half of the workers at both facilities were women; "Rosie the Riveter" was well represented at both locations. The air depot would eventually be renamed Tinker Field in honor of Oklahoma native and Osage Indian Army Air Corps general Clarence L. Tinker, who was killed in 1942. The Douglas Aircraft Company also established a bomber assembly plant in Tulsa. Work on the plant started soon after December 7, and the plant became operational in early 1943. The Tulsa plant produced the B-24 and the B-26 bombers.

In the early spring of 1942, the navy entered into talks with the University of Oklahoma to establish a flight training school at the university's Max Westheimer Field. The navy also expressed an interest in starting another facility for training aircraft mechanics. With the approval of the board of regents, the university leased Westheimer Field to the navy for the creation of the Naval Flight Training Center. The navy purchased additional land for the hangars, administrative buildings, quarters, and support buildings. The Naval Air Technical Training Center was established just south of campus. The university also secured contracts from the military to provide training programs, and funding was provided to construct housing for nine hundred military students, which would be named the Woodrow Wilson Center.

Beginning in the late 1930s, the government developed a program to train military pilots using civilian contract instructors. The goal of this program was to increase the number of qualified airmen as the United States rearmed. One of the first Oklahoma locations for flight training was the Spartan School of Aeronautics at Tulsa. As many as twenty thousand U.S. Army pilots along with Canadian and British airmen received their flight training at Chickasha, Miami, Ponca City, Cimarron Field near Mustang, and other locations across the state.

With the collapse of the Africa Corps in 1943, Oklahoma joined other states as a location for prisoner-of-war camps. Thousands of German and Italian POWs found themselves behind wire in camps spread throughout the state. The end of the war in 1945 witnessed the deactivation of a large portion of the military facilities spread across Oklahoma. While many defense workers lost their jobs as the need for military aircraft declined, many others continued to work for the military at Tinker Field, Fort Sill, and other locations.

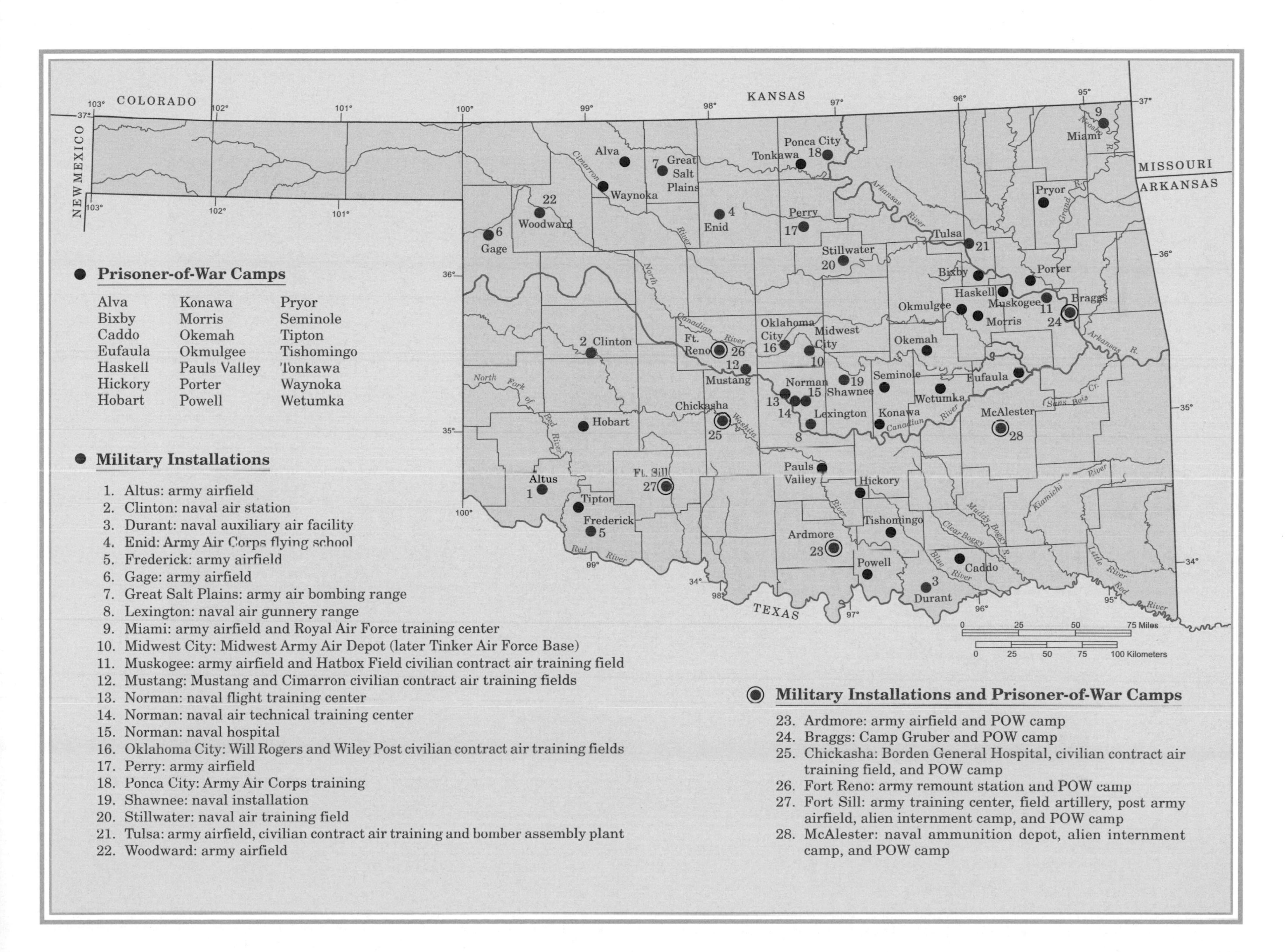

COLORADO
KANSAS
NEW MEXICO
MISSOURI
ARKANSAS
TEXAS
Prisoner-of-War Camps
Alva
Bixby
Caddo
Eufaula
Haskell
Hickory
Hobart
Konawa
Morris
Okemah
Okmulgee
Pauls Valley
Porter
Powell
Pryor
Seminole
Tipton
Tishomingo
Tonkawa
Waynoka
Wetumka
Military Installations
1. Altus: army airfield
2. Clinton: naval air station
3. Durant: naval auxiliary air facility
4. Enid: Army Air Corps flying school
5. Frederick: army airfield
6. Gage: army airfield
7. Great Salt Plains: army air bombing range
8. Lexington: naval air gunnery range
9. Miami: army airfield and Royal Air Force training center
10. Midwest City: Midwest Army Air Depot (later Tinker Air Force Base)
11. Muskogee: army airfield and Hatbox Field civilian contract air training field
12. Mustang: Mustang and Cimarron civilian contract air training fields
13. Norman: naval flight training center
14. Norman: naval air technical training center
15. Norman: naval hospital
16. Oklahoma City: Will Rogers and Wiley Post civilian contract air training fields
17. Perry: army airfield
18. Ponca City: Army Air Corps training
19. Shawnee: naval installation
20. Stillwater: naval air training field
21. Tulsa: army airfield, civilian contract air training and bomber assembly plant
22. Woodward: army airfield
Military Installations and Prisoner-of-War Camps
23. Ardmore: army airfield and POW camp
24. Braggs: Camp Gruber and POW camp
25. Chickasha: Borden General Hospital, civilian contract air training field, and POW camp
26. Fort Reno: army remount station and POW camp
27. Fort Sill: army training center, field artillery, post army airfield, alien internment camp, and POW camp
28. McAlester: naval ammunition depot, alien internment camp, and POW camp
0 25 50 75 Miles
0 25 50 75 100 Kilometers

The Oklahoma State Capitol, Oklahoma City. Constructed between 1914 and 1917, the building got its dome in 2002. (Photograph by John Elk III, courtesy of Elk Photography)

Part VI

You're Doing Fine, Oklahoma

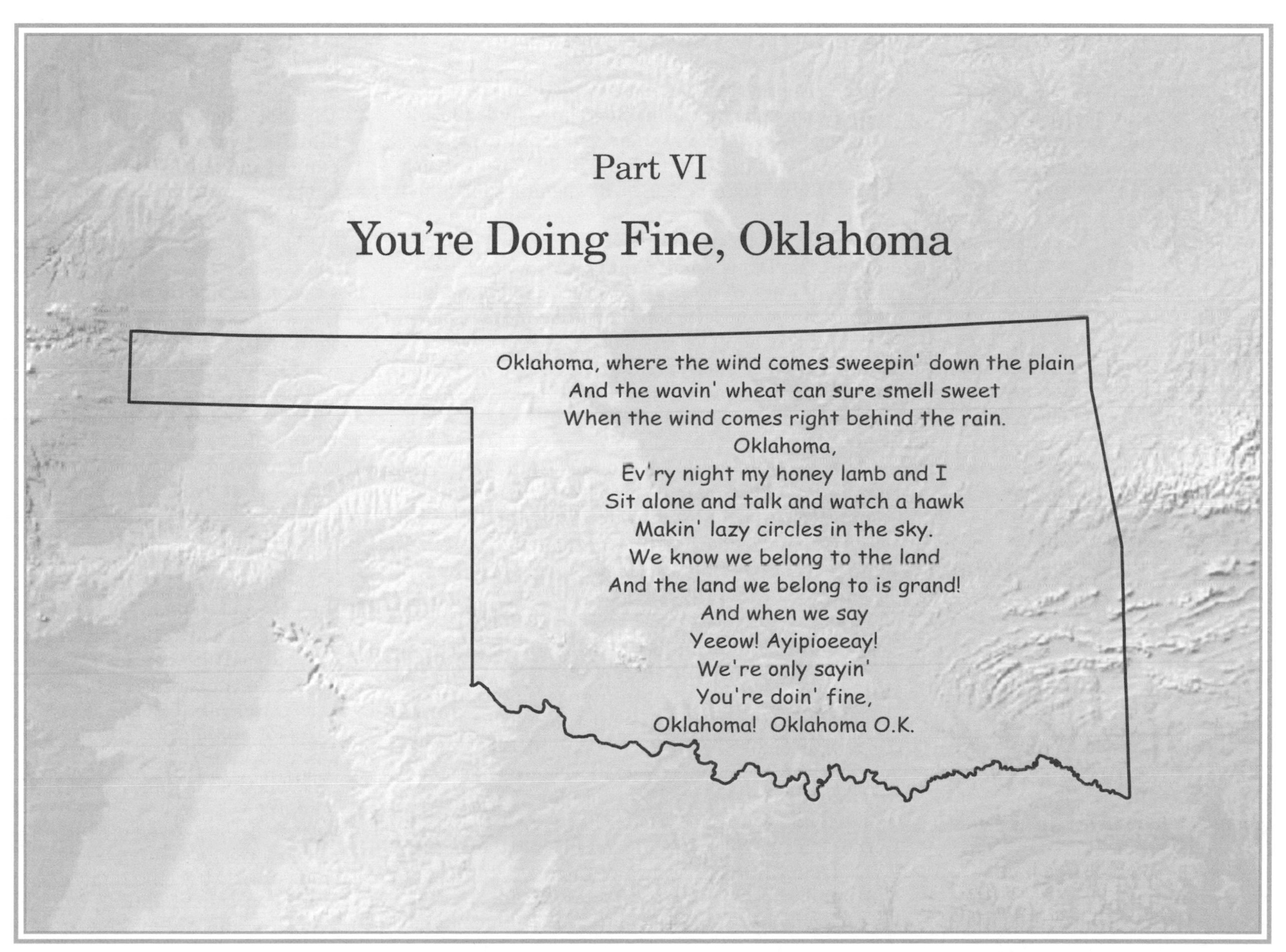

The state song, from the musical Oklahoma! *by Richard Rodgers and Oscar Hammerstein II, was adopted in 1953.*

90. RAILROADS, 1907–2000

Essay by *Bruce W. Hoagland & Danney Goble*

According to corporate magnates, the railroad regulation written into Oklahoma's "radical" statehood constitution would forever doom rail development; yet as it turned out, total railroad mileage peaked in that same year (1907), when trains roared across 6,678 miles of track to reach every corner of the state. Any relation between self-serving claims and historical records were, like reports of Mark Twain's death, greatly exaggerated. As of 1907, the federal Interstate Commerce Commission had existed for twenty years. Tough new legislation of 1906—followed by even stouter federal statutes in 1920, 1940, and 1958—had far greater impact on rail transport in Oklahoma than any state legislative assembly ever effected.

Local circumstances, not federal statutes, made the real difference. Transporting oil out of, into, or through a community was long the most compelling circumstance of all. The first shipment of crude oil left Bartlesville (site of Oklahoma's first commercial well) aboard a Santa Fe train bound for a Neodesha, Kansas, refinery. Thereafter, short-line railways matched oil-field openings almost one-for-one. Among the most successful was the Midland Valley, which linked the fabulous Glenn Pool oil field to the then-not-so-nearly-fabulous Tulsa. Subsequent lines were what put Tulsa at the nexus of the Cushing, Oilton, Jennings, and Drumwright fields. The sum of these made Tulsa into the self-proclaimed Oil Capital of the World.

Farther west, the transition from free-and-easy ranching to labor-intensive wheat growing called forth short rail lines as side effects. Commercial harvesting of southeastern Oklahoma's timber did the same. The region's main lumber company, the Choctaw Lumber and Coal Company (later renamed Dierks Lumber and Coal) controlled two of the southeastern lines, both of which were essential for the purpose of hauling timber into mills and shipping lumber out.

All of Oklahoma—not least its railroads—suffered the hard squeeze of the Great Depression. Nationally, the tonnage of materials transported by rail dropped by half between 1929 and 1932. Even absent the Depression, the mass availability of trucks and automobiles would have cut deeply into railroad profits. After all, their fall from a peak of $1,035,000,000 to $330,000,000 in 1933 began long before. Later state and federal spending for highways, bridges, airports, and waterways likewise would have had the same devastating consequences without the Depression. Oklahoma passenger service, following a slightly different trend, peaked during World War II, when the national call to move men and war materiel returned rail lines to something of their former splendor. As late as 1947, all seventy-seven counties had direct access to one or more of Oklahoma's seventeen railroads, nine of which were rated Class 1.

Thereafter, everything changed—for the worst, many said. Mergers, market losses, and federal deregulation (under the Staggers Act of 1980) led to what many considered an unmitigated disaster in states such as Oklahoma. Abandonment of formerly productive rail lines became both a symbol and a measure of this steep decline. Between 1970 and 1988 alone, 39,993 miles of railroad across the United States were simply cast off.

In Oklahoma, among the first to go was one of the first to have arrived: the Missouri, Kansas, and Texas (MK&T, or "Katy"). Starting in 1931, entire stretches of the Katy's tracks in western Oklahoma were abandoned and left to rust. Seven years later came a sudden and far greater blow: the liquidation of the Chicago, Rock Island, and Pacific (the mighty Rock Island line). Given that thirteen states and 7,610 miles of track were affected, people in other regions may have suffered more than Oklahomans. If so, Sooners were in no mood to hear about it. A thousand miles of tracks (then a fifth of the state's total) closed down. Forty-six communities—and who knows how many farmers—found themselves commercially stranded. In Canadian County, the unemployment rate doubled overnight.

As was often the way of things, the federal government thereupon attempted to relieve the pain that its policies had caused. The U.S. Treasury handed millions of dollars to states for rail planning. The Oklahoma Department of Transportation's new Rail Branch used most of its first federal check to buy up what had been the Rock Island's Hydro–Elk City section.

Over the long term, however, the inexorable trend toward mergers proved to be far more important than federal dollars. The many mergers led to a near-monopoly over rail service. When two of Oklahoma's pioneer railways—the Frisco and the Santa Fe—merged with the Burlington Northern (in 1980 and 1995, respectively), the resulting rail giant controlled 1,475 miles of Oklahoma tracks (over half of what little then remained).

Most of the cars of the Burlington Northern Santa Fe (and those of the twenty-one other railroads then running in Oklahoma) did no more than pass through, perhaps as fast as their deteriorating roadbeds would let them. Some carried Oklahoma products out. The few that carried something in mostly stuck to coal (for the state's public utilities) and grain (for its elevators, which have proven impervious both to climate and to economic change).

As for passengers, the declines of the 1960s terminated in 1979, when Amtrak's *Lone Star* made its final run. Twenty years and considerable politicking passed before the state got Amtrak service back, but the passenger line eventually returned. Every day since June 14, 1999, passengers could climb aboard the *Heartland Flyer* in Oklahoma City and head south, pulling into depots at Norman, Purcell, Pauls Valley, and Ardmore before crossing into Texas, Fort Worth–bound. Some got off here, others there. A few even got back on.

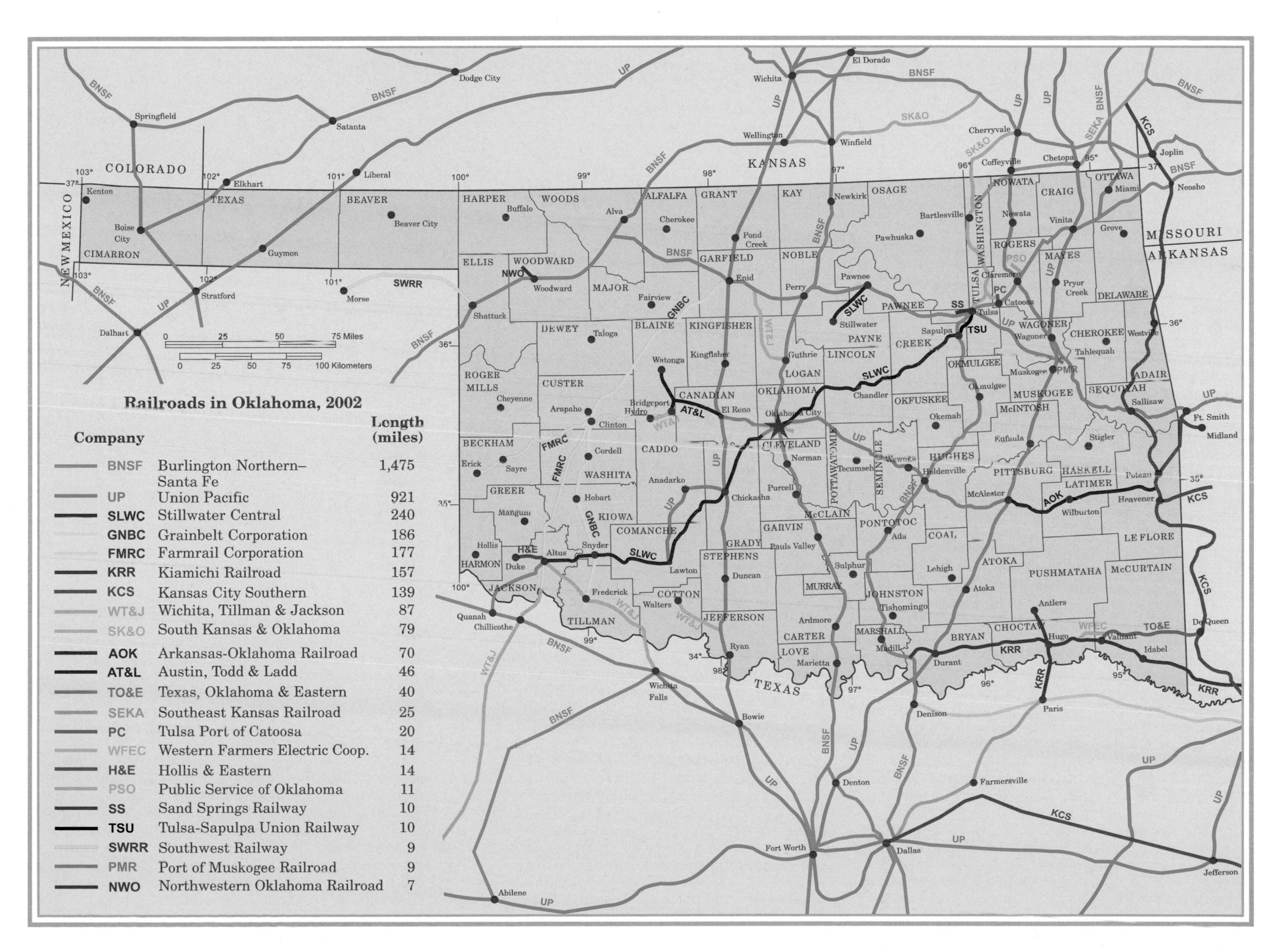
Railroads in Oklahoma, 2002
Company
Length (miles)
BNSF Burlington Northern–Santa Fe 1,475
UP Union Pacific 921
SLWC Stillwater Central 240
GNBC Grainbelt Corporation 186
FMRC Farmrail Corporation 177
KRR Kiamichi Railroad 157
KCS Kansas City Southern 139
WT&J Wichita, Tillman & Jackson 87
SK&O South Kansas & Oklahoma 79
AOK Arkansas-Oklahoma Railroad 70
AT&L Austin, Todd & Ladd 46
TO&E Texas, Oklahoma & Eastern 40
SEKA Southeast Kansas Railroad 25
PC Tulsa Port of Catoosa 20
WFEC Western Farmers Electric Coop. 14
H&E Hollis & Eastern 14
PSO Public Service of Oklahoma 11
SS Sand Springs Railway 10
TSU Tulsa-Sapulpa Union Railway 10
SWRR Southwest Railway 9
PMR Port of Muskogee Railroad 9
NWO Northwestern Oklahoma Railroad 7
0 25 50 75 Miles
0 25 50 75 100 Kilometers
COLORADO
KANSAS
NEW MEXICO
TEXAS
MISSOURI
ARKANSAS
Dodge City
Springfield
Satanta
Liberal
Elkhart
Kenton
Boise City
Guymon
Stratford
Dalhart
Morse
Wichita
El Dorado
Wellington
Winfield
Cherryvale
Coffeyville
Chetopa
Joplin
Neosho
Oklahoma City
Tulsa
Fort Worth
Dallas
Denton
Bowie
Wichita Falls
Abilene
Denison
Paris
Farmersville
Jefferson
Ft. Smith
Midland
De Queen
CIMARRON
TEXAS
BEAVER
HARPER
WOODS
ALFALFA
GRANT
KAY
OSAGE
NOWATA
CRAIG
OTTAWA
ELLIS
WOODWARD
MAJOR
GARFIELD
NOBLE
PAWNEE
WASHINGTON
ROGERS
MAYES
DELAWARE
DEWEY
BLAINE
KINGFISHER
PAYNE
CREEK
TULSA
WAGONER
CHEROKEE
ADAIR
ROGER MILLS
CUSTER
CANADIAN
LOGAN
LINCOLN
OKMULGEE
MUSKOGEE
SEQUOYAH
BECKHAM
WASHITA
CADDO
OKLAHOMA
CLEVELAND
OKFUSKEE
McINTOSH
POTTAWATOMIE
SEMINOLE
HUGHES
PITTSBURG
HASKELL
LATIMER
LE FLORE
GREER
KIOWA
COMANCHE
GRADY
McCLAIN
GARVIN
PONTOTOC
COAL
ATOKA
PUSHMATAHA
McCURTAIN
HARMON
JACKSON
TILLMAN
COTTON
STEPHENS
JEFFERSON
CARTER
MURRAY
JOHNSTON
MARSHALL
LOVE
BRYAN
CHOCTAW

91. INTERSTATE, TURNPIKE, AND MAJOR HIGHWAY SYSTEMS

Essay by *Danney Goble*

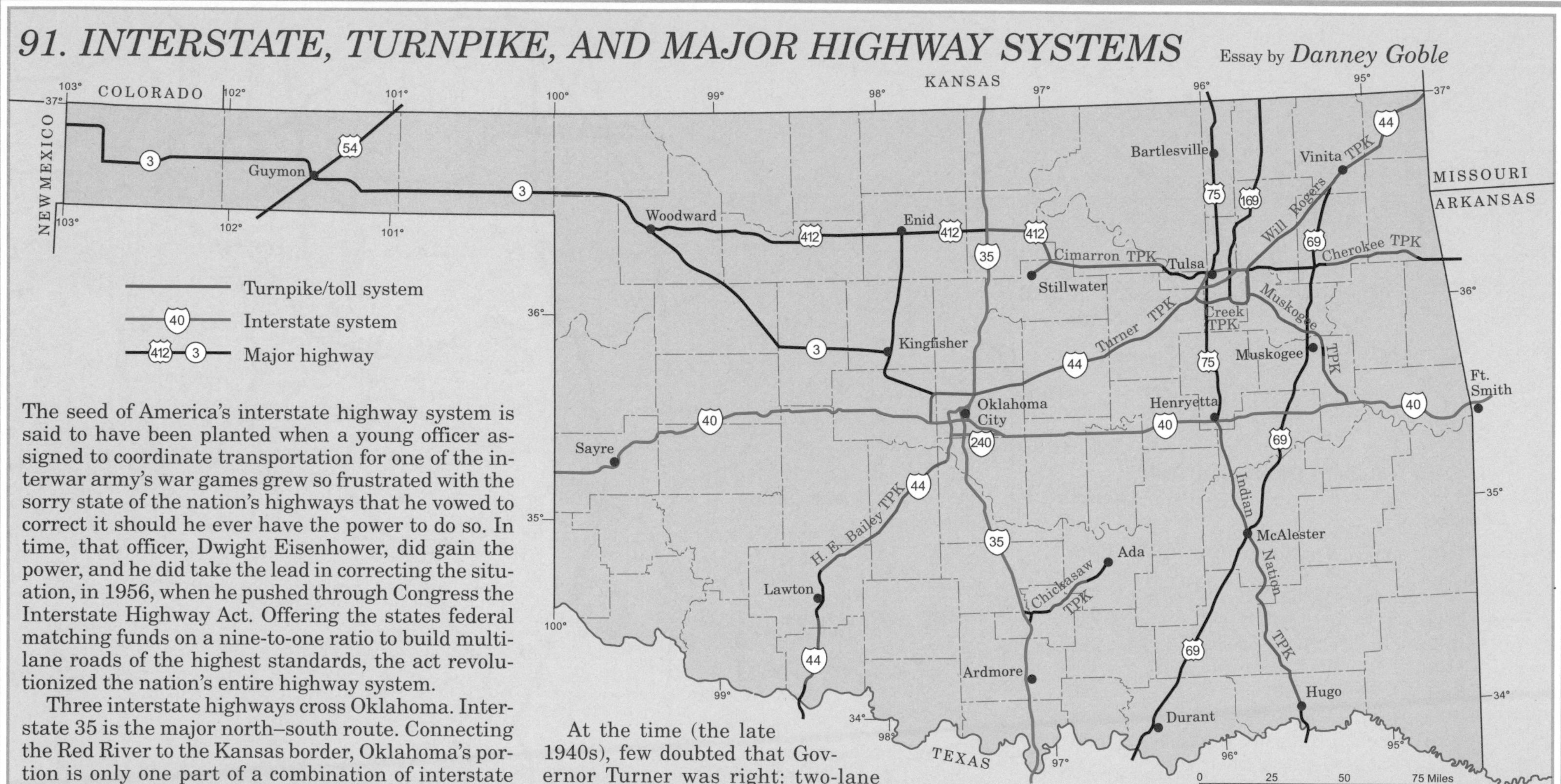

The seed of America's interstate highway system is said to have been planted when a young officer assigned to coordinate transportation for one of the interwar army's war games grew so frustrated with the sorry state of the nation's highways that he vowed to correct it should he ever have the power to do so. In time, that officer, Dwight Eisenhower, did gain the power, and he did take the lead in correcting the situation, in 1956, when he pushed through Congress the Interstate Highway Act. Offering the states federal matching funds on a nine-to-one ratio to build multilane roads of the highest standards, the act revolutionized the nation's entire highway system.

Three interstate highways cross Oklahoma. Interstate 35 is the major north–south route. Connecting the Red River to the Kansas border, Oklahoma's portion is only one part of a combination of interstate highways that ultimately links the U.S.-Mexican border to this country's boundary with Canada. Interstate 40 replaced the western portion of Route 66, past Oklahoma City, and creates a long mid-waist belt across Oklahoma that reaches from the state's border with Arkansas to the Texas panhandle. Interstate 44 essentially replaced the eastern diagonal of old US 66, which ran through Tulsa to Oklahoma City, and the interstate continues on a diagonal into southwestern Oklahoma.

The section of I-44 that connects Tulsa and Oklahoma City is the Turner Turnpike. Named for Governor Roy J. Turner, it is an object lesson in post–World War II politics as well as a vital link between the two metropolitan areas.

At the time (the late 1940s), few doubted that Governor Turner was right: two-lane Route 66 was not up to handling the traffic flow, both personal and commercial, between the two metropolises. Turner's opponents may have had neither reason nor fact on their side, but they did have power. The legislature still answered to lawmakers elected from small-town Oklahoma and expected to serve their hometowns well in Oklahoma City. Among the towns that would be affected by the proposed highway bypass were Sapulpa, Bristow, Stroud, and Chandler.

Legislative wrangling, legal maneuvering, constitutional amendments—all were employed during the struggle. Its end came through compromise. The affected towns were guaranteed separate exits, entrances, and toll booths. The sale of bonds to a consortium of three firms financed construction. Tolls ($1.40 was the original full-distance rate) would retire the bonds, at which point travel on the road was to become free.

Construction began in December 1949, and the four-lane superhighway opened in May 1953. The road is not and probably never will be "free." Although the bonds have long since been repaid, the tolls on the turnpike (which have long since increased, many times over) have been essential to finance and maintain Oklahoma's subsequent nine toll roads. None of them was as controversial or is as profitable.

92. AIRWAYS AND AIRPORTS

Essay by *Danney Goble*

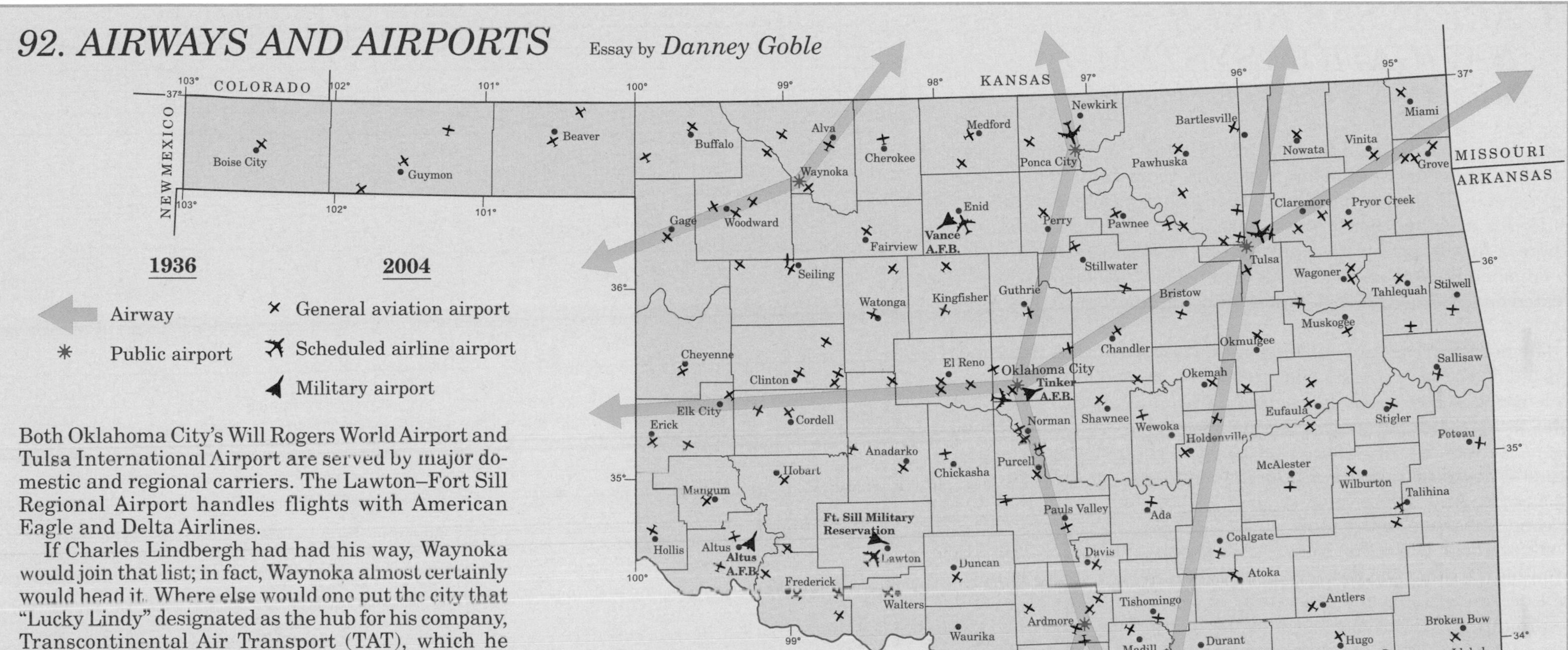

Both Oklahoma City's Will Rogers World Airport and Tulsa International Airport are served by major domestic and regional carriers. The Lawton–Fort Sill Regional Airport handles flights with American Eagle and Delta Airlines.

If Charles Lindbergh had had his way, Waynoka would join that list; in fact, Waynoka almost certainly would head it. Where else would one put the city that "Lucky Lindy" designated as the hub for his company, Transcontinental Air Transport (TAT), which he thought fated to revolutionize American travel?

Revolutionary it would have been. Coast-to-coast travel in a mere forty-eight hours? It had to be a dream—but not to Lindbergh and not to Waynoka either. Having traveled by train from New York City to Columbus, Ohio, where they would board a Ford Tri-motor with scheduled stops in Indianapolis, St. Louis, Kansas City, and Wichita, as many as ten passengers would descend from the skies every evening to reach Waynoka at 6:00 (the time being the reason for Lindbergh's choice), where they would enjoy fine meals at Waynoka's famed Harvey House before boarding the Santa Fe, bound for Clovis, New Mexico. Upon their arrival in Clovis the next day, a TAT aircraft would complete the westward journey, flying into Los Angeles, having made several stops en route.

In June 1929, the dream came true. Lindbergh and his bride of five weeks landed in Waynoka to dedicate the city's great TAT airport. Waynoka was mighty impressed with the couple; Anne Morrow Lindbergh could barely get over Waynoka herself. "I've never been in a place like it," she wrote her sister. The daughter of a Wall Street tycoon had never seen a place with "four or five paved streets and a hotel . . . the kind you see in an old western movie painted white with a large sign, 'Baths,' over the front door."

Passenger travel began a month later and continued for eighteen months, by the end of which TAT had lost $2.7 million along with two airplanes and all aboard. That was the end of TAT, which merged with Western Air Expressway to form a new company: Transcontinental and Western Airlines, the original TWA. On October 1, TWA landed the lucrative U.S. airmail contract that guaranteed the company's survival. Within the month, its managers announced the closing of Waynoka's airport and thereby ending that town's dreams.

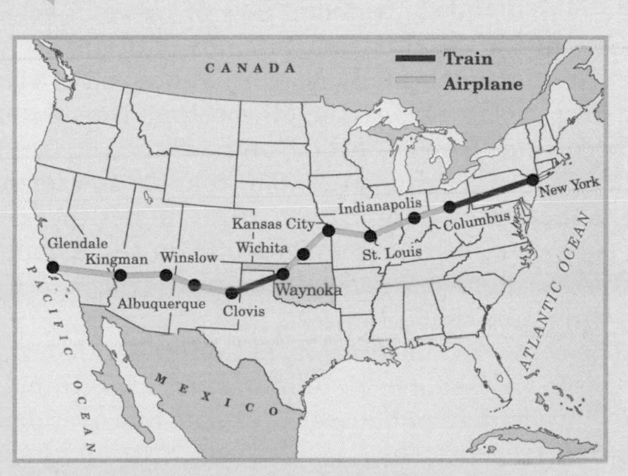

Coast to coast in 48 hours by combining rail and air travel. The first official cross-country trip began July 27, 1929.

93. ARKANSAS RIVER NAVIGATION SYSTEM

Danney Goble & Charles Robert Goins

For years people had said that the trouble with the Arkansas River was that it was too wet to plow and to dry to navigate. Then came real trouble. It started on May 7, 1946, when rain began falling, gentle for a while, then harder. Either way it just kept falling. When it finally let up, five days later, rain-swollen tributaries had pushed the Arkansas over its banks near Muskogee, where it crested at 38.3 feet, a foot and a half higher than it had ever reached.

The next day, the rain started again. It lasted a week this time. The old river rose out of its bed, crested at an incredible 48.2 feet, and roared across 1,448,400 acres. Flowing at a rate of 700,000 cubic feet of water per second, it had its way with everything standing in its way. By the time it returned to its bed, the river had ruined $31 million worth of property and killed at least twenty-six people. And before long, people were saying again that the Arkansas was too wet to plow.

Oklahoma's Governor Robert S. Kerr set out to fix that. He intended to tame the Arkansas, stabilize it, and make it navigable. Even with his determination, acquiring authorization and funding by the U.S. Congress and the focused efforts of the U.S. Army Corps of Engineers took sixteen years to produce the Arkansas River Navigation System.

Besides widening, deepening, and stabilizing the river's channel, the system depended on a series of artificial lakes to ensure a dependable and controllable flow of water. A series of locks (five in Oklahoma and thirteen more downstream, in Arkansas) made the river navigable all the way from the system's terminus—called the Port of Catoosa—to the Mississippi, New Orleans, the Gulf of Mexico, and the wide sea beyond.

The first inbound cargo, 650 tons of newsprint, arrived with great fanfare on January 18, 1971. To get there, it had traveled the system's entire 448 miles—398 on the Arkansas, the last 50 on the Verdigris—to reach Catoosa. Never before had there been anything like that.

The cost was substantial: $1.2 billion in federal funds for construction costs alone; $2 billion when everything was thrown in. Only one civilian public works project had ever demanded more of the U.S. Treasury: the Apollo Project. Putting a man on the moon—that alone cost more than getting that newsprint into Catoosa, Oklahoma.

And that is why there never will be anything like it again.

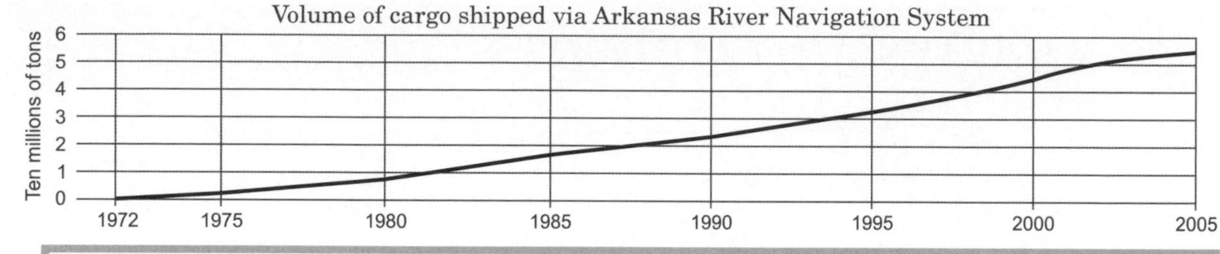

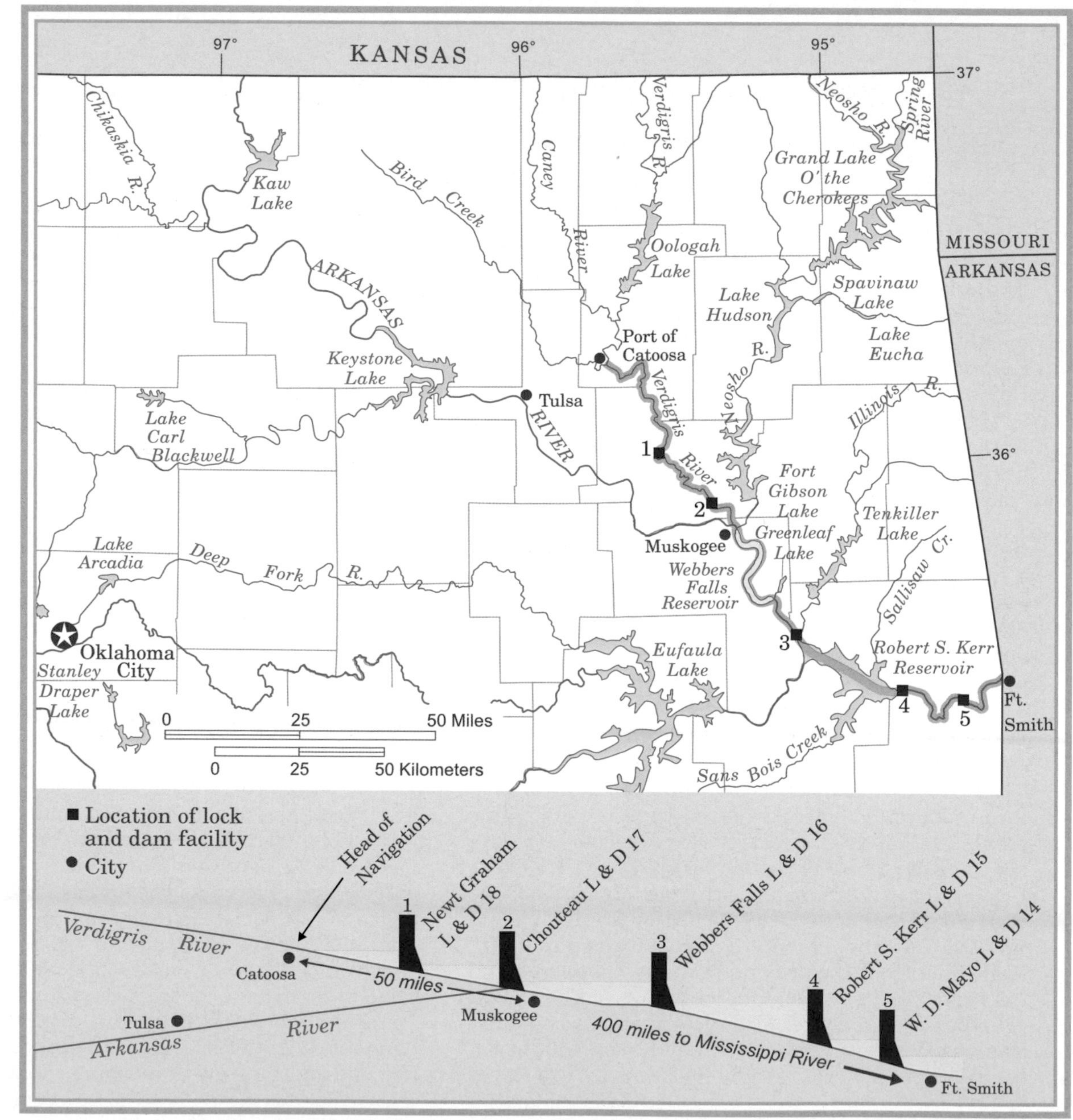

94. OKLAHOMA ASSOCIATION OF REGIONAL COUNCILS

Charles Robert Goins

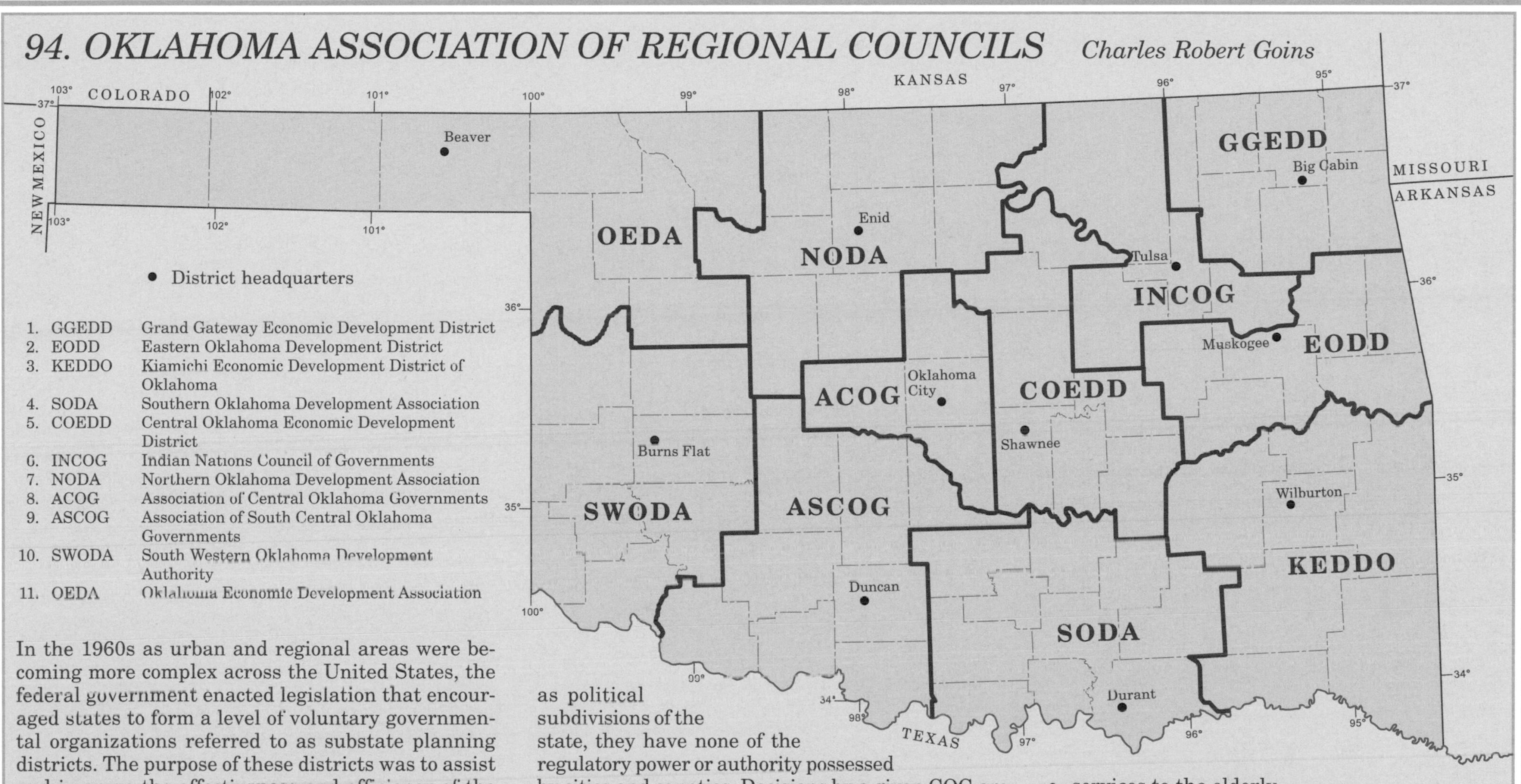

In the 1960s as urban and regional areas were becoming more complex across the United States, the federal government enacted legislation that encouraged states to form a level of voluntary governmental organizations referred to as substate planning districts. The purpose of these districts was to assist and improve the effectiveness and efficiency of the delivery of services by various levels of government.

In 1969, the Oklahoma Legislature approved Senate Bill 290, which provided that the Oklahoma Industrial Development and Park Commission be assigned the task of dividing the state into substate planning districts. On December 9, 1970, this agency announced the delineation of eleven districts, and by an executive order dated May 24, 1971, Governor David Hall recognized the eleven substate districts.

These districts are now referred to as Council of Government (COG) entities; they help manage and plan for issues that cross the boundaries of local and county governments. While they are defined by law as political subdivisions of the state, they have none of the regulatory power or authority possessed by cities and counties. Decisions by a given COG are not binding on member governments, and COGs are subject to state laws governing open meetings. Membership in the various councils consists of local governments of towns, cities, counties, conservation districts, and Indian nations (with cities and counties forming the majority of regional council membership). Each of the seventy-seven counties of Oklahoma is in one of the eleven COGs.

Each of the COGs has its own bylaws or articles of agreement and is managed by staff that carry out the policies of the governing bodies. The COGs have proven to be useful organizations in providing services in the following areas:

- services to the elderly
- economic development districts
- law enforcement planning and development
- areawide planning and development
- job training and workforce development
- development of emergency medical services
- development of rural fire defense
- resource conservation and development
- solid waste planning and development
- water resource development
- state cultural planning
- capital improvements planning
- hazard mitigation planning

95. POPULATION CHANGE BY COUNTY, 1990–2000

Charles Robert Goins

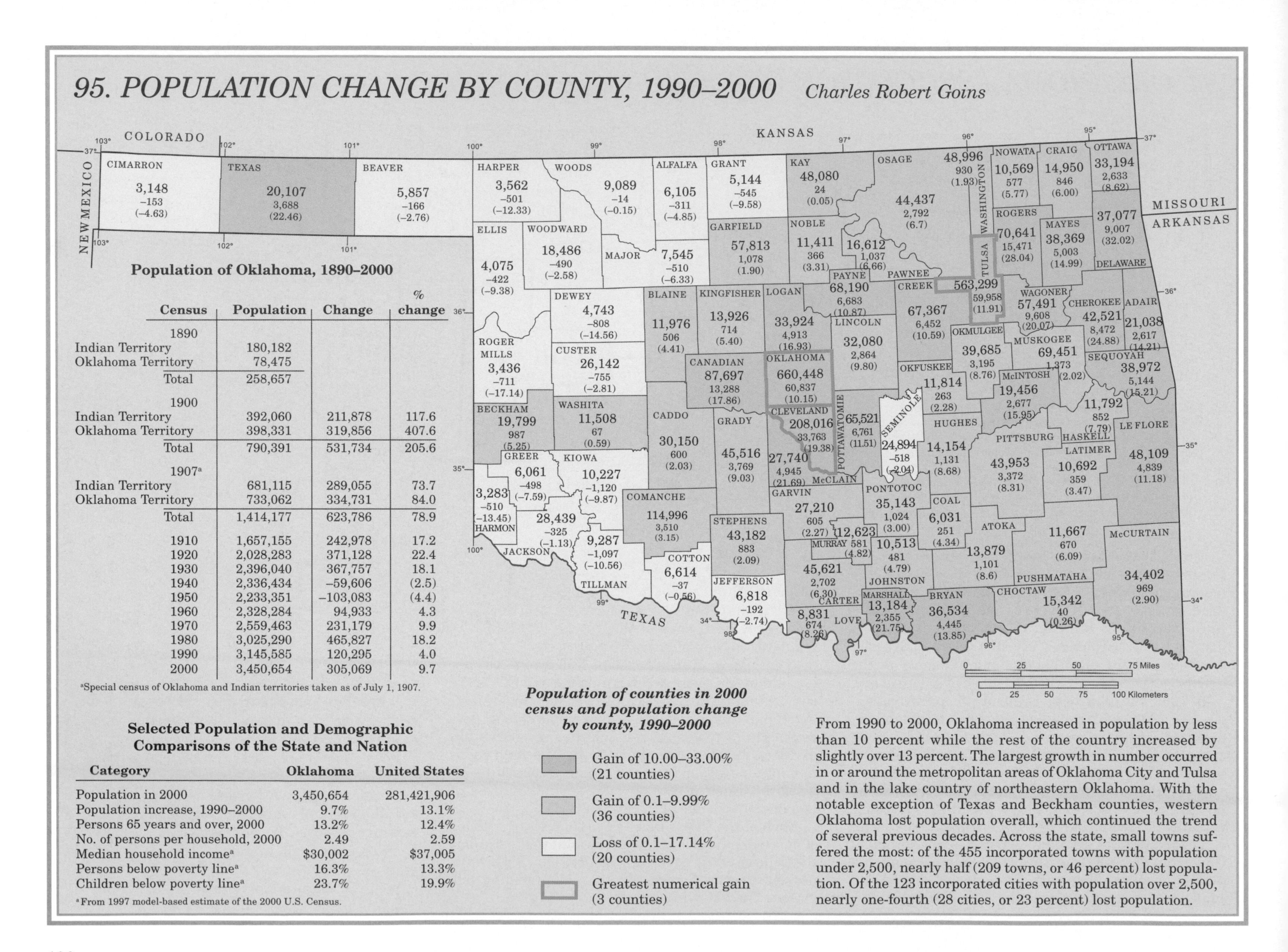

Population of Oklahoma, 1890–2000

Census	Population	Change	% change
1890			
Indian Territory	180,182		
Oklahoma Territory	78,475		
Total	258,657		
1900			
Indian Territory	392,060	211,878	117.6
Oklahoma Territory	398,331	319,856	407.6
Total	790,391	531,734	205.6
1907[a]			
Indian Territory	681,115	289,055	73.7
Oklahoma Territory	733,062	334,731	84.0
Total	1,414,177	623,786	78.9
1910	1,657,155	242,978	17.2
1920	2,028,283	371,128	22.4
1930	2,396,040	367,757	18.1
1940	2,336,434	–59,606	(2.5)
1950	2,233,351	–103,083	(4.4)
1960	2,328,284	94,933	4.3
1970	2,559,463	231,179	9.9
1980	3,025,290	465,827	18.2
1990	3,145,585	120,295	4.0
2000	3,450,654	305,069	9.7

[a]Special census of Oklahoma and Indian territories taken as of July 1, 1907.

Selected Population and Demographic Comparisons of the State and Nation

Category	Oklahoma	United States
Population in 2000	3,450,654	281,421,906
Population increase, 1990–2000	9.7%	13.1%
Persons 65 years and over, 2000	13.2%	12.4%
No. of persons per household, 2000	2.49	2.59
Median household income[a]	$30,002	$37,005
Persons below poverty line[a]	16.3%	13.3%
Children below poverty line[a]	23.7%	19.9%

[a]From 1997 model-based estimate of the 2000 U.S. Census.

Population of counties in 2000 census and population change by county, 1990–2000

- Gain of 10.00–33.00% (21 counties)
- Gain of 0.1–9.99% (36 counties)
- Loss of 0.1–17.14% (20 counties)
- Greatest numerical gain (3 counties)

From 1990 to 2000, Oklahoma increased in population by less than 10 percent while the rest of the country increased by slightly over 13 percent. The largest growth in number occurred in or around the metropolitan areas of Oklahoma City and Tulsa and in the lake country of northeastern Oklahoma. With the notable exception of Texas and Beckham counties, western Oklahoma lost population overall, which continued the trend of several previous decades. Across the state, small towns suffered the most: of the 455 incorporated towns with population under 2,500, nearly half (209 towns, or 46 percent) lost population. Of the 123 incorporated cities with population over 2,500, nearly one-fourth (28 cities, or 23 percent) lost population.

96. MINORITY POPULATION CHANGE, 1990–2000 *Charles Robert Goins*

Population Profile by Race of Oklahoma and the United States, 2000

Race	Population	Oklahoma % of total	United States % of total
White	2,628,434	76.2	75.1
American Indian	273,230	7.9	0.9
African American	260,968	7.5	12.3
Two or more races	155,985	4.5	2.4
Other race	82,898	2.4	5.5
Asian	46,767	1.4	3.6
Native Hawaiian and other Pacific Islander	2,372	0.1	0.1
Total	3,450,654	100.0	100.0

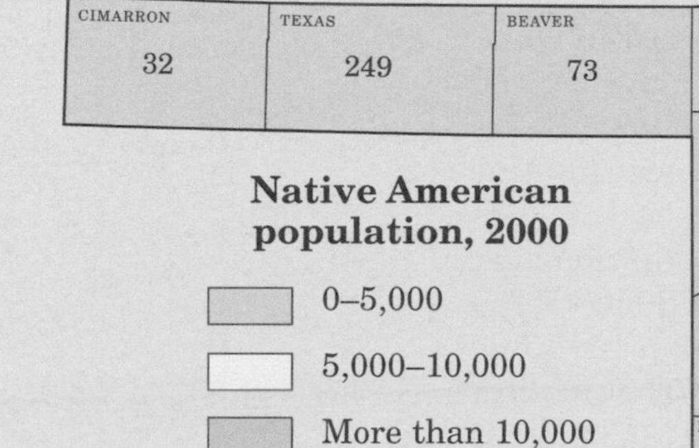

According to the U.S. census of 2000, Oklahoma has 1 percent more white population than the rest of the United States, which leaves the percentage of minority population almost equal to the U.S. percentage. The largest minority group in Oklahoma is that of the American Indian. Oklahoma (with a population of 273,230) is second only to California (333,346) in the number of American Indians. The African American population in Oklahoma is almost 5 percent lower than in the rest of the country. Oklahoma's percentage of Asian and other races is likewise lower than that of the United States generally. In the past ten years, the population of Hispanic people in Oklahoma has increased. Particularly noticeable has been the growth of Hispanic population in the city of Guymon. The growth of the pork-processing industry in the Panhandle has generated many jobs that have attracted Hispanic people to that area. Another major change in the past two decades has been the increase in the Vietnamese population, with many of these immigrants having settled in the Oklahoma City area.

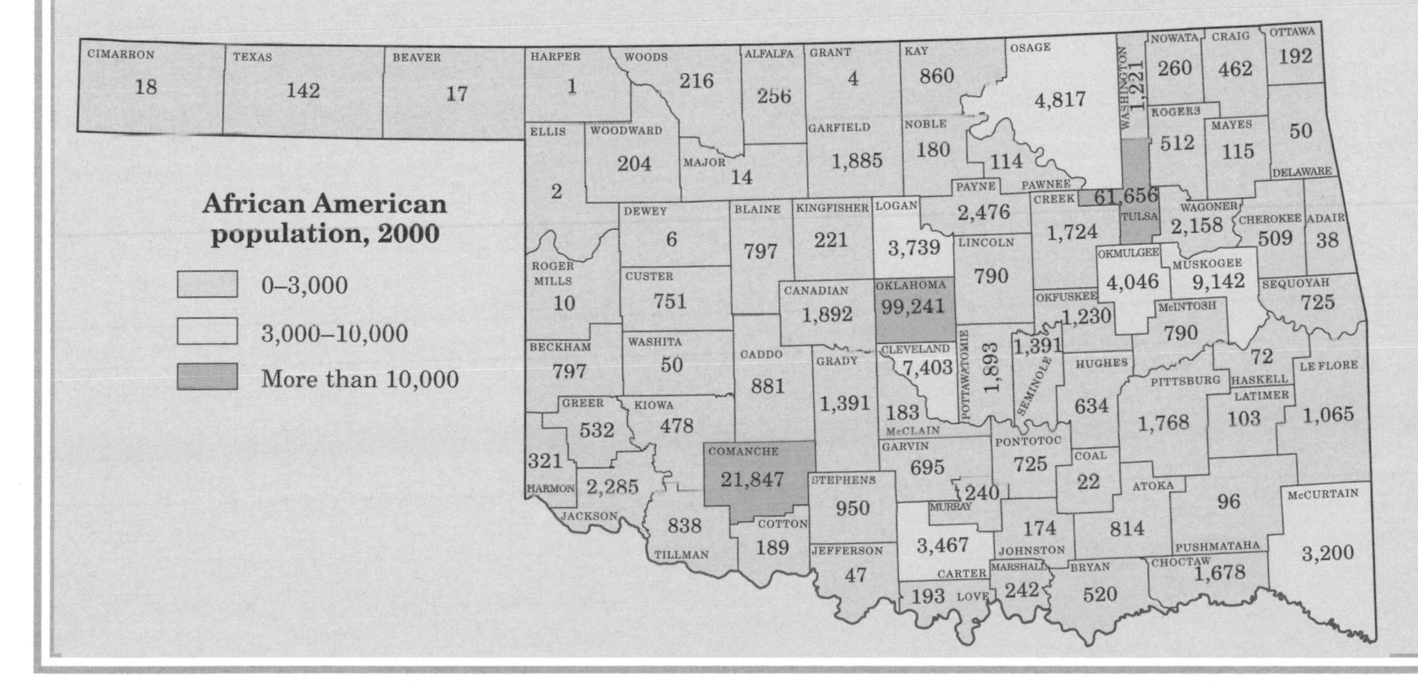

Population History of Native Americans and African Americans of Oklahoma

Census	Native Americans	% of state population	African Americans	% of state population
1907[a]	75,012	5.3	112,160	7.9
1910	74,825	4.5	137,612	8.3
1920	57,337	2.8	149,408	7.4
1930	92,725	3.9	172,198	7.2
1940	63,125	2.7	168,849	7.2
1950	53,769	2.4	145,503	6.5
1960	64,689	2.8	153,084	6.6
1970	98,468	3.8	171,892	6.7
1980	169,292	5.6	204,674	6.8
1990	252,420	8.0	233,801	7.4
2000	273,230	7.9	260,968	7.6

[a] Special census of Oklahoma Territory and Indian Territory, July 1, 1907.

97. NORTHWESTERN OKLAHOMA, 2000 *Charles Robert Goins*

From 1990 to 2000, the population of the sixteen counties that comprise northwestern Oklahoma increased by 8.7 percent, but virtually all of this growth occurred in Oklahoma County and the adjoining counties of Canadian and Logan. Oklahoma City and Edmond were the centers of the greatest growth, supplemented by the satellite cities of Mustang, Piedmont, and Midwest City. All of the ten westernmost counties within this quadrant of the state lost population.

In 2000 there were 25 cities in northwestern Oklahoma that had a population over 2,500; of these, a third (8, or 32 percent) lost population between 1990 and 2000. Of the 98 towns with population less than 2,500, the population loss is even more striking: nearly two-thirds (62, or 57 percent) lost population between 1990 and 2000. The smallest towns, with population less than 1,000, were the hardest hit: 52 out of 80 (65 percent) claimed losses, as compared to 10 out of 18 towns (55 percent) having populations between 1,000 and 2,500.

Population Change, 1990–2000, for Counties in Northwestern Oklahoma

County	Population 2000	Population 1990	Change	Percentage change
Alfalfa	6,105	6,416	–311	–4.8
Blaine	11,976	11,470	506	4.4
Canadian	87,697	74,409	13,288	17.9
Custer	26,142	26,897	–755	–2.8
Dewey	4,743	5,551	–808	–14.6
Ellis	4,075	4,497	–422	–9.4
Garfield	57,813	56,735	1,078	1.9
Grant	5,144	5,689	–545	–9.6
Harper	3,562	4,063	–501	–12.3
Kingfisher	13,926	13,212	714	5.4
Logan	33,924	29,011	4,913	16.9
Major	7,545	8,055	–510	–6.3
Oklahoma	660,448	599,611	60,837	10.1
Roger Mills	3,436	4,147	–711	–17.1
Woods	9,089	9,103	–14	–0.1
Woodward	18,486	18,976	–490	–2.6
Total	**954,111**	**877,842**	**76,269**	**8.7**

Population Change, 1990–2000, for Cities in Northwestern Oklahoma with Population over 2,500 in 2000

City	Population 2000	Population 1990	Change	Percentage change
Alva	5,288	5,495	–207	–3.8
Bethany	20,307	20,075	232	1.2
Choctaw	9,377	8,545	832	9.7
Clinton	8,833	9,298	–465	–5.0
Del City	22,128	23,928	–1,800	–7.5
Edmond	68,315	52,315	16,000	30.6
El Reno	16,212	15,414	798	5.2
Enid	47,045	45,309	1,736	3.8
Fairview	2,733	2,936	–203	–6.9
Guthrie	9,925	10,518	–593	–5.6
Harrah	4,719	4,206	513	12.2
Jones	2,517	2,424	93	3.8
Kingfisher	4,380	4,095	285	7.0
Midwest City	54,088	52,267	1,821	3.5
Mustang	13,156	10,343	2,813	27.2
Nichols Hills	4,056	4,020	36	0.9
Oklahoma City	506,132	447,719	58,413	13.0
Piedmont	3,650	2,522	1,128	44.7
Spencer	3,476	3,972	–496	–12.5
The Village	10,517	0	10,517	100.0
Warr Acres	9,735	9,288	447	4.8
Watonga	4,658	3,408	1,250	36.7
Weatherford	9,859	10,124	–265	–2.6
Woodward	11,853	12,340	–487	–3.9
Yukon	21,043	20,935	108	0.5
Total	**874,002**	**781,496**	**92,506**	**11.8**

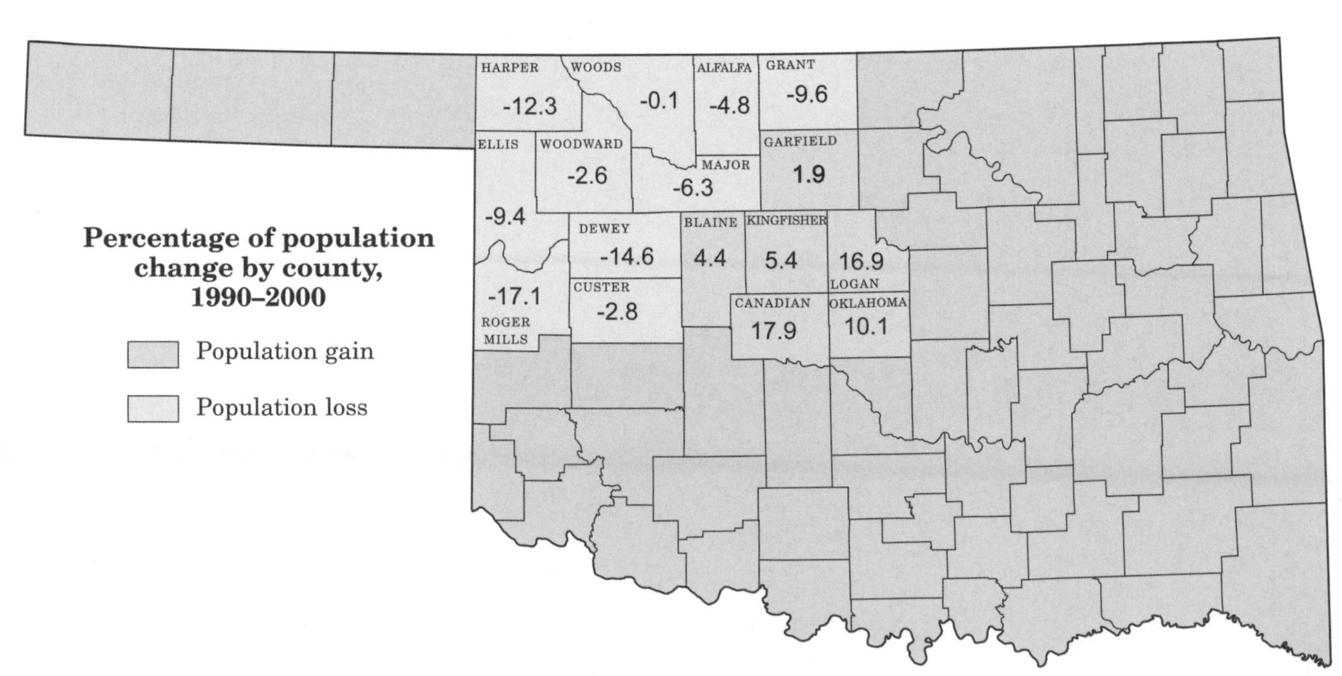

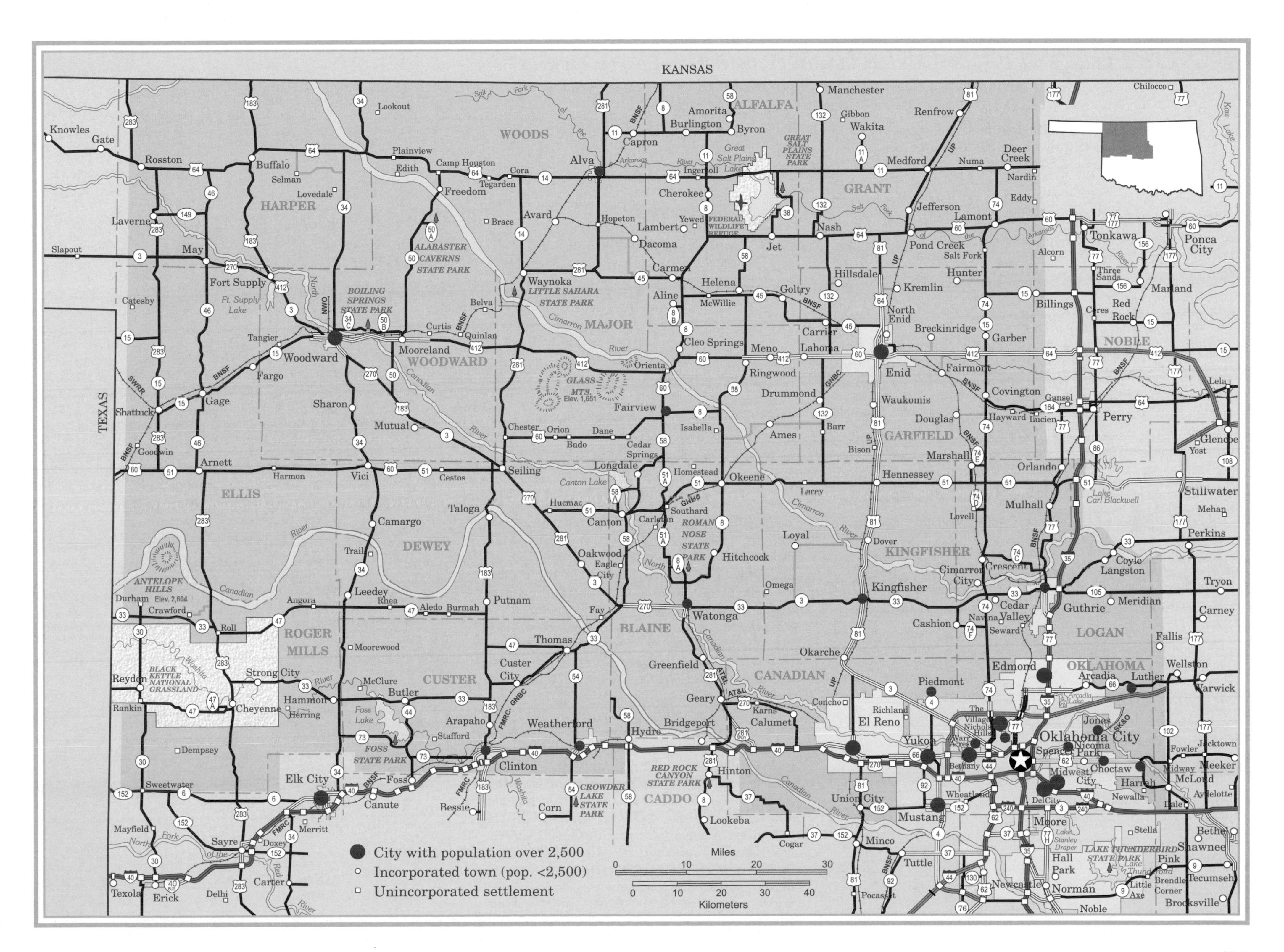
KANSAS
TEXAS
WOODS
ALFALFA
GRANT
HARPER
MAJOR
WOODWARD
NOBLE
GARFIELD
ELLIS
DEWEY
KINGFISHER
BLAINE
LOGAN
ROGER MILLS
CUSTER
CANADIAN
OKLAHOMA
CADDO
Knowles
Gate
Rosston
Buffalo
Selman
Lovedale
Laverne
Slapout
May
Fort Supply
Ft. Supply Lake
Catesby
Tangier
Woodward
Fargo
Gage
Shattuck
Goodwin
Arnett
Harmon
Vici
Sharon
Mutual
Lookout
Plainview
Edith
Camp Houston
Tegarden
Cora
Freedom
Brace
Avard
Alva
Hopeton
Capron
Amorita
Burlington
Byron
Cherokee
Ingersoll
Lambert
Yewed
Dacoma
Carmen
Aline
Helena
McWillie
Goltry
Jet
Great Salt Plains Lake
GREAT SALT PLAINS STATE PARK
FEDERAL WILDLIFE REFUGE
Manchester
Gibbon
Wakita
Renfrow
Medford
Numa
Deer Creek
Nardin
Eddy
Jefferson
Lamont
Nash
Pond Creek
Salt Fork
Hunter
Hillsdale
Kremlin
North Enid
Carrier
Lahoma
Breckinridge
Garber
Billings
Enid
Fairmont
Meno
Ringwood
Drummond
Waukomis
Covington
Douglas
Hayward
Lucien
Gansel
Perry
Chilocco
Tonkawa
Ponca City
Alcorn
Three Sands
Marland
Cares
Red Rock
Lela
Glencoe
Yost
Stillwater
Mehan
Perkins
Orlando
Lake Carl Blackwell
Mulhall
Lovell
Marshall
Hennessey
Bison
Barr
Ames
Isabella
Fairview
Orienta
Cleo Springs
Waynoka
LITTLE SAHARA STATE PARK
ALABASTER CAVERNS STATE PARK
BOILING SPRINGS STATE PARK
Belva
Curtis
Quinlan
Mooreland
GLASS MTS. Elev. 1,651
Chester
Orion
Bado
Dane
Cedar Springs
Longdale
Seiling
Canton Lake
Homestead
Okeene
Lacey
Cestos
Taloga
Hucmac
Canton
Carleton
Southard
ROMAN NOSE STATE PARK
Hitchcock
Loyal
Dover
Camargo
Trail
Leedey
Rhea
Oakwood
Eagle City
Omega
Kingfisher
Cimarron City
Crescent
Coyle
Langston
Guthrie
Meridian
Tryon
Carney
Cedar Valley
Navina
Seward
Cashion
Fallis
Wellston
Warwick
Luther
Arcadia
Edmond
Watonga
Fay
Putnam
Aledo
Burmah
Angora
ANTELOPE HILLS Elev. 2,604
Durham
Crawford
Roll
Thomas
Moorewood
Custer City
Greenfield
Geary
Okarche
Piedmont
Concho
Richland
El Reno
Calumet
Karns
Bridgeport
Hydro
Weatherford
Yukon
The Village
Nichols Hills
Warr Acres
Bethany
Oklahoma City
Spencer
Jones
Nicoma Park
Choctaw
Midwest City
Del City
Harrah
Newalla
Midway
McLoud
Dale
Aydelotte
Meeker
Jacktown
Fowler
Reydon
BLACK KETTLE NATIONAL GRASSLAND
Strong City
Cheyenne
Rankin
Hammon
Herring
McClure
Butler
Foss Lake
Arapaho
Stafford
FOSS STATE PARK
Clinton
Dempsey
Elk City
Foss
Canute
Bessie
Corn
CROWDER LAKE STATE PARK
RED ROCK CANYON STATE PARK
Hinton
Lookeba
Cogar
Union City
Minco
Mustang
Wheatland
Moore
Lake Stanley Draper
Stella
LAKE THUNDERBIRD STATE PARK
Lake Thunderbird
Hall Park
Norman
Noble
Little Axe
Brendle Corner
Pink
Bethel
Shawnee
Tecumseh
Brooksville
Newcastle
Tuttle
Pocasset
Sweetwater
Mayfield
Sayre
Doxey
Merritt
Texola
Erick
Delhi
Carter
Salt Fork of the Arkansas River
Cimarron River
Canadian River
North Canadian River
Washita
North Fork of the Red River
Red River
Kilometers
Miles
City with population over 2,500
Incorporated town (pop. <2,500)
Unincorporated settlement

98. NORTHEASTERN OKLAHOMA, 2000 *Charles Robert Goins*

Population Change, 1990–2000, for Cities in Northeastern Oklahoma with Population over 2,500 in 2000

City	Population 2000	Population 1990	Change	Percentage change
Bartlesville	34,748	34,256	492	1.4
Bixby	13,336	9,502	3,834	40.3
Blackwell	7,688	7,538	150	2.0
Bristow	4,325	4,062	263	6.5
Broken Arrow	74,859	58,043	16,816	29.0
Catoosa	5,449	2,954	2,495	84.5
Chandler	2,842	2,596	246	9.5
Checotah	3,481	3,290	191	5.8
Claremore	15,873	13,280	2,593	19.5
Cleveland	3,282	3,156	126	4.0
Collinsville	4,077	3,612	465	12.9
Commerce	2,645	2,426	219	9.0
Coweta	7,139	6,159	980	15.9
Cushing	8,371	7,218	1,153	16.0
Dewey	3,179	3,326	–147	–4.4
Drumright	2,905	2,799	106	3.8
Eufaula	2,639	2,652	–13	–0.5
Fort Gibson	4,054	3,359	695	20.7
Glenpool	8,123	6,688	1,435	21.5
Grove	5,131	4,020	1,111	27.6
Henryetta	6,096	5,872	224	3.8
Hominy	2,584	2,342	242	10.3
Jenks	9,557	7,493	2,064	27.5
Miami	13,704	13,142	562	4.3
Muldrow	3,104	2,889	215	7.4
Muskogee	38,310	37,708	602	1.6
Nowata	3,971	3,896	75	1.9
Okemah	3,038	3,085	–47	–1.5
Okmulgee	13,022	13,441	–419	–3.1
Owasso	18,502	11,151	7,351	65.9
Pawhuska	3,629	3,825	–196	–5.1
Perry	5,230	4,978	252	5.1
Ponca City	25,919	26,359	–440	–1.7
Pryor	8,659	8,327	332	4.0
Roland	2,842	2,481	361	14.6
Sallisaw	7,989	7,122	867	12.2
Sand Springs	17,451	15,346	2,105	13.7
Sapulpa	19,166	18,074	1,092	6.0
Skiatook	5,369	4,910	459	9.3
Stillwater	39,065	36,676	2,389	6.5
Stilwell	3,276	2,663	613	23.0
Stroud	2,758	2,666	92	3.5
Tahlequah	14,458	10,398	4,060	39.0
Tonkawa	3,299	3,127	172	5.5
Tulsa	393,419	367,302	26,117	7.1
Vinita	6,472	5,804	668	11.5
Wagoner	7,669	6,894	775	11.2
Total	**892,704**	**808,907**	**83,797**	**10.4**

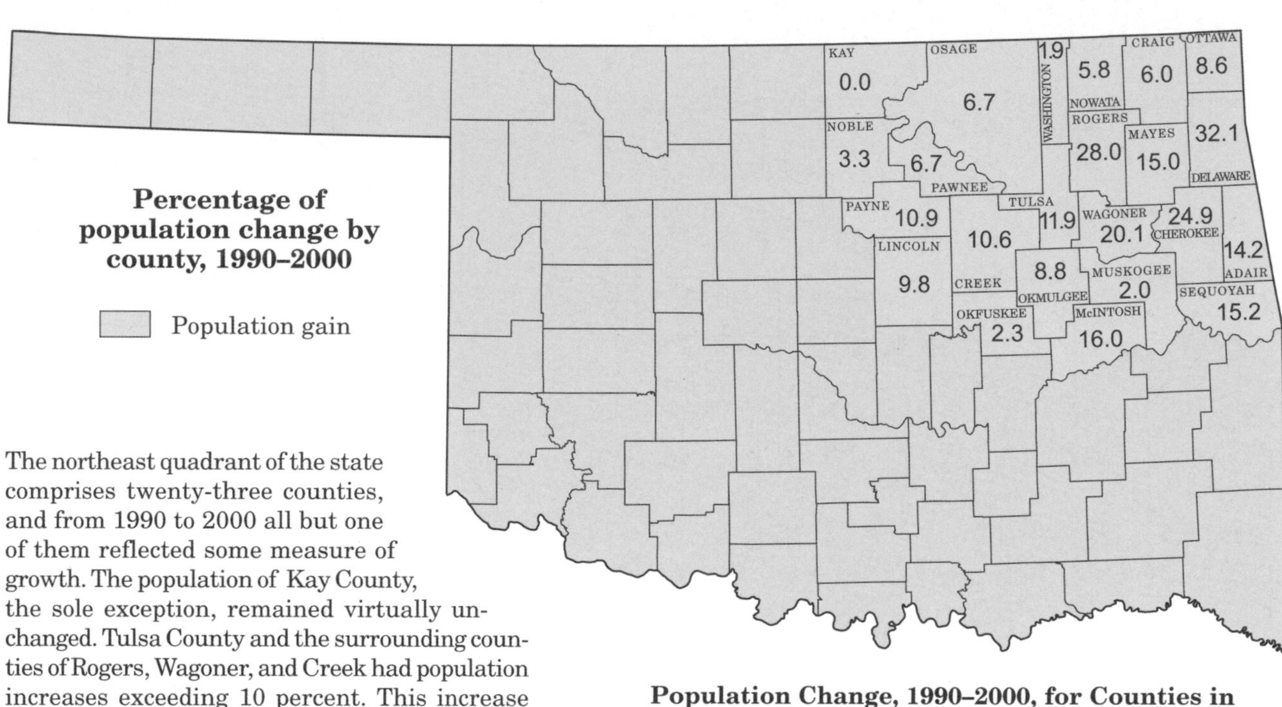

The northeast quadrant of the state comprises twenty-three counties, and from 1990 to 2000 all but one of them reflected some measure of growth. The population of Kay County, the sole exception, remained virtually unchanged. Tulsa County and the surrounding counties of Rogers, Wagoner, and Creek had population increases exceeding 10 percent. This increase in the Tulsa area is directly reflected in the strong growth of the city of Tulsa and the surrounding cities of Broken Arrow, Owasso, Bixby, Catoosa, and Jenks. The counties of Adair and Sequoyah—bordering the Arkansas state line and near the growing metropolitan areas of Fort Smith and Fayetteville, Arkansas—had growth rates of approximately 15 percent. Cherokee and Delaware counties, popular as recreation and retirement areas, had growth rates of 24.9 and 26 percent, respectively.

In 2000 there were 47 cities in northeastern Oklahoma with population over 2,500; 6 of them (12 percent) had lost a small percentage of population since 1990. In sharp contrast, of the 134 incorporated towns with population less than 2,500, there were 52 (39 percent) that had lost population between 1990 and 2000. As with the northwest quadrant, the smallest towns bore the brunt of population losses, with almost twice as many (46 of 109, or 42 percent) having lost residents, compared to those towns with population between 1,000 and 2,500 (6 of 25, or 24 percent) that show a decrease in the 2000 population.

Population Change, 1990–2000, for Counties in Northeastern Oklahoma

County	Population 2000	Population 1990	Change	Percentage change
Adair	21,038	18,421	2,617	14.2
Cherokee	42,521	34,049	8,472	24.9
Craig	14,950	14,104	846	6.0
Creek	67,367	60,915	6,452	10.6
Delaware	37,077	28,070	9,007	32.1
Kay	48,080	48,056	24	0.0
Lincoln	32,080	29,216	2,864	9.8
Mayes	38,369	33,366	5,003	15.0
McIntosh	19,456	16,779	2,677	16.0
Muskogee	69,451	68,078	1,373	2.0
Noble	11,411	11,045	366	3.3
Nowata	10,569	9,992	577	5.8
Okfuskee	11,814	11,551	263	2.3
Okmulgee	39,685	36,490	3,195	8.8
Osage	44,437	41,645	2,792	6.7
Ottawa	33,194	30,561	2,633	8.6
Pawnee	16,612	15,575	1,037	6.7
Payne	68,190	61,507	6,683	10.9
Rogers	70,641	55,170	15,471	28.0
Sequoyah	38,972	33,828	5,144	15.2
Tulsa	563,299	503,341	59,958	11.9
Wagoner	57,491	47,883	9,608	20.1
Washington	48,996	48,066	930	1.9
Total	**1,405,700**	**1,257,708**	**147,992**	**11.8**

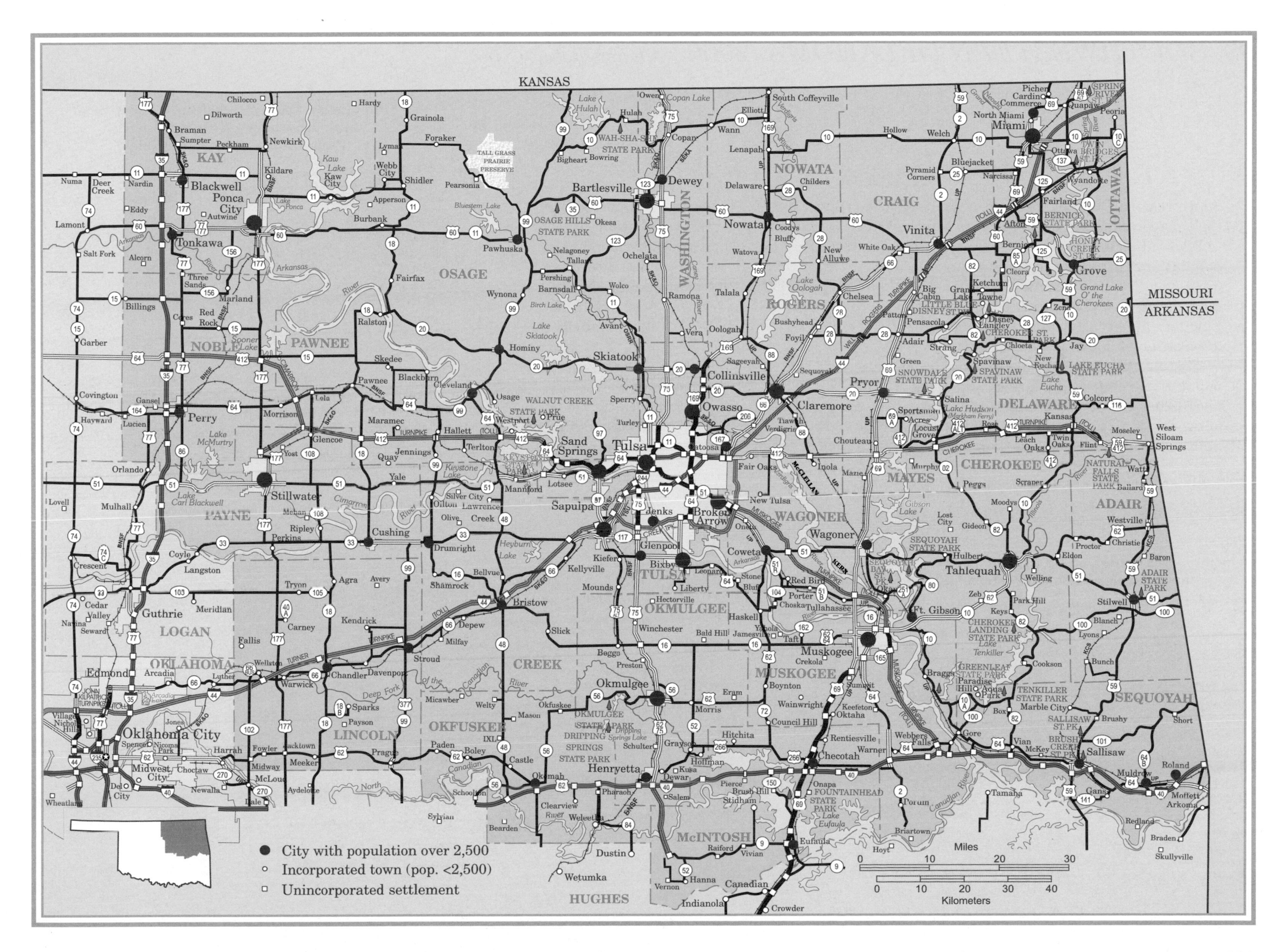
KANSAS
MISSOURI
ARKANSAS
KAY
OSAGE
WASHINGTON
NOWATA
CRAIG
OTTAWA
NOBLE
PAWNEE
ROGERS
DELAWARE
MAYES
PAYNE
CREEK
TULSA
WAGONER
CHEROKEE
ADAIR
LOGAN
OKLAHOMA
LINCOLN
OKFUSKEE
OKMULGEE
MUSKOGEE
SEQUOYAH
McINTOSH
HUGHES
Blackwell
Ponca City
Tonkawa
Bartlesville
Dewey
Pawhuska
Nowata
Vinita
Miami
Grove
Skiatook
Collinsville
Owasso
Claremore
Pryor
Perry
Stillwater
Cushing
Drumright
Sand Springs
Tulsa
Sapulpa
Jenks
Broken Arrow
Glenpool
Bixby
Coweta
Wagoner
Tahlequah
Stilwell
Guthrie
Edmond
Oklahoma City
Midwest City
Chandler
Bristow
Okmulgee
Henryetta
Muskogee
Ft. Gibson
Checotah
Eufaula
Sallisaw
Okemah
TALL GRASS PRAIRIE PRESERVE
OSAGE HILLS STATE PARK
WAH-SHA-SHE STATE PARK
KEYSTONE STATE PARK
WALNUT CREEK STATE PARK
SEQUOYAH STATE PARK
TENKILLER STATE PARK
FOUNTAINHEAD STATE PARK
Lake Oologah
Lake Eufaula
Keystone Lake
Tenkiller Lake
Grand Lake O' the Cherokees
City with population over 2,500
Incorporated town (pop. <2,500)
Unincorporated settlement
Miles
0
10
20
30
0
10
20
30
40
Kilometers

99. SOUTHWESTERN OKLAHOMA, 2000 *Charles Robert Goins*

Southwestern Oklahoma increased in population from 1990 to 2000 by only 1.8 percent. Of the thirteen counties that constitute southwestern Oklahoma, seven lost population.

Five out of the fourteen cities within the quadrant that have population over 2,500 lost population. Tuttle, Sayre, and Lawton are the only cities that reflected growth greater than 6 percent. Tuttle is within commuter distance of the Oklahoma City metropolitan employment area, and Sayre is enjoying growth spurred by oil and natural gas production, but Lawton's apparently substantial increase of 15 percent was largely the result of that city's annexation of housing areas of Fort Sill.

The incorporated towns with population between 1,000 and 2,500 followed the general population trend of their larger counterparts in this part of the state, with eight out of twenty-one (38 percent) losing population. Nearly three-quarters of the smallest communities, eight of twenty-one, lost population. All told, fifty of the eighty (62.5 percent) incorporated municipalities with population less than 2,500 lost population between the 1990 and 2000 censuses.

Population Change, 1990–2000, for Cities in Southwestern Oklahoma with Population over 2,500 in 2000

City	Population 2000	Population 1990	Change	Percentage change
Altus	21,447	21,910	–463	–2.1
Anadarko	6,645	6,586	59	0.9
Chickasha	15,850	14,988	862	5.8
Cordell	2,867	2,903	–36	–1.2
Duncan	22,505	21,732	773	3.6
Elk City	10,510	10,428	82	0.8
Frederick	4,637	5,221	–584	–11.2
Hobart	3,997	4,305	–308	–7.2
Lawton	92,757	80,561	12,196	15.1
Mangum	2,924	3,344	–420	–12.6
Marlow	4,592	4,416	176	4.0
Sayre	4,114	2,881	1,233	42.8
Tuttle	4,294	2,807	1,487	53.0
Walters	2,657	2,519	138	5.5
Total	**199,796**	**184,601**	**15,195**	**8.2**

Population Change, 1990–2000, for Counties in Southwestern Oklahoma

County	Population 2000	Population 1990	Change	Percentage change
Beckham	19,799	18,812	987	5.2
Caddo	30,150	29,550	600	2.0
Comanche	114,996	111,486	3,510	3.1
Cotton	6,614	6,651	–37	–0.6
Grady	45,516	41,747	3,769	9.0
Greer	6,061	6,559	–325	–7.6
Harmon	3,283	3,793	–498	–13.4
Jackson	28,439	28,764	–510	–1.1
Jefferson	6,818	7,010	–192	–2.7
Kiowa	10,227	11,347	–1,120	–9.9
Stephens	43,182	42,299	883	2.1
Tillman	9,287	10,384	–1,097	–10.6
Washita	11,508	11,441	67	0.6
Total	**335,880**	**329,843**	**6,037**	**1.8**

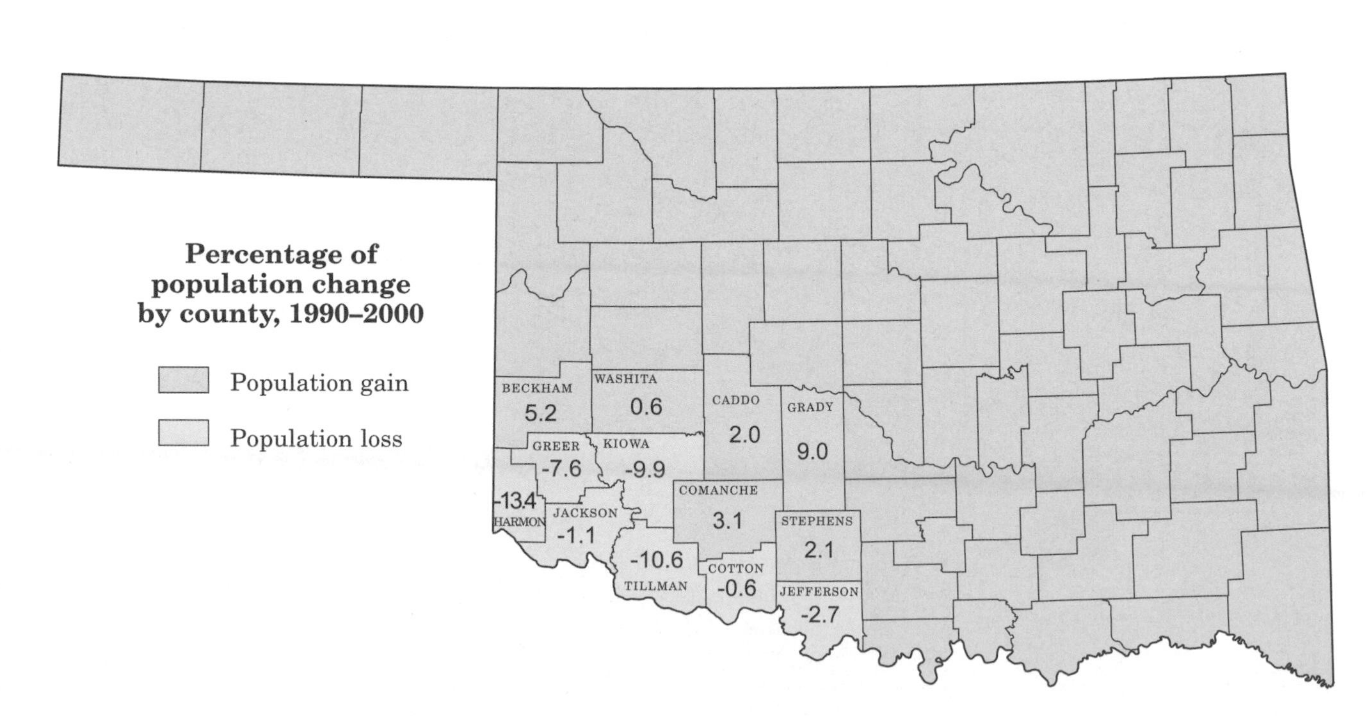

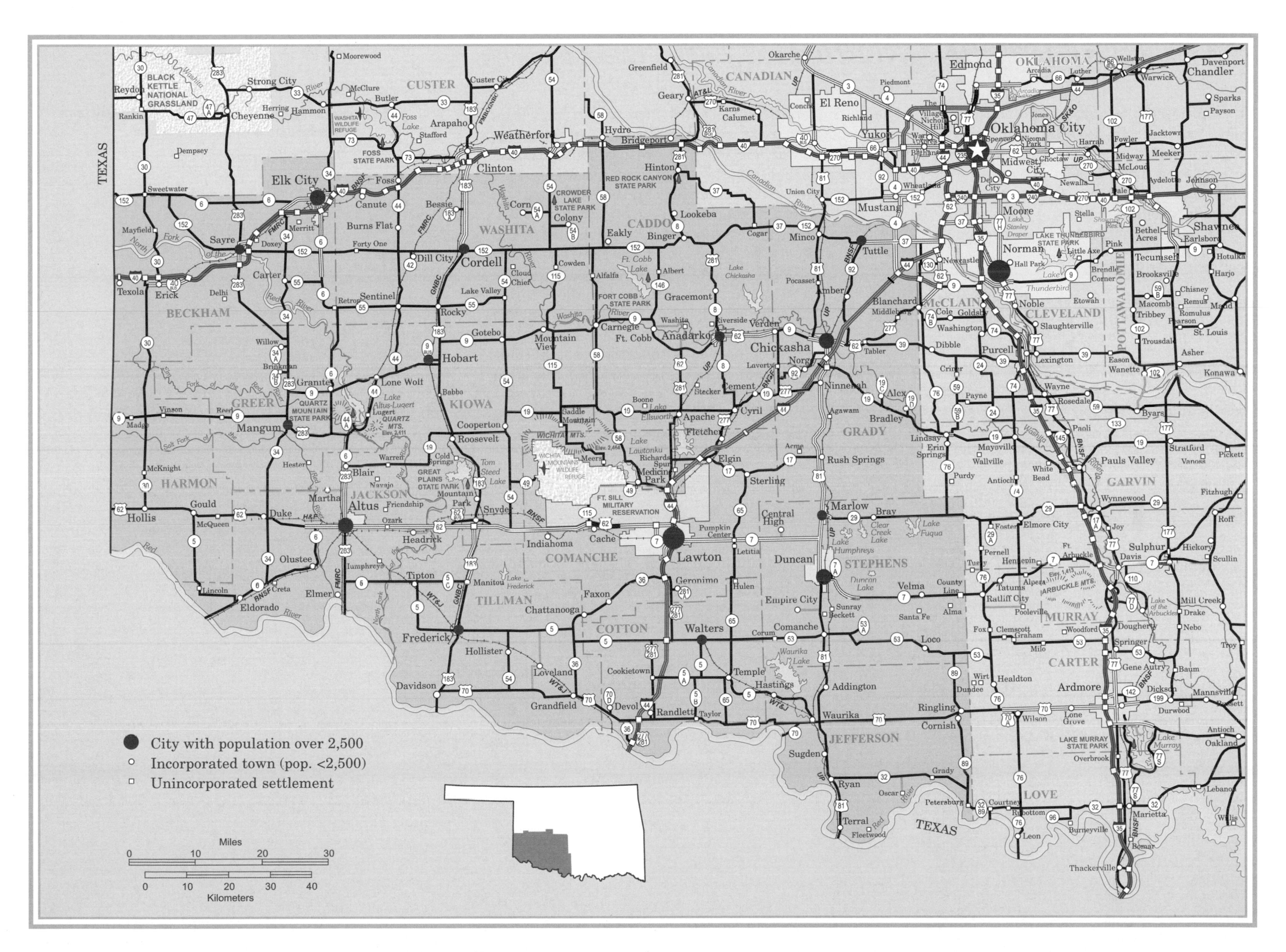
City with population over 2,500
Incorporated town (pop. <2,500)
Unincorporated settlement
Miles
Kilometers
TEXAS
Oklahoma City
Lawton
Norman
Elk City
Altus
Chickasha
Anadarko
Ardmore
Duncan
Moore
El Reno
Edmond
BECKHAM
CUSTER
WASHITA
CADDO
CANADIAN
GREER
KIOWA
HARMON
JACKSON
TILLMAN
COMANCHE
COTTON
STEPHENS
JEFFERSON
GRADY
McCLAIN
CLEVELAND
POTTAWATOMIE
GARVIN
MURRAY
CARTER
LOVE
OKLAHOMA

100. SOUTHEASTERN OKLAHOMA, 2000

Charles Robert Goins

The southeast quadrant of Oklahoma comprises twenty-two counties, all of which increased in population from 1990 to 2000 with the exception of Seminole County. The greatest growth occurred in Cleveland, Pottawatomie, and McClain counties, all part of the Oklahoma City metropolitan area, with growth rates ranging from more than 11 percent to nearly 22 percent. Norman was the major growth center, with a population increase of 15,623 (or 19.5 percent). In 2000, there were 35 cities in southeastern Oklahoma with population over 2,500; of these, 9 (approximately a quarter) lost population between 1990 and 2000. Of the 131 incorporated towns with population less than 2,500, there were 41 (or 31 percent) that lost population. In sharp contrast to the trends in the other three quadrants, here in the southeast, the smallest towns (those with population below 1,000) had a slightly lower proportion of population loss: only 31 of 105 (30 percent) of these communities lost residents, while 10 or the 26 (38 percent) mid-sized towns—those with population of 1,000–2,500—diminished in population.

Population Change, 1990–2000, for Cities in Southeastern Oklahoma with Population over 2,500 in 2000

City	Population 2000	Population 1990	Change	Percentage change
Ada	15,691	15,820	–129	–0.8
Antlers	2,552	2,524	28	1.1
Ardmore	23,711	23,079	632	2.7
Atoka	2,988	3,298	–310	–9.4
Bethel Acres	2,735	2,505	230	9.2
Blanchard	2,816	1,922	894	46.5
Broken Bow	4,230	3,961	269	6.8
Davis	2,610	2,543	67	2.6
Durant	13,549	12,823	726	5.7
Healdton	2,786	2,872	–86	–3.0
Heavener	3,201	2,601	600	23.1
Holdenville	4,732	4,792	–60	–1.3
Hugo	5,536	5,978	–442	–7.4
Idabel	6,952	6,957	–5	–0.1
Lindsay	2,889	2,947	–58	–2.0
Lone Grove	4,631	4,114	517	12.6
Madill	3,410	3,069	341	11.1
McAlester	17,783	16,370	1,413	8.6
McLoud	3,548	2,463	1,085	44.1
Moore	41,138	40,318	820	2.0
Newcastle	5,434	4,214	1,220	29.0
Noble	5,260	4,710	550	11.7
Norman	95,694	80,071	15,623	19.5
Pauls Valley	6,256	6,150	106	1.7
Pocola	3,994	3,664	330	9.0
Poteau	7,939	7,210	729	10.1
Purcell	5,571	4,784	787	16.5
Seminole	7,071	6,899	–72	–0.1
Shawnee	28,692	26,017	2,675	10.3
Slaughterville	3,609	1,843	1,766	95.8
Stigler	2,731	2,574	157	6.1
Sulphur	4,794	4,824	–30	–0.6
Tecumseh	6,098	5,750	348	6.1
Tishomingo	3,162	3,116	46	1.5
Wilburton	2,972	3,092	–120	–3.9
Total	**349,694**	**318,975**	**30,719**	**9.6**

Population Change, 1990–2000, for Counties in Southeastern Oklahoma

County	Population 2000	Population 1990	Change	Percentage change
Atoka	13,879	12,778	1,101	8.6
Bryan	36,534	32,089	4,445	13.9
Carter	45,621	42,919	2,702	6.3
Choctaw	15,342	15,302	40	0.3
Cleveland	208,016	174,253	33,763	19.4
Coal	6,031	5,780	251	4.3
Garvin	27,210	26,605	605	2.3
Haskell	11,792	10,940	852	7.8
Hughes	14,154	13,023	1,131	8.7
Johnston	10,513	10,032	481	4.8
Latimer	10,692	10,333	359	3.5
LeFlore	48,109	43,270	4,839	11.2
Love	8,831	8,157	674	8.3
McClain	27,740	22,795	4,945	21.7
McCurtain	34,402	33,433	969	2.9
Marshall	13,184	10,829	2,355	21.7
Murray	12,623	12,042	581	4.8
Pittsburg	43,953	40,581	3,372	8.3
Pontotoc	35,143	34,119	1,024	3.0
Pottawatomie	65,521	58,760	6,761	11.5
Pushmataha	11,667	10,997	670	6.1
Seminole	24,894	25,412	–518	–2.0
Total	**725,851**	**654,449**	**71,402**	**10.9**

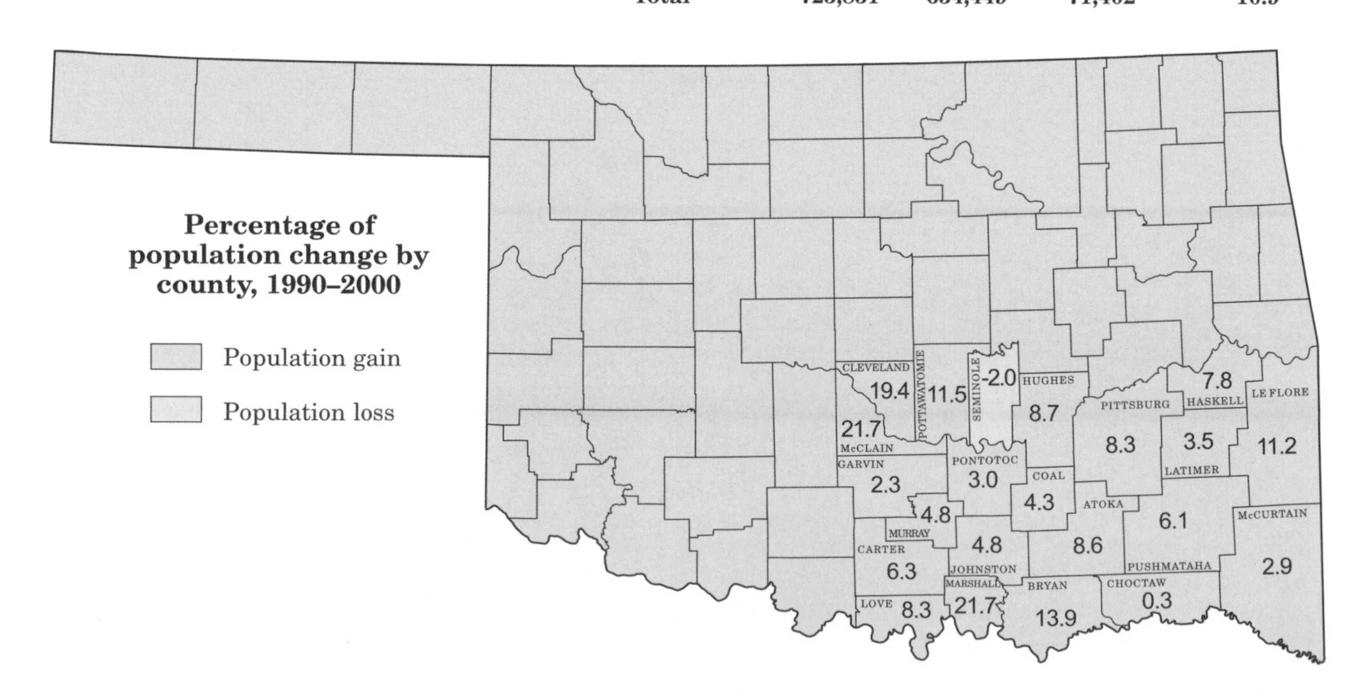

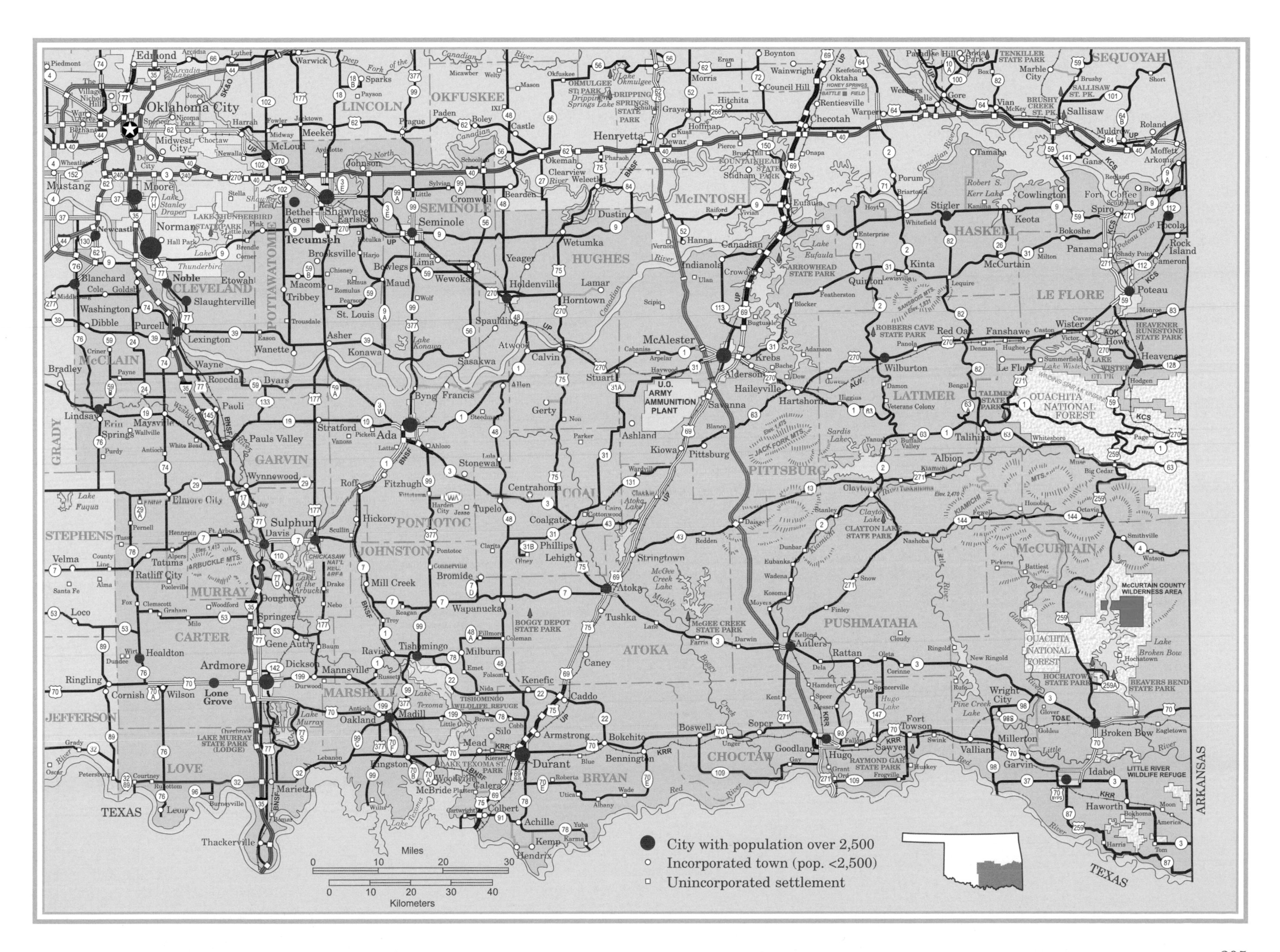

City with population over 2,500
Incorporated town (pop. <2,500)
Unincorporated settlement
Miles
0
10
20
30
Kilometers
0
10
20
30
40
LINCOLN
OKFUSKEE
SEQUOYAH
McINTOSH
SEMINOLE
POTTAWATOMIE
CLEVELAND
HUGHES
HASKELL
LE FLORE
McCLAIN
GRADY
GARVIN
PONTOTOC
COAL
PITTSBURG
LATIMER
STEPHENS
MURRAY
JOHNSTON
ATOKA
PUSHMATAHA
McCURTAIN
CARTER
JEFFERSON
LOVE
MARSHALL
BRYAN
CHOCTAW
TEXAS
ARKANSAS
Oklahoma City
Edmond
Midwest City
Moore
Norman
Noble
Shawnee
Tecumseh
Bethel Acres
Seminole
Henryetta
Okemah
Checotah
Eufaula
Stigler
Sallisaw
Muldrow
Spiro
Pocola
Poteau
Heavener
Wilburton
McAlester
Krebs
Holdenville
Wewoka
Ada
Purcell
Lexington
Blanchard
Slaughterville
Newcastle
Mustang
Lindsay
Pauls Valley
Sulphur
Davis
Ardmore
Healdton
Lone Grove
Marietta
Madill
Tishomingo
Durant
Atoka
Coalgate
Antlers
Hugo
Idabel
Broken Bow
Talihina
U.S. ARMY AMMUNITION PLANT
OUACHITA NATIONAL FOREST
McCURTAIN COUNTY WILDERNESS AREA
ROBBERS CAVE STATE PARK
CLAYTON LAKE STATE PARK
McGEE CREEK STATE PARK
BOGGY DEPOT STATE PARK
LAKE MURRAY STATE PARK (LODGE)
TISHOMINGO WILDLIFE REFUGE
LAKE TEXOMA ST. PARK
RAYMOND GARY STATE PARK
HOCHATOWN STATE PARK
BEAVERS BEND STATE PARK
LITTLE RIVER WILDLIFE REFUGE
ARROWHEAD STATE PARK
FOUNTAINHEAD STATE PARK
TENKILLER STATE PARK
BRUSHY CREEK ST. PK.
SALLISAW ST. PK.
HEAVENER RUNESTONE STATE PARK
LAKE WISTER ST. PK.
TALIMENA STATE PARK
CHICKASAW NAT'L REC. AREA
LAKE THUNDERBIRD STATE PARK
ARBUCKLE MTS.
JACK FORK MTS.
SANSBOIS MTS.
KIAMICHI MTS.
Lake Eufaula
Lake Texoma
Lake Murray
Sardis Lake
Clayton Lake
Hugo Lake
Pine Creek Lake
Lake Broken Bow
Lake Konawa
Lake Fuqua
Robert S. Kerr Lake
Canadian River
Red River

101. THE OKLAHOMA PANHANDLE, 2000 *Charles Robert Goins*

Population Change, 1990–2000, for Communities in Oklahoma Panhandle, 2000

City	Population 2000	Population 1990	Change	Percentage change
Beaver City	1,570	1,584	–14	–0.9
Boise City	1,483	1,509	–26	–1.7
Forgan	532	489	43	8.8
Gate	112	159	–47	–29.6
Goodwell	1,192	1,065	127	11.9
Guymon	10,472	7,803	2,669	34.2
Hardesty	277	228	49	21.5
Hooker	1,788	1,551	237	15.3
Keyes	410	454	–44	–9.7
Knowles	32	18	14	77.8
Optima	266	92	174	189.1
Texhoma	935	746	189	25.3
Tyrone	880	880	0	0.0
Total	**19,949**	**16,578**	**3,371**	**20.3**

Cimarron County and Beaver County, two of the three counties that comprise the largely rural Panhandle, lost population from 1990 to 2000. In 1950, Cimarron County had a population of 4,589, but the county has lost population in every census since the end of World War II, standing now at approximately half of its number of residents in 1907. Beaver County similarly has lost population since 1980, when its population was 6,806. However, the Panhandle's overall population increased by 13 percent between 1990 and 2000 as a result of a 22.5 percent increase in Texas County, a growth that has nearly restored this part of the state to its territorial population level. Of the increase in Texas County, 72 percent took place in the city of Guymon, the largest city in the Panhandle. The dramatic increase in the population of Guymon is largely attributable to the growth of agricultural industries related to the raising of cattle and hogs. As part of the overall increase in the employment base of Texas County, certain small communities near Guymon—such as Texhoma, Goodwell, Optima, Hooker, and Hardesty—have all had modest increases in population. Still, this region has the lowest population density of any of the five sections of Oklahoma.

Population Change, 1990–2000, for Counties in Oklahoma Panhandle

County	Population 2000	Population 1990	Change	Percentage change
Cimarron	3,148	3,301	–153	–4.6
Beaver	5,857	6,023	–166	–2.8
Texas	20,107	16,419	3,688	22.5
Total	**29,112**	**25,743**	**3,369**	**13.1**

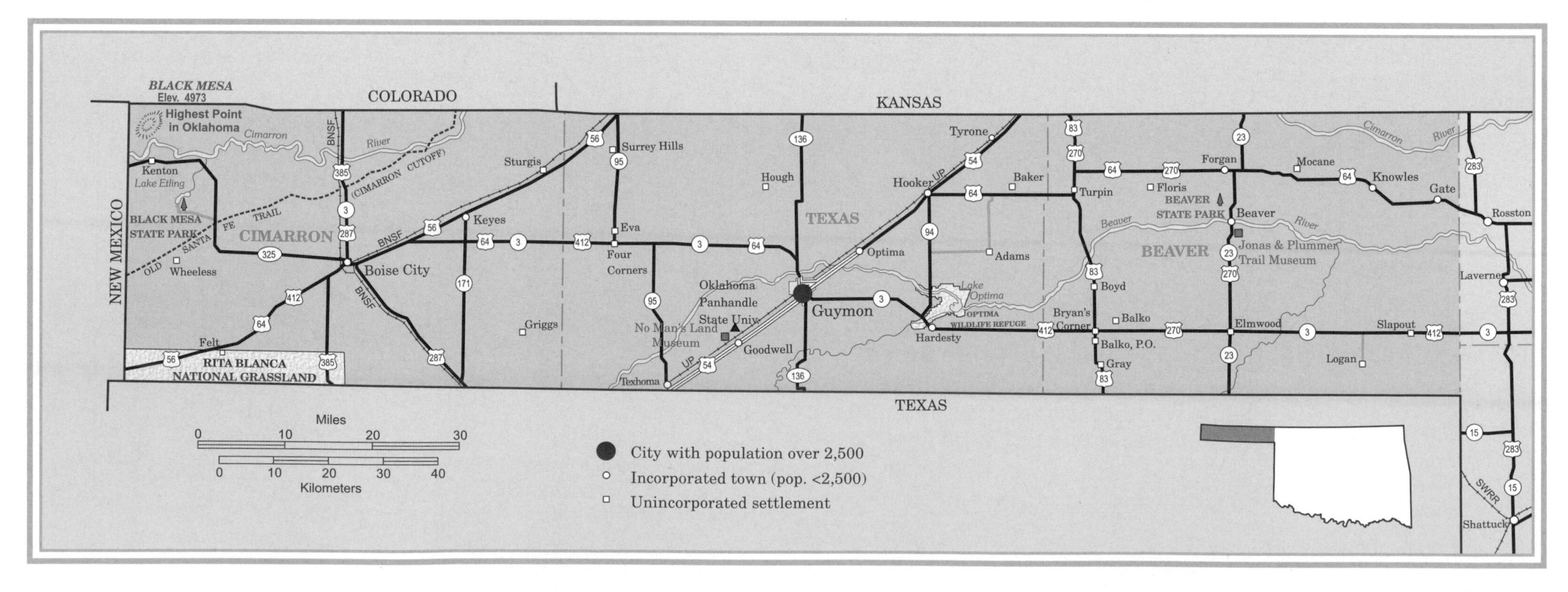

Caroline and Will at the time of their wedding in 1908. (Grandstaff Collection)

Population of Counties of the Panhandle, 1907–2000

Census	Cimarron	Beaver	Texas	Total
1907[a]	5,927	13,364	16,448	35,739
1910	4,553	13,631	14,249	32,433
1920	3,436	14,048	13,975	31,459
1930	5,408	11,452	14,100	30,960
1940	3,654	8,648	9,896	22,198
1950	4,589	7,411	14,235	26,235
1960	4,496	6,965	14,162	25,623
1970	4,145	6,282	16,352	26,779
1980	3,648	6,806	17,727	28,181
1990	3,301	6,023	16,419	25,743
2000	3,148	5,857	20,107	29,112

[a]Special census of Oklahoma Territory and Indian Territory, July 1, 1907.

Letters from the Dust Bowl *is a remarkable collection of letters and articles written by Caroline Henderson (1877–1966) about her life in Texas County. In 1907, at the age of thirty, Caroline Boa (educated at Mount Holyoke College) embarked upon a new life in a new state. Accepting a teaching position at Center, a country school near the settlement of Eva, Caroline established a claim on 160 acres across the road from the school. In 1908, she married Will Henderson (1877–1966), who would be her lifelong mate, and together they set about creating their dream of a Jeffersonian life of self-sufficiency by nurturing the soil. In 1910, their daughter Eleanor was born.*

Caroline and Will spent their lives on this homestead located where the characteristics of nature are always uncertain and where tomorrow's dreams will always be challenged. Over the years, Caroline wrote a prolific number of letters and articles, thus leaving a rich history of her life with Will and her unquenchable love of the land.

April 28, 1908: So here I am, away out in that narrow strip of Oklahoma between Kansas and the Panhandle of Texas, "holding down" one of the prettiest claims in the Beaver County strip. . . . The seventh of May I am to be married to Mr. W. E. Henderson. We have not known each other long for he found me here, yet we do not doubt that our whole lives have been preparing us for a new life together.

August 17, 1908: The day of the creation of our new world, May seventh, was one of the most perfect days I have ever seen. We had driven the thirty miles to Guymon (to be married) on the preceding day going in a prairie schooner. . . . A cook stove, table, two chairs and a few dishes had already been brought to the little "box" house, which contained just one room, 14×16, without lath or plaster or ceiling overhead—just one thickness of boards . . . lined with red building paper. This was our castle.

August 17, 1909: We worked so hard, both of us, early and late, putting in the crop, gardening etc. and did it all so hopefully and so happily.

April 13, 1919: . . . after a winter begun in November we have just this week had another dreadful blizzard, directly responsible for the loss of over a hundred cattle in its smothering drifts.

December 15, 1931: For several years now rain in the growing season has been scarce indeed and spring planted crops invariably fall short. Cattle, hogs, and poultry products have gone on down with wheat, so it is a real problem how to pay taxes and keep up expenses.

July 26, 1935: There are days when for hours at a time we cannot see the windmill fifty feet from the kitchen door. There are days when for briefer periods one cannot distinguish the windows from the solid wall because of the solid blackness of the raging storm . . . perhaps it is only because the dust is too dense and blinding.

August 1935: A short time ago a big tractor . . . accidentally hooked on to the cornerstone of the original survey and dragged it off up the road. All these many years that stone has marked the corner of our homestead.

December 20, 1938: . . . world conditions are so very painful, almost overwhelming to a person of any sensitiveness. Hitler seems the embodiment of the evil spirit.

December 13, 1944: It would be hard to find two people anywhere so little touched outwardly by the world's turmoil. Our nearest contact is with the young pilots of the Liberators or Flying Fortresses from the training field at Liberal, Kansas.

Spring 1947: We could make you more comfortable now, as we did manage in 1946 to get water piped into the house a small kitchen sink and bathroom filled up with all necessities even a heater for hot water!

April 14, 1957: I have seen the storms of fifty winters now in this particular spot but nothing approaching the fury and persistence of the blizzard of March 22 through March 25.

May 1, 1959: Truly a scene of Arctic desolation here this morning. . . . They said 8″ of snow . . . at Guymon and Dad thinks about the same here though hard to find a level pace for any accurate measurement.

December 12, 1965: I have a very dim hope of ever coming back to my long beloved home and have the burden of believing that the diagnosis was too long delayed and faulty, but that is over now and cannot be compensated for.

From *Letters from the Dust Bowl*, edited by Alvin O. Turner.

Left: *The Henderson home, ca. 1908. (Grandstaff Collection)*

Right: *The Henderson home, ca. 1930. (Grandstaff Collection)*

102. CONGRESSIONAL DISTRICTS AND PARTISAN VOTING, 1907–2004

Essay by *Danney Goble*

"The more things change, the more they stay the same." The French gave us the aphorism; Oklahomans have lived the experience. Consider politics, Sooner style.

At statehood, Oklahomans were so intense in their partisanship and so one-sided in their preferences that they brought to the union something of a one-party state. One party held both U.S. Senate seats. One party swept four of the new state's five congressional districts. At the first opportunity, in the presidential contest of 1908, one party walked away with Oklahoma's electoral votes, and that party kept doing so for decades.

And Oklahoma as it entered the twenty-first century? It, too, was something of a one-party state. One party held both of U.S. Senate seats; one party held sway in four of its five congressional districts. One party so dominated Oklahoma's quadrennial electoral college votes—and had done that for so long—that presidential contests had long since become no contest at all.

The only difference, come election day, is that statehood-era Oklahoma was under the Democrats' control, especially when it came to federal-level elections. A century later, it is Oklahoma's Republicans who are sitting pretty, particularly the ones sitting in Washington.

Why the change in party, yet the same singlemindedness?

The answer is simple in concept, if not execution: one political party, favored by fundamental demographic and cultural blessings, used economic circumstances to solidify its advantage over the other. The governing demographic and cultural factors shifted with time, and economic circumstances could turn on a dime. Thus, partisan fortunes rose and fell but the process itself never changed.

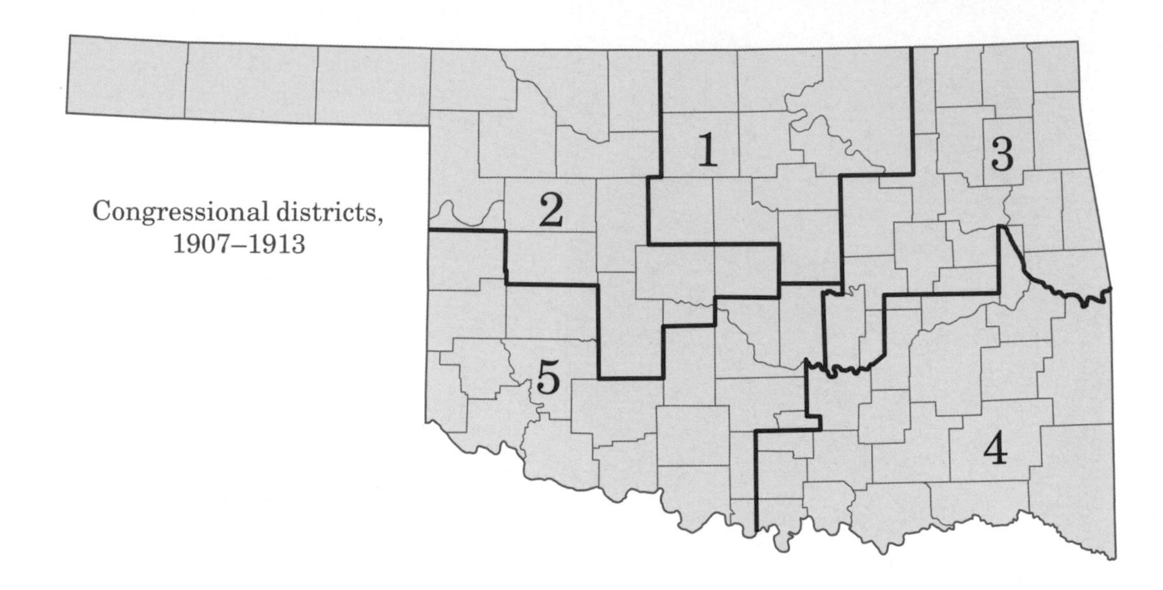

Congressional districts, 1907–1913

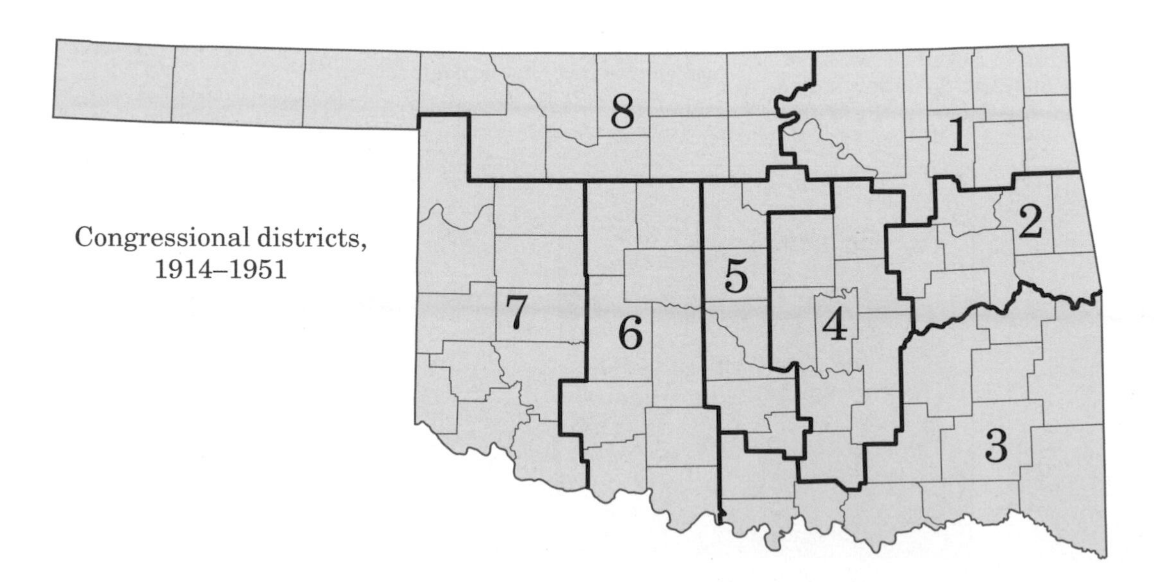

Congressional districts, 1914–1951

Start at statehood, start with political demography, and start with the fact that voters then routinely cast straight party ballots (independents being about as common as atheists, which partisans in both camps figured they were). The demographic truth was that more Democrats than Republicans had come to live—and vote—in Oklahoma.

Most of the new state's voters were recent arrivals. Already grown when they arrived, most came from nearby states. More had been born in Arkansas than in Indiana, more raised in Louisiana than Michigan, more came out of Texas than anywhere else. Given the prevailing equation of geography with party, the partisan effect was to bring Oklahoma politically closer to the Democratic South than to the Republican Midwest.

The state's continuing political geography has steadily mirrored that historical demography. Within the state, the farther north and west the voting, the greater have been Republican chances. The farther south and east, the less likely the GOP's prospects. In both respects, the explanation can be traced to national trends. Southeastern Oklahoma is an extension of the South, while northwestern Oklahoma belongs to the Midwest.

There were times in which nothing—not geography, not demography, not anything—added up to Republican victory. The Great Depression was one. Years after the Depression ended, an unmourned casualty of World War II, Oklahomans who endured it carried memories that could be especially sharp on election days. It took the war's conquering hero for them to put those memories aside.

In 1952 General Dwight Eisenhower's candidacy earned the GOP Oklahoma's electoral votes for the first time since 1928 (when pre-Depression Herbert Hoover had put away Catholic Democrat Al Smith). Ike's win turned out to be no mere aberration. On the contrary, it was the first of twelve (and counting) presidential sweeps for the GOP. Oklahoma, once dependably Democratic in presidential preferences, since 1952 has replaced Vermont as the nation's most reliably Republican state.

The Republican resurgence moved from presidential balloting downward, slowly but steadily, through the rest of the ticket. Starting with Henry Bellmon's victory in 1968 (at the time, only the fourth election of a Republican senator in state history), Republicans proceeded to win eleven of the next thirteen U.S. Senate contests, including every one since 1990. House seats took longer to come their way, but come they did. In 1994, Republicans took five of Oklahoma's six seats. Two years later, they had all six.

Measuring Oklahoma's partisan shift is easier than explaining it, but history shows where to look. Look first at demographic patterns, starting in traditional bastions of Democratic strength. Notice that the state's most heavily Democratic counties (those lying south of the Canadian River) lost, on average, a fifth of their population in just twenty-five years, beginning in 1950. If the pace slowed thereafter, it may have been only because every passing year ended with fewer to leave.

Some left Oklahoma for good. Others stayed in Oklahoma for better, and many found better in (or, increasingly, near) Oklahoma's biggest cities: Oklahoma City and Tulsa. With time, they constituted a generation entirely different from that which had suffered the Great Depression.

Predominately homeowning, white, middle class, and Protestant (of fundamentalist or charismatic leanings), they were at once contented and fearful. Both qualities went to work on election day—working to the advantage of the GOP, which was the party most responsive to their hopes and best attuned to their fears. Republicans were conservatives, and these were people who voted conservative because they had come to have much to conserve, just as they had much that they feared to lose. In modern Oklahoma, enough voters had enough and feared enough that Republicans had little to fear on election day.

They had enough to win.

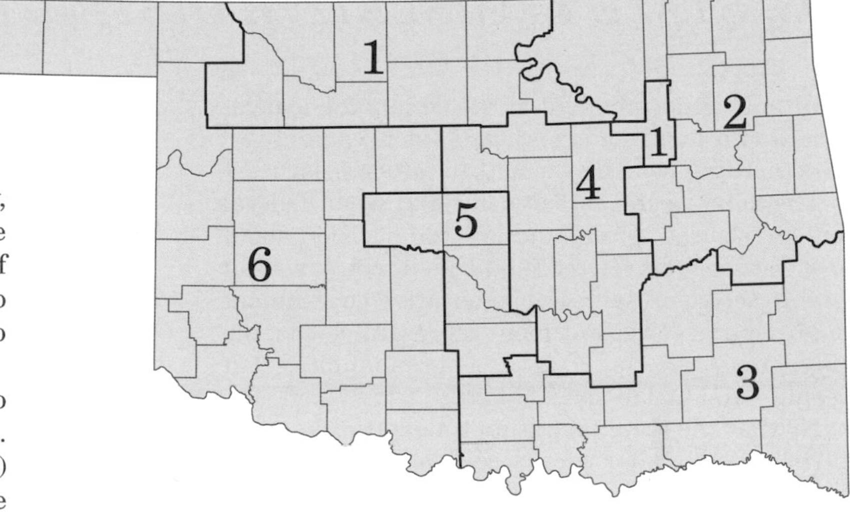

Congressional districts, 1952–2001

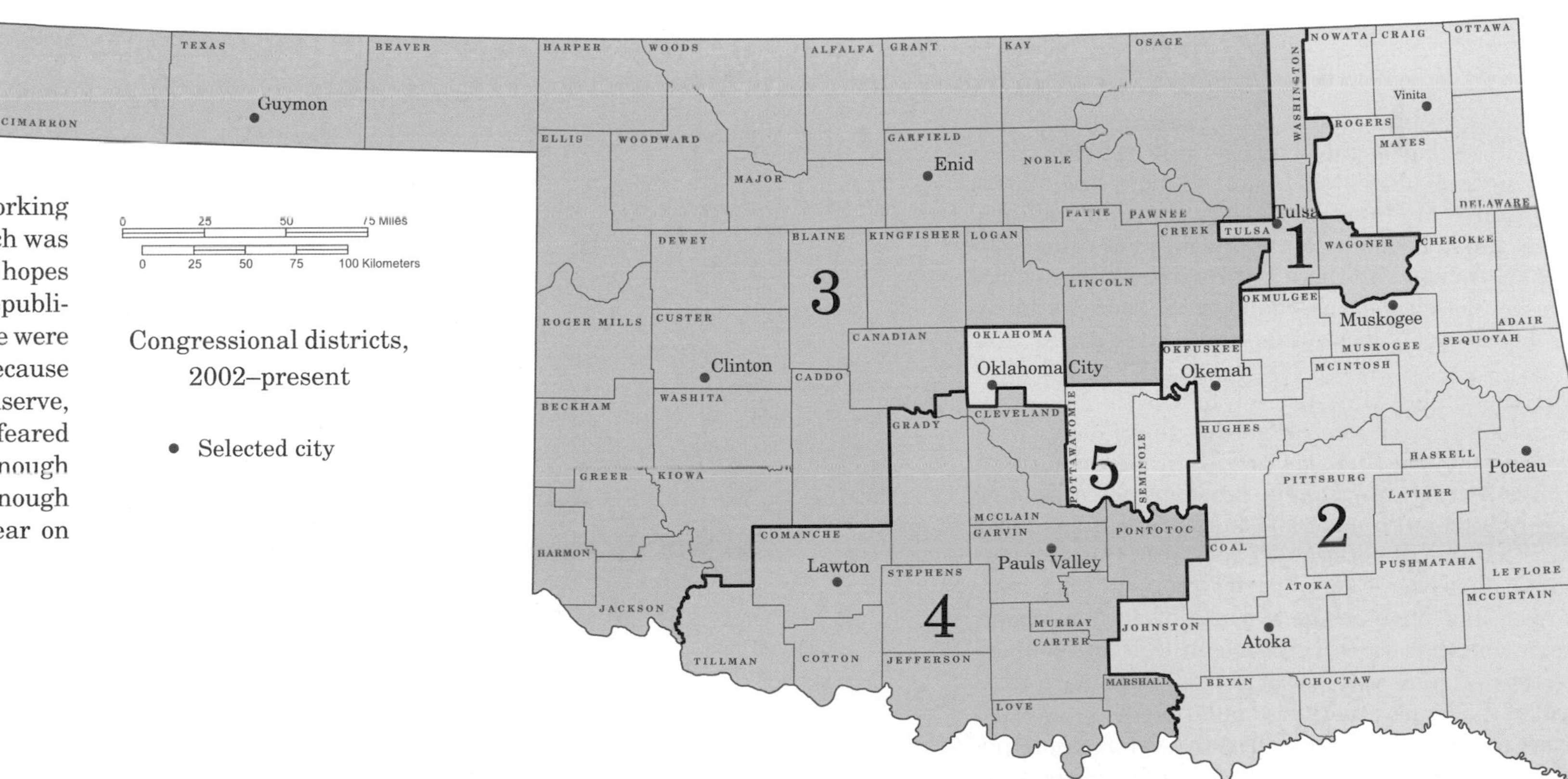

Congressional districts, 2002–present

103. STATE LEGISLATIVE DISTRICTS, 2005

Essay by *Danney Goble*

Equitable apportionment of the Oklahoma legislature was a long time coming. That it came at all owed nothing whatsoever to the state legislature.

The story began in August 1962, when federal judges released a brief and pointed decision about how Oklahomans elected their legislators. It was all wrong, the court said. Representative government required that the government represent people, the judges reasoned—not counties, not communities, but people—and Oklahoma's did not.

Neither the state constitution's explicit mandate of redistricting after each decennial census nor demographic shifts of nearly seismic proportions had shaken the legislators' rocklike insistence that their districts remain as they had been since statehood, in 1907. Federal judges told them, "No more": Oklahoma was guilty of "invidious discrimination" against every single urban voter. It was up to Oklahoma to fix the problem, and fixing it required that district lines for both legislative chambers be redrawn solely on the basis of "substantial numerical equality." The court gave the state until March 8, 1963, to do that—with the implicit threat, "Do it or else."

It took the "or else" to get anything done. With pauses to relieve themselves with tirades against all things federal, lawmakers put together a scheme barely in time to meet the March deadline. Their punctuality was noticeably superior to their computations, however. Every district's borders were rearranged, but none at the expense of an incumbent. Achieving that worthy goal meant that less than 30 percent of state voters would still elect more than half of the house and that populations of senate districts would vary by as much as five to one. Nonetheless, the lawmakers congratulated themselves for having met the court's test of "substantial numerical equality"—perhaps even with straight faces.

When the plan was dutifully submitted to the federal court, the judges found none of this funny or fair or acceptable. Instead, they showed Oklahoma what true redistricting would look like by imposing their own, which was based on work already accomplished by the University of Oklahoma's Bureau of Government Research. The professors' computations and the judges' insistence added up to a near-perfect equality in district populations for both houses, the fates of any or all incumbents be damned.

Again, there was much posturing, accompanied by a few evasive legal maneuvers—enough of the latter that the U.S. Supreme Court had no option but to void the results of an entire primary because it had been held under one of those ruses. As inconvenient as this voiding of an election was, it was effective. Their collective back immobilized against the wall of unyielding judicial authority, legislators at last gave in, accepted the inevitable, and hastily arranged a new, emergency round of elections based essentially on the court's original order. For many of the lawmakers—considerably over half—these elections were their last. New voters in new districts called them home.

Compared to those machinations, subsequent redistrictings became downright boring. Circum-

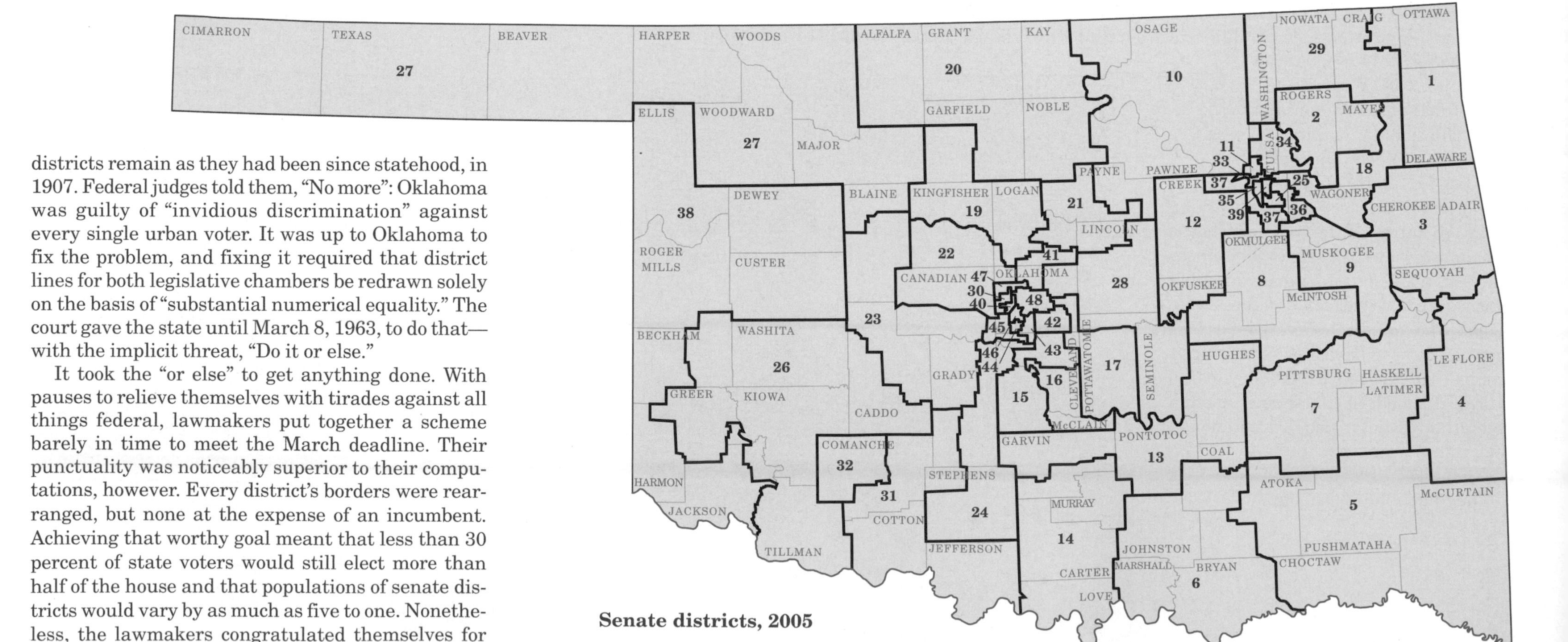

Senate districts, 2005

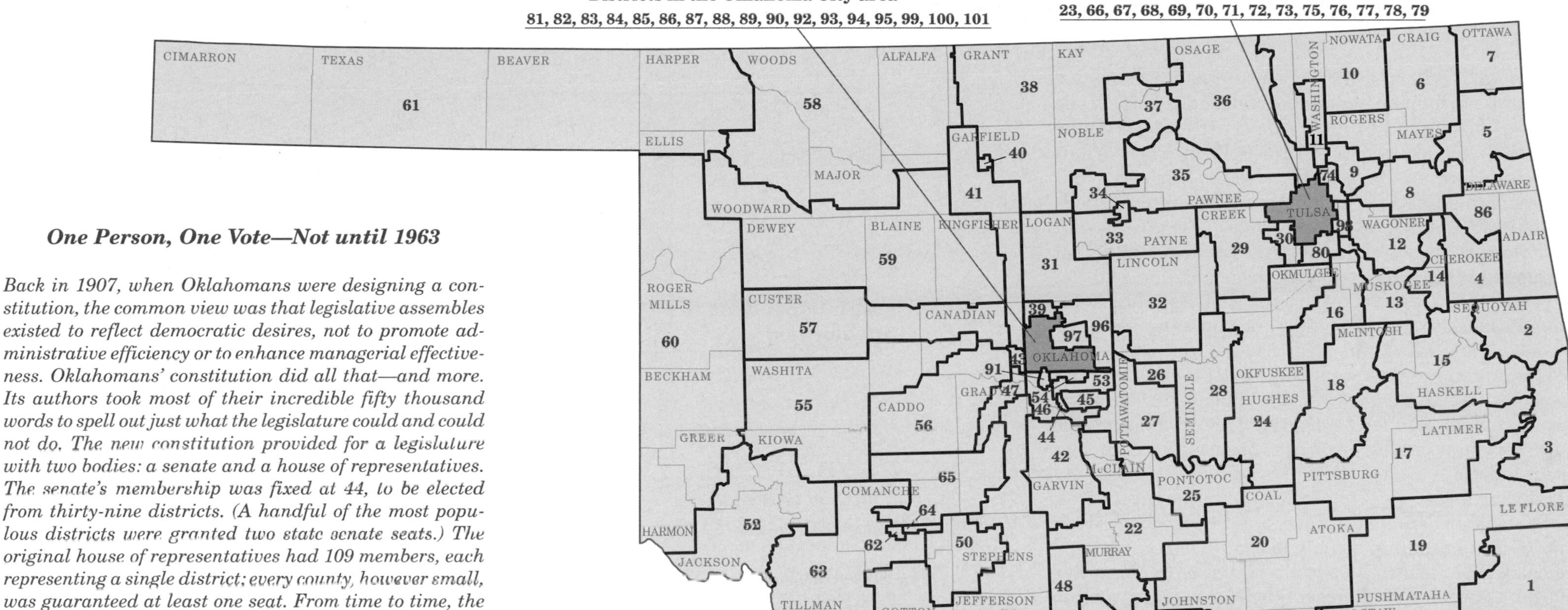

House districts, 2005

stances permitting, Republican governors could be expected to see things differently than did Democratic legislators. That could cause trouble, even a lawsuit, but neither side again carried the battle all the way to the Supreme Court, and judges never again had to throw out entire sets of election returns. When everything was said and done, much had been said but even more had been done.

How much more? Oklahoma entered the 1960s with legislative districts so inequitable that they were a national disgrace. It entered the next century with districts so finely balanced that they were a national model.

The sea-change in districting had to have made a difference, but it is hard to say how much of one. The number of legislators from urban areas increased dramatically, but the leadership in both chambers continued to come disproportionately from Oklahoma's smaller towns and rural districts. Particularly on the issues of spending and taxing, lawmakers could no longer afford to be openly hostile to urban interests, but neither did the legislature kowtow to them.

The one unquestionable difference was both unintended and unforeseen. Ever since its reapportionment (although not once before it), every legislative assembly has included both female and black lawmakers. Most have represented urban districts that had not existed previously. Their number remains too low to reach anything like proportional representation, but at least it is no longer stuck on zero. Surely that has to count for something.

One Person, One Vote—Not until 1963

Back in 1907, when Oklahomans were designing a constitution, the common view was that legislative assembles existed to reflect democratic desires, not to promote administrative efficiency or to enhance managerial effectiveness. Oklahomans' constitution did all that—and more. Its authors took most of their incredible fifty thousand words to spell out just what the legislature could and could not do. The new constitution provided for a legislature with two bodies: a senate and a house of representatives. The senate's membership was fixed at 44, to be elected from thirty-nine districts. (A handful of the most populous districts were granted two state senate seats.) The original house of representatives had 109 members, each representing a single district; every county, however small, was guaranteed at least one seat. From time to time, the total number of house members changed, as did the formulas used to select them.

In the early decades of the state's history, district boundaries scarcely changed. Over the years, the population of some districts grew to be large, while some grew hardly at all and still others grew but remained small. Whatever the difference in population, every district's representation remained as fixed as the constitution's words about the legislature's reapportionment—as fixed as the legislators' determination to do nothing at all about changing the situation. Some of the consequences could be measured precisely: by the mid-1950s, one voter in lonely Cimarron County had a greater impact on representation in the house of representatives than did ten residents of Oklahoma County, seven in Tulsa County, or five from either Canadian or Kay County. Things were even worse on the senate side. There, the nearly 40 percent of Oklahomans who lived in metropolitan Oklahoma and Tulsa Counties were served by only two of its forty-four members.

The question was, how to fit representation fairly with population. Legislators would never act, governors could never act, and judges, both state and federal, always refused to act—that is, until August 1962.

104. COLLEGES AND UNIVERSITIES

Essay by *Danney Goble*

Oklahoma Territory's first legislature had a heavy assignment—to fashion a complete civil and criminal code in a session limited to ninety days. After eighty-nine days, the lawmakers passed three bills into law. Whatever else, Norman would be home to the territory's university; Edmond, its normal (or teacher-training) school; and Stillwater, its land grant college.

Nothing could better demonstrate the importance that Oklahomans have attached to higher education—or that they have not always done so for the loftiest of reasons. Colleges brought towns payrolls and students. The more schools and sites, the more paychecks and customers. This motivation lay behind the First Legislature's obsession with obtaining institutes of higher education and subsequent assemblies' bequeathing the state those plus four more functioning or future colleges (not that anyone minded).

Lacking a tax base, Indian Territory brought the new state no publicly funded college, but the legislature took care of that situation, quickly placing five state-funded schools in five eastern sites plus a big prison in McAlester to even things up. Both geography and politics were no less decisive in the distribution of Oklahoma's unique two-year agricultural and mechanical (A&M) colleges. The constitution mandated their existence, but the legislature decided their number and locations: five, one for each judicial district. The wily lawmakers even had the presence of mind to name four for statesmen whom they needed to cultivate. As years passed, however, this tactic proved to be not providential but fatal, when Governor Robert L. Williams ordered that two—built to honor men he despised—be dispensed with.

Usually begun by religious denominations, Oklahoma's early private colleges are a case of many being called but few chosen. Their fates often depended less on the founders' faith than the fortunes of their locales: as Oklahoma City eclipsed Guthrie, for instance, the fall of the latter took four private schools down with it. Muskogee's Henry Kendall College was typical of many that survived and serves as an example of how some did. When Tulsa similarly eclipsed Muskogee in the east, the college packed up and moved, in 1917. Originally keeping the old name, it renamed itself the University of Tulsa in 1920.

PUBLIC UNIVERSITIES

1. **University of Oklahoma—Norman** Dec. 19, 1890
2. **Oklahoma State University—Stillwater** Dec. 25, 1890 (Oklahoma Agricultural and Mechanical College)
3. **University of Central Oklahoma—Edmond** Dec. 25, 1890 (Territorial Normal School of Oklahoma)
4. **Langston University—Langston** 1897 (Colored Agriculture and Normal School)
5. **Northwestern Oklahoma State University—Alva** 1897 (Northwestern Territorial Normal School)
6. **Southwestern Oklahoma State University—Weatherford** 1901 (Southwestern Normal School)
7. **University of Science and Arts of Oklahoma—Chickasha** 1908 (Oklahoma Industrial Institute and College for Girls; and in 1916, Oklahoma College for Women)
8. **Cameron University—Lawton** 1908 (Cameron State School of Agriculture)
9. **East Central University—Ada** 1909 (East Central State Normal School)
10. **Northeastern State University—Tahlequah** 1909 (Northeastern State Normal School; also, in 1846, Cherokee National Female Seminary)
11. **Southeastern Oklahoma State University—Durant** 1909 (Southeastern Normal School)
12. **Rogers State University—Claremore** 1909 (Eastern Oklahoma Preparatory School; and in 1923, Oklahoma Military Academy)
13. **Oklahoma Panhandle State University—Goodwell** 1909 (Pan-Handle Agriculture Institute)
14. **University of Oklahoma Health Sciences Center—Oklahoma City**
15. **Oklahoma State University Technical Branch—Okmulgee** 1946 (Oklahoma A&M College, School of Technical Training)
16. **Oklahoma State University—Oklahoma City** 1961 (OSU Technical Institute)
17. **OSU Center for Health Sciences—Tulsa** 1972 (Oklahoma College of Osteopathic Medicine and Surgery)
18. **Oklahoma State University—Tulsa** 1982 (University Center at Tulsa)
19. **University of Oklahoma, Schusterman Center—Tulsa** 1982 (University Center at Tulsa)

INDEPENDENT UNIVERSITIES

20. **Southern Nazarene University—Bethany** 1899 (Oklahoma Holiness College)
21. **Oklahoma Baptist University—Shawnee** 1910
22. **St. Gregory's University—Shawnee** 1915 (Sacred Heart Boys' School and College, 1875; St. Gregory's High School and College, 1915)
23. **Oklahoma City University—Oklahoma City** 1919 (Epworth University, 1904; Methodist University of Oklahoma, 1911)
24. **University of Tulsa—Tulsa** 1920 (Presbyterian School for Indian Girls—Muskogee, 1882; Henry Kendall College—Muskogee, 1894)
25. **Oklahoma Christian University—Oklahoma City** 1950 (Central Christian College)
26. **Oral Roberts University—Tulsa** 1963
27. **Oklahoma Wesleyan University—Bartlesville** 2001 (Bartlesville Wesleyan College, 1972)
28. **Southwestern Christian University—Bethany** 2002 (Southwestern Pentecostal Holiness College, 1946)

Dates indicate date of establishment; in parentheses are original names.

A surprising number of early Oklahoma communities once maintained two-year municipal colleges. More surprising still, many were founded in the financially strapped 1930s. This might seem an inexplicable coincidence except that it was no coincidence at all. They arose precisely when all income from property taxes was first devoted exclusively to local governments and school boards. Whatever the reason, several opened, most of them extensions of local high schools (often sharing the buildings).

In the succeeding decade—in the 1940s—three landmark constitutional amendments marked the beginnings of the modern university system. A pair of them established constitutional boards of regents: one for the University of Oklahoma, the other to oversee the state's many A&M colleges, starting with the big one, at Stillwater. The other amendment created the State Board of Regents for Higher Education. Responsible to no one school or to any set of schools, the state board was responsible for piecing together a coordinated system that embraced all of public higher education. The same amendment handed the new board the tool that made that possible: thereafter, the legislature had to deliver it a single, lump-sum appropriation for all of higher education. The state board and its full-time chancellor were to apportion the money as they saw fit.

Their chief goal was to ensure access to college of some kind—maybe any kind, as long as it was close to home. Opportunities steadily opened. Existing schools kept outgrowing their original forms. The old normal schools long since had matured into four-year regional colleges; with graduate programs attached, these took the name of universities. Some of the state's two-year schools passed through the status of four-year colleges en route to becoming regional universities, too. What was left of the old municipal schools became state-supported junior colleges, as did the new ones in Midwest City and southern Oklahoma City. Tulsa got its brand-new junior college and later a branch of Oklahoma State University, the modern form of Stillwater's original land grant college. Altogether, Oklahoma entered the twenty-first century funding twenty-five four-year colleges and universities, plus three higher education centers, in which several schools offered classes.

Private schools reached the century's end by way of a snarled and twisting path. Most never made it. Phillips University was the last casualty. After Phillips closed its Enid campus, only a handful of the independent schools remained. All but a few of those were left in or near Oklahoma's two principal cities.

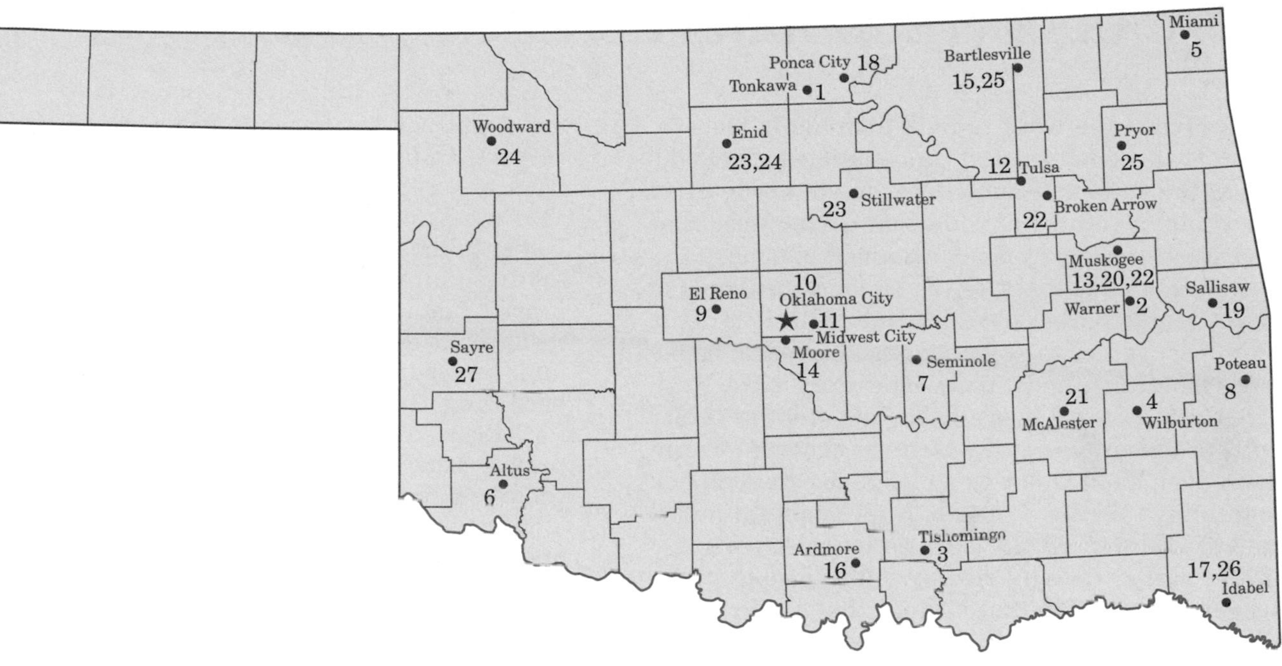

Public and Independent Colleges

PUBLIC COLLEGES

1.	**Northern Oklahoma College—Tonkawa** (University Preparatory School)	1901
2.	**Connors State College—Warner** (Connors State School of Agriculture)	1908
3.	**Murray State College—Tishomingo** (Murray State School of Agriculture)	1908
4.	**Eastern Oklahoma State College—Wilburton** (Oklahoma School of Mines and Metallurgy)	1908
5.	**Northeastern Oklahoma A&M College—Miami** (Miami School of Mines)	1919
6.	**Western Oklahoma State College—Altus** (Altus Junior College)	1926
7.	**Seminole State College—Seminole** (Seminole Junior College)	1931
8.	**Carl Albert State College—Poteau** (Poteau Junior College)	1933
9.	**Redlands Community College—El Reno** (El Reno Junior College)	1938
10.	**Oklahoma City Community College—Oklahoma City** (South Oklahoma City Junior College)	1970
11.	**Rose State College—Midwest City** (Oscar Rose Junior College)	1970
12.	**Tulsa Community College—Tulsa** (Tulsa Junior College)	1970

INDEPENDENT COLLEGES

13.	**Bacone College—Muskogee** (Indian University, 1880)	1910
14.	**Hillsdale Free Will Baptist College—Moore**	1959
15.	**Oklahoma Wesleyan College—Bartlesville** (Central Pilgrim College, 1959)	1972

HIGHER EDUCATION CENTERS

16.	**Ardmore Higher Education Program—Ardmore**	1974
17.	**McCurtain County Higher Education Program—Idabel**	1982
18.	**University Learning Center of Northern Oklahoma—Ponca City**	1999

SATELLITE PROGRAMS OF UNIVERSITIES AND COLLEGES

19.	**Carl Albert State College**	Sallisaw
20.	**Connors State College**	Muskogee
21.	**Eastern Oklahoma State College**	McAlester
22.	**Northeastern State University**	Broken Arrow Muskogee
23.	**Northern Oklahoma College**	Enid Stillwater
24.	**Northwestern Oklahoma State University**	Enid Woodward
25.	**Rogers State University**	Bartlesville Pryor
26.	**Southeastern Oklahoma State University**	Idabel
27.	**Southwestern Oklahoma State University**	Sayre

Year indicates date of establishment; in parentheses are original names.

105. CAREERTECH AREA CENTERS

Essay by *Danney Goble*

CareerTech—the word sounds thoroughly modern, and it is. It was not used officially until the year 2000. It was the up-to-date substitute for what people had been calling vocational education. Understood that way, it is very old, even older than Oklahoma.

Its roots reach back to the time of the Trails of Tears, to the treaties in which Indian nations of the Southeast agreed to exchange their ancestral homelands for strange and unknown territory in the West. The United States liberally sprinkled every treaty with promises, some of which the federal government even kept. One was a pledge to establish and maintain a series of schools where generations of Indian children would learn practical trades and useful skills. Usually run by white people, these schools taught only those things that white people thought practical and useful: largely, in those years, plowing and planting to boys, cooking and cleaning to girls. After the Civil War, when tribes native to the Great Plains and the arid Southwest were driven into Oklahoma, they, too, found schools anxious to greet them, to teach them, and to change them.

More praiseworthy were the so-called manual training schools, some of which were founded as territorial public schools. With statehood, Oklahoma began adding other types of vocational training. In fact, the state's constitution mandated that "agriculture, horticulture, stock feeding, and domestic science" be taught in "the common schools of the state."

A new era for vocational training in the United States opened with the Smith-Hughes Act of 1917. The law offered federal money to states, conditional upon their matching these funds with state dollars and agreeing to establish and maintain a state vocational system under the new law's standards. More than that, this act gave vocational education a very strict definition. For the next half century, vocational education meant formal schooling for both adults and secondary students in agriculture, home economics, or the so-called trades and industries.

Every state responded favorably, but not many acted as swiftly as Oklahoma, which took exactly twenty-nine days to accept the law, create a department, and ask for the money. In nearly every other respect, Oklahoma's program was little different from any state's, except perhaps in being worse than most and better than few until 1941, when J. B. Perky took over the department and proceeded to turn it into a national model. Every function improved, but none more quickly or dramatically than its agricultural component. A farm boy himself and later trained to teach vocational agriculture before becoming that division's long-time supervisor, Perky raised a dedicated corps of "ag" teachers, supervised them personally, and accepted nothing but their best professionally.

So consuming was Perky's devotion to agriculture above all else that not even World War II could diminish it. Granted, he put together a program for training "war production workers," which produced 120,505 highly skilled workers. That accomplished and the war won, however, Perky immediately dismantled the program and restored agriculture to its lofty status.

By then, that may have been the only thing about agriculture that was lofty. Every year, Oklahoma's farming population kept getting smaller, but every year its vocational system kept producing more would-be farmers, even though fewer and fewer of them ever would be farming.

A federal law eventually changed that moribund state of affairs. This law's title was pedestrian enough—the Vocational Education Amendments of 1968—but its effects were revolutionary, nowhere more so than in Oklahoma. This was the law that, half a century later, finally repealed Smith-Hughes. This was the law that took vocational training out of farm fields and home kitchens and placed it in modern offices and labs. This was the law that put vocational education in service to the needs of a modern (and increasingly urbanized) economy and made it sensitive to the pains of modern society.

Because J. B. Perky had retired the year before, the task of implementing the new law fell to his successor, Francis Tuttle. What J. B. Perky began, Francis Tuttle and his successors (each trained by him) have completely transformed. The most visible sign of this transformation exists in Oklahoma's remarkable series of technology centers. Nationally acclaimed, even internationally recognized, there were fifty-four of them by 2002, each a campus of one of Oklahoma's twenty-nine area vocational districts. No state has more; no state has better.

Moore Norman Technology Center, South Penn Campus. (Photo by Emily Dutcher)

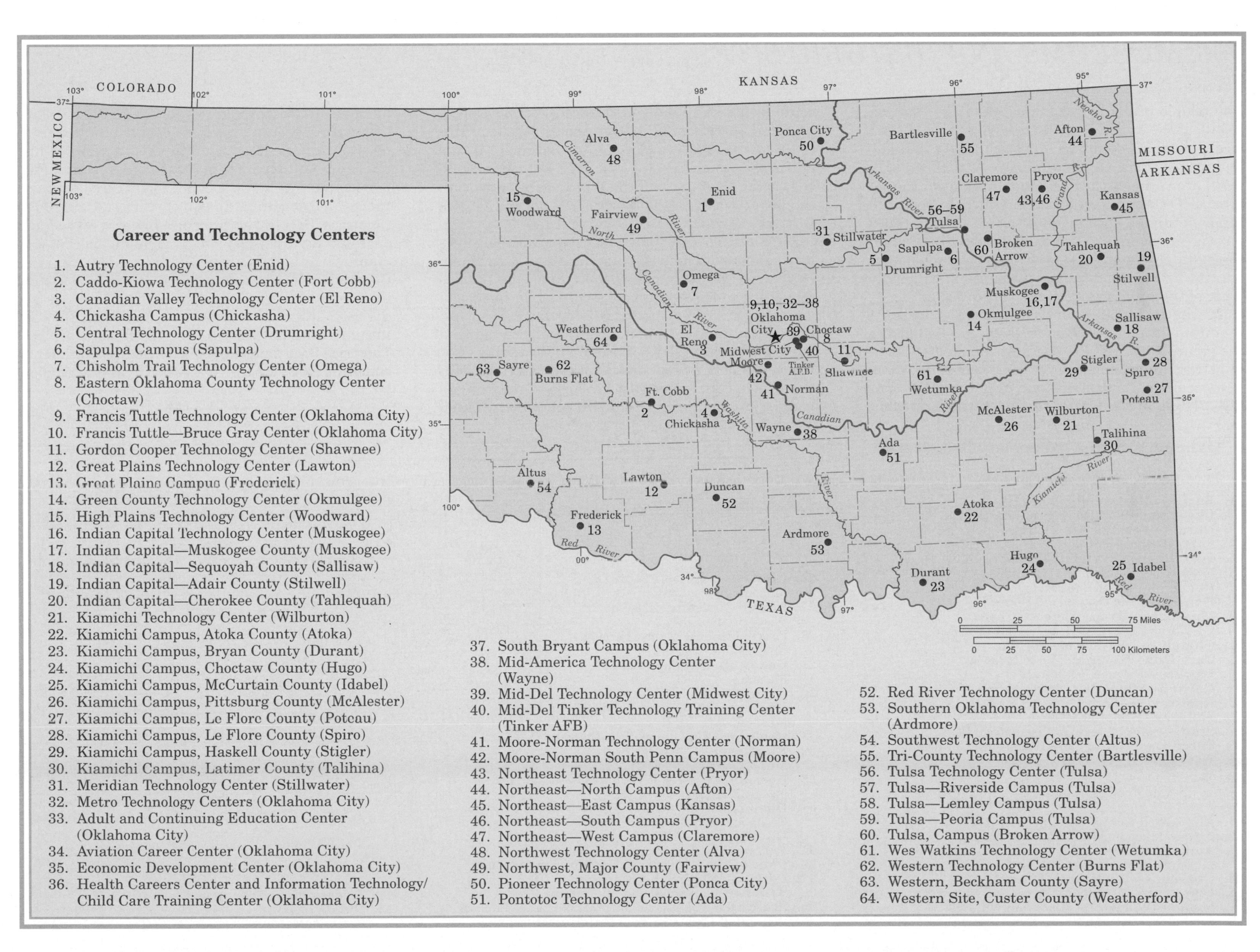
Career and Technology Centers
1. Autry Technology Center (Enid)
2. Caddo-Kiowa Technology Center (Fort Cobb)
3. Canadian Valley Technology Center (El Reno)
4. Chickasha Campus (Chickasha)
5. Central Technology Center (Drumright)
6. Sapulpa Campus (Sapulpa)
7. Chisholm Trail Technology Center (Omega)
8. Eastern Oklahoma County Technology Center (Choctaw)
9. Francis Tuttle Technology Center (Oklahoma City)
10. Francis Tuttle—Bruce Gray Center (Oklahoma City)
11. Gordon Cooper Technology Center (Shawnee)
12. Great Plains Technology Center (Lawton)
13. Great Plains Campus (Frederick)
14. Green County Technology Center (Okmulgee)
15. High Plains Technology Center (Woodward)
16. Indian Capital Technology Center (Muskogee)
17. Indian Capital—Muskogee County (Muskogee)
18. Indian Capital—Sequoyah County (Sallisaw)
19. Indian Capital—Adair County (Stilwell)
20. Indian Capital—Cherokee County (Tahlequah)
21. Kiamichi Technology Center (Wilburton)
22. Kiamichi Campus, Atoka County (Atoka)
23. Kiamichi Campus, Bryan County (Durant)
24. Kiamichi Campus, Choctaw County (Hugo)
25. Kiamichi Campus, McCurtain County (Idabel)
26. Kiamichi Campus, Pittsburg County (McAlester)
27. Kiamichi Campus, Le Flore County (Poteau)
28. Kiamichi Campus, Le Flore County (Spiro)
29. Kiamichi Campus, Haskell County (Stigler)
30. Kiamichi Campus, Latimer County (Talihina)
31. Meridian Technology Center (Stillwater)
32. Metro Technology Centers (Oklahoma City)
33. Adult and Continuing Education Center (Oklahoma City)
34. Aviation Career Center (Oklahoma City)
35. Economic Development Center (Oklahoma City)
36. Health Careers Center and Information Technology/Child Care Training Center (Oklahoma City)
37. South Bryant Campus (Oklahoma City)
38. Mid-America Technology Center (Wayne)
39. Mid-Del Technology Center (Midwest City)
40. Mid-Del Tinker Technology Training Center (Tinker AFB)
41. Moore-Norman Technology Center (Norman)
42. Moore-Norman South Penn Campus (Moore)
43. Northeast Technology Center (Pryor)
44. Northeast—North Campus (Afton)
45. Northeast—East Campus (Kansas)
46. Northeast—South Campus (Pryor)
47. Northeast—West Campus (Claremore)
48. Northwest Technology Center (Alva)
49. Northwest, Major County (Fairview)
50. Pioneer Technology Center (Ponca City)
51. Pontotoc Technology Center (Ada)
52. Red River Technology Center (Duncan)
53. Southern Oklahoma Technology Center (Ardmore)
54. Southwest Technology Center (Altus)
55. Tri-County Technology Center (Bartlesville)
56. Tulsa Technology Center (Tulsa)
57. Tulsa—Riverside Campus (Tulsa)
58. Tulsa—Lemley Campus (Tulsa)
59. Tulsa—Peoria Campus (Tulsa)
60. Tulsa, Campus (Broken Arrow)
61. Wes Watkins Technology Center (Wetumka)
62. Western Technology Center (Burns Flat)
63. Western, Beckham County (Sayre)
64. Western Site, Custer County (Weatherford)
COLORADO
KANSAS
NEW MEXICO
MISSOURI
ARKANSAS
TEXAS
0 25 50 75 Miles
0 25 50 75 100 Kilometers

106. MUSEUMS AND HISTORIC SITES

Essay by *Danney Goble*

The people of few other states have been as conscious of their history or as resolved to preserve it as are those of Oklahoma, despite the fact that only four states (Arizona, New Mexico, Alaska, and Hawaii) are younger than Oklahoma. Indeed, the origins of Oklahoma's official historical society—a publicly funded state agency with a private, dues-paying membership—are considerably older than the state. Begun in May 1893 as the Oklahoma Territorial Press Association, it was taken under the wing of the territorial government in 1895.

As the Oklahoma Historical Society (OHS), it maintains a payroll of more than 150 employees, the great majority of them at posts far from its headquarters in Oklahoma City. Most serve the many historical sites and museums that the OHS operates. These stretch from the No Man's Land Museum in the Panhandle to restored Fort Towson in the southeast, from Altus in the southwest (the Museum of the Western Prairie) to Claremore in the northeast (which has two—the J. M. Davis Arms and Historical Museum and the Will Rogers Memorial, the latter not to be confused with the Will Rogers Birthplace, which is in nearby Oologah).

OHS offices in Oklahoma City are themselves housed in a state museum: in *The* State Museum, in fact. Upon the state's 2007 centennial, the OHS is scheduled to move into new facilities, an interlocking complex of museums and other historical displays.

Other nationally and internationally recognized museums greatly enrich those run by the state. One, the National Cowboy and Western Heritage Museum, is in Oklahoma City. First called the Cowboy Hall of Fame, it originated with funds contributed by several western state governments. Tulsa's Gilcrease Museum is at least doubly unique. First, no other American museum equals its blend of historic and contemporary art (so-called western art in particular) with its vast collection of rare books, artifacts, and documents dating to the pre-Columbian Americas. Second, nothing else like it is owned and operated as a department of a municipal government. Originally assembled by oilman Thomas Gilcrease, it became city property in the 1950s, when the people of Tulsa voted a tax upon themselves lest the cash-strapped Gilcrease be forced to break up the museum's collection and sell it off piece by piece. The price they paid is irrelevant because what they bought is priceless.

Oklahoma Historical Society Resources

Historic Sites

1. **Bartlesville**—Frank Phillips House
2. **Cheyenne**—Washita National Battlefield
3. **Durant**—Fort Washita Historic Site
4. **Fort Gibson**—Fort Gibson Historic Site
5. **Fort Supply**—Fort Supply Historic Site
6. **Fort Towson**—Fort Towson Historic Site
7. **Heavener**—Peter Conser House
8. **Hominy**—Fred Drummond House
9. **Muskogee**—Thomas/Foreman Home
10. **Oklahoma City**—Henry Overholser House
11. **Okmulgee**—Nuyaka Mission Site
12. **Park Hill**—George M. Murrell House
13. **Pawnee**—Pawnee Bill Ranch
14. **Ralston**—White Hair Memorial
15. **Rentiesville**—Honey Springs Battlefield
16. **Sallisaw**—Sequoyah's Cabin
17. **Spiro**—Spiro Mounds Archaeological Ctr.
18. **Tulsa**—Jazz Hall of Fame/Greenwood Cultural Ctr.
19. **Watonga**—T. B. Ferguson House
20. **Yale**—Jim Thorpe House

Museum and Memorial Sites

21. **Aline**—Sod House Museum
22. **Altus**—Museum of the Western Prairie
23. **Atoka**—Confederate Memorial Museum and Cemetery
24. **Cheyenne**—Black Kettle Museum
25. **Claremore**—J. M. Davis Arms and Historical Museum; Will Rogers Memorial; Will Rogers Birthplace (Oologah)
26. **Clinton**—Oklahoma Route 66 Museum
27. **Dewey**—Tom Mix Museum and Western Theatre
28. **Enid**—Museum of the Cherokee Strip
29. **Goodwell**—No Man's Land Museum
30. **Guthrie**—Oklahoma Territorial Museum; State Capital Publishing Museum
31. **Healdton**—Healdton Oil Museum
32. **Kingfisher**—Chisholm Trail Museum/Seay Mansion
33. **Norman**—Sam Noble Oklahoma Museum of Natural History
34. **Oklahoma City**—45th Infantry Division Museum; Oklahoma City National Memorial; State Museum of History
35. **Perry**—Cherokee Strip Museum/Rose Hill School
36. **Ponca City**—Pioneer Woman Museum/Monument
37. **Poteau**—Robert S. Kerr Museum
38. **Salina**—Chouteau Memorial Museum
39. **Stillwater**—Oklahoma Museum of Higher Education
40. **Waurika**—Chisholm Trail Historical Museum

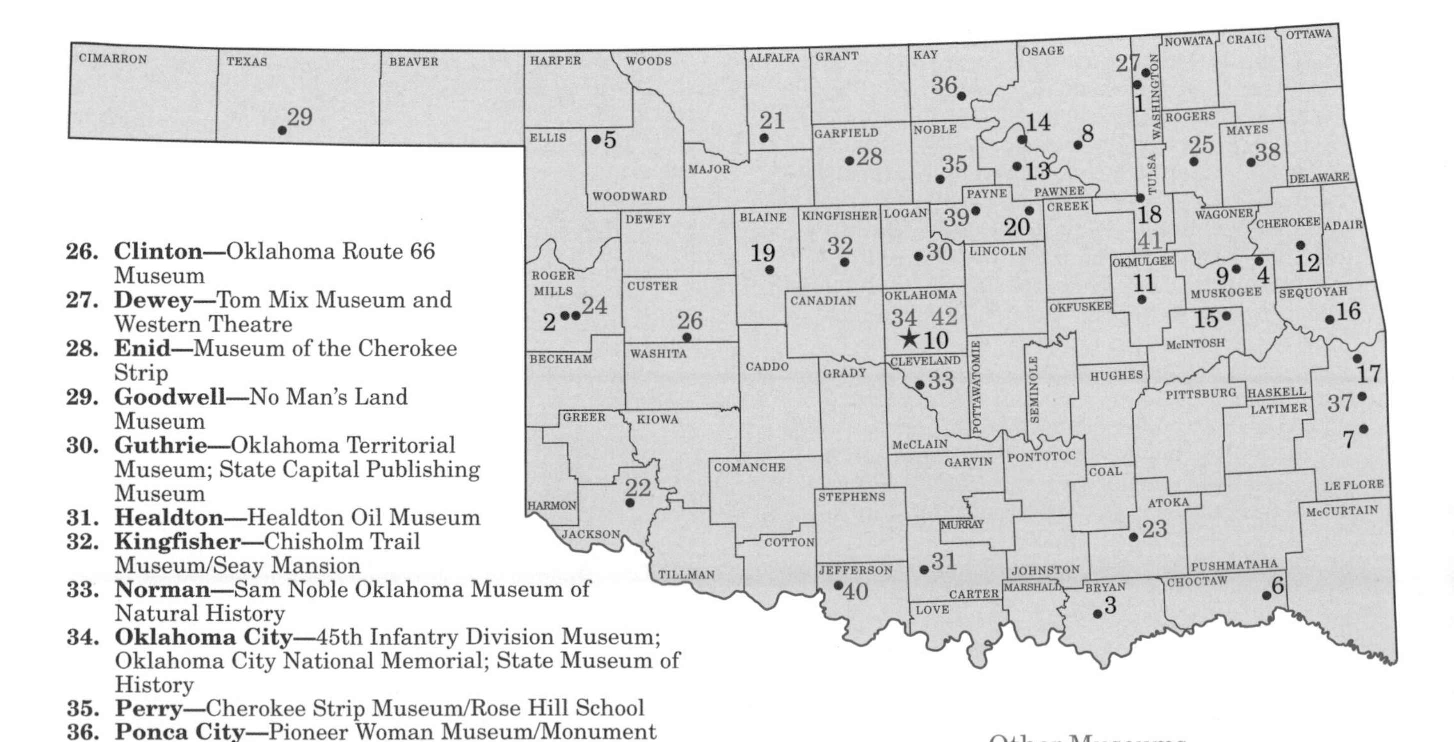

Other Museums

41. **Tulsa**—Gilcrease Museum
42. **Oklahoma City**—National Cowboy and Western Heritage Museum

107. STATE PARKS AND RECREATION AREAS

Essay by *Danney Goble*

Oklahoma's remarkable system of state parks was born in depression and grew to fruition during relative prosperity.

The state's first park dates to 1931, when the legislature appropriated $90,000 to buy sprawling acreage in far southern Oklahoma. Two years later, this purchase became the site for one of Oklahoma's earliest Civilian Conservation Corps (CCC) camps. The CCC put hundreds of volunteer corpsmen to work in clearing land, disposing of brush, and building an Oklahoma version of the early-twentieth-century national parks. The essence of the national parks movement was that a park was supposed to be built to preserve nature while also enhancing it—and certainly to leave it unmarred by modern frills and conveniences.

That pretty well describes Murray State Park (renamed Lake Murray State Park), opened in 1940, when CCC workers finished their labors on the land that had been bought nine years earlier. Six more parks—Osage Hills, Roman Nose, Beavers Bend, Robbers Cave, Boiling Springs, and Quartz Mountain—came right behind, likewise built as CCC projects and parklike in their deliberate rusticity.

Partly a consequence of changing tastes, partly a benefit of restored prosperity, and partly in response to the growth of leisure time, state parks changed notably beginning in the late 1940s. Lodges went up—and quickly filled up, too. The first opened at Lake Murray (the lake another New Deal product) in 1949, followed swiftly by others at Roman Nose and Quartz Mountain.

Thereafter came the effects of politics, especially of the Robert S. Kerr variety. First elected to the U.S. Senate in 1948, Kerr built an empire under his post on an obscure Senate subcommittee, the one that approved federal water projects. Money by the millions, then tens of millions, then hundreds of millions poured into Oklahoma—so much that Senator Kerr seemed to be set on putting a dam on every river and creek the state had.

He did not, not on every one. But he put up so many dams that created so many reservoirs that state parks almost had to follow. When they appeared, however—at Lake Eufaula, for example—they were anything but parks in the former meaning of the term. These were resorts, complete with swimming pools, eighteen-hole golf courses, and even aircraft landing fields. In short, they were packed with every modern frill and convenience imaginable.

They still are. They are occasionally packed with visitors, too.

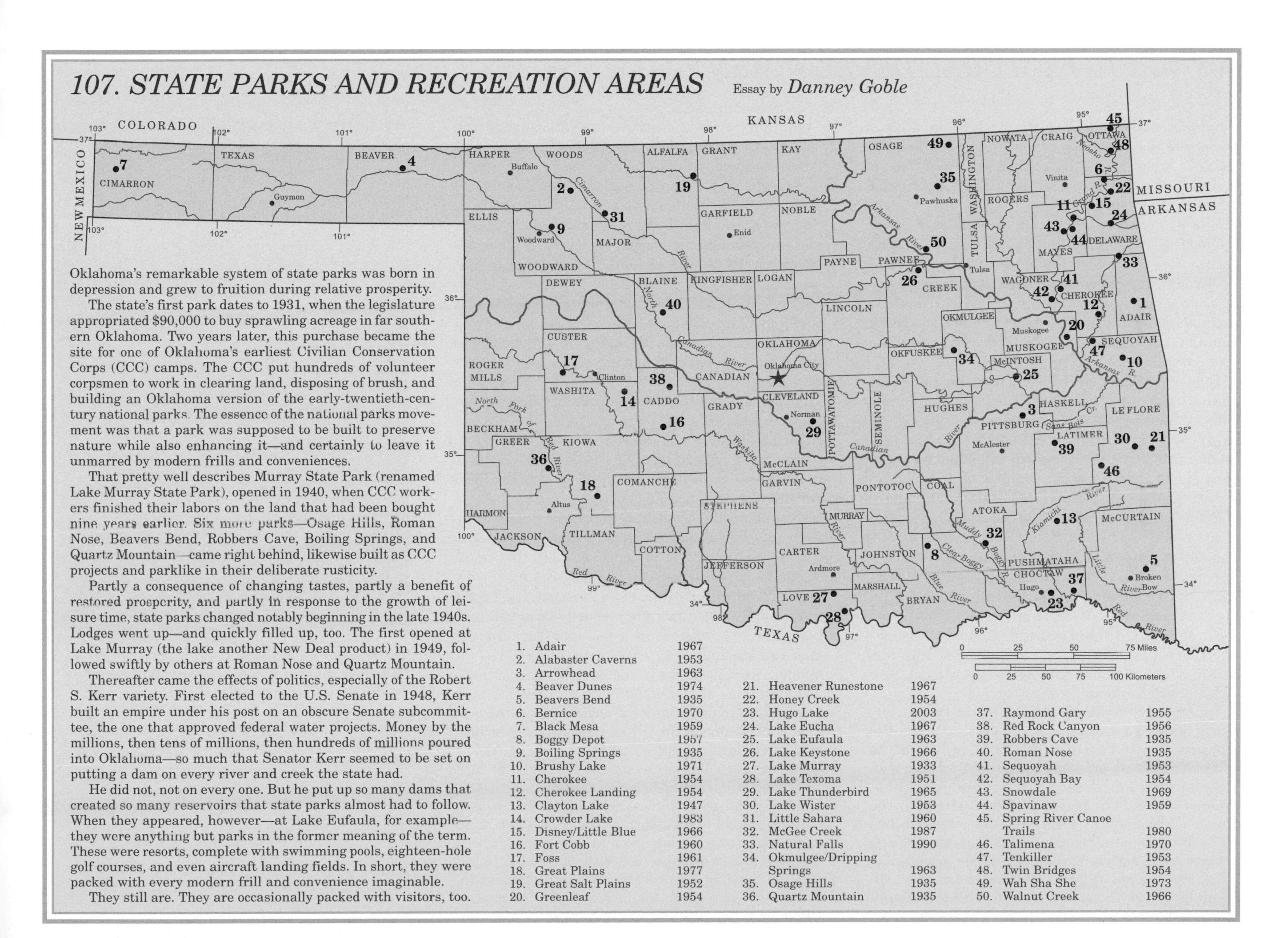

1. Adair 1967
2. Alabaster Caverns 1953
3. Arrowhead 1963
4. Beaver Dunes 1974
5. Beavers Bend 1935
6. Bernice 1970
7. Black Mesa 1959
8. Boggy Depot 1957
9. Boiling Springs 1935
10. Brushy Lake 1971
11. Cherokee 1954
12. Cherokee Landing 1954
13. Clayton Lake 1947
14. Crowder Lake 1983
15. Disney/Little Blue 1966
16. Fort Cobb 1960
17. Foss 1961
18. Great Plains 1977
19. Great Salt Plains 1952
20. Greenleaf 1954
21. Heavener Runestone 1967
22. Honey Creek 1954
23. Hugo Lake 2003
24. Lake Eucha 1967
25. Lake Eufaula 1963
26. Lake Keystone 1966
27. Lake Murray 1933
28. Lake Texoma 1951
29. Lake Thunderbird 1965
30. Lake Wister 1953
31. Little Sahara 1960
32. McGee Creek 1987
33. Natural Falls 1990
34. Okmulgee/Dripping Springs 1963
35. Osage Hills 1935
36. Quartz Mountain 1935
37. Raymond Gary 1955
38. Red Rock Canyon 1956
39. Robbers Cave 1935
40. Roman Nose 1935
41. Sequoyah 1953
42. Sequoyah Bay 1954
43. Snowdale 1969
44. Spavinaw 1959
45. Spring River Canoe Trails 1980
46. Talimena 1970
47. Tenkiller 1953
48. Twin Bridges 1954
49. Wah Sha She 1973
50. Walnut Creek 1966

108. ARCHITECTURAL DEVELOPMENT

Essay by *Arn Henderson*

When Coronado crossed western Oklahoma in 1541, he encountered a camp of Indians and commented on their architectural expression as one of dependency on the buffalo: "They have little field tents made of the hide of the cows, tanned and greased, very well made, in which they live as they travel around." Coronado had no way of knowing of the decline two hundred years earlier of the people of eastern Oklahoma, who had lived in permanent villages for a millennium. Remains from Spiro Mounds in the Poteau River valley reveal a complex of earth mounds over forty feet tall that served as platforms for houses, ceremonies, and burials.

Removal of the Five Tribes of the U.S. Southeast added a sedentary culture back onto the land. Fort Gibson, built of logs near the mouth of the Grand River, was constructed in 1824 to protect the new immigrants from their nomadic Plains Indian neighbors. It was the first major complex built in Indian Territory. Much of the early domestic architecture of the new settlers, both Indian and white, was also of log construction and reflected a pattern of vernacular buildings of earlier frontier settlements. Derivative from Appalachia, many of these single-room houses were simple gable-end cabins with a porch extending across the front. By contrast, some of the affluent Cherokee political leaders built homes at Park Hill in the popular Georgian style with furnishings and finished lumber brought from New Orleans by riverboat.

In the years following the Civil War, Indian Territory became a mosaic of tribal cultures with the creation of new reservations. The nations of the original removal process, devastated by the war, were forced to surrender lands for these new tribal groups. During the period of Reconstruction, the Creek, Chickasaw, Choctaw, and Cherokee nations all built new council houses in fashionable, eclectic architectural styles. While all of these are notable buildings, the native-stone Creek Council House in Okmulgee (now listed as a National Historic Landmark) is exceptional. In the western areas, the most significant construction of the reservation period was at Fort Sill during the 1870s, necessitated by escalating conflicts with Plains Indians.

The opening of the Unassigned Lands in 1889 brought unparalleled opportunities for growth. Spurred into action by land-hungry homesteaders and profit-hungry railroads, the U.S. Congress developed a policy of incremental openings of Indian lands by run, lottery, and auction. The impact of the Organic Act of 1890 created a prairie landscape of sod-house farmsteads accompanied by new towns and the establishment of Oklahoma Territory as a viable political entity. But there was a negative impact on tribal cultures: the disappearance of their lands foreshadowed a declining identity as they became an isolated minority scattered throughout the rural landscape.

The most important town—both politically and architecturally—of the new territory was Guthrie. Anticipating that it would be designated as the new territorial capital, thousands sought lots in the hilly town site in a mad and chaotic scramble. On the morning of April 22, 1889, there were only four small buildings in Guthrie, but by dark it was filled with tents. The transformation of the "instant city" began immediately. The next day, wooden buildings were being erected; within but a few months, fireproof masonry buildings were under construction. The individual responsible for the creation of many of these new buildings of stone and brick was the Flemish immigrant architect Joseph Foucart. He was the premier contributor to the urban landscape of Guthrie with his visions of eclectic Victorian architecture.

As the Twin Territories moved politically toward statehood, the rivalry between Guthrie and Oklahoma City for state capital designation intensified. Guthrie lost and languished as Oklahoma City, with its intersecting railroads, grew rapidly, and Foucart's architectural dominance was supplanted by that of Solomon Layton. With a career spanning several decades, Layton became the most prolific architect in Oklahoma; the effects can still be seen in his stun-

The Bavinger family home, 1950. (Goins and Morris Collection, courtesy Western History Collections, University of Oklahoma Libraries)

ning design of the 1911 Skirvin Hotel and the Oklahoma State Capitol of 1917. In this era, the Victorian style was abandoned, to be replaced by a resurgence of Neoclassicism. In domestic architecture, the Spanish Colonial and Mission Revival styles were popular in Oklahoma, while Craftsman-style bungalows became the dominant architectural expression of the middle class throughout America. The houses of the oil barons in the Sooner State—lavish with ornamentation and rare materials—symbolize these men's achievements and wealth. The city of Tulsa, in displays of civic pride during the oil boom, likewise saw creation of expressive architecture with construction of the downtown Philtower Building, the nearby Boston Avenue Methodist Church (by the youthful Bruce Goff), and an ensemble of exceptional Art Deco buildings. The effect of the Great Depression of the 1930s saw both the florescence of the Art Deco style and the emergence of new variations through buildings constructed under the aegis of federal programs.

The post–World War II years in Oklahoma witnessed the rise of Bruce Goff to international prominence with his design of the Bavinger House in Norman, while Frank Lloyd Wright created the remarkable Price Tower in Bartlesville. In recent years, the major cities have seen development of highly diversified and expressive movements in architecture and urban design. Oklahoma is a place of urban-rural duality, with a rich assemblage of high-style and vernacular architecture. Historic preservation, through a process of rehabilitation and adaptive reuse, clearly defines the continuing presence of buildings as metaphors of culture. Architecture reflects the essence of a placer's origins, its growth, and its purpose.

Selected Oklahoma Buildings and Urban Spaces

1. Sugg Clinic, *1947, Ada (NR; architect, Albert S. Ross)*: This streamlined Art Moderne design, a stylistic variant of the Art Deco movement, is notable for its elaborations of rounded forms veneered with light-green terra-cotta, an extensive use of glass block, corner windows, and dark-green decorative trim.

2. Price Tower, *1956, Bartlesville (NR; architect, Frank Lloyd Wright)*: Clad in copper and ivory-colored stucco, this landmark tower was Wright's only tall building. Structurally it was based on his "tap root" concept with all of the floors cantilevered from a central pier. Rich in variations of pattern with complex, angled geometry, it struck Wright as "the tree which escaped the crowded forest."

3. First Presbyterian Church, *1887, Beaver (NR)*: Simple white-painted, vernacular houses of worship were once ubiquitous throughout the rural Great Plains. The building of a church in No Man's Land was a testament to the tenacity of its people. In spite of the absence of political jurisdiction, it was home and they were here to stay.

4. Chandler Armory, *1935, Chandler (NR; architect, Bryan W. Nolan)*: Built by the CCC during the Depression, this monumental building has an arched-roof drill field abutting a smaller flat-roofed component of auxiliary functions. With exterior walls of rock-faced red sandstone rich in color and texture, the locally quarried stone evokes a sense of belonging to this place of central Oklahoma.

5. Route 66 Museum, *1995, Clinton (architect, Elliott & Associates)*: This museum on the "Mother Road" represents the transformation of an ordinary building into an imaginative artifact reflecting the popular culture of Route 66. The fusion of a rhythm of metal (like the tail fins on cars from the 1950s) on the roof, a portico defined by glass-block columns enclosing pink fluorescent tube lighting, and a prominent red neon sign amplify a reference to the past.

6. Washita County Courthouse, *1910, Cordell (NR; architect, Layton, Wemyss-Smith & Hawk)*: Located on a square block in the center of town on top of a hill, this landmark can be seen from miles away. The three-story brick building incorporates numerous Neoclassical elements with monumental Ionic porticoes on the east and west elevations and a raised dome clock tower supported by twelve Corinthian columns.

7. Kimmell Barn, *1906, Covington (NR)*: This stone barn with arched entries and distinctive angled cupola is a prominent landmark in the wheat belt of western Oklahoma. The presence of this vernacular building, a model of craftsmanship and elegance, resonates as an echo of the Jeffersonian ideal of an agrarian society.

8. Champlain House, *1938, Enid (NR; architects, Roy Shaw and Noris Wheeler)*: This visually complex example of Tudor Revival residential architecture with walls of rock-faced sandstone contrasting with smooth-cut decorative carvings, quoins, and lintels is both a landmark of that style and an expression of the affluence of oil developer Herbert Hiram Champlain.

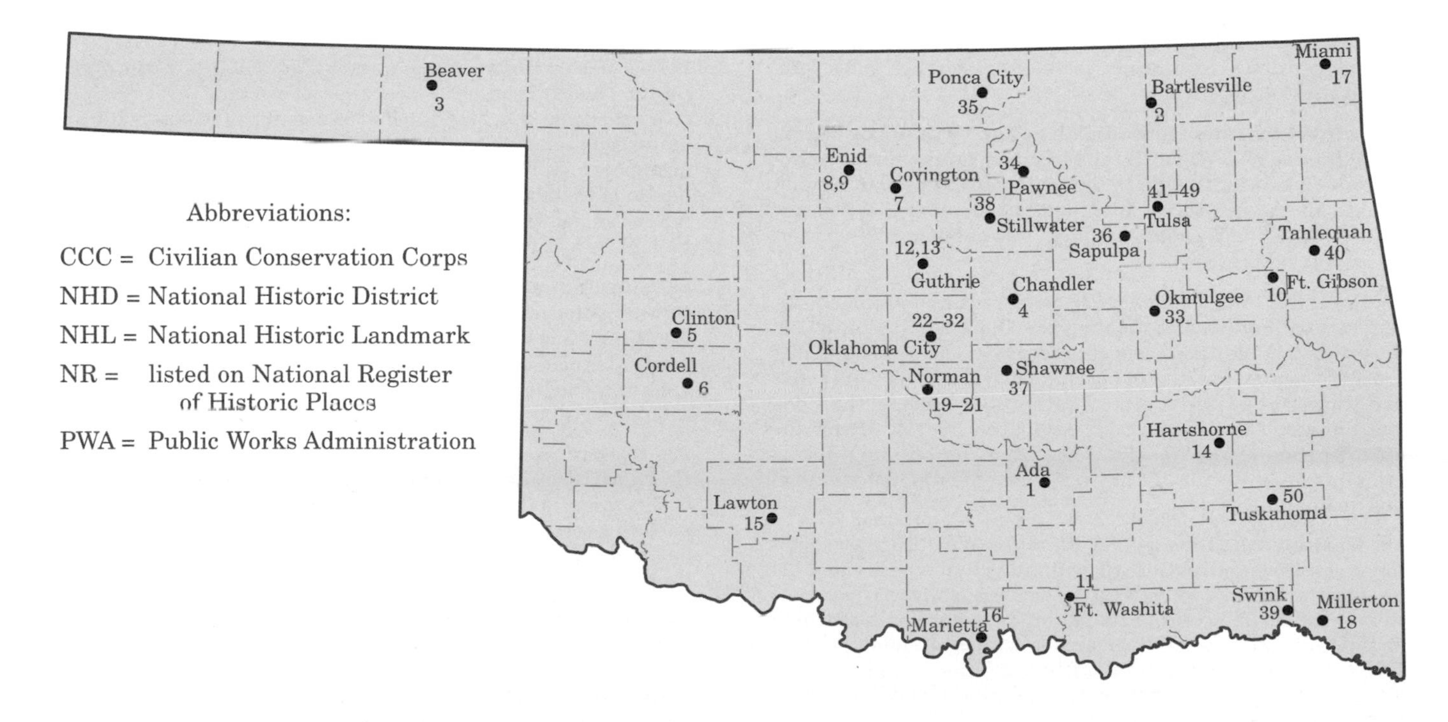

Abbreviations:

CCC = Civilian Conservation Corps
NHD = National Historic District
NHL = National Historic Landmark
NR = listed on National Register of Historic Places
PWA = Public Works Administration

9. Union Equity Elevator "B," *1947, Enid*: This monumental concrete structure, glistening white in sunlight and visible for miles, proclaims the importance of grain farming to the region and a tangible symbol of a way of life.

10. Fort Gibson, *1824, Fort Gibson (NHL)*: Established to restrain the quarreling Osage and Cherokee Indians, and protect white hunters in the area, this ensemble of vernacular log and stone buildings was the first military garrison in Indian Territory.

11. Fort Washita, *1842 (NHL)*: Built for the protection of the Chickasaws from marauding Texans and hostile Indians, the reconstructed Enlisted Men's Barracks suggests a Southern colonial stylistic influence with its hipped roof shading the continuous colonnade at the perimeter.

12. Cooperative Publishing Company, *1902, Guthrie (NR; architect*: Joseph Foucart): This eclectic building, now a museum, represents a masterful expression of nineteenth-century architectural ideals with its fusion of structural determinism and historicism. Reflecting the teachings of the architectural theorist Viollet-le-Duc, the structure is visualized by an extension of pilasters above the cornice and terminated by a rhythm of limestone finials. Contrasting with the massiveness of the brick box is the delicate tower, capped with a Russian dome, at the beveled entry corner.

13. Victor Block, *1893, Guthrie (NHD; architect, Joseph Foucart)*: Foucart's first major commission in Guthrie was the three-story, red-brick Victor Block. As with other corner buildings, he beveled the corner to define the entry and accent it with a projecting bay. Although he used a variety of window sizes and shapes, a sense of unity to the design arises from the restricted palette of materials, common sill heights, and a decorative sheet-metal cornice.

14. Saints Cyril and Methodius Russian Orthodox Church, *1916, Hartshorne*: When Ukrainian immigrants came to southeastern Oklahoma to work in the coal mines, they built a traditional church with three onion domes reflecting the vision of their faith. Though a small building, it is imbued with a powerful sculptural presence.

15. Fort Sill, *1869, Lawton (NHL)*: The continuum of barracks, commissary, and stables defining the Old Post Quadrangle of Ft. Sill reflect military design standards of the post–Civil War era. Developed as a base of operations against the Cheyennes and Kiowas and later to protect rather than subdue, the stone guardhouse of the garrison is best known historically for the incarceration of the Apache Geronimo. The building also is prominent architecturally, having a monumental scale that belies its diminutive size.

16. Washington House, *1888, Marietta (NR)*: Billy Washington epitomized the mythic, rugged individual who created his own destiny in the frontier West. His marriage with a Chickasaw woman gave him access to Indian lands to develop a ranching empire and build an eclectic mansion with an Italianate tower, Carpenter Gothic ornamentation, and exterior walls filled with gravel between the studs as protection from the bullets and arrows of marauders.

17. Coleman Theater, *1929, Miami (NR; architects, Boller Brothers)*: As the historic centerpiece of the central business district, this opulent Spanish Colonial Revival movie palace was developed by George L. Coleman, who acquired wealth through lead and zinc mining. Designed by prominent theater designers of the 1920s and 1930s, the architecture is characterized by a buff-colored stucco finish, ornate curvilinear gables, balconies with wrought-iron railings, and bell towers.

18. Wheelock Academy, *1884, Millerton (NHL)*: When Reverend Alfred Miller and his wife established Wheelock Mission in 1832, they founded both a church and a school. After fire destroyed the school, the present linear two-story building (with its façade defined by a continuous porch and bell tower) was constructed to become the prototype institution for Choctaw education.

19. Bavinger House, *1955, Norman (NR; architect, Bruce Goff)*: Emerging from the earth as a logarithmic spiral to wrap around a central mast, this house in the woods is an ode to nature. The "rooms" inside are platforms that ascend within a space that constantly changes as the stone walls narrow and the ceiling expands from the floor below—a collage of stone, plants, and pools of water with goldfish.

20. Bizell Memorial Library, *1929, Norman (NHL; architect, Layton, Smith & Forsyth)*: Located on a prominent site in the middle of the University of Oklahoma campus, this majestic library is the defining building of the South Oval. Built in a Collegiate Gothic style of red brick with generous limestone trim, the design is replete with gargoyles, battlements, and statuary. The interior of the Main Reading Room is equally impressive, with each bay filled with large windows facing the oval.

21. Ledbetter House, *1948, Norman (NR; architect: Bruce Goff)*: Built on a small corner lot near the OU campus, this ensemble of hard-edged, machine-finished elements contrasts with an undulating sandstone wall defining a garden as the eroded form disappears into the earth to reappear at another point. The façade of the house, forming a sawtooth rhythm, is a composition of angled panes of glass set in deep wood mullions inset with glass ashtrays to reflect the sun and the moon.

22. Cunningham House, *1962, Oklahoma City (architect, Herb Greene)*: Sited on a steeply sloping lot overlooking a golf course, the back of this house is defined by a two-story glass wall set on a brick-bermed terrace. Protecting the glass from the west sun are several angled and stepped brick piers with projecting curved tubular metal trellises as shading devices.

23. Kerr-McGee Tower, *1973, Oklahoma City (architects, Frankfurt Short Emery McKinley & Pietro Belluschi)*: The beauty of this tower is the simplicity of the design, with its innovative pattern expressed on the elevations defined by three zones of bay spacing. Gradation in the size of the bays ranges from the largest at the upper zone to the smallest at the lower zone.

24. Milk Bottle Grocery, *1930, Oklahoma City (NR)*: This diminutive triangular building (350 square feet) was originally a stop on the streetcar line. In 1948 an oversized milk bottle almost as tall as the building was placed on the roof as a form of advertisement of dairy products. The bottle with the grocery store pedestal continues to be viewed by citizens with affection as a symbol of everyday life.

25. Mummers Theater, *1971, Oklahoma City (architect, John M. Johansen & Associates)*: This theatre, now known as Stage Center, is a landmark of twentieth-century American architecture, with its fragmentation of components expressed as autonomous elements arranged to define an exterior central plaza. Towering above the plaza are boxlike forms that originally served as heating and cooling units. Collectively, the ensemble of painted steel and concrete forms amplifies an aesthetic of dissonance.

26. Myriad Botanical Gardens, *1975, Oklahoma City (architect, Conklin Rossant)*: The major feature of this urban park is the Crystal Bridge Tropical Conservatory. This translucent cylinder, 70 feet in diameter and 224 feet long, spans the lake as an abstract, machined object contrasting with the curved berms, meandering water, and lush foliage of the natural world.

27. Oklahoma City National Memorial, *2000, Oklahoma City (architects, Butzer Design Partnership and Sasaki Associates, Inc.)*: Selected through an international design competition, the memorial is defined by a reflecting pool with monumental bronze pylons at opposite entry points. To one side, where the Murrah Building stood, is an array of 168 bronze chairs set on glass pedestals honoring those who died. Rich with symbolism, the composition of transparent and translucent elements of water and glass played against frail, floating chairs is one of repose and dignity.

28. Oklahoma History Center, *2005, Oklahoma City (architects, Beck Associates & HOK, Inc.)*: Built as a new home for the expanding collections of the Oklahoma Historical Society, this curved linear composition is a lively interplay of concrete, limestone, glass, and onyx. The southwest elevation of the building, with its dominant rhythm of columns, is bisected by a projecting cylindrical glass atrium that faces the Oklahoma State Capitol.

Russian Orthodox Church in Hartshorne. (Courtesy Henderson Collection)

29. Oklahoma State Capitol, *1917, Oklahoma City (NR; architects, Layton & Smith 1917, Frankfort, Short, Bruza Associates 2002)*: This monumental Neoclassical building of cut limestone was originally designed to have a tall dome, but the dome was not constructed until the end of the century. With the inclusion of a bronze Native American warrior atop the dome gazing at a distant landscape, the state capitol is now an optimistic symbol of pride for Oklahomans.

30. Pollock House, *1957, Oklahoma City (NR; architect, Bruce Goff)*: Defined by a series of identical modules clustered together on a stone plinth, each of the modules of the Pollock House has a hipped roof with pyramidal skylights at the apex. A detached screen porch atop a studio with blue-green fiberglass panels in an angled configuration both contrasts and blends with the house.

31. Saint Patrick Church, *1962, Oklahoma City (architect, Murray Jones Murray with Felix Candela)*: This church represents a design of dualities. The interior of the glass-walled sanctuary has a roof of cantilevered thin-shell concrete vaults. Freestanding walls of concrete panels surround the sanctuary, providing a visual barrier. The interior face of each panel is deeply incised with an abstract image of the patron saint.

32. Skirvin Hotel, *1911, Oklahoma City (NR; architect, Layton, Smith & Hawk)*: The geometric variations of the façade of this hotel—with a rhythm of rectilinear bays contrasting with recessed curved bays—gives the building a distinctive verticality. The design is one of the very best of Solomon Layton's.

33. Creek National Capitol, *1878, Okmulgee (NHL)*: Located on a landscaped city block in the center of town, the symmetrical Italianate building has walls of rock-faced sandstone with paired brackets at the cornice and a hipped roof with a cupola. In the mid-1920s, town leaders wanted to demolish the building, but the famous Will Rogers publicly opposed that idea when he said, "This is the only town in the world where you can find a Creek National Council House."

34. Blue Hawk Peak, *1910, Pawnee (NR)*: Gordon W. Lillie, the developer and star attraction of Pawnee Bill's Wild West Show, constructed a rustic, asymmetrical stone house on his ranch near Pawnee. With its red-tiled roof, half-timbered stucco gables, and generous terraces, the design is a stylistic hybrid with mixed elements of Craftsman and English Tudor styles.

35. Marland Mansion, *1920, Ponca City (NHL; architect, John Duncan Forsyth)*: This mansion symbolizes the often similar rags-to-riches stories of Oklahoma oil barons. Developer of the Ponca oil field, Marland built a lavish 26-room, three-story stone mansion modeled on Italian Renaissance design ideals.

36. Frank House, *1955, Sapulpa (NR; architect, Bruce Goff)*: The curved walls of this house establish a duality of intentions—the outer wall of the curve, facing the street, is sheathed with terra-cotta tile, suggesting ruggedness and protection; the inner wall, defining the entry courtyard, evokes intimacy and delicacy. The brick and tile on the inner wall were all glazed with standard colors from Frankhoma Pottery for his artist friend John Frank, founder of Frankhoma.

37. Santa Fe Depot, *1903, Shawnee (NR)*: This Romanesque Revival–style building with rock-faced stone walls is a diverse composition of varied geometric forms rich in texture and pattern. The multiple arches defining a rounded portico intersecting a tall, battered tower dramatically contrast with the stepped wall gables of the rectangular forms.

38. Old Central, *1894, Stillwater (NR)*: Constructed as the first permanent building on the campus of Oklahoma A&M College (to house the library and administrative offices), the eclectic design is a proud symbol of Oklahoma State University. With massive walls of red sandstone and brick, hipped and gabled roofs, and a prominent belfry tower, the building appears larger than it actually is.

39. Choctaw Chief's House, *1837, Swink (NR)*: The "dogtrot," a vernacular house-form prominent in Appalachia, is defined by two rooms separated by an open passage between them. A continuous roof over both rooms and passage provided a sheltered, multipurpose outdoor space. This two-story log dogtrot was built by the federal government for Greenwood LeFlore, one of the three district chiefs of the Choctaw Nation.

40. Cherokee National Capitol, *1869, Tahlequah (NHL; architect, C. W. Goodlander)*: Built during the period of Reconstruction, this building replaced an earlier one destroyed by intertribal factionalism during the Civil War. Designed in the popular Italianate style, each of the four elevations is defined as a tripartite scheme with a pedimented center pavilion flanked by secondary wall surfaces.

41. Boston Avenue Methodist Church, *1928, Tulsa (NHL; architects, Bruce Goff with Rush Endicott & Rush and Adah Robinson)*: Known internationally, the design of this Neo-Gothic church was a collaboration of the youthful Bruce Goff and his former art teacher and client, who designed the decorative motifs. The sculptor Robert Garrison designed the terra-cotta sculpture over the major entrances. With exterior walls clad in cut limestone and terra-cotta spandrels, the tower, terminated with copper and glass fins, rises to a height of 255 feet.

42. Christ the King Church, *1926, Tulsa (architects, Byrne and Ryan)*: This buff-brick church has pronounced corners with sawtooth clusters of vertical brick shafts. Although Byrne had apprenticed with Frank Lloyd Wright, he drew inspiration for the church from European expressionism "to give a feeling of aspiration suitable to its purpose." The ivory-colored terra-cotta pinnacles, rhythmic coping, and stained glass windows were designed by the Chicago sculptor Alfonso Iannelli.

43. Mid-continent Tower, *1984, Tulsa (architects, Hoyt Price & Barnes 1918, HTB, Inc., 1984)*: The transformation of a 1918 downtown midrise building into a tall tower over sixty years later is a unique example of historic preservation. With the base of the tower built on property adjacent to the original building, the tower cantilevers over the earlier structure to join it seamlessly and rise into the sky to a height of thirty-six floors. The exterior walls of the tower are clad in terra-cotta identical in form and color to the original building.

44. Philbrook Art Museum, *1927, Tulsa (NR; architect, Edward Buehler Delk)*: This museum, originally the home of oil tycoon Waite Phillips, owes its stylistic origins to the Italian Renaissance. The palatial stone villa, built on a 23-acre site, is opulent, with stained-glass windows, decorative ironwork, and murals on the walls and ceiling. A terrace at the back of the mansion overlooks a large formal garden designed by the landscape architect Herbert Hare.

45. Philtower Building, *1928, Tulsa (NR; architects, Edward Buehler Delk with Keene & Simpson)*: This Neo-Gothic tower of brick and terra-cotta with its distinctive shingle-tiled roof is a landmark in the Tulsa skyline. Built by oilman Waite Phillips, the lobby of the building is opulent, with specialty stones and a sculptured ceiling exhibiting English fan-vaulted tracery.

46. Temple Israel, *1955, Tulsa (architect, Percival Goodman)*: This temple is, for the most part, a subtle understatement of the Modern movement with its orthogonal plan arrangement and crisp geometry. Dominating the façade are two massive concrete pierlike boxes in an angled configuration and engraved with the Ten Commandments. These expressive sculptural "tablets" provide a visually powerful focal point as a proclamation of faith.

47. Tulsa Fire Alarm Building, *1931, Tulsa (NR; architects: Frederick V. Kershner with Smith & Senter)*: This small building, a masterpiece of Art Deco architecture, was the nerve center of the Tulsa alarm system. Although the plan organization and massing are derived from classical design principles, the imaginative ornamental terra-cotta frieze combines exotic Maya temple motifs with a centerpiece of a heroic, shirtless dispatcher holding fire alarm tape with lightning bolts emanating from his hands.

48. Westhope, *1930, Tulsa (NR, architect: Frank Lloyd Wright)*: Westhope, one of three buildings in Oklahoma by Wright, was designed for his cousin Richard Lloyd Jones, founder and publisher of the *Tulsa Tribune.* The large rambling house (about 12,000 square feet) was built of concrete block molded at the site and was the last of Wright's patterned "textile block" designs, developed earlier in California.

49. Will Rogers High School, *1939, Tulsa (architects, Joseph R. Koberling, Jr., and Leon B. Senter)*: With its asymmetrical massing enlivened by a composition of horizontal and vertical elements, this school was one of the first PWA projects in Oklahoma. Rich with stylized Art Deco ornament on the exterior and interior, the design represents a collaboration of architects and artisans in creating a durable monument reflecting the aspirations of the era.

50. Choctaw Council House, *1884, Tuskahoma (NR)*: Built at the foot of the forested Kiamichi Mountains as the seat of government for the Choctaw Nation, this building combines a French Second Empire mansard roof with an Italianate cornice and windows. The council house, now a museum, continues to serve as a proud symbol of tribal determination to maintain their own identity as a people.

109. BOMBING OF THE ALFRED P. MURRAH FEDERAL BUILDING, 1995

Essay by *Hans Butzer*

On April 19, 1995, at 9:02 A.M., a two-ton fertilizer bomb exploded in front of the Alfred P. Murrah Federal Building in downtown Oklahoma City. The bomb's impact was felt across the state of Oklahoma—and the entire country. All totaled, 168 people, including 19 children, were killed. In addition, 30 children were orphaned and 219 children lost at least one parent. In the hours and days that followed, 12,384 volunteers and rescue workers (both local and national) participated in the rescue and recovery effort. After six weeks of the rubble's being searched for victims, what remained of the Alfred P. Murrah Federal Building was cleared from the site.

The nature of the bombing's impact and the large number of deaths caused by a terrorist attack exposed American society to a reality that had already been experienced in most other parts of the globe. In retrospect, the bombing of the Alfred P. Murrah Federal Building in 1995 also prepared the nation for the transition to an even greater scale of death, destruction, and threat to national security in the wake of the attacks of September 11, 2001. Organized efforts by Oklahomans, with the aid of many across the country, led to the nationwide development of new response standards in the wake of terrorist attacks. The complexity of insurance claims involving the building damages in downtown Oklahoma City foreshadowed the even more complex cases created by the 9/11 attacks. New safety standards for government buildings were introduced to reduce the potential for injuries of the type suffered in Oklahoma City.

In the courts, the trials of those accused of planning and carrying out the Oklahoma City attack dominated headlines for years. In June 2001, Timothy McVeigh was executed for his role in masterminding the attack, while his accomplice, Terry Nichols, was sentenced in 2004 to life imprisonment for his role in the attack.

With the impact of the bombing came widespread recognition that those who survived the attack but suffered from resulting physical and/or psychological illnesses were also to be considered victims. In addition, the memorialization process in American culture was impacted; at a large scale, the notion was accepted that the process of conceiving of and building a memorial should include not just designers and politicians but also victims' families, survivors, and rescuers. The outdoor symbolic memorial dedicated in Oklahoma City in 2000 continues to visibly influence memorials subsequently built elsewhere in the United States.

In the summer of 1995, Oklahoma governor Frank Keating authorized the establishment of a task force with the expressed goal of creating a memorial to the victims of the bombing. Family members,

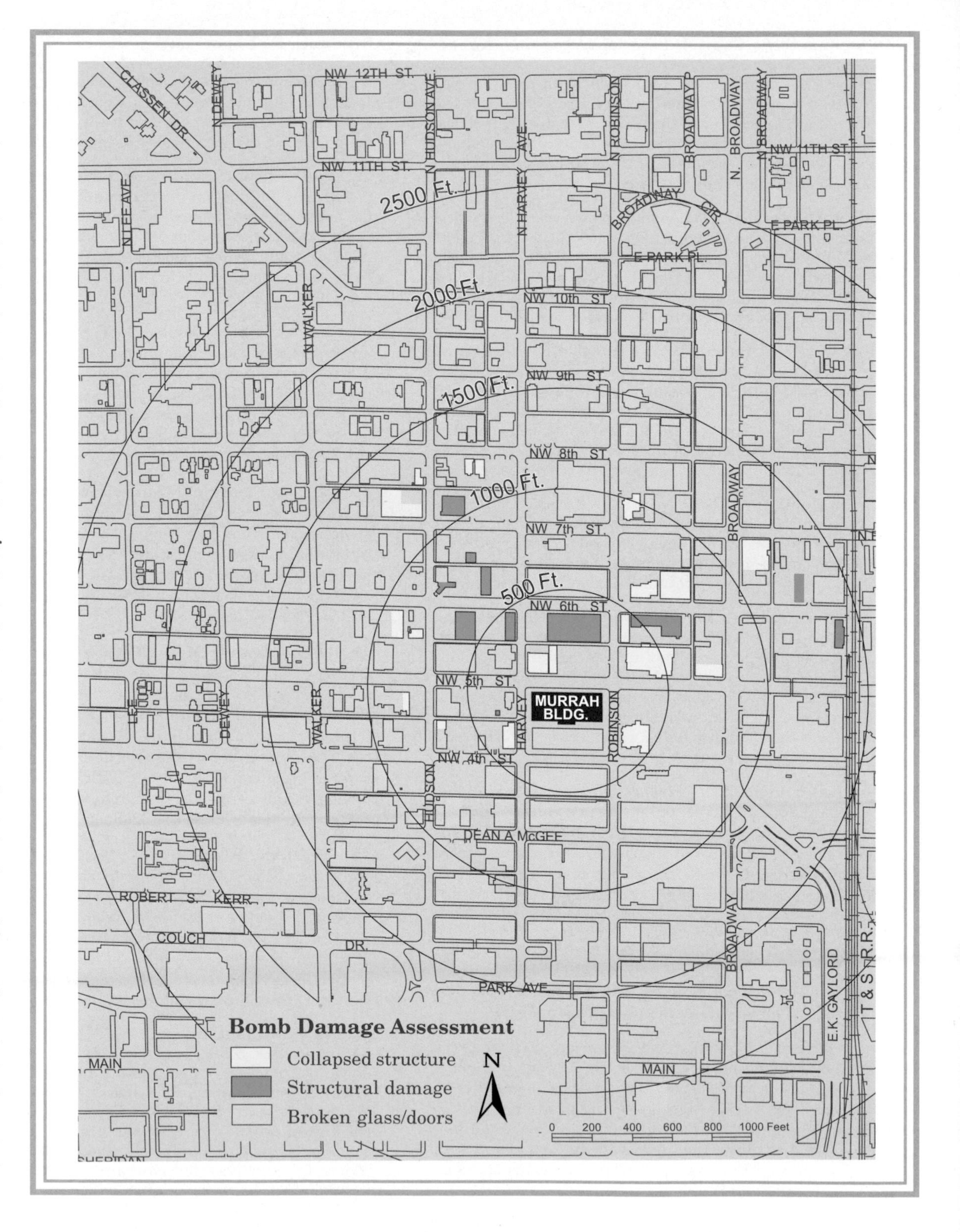

survivors, and volunteers worked together as the Oklahoma City Memorial Foundation, a private nonprofit organization. In 1996, the Memorial Foundation created three parallel-functioning efforts to carry out its mission: the Oklahoma City National Memorial, the Memorial Museum, and the Institute for the Prevention of Terrorism. All three entities (the last being dedicated in 2004) are located together in downtown Oklahoma City.

In September 1996, a two-stage international competition for the design of the outdoor symbolic memorial was announced. By March 1997, 624 design entries had been submitted. Proposals came from all fifty states and twenty-three foreign countries.

On July 1, 1997, the design submitted by Hans Butzer and Torrey Butzer with Sven Berg was selected by unanimous decision as the design for the Oklahoma City National Memorial. Conceived as a story, the design of the Butzer Design Partnership uses entry gates, terraces, orchards, a reflecting pool, and 168 empty chairs to explicate the events of April 19, 1995. Built at a cost of $7.82 million, most of it provided by private donations, the Oklahoma City National Memorial was dedicated on April 19, 2000, to international acclaim. It has received numerous national awards and was listed in *Time* magazine's Top Five Best Designs for 2000.

Above: *The Alfred P. Murrah Federal Building a few days after the bombing in 1995. (Courtesy Oklahoma City National Memorial Foundation)*

Left: *The completed Oklahoma City National Memorial. (Courtesy Allproof/ Anthony L. Lindsey)*

110. RELIGIOUS TRADITIONS AND INFLUENCES

Essay by *Alvin O. Turner*

Religious forces have both shaped and mirrored much of Oklahoma's history. Developments as varied as the different American Indian responses to the Civil War, constitutional prescriptions for prohibition, and the growth of the state's Asian populations after 1970 were all affected by religion. Oklahoma's unique cultural history explains why the state's residents are seven times more likely than other Americans to identify themselves as Baptist and are correspondingly much less often associated with other religious groups. Yet Baptists are not as dominant in Oklahoma as they are in many surrounding states. At the same time, the state's religious mix is made even richer by the continuing presence of American Indian beliefs and practices.

Long before historical developments shaped present patterns, Caddoan mound builders created a regional political and religious center at Spiro. That culture's rituals vanished with Spiro's abandonment, but subsequent indigenous traditions defined religion for successive Native populations until the early nineteenth century. Thereafter, Christian influences became increasingly dominant, but tribal practices still influence many American Indians, who retain a deep respect for nature or exhibit a continuing commitment to traditional religious observations. Similarly, some rituals in the Native American Church stem directly from the Plains Indians' Sun Dance ceremony.

Many within the Five Tribes had already adopted Christianity by the time of the Trails of Tears. Missionaries (who frequently accompanied the tribes on their forced migrations to Indian Territory) established missions and schools, translated tribal languages, published Bibles and other Native-language materials, and promoted temperance and other programs that they believed would benefit the tribes. Abolitionism divided the missionary groups and their tribal followers, and these divisions largely defined tribal responses to the slavery issue and the Civil War.

New cultural forces moved into the state after the war. President Ulysses S. Grant's peace policy encouraged Mennonites, Quakers, and other religious groups to work as Indian agents among these tribes in western Oklahoma. The efforts of such diverse groups led to relocation of religious communities as well as the spread of their teachings among the tribes.

Territorial-era migrations contributed to the state's ethnic and religious mix. African American migrations to the Twin Territories augmented already significant numbers of tribal freedpersons and their descendants, who clustered in all-black towns, where African Methodists, Episcopalians, Baptists, and similar groups dominated. In Indian Territory, coal mining drew southern and eastern European populations, many with Roman Catholic or Orthodox religious convictions. The ancestors of much of the state's present Jewish population arrived during the same period. Saints Cyril and Methodius, a Russian Orthodox church at Hartshorne, reflects the regional diversity of eastern Oklahoma. In western Oklahoma, many communities contain other ethnic churches, such as those established by Mennonites and other denominations characteristic of the Germans from Russia.

Poverty and corresponding pressures on institutions in the territorial and early statehood eras increased the importance of church-related work in many fields and bolstered the cultural influence of these churches. Even those denominations that struggled to gain a foothold in Oklahoma often made valuable contributions to the well-being of the state's residents by creating hospitals, orphanages, and schools. The contribution of various Catholic orders, which often provided the principal source of medical care to many communities, was especially significant.

Similarly, church-based programs (from newspapers to orphanages and colleges) provided vital services to many communities. Baptist groups alone established five colleges before statehood, of which Oklahoma Baptist University and Bacone College remain. Such forces also played a key role in supporting a constitutional mandate for Prohibition—a major influence in state politics until its repeal in 1959. Prohibition reflected a Protestant social-political synthesis typical of the South that gave religious sanction to prevailing cultural norms. That synthesis went largely unchallenged for decades in Oklahoma as Southern Baptists and similar groups followed successive population movements from farms to towns, thence to cities and on to the suburbs.

By the time of the cold war, the Southern Baptists' initial advantages were augmented by the gradual decline of the older major denominations and the more conservative church groups' ability to link their teachings with prevailing anticommunist concerns of the era. In the same period, Oral Roberts moved from Pentecostal tent meetings and healing crusades to nationwide television ministries and subsequently founded the Tulsa university bearing his name.

Despite the continuing impact of such historic patterns, diverse religious traditions have persisted. In fact, that synthesis provided an impetus for increasing diversity during the 1970s, when Oklahoma's churches rallied to provide homes to Vietnamese refugees. In the meantime, the countercultural movement and a significant increase in Hispanic and other migrations added to the religious as well as the ethnic profile of the state. At the end of the twentieth century, the state's larger cities provided homes to Islamic mosques and Buddhist temples alongside the churches that for so long dominated the religious and cultural roots of the state.

Selected Religious Sites

1. Spiro Mounds, remnants of a flourishing religious center (850–1450 A.D.). This is the westernmost extension of cultures whose mounds are also found at sites such as Cahokia, Illinois, and Natchez, Mississippi.

2. Union Mission, a mission for the Osages, opened in September 1821 by the United Foreign Mission Society. This is the location of the first printing press in Oklahoma and also the site of the oldest marked grave, that of Rev. Epaphras Chapman, dated June 7, 1825.

3. Dwight Mission was established in Indian Territory in 1829 by the American Board of Foreign Missions as a mission to the Western Cherokees.

4. Baptist Mission was established in 1839 by Rev. Jesse Bushyhead. In 1844 it was the site of the publication of the "Cherokee Messenger," the first newspaper to be published in Oklahoma. In 1867 the mission moved to Tahlequah, where Bacone Indian University was established in 1879, and to Muskogee six years later.

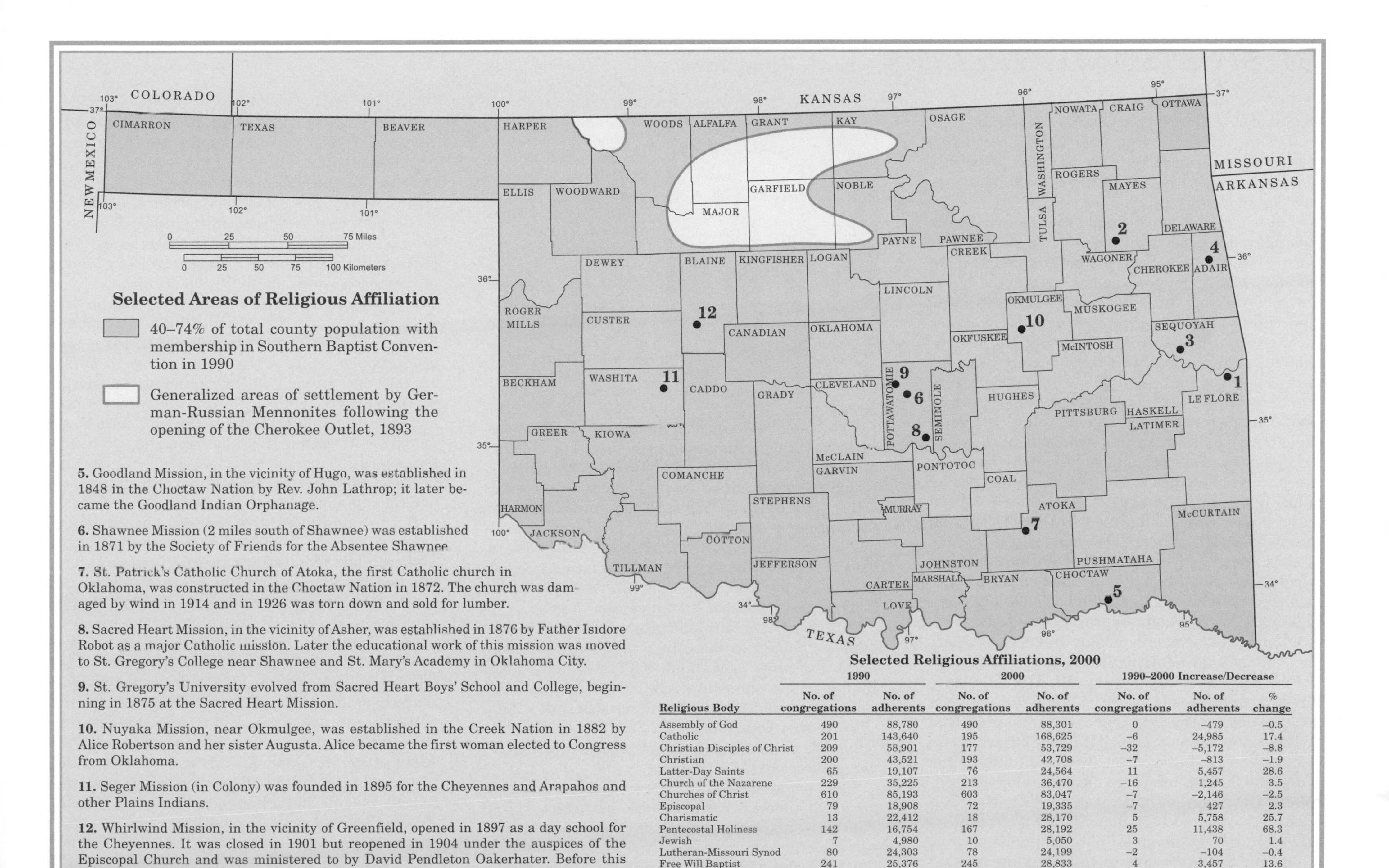

5. Goodland Mission, in the vicinity of Hugo, was established in 1848 in the Choctaw Nation by Rev. John Lathrop; it later became the Goodland Indian Orphanage.

6. Shawnee Mission (2 miles south of Shawnee) was established in 1871 by the Society of Friends for the Absentee Shawnee.

7. St. Patrick's Catholic Church of Atoka, the first Catholic church in Oklahoma, was constructed in the Choctaw Nation in 1872. The church was damaged by wind in 1914 and in 1926 was torn down and sold for lumber.

8. Sacred Heart Mission, in the vicinity of Asher, was established in 1876 by Father Isidore Robot as a major Catholic mission. Later the educational work of this mission was moved to St. Gregory's College near Shawnee and St. Mary's Academy in Oklahoma City.

9. St. Gregory's University evolved from Sacred Heart Boys' School and College, beginning in 1875 at the Sacred Heart Mission.

10. Nuyaka Mission, near Okmulgee, was established in the Creek Nation in 1882 by Alice Robertson and her sister Augusta. Alice became the first woman elected to Congress from Oklahoma.

11. Seger Mission (in Colony) was founded in 1895 for the Cheyennes and Arapahos and other Plains Indians.

12. Whirlwind Mission, in the vicinity of Greenfield, opened in 1897 as a day school for the Cheyennes. It was closed in 1901 but reopened in 1904 under the auspices of the Episcopal Church and was ministered to by David Pendleton Oakerhater. Before this time, Oakerhater had been a warrior leader of the Cheyennes; he had been imprisoned and sent to Florida and then to upstate New York. During this period, he was baptized in the Episcopal Church. He returned to the Cheyenne Reservation and served as a deacon for 50 years, until his death in 1931. In 1985, the Episcopal Church elected him to the Calendar of Saints, one of the very few so honored from the United States.

Selected Religious Affiliations, 2000

	1990		2000		1990–2000 Increase/Decrease		
Religious Body	No. of congregations	No. of adherents	No. of congregations	No. of adherents	No. of congregations	No. of adherents	% change
Assembly of God	490	88,780	490	88,301	0	–479	–0.5
Catholic	201	143,640	195	168,625	–6	24,985	17.4
Christian Disciples of Christ	209	58,901	177	53,729	–32	–5,172	–8.8
Christian	200	43,521	193	42,708	–7	–813	–1.9
Latter-Day Saints	65	19,107	76	24,564	11	5,457	28.6
Church of the Nazarene	229	35,225	213	36,470	–16	1,245	3.5
Churches of Christ	610	85,193	603	83,047	–7	–2,146	–2.5
Episcopal	79	18,908	72	19,335	–7	427	2.3
Charismatic	13	22,412	18	28,170	5	5,758	25.7
Pentecostal Holiness	142	16,754	167	28,192	25	11,438	68.3
Jewish	7	4,980	10	5,050	3	70	1.4
Lutheran-Missouri Synod	80	24,303	78	24,199	–2	–104	–0.4
Free Will Baptist	241	25,376	245	28,833	4	3,457	13.6
Presbyterian	162	41,615	147	35,211	–15	–6,404	–15.4
Southern Baptist Convention	1,490	964,615	1,578	967,223	88	2,608	0.3
United Methodist	681	326,294	636	322,794	–45	–3,500	–1.1
Black Baptist estimate		83,619		n/a			

Source: *Churches and Church Memberships in the United States, 1990* and *Religious Congregations and Membership in the United States, 2000* (Nashville: Glenmary Research Center).
The population of Oklahoma in 1990 was 3,145,585; in 2000 it was 3,450,654. The total population increased 9.7%. The population unclaimed by any religious affiliation thus represents 39.2% of the total population in 2000.

111. SPORTS AND ATHLETES

Essay by *Berry Tramel*

Oklahoma Territory began with its own athletic festival. The great Land Run of 1889 was part horse race, part track meet, part chariot dash. Probably some boxing and wrestling were thrown in, too, as new Oklahomans wrangled for land.

Call it a harbinger of things to come, for sports have played a huge role in Oklahoma culture ever since. From the 1888 birth of Jim Thorpe in Indian Territory and Bullet Joe Rogan's birth in the boomtown of Oklahoma City a few months after the initial land run to the development of legendary coaches such as Henry Iba and Bud Wilkinson, to the outstanding performances of 1990s Olympians Shannon Miller and John Smith, Oklahoma has produced athletic heroes and heroines who have inflamed the passions of fans whose very identity often is tied to exploits on a ball field or in a gymnasium.

University of Oklahoma football offers the greatest example. No other state institution—not the oil fields, not country music, not even the Dust Bowl legacy—is as closely identified with the state. And that is by design. When OU regents met in 1945 to discuss filling the school's football coaching vacancy, regent Lloyd Noble of Ardmore hatched the historic idea that if OU hired a coach who could produce a big-time winner, it might improve the state's morale, as Oklahoma then was cursed by an inferiority complex (fallout from John Steinbeck's *Grapes of Wrath*).

Few plans ever worked so well. The university hired an experienced winner in Jim Tatum—in part because of a charming young assistant named Bud Wilkinson who accompanied Tatum to Norman on his visit. A year later, when Tatum left to take the Maryland job, regents were quick to offer the position of OU head football coach to Wilkinson. Recruiting boys from Oklahoma City's high schools and western Oklahoma oil-patch hamlets such as Hollis and athletic-crazy towns including Muskogee, Wilkinson fashioned one of the great dynasties in sports history. In his seventeen years as head coach, OU won three national titles and between 1953 and 1957 unleashed an epic forty-seven-game winning streak.

James Francis "Jim" Thorpe was born on the Sac and Fox Reservation near present-day Prague. His mother gave him the Indian name of Wa-tho-huck, meaning "bright path." (Courtesy Western History Collections, University of Oklahoma Libraries)

The state was hooked. From wheat fields in the southwest to gas stations in the Jack Fork Mountains to the urban centers of Tulsa and Oklahoma City, Sooner football became the language of the state. Today, the passion has not subsided—as is evident in the ever-expanding and full stadium on campus (now holding more than 80,000 fans), the political offices held by former football stars, the exorbitant salaries paid to successful coaches. The sport's status in the state is clear; the Dust Bowl mentality is gone.

But Oklahoma's athletic prowess never was tied solely to Sooner football. In Stillwater, Oklahoma A&M University (now Oklahoma State) built NCAA championship teams in wrestling (under coach Ed Gallagher) and basketball (under coach Henry Iba), using mostly Oklahoma kids. Fittingly, OSU today remains a national power in both sports, which compete in Gallagher-Iba Arena.

Even before collegiate sports became a cultural force, Oklahoma turned out supreme athletes. Jim Thorpe, by many measurements the greatest American athlete ever, grew up in the Prague-Yale area (in the Sac and Fox Nation) and went on to reach the pinnacle of two sports. He was the 1912 Olympic champion in both the decathlon and the pentathlon, and he was the first megastar in a fledgling enterprise called the National Football League. Joe Rogan was born a year after Thorpe and lived for nineteen years in Oklahoma City; he then moved to Kansas City, Kansas, and became one of the greatest baseball stars of the Negro Leagues. In truth, Oklahoma's baseball history surpasses its football status. Rogan is joined in the Baseball Hall of Fame (in Cooperstown, New York) by five other Oklahoma-bred players: the Waner brothers, Paul and Lloyd, of Harrah; Carl Hubbell of Meeker; Mickey Mantle of Commerce; and Johnny Bench of Binger.

Nowhere is athletic spirit more prevalent than in the small towns throughout Oklahoma that embrace their high school teams. Small-town high schools have replaced the town-team concept of a century ago, serving as the community gathering place on Friday nights in autumn and winter. Towns such as Ada, Clinton, Davis, Jenks, and Tulsa house football-rich schools that have won championships for generation after generation. Similarly, mention of Byng and Boynton automatically conjures basketball among the sports-minded.

Such commitment to sports can have its drawbacks, however. School funding is a constant battle, and scandals (from drugs to rule breaking) have plagued both college and high school levels. But sports also have pulled the state forward. A state solidly Jim Crow in its racial relations has been ahead of the curve athletically. Prentice Gautt of Oklahoma City's Douglass High School broke the OU football color line in 1957, a dozen years before the barrier fell at the culturally similar universities of Texas and Arkansas. And whereas widespread girls' athletics did not come to most states until the 1960s or 1970s, Oklahoma has had a long and rich history of girls' basketball, particularly in the small schools, staging state championships as early as the 1920s. Bertha Frank Teague, the legendary girls coach at Byng from 1927 to 1969, is in the National Basketball Hall of Fame as a special contributor.

All told, the state has experienced quite an unexpected result from that April day in 1889, when the wagons raced and the horses galloped and even mighty souls on foot sprinted. New Oklahomans competed that day, just as their descendants compete still.

Selected Athletes and Coaches

1. Elvan George, *1913–1974, Ada (football)*: Perhaps the greatest high school coach in Oklahoma history, George built the Ada dynasty, winning six state championships in the 1950s and compiling a 174–52–9 record in 19 years. He then coached 11 seasons at Ada's East Central University, his alma mater, and had a record of 93–36–5.

2. Johnny Bench, *1947– , Binger (baseball)*: One of the greatest catchers in baseball history, Bench signed with the Cincinnati Reds out of Binger High School and became one of the cornerstones of Cincinnati's "Big Red Machine." He was elected to the Baseball Hall of Fame in 1989, his first year of eligibility, with the third-highest total of votes in history. Bench was a two-time National League most valuable player.

3. Bertha Frank Teague, *1906–1991, Byng (basketball)*: In 1985, Teague became the first woman coach inducted into the National Basketball Hall of Fame. Her record was hard to ignore. In 43 years at Byng High School (1927–1969), Teague won eight state championships and compiled a record of 1,157–115.

4. Andy Payne, *1907–1977, Claremore (track)*: Payne became a national celebrity in 1928 when he won the first International Trans-Continental Foot Race, a 3,422-mile event that drew 275 runners from around the world and snaked through 10 states, from Los Angeles to New York. Payne, 20 years old at the time, was one of only six Americans in the race. He averaged 60 miles a day and beat his nearest competitor by 15 hours. Payne later was elected Clerk of the Supreme Court of Oklahoma and held the position for 38 years.

5. Billy Vessels, *1931–2001, Cleveland (football)*: Oklahoma's first Heisman Trophy winner, in 1952, Vessels was declared by legendary coach Bud Wilkinson to be that coach's greatest Sooner player. Vessels became the University of Oklahoma's first single-season 1,000-yard rusher. He also was a ferocious defensive player.

6. Mickey Mantle, *1931–1995, Commerce (baseball)*: An Oklahoma legend, Mantle's athleticism and exploits on the baseball field still are hallowed in New York, where he spent 18 seasons with the Yankees. Mantle hit 536 home runs and was one of the fastest players in the game until injuries slowed him; he played in 12 World Series, hitting a record 18 home runs. Mantle, who grew up in the mining community of Commerce, was a three-time American League most valuable player.

7. Hubert "Geese" Ausbie, *1938– , Crescent (basketball)*: The "Clown Prince of Basketball" was one of the most beloved Harlem Globetrotters. He grew up in Crescent and in one tournament for Douglass High School scored 70, 54, and 62 points in consecutive games. He attended Philander Smith College in Arkansas and then won a tryout with the Globetrotters, with whom he played for 24 years.

8. John Smith, *1965–, Del City (wrestling)*: The greatest American wrestler ever, Smith won six World Championship titles, including two Olympic gold medals. Smith's legacy continues, as he coached his alma mater, Oklahoma State University, to NCAA championships in 1994, 2003, 2004, and 2005. Smith—part of a wrestling family dynasty at Del City High School and OSU—has three brothers who were champions at both schools.

9. Shannon Miller, *1977– , Edmond (gymnastics)*: The most decorated American gymnast ever, Miller won seven Olympic medals and eight World Championship medals. Miller helped lead the U.S. women to the team gold medal in the 1996 Olympics at Atlanta and also won a gold medal in the balance beam event. Miller twice won the gold medal in the World Championship all-around competition.

10. Don Haskins, *1930–, Enid (basketball)*: Coach of perhaps the most important game in college basketball history, Haskin took his Texas Western Miners to the 1966 NCAA championship with a 72–65 victory over mighty Kentucky. It was the NCAA's first title game matching an all-black starting lineup (Texas Western, now Texas–El Paso) against an all-white lineup. Haskins was an all-state basketball player in Enid and played on two NCAA semifinal teams at Oklahoma A&M. He has been inducted into the National Basketball Hall of Fame.

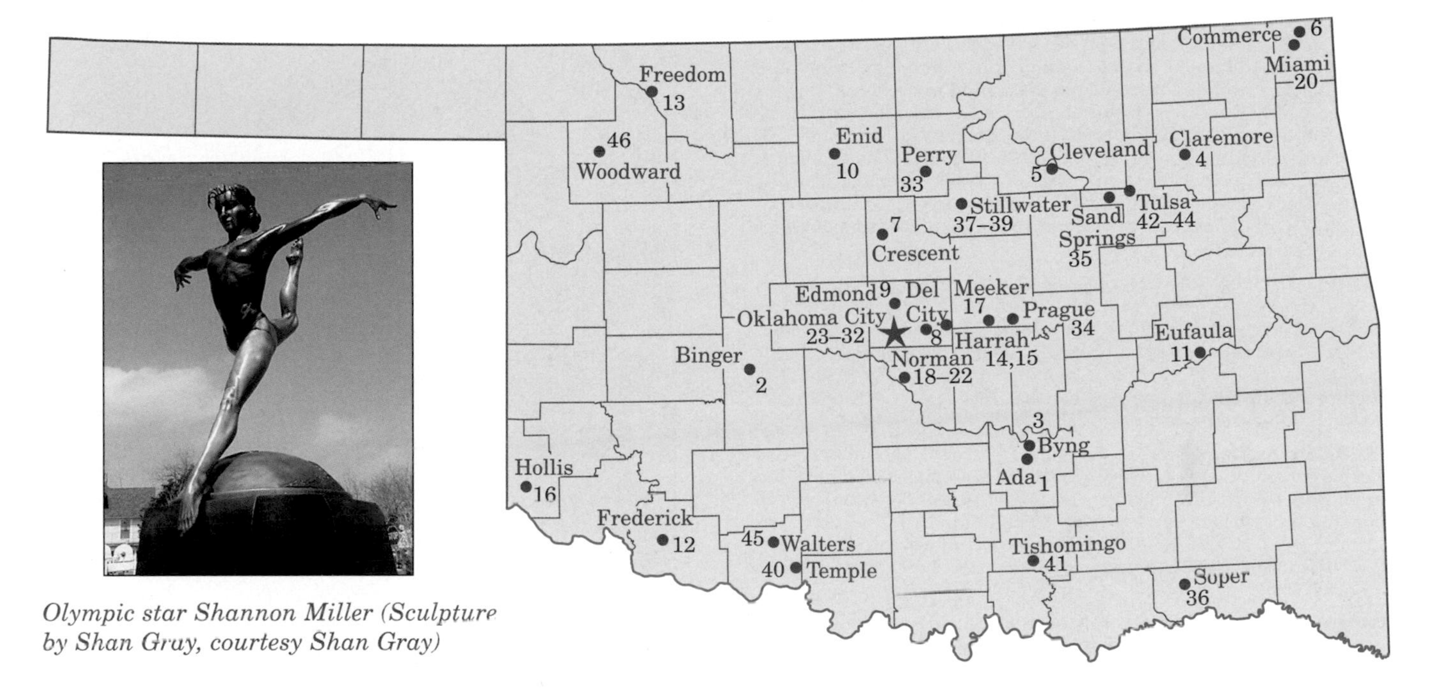

Olympic star Shannon Miller (Sculpture by Shan Gray, courtesy Shan Gray)

11. Lee Roy Selmon, *1954– , Eufaula (football)*: One of the most decorated Native Oklahomans in football history, Selmon was the best of three legendary brothers who played for the University of Oklahoma. Lee Roy, Dewey, and Lucious Selmon played together on the 1973 OU defensive line that anchored one of the greatest defenses in college football history. Lee Roy became the No. 1 overall pick in the National Football League draft and spent 10 years with the Tampa Bay Buccaneers. He was elected to the Pro Football Hall of Fame.

12. Glenn Dobbs, *1920–2002, Frederick (football)*: Best known as the University of Tulsa football coach when TU led the nation in passing for five straight years, Dobbs was quite the player himself. Told he was too small (5-foot-8) to play at Frederick High School, he became a star not just there but also at TU, making All-American as a tailback. Dobbs then became an all-pro in the All-America Football Conference for the Brooklyn Dodgers.

13. Steve Owen, *1898–1964, Freedom (football)*: One of the greatest coaches in National Football League history, Owen spent 23 years leading the New York Giants and developing some of the standard defenses still in use. Owen attended Aline High School, which offered only basketball, but Phillips University coach Johnny Maulbetsch introduced Owen to football. He became a star and went on to the NFL. He became the Giants' head coach in 1931 and in 23 years won two league titles and amassed a record of 153–108–17. His innovations include the "umbrella" defense, the forerunner of the modern zone defense.

14. Lloyd Waner, *1906–1982, Harrah (baseball)*: Called "Little Poison," Lloyd teamed with his brother, Paul, to form a Hall of Fame duo in the Pittsburgh Pirates outfield. They are the only brother duo enshrined in the Baseball Hall of Fame. Their combined hit total of 5,611 is the most of any brothers in baseball history—almost 1,000 more than the five Delahanty brothers and 500 more than the three DiMaggio brothers.

15. Paul Waner, *1903–1965, Harrah (baseball)*: With the nickname "Big Poison," Paul was the more accomplished of the two Waner brothers, both enshrined in the Baseball Hall of Fame. He finished his career with 3,152 hits (still 16th-best in history) and a .333 batting average. Waner was the 1927 National League's most valuable player and three-time National League batting champion.

16. Darrell Royal, *1924–, Hollis (football)*: An All-American at the University of Oklahoma, Royal became one of the greatest coaches in college football history, for the University of Texas. Royal, one of many Hollis stars from the post–World War II era, was a quarterback, defensive back, and punter at OU for Bud Wilkinson. He later became Wilkinson's chief nemesis. Royal in 1957 was hired as head coach at Texas and lost to the Sooners that first season. Royal then won eight straight from OU and built a dynasty. Texas won national titles in 1963 and 1969.

17. Carl Hubbell, *1903–1988, Meeker (baseball)*: "King Carl" they dubbed the perfector of the screwball, a funky pitch that broke opposite of a curveball and lifted Hubbell into the pantheon of great baseball pitchers. Hubbell set a major-league record with a 24-game winning streak and pitched 16 years with the New York Giants, finishing almost 100 games above .500, with a 253–154 record. He was a two-time National League most valuable player.

18. Bruce Drake, *1905–1983, Norman (basketball)*: One of the most influential basketball coaches of his time, Drake was known for his offensive innovation, the Drake Shuffle, which became a standard in the game, giving smaller opponents a counter to size. Drake played basketball at the University of Oklahoma and later was OU head coach for 17 years. In 1971, Drake was inducted into the National Basketball Hall of Fame.

19. John Jacobs, *1892–1978, Norman (track)*: During the four years he competed as a track and field athlete at the University of Oklahoma, he won the trophy as outstanding athlete and high point man. He also held the state intercollegiate record in four events. He was selected Knute Rockne Club National Track Coach of the year, member of the Helm Foundation and Drake Relays Hall of Fame, OK Athletic, and four other OK Sports Halls of Fame. The OU Track and Field facility and the Annual Outdoor Track Meet also bear his name. After coaching at OU for 45 consecutive years, he retired in 1967. John was known for his humor, sportsmanship, and development of fine athletes.

20. Steve Owens, *1947–, Miami and Norman (football)*: Oklahoma's second Heisman Trophy winner, Owens went from Miami High School to a record-breaking career at the University of Oklahoma. In three Sooner seasons, he broke 13 school records, 9 Big Eight records, and 7 NCAA records. Owens went on to play in the National Football League and became the Detroit Lions' first single-season 1,000-yard rusher.

21. Barry Switzer, *1937– , Norman (football)*: One of only two coaches to lead teams to both a national collegiate championship and a Super Bowl title, Switzer led the University of Oklahoma to amazing success between 1973 and 1988. In his 16 years at OU, the Sooners went 157–29–4. After leaving OU, he was hired to coach the Dallas Cowboys, who under Switzer won Super Bowl XXX in January 1996.

22. Bud Wilkinson, *1916–1994, Norman (football)*: The architect of college football's greatest dynasty, Wilkinson turned University of Oklahoma football into the cultural icon it is today. In his 17 seasons as the Sooner coach (1947–1963), OU won 145 games, lost 29, and tied 4. Wilkinson's teams won three national championships. The Sooners' 47-game winning streak of 1953–1957 remains one of the greatest achievements in sports. Wilkinson grew up in Minnesota and came to OU in 1946.

23. Alvan Adams, *1954– , Oklahoma City (basketball)*: A star on every level, Adams established himself as one of the state's three greatest players, along with Mark Price and Wayman Tisdale. Adams led Putnam City High School to a state championship in 1972, set records in a 3-year career at the University of Oklahoma, and then played for 13 years in the NBA with the Phoenix Suns, where he began by being named the league's rookie of the year.

24. Susie Maxwell Berning, *1941– , Oklahoma City (golf)*: One of only three women to win the U.S. Open three times, Berning learned the game at Lincoln Park in Oklahoma City and went on to win three straight high school state championships and three straight Oklahoma City Women's Amateur championships. She then received a scholarship to Oklahoma City University and played on its men's team before joining the Ladies Professional Golf Association.

25. Tom Churchill, *1908–1963, Oklahoma City (track and field)*: Churchill gave Jim Thorpe a good run as Oklahoma's most diversified athlete. Churchill, who graduated from Central High School in Oklahoma City, was an Olympic decathlete and a two-sport All-American at the University of Oklahoma and also played professional baseball. At OU, Churchill was all-conference in basketball and all-American in football. He placed fifth in the decathlon at the 1928 Olympics in Amsterdam.

26. Prentice Gautt, *1938–2005, Oklahoma City (football)*: Chosen by Oklahoma City black professionals and University of Oklahoma football coach Bud Wilkinson to break the Sooners' color barrier, Gautt became a two-time All-American and cleared the way for quick athletic desegregation. Gautt, who attended Douglass High School, played for seven years in the National Football League and later became association commissioner of the Big 8 and Big 12 conferences.

University of Oklahoma tailback and Heisman Trophy winner Steve Owens, 1969. (Courtesy Western History Collections, University of Oklahoma Libraries)

27. Steve Largent, *1954–, Oklahoma City (football)*: Largent went from Putnam City High School and the University of Tulsa to breaking records in the National Football League. At Tulsa, Largent twice led the NCAA in touchdown catches. He then played 14 seasons with the Seattle Seahawks and retired as the league's all-time leader in catches, receiving yards, and touchdown catches. Largent later was elected to the U.S. House of Representatives from Oklahoma's first district.

28. Don McNeil, *1918–1996, Oklahoma City (tennis)*: The greatest tennis player ever from Oklahoma, McNeil won the 1939 French Open singles, beating tournament favorite Bobby Riggs. McNeil, born in Chickasha, grew up in Oklahoma City and won five state tennis titles for Classen High School. McNeil played at Ohio's Kenyon College, a national power at the time. He lost several of his prime years to World War II, in which he served as a U.S. Navy intelligence officer.

29. Orville Moody, *1933– , Oklahoma City (golf)*: Known as "Sarge," Moody spent 14 years in the U.S. Army; and 15 months after his discharge, he became one of the great underdog stories in U.S. Open history. Moody's first PGA Tour victory came in the 1969 U.S. Open at Champions Golf Club in Houston. Moody, the son of a golf course superintendent, attended Capitol Hill High School and won the 1952 state championship.

30. Sean O'Grady, *1959– , Oklahoma City (boxing)*: The only world champion boxer from Oklahoma, O'Grady was a teenage fight sensation who in 1981 reached the peak of the sport with a 15-round decision over Hilmer Kenty for the World Boxing Association lightweight championship. O'Grady turned pro at the age of 15 and retired in 1983 with a professional record of 81–6.

31. Allie Reynolds, *1917–1994, Oklahoma City (baseball)*: "Superchief," as he was nicknamed, went from Capitol Hill High School and Oklahoma State University to a legendary pitching career in major-league baseball. Reynolds was the best pitcher on the most successful team of all time, the 1949–1953 Yankees, which won five straight World Series. Reynolds' 13-year career included a record of 182–107 and two no-hitters. His World Series record was 7–2.

32. Wayne Wells, *1946– , Oklahoma City (wrestling)*: Wells's final competition was his best—the 1972 Munich Olympics, in which Wells won all seven of his matches to capture the gold medal. Wells was a two-time state champion at John Marshall High School in Oklahoma City and the 1968 NCAA champion for the University of Oklahoma. While training for the Olympics, he finished law school and passed the Oklahoma bar exam.

33. Danny Hodge, *1932– , Perry (wrestling)*: One of the greatest wrestlers in Oklahoma history, Hodge won all 46 of his matches at the University of Oklahoma and captured a silver medal in the 1956 Melbourne Olympics. Hodge, a state champion at Perry High School, became the first wrestler featured on a *Sports Illustrated* cover. In 1976, he was one of 14 charter members of the Wrestling Hall of Fame in Stillwater.

University of Oklahoma coach Barry Switzer on the Sooner sideline, 1980s. (Courtesy Western History Collections, University of Oklahoma Libraries)

Left: *University of Oklahoma football coach Bud Wilkinson, with Buck McPhail* (left) *and Billy Vessels* (right)*, 1952. (Courtesy Western History Collections, University of Oklahoma Libraries)*

Bottom Left: *Ed Gallagher, Oklahoma State University wrestling coach. (Courtesy Special Collections and University Archives, Oklahoma State University Libraries)*

Bottom Right: *Henry Iba, Oklahoma State University basketball coach. (Courtesy Special Collections and University Archives, Oklahoma State University Libraries)*

34. Jim Thorpe, *1888–1953, Prague (football, baseball, track)*: The world's greatest athlete of his time and maybe still, Thorpe won Olympic gold medals in decathlon and pentathlon in 1912 and then became the first pro football superstar. For good measure, he also played major-league baseball. He left Oklahoma to attend Carlisle Indian Institute in Pennsylvania, where he became one of the first stars of college football. A statue of Thorpe stands at the entrance to the Pro Football Hall of Fame, with a plaque proclaiming him "the first great performer" of the National Football League.

35. Marques Haynes, *1926– , Sand Springs (basketball)*: Known as "The World's Greatest Dribbler," Haynes became an international star with the Harlem Globetrotters after a stunning school career in Oklahoma. Haynes led Booker T. Washington High School in Sand Springs to the 1941 national high school championship for segregated schools. Haynes led Langston University to a 112–3 record in four seasons, including a 59-game winning streak. In a five-decade career with the Globetrotters and his own Harlem Magicians, Haynes played in more than 12,000 games and 97 nations. He was the first Globetrotter elected to the National Basketball Hall of Fame.

36. Freckles Brown, *1921–1987, Soper (rodeo)*: Brown became a rodeo legend with one bull ride. Brown already was a cowboy star, winning the 1962 bull-riding title at the National Finals Rodeo. But in the 1967 NFR, Brown rode the unrideable bull Tornado (owned by rodeo legend Jim Shoulders), which had gone unridden for 220 professional rides, in Oklahoma City's State Fair Arena. Brown grew up in Wyoming and Arizona but was stationed at Fort Sill during World War II and made Oklahoma his home.

37. Ed Gallagher, *1887–1940, Stillwater (wrestling)*: Ed Gallagher never wrestled a match in his life, but he impacted the sport by establishing a peerless tradition. Gallagher started the varsity program at Oklahoma A&M and coached for 23 years, winning 13 NCAA titles. Gallagher twice (1932, 1936) was the U.S. Olympic coach. OSU's historic coliseum, Gallagher-Iba Arena (formerly Gallagher Hall), bears his name.

38. Henry Iba, *1904–1993, Stillwater (basketball)*: One of the great innovators of the game, Iba instigated Oklahoma State University's basketball tradition. In his 36 seasons coaching the Cowboys, Iba's teams won 655 games. His 41-year coaching career consisted of a record of 767–338. Iba's teams won the NCAA title in 1945 and 1946 and reached the national semifinals in two other years. Iba grew up in Missouri.

39. Eddie Sutton, *1936–, Stillwater (basketball)*: Sutton has bridged the gap between Oklahoma State University's two great basketball eras. Sutton played for legendary coach Henry Iba from 1955 through 1957 and returned to his alma mater in 1990 to usher in another successful stretch for the Cowboys. Sutton—who also coached teams at Creighton, Arkansas, and Kentucky to the NCAA Tournament—led OSU to the Final Four in 1995 and 2004.

40. Pepper Martin, *1904–1965, Temple (baseball)*: John Leonard Roosevelt Martin spent 13 seasons with the St. Louis Cardinals and was a ringleader of the "Gashouse Gang," one of the most famous baseball teams in history. Martin moved from Temple to Oklahoma City as a boy and played sandlot ball. He was spied by a Cardinal scout and signed to a contract. Martin became a star in the 1931 World Series, when he had 12 hits in 24 at-bats. Martin also shined in the 1934 World Series, with a .355 batting average.

41. Neill Armstrong, *1926– , Tishomingo (football)*: Head coach of the Chicago Bears 1978–1981, Armstrong began his football career in Tishomingo and continued it at Oklahoma A&M, where he led the nation in pass receptions in 1943 and 1946. Armstrong was a first-round draft choice of the NFL's Philadelphia Eagles in 1947 and played on two league title teams in the next five years. He then became a Canadian Football League all-star before starting a coaching career.

42. Kenny Monday, *1961– , Tulsa (wrestling)*: Monday became a champion at every level of wrestling. He was a rare four-time state champion at Tulsa's Booker T. Washington High School, and then he won three NCAA titles at Oklahoma State University. Monday's freestyle career included World Championship gold medals in 1983 and 1987. He was an Olympic silver medalist in 1992.

43. Jim Shoulders, *1928– , Tulsa (rodeo)*: Shoulders didn't have a ranch background, but at the age of 14, he tried rodeoing and became one of the greatest cowboy champions. He won 16 Rodeo Cowboys Association championships between 1949 and 1959, including five all-around titles. Shoulders also won seven bull-riding national titles and four bareback championships.

44. Wayman Tisdale, *1964– , Tulsa (basketball)*: The first first-team All-American as an NCAA freshman, Tisdale broke Alvan Adams's scoring records at the University of Oklahoma, then played 13 years in the National Basketball Association. Tisdale was a star at Tulsa's Booker T. Washington High School and later helped win a team gold medal for the United States in the 1984 Los Angeles Olympics.

45. Abe Lemons, *1922–2002, Walters (basketball)*: One of the funniest men ever, Lemons also was quite the coach. In 34 seasons, he amassed 599 wins and seven times took Oklahoma City University to the NCAA Tournament. Lemons also was head coach at Pan American University and the University of Texas.

46. Bob Fenimore, *1925– , Woodward (football)*: The "Blonde Bomber" was the best player on Oklahoma A&M's powerhouse teams of the 1940s. He was named All-American in both 1944 and 1945, when he led the nation in total offense and ignited the Cowboys to victories in the Cotton and Sugar bowls. When his eligibility ended, Fenimore was college football's all-time total offense leader.

112. LITERARY PEOPLE

Essay by *Lawrence R. Rodgers*

Although the Oklahoma region lacks a major native writer akin to Mississippi's William Faulkner, it nonetheless can lay claim, over the past several centuries, to a surprisingly rich literary tradition. The tradition's varieties of texts are unified by prominent themes and subjects that mirror Oklahoma's terms of identity: western migration and settlement, Indian affairs, agriculture, ranching, outlaw culture, oil exploration, athletics, and rural and small-town matters. The dominant subject—found in many narratives, stories, and poems—seems to be how people have confronted the challenges of the region's natural features. Whether about exploration, settlement, farming, or nature, Oklahoma literature has emphasized the land, defining itself more by spatial and ethnic images and metaphors than by an interest in abstract ideas and high culture. Writers within the state have favored realistic modes of expression over philosophy and romance. They have also showcased the diverse nature of the population (and the conflicts that such diversity generates), with special attention being paid to American Indian life.

The Best Picture of 1931, Cimarron, *adapted from Edna Ferber's sweeping novel, tracks the growth of an Oklahoma town and the homesteaders who came there beginning in 1889. (Courtesy Western History Collections, University of Oklahoma Libraries)*

The area's earliest stories are preserved in the stone-wall pictographs made by pre-Columbian Plains Indians in present-day Black Mesa State Park. The earliest literature is found in the diaries, memoirs, and official chronicles of travelers and explorers. Coronado, who crossed the Panhandle region in 1541, was the first European visitor to record his presence. His brief account was followed by a string of travelogues by Spanish, French, and eventually English visitors. Among the more memorable are Thomas Nuttall's 1819 journal recording Oklahoma's first scientific exploration and Josiah Gregg's 1839 *Commerce of the Prairies*, a lively record of economic life along the Santa Fe Trail. Oklahoma's most famous travel chronicle of early days is Washington Irving's *Tour of the Prairies* (1835), an account of travels from Fort Gibson through the central Oklahoma region with Indian Commissioner Henry Ellsworth. Although Irving represents the journey as a pleasurable lark, his dilettante's enthusiasm for exploration masks the more serious purpose behind the trip, which was to scout lands in which to settle the Indian nations that were to be removed from the U.S. Southeast.

Irving's narrative joins three other works—all by non-Oklahomans and preceding post–World War II prosperity—that together have come to embody literature about the state: Edna Ferber's *Cimarron* (1929), John Steinbeck's *Grapes of Wrath* (1939), and Richard Rodgers and Oscar Hammerstein's musical *Oklahoma!* (1943). Their only state rivals in popularity are folk musician Woodie Guthrie and

Oklahoma Poets, Inc.

In the decades following statehood, the University of Oklahoma hosted an especially lively literary scene. Built on the influence of distinguished lyric poets Muna Lee and John McClure (whom H. L. Mencken labeled the "finest lyric poet the United States has produced in fifty years"), a cadre of poets emerged whom English professor Benjamin Botkin christened "Oklahoma Poets Inc." Three celebrated university anthologies emerged from this group and led Mencken to announce in American Mercury *an "Oklahoma manner" of writing. Included in this group were May Frank, longtime literary editor of the* Daily Oklahoman, *and William Cunningham, head of the 1935–1938 Oklahoma Writers' Project. Fellow student George Milburn gained later distinction as a novelist and short story writer and was compared favorably to Sherwood Anderson for his best known collection,* Oklahoma Town *(1931).*

World Literature Today

In 1927, Books Abroad, *the state's most prestigious literary journal, was founded by Roy Temple House at the University of Oklahoma. Later renamed* World Literature Today, *it has played host to the biennial Neustadt International Prize for Literature, a literary honor second only to the Nobel Prize.*

University of Oklahoma Press

The University of Oklahoma Press, the state's most lasting literary legacy, was founded in 1928 by Joseph Brandt. The first volume—an anthology of regional writing called Folk Say, *one of four regional miscellanies edited by Botkin—set the tone for the long lineage of books that continue to appear, many of which address themes and subjects pertinent to the region.*

Western History Collection

In 1927, University of Oklahoma history professor Edward E. Dale's dream of a library collection for western history became a reality. With encouragement from OU president William Bennett Bizzell and attorney Patrick Hurley and the financial generosity of Frank Phillips, the Phillips Collection began. In 1948, with the assistance of a Rockefeller Foundation grant, the Manuscript Division of the library was created. These two special collections were merged in 1967 into the highly respected Western History Collection of the University of Oklahoma.

humorist Will Rogers. *Cimarron*, a larger-than-life tale set in the rowdy pioneering days surrounding statehood, was a national sensation that emerged as number one on the best-seller list for all of 1930. Its movie version won the 1931 Oscar for best picture. A very different state image was set forth in *The Grapes of Wrath* (which, as one of the best-selling novels of all time, has sold over fourteen million copies). Steinbeck's portrait of the Joad family—California-bound migrant laborers dispossessed during the Great Depression—laid the groundwork for Oklahoma's becoming a land of "Okies," perhaps the state's most enduring, if disparaging, image. Steinbeck had briefly driven along Route 66 and met Oklahoma migrants in California, but he located the Joad family home near tree-covered Sallisaw in the eastern Oklahoma Ozarks, labeled it the "dustbowl," and commenced a fury about the book's inaccuracies and stereotypes among native Oklahomans that has yet to subside. *Oklahoma!* has perpetuated its own lasting set of clichés about the state, but they are more positive and therefore less contested.

The popularity of these outsiders-looking-in has obscured the impressive tradition of writing by Native-born authors. As Oklahoma became more settled and moved toward statehood, it began to lay claim to a traditional lineage of poetry, novels, drama, and autobiography. Creek Indian writer and journalist Alexander Posey (1873–1908) together with John Rollin Ridge, the foremost Cherokee poet, initiated Oklahoma's tradition of excellent poets. Other notable writers with tribal affiliations include Lynn Riggs (whose folk drama *Green Grow the Lilacs* was the basis for *Oklahoma!*), John Milton Oskison (author of *Black Jack Davy* and *Brothers Three*), and John Joseph Mathews (who penned *Sundown*, an under-praised gem about assimilation). Contemporary writers include Rhodes Scholar Carter Revard (Osage), N. Scott Momaday (Kiowa), Joy Harjo (Muscogee), Jim Barnes (Choctaw), Linda Hogan (Chickasaw), and Lance Henson (Cheyenne/Oglala).

Although Oklahoma's most distinguished literary name, Ralph Ellison, left the state as a teenager (settling permanently in New York City in his twenties), the imprint of his Oklahoma City childhood is fully etched into his 1952 masterpiece, *Invisible Man*. Melvin Tolson (poet and longtime Langston professor), historian John Hope Franklin, autobiographer and lawyer Ada Lois Sipuel Fisher, and children's writer Joyce Carol Thomas point to the range of distinguished African American writers with Oklahoma affiliations.

Oklahoma farm life—and its institutions—has occupied a significant group of novelists, including Nola Henderson (*This Much Is Mine,* 1934), Dora Aydelotte (*Long Furrows,* 1935), William Cunningham (*Green Corn Rebellion*, 1935); Alice Lent Covert (*Return to Dust*, 1939, and *Months of Rain*, 1941); Texan Edwin Lanham (*The Stricklands*, 1939); and Cecil Brown Williams (*Paradise Prairie*, 1953).

During the past few decades, Oklahoma's most recognized literary voices have been its genre writers. Harold Keith, Helen Roney Satler, Bill Wallace, and S. E. Hinton (whose *Outsiders* remains one of the most popular adolescent novels of all time) all join Thomas as distinguished writers for young readers. Tulsa bookstore owner Lewis Meyer's humorous memoirs of his Sapulpa boyhood, *Preposterous Papa* and *Off the Sauce*, have sold over a million copies each. Anadarko's Jim Thompson remains one of the twentieth century's preeminent pulp/crime novelists, and Hugo Award–winning Tulsan R. A. Lafferty is an equally distinguished science fiction writer. The country's most dominant western writer, Louis L'Amour, claimed Oklahoma ties during the Depression. Tony Hillerman's Navajo-themed mysteries place him among the top-selling mystery writers of all time. Billie Letts's 1996 Oprah selection *Where the Heart Is* was joined by *The Honk and Holler Opening Soon* (1999) to turn anything Letts writes into a surefire best seller. Like Letts, Rilla Askew has won the Oklahoma Book Award. Her impressive novels, including *The Mercy Seat* (1997) and *Fire in Beulah* (2002), offer evidence that Oklahoma continues to offer a tradition of writers of genuine distinction.

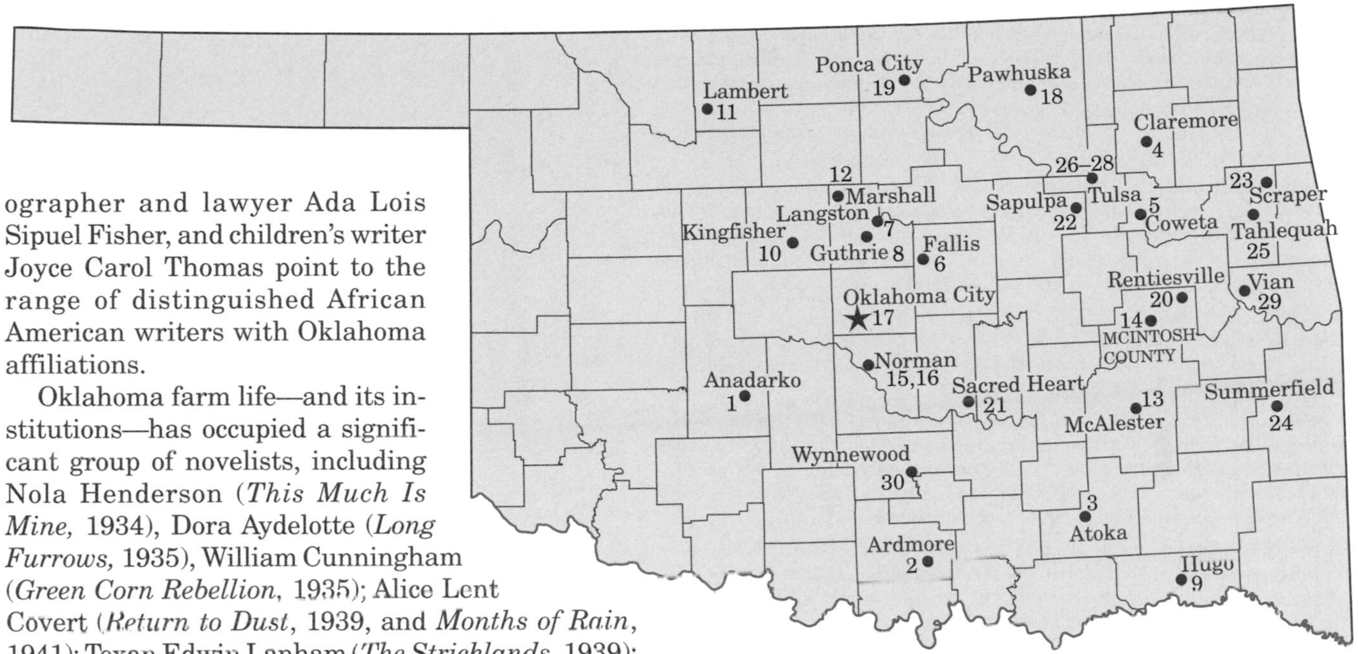

Selected Literary People

1. Jim Thompson, *1906–1976, Anadarko (novelist)*: Alongside Dashiell Hammett and Raymond Chandler, Jim Thompson is one of the country's greatest pulp crime writers. Arising from his troubled early years, Thompson's novels focus on a range of disenchanted outsiders who populate America's small, out-of-the-way towns.

2. John McClure, *1893–1956, Ardmore (poet)*: Noted for lofty subject matter, classical references, and simple lines, McClure's poetry contrasts with many of his contemporaries' experimental, modernist verse. In 1918 McClure saw the publication of his best-known work, *Airs and Ballads,* which became the inspiration over the next decade for a talented group of Oklahoma student poets.

3. Todd Downing, *1902–1974, Atoka (author)*: Downing was born to a prominent Choctaw family. Author of 10 popular mystery novels, he also wrote *Mexican Earth,* a Mexican history from an indigenous point of view. After working as a teacher in Philadelphia and Woodstock, Virginia, in the 1950s, he returned to Oklahoma, where he taught at Atoka High School, later becoming a professor of Choctaw language at Southeastern Oklahoma State University. In 1971 his *Chahta Anompa: An Introduction to the Choctaw Grammar* was published.

4. Lynn Riggs, *1899–1954, Claremore (playwright)*: Enrolled in the Cherokee Nation, Riggs is best known as the author of *Green Grow the Lilacs,* which had a New York stage run of 64 performances and was later adapted for the musical *Oklahoma!* Praised for his ability to capture Oklahoma dialect and folk culture, Riggs wrote 21 full-length stage plays.

5. George Milburn, *1906–1966, Coweta (author)*: In the tradition of Sherwood Anderson and Sinclair Lewis, Milburn authored trenchant satires about small-town Oklahoma life. *Oklahoma Town* (1931), a series of 36 sketches, was followed by a range of other novels and short story collections.

6. Vingie E. Roe, *1879–1958, Fallis (novelist)*: In 1939, Oklahoma literary scholars Marable and Boylan labeled Roe "the most widely known early Oklahoma writer." Born in Oxford, Kansas, Roe grew up in Guthrie, Carney, and Fallis. Although she left Oklahoma while still young, she regarded herself as an Oklahoman. She became a celebrated popular novelist who wrote prolifically on a variety of locales, each underscoring the reading public's fascination with westward expansion in a romantic vein.

7. Melvin Tolson, *1898–1966, Guthrie / Langston (poet)*: A longtime English professor at Langston College, Tolson is recognized as an erudite practitioner of modernist poetry in an African American vein. Emphasizing black vernacular and characterization, Tolson's "Harlem Gallery" (among others) confirms his poetic eclecticism and brilliance. He was named poet laureate of Liberia.

8. Guthrie: The state's first novel—Thompson B. Ferguson's *Jayhawkers, a Tale of the Border War* (State Capital Printing Co.)—was published here in 1892.

9. Muna Lee, *1895–1965, Hugo (author / poet)*: Born in Mississippi, raised in Hugo, and living for a time in Sulphur and Oklahoma City, Lee was a translator, coauthor of several mystery novels, and author of five works of nonfiction. She was also a poet and viewed her many published lyric verses and her single 1923 collection *Sea-Change* as her most significant writing.

10. Don Blanding, *1894–1957, Kingfisher (poet)*: Born in Kingfisher, Blanding graduated from high school in Lawton before eventually gravitating to Hawaii, where he became the island's unofficial poet laureate during the 1920s and 1930s. His best-known work, *Vagabond's House,* paired informal celebrations of life in Hawaii with his whimsical pen-and-ink illustrations to sell more than 150,000 copies.

11. Harold Keith, *1903–1998, Lambert (author)*: In addition to his primary job as the University of Oklahoma's sports publicity director from 1930 until 1969, which led him to write books about Oklahoma athletics, Keith was also a prolific author for young adults. His novel *Rifles for Waite* won the 1958 Newberry Award, children's literature's most distinguished honor.

12. Angie Debo, *1890–1988, Marshall (historian / author)*: A pioneering historian of the Southwest, Debo was born in Kansas and moved to Marshall at the age of nine. Debo's portrait hangs in the Oklahoma state capitol building in recognition of a lifetime of historical scholarship on Oklahoma. Holding degrees from the University of Chicago and OU but unable to secure a university teaching position, Debo supported herself from her hometown of Marshall through writing. She authored major revisionist works on Indian history, including *The Rise and Fall of the Choctaw Republic* (1934), which won the John H. Dunning Prize, and her most famous (and controversial) work, *And Still the Waters Run* (1940), an account of land usurpation from the Indians in Indian Territory. She also wrote a novel, *Prairie City* (1944).

13. John Berryman, *1914–1972, McAlester (poet)*: Born John Allyn Smith, Jr., in McAlester, Berryman was a major modern poet best known for *The Dream Songs,* which won the 1964 Pulitzer Prize. Though crippled by alcoholism, Berryman produced a large corpus of verse characterized by its lyrical intensity and colloquial use of American English.

14. Alexander Lawrence Posey, *1873–1908, McIntosh County (poet)*: Born to a prominent Creek family, Posey spoke only Creek until he was 12. After learning English, he became interested in poetry, adopting the pseudonym Chinnubbie Harjo, a character of Muskogee mythology. He is best known for the "Fus Fixico Letters"—satirical portraits of Indian mistreatment written in dialect. Tragically, he drowned crossing the North Canadian River in 1908.

15. Edward Everett Dale, *1879–1972, Norman (historian / author)*: Oklahoma's preeminent historian, Dale was born in northern Texas in 1879 and moved to Oklahoma Territory in his youth. After completing degrees from Central State in Edmond, the University of Oklahoma, and Harvard, he began in 1922 a long career as a faculty member in OU's history department. In addition to his many books on Oklahoma and western history, he had a collection of short stories, a volume of poetry, and two autobiographies published.

Dr. Edward Everett Dale, participant in the land lottery of 1901 and professor of history at the University of Oklahoma from 1914 to 1952. (Courtesy Western History Collections, University of Oklahoma Libraries)

16. Arrell Morgan Gibson, *1921–1987, Norman (historian)*: Born in Pleasanton, Kansas, Gibson earned his Ph.D. from the University of Oklahoma in 1954. Starting as a professor of government and history at Phillips University, he moved to OU, where he became a distinguished professor of history. He published widely on Indian and western history and authored a definitive history of the state: *Oklahoma: A History of Five Centuries* (1965, 1981).

17. Ralph Ellison, *1912–1992, Oklahoma City (novelist)*: Ellison grew up in Oklahoma City's vibrant African American cultural center, known as "Deep Deuce." Oklahoma's most distinguished native writer, Ellison's *Invisible Man* (1952) is widely considered one of the twentieth century's greatest works of literature.

18. John Joseph Mathews, *1895–1979, Pawhuska (author)*: Born in Pawhuska, Mathews was educated at the University of Oklahoma and Oxford. One-eighth Osage, he wrote sensitively about Indian assimilation. He is best remembered for two books, *WahKon-tah: The Osage and the White Man's Road* (a Book-of-the-Month Club selection, 1932) and *Sundown* (a novel about a character alienated from both his tribal heritage and American culture, 1934).

Oklahoma Historians

The humanities in Oklahoma have been shaped not only by creative writers but also by several generations of distinguished historians. Among their key contributions have been to establish the details of Oklahoma's patterns of settlement alongside its social and political history. Whether tracing the state's roots as a territorial borderland, a long term target of European occupation, a strategic military locale, or, most controversially, a zone of Indian colonization, historians have set out the ways in which Oklahoma's development is as unique as it is fascinating.

Marion Tuttle Rock is credited with producing the first state history in 1890. Muriel Wright's Story of Oklahoma *(1929), Grant Foreman's* History of Oklahoma *(1943), Edward E. Dale and Morris Wardell's* History of Oklahoma *(1942), Edwin McReynolds's* Oklahoma: A History of the Sooner State *(1954, rev. 1964), and Arrell Gibson's* Oklahoma: A History of Five Centuries *(1965, rev. 1981) represent a progression of general state histories.*

Among these, Wright, Dale, and Gibson join Angie Debo in deserving special mention. Wright was the granddaughter of Choctaw chief Alan Wright, best known for naming Oklahoma. As a leading Indian authority, Murial Wright edited the primary historical journal of record, Chronicles of Oklahoma, *from 1924 to 1973. Dale, considered by many to be the state's premier historian, graduated from Harvard and joined the OU History Department, serving as chairman from 1924 to 1942. In addition to numerous books on Oklahoma and the West, he penned two autobiographies:* The Cross Timbers: Memories of a North Texas Boyhood *(1966) and* The West Wind Blows *(posthumous, 1984). Debo was also a pioneering scholar of American Indians. Ahead of her time, she set out history from an Indian perspective that met with stiff resistance from readers uncomfortable with the unvarnished details of white exploitation. Her work* And Still the Waters Run *(1940), which describes the theft of Indian lands by resource-hungry settlers abetted by governmental bodies, remains a definitive historical account.*

Violet McDougal. (From the photograph collection of The Oklahoma Publishing Company)

19. Joyce Carol Thomas, *1938–, Ponca City (novelist, poet, playwright)*: A prolific and widely celebrated African American children's and adolescent novelist, Thomas began her writing career as a poet and playwright. Focusing on black children and their families, her novels consistently emphasize the centrality of community in African American experience.

20. John Hope Franklin, *1915–, Rentiesville (historian)*: Franklin, a prominent African American historian and educator, was raised in Rentiesville, a mostly black community near Tulsa, and was educated at Fiske and Harvard. His best-known book, among many, is *From Slavery to Freedom: A History of African Americans,* which has gone through seven editions. He was awarded the Presidential Medal of Freedom in 1995.

21. Tony Hillerman, *1925–, Sacred Heart (novelist)*: Born in Sacred Heart near Konawa, Hillerman is one of the country's most popular mystery novelists. He attended Oklahoma State and graduated from the University of Oklahoma, eventually settling in New Mexico. Raised among Pottawatomie and Seminole Indians, his novels—the most successful of which revolve around two members of the Navajo Tribal Police—draw on Native American culture.

22. Violet McDougal, *1893–1989, Sapulpa (poet)*: Born in Tennessee, McDougal spent her childhood in Sapulpa. She was named Oklahoma's first poet laureate by Governor J.C. Walton in 1923, a post she retained until 1931.

23. Wilson Rawls, *1913–1984, Scraper (novelist)*: Rawls grew up in extreme poverty in Scraper. Two of his heavily autobiographical novels, *Where the Red Fern Grows* (1961) and *Summer of the Monkeys* (1976), are beloved classics of adolescent literature.

24. Jim Barnes, *1933–, Summerfield (poet/author)*: A professor of comparative literature and creative writing for three decades, Barnes is an award-winning poet, translator, and autobiographer. *On Native Ground: Memoirs and Impressions,* which won an American Book Award for 1998, addresses his Oklahoma boyhood via his Choctaw and Welsh ancestry.

25. John Milton Oskison, *1874–1947, Tahlequah (author)*: Born to an English father and part Cherokee mother, Oskison was raised on the family's cattle ranch. He attended Stanford, from which he received a B.A. in 1898. A writer whose work spanned journalism, editing, and fiction, he had many short stories and six books published and also edited two books. Among his notable novels are *Wild Harvest* (1925), *Black Jack Davy* (1926), and *Brothers Three* (1935). His writings show keen insight into the challenges of maintaining a balance between the white world and tribal affiliations and heritage.

26. Daniel J. Boorstin, *1914–2004, Tulsa (historian)*: Boorstin grew up in Tulsa, graduating from Tulsa Central High School. As a distinguished historian, he served as the Librarian of Congress from 1975 to 1987. He won the 1974 Pulitzer Prize for History for *The Americans: The Democratic Experience.*

Tony Hillerman. (Copyright 1991, The Oklahoma Publishing Company)

Angie Debo. (Courtesy Western History Collections, University of Oklahoma Libraries)

27. S. E. Hinton, *1952–, Tulsa (novelist)*: Susan Eloise Hinton was a student at Will Rogers High School when she began a novel about divisions among adolescent social classes. *The Outsiders* (1969), published when she was 17, set a new standard for its honest account of teenage life. Over 8 million copies have been sold. Her subsequent books found equal acclaim, and Hinton received the American Library Association's Margaret A. Edwards Award.

28. Tulsa: Home to the celebrated literary journal *Nimrod,* edited by Tulsa poet Fran Ringold.

29. Maggie Culver Fry, *1900–1997, Vian (poet)*: Fry's grandparents traveled the Trail of Tears. She was an original enrollee in the Cherokee Nation and was poet laureate emeritus of Oklahoma at her death. A lifelong writer, she was especially interested in topics involving her heritage and Indian lore.

30. Mark Turbyfill, *1896–1966, Wynnewood (poet)*: Although Turbyfill is best known as a celebrated ballet dancer and art critic, he was also a gifted modernist poet. His magnum opus, a 32-page poem "A Marriage with Space" (published in *Poetry* in 1926), was awarded the magazine's Helen Haire Levinson Prize, for many years one of American poetry's most distinguished awards.

113. THEATRICAL AND MOVIE PEOPLE

Essay by *Guy W. Logsdon*

Oklahoma's contributions to the performing arts and entertainment in general are broad and extensive, with some personalities performing in different entertainment and communication genres. Will Rogers is our greatest example, for as a trick roper and humorist he performed in Wild West shows, on the vaudeville stage, as a radio commentator, as a public speaker, and as a movie star. Similarly, Gene Autry was a radio, recording, movie, and television singing cowboy star. William Boyd, known as Hopalong Cassidy, performed as an actor in the movies and television as well as over the radio. Not all were in the western genre, and not all were performers, for Lynn Riggs was a playwright with popular Broadway plays to his credit and Paul Harvey is a radio commentator who cannot be ignored as a popular influence in the nation's daily life. Not all who are associated with Oklahoma were native born. Some—such as Gene Autry, Jimmy Wakely, Chuck Norris, and Tom Mix—came through the state on their way to success. Many well-known stars first performed with community theaters in Oklahoma.

The training of potentially successful performers has also been of importance in many communities across the state, along with other outlets for those wanting experience. Speech and drama classes were once found in most high schools, with junior and senior plays an anticipated and popular community activity, and school talent shows provided a welcome opportunity for students who were not in organized activities. Most schools of higher education taught dramatic acting and musical presentation as well as production, and they staged shows each year; some of the graduates, such as the University of Tulsa's Rue McClanahan, went on to highly successful acting careers. James Garner (of *Maverick* and *The Rockford Files*) left high school to join the merchant marine. Later he was drafted and served in the Korean War. In 2002 he donated $500,000 to the University of Oklahoma to endow the James Garner Chair in Drama in the School of Drama.

Community playhouses were not uncommon; the Mummers Theater in Oklahoma City enjoyed a national reputation. Tulsa Little Theatre, now known as Theatre Tulsa, has produced many successful shows and is the oldest community theatre west of the Mississippi; organized in 1921, it is the seventh-oldest community theatre in the nation and has won more national first-place awards at festivals than any other theatre. At the Spot Light theatre, *The Drunkard* and other productions have provided years of entertainment and experience in Tulsa. Since the early 1960s, the Lyric Theatre in Oklahoma City has been a connection with Broadway, and the Oklahoma Community Theatre Association (based in Oklahoma City) is an organization of over twenty-five theatre groups from across the state that are nationally recognized for excellence, along with some university theatre departments.

Numerous American Indian theatrical productions and organizations, such as the Tulsa Indian Actors Workshop, are also enjoyed throughout the state. Actors, actresses, and musicians from Oklahoma who are of American Indian descent are numerous, with Will Rogers leading the way; the well-known Indian character actor Iron Eyes Cody was born in Oklahoma, as were Will Sampson and the popular contemporary actor Wes Studi. Those of African American descent such as Alfre Woodard are also seen on screens around the world.

Possibly the first "theatrical" presentations in Oklahoma were on the outdoor stages, as presented by Wild West shows, for the Millers Brothers' Wild West Show and the Pawnee Bill Wild West Show (and lesser-known shows) provided western drama and entertainment worldwide, often using Native Oklahomans in their presentations. Small privately owned Oklahoma theatrical troupes traveled throughout the Southwest, and Oklahoma also became the winter station for a few circuses and carnivals. Oklahomans have influenced the entertainment world in numerous venues as well as through outstanding individual entertainers.

It is impossible to list all of the individuals and communities that are worthy of note in the large arena of Oklahoma entertainers, both past and present. A short list of well-known contemporary movie stars alone might include Ed Harris, Leslie Nielsen, Chuck Norris, and many more. The following, however, represent the ethnic and cultural diversity and beauty of the state's population.

Will Rogers. (Courtesy Western History Collections, University of Oklahoma Libraries)

Selected Theatrical and Movie People

1. Will Rogers, *1879–1935, Oologah (actor, cowboy, humorist)*: Born William Penn Adair Rogers, he left Indian Territory at the age of 21 as a cowboy and found popularity as the "Cherokee Kid" doing rope tricks in a traveling Wild West show. His career climbed in vaudeville, earning him top billing in the Ziegfeld Follies. In

1918 he started his silent film career and was the hero in 50 silent films; he later starred in 21 Twentieth Century Fox movies, ad-libbing most of his lines. In the movies, newspaper columns, and books as well as on stage, he always portrayed himself as the common man and was extremely proud of his Cherokee heritage.

2. Vera Miles, *1929– , Boise City (actress)*: Born Vera Ralston in Boise City, she started her acting career with a beauty contest, followed by live television dramas in the early 1950s. She has appeared in over 40 films and television movies; her star quality was recognized in John Ford's *Searchers* (1956).

3. Kristin Chenoweth, *1968– , Broken Arrow (musical actress)*: After graduating from high school, Chenoweth attended Oklahoma City University, an academic institution with a reputation for musical studies. She made her way to Broadway and quickly gained international attention with her acting and singing talents. She won a Tony Award in 1999 for the Best Performance by a Featured Actress, and she has received other nominations. She has performed musically across the nation.

4. Lynn Riggs, *1899–1954, Claremore (playwright, poet)*: Born Rollie Lynn Riggs, he became a major contributor to American theatre in the Depression and post-Depression era. His Cherokee ancestry and Oklahoma background were often expressed in plays, poems, and short stories, with his most lasting influence found in his *Green Grow the Lilacs,* produced as a Broadway play in 1931and the inspiration for the musical *Oklahoma!*—the source of the state's official song, "Oklahoma!"

Tom Mix. (Courtesy Guy W. Logsdon Collection)

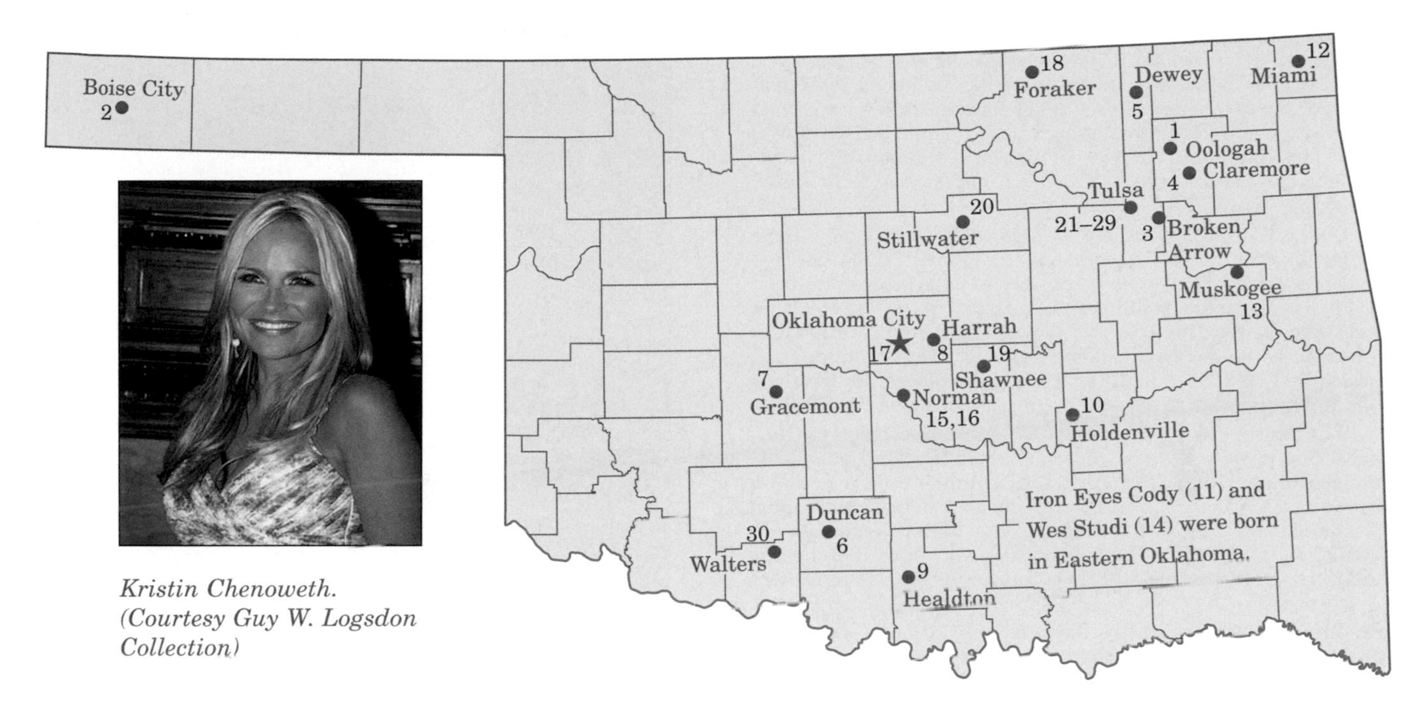

Kristin Chenoweth. (Courtesy Guy W. Logsdon Collection)

5. Tom Mix, *1880–1940, Dewey (actor)*: Born in Mix Run, Pennsylvania, he dropped out of school after the fourth grade; in 1906 he joined the Miller Brothers' 101 Ranch Wild West Show, based in Oklahoma. By 1909 he was in Hollywood, where he helped create the standard formula for westerns. He starred in over 800 films before leaving the silent screen. He returned to the movies in 1932, after the incorporation of sound, but never regained his earlier popularity; he made his last movie in 1935. Since he worked in Dewey, the Tom Mix Museum was established there to house a great Mix collection.

6. Ron Howard, *1953– , Duncan (actor, director, producer)*: Howard made his first professional appearance in Baltimore at the age of two with his parents, Rance and Jean Howard, and made several appearances in Hollywood screen roles as a child actor before becoming Opie Taylor in the television series *The Andy Griffith Show.* After playing Richie Cunningham in *Happy Days,* he returned to screen appearances and then to directing movies. He and a friend organized Imagine Films Entertainment, which is a highly successful independent production company.

7. Sunset Carson, *1922–1990, Gracemont (actor)*: Born with the name Winifred Maurice Harrison, he moved with his family to Texas when he was young; his father worked as a rodeo performer in the Tom Mix Circus. As a teenager he rodeoed before Tom Mix encouraged him to try the movies. He appeared using his birth name in a 1943 movie. Since he looked good on a horse, he made a series of movies in 1945–1946 for Republic using the name Sunset Carson, and he became eighth in popularity as a cowboy actor. In later life, though, he had few (and limited) roles.

8. Dale Robertson, *1923– , Harrah (actor)*: This farm boy became a teenage boxer to help support the family before joining the army at the beginning of World War II. He reached the rank of second lieutenant before being wounded and discharged. Hollywood agents saw a photo of him and encouraged him to go to Hollywood; he appeared in movies of different genres but became best known in westerns, including approximately 430 television shows. His own *Tales of Wells Fargo* ran for six years. He also recorded a few songs, and in the late 1990s he issued a compact disc entitled *When I Was Young.*

9. Rue McClanahan, *1934– , Healdton (actress and producer)*: Born Eddi-Rue McClanahan, she developed a love of acting and dancing at an early age. After high school she attended the University of Tulsa, graduating cum laude with majors in German and theatre arts. In the late 1950s, she went to New York City, where she landed roles in *All in the Family* and *Maude.* She has had featured roles in approximately 65 movies and television shows and has made guest appearances in at least 41 additional shows, occasionally being billed as Patti Leigh. She won awards for her role in *The Golden Girls* and has received other nominations.

10. Clu Gulager, *1928– , Holdenville (actor)*: The son of John Gulager, a Broadway actor, Clu was given the name William Martin Gulager at birth. The nickname "Clu" ("red birds") was given to him by his father for the clu clu birds nesting near their home when Clu was born. Clu grew up on his uncle's farm near Tahlequah and is reported to be a relative of Will Rogers. He started his acting career in the early 1960s and played a major role in *The Last Picture Show* (1971). In the 1980s, he worked in many horror films.

11. Iron Eyes Cody, *1907–1999, Indian Territory (actor)*: Born in Indian Territory (the site has not been documented) as Oskie Cody, he followed his father, working in Wild West shows and circuses; he first appeared in movies at the age of 12 as an extra. He was a consultant about American Indian lore and life for movies and appeared in over 40 movies. He probably was best known as the American Indian shedding a tear in the ads about the destruction of the environment.

12. Lucien Ballard, *1908–1988, Miami (cinematographer)*: Born in Miami, Ballard was of Cherokee descent and attended the University of Oklahoma. In his early 20s he joined the Paramount organization as an assistant cameraman and soon gained a reputation as a master of photography and lighting. He moved from black-and-white interior filming into outdoor color westerns such as *Nevada Smith, True Grit, The Sons of Katie Elder,* and many others.

13. Chief Thundercloud, *1899–1955, Muskogee (actor)*: Born in Muskogee with the birth name Victor Daniels, this Cherokee was not a chief; however, he is reported to have been a full-blood Indian. He became a stunt man and an extra in the late 1920s; in the 1930s, he was Tonto in two Lone Ranger series. In his film appearances he portrayed chiefs Crazy Horse, Geronimo, and Sitting Bull, and through the years, he often played leading roles in many Indian theme movies. He died in Muskogee in 1955.

14. Wes Studi, *1947– , Nofire Hollow (actor, director)*: This full-blood Cherokee—an actor, director, musician, and artist—attended Chilocco Indian School and Tulsa Junior College and also served in the Vietnam War. He became an American Indian activist and started his own Indian-oriented newspaper before appearing in his first film, *Pow Wow Highway.* Since 1989 he has had roles in 20 movies and is best known for his role in *Dances with Wolves.*

15. James Garner, *1928– , Norman (actor)*: Born James Scott Bumgarner in Norman, at the age of 16 he dropped out of high school and joined the merchant marines. During the Korean War, he was wounded and awarded two Purple Hearts; he returned to Norman but left to join his father in Los Angeles, where he worked odd jobs and attended Hollywood High. A friend offered him a nonspeaking role in a Broadway production, and with that, Garner's acting career started. By 1957 he had gained enough stature to land the starring role in the television series *Maverick,* and his popularity expanded into the *Rockford Files.* He has received numerous awards for his roles in both film and television and was honored with a 2004 Screen Actors Guild Life Achievement Award.

16. Max Weitzenhoffer, Jr., *1939– , Norman (producer)*: Born in Oklahoma City and a graduate of the University of Oklahoma's School of Drama, he gained international acclaim as an independent producer, winning awards for his productions in New York and London. His two Tony Awards were for producing *The Will Rogers Follies* and *Dracula.* He is an adjunct professor and producing director in the Weitzenhoffer Department of Musical Theatre and the Max Weitzenhoffer Theater of the University of Oklahoma. He was inducted into the Oklahoma Hall of Fame in 1994 and is a member of the University Of Oklahoma Board of Regents.

17. Lon Chaney, Jr., *1906–1973, Oklahoma City (actor)*: This noted actor was born Creighton Chaney in Oklahoma City. In 1932, when he started his screen career, he used his real name, but in 1935 he changed his name to that of his legendary actor-father, Lon Chaney. In 1940 he played the role of Lennie in *Of Mice and Men,* and he played the role of a villain or monster in approximately 150 movies, ranging from vampire and horror films to westerns.

18. Ben Johnson, Jr., *1918–1996, Foraker/Pawhuska (actor)*: The son of a world champion steer roper (and foreman of the legendary Chapman-Bernard Ranch in Osage County), Ben grew up as a genuine working cowboy. He went to Hollywood in the early 1940s wrangling horses for Howard Hughes in *The Outlaw,* and he worked as a double and stuntman as well as teaching some stars how to ride a horse. In Oklahoma he rodeoed and won the 1953 world championship in team roping; he returned to Hollywood, where John Ford started using him in the movies. Johnson won an Oscar in 1971 as best supporting actor in *The Last Picture Show.* He appeared in many movies, not just westerns.

James Garner. (Courtesy James Garner Studio)

19. Brad Pitt, *1963– , Shawnee (actor)*: In his mid-20s, he was given a role in *The Dark Side of the Sun,* and in 1991 he won acclaim as a drifter in *Thelma and Louise.* He earned an Oscar nomination for best supporting actor in *Twelve Monkeys* (1995) and has become a major Hollywood actor, appearing in more than 20 movies.

20. Art Acord (Accord), *1890–1931, Stillwater (actor)*: This silent movie star may have been born in Utah, but since he started his career in Wild West shows it is probable that Stillwater is correct. He became a stuntman in 1909 for a film company in New Jersey, and in 1914 he became Buck Parvin, a silent film hero; later the producers gave him other names. He served in France during World War I, and upon his return, he became the major silent movie cowboy for Universal Studio. The entry of sound movies along with many personal problems ended his career.

21. William Boyd, *1895–1972, Tulsa (actor, producer)*: Born in Ohio, he moved with his family in 1906 to Tulsa, where he delivered groceries as a young boy. His father was killed in 1912 working for the Tulsa Water Department; the following year, Boyd started his westward trek. He became a Cecil B. DeMille favorite in silent movies starting in 1919. In 1935 he started his Hopalong Cassidy series, eventually starring in 66 films and producing the last 12. He was the first to introduce a cowboy series to television viewers, and he also had a radio series; he often returned to Tulsa to visit friends and relatives.

22. Gary Busey, *1944– , Tulsa (actor)*: Born in Texas but reared in Oklahoma, Busey (who is of American Indian descent) worked on a ranch, had a band while a student at Oklahoma State University, worked as a drummer for such individuals as Leon Russell and Willie Nelson, and started his acting career in Tulsa as Teddy Jack Eddy (with Gailard Sartain) on the television show *Mazeppa's Uncanny Film Festival & Camp Meeting.* He has appeared in over 90 movies as well as numerous television shows, and he received an Oscar nomination for his role in *The Buddy Holly Story.*

23. Blake Edwards, *1922– , Tulsa (screenwriter, actor, producer, director)*: Born in Tulsa with the birth name William Blake McEdwards, he is the son and grandson of individuals already established in the movie business. His career started as an actor, but he became a director, screenwriter, and producer for television as well as movies. He is well known for the Pink Panther series as well as many other popular movies. He is also a painter and sculptor.

William Boyd. (Courtesy Guy W. Logsdon Collection)

Dale Robertson. (Courtesy Western History Collections, University of Oklahoma Libraries)

24. Paul Harvey, *1918–, Tulsa (radio and television commentator)*: Born Paul Aurandt in Tulsa, as a student at Central High and later while a student at the University of Tulsa, Harvey worked at KVOO radio. He worked for stations in Kansas, Oklahoma City, and St. Louis. He enlisted in the U.S. Army Air Corps during World War II. After being discharged, he moved to Chicago to work for the ABC affiliate and became known as Paul Harvey. His voice and popular "The Rest of the Story" have made him the most-listened-to commentator in the nation and have garnered many awards; he has been heard on over 1,200 radio stations, and his column appears in approximately 300 newspapers.

25. Jennifer Jones, *1919–, Tulsa (actress)*: Born Phyllis Lee Isley to parents who owned a small vaudeville touring tent show that operated out of Tulsa, she soon decided to become an actress. She and her family moved to Oklahoma City, where she graduated from high school, and then they returned to Tulsa. She went to Hollywood and worked in a few westerns using her own name before David O. Selznick changed her name to Jennifer Jones. She won an Oscar for her starring role in *Song of Bernadette* (1943) and received other nominations through her years in a wide variety of movies.

26. Mary Kay Place, *1947–, Tulsa (actress, scriptwriter, singer/songwriter)*: One of three children born to artistically talented parents, she studied media production at the University of Tulsa before using her excellent sense of humor as a scriptwriter for major sitcoms of the 1970s. She has appeared in movies and television, winning an Emmy for her supporting role as Loretta Haggars in *Mary Hartman, Mary Hartman.* Her film appearances (in over 20 movies) range from *Bound for Glory* and *The Big Chill* to *Committed.* In the 1980s, her singing and songwriting talents were issued on recordings, with some songs recorded with Willie Nelson.

Tony Randall. (Copyright 1994, The Oklahoma Publishing Company)

27. Tony Randall, *1920–2004, Tulsa (actor)*: Born Leonard Rosenberg in Tulsa, he became interested in acting after seeing touring shows that came to town. After graduating from Central High, he attended Northwestern University and then Columbia University; in 1941 he appeared in the Neighborhood Playhouse's staging of *The Circle of Chalk.* He served in the Signal Corps during World War II and has appeared (usually as an urban comedian) on stage, radio, movies, and television. His role in *Will Success Spoil Rock Hunter?* won him a nomination for a Golden Globe Award in 1957 (he received five such nominations over his career). He is perhaps best known for his role in *The Odd Couple.*

28. Jeanne Tripplehorn, *1963–, Tulsa (actress)*: A graduate of the Juilliard School of Drama in New York City, she appeared in stage shows before some television appearances. Her role in the movie *The Firm* (1993) gained her critical acclaim; she has been in approximately 15 movies.

29. Alfre Woodard, *1953–, Tulsa (actress)*: This African American actress was active in high school plays and was a cheerleader in Tulsa. She attended Boston College, studying drama, before going to Washington, D.C., to work in the Arena Stage productions. From there she went to Los Angeles in 1978 to work in movies and television productions. She earned an Academy Award nomination for her work in Cross Creek; she has won Emmys, a Golden Globe Award, and a Screen Actors Guild Award along with other awards and recognition for her acting skills in both drama and comedy.

30. Van Heflin, *1910–1971, Walters (actor)*: Born Emmett Evan Heflin, Jr., in Walters, he was the son of a dentist who moved the family to California before returning to Oklahoma City; they then moved to Norman, where Van Heflin attended the University of Oklahoma and graduated in 1932. He was recommended for an MGM movie appearance; he became known as an "actor's actor." He won an Oscar for best actor in a supporting role in *Johnny Eager* (1942). He served in the military during World War II, and afterwards he worked for different studios. His sister Frances Heflin Kaplan, born in Oklahoma City (1922), also had a lengthy career as a stage, screen, and television actress.

Van Heflin. (Courtesy Western History Collections, University of Oklahoma Libraries)

114. COUNTRY, WESTERN, AND FOLK MUSIC

Essay by *Guy W. Logsdon*

Oklahoma's heritage in the different genres of musical expression is vast in scope and influence, including songwriters, composers, instrumentalists, singers and dancers, and major musical organizations and events. This musical heritage encompasses spirituals, gospel, classical, ballet, blues, jazz, pop, country-western, bluegrass, western swing, rock, and folk—in other words, most if not all musical genres. Indeed, the first song in the English language documented to have come from Oklahoma (when it was Indian Territory) was a Negro spiritual.

The Choctaw Nation established Spencer Academy as a boys' school near Doaksville in the early 1840s and contracted with the Presbyterian Church for educational leadership. In the late 1840s, Reverend Alexander Reid was assigned to the academy as superintendent. Brett Willis, a white man, was married to a Choctaw woman and ran a huge cotton plantation in the southern Choctaw Nation along the Red River; he owned a large number of slaves. Willis loaned two of his slaves—Uncle Wallace and Aunt Minerva Willis—to Spencer Academy. Reid heard them sing as they did kitchen and cooking chores, and he learned some of their songs; after the Civil War in 1871, he taught "Swing Low, Sweet Chariot," "Steal Away to Jesus," and four other Willis spirituals to the Fisk Jubilee Singers of Fisk University in Nashville, Tennessee. They took these now-beloved spirituals around the world.

The European form of round notes for musical notation is the standard method of teaching and reading music; however, in the late 1700s in the New England region, a form of musical notation called shape note was developed to help congregations of frontier churches learn church songs. Each note in the seven-note scale had a different shape or form. The traveling shape-note singing teacher became a frontier figure, and the "Fa So La" method spread into southern states. By the 1870s it was a common activity in Indian Territory, which was the westernmost expansion of shape-note singing. African American freedpersons organized singing groups such as the New Harmony Singers, keeping the tradition going well into the latter part of the twentieth century.

Folk or traditional music is handed informally from one generation to another; it can be fiddle music, cowboy songs, out-

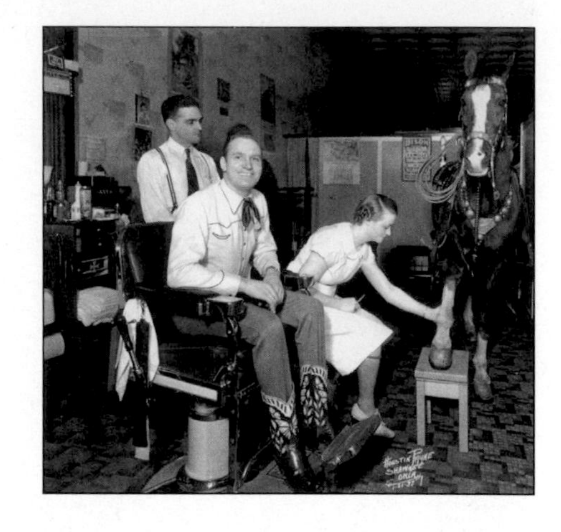

Gene Autry and his horse, Champion, get a haircut and manicure in a Shawnee barbershop, 1937. (Courtesy Western History Collections, University of Oklahoma Libraries)

Selected Musicians and Musical Influences

1. Tom Paxton, *1937– , Bristow (folksinger/songwriter)*: Born in Chicago, Paxton moved to Bristow with his family when he was 10 years old. When he was 16, he was given a guitar and learned to play it, but he wanted to become an actor. After graduating from high school he enrolled at the University of Oklahoma majoring in drama, but by the time he graduated in 1960, he had written a few songs in the folk genre. He went to New York as a participant in the folk music movement. His first album was *Ramblin' Boy*; since then, he has had many albums and CDs released with a diversity of children's songs, love songs, and protest songs. He continues to write, record songs, and entertain audiences around the world.

2. KFRU/KVOO, *1925–1990s, Bristow (country/western radio)*: In the fall of 1924, E. H. Rollestone started one of Oklahoma's earliest radio stations, KFRU (Kind Friends Remember Us), in Bristow; that 500-watt station officially went on the air in January 1925 and became well known nationally. Any Oklahoma town could spend one day, at no cost, promoting their community, so in 1926 the call letters were changed to KVOO, the Voice of Oklahoma. W. G. Skelly of the Skelly Oil Company invested in the station, and in September 1928 it was moved to Tulsa, where it became one of the most influential stations in the nation. However, in the 1990s it was purchased by a media conglomerate and the call letters were changed; it became a talk show station and no longer is a musical influence.

3. Gene Autry, *1907–1998, Chelsea (singer, songwriter, movie star)*: Born Orvon Gordon Autry in Tioga, Texas, Autry started his singing career as a five-year-old soprano in his grandfather's church choir, and he later purchased a Sears Roebuck guitar. He became the premier cowboy/western singer, and as a wise manager of money, he became one of the nation's wealthiest men. As a young man he earned a position as relief telegrapher for the Frisco railroad, with temporary work in Chelsea as well as in towns up and down the line. In Chelsea, Will Rogers encouraged him to become a professional entertainer. Autry sang over KVOO as well as to any organization that would listen. He went to Chicago and the influential WLS radio station in the late 1920s as "Oklahoma's Yodeling Cowboy," and in 1934, he was hired to appear in Ken Maynard's *In Old Santa Fe*. The concept of a singing-cowboy movie was developed for him, and the first movie in this new genre of singing westerns was Gene Autry's *Tumbling Tumbleweeds* (Republic Pictures, 1935). During the following years, he starred in at least 90 movies, recorded hundreds of songs that placed him as one of the top-selling artists in recording history, served in the U.S. Army Air Corps, starred on radio and television, purchased radio and television stations, became a major league baseball club owner, and created the Gene Autry Western Heritage Museum in Los Angeles.

4. Merle Kilgore, *1934– , Chickasha (country singer/songwriter)*: Wyatt Merle Kilgore was born in Chickasha but grew up in Shreveport, Louisiana (where, as a teenager, he knew the iconic Hank Williams). Kilgore wrote his first song at the age of 18. He became a disc jockey before becoming a performer and songwriter and taking on other music business responsibilities. As a performer he was the opening act for Hank Williams, Jr., and he was also vice president of Hank Williams, Jr., Enterprises. His songwriting credentials include such well-known songs as "Johnny Reb," "Wolverton Mountain," and "Ring of Fire," which was written with June Carter. In 2004 he was inducted into the Oklahoma Music Hall of Fame.

5. Reba McEntire, *1954– , Chockie (country music star, actress)*: Born Reba Nell McIntire, she grew up on a large ranch with a rodeo-champion father and a singing mother. she and her siblings had a family ranch singing group during those growth years. She participated in rodeo activities, both riding and singing. Red Steagall heard her at the National Finals Rodeo in Oklahoma City and became a primary backer supporting her singing career. She soon became a major female country music star with numerous well-deserved awards to her credit.

Reba McEntire. (Guy W. Logsdon Collection)

law ballads, children's songs, protest songs, union songs, or songs from a wide variety of genres. Woody Guthrie was Oklahoma's most creative native son, and he wrote many songs that have become traditional; people sing them not knowing who wrote them. The Woody Guthrie Coalition in Okemah produces the Woody Guthrie Free Festival, which attracts fans from around the world. Many other folk singer/songwriters such as Tom Paxton have their roots in Oklahoma, as do many who are currently gaining recognition, including Jimmy LaFave, Tom Skinner, the Red Dirt Rangers, Larry Sparks, and countless others.

The country music genre went through a variety of names before becoming called simply country, predominantly with the Nashville sound. In the western states, an earlier version was known as country-western music, and the eastern mountain sound of the same time was referred to as hillbilly. Most musicians who started their careers in Oklahoma had roots in western rather than in hillbilly sounds. Individuals and groups who achieved fame with such music include Gene Autry, Otto Grey and His Oklahoma Cowboy Band, Jimmy Wakely, Johnny Bond, Jack Guthrie, and numerous others. One very popular group in the late 1920s and 1930s was Jimmie Wilson and His Cat Fish String Band, mixing western and hillbilly sounds. As the industry became known as country, many Oklahomans such as Roger Miller went east instead of west. Particularly as bluegrass music emerged out of the eastern mountains in the 1960s, that genre became popular among many Oklahoma musicians. Bill Grant established a bluegrass festival in Hugo, and Byron Berline started another major bluegrass festival in Guthrie. Vince Gill emerged as a country star after starting his career in Oklahoma bluegrass.

Western swing may have been born in Texas, but it grew to maturity in Oklahoma. Bob Wills and the Playboys made Tulsa their home in 1934; it was a few years later when they added the word "Texas" in front of "Playboys." Johnnie Lee Wills and His Boys, Leon McAuliffe and the Cimarron Boys, the Alabama Boys, Al Clauser and His Oklahoma Outlaws, Hank Thompson and His Brazos Valley Boys, and Merl Lindsay and His Oklahoma Night-Riders were just a few of the western swing groups to make Oklahoma their home. Spade Cooley was born in the state but developed his style along the West Coast.

There are so many outstanding folk, country, western, and bluegrass musicians and musical groups with strong roots in Oklahoma that listing or even mentioning all of them would be impossible. A short list would have to include Merle Haggard, who is associated with Oklahoma but was born in California, and Blake Shelton, who is an up-and-coming country star from Ada.

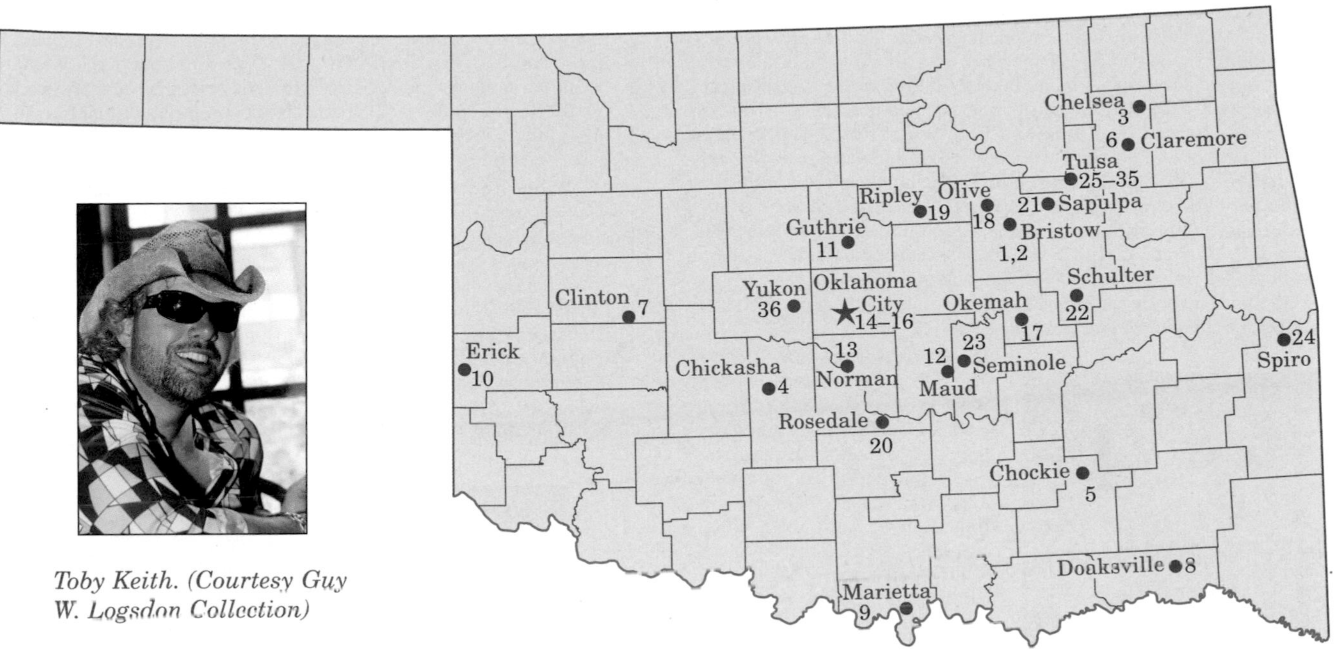

Toby Keith. (Courtesy Guy W. Logsdon Collection)

6. Tommy Allsup, *1931– , Claremore (guitarist)*: Born Tommy Douglas Allsup near Owasso, he was the twelfth of thirteen children in a musical family who were of Cherokee descent. The family moved to Claremore when he was young. In 1947 as a sophomore in high school, Tommy and friends organized the Oklahoma Swing Billies; later he worked with Art Davis, Johnnie Lee Wills, and numerous Oklahoma-based groups, and he fronted his own band in the Southern Club in Lawton. In 1958 Buddy Holly asked Tommy to record with him; Allsup was the first to play a guitar solo on a Holly recording. He toured with Holly and was the person who had flipped the coin with Richie Valens for the seat on Holly's plane on the fateful day that it crashed; he lost, but won. Tommy became a country music producer and promoter and recording artist, and he leads the current Texas Playboys. He was inducted into the Oklahoma Music Hall of Fame in 2005.

7. Toby Keith, *1961– , Clinton (country singer/songwriter)*: Born in Clinton as Toby Keith Covel, he started playing the guitar at eight years of age. He enjoyed playing football, and his height (6′4″) allowed him to play semipro football in Oklahoma City. He also participated in rodeos and worked in the oil fields before becoming an award-winning country music star. In 1984 he became the lead singer in the Easy Money Band, an Oklahoma City group. His singing earned him a recording contract in Nashville. He released his first album, *Toby Keith,* in 1993 on the Mercury label and went platinum. *Billboard Magazine* named him Top New Country Artist, and over the years, he has received numerous other awards, including induction into the Oklahoma Music Hall of Fame in 2005.

8. Uncle Wallace and Aunt Minerva Willis, *active in the 1830s–1840s, Doaksville (spirituals)*: The Civil War emancipated this African American slave couple. The spirituals learned from them and spread across the world include "Swing Low, Sweet Chariot," "Steal Away to Jesus," and "I'm A-Rollin', I'm A-Rollin'. They are buried in an African American graveyard at Doaksville, near Hugo.

9. Johnny Bond, *1915–1978, Enville/Marietta (western singer/songwriter, author)*: Born in Enville as Cyrus Whitfield Bond, he moved with his family to nearby Marietta, where he attended school. He moved to Oklahoma City in 1934, and in 1937, he, Jimmy Wakely, and Scotty Harrell he started The Bell Boys trio. When he took the name "Johnny" is speculation. He composed his western classic, "Cimarron," while the trio lived in the Oklahoma City YMCA. In 1940 the trio joined Gene Autry in Hollywood; there Johnny earned a reputation for humor and musical skills by working in 38 movies and other categories of entertainment. He recorded as Johnny Bond and His Red River Valley Boys, wrote over 500 songs, and authored a biography of Tex Ritter and his own autobiography.

10. Roger Miller, *1936–1992, Erick (multitalented country musician and songwriter)*: Born Roger Dean Miller in Fort Worth, Texas, at the age of three he was taken to Erick to live with an uncle. In time, he wanted a life different from farming; he turned to music. He traveled across Oklahoma and Texas as a wandering musician, singing and playing the guitar and fiddle. He was drafted during the Korean War, and after being discharged, he went to Nashville and slowly worked his way up as a songwriter and recording artist. He won numerous Grammys and a Tony Award. His hits include "Dang Me," "King of the Road," and "Me and Bobbie McGee." In 2004 he was inducted into the Oklahoma Music Hall of Fame.

Roger Miller. (Courtesy Guy W. Logsdon Collection)

11. Byron Berline, *1944– , Guthrie (bluegrass and swing fiddler)*: Born in Caldwell, Kansas, to musical parents, Berline was playing the fiddle by the age of five. His father was an old-time fiddler who taught him to play, and he won his first fiddling contest at the age of ten. He played football for the University of Oklahoma, where he and friends formed the Cleveland County Ramblers. He began to play bluegrass and worked with major bands before military service in 1967; after his discharge in 1969, he settled in California, where he worked with major bluegrass bands and became a successful session musician, playing jazz, pop, blues, and rock as well as traditional fiddling. In the 1990s, he returned to Oklahoma and established a music store in Guthrie, where he promotes the annual Oklahoma International Bluegrass Festival. In 1999 he was inducted into the Oklahoma Music Hall of Fame.

Wanda Jackson. (Courtesy Guy W. Logsdon Collection)

12. Wanda Jackson, *1937– , Maud (country/rockabilly star)*: Born in Maud, Wanda Lavonne Jackson started her singing career in Oklahoma City, starting her radio singing and television appearances before her graduation from high school in 1955. She worked with a variety of musicians and singers; her first recording was in 1954. She hired a mixed-race band, for she moved back and forth between country and rock & roll—thus, she became known as a rockabilly star. She later turned primarily to religious musical expression. In 2000 she was inducted into the Oklahoma Music Hall of Fame.

13. Vince Gill, *1957–, Norman (country music star)*: Born in Norman, Vincent Grant Gill learned from his father how to play the banjo, and he soon became an avid bluegrass musician, also mastering the guitar and other stringed instruments. He worked in a variety of bands, such as Pure Prairie League, within a style often referred to as "new grass." By the mid-1980s, he had a few releases of his own while he worked as a session musician with numerous country stars. His first album in 1991 sold one million copies, and from there, his mellow tenor voice and musical skills have kept him at the top of the charts in popularity. In 1999 he was inducted into the Oklahoma Music Hall of Fame.

14. Merl Lindsay, *1915–1965, Oklahoma City (western swing bandleader)*: Born Merle Lindsay Salathiel in Oklahoma City, he started his career in 1936 in the family-owned dance hall, Salathiel's Barn. Two years later, he formed his own band, Merle Salathiel and the Barnyard Boys; in 1941 they moved to California as the Oklahoma Night-Riders. He decided to drop Salathiel and changed his professional name to Merl Lindsay and His Oklahoma Night-Riders. They returned to Oklahoma City in 1947, started a noonday broadcast over WKY, and eventually developed a television show. When the family dance hall burned, he and the Night-Riders worked a variety of dance halls until he opened his own ballroom. In 1957 Red Foley featured them on his *Ozark Jubilee* television show and hired them as the regular show band, at which point they changed their name to the Ozark Jubilee Band.

15. Conway Twitty, *1933–1993, Oklahoma City (songwriter, rockabilly star)*: Born Harold Lloyd Jenkins in Friars Point, Mississippi, he eventually found his success in Oklahoma; however, his early radio appearance was in Arkansas when he was 12. He served in the military, and later changed his name to reflect Conway, Arkansas, and Twitty, Texas. Through the influence of rock music, he became a male rockabilly star and songwriter, with songs such as "Hello Darlin'" and "Tight Fittin' Jeans" as well as numerous other hits. During those formative years, he made Oklahoma City his home base, performing there with his band regularly.

16. Wiley and Gene, *1911–1966 and 1914–1984, Oklahoma City (country duet)*: In the late 1940s and 1950s, "Wiley and Gene" were almost household words throughout most of Oklahoma, for they had very popular early-morning radio shows and a noonday television show emanating from Oklahoma City. Wiley Walker was born in Laurel Hill, Florida, and Gene Sullivan was born in Carbon Hill, Alabama. Wiley was a fiddler, and Gene played the guitar and was the humorist. They met while performing in Louisiana and started singing as a duet; they moved to Oklahoma City in 1940, and soon afterwards, their efforts produced a country music classic, "When My Blue Moon Turns to Gold Again."

Woody Guthrie. (Courtesy Guy W. Logsdon Collection)

17. Woody Guthrie, *1912–1967, Okemah (folk singer/songwriter, author)*: Born in Okemah as Woodrow Wilson Guthrie on July 4, 1912, Woody Guthrie became Oklahoma's best-known, most influential, and most creative native son. His creative efforts included approximately 3,000 songs and poems written by him, two autobiographical novels, numerous essays and letters, over 500 illustrations, and over 300 recorded songs—both his own and traditional folk songs. His "This Land Is Your Land" remains one of the most widely sung songs in the nation and around the world. He played the guitar, fiddle, mandolin, harmonica, and bass fiddle, and he accomplished most of this in approximately 17 years of creativity before Huntington's disease defeated him. After 15 years of hospitalization, Woody died on October 3, 1967. In 1997 he was inducted into the Oklahoma Music Hall of Fame.

18. Jack Guthrie, *1915–1948, Olive (western singer)*: Born Leon Jerry Guthrie in Olive, Jack is best known as the recording artist who introduced the classic western song and Oklahoma's official folk song, "Oklahoma Hills." (However, his cousin and good friend Woody Guthrie composed it in 1937.) Jack recorded it for Capitol Records; it became a number-one hit in 1945. The copyright is registered in Jack's and Woody's names, and Jack played western dances up and down the West Coast. He died, as his idol Jimmie Rodgers died, from tuberculosis on January 15, 1948.

19. Otto Gray and the Oklahoma Cowboys, *active 1921–1935, Ripley (cowboy band)*: This outstanding cowboy entertainment troupe was the most popular country/western stage act in the nation in the late 1920s and early 1930s. They were the first touring cowboy/western stage show featuring genuine cowboy songs, and they were probably the first touring group to use large, custom-made Cadillacs for transportation. Originally called the Billy McGinty Cowboy Band (in Ripley), they were one of the first groups to perform on KFRU in Bristow. As their popularity expanded, they brought in Otto Gray as their manager and announcer; he and his wife were trick ropers, and he had the additional skills of being a promoter and manager. He made "Otto Gray and His Oklahoma Cowboy Band" a hot radio/stage act, and eventually they worked their way to New York City and the Roxy Theatre, and playing the show circuits such as Loew, RKO, and Fox. More than 100 radio stations carried their shows. Otto Gray became the first country/western performer to have his portrait on the front cover of *Billboard Magazine*. In 1935, they first reduced their activities and then disbanded.

20. Jimmy Wakely, *1914–1982, Rosedale (western movie, radio, and recording star)*: Born James Clarence Wakely near Mineola, Arkansas, he moved with his family to southeastern Oklahoma when he was three; later they moved to Rosedale. He learned to play the guitar and piano, skills that in 1937 landed him a job with Merl Lindsay and later in the Bell Trio on WKY in Oklahoma City. In 1940 Gene Autry heard them in a show in Okemah and took them to Hollywood as members of his CBS Melody Ranch Show. Wakely was one of the few saddle serenaders in the 1940s and 1950s to enjoy success in the movies, on the stage, over the radio, and on phonograph records.

21. Jimmy Wilson and His Cat Fish String Band, *1920–1938, Sapulpa (humorist, string band musician and bandleader)*: In 1920 a few Rotarians in Sapulpa organized a band to entertain and raise money for charitable purposes; they were led by local businessman, humorist, and Rotarian Jimmy Wilson. When KFRU (Bristow) went on the air, this band became known across the country; they always proudly claimed to be the first to use sound effects over the airwaves, but most important, they were the first to use the airwaves to raise money for charity. In 1929 a mining disaster killed some 60 miners near McAlester, and this band went on KVOO and broadcast for 12 hours, raising $40,000 for the widows and children.

Jimmy Wilson and his Cat Fish String Band. (Courtesy Guy W. Logsdon Collection)

22. Willis Brothers, *1915–1995, Schulter (country music stars)*: Only the youngest, Vic (John V.), was born in Schulter, but he and his brothers Guy and Skeeter grew up in Schulter and became known on the Grand Ole Opry as the Oklahoma Wranglers; years later they became the Willis Brothers. Among them they played the fiddle, guitar, and accordion from a very young age, and they were the first to accompany Hank Williams on a recording. They traveled with Eddie Arnold and others and recorded for a variety of labels.

23. Stoney Edwards, *1929–1997, Seminole (country singer)*: Born near Seminole and given the name Frenchy Edwards, this African American experienced rough years during the Great Depression. He did not go to school and could not read or write, but he did listen to Bob Wills and the Grand Ole Opry on the radio. He taught himself how to play the guitar and started singing country songs. After moving to California as a common laborer in the early 1950s, Stoney was discovered as a country singer and songwriter, and he became a popular recording artist—exhibiting that African Americans could participate in and contribute to country music.

24. Albert Brumley, *1905–1977, near Spiro (gospel songwriter and publisher)*: Albert Edward Brumley, who became known as the dean of gospel songwriters, was born the son of tenant farmers near Spiro in what was then the Choctaw Nation. He grew up in the shape-note tradition. Brumley wrote popular country gospel songs such as "Turn Your Radio On" and "I'll Fly Away," along with hundreds of other gospel songs, many of them for the Stamps-Baxter organization. He also operated a publishing firm in Powell, Missouri. Since many of his well-known songs were written during the Great Depression, in a study of gospel music the Smithsonian Institution wrote that he was the "greatest white gospel songwriter before World War II." He has been honored in many halls of fame, including the Oklahoma Music Hall of Fame (inducted in 1998).

25. Alabama Boys, *active 1935–1942, Tulsa (western swing band)*: Don Ivey was an early member of the Texas Playboys in Tulsa, but Bob Wills fired him. It was 1935, and Ivey decided to organize a band to compete with Wills. He hired some excellent musicians, such as Eldon Shamblin, and began radio broadcasting and playing dances in the Playmore Ballroom. Ivey could not get along with the band members, though; he left the band, and Allen Franklin became the manager. They were successfully competing with Wills when Franklin left the group. An inexperienced grocery man, David T. Edwards, took over their promotion and management, and many of the members left to become Texas Playboys and, later, major members of Johnnie Lee's band. They broadcast over KTUL and recorded a few sides for Decca Records, but they never regained their popularity. In 1942, the Alabama Boys disbanded.

Roy Clark. (Courtesy Guy W. Logsdon Collection)

26. Roy Clark, *1933– , Tulsa (country music star, actor, comedian)*: Roy Linwood Clark often credits Jim Halsey as the man who made him a successful star in country music. Born Roy Linwood Clark in Meherrin, Virginia, he grew up in a variety of eastern states, for his father moved often; his parents were musical, so he grew up learning to master a variety of instruments. He started his professional career as a teenager and worked in many different bands; in 1960 Wanda Jackson recruited him to work with her. In 1962 Jim Halsey became his agent, and Clark became an all-around entertainer: singer, instrumentalist on a variety of instruments, comedian, and actor. As his popularity increased, he moved to Tulsa; in 2000 he was inducted into the Oklahoma Music Hall of Fame.

27. Al Clauser and the Oklahoma Outlaws, *1911–1989, Tulsa (western swing band)*: Henry Alfred "Al" Clauser started his musical career in Illinois while in high school. His trio grew larger with musicians who played two or more instruments and could play with a jazz sound. He chose the name "Oklahoma Outlaws," for they needed a western name. In 1942 they moved to Tulsa, where they broadcasted daily over station KTUL and introduced 12-year-old Clara Ann Fowler, who became known professionally as Patti Page. They disbanded in the early 1920s.

28. The Collins Kids, *1950s–1960s, Tulsa (country music duo)*: This family duo no longer performs together, but in the mid-1950s and 1960s, they were a very popular duo across the West Coast even though their recordings were only marginally successful. Lawrencine "Lorrie" May Collins was born in Tulsa on May 7, 1942, and her brother, Lawrence "Larry" Albert Collins, was born October 4, 1942. Leon McAuliffe was hosting a talent show in Tulsa when Lorrie was eight years old; she won the contest, and McAuliffe recommended that her take her to California where opportunities were greater. Larry developed his guitar and singing skills, and their sound set early patterns for rockabilly music.

29. Joe Diffee, *1958– , Tulsa (country singer)*: Born Joe Logan Diffee in Tulsa, he was singing harmony at an early age, and his father taught him to play guitar when he was eight. He sang in a gospel group on weekends, and he later turned to bluegrass. In the mid-1980s, the oil industry went downhill; he lost his weekday job, so he moved to Nashville and became a popular demonstration record singer. In 1990 his first solo recording was released and became the #1 recording in the charts; other recordings followed with great success. In 2002 Diffie was inducted into the Oklahoma Music Hall of Fame.

30. Ronnie Dunn, *1953– , Tulsa (half of country music duo)*: Ronnie Gene Dunn was born in Coleman, Texas. After studying theology in Texas, he moved with his parents to Tulsa, where he soon was fronting a band at a popular nightclub. He recorded for Churchill Records, which was owned by Jim Halsey in Tulsa. He won a Marlboro country music talent contest and toured with the Marlboro Country Music Tour. He joined with Kix Brooks to form the duo Brooks and Dunn, with Dunn singing most of the lead vocals. They have gained great popularity and have been given many awards. In 2003 he was inducted into the Oklahoma Music Hall of Fame.

31. Jim Halsey, *1930– , Tulsa (country music manager/promoter)*: Born in Independence, Kansas, James Albert Halsey became a major influence in the country music industry; he started promoting shows as a teenager in his hometown. In 1951 he became Hank Thompson's agent and moved his Halsey Agency to Tulsa in the 1960s. He added Roy Clark, the Oak Ridge Boys, Merle Haggard, Minnie Pearl, Mel Tillis, and many more to his stable of stars through the years. He was a pioneer in booking country music in Las Vegas, on television, and in foreign countries. In the late 1980s, he moved his agency to Nashville, where he merged it with the William Morris Agency. He moved back to Oklahoma in the 1990s and taught the music business in Oklahoma City and Tulsa. In 2000 he was inducted into the Oklahoma Music Hall of Fame.

32. Leon McAuliffe, *1917–1988, Tulsa (western swing artist)*: William Leon McAuliffe was born in Houston, Texas. When Bob Wills on the 1936 recording of "Steel Guitar Rag" said, "Take it away, Leon," he started a saying that is still heard—and created a star. Leon became a major western swing bandleader as well as a steel guitar pioneer. In 1935 at the age of 18, he was hired by Bob Wills as a member of the Playboys in Tulsa. He joined the navy during World War II, and following his discharge, he organized his own western swing band in Tulsa. He competed with Johnnie Lee Wills and Cain's Ballroom for dance popularity. He became a licensed pilot and the owner of radio station KAMO in Rogers, Arkansas, before disbanding in 1968. He led the Original Texas Playboys in the 1970s and 1980s; he died in Tulsa.

33. Hank Thompson, *1925– , Tulsa (western swing artist)*: Born Henry William Thompson in Waco, Texas, he is the only western artist to perform and record over a seven-decade period; as a giant in western swing, he also helped transform music into an industry. As a teenager, he had his own radio show. In 1943 he signed up for service in the navy, and after he was discharged, he returned to Waco and his own radio show. He organized his western swing band, naming them the Brazos Valley Boys. After recording some regional hits, in 1948 he was signed to a recording contract with Capitol Records and proceeded to record innumerable hits. In 1952 he moved his band to Oklahoma City; a few years later, he moved to Tulsa and worked out of there for over 30 years. He became the first to take live western swing into foreign countries; he was the first country/western artist to record in high fidelity and in stereo. He also became the first to record a live album: *Live at the Golden Nugget*. In the 1990s, he returned to Texas, and in 2002, he was inducted into the Oklahoma Music Hall of Fame.

34. Bob Wills, *1905–1975, Tulsa (western swing legend)*: Born James Robert (Jim Rob) Wills in Limestone County, Texas, in a family of fiddlers, he became the "Daddy of Western Swing." He learned to play the fiddle as a youngster, and in the early 1930s, he and two others formed the original Light Crust Doughboys. Wills left and organized his own band and in early 1934 started playing over KVOO (Tulsa). Wills was buried in Tulsa, and in 2001 Bob Wills and the Texas Playboys were inducted into the Oklahoma Music Hall of Fame.

Bob Wills. (Courtesy Guy W. Logsdon Collection)

35. Johnnie Lee Wills, *1912–1984, Tulsa (western swing bandleader)*: Born in Hall County, Texas, Johnnie Lee was the second of four sons born to John and Emma Wills, who were tenant cotton farmers. As a tenor banjo player he was with his brother Bob when the band moved to Tulsa, and later Bob told him to form his own band and to take over the KVOO shows, Cain's Ballroom dances, and the Annual Rodeo. He made Tulsa his home for 50 years.

36. Garth Brooks, *1962– , Yukon (country music star)*: Born Troyal "Garth" Brooks in Luba, Oklahoma, he moved with the family to Yukon when he was young. As a student at Oklahoma State University, he started playing clubs around the Stillwater area. His trip to Nashville in 1985 was a disappointment, but he returned in 1987. His first recording was only marginally successful, but in 1990 after the release of "The Dance," his popularity expanded greatly. By 1991 three of his albums had sold 30 million copies; his albums have sold more than those of any other musician in musical history. He now lives near Owasso.

115. CLASSICAL AND POPULAR MUSIC AND DANCE

Essay by *Guy W. Logsdon*

Grouping classical, popular, jazz, and blues styles together may seem an awkward mix, but Oklahoma is the home of a multitude of musical entertainers and annual events whose musical style is more formal than that of the folk-derived country, western, and bluegrass. In classical music, Bartlesville has the annual OK Mozart musical fest, attracting performers and visitors from around the world. Five American Indian ballerinas toured internationally, representing the diversity of Oklahoma's population and musical heritage. The Tulsa Ballet Theatre was organized in the 1950s and has gained worldwide respect, as has Ballet Oklahoma in Oklahoma City.

Opera likewise has enjoyed Oklahoma's contributions, featuring such vocalists as Joseph Benton, who sang opera in Europe under the name Guiseppe Bentonelli and ended his career as a voice teacher at the University of Oklahoma. In 1906 Tulsa had its "Grand Opera House," where numerous international opera stars performed, but during the Great Depression and World War II, performances there were ended. In 1948 the Tulsa Opera Club brought opera back to Tulsa, which remains a national opera venue. The Oklahoma City Philharmonic Orchestra has had over seventy-five years of successful and popular concerts and musical supportive roles. As but a single example of popular music, Broadway musicals on tour have for many years enjoyed a strong presence in the theatre of many Oklahomans.

Oklahoma pays tribute to many of its musical performers through the Oklahoma Music Hall of Fame in Muskogee and the Oklahoma Jazz Hall of Fame in Tulsa; Guthrie has a Four String Banjo Museum that exhibits an outstanding collection of four-string banjos—once played in minstrel shows and banjo orchestras, the popular music of long-ago days. Jazz and blues festivals are held across the state, with the Dusk Til Dawn Blues Festival in Rentiesville (produced by D. C. and Selby Minner) attracting musicians and fans from across the nation.

Flight of Spirit *by Mike Larsen. (Courtesy Oklahoma Arts Council)*

Selected Classical Musicians and Dancers

The Five Native American Ballerinas

1. Rosella Hightower, *1920– , Durwood (ballerina)*: Born in southern Oklahoma, this star ballerina of Choctaw heritage was five when the family moved to Kansas City; it was there a few years later when she saw her first ballet and decided that she wanted to be a ballerina. After a few years of training, in 1938, at the age of 18 she made her debut with Ballet Russe de Monte Carlo. She became an international star, receiving numerous honors. In 1962 she reduced her appearances to establish a ballet school in Cannes, France.

2. Moscelyne Larkin, *1926– , Miami (ballerina)*: This ballerina of Shawnee and Peoria heritage along with Russian ancestors was born in Miami. She started ballet training at an early age and in 1941 debuted with the Colonel W. De Basil's Original Ballet Russe; at the age of 19 she married Roman Jasinsky, a Perier danseur. In 1948 they joined the Ballet Russe de Monte Carlo, and after worldwide performances, she and her husband decided to settle in Tulsa, where they helped form the Tulsa Ballet Theatre. She also produced three popular Oklahoma Indian Ballerina festivals.

3. Maria Tallchief, *1925– , Fairfax (prima ballerina)*: Born as Elizabeth Marie Tall Chief, this ballerina of Osage descent started dancing as a child, but traditional Osage dance was never a part of her life. In Fairfax she studied piano and dance and became a promising student at both. For more professional training, her parents moved Marie and her sister, Marjorie, to California to study ballet. She joined the Ballet Russe de Monte Carlo in 1942 and later joined other ballet companies before becoming one of America's greatest ballerinas. She retired in 1965.

4. Marjorie Tallchief, *1927– , Fairfax (ballerina)*: Marjorie had the same early life experiences as her older sister, Marie; while she was in Fairfax, dancing became her favorite creative outlet. In California she studied with the same individuals, but she started her career with the American Ballet Theatre. In 1946 she became a member of the Ballet Russe de Monte Carlo and joined Maria. She became a popular premier ballerina in France and performed with other ballet organizations; she retired in 1966. She helped found the Dallas Civic Ballet Academy and taught there. In 1980 she joined Maria in Chicago to assist in the founding of the Chicago City Ballet.

5. Yvonne Chouteau, *1929– , Vinita (ballerina)*: Myra Yvonne Chouteau was born in Fort Worth, Texas, much to her Cherokee/Shawnee relatives' disappointment, but she was soon back in Vinita. Her early exposure to dance was the traditional dances of American Indians, and after the family moved to Oklahoma City, she gained much recognition as a young traditional dancer and also decided that she wanted to be a ballerina. At the age of 12, her parents took her to New York, where she soon earned recognition as a ballet student. In 1943 she debuted with the Ballet Russe de Monte Carlo. After years of fame as a ballerina, she returned to Oklahoma City and helped create the Ballet Oklahoma organization as well as a dance program at the University of Oklahoma.

Patti Page. (Courtesy Guy W. Logsdon Collection)

Selected Musicians and Composers

6. Patti Page, *1927– , Claremore (pop singer)*: Clara Anne Fowler, the daughter of a railroad worker, was born in Claremore; at an early age, her vocal skills became obvious. In nearby Tulsa, there was a radio show featuring Al Clauser and the Oklahoma Outlaws, sponsored by the Page Milk Company; the female singer was named Patti Page. When they needed a new Patti Page, as a teenager Clara Anne Fowler auditioned for the role. She was a hit and recorded her first song in Tulsa; when she left to pursue her singing career, she kept the name Patti Page and embarked on a career in music and motion pictures spanning more than 50 years. She accumulated 15 gold records while selling over 100 million records, and she was the most popular female singer in the 1950s, recording 130 albums in a variety of genres spanning pop, jazz, country, and religious. Her performance at Carnegie Hall won her a Grammy Award in 1999. She was a 1992 recipient of the Living Legacy Award, celebrating women for their contributions to humanity, and she was a 1997 inductee into the Oklahoma Music Hall of Fame.

Kay Starr. (Courtesy Guy W. Logsdon Collection)

7. Kay Starr, *1922– , Dougherty (pop singer)*: Born in Dougherty as Katherine LaVerne Starks, she moved with her family to Dallas, where her full-blood Iroquois father could find work. They had chickens, and each afternoon after school she would sing to the chickens. She won a radio talent show so many times that they gave her time for her own show, and then the family moved to Memphis. Again she earned a radio show, being dubbed the "Kid"; however, her fan mail had so many misspellings that she took the name Kay Starr. Legendary jazz musician Joe Venuti needed a female singer and hired her at the age of 15, but she could only work in the summers while school was out. After graduating from high school, she continued to rise in popularity and became one of the all-time most popular female singers, with songs including "Bonaparte's Retreat" and "Wheel of Fortune." She was a 2002 inductee into the Oklahoma Music Hall of Fame.

8. Leona Mitchell, *1948– , Enid (opera singer)*: This African American was born in Enid as the 10th of 15 siblings. Her father was the minister of the Antioch Baptist Church, where she started singing at an early age. After high school, she studied music with scholarship support at Oklahoma City University, graduating in 1971; in the following years, she received awards to continue her music studies and debuted in San Francisco in 1973. Within two years, she was performing in the Metropolitan Opera Company in New York City, and from there her popularity as a lyric soprano has taken her to numerous opera venues, concerts, and recitals around the world. She was inducted into the Oklahoma Music Hall of Fame in 2001.

Leona Mitchell. (Courtesy Guy W. Logsdon Collection)

9. Lee Wiley, *1915–1975, Fort Gibson (jazz singer)*: This Oklahoman, born in Fort Gibson, became a highly respected singer with a "little girl sound" and a "great respect for lyrics." She left home as a teenager to sing with the Leo Reisman band and later the Paul Whiteman orchestra. She cowrote songs such as "Got the South in My Soul" and through the years recorded with many popular small jazz bands. She recorded into the 1960s and was considered by musicians of her time to be one of the greatest jazz singers. She died in New York City.

10. Flash Terry, *1935–2004, Inola / Tulsa (blues musician)*: Flash Terry was born in Inola and moved to Tulsa in the 1950s so that he could work and play music. He was born into a musical family and by 1958 made music his career. For a few years he toured with popular bands and recorded for different labels. When he returned to Tulsa, he worked for the Tulsa Transit Authority and became known as the "Bus Driver Bluesman." He organized the Flash Terry and the Uptown Blues Band. In 1988 Governor Henry Bellmon honored them with the state of excellence award, and the state senate designated them "Oklahoma's Favorite Blues Band." In 1994 Terry was inducted into the Oklahoma Jazz Hall of Fame and in 2003 into the Oklahoma Music Hall of Fame.

11. Ridge Bond, *1922–1997, McAlester (Broadway performer)*: Ridge Bond was called "the best cowhand in 17 counties," for he played the role of Curly in the Broadway show *Oklahoma!* He is reported to have appeared in over 2,600 presentations not only on Broadway but also in Germany and Canada. He played roles in other musicals such as *Kiss Me Kate* and *Annie Get Your Gun.* He attended the University of Tulsa, where he appeared in plays such as *Green Grow the Lilacs,* and it has been stated that he sang "Oklahoma" to the legislature to encourage them to adopt it as the state song.

12. Ralph Blane, *1914–1995, Broken Arrow (songwriter)*: Born in Broken Arrow with the name Ralph Uriah Hunsecker, he attended school in Broken Arrow and Tulsa and later studied music in New York City, where he became Ralph Blane. He teamed with Harry Warren and wrote "Buckle Down, Winsocki"; he composed for Broadway musicals and also for Hollywood musicals such as *Meet Me in St. Louis* that introduced songs he co-composed, including "The Trolley Song," "Meet Me in St. Louis," and "Have Yourself a Merry Little Christmas." He retired to Broken Arrow.

Buckle Down, Winosocki

Meet Me in St. Louis

Have Yourself a Merry Little Christmas

Ralph Blane. (Copyright 1974, The Oklahoma Publishing Company)

13. Don Byas, *1912–1972, Muskogee (jazz saxophonist)*: Carlos Wesley Byas was born in Muskogee. He was a black tenor saxophone player who had an influence on swing music and on bebop music. He worked with many legendary musicians and famous bands; his improvisation skills and phrasing made him popular among musicians.

14. Barney Kessel, *1923–2004, Muskogee (jazz guitarist, songwriter, music director)*: This legendary guitarist was born in Muskogee; he taught himself to play the guitar by listening to radio broadcasts of western swing musicians. At the age of 14, he left school and worked as a young white guitar player in an all-black band playing black clubs in Oklahoma. He was influenced by the guitar style of black guitarist Charlie Christian, and after they met, Christian encouraged him to move to California, where Kessel joined the Chico Marx Orchestra. Through the years, his reputation expanded around the world; he recorded over 60 albums, wrote songs, played on movie sound tracks, was music director for television shows, wrote music columns, and influenced many famous musicians. He is a member of the Jazz Hall of Fame and a 1999 Oklahoma Music Hall of Fame inductee.

15. Claude Williams, *1908–2004, Muskogee (jazz fiddler)*: Born in Muskogee, Claude "Fiddler" Williams could play four instruments at a very young age; he was approximately ten years old when he heard swing fiddling and added the fiddle to his skills. He worked with different groups in Muskogee until he moved to Kansas City in 1928. Through the years he worked in many different bands (including playing guitar in the Count Basie Orchestra), but the fiddle became his trademark. In 1982 he was a member of the Oklahoma Diamond Jubilee representatives, who entertained at the Smithsonian Folklife Festival. He was a 1989 inductee into the Oklahoma Jazz Hall of Fame and a 1997 inductee into the Oklahoma Music Hall of Fame.

16. Pinky Tomlin, *1907– , Durant (songwriter)*: Born in Arkansas as Truman Virgil Tomlin, he soon became known as Pinky because of his light red hair. In 1913 his family moved to Durant, where he quickly became interested in music. He worked his way through the University of Oklahoma before heading to Hollywood; there he sold his first song, "The Object of My Affection." He became a writer and singer of songs in Hollywood films; his numerous songs were varied, including "The Love Bug Will Bite You If You Don't Watch Out" and "In Ole Oklahoma." He grew tired of traveling and turned to the oil industry as the owner and operator of the Pinky Tomlin Oil Properties.

The Object of My Affection

In Ole Oklahoma

The Love Bug Will Bite You If You Don't Watch Out

Pinky Tomlin. (Courtesy Guy W. Logsdon Collection)

17. Jay McShann, *1916– , Muskogee (jazz pianist)*: Born in Muskogee, James Colombus McShann as a young child taught himself to play the piano. He worked with Don Byas in the Muskogee area before attending the Tuskegee Institute, and in 1936 he moved to Kansas City because "liquor hunting sheriffs pushed" him out of Oklahoma. Through the years he worked with many big bands before organizing his own band and becoming known as Jay "Hootie" McShann; in the 1950s in Kansas City, he studied music at the University of Missouri campus. He recorded for numerous companies and in 1996 received the Rhythm and Blues Foundation's Pioneer Award.

18. Charlie Christian, *1916–1942, Oklahoma City (jazz guitarist)*: One of the all-time most influential guitarists, Charles "Charlie" Henry Christian was born into a musical family in Bonham, Texas, but they soon moved to Oklahoma City, where he grew to maturity. Zelia Breaux, a music teacher at Douglas High School who encouraged many young black musicians in Oklahoma City, tried to make him into a horn player, but the guitar held him captive. His older brothers told him that if he wanted to be a professional he would have to learn to "read them dots." At the age of 19, in 1939 he joined the Benny Goodman organization and became the first to record the electric guitar as a solo/lead instrument in big bands. In Harlem jam sessions, he was a participant in what became known as bebop music.

19. Jimmy Rushing, *1903–1972, Oklahoma City (jazz/blues singer)*: This short and wide singer became known in the music world as "Mr. Five by Five"; he was born into a musical family as James Andrew Rushing in Oklahoma City. He trained on the piano and violin in his youth, but his dynamic voice led him into singing. He worked in the Blue Devils and later in the Bennie Moten Band. He stayed with Count Basie when Moten died in 1935 and continued with Basie until 1950. Later he sang with well-known musicians in recording sessions and recorded solo albums and appeared on a variety of television shows.

20. Jimmy Webb, *1946, Elk City (songwriter)*: This son of a Baptist minister, born in Elk City, is one of the rare rock songwriters to gain fame as a songwriter instead of a recording artist; he grew up playing the organ in the Baptist Church, but his creativity carried him further. He went to Los Angeles and became a successful songwriter. He has won numerous Grammys for songs such as "By the Time I Get to Phoenix," "Up, Up and Away," "Wichita Lineman," "MacArthur Park" and others. His recordings with other performers were received better than those that he recorded alone.

By the Time I Get to Phoenix

Up, Up and Away

Wichita Lineman

MacArthur Park

Jimmy Webb. (Copyright 1989, The Oklahoma Publishing Company)

21. The Oklahoma Blue Devils, *popular in late 1920s, Oklahoma City (jazz band)*: This organization, which started in Kansas City in 1923, became famous for its music and entertainment after moving to Oklahoma City in 1925 with Walter Page as the leader. Many black musicians who later became renowned performers—such as Jimmy Rushing, Don Byas, and Count Basie—gained experience in the Blue Devils organization. The Blue Devils were known as a territorial band because they monopolized the bookings in their "territory." They were not a band of national reputation, but many members became the heart of other nationally recognized bands, such as the Bennie Moten Band that evolved into the Count Basie Orchestra.

22. Louis Ballard, *1931–, Quapaw (composer and music educator)*: Dr. Louis Ballard, an American Indian whose Cherokee and Quapaw ancestors were leaders in their nations, was born near Quapaw. After attending high school with a strong musical background, he studied music theory and composition at the University of Oklahoma and the University of Tulsa. His masterful blending of American Indian traditional music with the sounds and styles of Western European compositions resulted in international praise and popularity. As a composer and music educator with strong American Indian values, he is dedicated to preserving, blending, and sharing musical cultures. He has received numerous awards and grants and was a 2004 inductee into the Oklahoma Music Hall of Fame.

Cover of the original-cast recording of Oklahoma! *(Courtesy Decca U.S.)*

23. D. C. Minner, *1935–, Rentiesville (blues musician)*: D. C. Minner was reared by his grandmother in Rentiesville. She sold corn liquor when Oklahoma was still dry, and it is this property where D. C. and his wife Selby produce their annual Dusk 'Til Dawn Blues Festival and where he first heard live music. After serving in the military, he became a bass player in Oklahoma City and later in California (where he and Selby met; she became his bass player). After touring for years, in 1988 they returned to his old home, known as the Cozy Corner, and reopened it as the Down Home Blues Club. Later he inaugurated the Oklahoma Blues Hall of Fame. They have received a variety of awards, and in 1999 he was inducted into the Oklahoma Jazz Hall of Fame and in 2003 the Oklahoma Music Hall of Fame.

24. J. J. Cale, *1938–, Tulsa (songwriter and rock musician)*: Born in Oklahoma City, as a child John W. Cale moved with the family to Tulsa. He and other Tulsans became well-known performers, songwriters, and recording stars in the 1960s–1970s. Cale was given the nickname "J. J." while in California—in Tulsa he was known as Johnny Call. He made a little money playing in Tulsa clubs, but he eventually moved to California, where his songs were and are recorded by many stars and his guitar style influenced others.

25. David Gates, *1940–, Tulsa (rock musician, songwriter, producer)*: Born in Tulsa to musical parents, David A. Gates became a man with many talents—keyboardist, songwriter, producer, composer, and actor. In high school he was adept at the piano, guitar, and bass and had written his first hit, "Jo-Baby." After attending the University of Oklahoma, he moved to Los Angeles in 1961 and worked as a songwriter and producer before organizing David Gates and Bread in 1968; they were popular as soft rock performers. After the group disbanded, he continued to compose scores for movies and appeared in some as well as making appearances on television.

26. Leon Russell, *1941–, Tulsa (composer and rock musician)*: Claude Russell Bridges was born in Lawton and grew up in Tulsa. He studied classical music for many years before turning to rock and roll. He was a young, talented participant in what became known as the Tulsa Sound, and during those years he backed many well-known musicians who came to Tulsa. Jerry Lee Lewis hired Leon's Tulsa band to tour with him for two years. He became Leon Russell, a popular production man and session musician, recording with numerous artists in different musical genres, including symphony orchestras; he even recorded in the country genre as Hank Wilson. His songs won Grammies for many stars along with his own recordings. He returned to Tulsa and established a recording studio and Shelter Records. As a musician, producer, and songwriter, Leon Russell became a legend.

27. The Tractors, *1990s, Tulsa (eclectic)*: It is hard to place The Tractors into a musical genre, for they represent many. Tulsa and surrounding communities produced an amazing number of talented musicians, and some styles have diminished in popularity. Steve Ripley—who has worked and toured as a guitarist with legends such as Bob Dylan—purchased the Leon Russell recording company in Tulsa and named it the Church Studio. He decided to call together veterans of the Tulsa Sound and other genres to record their blend of music; Steve and a few others were not from the Big City, so they called themselves The Tractors. They represent Oklahoma musical sounds both past and present.

28. Chet Baker, *1929–1988, Yale (jazz trumpeter)*: An Oklahoman who grew up with music as a family tradition or a religious activity, Chesney Henry Baker was born in Yale; he was 11 when the family moved to California. His mother wanted him to be a singer, but his father bought him a trumpet that he learned to play by ear. He quit school when he was 16, joined the army, and became a member of the 298th Army Band. Later he worked in various bands in the United States and Europe; his influence was great in Europe, where he was the most frequently recorded American jazzman, with over 200 recordings. He died in Holland.

Chet Baker. (Photo by William Claxton, courtesy Guy W. Logsdon Collection)

116. NATIVE AMERICAN ART AND ARTISTS Essay by *Mary Jo Watson*

American Indian art has a lengthy history in Oklahoma, but its critical study within the field of art history is quite recent. Although the early people of Oklahoma would not have had the same concept of art as contemporary Westerners, their manufacture of utilitarian items with symbolic meaning according to their cosmology exhibit surpassing excellence and express a sense of deeply held aesthetics. During the twentieth century, especially after World War II, academics, the Indian community, and non-Indians alike developed a wider view of art and aesthetics, which provoked appreciation of and provided validity to the study of American Indian art. A newly formed sensitivity to the works of non-Western people enables us to appreciate different philosophies and the artistic creativity of other cultures–especially, in Oklahoma, that of American Indians.

Careful observation provides a record of distinctive, recognizable cultural and tribal arts that during the past five hundred years were perpetually dynamic. This resilience and brilliance of adaptation (especially in the traditional arts) has helped maintain the identity, culture, and belief systems of each Indian nation. Oklahoma Native American art is quite varied.

On the western side of the state, Plains village farmers (A.D. 600–1400) left remains of their homes, undecorated pottery, small figurines, typical clothing, and sophisticated chipped points. In eastern Oklahoma, Mississippian Caddoan mound builders, the Spiro people, inhabited lands close to the Arkansas River boundary. From A.D. 900 until about 1450, they built monumental earthen mounds surrounded by great ceremonial plazas. Found at this site were large shells with incised motifs such as the hawk warrior and the circle-and-cross symbol for the four directions, stone pipes, embossed coppers, beaded jewelry, exquisitely worked flints, and stone celts. Some of the pieces were acquired in trade with other Mississippian mound sites. Remains of basketry and woven fabric, including delicate lace stitching, were also found. All of the arts combine to reveal an artistic and aesthetic expression of their belief system.

After the dispersal of the mound peoples by A.D. 1541, the Wichitas and affiliated tribes moved to the banks of the Red and Arkansas rivers and the Quapaws lived near the former territory of the Spiro people. They created personal adornments including tattoos, gorgets, and jewelry. Undecorated pottery and stone carvings were also found in this area.

Passing in and out of Oklahoma were the Plains Apaches, the Comanches, and the Osages. All were adept at working hides, with some excelling at carving stone bone and making fine points. The creation of personal adornments, of painted hides and feathers and jewelry, proliferated.

The movement of many other American Indian peoples to Oklahoma in the early part of the nineteenth century was propelled by the Indian Removal Act of 1830. More than sixty Indian tribes were removed from their homelands and forced to relocate. This diaspora brought together diverse people who had different languages, different belief systems, and different arts. All were subject to white influences and governance, though they had been promised otherwise. But even as refugees—and to survive politically and culturally—the Indian peoples continued to make works of important symbolism and beauty.

Owing to the great diversity of tribes, generations of creative visual artists provide a cross section of national American Indian art history in painting, sculpture, architecture, pottery, weaving, carving, and jewelry making. The materials and forms varied from area to area, depending on the availability of materials needed for making a particular art form. One early adaptation of Plains Indian art to Euro-American materials included painting and drawing on paper instead of hides.

In 1875, the U.S. government arrested and imprisoned seventy-two Indians from Indian Territory in Fort Marion at St. Augustine, Florida. Many of these prisoners, who had a long history of painting on hides, commenced using the new materials of their white captors. This "Ledger Art" on ruled and lined ledger paper represents a time of transition and was made by both the Fort Marion prisoners and later by Indian artists in Oklahoma. Thus they demonstrated their adaptability and survival skills in all facets of life—including the arts.

A Kiowa artist who created an extraordinary number of paintings and drawings in Oklahoma between the 1870s and 1910 was Silver Horn, or Haun-gooah, whose images are replete with Kiowa narrative history, calendars, and Sun Dance ceremonials. Use of the new materials was accepted by succeeding generations, particularly among the Kiowas in Oklahoma during the 1920s. A group of five artists (including one woman for a short while, making six in total) found encouragement by Kiowa field matron Susie Peters. By special arrangement they came to the University of Oklahoma; under the tutelage of Oscar B. Jacobson and Edith Mahier, they developed a flat two-dimensional style that became, to many non-Indian collectors and patrons, the quintessential Indian style of painting.

Another area of early intensive formal artistic training was at Bacone Indian University in Muskogee, where Ataloa McLendon was a prime force in establishing an Indian art and music center. Acee Blue Eagle (Creek/Pawnee), who had studied under Jacobson, was the first director of the art school, and many eastern Oklahoma Indians followed as the directors. Dick West (Cheyenne) was chairman of the Art Department from 1947 to 1970. His son W. Richard West Jr. (Southern Cheyenne) is the founding director of the National Museum of the American Indian that was opened in the fall of 2004 in Washington, D.C.

As the twentieth century unfolded and as Indian men and women returned from World War II, the Philbrook Museum of Art in Tulsa became a center of national Indian participation in the arts. Also, many Oklahoma Indian artists attended the Institute of American Indian Arts in Santa Fe, New Mexico, and had the opportunity to expand their artistic knowledge. During the later part of the twentieth century, Indian artists also worked in film, video, and photography.

Currently Oklahoma Native artists continue to reflect their tribal heritage and traditional concepts with the framework of traditional and contemporary styles and materials. The ability of Native people to respond artistically to new materials and external influences is reflective of centuries of adaptation to cultural and environmental changes. The concepts of particular belief systems and cosmology are retained, and at the same time, Indian artists have the freedom to experiment and communicate their aesthetic responses to their experiences in the twenty-first century.

Selected American Indian Visual Artists and Educators

1. Spencer Asah, *Kiowa*, *1905–1954, Anadarko (painter)*: Asah is one of the Kiowa Five artists who studied under Jacobson at the University of Oklahoma. His work includes traditional dancers, flute players, and men in traditional Kiowa dress.

2. James Auchiah, *Kiowa*, *1906–1974, Anadarko (painter)*: In addition to painting, Auchiah worked on murals in Oklahoma. He was a teacher, and his work features scenes of Kiowa life of the 19th century. Strong color and flat painting define the people and events he depicts.

The Flute Player, *by Stephen Mopope. (Oklahoma Indian Art Gallery, courtesy Vanessa Jennings)*

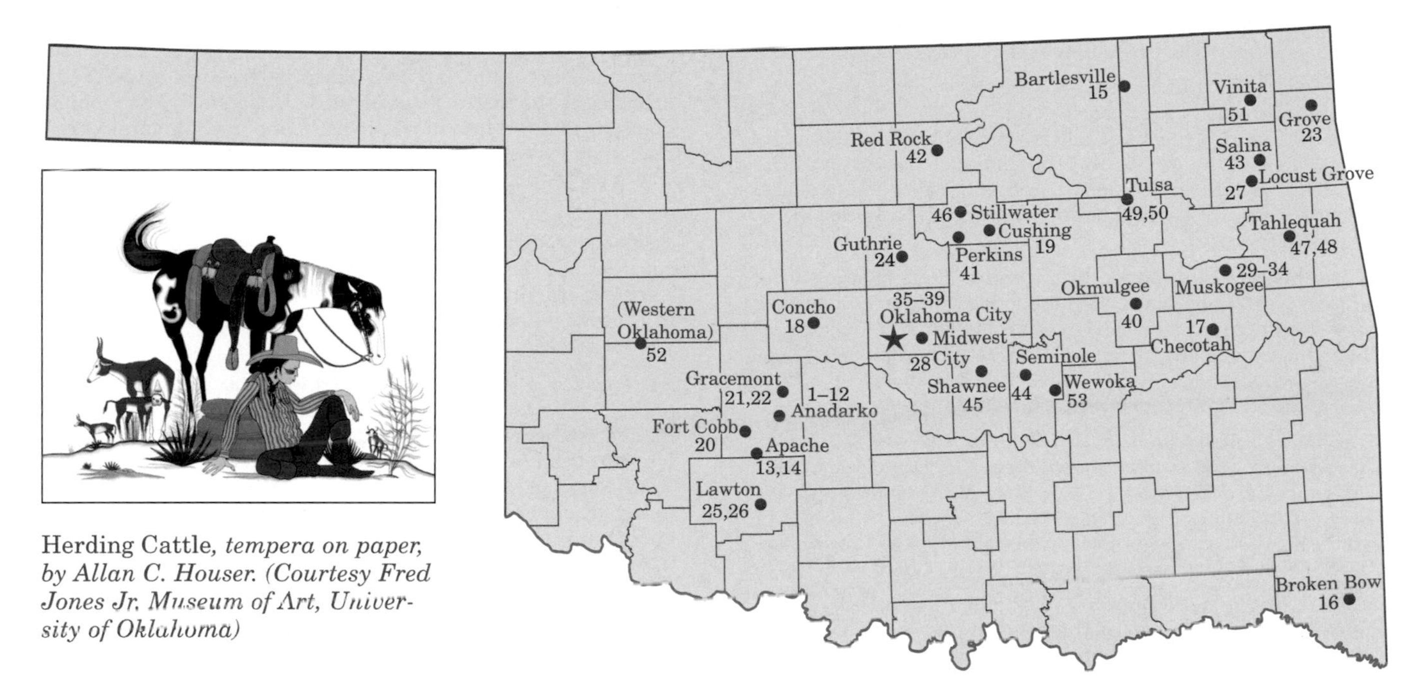

Herding Cattle, *tempera on paper, by Allan C. Houser. (Courtesy Fred Jones Jr. Museum of Art, University of Oklahoma)*

3. Blackbear Bosin, *Kiowa/Comanche*, *1921–1980, Anadarko (painter)*: Bosin represents an important generation of artists whose influence is far reaching. His realistic and idealistic images of Indian life are illuminated in both painting and murals. Perhaps the most reproduced Indian painting of the 20th century is his rendering of "Prairie Fire" (c. 1953), which is now located in the Gilcrease Museum in Tulsa.

4. Bruce Ceasar, *Pawnee/Sac and Fox*, *1952– , Anadarko (jeweler)*: Following in his famous father's work, Bruce Ceasar is a nationally recognized jeweler in German (or nickel) silver. The National Heritage Fellowship, Folk and Traditional arts program for the National Endowment of the Arts recognized Bruce as a Master Traditional Artist at the Kennedy Center in Washington, D.C., in 1998.

5. Julius Ceasar, *Pawnee*, *1910–1982, Anadarko (jewelry artist)*: Ceasar grew up in Pawnee and was an apprentice to the well-known Pawnee silversmith Hiram Jake. Ceasar's work is some of the finest German silver that was made during the 20th century in the United States and is found in museums throughout Europe.

6. Alice Littleman, *Kiowa*, *1910–2000, Anadarko (beading artist)*: Littleman, a premier bead worker and dressmaker, was taught by her mother, Anna Konad. She tanned deer hide and cut, sewed, and beaded more than 50 ceremonial hide dresses. She was instrumental in nurturing and teaching traditional Kiowa beadwork to new generations of women and men.

7. Marlene Riding-In Marneah, *Pawnee*, *1933– , Anadarko (jeweler)*: Early on, Marneah studied painting, but it is through her metalwork that she has received respect and awards, both in Oklahoma and nationally. Among her metalworks are pins, tie slides, and necklaces with images important to the Native American Church. She works in German silver and brass.

8. Stephen Mopope, *Kiowa*, *1898–1974, Anadarko (painter)*: Mopope was well known for his painting and work on WPA murals. The flat surface was organized in both smaller paintings and the murals. He applied dramatic colors and movement in much of his work.

9. Vanessa Paukeigope Morgan, *Kiowa/Pima*, *1952– , Anadarko (beadworker, cradleboard maker)*: Morgan is an excellent beader and has perpetuated the skills of Kiowa cradleboard making. She has received awards from across the United States, including Santa Fe Indian Market and Red Earth, Inc. Her work has been featured in many exhibitions.

10. Horace Poolaw, *Kiowa*, *1906–1984, Anadarko (photographer)*: Throughout his life, Poolaw was fascinated with the camera. In following his passion, he recorded images of Indians throughout most of the 20th century. He has received national recognition for his images of western Oklahoma and those that were made when he was in the U.S. Army Air Corps during World War II, where he taught aerial photography.

11. Lois Smokey, *Kiowa*, *1907–1981, Anadarko (painter)*: Smokey is an important figure in Oklahoma Indian art history as the first woman to step out of a traditional tribal role; she attended painting classes with the Kiowa Five artists. Her subjects were women and children. Although her time at the University of Oklahoma was short, her presence reverberated throughout the 20th century.

12. Nettie Standing, *Kiowa*, *1917–1987, Anadarko (beading artist)*: A premier beader, Nettie Standing was associated with the Craft Cooperative at the Southern Plains Indian Museum in Anadarko for many years. He influence is seen in her teaching and especially the continuing work of her family members and other students.

13. Allan Houser, *Chiricahua Apache,* *1915–1994, Apache (sculptor)*: Commencing as a painter, Houser later began sculpting in stone and bronze. He was the sculpture instructor at the Institute of American Indian Art in Santa Fe for many years. His work is some of the best known artwork of any Indian artist of the 20th century.

14. Doc Tate Nevaquaya, *Comanche,* *1912–1996, Apache (painter)*: Nevaquaya was a talented dancer, singer, and painter and was recognized as a master flute player. His artwork includes images of Plains Indians. He was named a Living Legend by the Oklahoma Arts Council in 1990 and gave a flute performance that same year at Carnegie Hall in New York.

15. C. Terry Saul, *Choctaw/Chickasaw,* *1921–1976, Bartlesville (painter)*: Saul studied under Acee Blue Eagle and Woody Crumbo. He later received a BFA and an MFA from the University of Oklahoma and studied at the Arts Students League in New York. His work in watercolor depicted stories of the Southeast and especially Choctaw customs.

16. Elsie Battiest, *Choctaw,* *1914–1999, Broken Bow (basket maker)*: Battiest was one of the 20th century's most capable Choctaw basket makers. She used traditional materials, including river cane, which she processed by splitting, stripping, and dyeing to make the weavers. Her baskets are now in many collections and museums.

17. Woodrow Wilson Crumbo, *Pottawatomie,* *1912–1989, Checotah (painter)*: As both a printmaker and a painter Crumbo transformed the Kiowa style into his unique imagery with watercolors. He continued using brilliant color but added movement, developing his own style to portray animals and tribal peoples.

18. Charles Pratt, *Arapaho/Sioux/Cheyenne,* *1937– , Concho (painter, sculptor)*: Early on in his career, Charles Pratt's work included experimentation with a combination of traditional and contemporary materials in three-dimensional forms. Use of bronze and metals combined with turquoise in replicas of cornstalks were but one of his innovations. He was named The Honored One at Red Earth in 2000.

19. Archie Blackowl, *Cheyenne,* *1911–1992, Cushing (painter)*: Customs of Cheyenne society and ceremonies were the subjects of Blackowl's work. He rendered exacting details of the Sun Dance, Cheyenne buffalo hunters, and burial scenes, among others.

20. Jack Hokeah, *Kiowa,* *1902–1969, Fort Cobb (painter)*: Hokeah attended St. Patrick's Mission School in Anadarko and attended the University of Oklahoma under Jacobson. His work included images of dancers with strong colors and delicate lines. Portraits in watercolors and tempera expressed strength and traditional dress.

21. Ronald Anderson, *Choctaw,* *1937– , near Gracemont (painter)*: Creative and brilliant, Anderson's work is reflective of his continual study of both traditional and contemporary art forms. He is nationally recognized for his monumental sculptures and evocative realistic and conceptual paintings.

22. T. C. Cannon, *Caddo/Kiowa,* *1946–1978, Gracemont (painter)*: This Oklahoma artist is recognized as one of the more prominent artists of the 20th century. His work under Fritz Scholder at the Institute of American Indian Arts was groundbreaking and revolutionary for the Indian art community. Well read in philosophy and art history, Cannon produced important works before his untimely death.

23. Bill Glass, *Cherokee,* *1950– , Grove (pottery artist)*: Glass creates powerful clay pieces that reference the ancient mound cultures and those of contemporary life. He fashions clay into the hawk-warriors of the Spiro people and adds color and stone to the image. His work is seen in Oklahoma and across the United States.

24. Harvey Pratt, *Southern Cheyenne,* *1941– , Guthrie (painter, sculptor)*: Pratt is from a distinguished Cheyenne family and is a painter and wood sculptor. He is also a successful forensic artist for the Oklahoma State Bureau of Investigation. Pratt works in a traditional narrative style of painting and has received numerous awards, including being named The Honored One at the June 2005 Red Earth festival.

25. Carl Sweezy, *Arapaho,* *1881–1953, Lawton (painter)*: Sweezy worked in oils, watercolor, and enamel. His art education was limited, but he excelled at creating images of an older time of Cheyenne-Arapaho life. He worked for the anthropologist James Mooney, who had some influence on his art.

26. Josephine Wapp, *Comanche,* *1912–, Lawton (finger weaving, wall hangings)*: Wapp has a long, distinguished career as an educator and artist. After receiving her bachelor's degree from Oklahoma State University, she taught at the Santa Fe Indian School, Chilocco Indian School, and the Institute of American Indian Arts in Santa Fe and other schools. She continues to create and teach the skills for finger-woven sashes and elaborate wall hangings.

27. Willard Stone, *Cherokee,* *1916–1985, Locust Grove (sculptor)*: Stone is considered one of the foremost wood sculptors of the 20th century. Elegant three-dimensional figures of animals and people are executed in walnut, sassafras, cherry, and Oklahoma red cedar. His images in wood are delicate and precise. He was named a Master Artist by the Five Civilized Tribes Museum and was an artist in residence for several years at the Gilcrease Museum in Tulsa.

28. Mavis Doering, *Cherokee,* *1929– , Midwest City (basket maker)*: Doering revitalized Cherokee basket making and became a national award-winning artist. Her creativity included baskets in the shapes of Hopi pots, and her baskets are in major museums and private collections throughout the United States. One of her Cherokee double-walled baskets is now in the Oklahoma State Arts Collection.

29. Fred Beaver, *Creek,* *1911–1980, Muskogee (painter)*: Exhibited in much of Beaver's art is a passionate interest in the life and culture of the Florida Seminoles. He was designated a Master Artist by the Five Civilized Tribes Museum in Muskogee in 1973. Like other artists of the 20th century, he painted scenes of tribes from the southern plains.

30. Acee Blue Eagle, *Creek/Pawnee,* *1907–1959, Muskogee (painter)*: Acee Blue Eagle was the first director of the Art Department at Bacone University in Muskogee. He was a painter and a lecturer. He studied at the University of Oklahoma under Jacobson and took classes at Oxford in England. He was named the outstanding Indian in the United States in 1958 and was one of the most celebrated Indian artists of his time. He was honored posthumously by the Oklahoma legislature in 1959.

31. Joan Hill, *Creek/Cherokee,* *1930– , Muskogee (painter)*: Hill is one of the strongest women painters of her times. Her award-winning work consists of a wide variety of traditional images of Southeastern Indians and contemporary approaches to figures and landscapes.

32. Knokovtee Scott, *Creek/Cherokee,* *1951– , Muskogee (jeweler)*: Scott was instrumental in the 20th century in the reinstitution of a traditional Southeastern art form in Oklahoma. His jewelry is made from the shiny surfaces found in mussels and shell. This pink material is found in his pendants, necklaces, and earrings and has brought national attention to his work.

33. Jerome Tiger, *Creek/Seminole,* *1941–1967, Muskogee (painter)*: Jerome Tiger developed a riveting and independent style of work during the mid-20th century. His sensitive treatment of scenes of removal brought him national and international fame.

The Guardian Spirit, *by Jerome Tiger.*
(Oklahoma Indian Art Gallery, courtesy Peggy Tiger)

34. W. Richard West, *Cheyenne,* *1912–1996, Muskogee / Tijeras, N.Mex. (painter)*: West was a powerful force in his artwork and in training succeeding generations of artists at Bacone University in Muskogee. His images included traditional ceremonies and 19th-century life, and he later experimented with cubist and abstract styles of painting.

35. Richard Aitson, *Kiowa,* *1953– , Oklahoma City (beading artist)*: Aitson excels at beading cradleboards, medallions, and dance accessories. He uses small beads that are meticulously applied and is creative within a traditional framework. His work is recognized as superior across Oklahoma and the United States.

36. Benjamin Harjo, Jr., *Seminole/Shawnee,* *1945– , Oklahoma City (painter)*: Harjo has a unique and appealing style of painting that involves brilliant colors and unusual combinations of geometric and figural images. He studied at the Institute of American Indian Arts in Santa Fe and received a BFA from Oklahoma State University. He was designated a Master Artist by the Five Civilized Tribes in 1988 and is collected internationally.

37. Sharron Ahtone Harjo, *Kiowa,* *1945– , Oklahoma City (painter)*: Ahtone Harjo is the second major female Kiowa painter of the 20th century. She has a strong background in academics and art and is an expert basketmaker. Her work is traditional and deals with Kiowa life and legends; it can be found in museums, galleries, and private collections.

38. Edgar Heap of Birds, *Cheyenne,* *1954– , Oklahoma City (painter, sculptor, conceptual artist)*: Heap of Birds is one of Oklahoma's best-known contemporary artists for his political commentary using both paint and text. His work deals with past and present experiences of being an American Indian. His paintings are found throughout the United States and other countries.

39. Richard Ray Whiteman, *Yuchie,* *1949– , Oklahoma City (painter, photographer)*: During the last three decades of the 20th century, Whiteman became one of the most well known artist/activists in Oklahoma and throughout the United States. His photographs were intimate portraits of Indian people and were effective in breaking the stereotypical images that had proliferated during the past century.

Prayer for the Mother, *watercolor, by Archie Blackowl. (Courtesy Fred Jones Jr. Museum of Art, University of Oklahoma)*

40. Ruthe Blalock Jones, *Delaware/Shawnee/Peoria,* *1939– , Okmulgee (painter)*: Jones studied under Richard West at Bacone University in Muskogee and succeeded him as director of the Art Department. She has received awards for her traditional images of tribal culture. Jones received the Oklahoma Governor's Arts Awards, Art and Education Award, in 1993.

41. Mike Larsen, *Chickasaw,* *1944– , Perkins (painter)*: This painter's work is noted for the murals located in the Oklahoma State Capitol rotunda and the Donald W. Reynolds Performing Arts Center at the University of Oklahoma. He is recognized for his unique painting style depicting individuals and historic figures.

42. Monroe Tsatoke, *Kiowa,* *1904–1937, Red Rock (painter)*: Tsatoke was born near Saddle Mountain in western Oklahoma. His work is filled with images of the Native American Church and traditional image of warriors. Like the other Kiowa Five artists, Tsatoke was also a singer and dancer.

43. Ella Mae Blackbear, *Cherokee,* *1930–1991, Salina (basket maker)*: Ella Mae Blackbear was named the Master Craftsperson Cherokee Living National Treasure in 1990 for her basketry. She collected her own material, produced the natural dyes, and taught numerous generations of basket makers traditional Cherokee techniques.

44. Enoch Kelly Haney, *Seminole,* *1940– , Seminole (painter)*: The legacy of Kelly Haney will continue not only through his painting but also because of his sculpture that sits atop the Oklahoma State Capitol dome: "The Guardian," a 17′ bronze sculpture of an Indian warrior, represents all Oklahoma tribes. Haney is also widely known for his realistic paintings of historic and contemporary Indian figures.

45. Ernest Spybuck, *Shawnee,* *1883–1949, Shawnee (painter)*: A self-taught artist, Spybuck provided intimate details of early-day life of the Shawnees in central Oklahoma. His paintings are filled with great numbers of people and action.

46. Anita Fields, *Osage,* *1951– , Stillwater (pottery artist)*: Fields is a nationally recognized artist who uses tribal dress and everyday objects to make expressive clay pieces. Swaying dresses and traditional designs are incorporated with abstracted images that reference her family and culture.

47. Cecil Dick, *Cherokee,* *1915–1992, Tahlequah (painter)*: Cecil Dick spent his painting career depicting the stories and history of the Cherokees. Dick studied at Chilocco Indian School and Bacone College in Oklahoma and at the Santa Fe Indian School in New Mexico. His style is reminiscent of the flat "Kiowa" style of color with a great deal of action in many of his works. Recognized for his contribution to the Oklahoma Indian art community, he was named The Honored One by Red Earth shortly before his death.

48. Jane Osti, *Osage,* *1945– , Tahlequah (pottery artist)*: Osti studied under Anna Mitchell and creates pottery that reflect her Southeastern and Cherokee culture. The well-educated Osti received a BFA from Northeastern State University and a master's of science education. Her pieces are found in art markets in the United States and Europe.

49. Valjean Hessing, *Choctaw,* *1934– , Tulsa / Onarga, Ill. (painter)*: As an adult, Hessing commenced her painting career and developed a flat, colorful style that was adopted by other painters. Her subjects included the Trail of Tears and some paintings that hold great humor. She was adept at watercolor, acrylic, pencil, and pen and ink.

50. Solomon McCombs, *Creek,* *1913–1980, Tulsa (painter)*: At Bacone, McCombs studied under Acee Blue Eagle. He considered his painting a record of Creek life. His images included scenes of stickball games, Indian burials, and the Ribbon Dances of Creek women.

51. Anna Belle Sixkiller Mitchell, *Cherokee,* *1926– , Vinita (potter)*: Mitchell taught herself how to make pottery by visiting museums and traveling to North Carolina to see firsthand how her relatives make Cherokee pottery. Using designs from nature and shapes from the ancient mound cultures, Mitchell is now recognized as a leading traditional potter and has helped to revitalize this form through her students. Her work has been recognized by the Smithsonian.

52. Haun-gooah (Silver Horn), *Kiowa,* *1860–1941, western Oklahoma (painter)*: Silverhorn was an uncle of Stephen Mopope's and was an expert in Kiowa graphic art and traditions. He is recognized as one of the great transitional artists between the 19th and 20th centuries.

53. June Lee, *Seminole,* *1933, Wewoka / Midwest City (textile artist)*: June Lee taught herself the art of Seminole patchwork and passed this technique on to succeeding generations. Well known throughout the state and nation, Lee continues to develop exquisite patchwork with both traditional and contemporary designs.

Honor, Serve, Protect, *by Robert Taylor.* Left to right*: Quanah Parker, Bass Reeves, Bud Ledbetter. Artist's study for a major triptych painting in the Attorney General's Office. (Courtesy Robert Taylor, Attorney General Drew Edmondson, Oklahoma Arts Council, and Oklahoma Centennial Commission)*

117. OTHER TRADITIONS OF VISUAL ARTS AND ARTISTS

Essay by *Byron Price*

An exploring expedition led by Colonel Stephen Long brought the first European-American artists to present-day Oklahoma in 1820. What works, if any, that Philadelphian Titian Peale and English-born Samuel Seymour may have completed during their brief sojourn, however, remain unknown.

More than a decade passed before another artist from the United States entered the region. Convinced that the Native inhabitants of the West were destined to disappear, George Catlin had set out in 1833 to document as many Indian tribes as possible. The following year, his quest led him to Fort Gibson, where he joined a military expedition to the Wichita Mountains. During his foray through Indian Territory, Catlin managed to paint bands of Osages, Cherokees, Comanches, Kiowas, and Wichitas and to depict a landscape teeming with wildlife.

Artist John Mix Stanley arrived in Oklahoma in the fall of 1842 and became the first artist to establish a studio there. During his three-year stay among the Five Nations, Stanley painted numerous portraits and genre scenes. He documented the famous Indian council held at Tahlequah in June 1843 and created a body of work that he later exhibited as an Indian gallery.

In the years that followed, explorer-artists continued to document the landscape and inhabitants of Oklahoma. Lieutenant James W. Abert of the U.S. Corps of Topographical Engineers, for example, produced sketches of a reconnaissance along the Canadian River in 1845. Eight years later, Lieutenant Amiel W. Whipple's Pacific Railroad Survey along the thirty-fifth parallel brought civilian artist and topographer Heinrich B. Möllhausen to Oklahoma. Some of the German-born artist's drawings and watercolors illustrated published accounts of the expedition.

After the Civil War, the continuing desire to document the tribes of the southern plains attracted several new artists to what later became Oklahoma, among them U.S. Indian commissioner and watercolorist Vincent Coyler, who toured reservations and military posts in 1868–1869. Nearly two decades later, on the eve of the opening of the Unassigned Lands to settlement, nationally known illustrators Frederic Remington and Rufus F. Zogbaum visited the region. Drawings and paintings based on their Oklahoma experiences appeared in such magazines as *Harper's Weekly* and *The Century* throughout the 1890s. The opportunity to paint Indians likewise drew artists Julian Scott and Elbridge Ayer Burbank to the Twin Territories during the same period. Burbank's visits to Fort Sill yielded portraits of the captive Apache leader Geronimo and several members of the Kiowa, Cheyenne, and Arapaho tribes.

During the first decade of the twentieth century, art instruction became part of the public school curricula in both Oklahoma City and Tulsa, and the University of Oklahoma began to offer art classes under the direction of Oscar B. Jacobson. In 1916 Jacobson and more than a dozen other painters and sculptors organized the Association of Oklahoma Artists and began to offer annual shows. Three years later, a museum housing art treasures collected by Father Gregory Gerrer opened at St. Gregory's College in Shawnee.

The onset of the Great Depression stimulated an explosion of public artworks financed by the U.S. government. Between 1933 and 1943, artists employed by several federal agencies painted more than forty murals in public buildings throughout the state. Although Oklahoma-based artists finished two-thirds of the work, such distinguished American painters as Oscar E. Berninghaus, Ila McAfee Turner, Joseph A. Fleck, and Randall Davey also completed murals in the state. Rendered in a representational style, most such works depicted events and scenes from Oklahoma's Indian and pioneer past.

In 1936, the Works Progress Administration opened a federally funded art center in Oklahoma City. The new facility offered art classes, lectures, and exhibitions and housed the permanent collection of the Oklahoma Art League, organized in Oklahoma City in 1910. The 1930s also witnessed the opening of art museums in Tulsa and in Norman at the University of Oklahoma.

The Horse, *by Joe Taylor.*
(Goins Collection, photo by Emily Dutcher)

During the post–World War II era, many Oklahoma artists embraced national artistic trends toward abstract expressionism and the avant-garde. Fortunes made from Oklahoma's oil industry, meanwhile, enabled such entrepreneurs as Frank Phillips and Thomas Gilcrease to develop nationally renowned art collections. Both men eventually established museums and shared their holdings with the public. Thanks to these and a few other Oklahoma visionaries, the state now houses the largest collection of art of the American West in the nation.

In 1965 the Oklahoma Arts and Humanities Council was created to take advantage of federal arts funding through the National Endowment for the Arts. Today, the Oklahoma Arts Council (under the leadership of Betty Price) provides leadership and support to some eight hundred arts programs of all types, statewide.

Oklahoma's vibrant contemporary fine arts community includes some of the most outstanding artists and museums in the nation. Nearly four hundred outdoor sculptures in a variety of media and styles grace the state's landscape. Perhaps the most famous monument is Ponca City's *Pioneer Woman,* created by Bryant Baker in 1927. Dozens of sculptures line the Arkansas River in Tulsa's Riverside Park alone.

Renovations and additions to the state capitol at the turn of the twenty-first century included many stunning new works of art, among them Wilson Hurley's magnificent Centennial Suite of Oklahoma landscapes. The state's artistic legacy will be further enriched by the installation of sculptor Paul Moore's massive Centennial Land Run Monument in Oklahoma City and by the continued creativity, energy, and vision of Oklahoma's many artists.

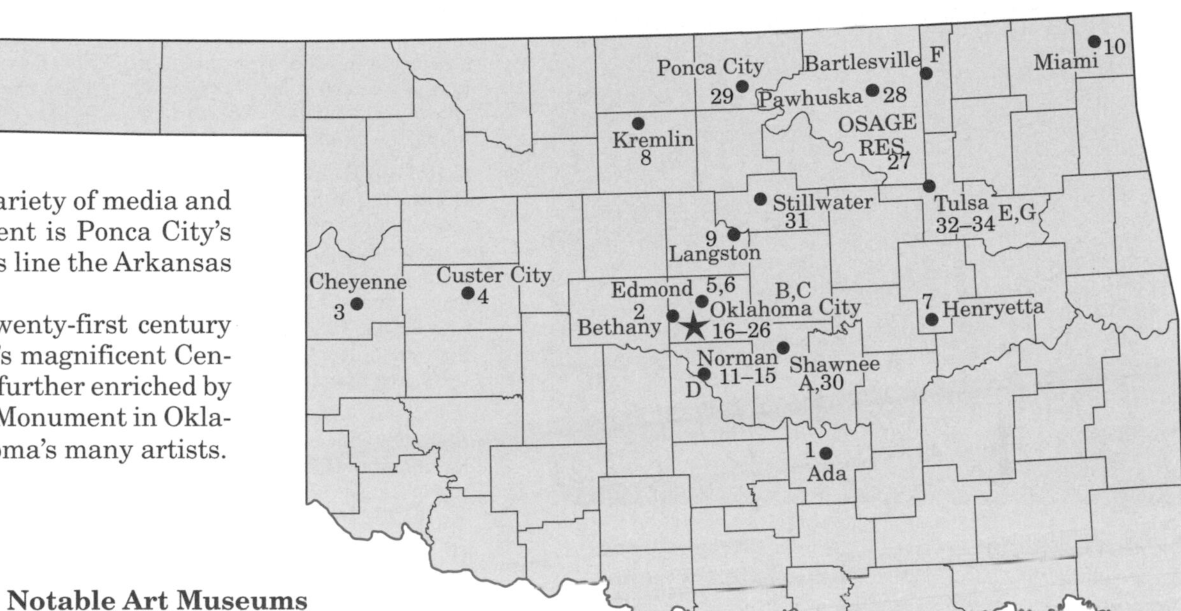

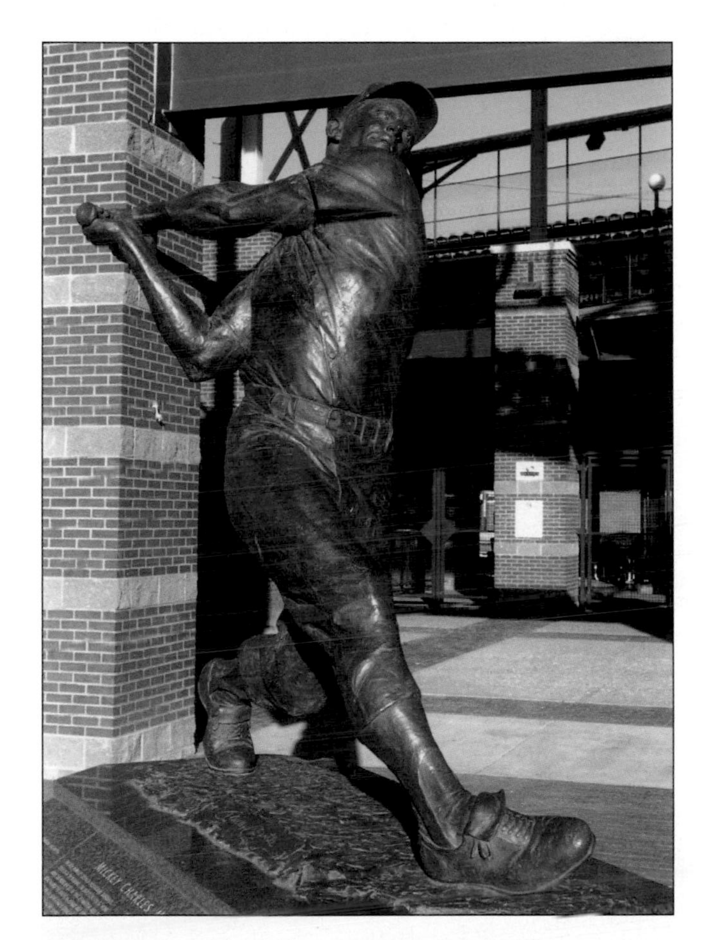

Mickey Mantle, sculpture by Blair Buswell. (Courtesy Oklahoma Centennial Commission, photo by Emily Dutcher)

Notable Art Museums

A. Mabee Gerrer Museum, *Shawnee*: Founded in 1914 on the campus of St. Gregory's College in Shawnee, St. Gregory's Museum and Art Gallery opened to the public in 1919 and ranks as one of the oldest museums in the state. Renamed the Mabee Gerrer Museum of Art, the museum moved to its present facility in 1979 and contains a diverse array of art objects from all over the world.

B. Oklahoma City Art Museum, Oklahoma City: Established as a federally supported art center in 1936, the Oklahoma City Art Museum now occupies part of the Donald W. Reynolds Visual Arts Center downtown. The museum maintains a broad collection of European, Asian, and American art, with the collection numbering more than 3,000 works.

C. National Cowboy and Western Heritage Museum, *Oklahoma City*: Opened in 1965 as the National Cowboy Hall of Fame and Western Heritage Center, the museum maintains a superb collection of art of the American West, including nearly 100 works by artists Frederic Remington and Charles M. Russell and more than 2,500 Native American paintings. The museum's research center actively collects the papers of historic and contemporary western and Native American artists.

D. Fred Jones Jr. Museum, University of Oklahoma, *Norman*: Established in 1936, the University of Oklahoma Museum of Art and Exhibitions was redesignated the Fred Jones Jr. Museum of Art in 1992. The museum boasts a collection of more than 8,000 objects, including the Weitzenhoffer Collection of French Impressionism and important works by the Taos Society of Artists. In 2005 the museum opened a new wing designed by renowned architect Hugh Newell Jacobsen.

E. Philbrook Museum, *Tulsa*: In 1938 Oklahoma oilman Waite Phillips donated his 23-acre Tulsa estate and 72-room mansion to the City of Tulsa for use as an art center. The villa was opened to the public as a museum the following year and now has more than 8,600 art works. In addition to American and European masterpieces, the museum owns a significant collection of Native American art and artifacts.

F. Woolaroc Museum, *located near Bartlesville*: Founded as a private collection in 1929 on the Frank Phillips Ranch near Bartlesville, the Woolaroc Museum opened to the public in 1944. A superb array of fine art of the American West, firearms, and Native American artifacts characterizes its collections.

G. Gilcrease Museum, *Tulsa*: In 1949 Tulsa oilman Thomas Gilcrease opened his vast collection of fine art, books, and other objects to the public. Gilcrease fell into debt, however, and offered the collection to the city, which secured it in a bond election in 1954. The Gilcrease Museum houses a broad-ranging collection of American art, including an unsurpassed collection of more than 10,000 works relating to the American West and representing some 400 artists.

Selected Artists and Art Educators

1. D. J. Lafon, 1929– , *Ada*: Born and raised in Utah, D. J. Lafon is known in Oklahoma as a distinguished painter and art educator. He chaired the art department of East Central University in Ada for two decades and has served as visual arts director for the Oklahoma Summer Arts Institute and as a guest artist at Wichita State University.

2. Sunni Mercer, 1957– , *Bethany*: Since earning an MFA in fine art at the University of Oklahoma in 1993, Mercer has earned a national reputation as a painter and mixed media artist and teacher. She is best known for imaginative assemblages that incorporate found objects and abstract and figurative forms in symmetrical compositions.

Oklahoma Autumn in the Distance, *by Oscar Brousse Jacobson (1954). (Courtesy Phyllis Melton Dowling Collection, photo by Emily Dutcher)*

3. Augusta J. Metcalf, 1881–1971, *Antelope Hills, west of Cheyenne*: Called the "Sage Brush Artist," Metcalf was sometimes compared to the famous Grandma Moses. The self-taught artist's straightforward images of ranch life in western Oklahoma took prizes at the fairs in Oklahoma and Texas and appeared in *Life* magazine in 1950. Lacking formal education and art lessons, she sketched in between chores on the homestead she built and managed with her mother, while as a single parent raising a son. Metcalf became a member of the Oklahoma Hall of Fame in 1968.

4. Joan Marron-Larue, 1934– , *Custer*: Born in Custer City, Marron LaRue now makes her home in Arizona. Although noted for her intimate plein air landscapes, Marron LaRue has also executed murals at Mercy Health Center and the Senate Chamber in the capitol in Oklahoma City. In 1992 judges awarded her work best of show at the Cheyenne Frontier Days Art Show in Wyoming.

5. Shan Gray, 1956– , *Edmond*: Gray is strongly rooted in the tradition of classical Renaissance sculpture and has honed his technique to the finish and polish of early Florentine work. His recent works include statues of Shannon Miller, Warren Spahn, Billy Vessels, and at Oklahoma City University, three Miss Americas: Jane Jayroe, Susan Powell, and Shawntel Smith. His current works include :"James Garner" and "The American," a sculpture planned for Tulsa that will be more than 21 stories high.

6. David Phelps, 1956– , *Edmond*: Sculptor David Phelps grew up in California. In 1987 he was awarded a residency at the Kohler Co. Arts in Industry program, where he learned to work with vitreous china and cast iron. Phelps earned an MFA in 1994 from the University of Oklahoma and has taught sculpture at the University of Central Oklahoma. He has received numerous large scale public art commissions, including one for McCarran International Airport in Las Vegas, Nevada, in 1995.

7. Barbara Vaupel, 1939– , *Henryetta*: Self taught painter and illustrator Barbara Vaupel moved to Oklahoma from her native California in 1968, eventually settling in Henryetta. Her paintings of western subjects, especially horses, have won awards in shows from Texas to Wyoming, and several have appeared on magazine covers.

8. Harold Holden, 1940– , *Kremlin*: Born in Enid, Harold "H" Holden began his career as a commercial artist before turning to sculpture and easel painting in 1973. He has sculpted nearly a dozen major bronze monuments, in Oklahoma, Texas, and Kansas. Dedicated in 2005, Holden's "Will Rogers on Teddy" adorns the grounds of the Will Rogers World Airport in Oklahoma City. In 1993 he was commissioned by the U.S. Postal Service to design a stamp commemorating the opening of the Cherokee Strip to settlement.

9. Eugene Jesse Brown, 1897–1963, *Langston*: African American artist educator Eugene Brown was born in 1897 in Arkansas. He moved to Oklahoma as a child and studied art at the University of Kansas and at Carnegie Tech, in Pittsburgh, before founding the Art Department at Langston University in 1924.

10. Charles Banks Wilson, 1918– , *Miami and Tahlequah*: Born in Arkansas and raised in Miami, Oklahoma, Wilson studied painting and lithography at the Art Institute of Chicago, then embarked on a career in illustration. He taught art at Northeastern A&M College in Tahlequah before becoming a full-time painter in 1960. Several of his portraits and murals hang in the state capitol. Honored with the Governor's Art Award and inducted into the Oklahoma Hall of Fame, Wilson was named an Oklahoma Cultural Treasure by Governor Frank Keating.

11. Samuel I. Holmberg, 1885–1911, *Norman*: A student of Sven Birger Sandzen's at Bethany College in Kansas, Holmberg also studied in Paris before becoming the first regular member of the art faculty at the University of Oklahoma. Academic responsibilities and illness cut short his promising career as an educator and artist.

12. Oscar B. Jacobson, 1882–1966, *Norman*: Jacobson came to the United States from his native Sweden in 1890. A gifted painter, he studied at the Louvre in Paris and earned a degree from Yale University in 1916. He directed the University of Oklahoma's School of Art from 1915 to 1945, and its art museum from 1936 to 1950.

13. Paul Moore, 1957– , *Norman*: Named artist in residence at the University of Oklahoma School of Art in 1997, Moore reestablished the school's long dormant figurative sculpture program. He has completed more than 60 commissions, including "Johnny Bench" at the Bricktown Ball Park in Oklahoma City and "On the Chisholm Trail" in McCasland Park in Duncan. When completed, Moore's Oklahoma Centennial Land Run Monument" in Oklahoma City will rank as one of the world's largest bronze sculptures.

The Run of '89, *sculpture by Paul Moore. (Courtesy Oklahoma Centennial Commission, photo by Emily Dutcher)*

14. Joseph R. Taylor, 1907–1999, *Norman*: A native of Washington State, Taylor joined the art faculty at the University of Oklahoma in 1932 and enjoyed a stellar career as a teacher and sculptor. His bronzes and wood carvings won many honors and were exhibited at such prestigious venues as the Pennsylvania Academy of Art and the Metropolitan Museum of New York.

15. Mike Wimmer, 1961– , *Norman*: One of Oklahoma's most successful commercial artists and illustrators, Wimmer grew up in Muskogee and earned an art degree from the University of Oklahoma in 1981. He has illustrated books and created advertising art for such national companies as AT&T, Procter & Gamble, and Kimberly Clark. Several of his easel paintings adorn the Oklahoma state capitol.

16. Gloria Abella de Duncan, 1943– , *Oklahoma City*: Born and raised in Bogota, Colombia, Abella de Duncan is an internationally known studio artist and an adjunct art professor at Oklahoma Baptist University. She holds an advanced degree in art from the State University of New York–Buffalo and studied at the National University in Mexico City. Her award-winning paintings can be found in public and private collections throughout the Americas and Europe and have earned her recognition from UNESCO and the National Endowment for the Arts.

17. Martha Avey, 1872–1943, *Oklahoma City*: A native of Arcola, Illinois, Avey studied art in Chicago, New York, and Europe before accepting a position as the first supervisor of art in the public schools of Oklahoma City. She was later named art director for Oklahoma City University.

18. Wayne Cooper, 1942– , *Oklahoma City*: A native of Depew, Oklahoma, and a professional artist since 1964, Cooper trained with Native American artist Woody Crumbo and at the Famous Artist School and the American Atelier in New York. The artist's paintings and sculpture of western and Indian subjects have attracted patrons and exhibitions around the world.

19. Emil Lenders, 1864–1934, *Oklahoma City*: Born in London, England, Lenders became captivated by American Indians as a child in Germany. After immigrating to the United States, he joined Buffalo Bill's Wild West troupe and later visited the Miller Brothers 101 Ranch, near Ponca City, where he painted local Indians and wildlife, especially bison.

20. Leonard D. McMurry, 1913– , *Oklahoma City*: McMurry earned a fine arts degree in sculpture at Washington University in St. Louis. He is best known for creating monuments depicting western themes. "The 89er" in downtown Oklahoma City, "Buffalo Bill" at the National Cowboy and Western Heritage Museum, and "Praying Hands" at Oral Roberts University in Tulsa are typical of his work. In 1981 McMurry was inducted into the Oklahoma Hall of Fame.

21. Jean Richardson, 1940– , *Oklahoma City*: A painter, sculptor, graphic artist, and muralist, Richardson studied art at Wesleyan College in Macon, Georgia, and at the Art Students League in New York. Her abstract expressionist works have been exhibited at the National Academy of Design and are represented in several corporate collections and in the U.S. Embassy in Denmark.

22. Nan Sheets, 1889–1976, *Oklahoma City*: Illinois native Nan Sheets earned her living as a pharmacist in Utah before becoming an artist, teacher, and arts administrator in Oklahoma City. She became the first director of the Oklahoma Art Center in 1936 and served in that capacity for more than three decades.

23. Nellie Shepherd, 1877–1920, *Oklahoma City*: Considered one of Oklahoma's first resident professional artists, Kansas born Nellie Shepherd trained at the Art Academy of Cincinnati and four years in Paris before returning to the United States in 1910. She settled in Oklahoma City but spent several years painting in Arizona. Illness claimed her life at the age of 43.

24. Michi Susan, 1935– , *Oklahoma City*: Born in Tokyo, Japan, Michi Susan attended Japan's Women's University and Hosei University before arriving in Oklahoma in the late 1970s. Her colorful collage and mixed media "landscapes" have garnered Susan an international reputation.

25. Shirley Thompson-Smith, 1929– , *Oklahoma City*: Although attracted to art at an early age, she did not make sculpture her profession until 1980. Five years later, she was accepted as a member of the National Academy of Western Art. Smith's sculptural portrayals of strong and dignified women from diverse cultures have gained a devoted following. The Gilcrease Museum featured the St. Louis native's work in its "2001 Rendezvous" exhibition.

26. Corazon Watkins, 1948– , *Oklahoma City*: A native of the Philippines, Watkins works in oil and mixed media. She earned an MFA at the University of Oklahoma, received a fellowship from the National Endowment for the Arts, and has enjoyed residencies at the Julia and David White Artists' Colony and the Ragdale Foundation at Lake Forrest, Chicago.

27. John Noble, 1874–1935, *Osage Reservation*: Born in Wichita, Kansas, Noble took part in the opening of the Cherokee Strip in 1893. Noble's painting "The Run," commemorating the event, hung in Governor E. W. Marland's office and is presently in the collection of the Woolaroc Museum. Noble later became a member of the National Academy of Design and was best known for his seascapes.

28. May Todd Aaron, 1879–1967, *Pawhuska*: Born in La Celle, Iowa, Aaron attended the Chicago Art Institute (1901–1902) before opening a studio in Pawhuska. She painted primarily landscapes and Indians, particularly the Osage tribe.

29. Jo Saylors, 1932– , *Ponca City*: Tennessee born Jo Saylors has exhibited her lifelike bronze sculptures at the National Audubon Society, the National Museum of American Art in Washington, D.C., and in numerous Oklahoma venues. Her monument "Lady of Justice" beautifies the grounds of the Oklahoma Bar Foundation in Oklahoma City, and "Through the Eyes of a Child" greets patrons of the Ponca City Library.

30. Father Gregory Gerrer, 1867–1946, *Shawnee*: Francis Xavier Gerrer immigrated to America from his native Alsace in 1872 and moved to Guthrie, Oklahoma Territory, in 1892. He was ordained a Catholic priest in 1900, studied art in Europe, served as the first president of the Association of Oklahoma Artists, and taught summer art classes at the University of Notre Dame for more than a decade. In 1931 Gerrer was inducted into the Oklahoma Hall of Fame.

31. Doel Reed, 1894–1985, *Stillwater*: Raised in Indianapolis, Reed headed the art department at Oklahoma A&M College from 1924 to 1959. Considered the premier American printmaker of his time, Reed produced etchings and aquatints that gained him international fame and membership in the National Academy of Design.

32. Henrietta Clopath, 1862–1936, *Tulsa*: Born in Switzerland, Clopath directed art departments at both the American College in Constantinople, Turkey, and the University of Minnesota before establishing a studio in Tulsa in 1913. Her work earned a gold medal at the first Association of Oklahoma Artists exhibition in 1916.

33. Alexandre Hogue, 1898–1994, *Tulsa*: Missourian Alexander Hogue gained fame during the Great Depression for his powerful evocations of the trauma and despair of the Dust Bowl. During this period, his work gained wide exposure in *Life* and *Time* magazines. In 1945, Hogue became director of the Art Department at Tulsa University.

34. Wilson Hurley, 1924– , *Tulsa*: One of America's premier landscapists, Hurley was born in Tulsa but has lived most of his life in New Mexico. A graduate of West Point, Hurley was a military pilot and an attorney before becoming a full-time artist in the mid 1960s. Hurley won the prestigious Prix de West Purchase Award at the National Cowboy and Western Heritage Museum in 1984 and in 1996 completed work on five mammoth triptychs for the museum's special events center.

Flowers, *by Nan Sheets. (Courtesy Fred Jones Jr. Museum of Art, University of Oklahoma)*

118. WOMEN AS PARTNERS ON THE LAND

Essay by *Linda W. Reese*

Oklahoma women, from the beginning, have understood themselves to be partners with men in the creation of the state. Near the end of the 1939 Academy Award–winning motion picture *Cimarron,* the heroine of the story, Sabra Cravat, explained to an assembled audience of notable Oklahomans, "The women of Oklahoma have helped build a prairie wilderness into the state of today." This motion picture and Sabra Cravat—modeled by novelist Edna Ferber after the life of Elva Shartel Ferguson, First Lady of territorial Oklahoma—represent the symbolic image of the history of Oklahoma women. But long before statehood, women had made their imprint on the land and the historical record with their presence.

Women of the Five Nations, forcibly removed to Indian Territory in the 1830s and 1840s, exercised considerable influence in the direction of tribal affairs even though their governments reflected U.S. patterns of power. The matrilineal clan kinship structure and female role as the agriculturalists of their communities granted women a voice. Senior women of exceptional ability, known in the Cherokee Nation as "Beloved Woman," often counseled the chiefs in major decisions. In addition, the federal government early recognized Indian women as effective agents of acculturation, for through their adaptation of material products, intermarriage with white men, and acceptance of Christianity and American education, women created corridors of cultural accommodation that influenced positive political interaction. Separate academies for females (such as Bloomfield, New Hope, and the Cherokee National Female Seminary) educated the elites who provided the leadership model for the future.

Scores of white missionary women either accompanying their husbands or sent singly by the American Board of Commissioners for Foreign Missions struggled to build and develop the Oklahoma mission stations, staffed the mission schools, demonstrated homemaking skills, nursed the sick, and built bridges of cooperation and respect with the Indian people. Some, such as Ann Eliza Worcester Robertson, were instrumental in translating biblical texts into the Indian languages.

African American women added to the racial and cultural diversity of Indian Territory as well. Slaves of the Five Nations—particularly through their household and field labor—contributed to the wealth of Indian-held lands. Intermarriage with members of some of the Indian nations also established kinship ties. The beginning of the Civil War shattered the peaceful, productive lives enjoyed by many families, however. Confederate sympathizers sold their slaves (thus separating husbands, wives, and children) or removed them to camps across the Red River. As men went to war, women either stayed in the territory, managing the farms alone, or retreated with the slaves to refugee camps for the duration. Supporters of the Union and runaway slaves fled to the North. All sides suffered destruction, hunger, and death.

Peace treaties with the Five Nations after the Civil War opened the territory to newcomers and signaled the end of an Indian domain and sovereignty. Plains Indians, commercial developers, outlaws, freed slaves, European immigrants, and "Boomer" colonists (all groups including women from a variety of backgrounds) entered the area and stayed. The land runs beginning in 1889 and later lotteries enabled single women over the age of twenty-one to acquire both a homestead and a town lot, thus attracting a wave of female homesteaders with and without family attachments. Elva Ferguson was one of many who participated in more than one land run. Their sacrifices, hard work, and commitment to the land are commemorated by the "Pioneer Woman Statue," dedicated in 1930 in Ponca City.

Women significantly influenced the constitution and governmental structures of the state of Oklahoma in 1907. The state was symbolically created through the mock wedding of Miss Indian Territory and Mr. Oklahoma Territory. The Oklahoma Federation of Women's Clubs and charismatic reformer Kate Barnard pressured members of the convention for provisions protecting children, families, the handicapped, and workers. An exclusively male electorate voted Barnard into the office of commissioner of charities and corrections, giving her more votes than any other candidate.

Nevertheless, Oklahoma denied woman suffrage (in spite of numerous referendums) until 1918. Reflecting the conservative political climate, residents of the state have elected only one woman—Alice M. Robertson, in 1920—to the U.S. Congress to date; and voters rejected the Equal Rights Amendment. Oklahoma women have, however, held office at every level of state government (with the exception of governor) and have effectively promoted justice on behalf of the poor, children, and families. Female Oklahoma activists have also initiated change in attitudes and policies regarding race and gender.

The Great Depression and the Dust Bowl conditions of western Oklahoma failed to defeat the spirit of Oklahoma women who stayed on the land, inspiring subsequent generations. When World War II began, women stepped into agriculture and factory jobs as well as joining the war effort as nurses and as members of the Women's Army Corps (WAC) and Women Air Service Pilots (WASP). Oklahoma women have since then engaged in every field of endeavor and have brought honor to the state in both the arts and sciences. Five internationally famous ballerinas, four Miss Americas, numerous Grammy Award–winning entertainers and Hollywood actresses, nationally recognized historians and authors, the first female United Nations ambassador, and the astronaut with the longest duration of space flight all are women who claim an Oklahoma heritage. This historical record of Oklahoma women documents an impressive partnership with men in the development of the state.

Selected Women of Oklahoma

1. Molly Shi Boren, *1943– , Ada (state leader)*: A University of Oklahoma law graduate, Boren established a law practice in Ada, becoming one of the youngest women judges in Oklahoma history and the first woman to serve on the board of trustees of the Oklahoma Bar Foundation. A past director of the Oklahoma Arts Institute, the Sarkeys Foundation, and the Gilcrease Museum of Art, she has served in a leadership role for several major corporations. Boren was instrumental in establishing the National Tallgrass Prairie Preserve and was recognized for her role in improving landscaping and building restoration as OU's First Lady. A recipient of the national ATHENA award for her contributions to leadership opportunities for women, she was inducted into the Oklahoma Hall of Fame in 2004.

2. Rosemary Hogan, *1912–1964, Ahpeatone (career military service)*: Known as the "Angel of Bataan," Hogan served in the U.S. Army Nurse Corps in the Philippines during World War II, establishing field hospitals and training nurses. She was injured during evacuation of the Philippines, was captured by the Japanese, and remained a POW until 1945. She was one of the first women to be awarded a Purple Heart and to achieve the rank of colonel in what became the U.S. Air Force after the war.

3. Annette Ross Hume, *1858–1933, Anadarko (photographer, civic leader)*: In 1890 Hume accompanied her physician husband to the Kiowa Agency in Anadarko, where she became a leading education, philanthropic, and civic leader. Her passion for photography left a legacy of approximately 750 negatives capturing early Oklahoma development and Native Americans.

4. Mildred Imache Cleghorn, *1910–1997, Apache (activist, Apache leader)*: Cleghorn—a descendant of Geronimo's band, captured in 1886—was born a prisoner of war at Fort Sill. She completed a bachelor's degree at the University of Oklahoma, traveled the world as an ambassador for women's issues, and in 1977 became the first woman chief of the Fort Sill Apaches.

Belle Starr was an infamous Indian Territory outlaw. (Courtesy Western History Collections, University of Oklahoma Libraries)

Molly Shi Boren. (Courtesy Office of the President, University of Oklahoma)

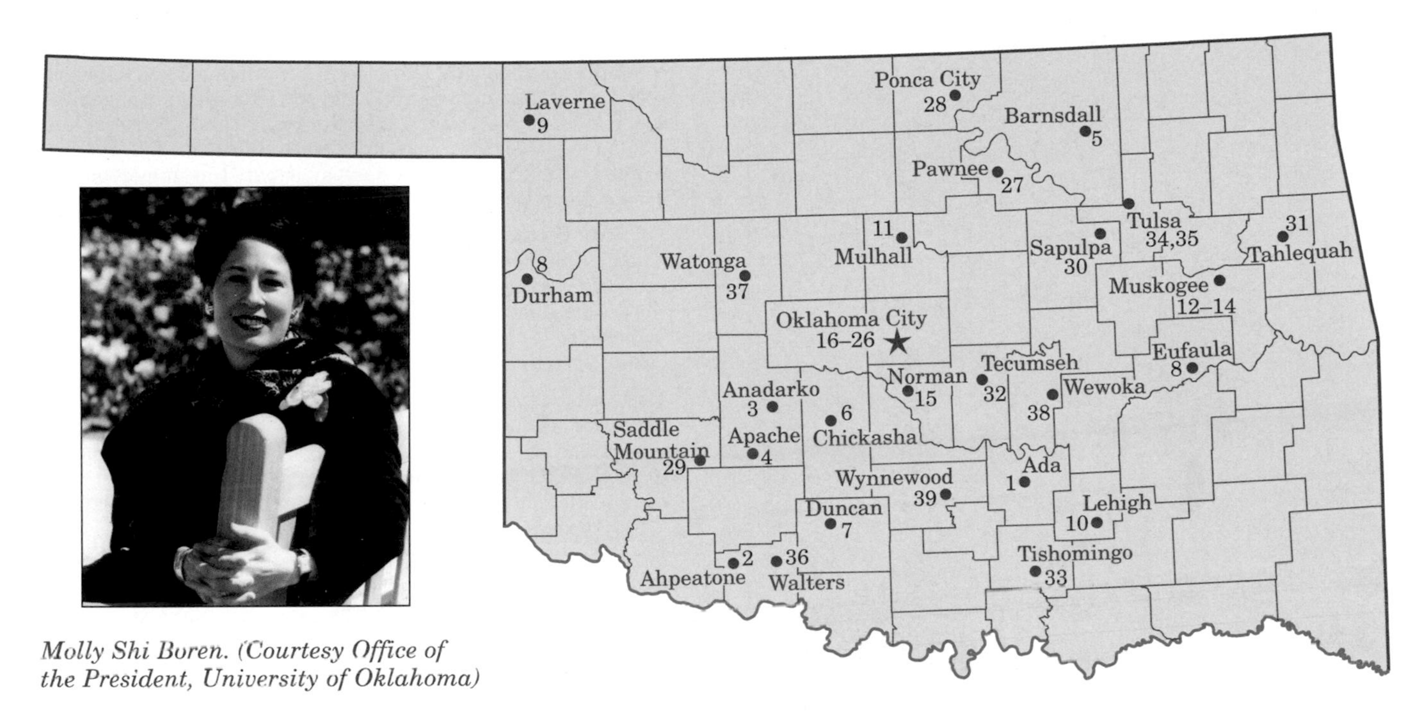

5. Anita Bryant, *1940– , Barnsdall (entertainer)*: Bryant placed third at the Miss America pageant in 1958, but she emerged as a major popular music presence, with three top-20 hits in 1960–1961. She later turned to recording religious music and became an outspoken opponent of gay and lesbian rights.

6. Ada Lois Sipuel Fisher, *1924–1995, Chickasha (attorney, educator)*: Fisher's landmark U.S. Supreme Court case argued by Thurgood Marshall in 1949 brought the end of segregation in higher education in Oklahoma. Fisher became an attorney, educator, and a regent for the University of Oklahoma, which had denied her admission to law school.

7. Jeane Kirkpatrick, *1926– , Duncan (educator, policy maker)*: Kirkpatrick earned a Ph.D. from Columbia University in 1968 and taught political science at Georgetown University, where she became a prolific writer on foreign policy. President Reagan appointed her the first woman U.S. ambassador to the United Nations in 1981, and she advised the Reagan administration on foreign policy decisions until 1985, when she returned to teaching and writing.

8. Belle Starr, *1848–1889, Eufaula (outlaw)*: Starr became infamous in national tabloids and folklore during territorial days. Marrying often, she opened her home near Eufaula to horse and cattle rustlers and various outlaws. The identity of the assassin who murdered the "Bandit Queen," as she was called, is still unknown.

9. Jayne Jayroe, *1946– , Laverne (state leader, news anchor)*: In 1968 Jayroe won the title of Miss America, which, along with her academic degrees, propelled her into a public career in education, television broadcasting, and appointive offices in state government.

10. Muriel Wright, *1889–1975, Lehigh (historian, educator, activist)*: Best known as editor of the scholarly history journal *The Chronicles of Oklahoma* from 1943 until 1973, Wright also wrote 12 books on Oklahoma and Indian history, her research capturing the places, voices, and symbols of the earliest recorded days of the area. She taught many years in rural Oklahoma schools and was a lifelong activist on behalf of the Choctaw Nation.

11. Lucille Mulhall, *1885–1940, Mulhall (rodeo performer)*: The nation's first designated "cowgirl," Mulhall performed for her father's Wild West show, traveled with Will Rogers in the Pawnee Bill Lillie Show, and at age 17 defeated all male contenders in rodeo steer-roping competitions.

12. Carolyn Foreman, *1872–1967, Muskogee (historian)*: Foreman worked in conjunction with her more famous husband, Grant, in researching and writing the history of early Oklahoma and Native Americans. She contributed numerous articles to the history journal *The Chronicles of Oklahoma* that located obscure sites and captured the essence of individuals and events concerning life in the area.

13. Alice M. Robertson, *1854–1931, Muskogee (educator, politician)*: Alice Robertson, granddaughter of Samuel Austin Worcester, missionary to the Cherokees, devoted her life to Indian education as a teacher and superintendent of the Creek Nation schools. She was instrumental in the founding of the University of Tulsa, and at the age of 66, she won election to the U.S. House of Representatives—and still holds the dubious distinction of being Oklahoma's only female congresswoman these many decades later.

Kate Barnard led reform crusades on behalf of children and was a pioneering advocate for women's rights. (Courtesy Western History Collections, University of Oklahoma Libraries)

14. Ann Eliza Worcester Robertson, *1826–1905, Muskogee (missionary)*: Robertson (with her husband, William) built the substantial Presbyterian Tullahassee mission station and school in the Creek Nation. An exceptionally talented linguist, Robertson translated the Bible and other religious literature into the Creek language.

15. Laura Boyd, *1949– , Norman (politician)*: Boyd served in the Oklahoma House of Representatives (1993–1998), standing for issues of education, family, and children's rights. She continued to be active in the Democratic Party, campaigning for governor in 1998 and lieutenant governor in 2002.

16. Freda Hogan Ameringer, *1892–1988, Oklahoma City (publisher)*: Ameringer and her husband, Oscar, were the most effective spokespersons and organizers for the Socialist Party in Oklahoma during the 1920s–1940s, publishing a number of newspapers, the most significant being the *American Guardian*. She continued to publish the *Oklahoma City Advertiser*, promoting health care, education, and veteran benefits, long after her husband's death.

17. Hannah Diggs Atkins, *1923– , Oklahoma City (politician)*: Atkins served six terms in the Oklahoma House of Representatives beginning in 1968, becoming the first woman to chair a committee in that body. Governor Henry Bellmon appointed her secretary of human resources, and she administered that office concurrently as secretary of state, being the highest-ranking woman in state government until 1991. She was a U.S. delegate to the United Nations and has participated in numerous governmental, civic, and humanitarian councils.

18. Kate Barnard, *1875–1930, Oklahoma City (reformer, politician)*: An inspiring campaigner, Barnard became the leading voice of reform on behalf of children and the underprivileged in the debates surrounding the Oklahoma State Constitution. She was elected to office before women could vote and initiated much of the protective legislation and institutions of early statehood.

19. Linda Cavanaugh, *1952– , Oklahoma City (news anchor)*: News anchor for KFOR, Cavanaugh has earned more than 30 national awards, including 11 Emmys. Her investigative reporting and extended series such as "Strangers in Their Own Land," about Oklahoma's Indian tribes, have won widespread acclaim.

20. Gertrude Sober Field, *1869–1949, Oklahoma City (geologist)*: Field left a secretarial job to prospect in the Arbuckle Mountains in 1907. Following two years of solitary effort, her discoveries of zinc resulted in the Indian Mining and Development Company. Late in life she earned a degree in geology from the University of Oklahoma and was posthumously inducted into the Miners Hall of Fame in 1988.

21. Edith Cherry Johnson, *1879–1961, Oklahoma City (journalist)*: Johnson's column on the editorial page of the *Daily Oklahoman* appeared from 1908 to 1958, bringing to generations of Oklahoma women commentary on state and national affairs, advice about marriage and family, and discussion about the changing role of women in America.

22. Vicki Miles LaGrange, *1953– , Oklahoma City (judge)*: LaGrange was the first African American woman elected to the Oklahoma Senate (1986–1993) and the first African American woman to serve as U.S. Attorney in Oklahoma. In 1994, President Clinton appointed her to the U.S. District Court for the Western District.

23. Shannon Lucid, *1943– , Oklahoma City (astronaut)*: NASA administrators chose Lucid in 2002 to serve on a three-person council that will shape the future of space exploration in the United States. Lucid holds the record for single-mission space flight endurance—188 days—and is the only woman to receive the Congressional Space Medal of Honor.

24. Clara Luper, *1923– , Oklahoma City (activist)*: A public school teacher, Luper organized a group of NAACP Youth Council members for a sit-in at a lunch counter in downtown Oklahoma City in 1958 that led—six years and many demonstrations later—to the integration of public facilities in Oklahoma. Luper has been an instrumental advocate of black justice issues.

25. Perle Skirvin Mesta, *1892–1975, Oklahoma City (politician)*: Daughter of a formidable Oklahoma City oil man and real estate developer, Mesta supported Democrat Party politics during World War II and received an appointment from Harry Truman as ambassador to Luxembourg in 1949. Mesta became famous for her ability to orchestrate large political parties and celebrations both in Washington, D.C., and around the world.

Lucille Mulhall learned to ride and rope on her family's Oklahoma ranch. (Courtesy Western History Collections, University of Oklahoma Libraries)

26. Alma Wilson, *1917–1999, Oklahoma City (judge)*: Governor George Nigh appointed Wilson to the Oklahoma Supreme Court in 1982, the first woman to serve in this capacity and that of chief justice, which position she held between 1995 and 1997. She was honored as Appellate Judge of the Year in 1986 and 1989.

27. May Lillie, *1872–1936, Pawnee (rodeo performer)*: In the 1890s, May Lillie's expertise as a cowgirl rider and sharpshooter in the Wild West shows rivaled that of Annie Oakley and Lucille Mulhall. She performed in her husband's Pawnee Bill Lillie Show and was featured in the motion picture *May Lillie, Queen of the Buffalo Ranch*.

28. Jerri Cobb, *1931– , Ponca City (aviator)*: An airplane pilot at age 16, Cobb graduated to testing aircraft and won numerous awards—breaking speed, distance, and altitude records by age 29, when NASA invited her to be part of the Mercury 13 female

Jerrie Cobb. (Copyright 1957, The Oklahoma Publishing Company)

astronaut experiment. When the project was discontinued because the women lacked jet training, Cobb devoted her energies to missionary work in the Amazon jungles. She was nominated for the Nobel Peace Prize in 1981.

29. Isabel Crawford, *1865–1961, Saddle Mountain (missionary)*: The nearly completely deaf Crawford arrived to minister to the Kiowas in 1893 after graduating from the Female Baptist Missionary Training School. She remained with them for 13 years and earned their trust by living alongside them and suffering their hardships. The Saddle Mountain Baptist Church, Kiowa built and administered, resulted largely from her efforts.

30. Mabel Bourne Bassett, *1876–1953, Sapulpa (politician)*: Bassett served six consecutive terms as commissioner of charities and corrections (1923–1947), improving conditions in the state's prisons. She was defeated in a bid for the U.S. Congress on the Democratic ticket in 1932.

31. Wilma Mankiller, *1945– , Tahlequah (Cherokee leader, activist)*: Like many other Indian families, the Mankillers were relocated to California by the Bureau of Indian Affairs when Wilma was a child. She returned to Oklahoma after college graduation and worked to build the economy of her tribe, winning election as deputy chief in 1983 and in 1987 becoming chief of the Cherokee Nation. She is recognized as a leading authority on Indian affairs, an author, and an activist.

32. Mary Fallin, *1955– , Tecumseh (politician)*: Fallin was elected to the Oklahoma House of Representatives in 1990, serving until 1994. In that year she was elected the first woman (and first Republican) lieutenant governor; she was reelected to that office in 2002.

33. Te Ata Fisher, *1895–1995, Tishomingo (entertainer)*: Educated at the Oklahoma College for Women in Chickasha, Fisher developed a talent for storytelling and interpretative dance about the folklore of American Indians. Her one-woman show caught the attention of President Franklin Roosevelt and Eleanor Roosevelt, and Fisher often performed at the White House. In 1987 she was proclaimed a State Treasure.

34. Anita Hill, *1954– , Tulsa (law professor)*: An Oklahoma State University and Yale Law School graduate, Hill established herself at the University of Oklahoma Law School. In 1991, her testimony in televised hearings before the U.S. Senate on the Supreme Court nomination of Clarence Thomas produced a furor over the issue of sexual harassment. Hill, an author and a national authority on women's rights, now teaches at Brandeis University.

35. Lilah Denton Lindsey, *1860–1943, Tulsa (educator)*: When Lindsey graduated from college in 1883, she became the first Creek woman to earn a baccalaureate degree. She spent the remainder of her life teaching in mission and public schools near Tulsa, organizing relief and temperance societies, and participating in Republican Party campaigns.

36. LaDonna Harris, *1931– , Walters (activist)*: Harris founded Americans for Indian Opportunity in 1970 to develop Indian-owned resources throughout the United States. Gaining influential contacts with the nation's capital during the tenure of her husband, Fred Harris, as U.S. senator from Oklahoma, LaDonna has been appointed an advisor to many presidential administrations, beginning in 1967 with that of Lyndon Johnson, who asked her to chair the National Women's Advisory Council of the war on poverty.

37. Elva Shartel Ferguson, *1867–1947, Watonga (publisher, state leader)*: Elva Ferguson became the model for Edna Ferber's fictional heroine, Sabra Cravat, in the novel *Cimarron,* depicting the creation of the new state of Oklahoma. She participated in the Oklahoma land runs with her husband, Thompson B. Ferguson, and became a territorial First Lady during his tenure as governor. Elva continued to influence Oklahomans through their newspaper, and she remained active in Republican politics after the death of her husband.

38. Alice Brown Davis, *1852–1935, Wewoka (Seminole leader)*: Because of her fluency in the Seminole language, Davis served as an interpreter for the U.S. government in relations with Seminole factions in both Florida and Mexico. After the discovery of oil on Seminole land, she was instrumental in negotiations between oil companies and the Seminole people. Her expertise was rewarded by her appointment as chief in 1922, in which position she remained until her death.

39. Donna Shirley, *1942– , Wynnewood (aerospace engineer)*: Winner of numerous achievement awards including the NASA Outstanding Leadership Medal, Shirley was instrumental in development of the Mars Pathfinder Rover. An aerospace engineer and author, she now teaches at the University of Oklahoma.

Ada Lois Sipuel (later Fisher), the first African American to attend the University of Oklahoma Law School, with (left to right) *Amos T. Hall, counsel for the NAACP; Thurgood Marshall, attorney of the NAACP; Dr. H. W. Williamston, state president of the Oklahoma NAACP (Courtesy Western History Collections, University of Oklahoma Libraries)*

119. MEN AS PARTNERS ON THE LAND

Essay by *Danney Goble*

Take out every one of the musicians, the writers, the actors, the entertainers, the athletes, even the women who have played these roles and others—leave out all of these who have taken Oklahoma's influence to the nation, and what would be left? Plenty.

Of course, there would have to be politicians, maybe even a statesman from time to time. This being Oklahoma, there would have to be rich oilmen, a few philanthropists among them. Then there would have to be journalists and ministers; educators and agitators; sailors, soldiers, and airmen. These men could be anything and everything. They would come from all over Oklahoma. Some would stay in Oklahoma all their lives. Others would travel the world. A few would even go into space.

Wherever they came from and wherever they went, they remained Oklahomans. They saw themselves (and others saw them) as Oklahomans. As such, they have made Oklahoma's history part of the nation's.

The list that follows contains no more than some of their names and describes just a few of their deeds. Other names could be added. Let us leave it at this, then: our own list starts here.

Robert S. Kerr. (Courtesy Carl Albert Center Congressional Archives, University of Oklahoma)

1. Robert S. Kerr, *1896–1963, Ada (politician)*: Kerr may one day be footnoted in history as the last candidate for president of the United States to claim birth in a log cabin (a faithful replica of which stands near Ada). As a young man, he intended to attain three things in life: a family, a million dollars, and the governorship of Oklahoma. He got all that and more, earning him the nickname "Uncrowned King of the United States Senate" and acquiring untold billions of dollars in federal spending for the state.

2. Oral Roberts, *1918– , Ada (religious leader)*: Born near Ada, Roberts nearly died of tuberculosis while in high school but recounts how his life was divinely spared after his desperate family took him to a traveling evangelist/faith healer. As a young man, Roberts went into the ministry and pastored a series of small Pentecostal churches, the final one in Enid, before becoming an itinerant minister and healer. He began purchasing blocks of television time to broadcast his miracles and messages of inspiration. Eventually he outgrew the tent, founded the Oral Roberts Evangelistic Association, and put its headquarters on the campus of Oral Roberts University in Tulsa (at 7777 South Lewis Avenue, to be precise, since Roberts has long associated the number seven with the deity's all-encompassing power).

3. Lloyd Noble, *1896–1950, Ardmore (oilman and philanthropist)*: Noble is known for giving away more than $233 million in support of medical research, education, and the arts. Established on the family farm, Noble Drilling was an oil business as innovative as it was successful, offering a profit-sharing plan to employees before the term was even known.During World War II, Noble accepted federal contracts to deliver oil from the Arctic Circle subject to one condition: his company would accept no profit.

4. Frank Phillips, *1873–1950, Bartlesville (businessman)*: Although Frank Phillips was born in Cherry County, Nebraska, and began his working life as a barber, his name will forever be linked with Bartlesville and Phillips Petroleum. His identification with both dates to 1917, when he and his brother L.E. arrived in Bartlesville to found what would become Phillips Petroleum. Perhaps no Oklahoma-based company has done as well (by the late 1960s, Phillips was the 38th-largest corporation in the United States)—and certainly none has had a greater impact upon its hometown.

5. Quanah Parker, *1845–1911, Cache (Comanche leader)*: His last name came from his mother, Cynthia Ann Parker. His first meant "fragrance" in the tongue of those who captured her and raised him to follow his father's path as a Comanche war chief. As a young man, he took that path and resolutely followed it to its one, unavoidable end—surrender and confinement to a government reservation outside Fort Sill, in 1875. His leadership did not end then or there, however. Instead, it took a new, vital, and creative form. Quanah Parker became the one man most adept first at reconciling with and then in leading his mother's people and his father's as well.

6. T. Howard McCasland, Sr., *1895–1979, Duncan (businessman)*: "He came, he saw, he conquered all our hearts; man so handsome, bashful, brave; man of many parts," was a quote from the 1916 Sooner Yearbook that not only reflected the immediate past but also characterized the future life of this young man born near Duncan, Indian Territory, in February 1895. Following graduation in 1916, McCasland served for a year as athletic director and coach at what is now Northern Oklahoma College, at Tonkawa, before serving 18 months in the U.S. Army during World War I. Back home in Duncan, he opened a real estate and oil-lease brokerage office; then he purchased a small rotary rig and joined the hunt for oil and gas. In 1945, he organized the Mack Oil Company and was one of the lucky ones to amass a personal fortune relatively early in life. Eager to share his success, he organized the McCasland Foundation, which strongly supports higher-education opportunities for young people.

Quanah Parker. (Courtesy Western History Collections, University of Oklahoma Libraries)

7. Carl Albert, *1908–2000, McAlester (politician)*: Called "The Little Giant from Little Dixie," Albert was the first-born son of barely schooled parents; he went all eight grades at Bugtussle, graduated from high school in McAlester, and left the University of Oklahoma for Oxford with diploma in hand and a Rhodes scholarship as his ticket. He went on to serve as U.S. congressman from 1947 to 1977. As House Speaker, he presided over a long-past-due overhaul of the House of Representatives' internal workings, then directed the House through the century's greatest constitutional crisis. Watergate ended Nixon's presidency, but it also affirmed how much Oklahoma and the nation were indebted to this "Little Giant"—all 5′ 2³/₈″ of him.

Carl Albert. (Courtesy Carl Albert Center Congressional Archives, University of Oklahoma)

8. George L. Cross, *1905–1998, Norman (university administrator)*: George L. Cross may be remembered as the University of Oklahoma's longest-serving president; he almost certainly will always be identified with hiring Bud Wilkinson as football coach. His true legacy is far greater, however. In the late 1940s, he did everything the state constitution and statutes required of him; he refused to admit a single black applicant to OU. He also put into writing that he was refusing to admit otherwise qualified applicants entirely because of their race. As honest as it was calculated, his statement put Oklahoma's racist and segregated acts directly before the U.S. Supreme Court. The court overruled the state and the university and its president and in so doing, opened the way to changes that were long overdue in Oklahoma and across the nation.

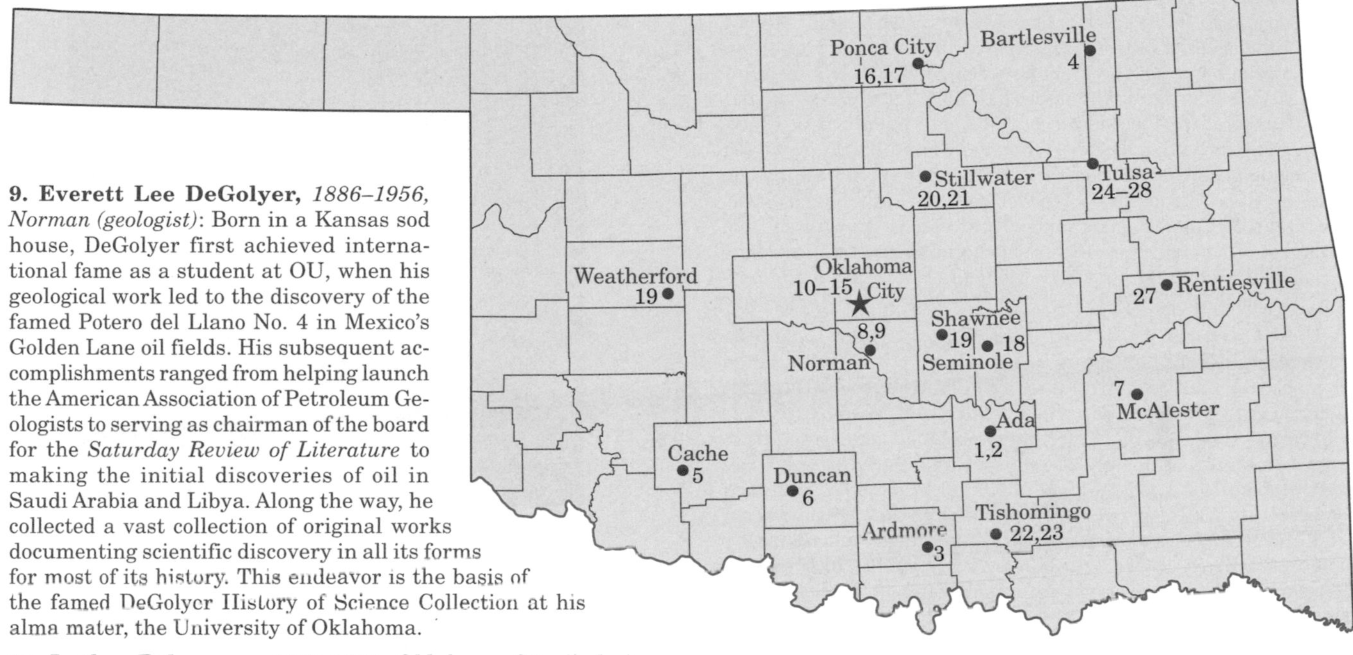

9. Everett Lee DeGolyer, *1886–1956, Norman (geologist)*: Born in a Kansas sod house, DeGolyer first achieved international fame as a student at OU, when his geological work led to the discovery of the famed Potero del Llano No. 4 in Mexico's Golden Lane oil fields. His subsequent accomplishments ranged from helping launch the American Association of Petroleum Geologists to serving as chairman of the board for the *Saturday Review of Literature* to making the initial discoveries of oil in Saudi Arabia and Libya. Along the way, he collected a vast collection of original works documenting scientific discovery in all its forms for most of its history. This endeavor is the basis of the famed DeGolyer History of Science Collection at his alma mater, the University of Oklahoma.

10. Luther Bohannon, *1902–2003, Oklahoma City (judge)*: Bohannon was a student of OU's charismatic speech professor Josh Lee. With fellow OU law students Alfred P. "Fish" Murrah and Royce Savage, the three became Lee's Rover Boys. Lee moved from the classroom to the U.S. Senate, and each of the Rover Boys was eventually appointed to a federal judgeship in Oklahoma. Bohannon's rulings and orders, particularly those promoting racial desegregation and school busing, had a substantial and long-lasting impact—and prompted widespread controversy.

11. William J. Crowe, Jr., *1925– , Oklahoma City (career military service)*: Crowe's father, a native Oklahoman, moved the family home to Oklahoma, from Kentucky, when young William was four. Crowe went on to attend an Oklahoma City high school (Classen) with few if any equals in competitive forensics, particularly debate, which was approached as something of a blood sport. What Crowe learned behind the podiums of Classen High fueled an Annapolis degree, 47 years of naval service, the rank of admiral—with Crowe becoming the highest-ranking military officer that Oklahoma has ever produced—and appointment by Presidents Reagan and Clinton as chairman of the Joint Chiefs of Staff. Even then, Crowe was not finished, for his rare military career was followed with a singular diplomatic honor: ambassador to the Court of Saint James in England.

12. Roscoe Dunjee, *1883–1965, Oklahoma City (newspaperman, activist)*: Dunjee shared his first real home in Oklahoma Territory with 1,500 books, each read and owned by his father, the Reverend John William Dunjee. After graduating from Langston (where he also learned the printer's trade), on November 5, 1915, Roscoe launched Oklahoma City's *Black Dispatch.* Every Thursday for years to come, as many as 20,000 readers eagerly turned to his weekly editorials. In 1931, Dunjee formed the Oklahoma conference of the National Association for the Advancement of Colored People and committed it to judicial combat against legalized racism defeating educational segregation, the exclusion of blacks from juries and voter registration, and numerous other cases against the State of Oklahoma in one form or another.

13. Edward King Gaylord, *1873–1974, Oklahoma City (media businessman)*: Even if apocryphal the story is so appropriate that it has to be true: in 1898 young E. K. Gaylord, with $5,000 in poker winnings in hand, traveled from one western city to another, in search of the one most appropriate for the kind of newspaper he envisioned. Oklahoma City was his choice. Why? Because even though the city was so young and raw that its sidewalks consisted of no more than boards lying loose in the mud, its downtown stores offered magnificent grand pianos in their front windows. Any city that would sell pianos to rich folks before paving its own sidewalks, he reputedly reasoned, was his kind of city. From then until his death at 101 years old, Gaylord built an empire: the Oklahoma Publishing Company, WKY radio and television, Mistletoe Express.

14. John Kirkpatrick, *1908– , Oklahoma City (career military service, businessman, philanthropist)*: Born to the family of an Oklahoma City dentist, Kirkpatrick might have been spared from service in World War II had he chosen not to serve his country. Rising to the rank of admiral, he earned two Silver Stars and also served as executive officer aboard the heavy cruiser U.S.S. *Oklahoma City.* Restoration of peace permitted his plunge into the oil business, in which he quickly amassed a fortune and almost as quickly began giving it away, largely in grants that totaled millions of dollars to Oklahoma County's cash-strapped nonprofits. The giving and the spirit of sacrifice continues through the Kirkpatrick Foundation, which he founded in 1955.

15. Dean McGee, *1904–1989, Oklahoma City (geologist, oilman, philanthropist)*: Robert S. Kerr knew a lot about oil, more about politics, but most about the importance of having the right man in the right place for the right job. So convinced was he that Dean McGee was the right man that Kerr lured the geologist away from Phillips Petroleum, put McGee's talents at work expanding and enriching Kerwyn Oil, and ultimately acknowledged what made possible the resulting energy giant by renaming the company Kerr-McGee. As Kerr-McGee's CEO and board chairman, Dean McGee was also in the right place to put his gifts to public benefit, mostly notably with the millions of dollars that he poured into Oklahoma City's Medical Center and made possible its Myriad Gardens.

16. E. W. Marland, *1874–1941, Ponca City (geologist, businessman)*: Born in Pennsylvania, Ernest Whitworth Marland made his mark in Ponca City. After a series of failures, the self-taught geologist hit black gold with his original well, Willie Cries-for-War No. 1. By the mid-1920s, Marland Oils was estimated to control one-tenth of the world's supply. By the decade's end, however, Marland had lost control of his own company, renamed Conoco after Wall Street bankers forced him out. He pursued a brief and inglorious career in politics and died with relatively little of his previous wealth. His legacy is visible in the mansions, public buildings, and exotic landscaping that his money had brought Ponca City.

17. Zack Miller, *1877–1952, Ponca City (rancher)*: E. W. Marland's discovery well (Willy Cries-for-War No. 1) lay just below the Ponca tribal cemetery, where it met a corner of Zack Miller's vast 101 Ranch. The ranch, in turn, consisted of land that Miller leased from the Ponca tribe—not for cash, but with 50,000 pounds of bacon. Pronounced the "hundred-and-one," the name stood not for its vast size but as a reminder to its cowhands of a similarly named San Antonio saloon notorious for the pains its wares inflicted upon the indolent and irresponsible. Neither Miller nor his sons, who later took it over, were either. On the contrary, they built what might have been called the world's first fully integrated agribusiness, if only the term had been invented. The ranch raised its own cattle and processed and sold milk, flesh, and tanned hides. The 101's wells pumped crude oil, refined the oil on the ranch, and dispensed the products from its own gas pumps. Last but hardly least, its globe-trotting Wild West show forever defined the myth of America's frontier past.

18. David L. Boren, *1941– , Seminole (politician, university administrator)*: One would be hard pressed to name an Oklahoman who has had greater positive impact upon his state than David Boren. Son of a Depression-era Oklahoma congressman and father of another, he comes from a family devoted not to politics, but to public service. Boren served briefly in the state legislature and was then elected to a term as governor, followed by 20 years in the U.S. Senate. In 1994, Senator Boren voluntarily walked away from power in the Senate—even the much-discussed possibility of a future presidential candidacy—to serve in the one capacity most important to him: president of the University of Oklahoma. Both OU and the entire state will forever be beneficiaries of David Boren and his most revealing choice.

19. Gordon Cooper, *1927–2004, Shawnee; and* **Thomas Stafford,** *1930– , Weatherford (astronauts)*: All of the 24 men who have set foot on the moon have been Americans, among their elite

David L. Boren. (Courtesy Office of the President, University of Oklahoma)

ranks an Oklahoman. Cooper, the last of the original seven Mercury astronauts to go into space, circled the earth 22 times in 1963 (aboard Faith 7), thus going further, farther, and faster than man had ever gone before. He then commanded Gemini V on an eight-day endurance mission. Following the success of the Mercury project, Stafford (aboard Gemini VI in 1965, Gemini IX in 1966, and commanding Apollo X in 1969) and others made possible Neil Armstrong's historic "giant step for mankind" on the moon's surface. Stafford's last space flight came in 1975 as commander of the first joint American-Soviet Apollo-Soyuz test project. Upon retirement as an air force lieutenant general, Stafford had added to his 7,000 flight hours another 500 hours of space time, earning him the Congressional Space Medal of Honor.

20. Henry G. Bennett, *1901–1951, Stillwater (university administrator, public servant)*: Although born in Arkansas and best known as president of Oklahoma Agricultural and Mechanical College, Henry Bennett's influence reached across all of Oklahoma, toward every corner of the world. Moreover, Bennett began the refashioning of an obscure Aggie college into a world-class research university. Six years after his death, its name was officially changed to Oklahoma State University—state legislators took that long to catch up to what Bennett had done. His death came, not on the prairies of his beloved Stillwater, but over the sands of distant Iran, where his plane crashed while he was traveling as President Truman's personal representative as well as head of the administration's Point Four program of foreign technical aid.

21. Francis Tuttle, *1921–1997, Stillwater (vocational education administrator)*: What is now called CareerTech training owes its origins largely to Wellston-born FFA member, Oklahoma A&M graduate, and early "ag" teacher at tiny Gotebo: Francis Tuttle. After inheriting an archaic state vo-tech department based in Stillwater, in 20 years Tuttle made his department a national model as well as an international resource. Every week, it ships curriculum materials across the world, and every year, educators come from across the globe to visit one or more of its many campuses.

22. Bill Anoatubby, *1945– , Tishomingo*: From being high school's "all-around boy" to being the leader of the more than 38,000-member Chickasaw Nation took Anoatubby only 23 years. In 1987, the newly elected 30th governor of the Chickasaw Nation was faced with a financial crisis, but under his financial leadership, the nation became one of the first tribal governments in the United States to be certified with superior ratings for management and fiscal controls. This is no surprise when the almost-bankrupt $11 million annual budget in 1987 is compared with the $300 million budget in 2005 and the presence of employees in 48 states. With strong tribal support, Anoatubby's commitment continues to be funding higher-education scholarships, providing Indian health services, preserving Chickasaw natural resources and the Chickasaw language, and expanding economic development. He is chairman of the Native American Culture on Educational Authority, which is developing an Oklahoma City world-class facility focused on the tribes located in Oklahoma.

23. William H. Murray, *1869–1956, Tishomingo (politician)*: He was a man of many nicknames—among them "Cocklebur Bill," "Alfalfa Bill," and the "Sage of Tishomingo"—and even more opinions, which covered every subject from crops to constitutions. President of the state's constitutional convention, House Speaker of its First Legislature, two-term congressman, and Depression-era governor, Murray managed to make many of those opinions public policy. At statehood, he orchestrated the new constitution's populist tone. In the 1930s, however, his eccentric deeds (such as his offer of a full pardon to any convict

Henry G. Bennett. (Courtesy Special Collections and University Archives, Oklahoma State University Libraries)

Daniel Boorstin. (Copyright 1993, The Oklahoma Publishing Company)

who would leave the state, which had the effect of exporting 2,216 criminals to Oklahoma's neighbors) led many to view Oklahoma as a rustic, backwater state governed by cranks and hicks.

24. Thomas Gilcrease, *1890–1962, Tulsa (oilman, philanthropist)*: When the Creek Nation was broken up as allotments, only a few Creek citizens were lucky enough to be assigned lands later found to be rich with oil. In 1954, Gilcrease, one of the fortunate ones, sold to the City of Tulsa the 200,000 pieces of art and artifacts that his oil money had bought. Tulsa paid him $2,250,000, a pittance of the priceless collection's worth. Because he threw in half interest in his East Texas oil holdings as an endowment, Gilcrease must be said to have repaid Tulsa every penny and more that it had given him.

25. Waite Phillips, *1883–1964, Tulsa (oilman, philanthropist)*: Like his older brothers of Bartlesville fame, Waite Phillips established an oil company, this one in Tulsa. In 1926, Phillips hired architects Jesse Claude Nichols and Edward Buehler Delk to build him a house. The result was Villa Philbrook, perhaps the state's most magnificent private residence. Phillips and his wife, Genevieve, raised two children there before handing the mansion and grounds over to the city in 1938. To maintain and fund both, he threw in the Beacon Building, a nine-story, high-rent downtown office structure. Thus Tulsa acquired the Philbrook Art Center, which is, like the Gilcrease Museum, one of the nation's premier art institutions.

26. Julian Rothbaum, *1913–2003, Tulsa (philanthropist)*: This son of a Jewish back-peddler in the Krebs-Hartshorne coal fields was a devoted contributor to the Democratic Party, but his endowments, awards, and lecture series at his beloved alma mater, the University of Oklahoma, have proved an even more enduring legacy. The Irene Rothbaum Award honors the university's outstanding assistant professor in his wife's name. In the name of his lifelong friend Carl Albert, Rothbaum endowed the school's most prestigious student award, the Carl Albert Award, which honors the College of Arts and Sciences' top graduate. It also has exact parallels at both McAlester High School and Oxford University, the other schools that issued diplomas to Rothbaum's great friend. Every other year, the Julian Rothbaum Lecture Series brings to campus one of the most respected of the nation's political scientists to visit classes and present a series of public lectures on the general topic of representative government. Published thereafter by the University of Oklahoma Press, books in the resulting series have collected national as well as international awards, both for their contributions to scholarship and for their encouragement to the spread of democratic institutions around the world.

John Hope Franklin. (Courtesy University of Oklahoma)

27. John Hope Franklin, *1915– , Rentiesville (historian)*; **Daniel J. Boorstin,** *1914–2004, Tulsa (historian)*: Think of it like this: Rarely has one relatively small American city produced two men of such stunning intellectual achievements. Rarer still, these two were almost exact contemporaries. Both attended Tulsa high schools at the same time. Both left to begin college work at the same time. Both earned doctorates in American history. They even briefly worked side by side at the same school: the University of Chicago.

The difference was this: John Hope Franklin was black, son of a black attorney, born in all black Rentiesville; arriving in all black north Tulsa just after the 1921 race riot, he graduated from Tulsa's Booker T. Washington High School and from all black Howard University, and was among the earliest of Harvard's black Ph.D.'s. Daniel Boorstin was white, the son of a Jewish family who had fled Georgia for Tulsa in the aftermath of Leo Frank's lynching; he was a graduate of Tulsa Central High School and of Oxford University, the latter as a Rhodes scholar.

The similarities were these: Both had brilliant academic careers. Both produced books that are permanent landmarks in American history: Franklin's *From Slavery to Freedom: A History of African Americans* and Boorstin's trilogy *The Americans*. Both reached the very top of their profession and graciously devoted their professional achievements to national service. The first black American elected president of the American Historical Association, John Hope Franklin was later recipient of the Medal of Freedom and was President Bill Clinton's choice to head a national dialogue on race. Upon leaving the classroom and seminar study, Boorstin took over the Smithsonian Institution, then served as Librarian of Congress.

John Hope Franklin and Daniel Boorstin—how irrelevant that they happened to come from two minorities. How telling that they became everlasting credits to one city, one state, and one America.

28. William G. Skelly, *1878–1957, Tulsa (businessman, community leader)*: Called "Mr. Tulsa," Bill Skelly's touch can be seen throughout the city. Skelly, who was among the early leaders of the city's chamber of commerce, helped water the city with the Spavinaw dam and water system, an engineering marvel that as a municipal public project ranked second in cost only to New York's Holland Tunnel. Founder of Skelly Oil, he included among his protégés young J. Paul Getty, who founded Getty Oil. Skelly's Spartan Aircraft and Spartan School of Aeronautics were major players in early aviation and critical factors in the War Department's choice of Tulsa as the site for two major World War II bomber plants. Then there is the University of Tulsa, with its athletic fields (Skelly Stadium) at one end, its public radio station (KWGS, with call letters for William Grove Skelly) at the other.

Julian Rothbaum. (photo by Paul Esserman, courtesy Carl Albert Center Congressional Archives, University of Oklahoma)

Bibliography

Archival Sources

Constitution of the State of Oklahoma. Article 17: Counties and County Seats.
Oklahoma City National Memorial Foundation. Biographies.
Oklahoma Corporation Commission, Records Department.
Oklahoma Department of Commerce, Records Department.
Oklahoma Jazz Hall of Fame. Biographies.
Oklahoma Music Hall of Fame. Biographies.
Oklahoman, The. Newspaper archives.
Oklahoma Sports Hall of Fame. Biographies.
University of Oklahoma Libraries, Western History Collections, Manuscripts Division. Manuscript Collections and Map Collections.
U.S. Department of Agriculture, Bureau of Agricultural Economics.
U.S. Department of Energy, Energy Information Administration. "Annual Energy Review, 1998"; "Coal Industry Annual, 1999"; "Inventory of Electric Utility Power Plants in the United States, 1999"; "Inventory of Non-utility Electric Power Plants in the United States, 1999"; "State Electricity Profiles, 1999"; "State Energy Data Report, 1999"; and Keystone Coal Industry Manual, 2001. See EIA Web site: www.eia.doe.gov.

Secondary Sources

Aandahal, Andrew R. *Soils of the Great Plains: Use, Crops, and Grasses.* Lincoln: University of Nebraska Press, 1982.
Abel, Anne H. *The Slaveholding Indians.* 3 vols. Cleveland: Arthur H. Clark, 1915–25.
Able, Annie Heloise. *The American Indian as a Participant in the Civil War, 1862–1865.* Cleveland: Arthur H. Clark, 1915.
Adair, James. *The History of the American Indians.* London: Edward and Charles Dilly, 1775. (Reprinted as *Adair's History of the American Indians,* ed. Samuel C. Williams. Johnson City, Tenn.: Watauga Press, 1930.)
Agnew, Brad. *Fort Gibson: Terminal of the Trail of Tears.* Norman: University of Oklahoma Press, 1980.
Alexander, Charles C. *The Ku Klux Klan in the Southwest.* Lexington: University of Kentucky Press, 1965.
American Horse Council. "The Economic Impact of the Horse Industry in the United States." Report commissioned in 2005.
Anonymous. *Pasture and Range Plants.* Hayes, Kans.: Fort Hayes State University, 1989.
Anonymous. *Thunderbird Review.* Atlanta: Albert Love Enterprises, 1952.
Asplin, Ray. "A History of Council Grove in Oklahoma." *Chronicles of Oklahoma* 45, no. 4 (Winter 1967–68): 433–50.
Autry, Gene, and Mickey Herskowitz. *Back in the Saddle Again.* Garden City, N.Y.: Doubleday, 1978.
Babcock, Sidney, and John Y. Bryce. *The History of Methodism in Oklahoma.* N.p., 1935.
Bailey, M. Thomas. *Reconstruction in Indian Territory.* New York: Kennekat Press, 1972.
Baird, W. David. "Cathedrals of the Plains: The Grain Elevators of Oklahoma." *Chronicles of Oklahoma* 70, no. 1 (Spring 1992): 4–25.
Baird, W. David. *The Chickasaw People.* Phoenix: Indian Tribal Series, 1974.
Baird, W. David. *The Choctaw People.* Phoenix: Indian Tribal Series, 1973.
Baird, W. David. *Peter Pitchlynn: Chief of the Choctaws.* Norman: University of Oklahoma Press, 1972.
Baird, W. David. "Spencer Academy, Choctaw Nation, 1842–1900." *Chronicles of Oklahoma* 45, no. 1 (Spring 1967): 25–43.
Baird, W. David, and Danney Goble. *The Story of Oklahoma.* Norman: University of Oklahoma Press, 1994.
Baker, Elmer LeRoy. *Gunman's Territory.* San Antonio: Naylor, 1969.
Baker, T. Lindsay, and Julie P. Baker. *The WPA Oklahoma Slave Narratives.* Norman: University of Oklahoma Press, 1996.
Balyeat, Frank A. "Joseph Samuel Murrow, Apostle to the Indians." *Chronicles of Oklahoma* 35 (Fall 1957): 297–314.
Bell, Robert E. *Oklahoma Prehistory.* New York: Academic Press, 1984.
Bement, Leland C. *Bison Hunting at Cooper Site: Where Lightning Bolts Drew Thundering Herds.* Norman: University of Oklahoma Press, 1999.
Berkhofer, Robert F., Jr. *The White Man's Indian: Images of the American Indian from Columbus to the Present.* New York: Random House, 1978.
Berlo, Janet C., ed. *The Early Years of Native American Art History.* Seattle: University of Washington Press, 1992.

Berlo, Janet C., and Ruth B. Phillips, eds. *Native North American Art.* New York: Oxford University Press, 1998.
Berthrong, Donald J. "Cattlemen on the Cheyenne-Arapaho Reservation, 1883–1885." *Arizona and the West* 13, no. 1 (1971): 5–32.
Berthrong, Donald J. *The Cheyenne and Arapaho Ordeal: Reservation and Agency Life in the Indian Territory, 1875–1907.* Norman: University of Oklahoma Press, 1976.
Bittle, William E., and Gilbert Geis. *The Longest Way Home: Chief Alfred C. Sam's Back-to-Africa Movement.* Detroit, Mich.: Wayne State University Press, 1964.
Blackburn, Bob L. *Images of Oklahoma: A Pictorial History with Text.* Oklahoma City: Oklahoma Historical Society, 1984.
Bollinger, C. J. *The Geography of Oklahoma.* Chicago: Rand McNally, 1930.
Bowman, Isaiah. "An American Boundary Dispute: Decision of the Supreme Court of the United States with Respect to the Texas-Oklahoma Boundary." *Geographical Review* 13 (1923): 161–89.
Braunlich, Phyllis Cole. *Haunted by Home: The Life and Letters of Lynn Riggs.* Norman: University of Oklahoma Press, 1988.
Brill, Charles J. *Custer, Black Kettle and the Fight on the Washita.* Norman: University of Oklahoma Press, 2002.
Britton, Wiley. *The Union Indian Brigade in the Civil War.* Kansas City: F. Hudson Publishing, 1992.
Brown, James A. *The Spiro Ceremonial Center: The Archaeology of Arkansas Valley Caddoan Culture in Eastern Oklahoma.* 2 vols. Memoir 29. Ann Arbor: Museum of Anthropology, University of Michigan, 1996.
Brown, Opal H. *Indomitable Oklahoma Women.* Oklahoma City: Oklahoma Heritage Association, 1994.
Bureau of the Census. *Thirteenth Census of the United States.* Washington, D.C.: Government Publication Office, 1912.
Burke, Bob, Betty Crow, and Sandy Meyers. *Art Treasures of the Oklahoma State Capitol.* Oklahoma City: Oklahoma State Senate Historical Preservation Fund, 2003.
Butler, William. *Tulsa 75.* Tulsa: Metropolitan Tulsa Chamber of Commerce, 1975.
Calhoun, Frederick S. *The Lawmen: United States Marshals and Their Deputies, 1789–1989.* Washington, D.C.: Smithsonian Institution Press, 1989.
Campbell, O. B. *Mission to the Cherokees.* Oklahoma City: Metro Press, 1973.
Carlile, Glenda. *Petticoats, Politics, and Pirouettes: Oklahoma Women, 1900–1950.* Oklahoma City: Southern Hills Publishing, 1995.
Carney, George. *Oklahoma Jazz Artists: A Biographical Dictionary.* Stillwater, Okla.: N.p., 1992.
Carney, George O., and Hugh W. Foley, Jr. *Oklahoma Music Guide: Biographies, Big Hits and Annual Events.* Stillwater, Okla.: New Forums Press, 2003.
Carroll, John M. *General Custer and the Battle of the Washita: The Federal View.* Bryan, Okla.: Guidon Press, 1978.
Cassal, Reverend Hillary. "Missionary Tour in the Chickasaw Nation." *Chronicles of Oklahoma* 34, no. 4 (Winter 1956–57): 397–416.
Chandler, Allison, and Stephen D. Maguire. *When Oklahoma Took the Trolley.* Glendale, Calif.: US Interurbans, 1980.
Chapman, Berlin B. "Establishment of the Iowa Reservation." *Chronicles of Oklahoma* 21, no. 4 (December 1943): 366–77.
Chapman, Berlin B. "How the Cherokees Acquired and Disposed of the Outlet (Part Two)." *Chronicles of Oklahoma* 15, no. 2 (June 1937): 205–25.
Clark, Blue. "Delegates to the Constitutional Convention." *Chronicles of Oklahoma* 48, no. 4 (Winter 1970–71): 400–15.
Clark, Joseph Stanley. *The Boundaries of Oklahoma.* Master's thesis, University of Oklahoma, 1932.
Clark, Joseph Stanley. "The Eastern Boundary of Oklahoma." *Chronicles of Oklahoma* 11, no. 4 (December 1933): 1084–1110.
Coleman, Louis. "Cyrus Byington: Missionary to the Choctaws." *Chronicles of Oklahoma* 62, no. 4 (Winter 1984–85): 360–87.
Cooper, Charles M. "The Big Pasture." *Chronicles of Oklahoma* 35, no. 2 (Summer 1957): 138–46.
Corkran, David H. *The Creek Frontier, 1540-1783.* Norman: University of Oklahoma Press, 1967.
Cotterill, R. A. *The Southern Indians: The Story of the Civilized Tribes before Removal.* Norman: University of Oklahoma Press, 1954.
Crane, Verner W. *The Southern Frontier, 1670-1732.* Durham, N.C.: Duke University Press, 1929.
Cray, Ed. *Ramblin' Man: The Life and Times of Woody Guthrie.* New York: W. W. Norton, 2004.
Cross, George L. *Blacks in White Colleges.* Norman: University of Oklahoma Press, 1975.
Cross, George Lynn. *The University of Oklahoma and World War II: A Personal Account, 1941–1946.* Norman: University of Oklahoma Press, 1980.
Crowder, James L., Jr. "More Valuable Than Oil: The Establishment and Development of Tinker Air Force Base, 1940–1949." *Chronicles of Oklahoma* 70, no. 3 (Fall 1992): 228–57.
Cubage, Annie Rosser. "Engagement at Cabin Creek, Indian Territory, July 1 and 2, 1863." *Chronicles of Oklahoma* 10, no. 1 (March 1932): 44–51.
Culberson, James. "The Fort Towson Road." *Chronicles of Oklahoma* 5, no. 4 (December 1927): 414–21.
Cunningham, Hugh T. "A History of the Cherokee Indians." *Chronicles of Oklahoma* 8, no. 3 (September 1930): 291–314.
Cunningham, William. *The Green Corn Rebellion: A Novel.* New York: Vanguard Press, 1935.
Dale, Edward Everett. *The Range Cattle Industry: Ranching on the Great Plains from 1865 to 1925.* Norman: University of Oklahoma Press, 1960.
Dale, Edward Everett. "The Cherokee Strip Livestock Association." *Chronicles of Oklahoma* 5, no. 1 (March 1927): 58–78.
Dale, Edward Everett. "Ranching on the Cheyenne-Arapaho Reservation." *Chronicles of Oklahoma* 6, no. 1 (March 1928): 35–59.

Dale, Edward Everett, and Morris L. Wardell. *History of Oklahoma.* New York: Prentice Hall, 1948.

Davidson, Marshall B. *Life in America.* Boston: Houghton Mifflin, 1954.

Davis, Caroline. "Education of the Chickasaws." *Chronicles of Oklahoma* 15, no. 4 (December 1937): 415–48.

Davison, Oscar W. "Oklahoma's Educational Heritage." *Chronicles of Oklahoma* 27, no. 4 (Winter 1949–50): 354–72.

Debo, Angie. *And Still the Waters Run: The Betrayal of the Five Civilized Tribes.* Princeton, N.J.: Princeton University Press, 1940.

Debo, Angie. "Education in the Choctaw Country after the Civil War." *Chronicles of Oklahoma* 10, no. 3 (September 1932): 383–91.

Debo, Angie. *A History of the Indians of the United States.* Norman: University of Oklahoma Press, 1934. Reprint, Norman: University of Oklahoma Press, 1970.

Debo, Angie. *Oklahoma: Foot-Loose and Fancy-Free.* Norman: University of Oklahoma Press, 1949.

Debo, Angie. *Prairie City: The Story of an American Community.* New York: Alfred A. Knopf, 1944.

Debo, Angie. "Realizing Oklahoma's Literary Potential." *Oklahoma Libraries* 16 (July 1966): 67–75.

Debo, Angie. *The Rise and Fall of the Choctaw Republic.* Norman: University of Oklahoma Press, 1934.

Debo, Angie. *The Road to Disappearance.* Norman: University of Oklahoma Press, 1941.

Debo, Angie, and John M. Oskison, eds. *Oklahoma: A Guide to the Sooner State.* Compiled by Writers' Program of the Work Projects Administration in the State of Oklahoma. American Guide Series. Norman: University of Oklahoma Press, 1941. Reprint, Norman, University of Oklahoma Press, 1947.

DeLong, David G. *Bruce Goff: Toward Absolute Architecture.* New York: Architectural History Foundation, 1988.

DeLong, Lea Rosson. *Nature's Forms / Nature's Forces: The Art of Alexandre Hogue.* Tulsa: Philbrook Art Center, and Norman: University of Oklahoma Press, 1984.

DeMarco, Mario. *William Boyd: "Hopalong Cassidy—Knight of the West."* N.p.: privately published, 1983.

DeRosier, Arthur H. *The Removal of the Choctaw Indians.* Knoxville: University of Tennessee Press, 1970.

Dillehay, Tom D., and David J. Meltzer, eds. *The First Americans: Search and Research.* Boca Raton, Fla.: CRC Press, 1991.

Dippie, Brian W. *Catlin and His Contemporaries, The Politics of Patronage.* Lincoln: University of Nebraska Press, 1990.

Dott, Robert H. "Lieutenant Simpson's California Road through Oklahoma." *Chronicles of Oklahoma* 38, no. 2 (Summer 1960): 154–79.

Doyle, Thomas H. "Single Versus Double Statehood," *Chronicles of Oklahoma* 5, no. 2 (June 1927): 18–41.

Droze, Wilmon H. *Trees, Prairies, and People: A History of Tree Planting in the Plains States.* Denton: Texas Woman's University, 1977.

Duck, Lester G., and Jack B. Fletcher. *A Game Type Map of Oklahoma.* Oklahoma City: State of Oklahoma Game and Fish Department, 1945.

Duck, Lester G., and Jack B. Fletcher. *A Survey of the Game and Furbearing Animals of Oklahoma.* Oklahoma City: Oklahoma Department of Wildlife Conservation, 1945.

Dye, Karen. "Politics and Greed? Allotments and Town Building Schemes in the Cherokee Outlet." *Chronicles of Oklahoma* 73, no. 3 (1995): 308–21.

Eastman, James N., Jr. "Location and Growth of Tinker Airforce Base and Oklahoma City Air Materiel Area." *Chronicles of Oklahoma* 50, no. 3 (Fall 1972): 326–46.

Eaton, Rachel C. "The Legend of the Battle of Claremore Mound." *Chronicles of Oklahoma* 8, no. 4 (December 1930): 369–77.

Ellis, A. H. *History of the Oklahoma Constitutional Convention.* Muskogee: Economy Printing, 1923.

England, Gary. *Oklahoma Weather.* Oklahoma City: England and May, 1975.

Epple, Jessee C. *Custer's Battle of the Washita and a History of the Plains Indian Tribes.* New York: Exposition Press, 1970.

Espenshade, Edward B., Jr., ed. *Goode's World Atlas.* Chicago: Rand McNally, 1974.

Fairbanks, Charles W. *The Florida Seminole People.* Phoenix: Indian Tribal Series, 1973.

Faulk, Odie B., Kenny A. Franks, and Paul Lambert. *Early Military Forts and Posts in Oklahoma.* Oklahoma City: Oklahoma Historical Society, 1978.

Fessler, W. Julian. "Captain Nathan Boone's Journal." *Chronicles of Oklahoma* 7, no. 1 (March 1929): 58–105.

Fessler, W. Julian. "Jacob Fowler's Journal (Oklahoma Section)." *Chronicles of Oklahoma* 8, no. 2 (June 1930): 181–88.

Fischer, LeRoy Henry. *The Civil War Era in Indian Territory.* Los Angeles: L. L. Morrison, 1974.

Fischer, LeRoy H. "Honey Springs Battlefield Park." *Chronicles of Oklahoma* 47, no. 1 (Spring 1969): 515–30 [22–37].

Fischer, LeRoy Henry, and Muriel H. Wright. "Civil War Sites in Oklahoma." *Chronicles of Oklahoma* 44, no. 2 (Summer 1966): 158–215.

Fisher, Ada Lois Sipuel, with Danney Goble. *A Matter of Black and White: The Autobiography of Ada Lois Sipuel Fisher.* Norman: University of Oklahoma Press, 1996.

Fite, Gilbert C. "Development of the Cotton Industry by the Five Civilized Tribes in Indian Territory." *Journal of Southern History* 15 (1949): 342–53.

Fitzgerald, David. *Oklahoma.* Rev. ed., Portland, Ore.: Graphic Arts Center Publishing, 1989.

Fitzgerald, David, with George Nigh. *Oklahoma II.* Portland, Ore.: Graphic Arts Center Publishing, 1994.

Fly, Shelby M. *The Saga of the Chouteaus of Oklahoma: French Footprints in the Valley Grand.* Norman, Okla.: Levite of Apache, 1988.

Fogelson, Raymond D. *The Cherokees: A Critical Bibliography.* Bloomington: Indiana University Press, 1978.

Forbes, Gerald. "History of the Osage Blanket Lease." *Chronicles of Oklahoma* 19, no. 1 (March 1941): 70–81.

Foreman, Carolyn Thomas. "Nathan Boone." *Chronicles of Oklahoma* 19, no. 4 (December 1941): 322–47.

Foreman, Grant. *Down the Texas Road.* Norman: University of Oklahoma Press, 1936.

Foreman, Grant. "Early Trails through Oklahoma." *Chronicles of Oklahoma* 3, no. 2 (June 1925): 99–119.

Foreman, Grant. *The Five Civilized Tribes.* Norman: University of Oklahoma Press, 1934.

Foreman, Grant. "Historical Phases of the Grand River Valley." *Chronicles of Oklahoma* 25 (Summer 1947): 141–52.

Foreman, Grant. *History of Oklahoma.* Norman: University of Oklahoma Press, 1942.

Foreman, Grant. *Indian Removal.* Norman: University of Oklahoma Press, 1932, 1953.

Foreman, Grant. *Indians and Pioneers: The Story of the American Southwest before 1830.* Norman: University of Oklahoma Press, 1930.

Foreman, Grant. *Indians and Pioneers.* Norman: University of Oklahoma Press, 1937.

Foreman, Grant. *The Last Trek of the Indians.* Chicago: University of Chicago Press, 1946.

Foreman, Grant. *Marcy and the Gold Seekers: The Journal of Captain R. B. Marcy: With an Account of the Gold Rush over the SouthernRoute.* Norman: University of Oklahoma Press, 1939.

Foreman, Grant. *Muskogee: The Biography of an Oklahoma Town.* Norman: University of Oklahoma Press, 1943.

Franklin, Jimmie Lewis. *Journey Toward Hope: A History of Blacks in Oklahoma.* Norman: University of Oklahoma Press, 1986.

Franks, Kenny. "Among the Plains Tribes in Oklahoma with Frederic Remington." *Chronicles of Oklahoma* 52, no. 4 (Winter 1974–75): 419–38.

Franks, Kenny A. *Citizen Soldiers: Oklahoma's National Guard.* Norman: University of Oklahoma Press, 1984.

Franks, Kenny. *The Oklahoma Petroleum Industry.* Norman: Published for the Oklahoma Heritage Association by the University of Oklahoma Press, 1980.

Franks, Kenny A., George H. Shirk, and Muriel H. Wright. *Mark of Heritage.* 2nd ed. Oklahoma City: Oklahoma Historical Society, 1976.

Frazer, Robert W. *Forts of the West: Military Forts and Presidios and Posts Commonly Called Forts West of the Mississippi River to 1898.* Norman: University of Oklahoma Press, 1965.

Freeman, Charles R. "The Battle of Honey Springs." *Chronicles of Oklahoma* 13, no. 2 (June 1935): 154–68.

French, Benjamin F. *Historical Collections of Louisiana.* New York: Wiley and Putnam, 1846–53.

Garbarino, Merwyn S. *The Seminole.* New York: Chelsea House, 1989.

Gard, Wayne. *The Chisholm Trail.* Norman: University of Oklahoma Press, 1954.

Gardner, Charles. *Railroad Abandonment in Oklahoma.* Master's thesis, University of Oklahoma, 1958.

Gaskin, J. M. *Baptist Milestones in Oklahoma.* Messenger Press, 1966.

Gates, Eddie Faye. *They Came Searching: How Blacks Sought the Promised Land in Tulsa.* Austin, Tex.: Eakin Press, 1997.

Gibson, Arrell M. *The American Indian: Prehistory to the Present.* Lexington, Ky.: D.C. Heath, 1980.

Gibson, Arrell M., ed. *America's Exiles: Indian Colonization in Oklahoma.* Oklahoma City: Oklahoma Historical Society, 1976.

Gibson, Arrell M. *The Chickasaws.* Norman: University of Oklahoma Press, 1971.

Gibson, Arrell M. *Oklahoma: A History of Five Centuries.* Norman: Harlow, 1965.

Gibson, Arrell M. *Oklahoma: A History of Five Centuries.* 2nd ed. Norman: University of Oklahoma Press, 1981.

Gibson, Arrell M. *The Oklahoma Story.* Norman: University of Oklahoma Press, 1978.

Gilbert, Claudette Marie, and Robert L. Brooks. *From Mounds to Mammoths: A Field Guide to Oklahoma Prehistory.* 2nd ed. Norman: University of Oklahoma Press, 2000.

Gittinger, Roy. *The Formation of the State of Oklahoma.* Norman: University of Oklahoma Press, 1939.

Glenmary Research Center. *Churches and Church Membership in the United States.* Nashville, Tenn.: Glenmary Research Center, 1990.

Glenmary Research Center. *Religious Congregations and Membership in the United States.* Nashville, Tenn.: Glenmary Research Center, 2000.

Goble, Danney. *Tulsa! Biography of the American City.* Tulsa: Council Oak Books, 1998.

Goins, Charles R., Edwin C. McReynolds, and John W. Morris. *Historical Atlas of Oklahoma.* 3rd ed. Norman: University of Oklahoma Press, 1986.

Good, Leonard. "Oklahoma's Art in the 1930s: A Remembrance." *Chronicles of Oklahoma* 70, no. 2 (Summer 1992): 194–209.

Goodwin, Dan E. *Remembrances of Durham, Oklahoma.* Unpublished manuscript. Stillwater, Okla., 2004.

Gould, Charles N. "Dedication of the Monument on Black Mesa." *Chronicles of Oklahoma* 7, no. 1 (March 1929): 34–54.

Gould, Charles N. *Geography of Oklahoma.* Ardmore, Okla.: Bunn Brothers, 1909.

Graebner, Norman A. "History of Cattle Ranching in Eastern Oklahoma." *Chronicles of Oklahoma* 21, no. 3 (September 1943): 300–311.

Gray, Fenton, and Harry M. Galloway. *Soils of Oklahoma.* Miscellaneous Publication 56. Stillwater: Oklahoma State University Agricultural Experiment Station, 1959.

Grazulis, Thomas P. *Significant Tornadoes, 1880–1989.* Vol. 2, *A Chronology of Events.* Johnsberry, Vt.: Environmental Films, 1990.

Green, Donald Edward. "Beginnings of Wheat Culture in Oklahoma." In *Rural Oklahoma,* ed. Donald Edward Green. Oklahoma City: Oklahoma Historical Society, 1977.

Green, Donald E. *The Creek People.* Phoenix: Indian Tribal Series, 1973.

Green, Michael D. *The Creeks.* New York: Chelsea House, 1990.

Green, Michael D. *The Creeks: A Critical Bibliography.* Bloomington: Indiana University Press, 1979.

Green, Michael D. *The Politics of Indian Removal: Creek Government and Society in Crisis.* Lincoln: University of Nebraska Press, 1982.

Gregg, Josiah. *Diary and Letters.* 2 vols., ed. Maurice Garland Fulton. Norman: University of Oklahoma Press, 1941, 1944.

Gregory, Robert. *Oil in Oklahoma.* Muskogee: Leake Industries, 1976.

Griffith, Richard. *The Movie Stars.* Garden City, N.Y.: Doubleday, 1970.

Guthrey, E. Bee. "Early Days in Payne County." *Chronicles of Oklahoma* 3, no. 1 (April 1925): 74–80.

Hagan, William T. *Taking Indian Lands: The Cherokee (Jerome) Commission, 1889–1893.* Norman: University of Oklahoma Press, 2003.

Hale, Douglas. "European Immigrants in Oklahoma: A Survey." *Chronicles of Oklahoma* 53, no. 2 (Summer 1975): 179–203.

Haley, James L. *The Buffalo War: The History of the Red River Indian Uprising of 1874.* Norman: University of Oklahoma Press, 1985.

Harrel, Melvin, ed. "My Life in Indian Territory—Augusta C. Metcalf." *Chronicles of Oklahoma* 33, no. 1 (March 1955): 49–62.

Harris, Phil. *This Is the Three Forks Country.* Muskogee, Okla.: Hoffman Printing, 1965.

Hastings, James K. "The Opening of Oklahoma." *Chronicles of Oklahoma* 27, no. 1 (Spring 1949): 70–75.

Henderson, Arn. "Joseph Foucart, Territorial Architect." In *Of the Earth: Oklahoma Architectural History,* ed. H. and M. Meredith. Oklahoma City: Oklahoma Historical Society, 1980.

Henderson, Arn. "Low-Style/High-Style: Oklahoma Architectural Origins and Image Distortion.–" In *The Culture of Oklahoma,* ed. H. Stein and R. Hill. Norman: University of Oklahoma Press, 1993.

Henderson, Arn, Frank Parman, and Dortha Henderson. *Architecture in Oklahoma: Landmark and Vernacular.* Norman: Point Riders Press, 1978.

Henderson, Caroline. *Letters from the Dust Bowl.* Ed. Alvin O. Turner. Norman: University of Oklahoma Press, 2003.

Hewes, Leslie. "Cherokee Occupance in the Oklahoma Ozarks and the Prairie Plains." *Chronicles of Oklahoma* 22, no. 3 (Autumn 1944): 324–37.

Hirsch, James S. *Riot and Remembrance: The Tulsa Race War and Its Legacy.* Boston: Houghton Mifflin, 2002.

Hoig, Stan. *The Battle of the Washita: The Sheridan-Custer Indian Campaign of 1867-69.* Lincoln: University of Nebraska Press, 1979.

Hoig, Stan. *The Oklahoma Land Run of 1889.* Oklahoma City: Oklahoma Historical Society, 1984.

Holland, Reid. "Life in Oklahoma's Civilian Conservation Corps." *Chronicles of Oklahoma* 48, no. 2 (Summer 1970): 224–34.

Hornbeck, Lewis N. "The Battle of the Washita," *Sturms Oklahoma Magazine* 5, no. 5 (January 1908).

Hudson, Charles M. *The Southeastern Indians.* Knoxville: University of Tennessee Press, 1976.

Irving, Washington. *A Tour on the Prairies.* Vol. 16 of *Early Western Travels, 1748–1846,* 32 vols, ed. R. G. Thwaites. Cleveland: Arthur H. Clark, 1904–7.

Jacobson, O. B., and Jeane d'Ucel. "Art in Oklahoma." *Chronicles of Oklahoma* 32, no. 3 (Autumn 1954): 263–77.

Jacobson, O. B., and Jeane d'Ucel. "Early Oklahoma Artists." *Chronicles of Oklahoma* 31, no. 2 (Summer 1953): 122–30.

James, Edwin. *The Stephen H. Long Expedition.* Vols. 14–17 of *Early Western Travels, 1748–1846,* 32 vols, ed. R. G. Thwaites. Cleveland: Arthur H. Clark, 1904–7.

James, Marquis. *The Cherokee Strip: A Tale of an Oklahoma Boyhood.* New York: Viking Press, 1945.

Jennings, Francis. *The Invasion of America: Indians, Colonialism and the Cant of Conquest.* Chapel Hill: University of North Carolina Press, 1975.

Johnson, Carol Newton. *Tulsa Art Deco.* Tulsa: Junior League of Tulsa, Oklahoma, 1980.

Johnson, Howard L., and Claude E. Duchon. *Atlas of Oklahoma Climate.* Norman: University of Oklahoma Press, 1995.

Johnson, Kenneth S. "Geology and Industrial-Mineral Resources of Oklahoma." Pp. 1–12 in *Proceedings of the 34th Forum on the Geology of Industrial Minerals,* ed. Kenneth S. Johnson. Circular 102. Norman: Oklahoma Geological Survey, 1999.

Johnson, Kenneth S. "Geology of Oklahoma." Pp. 1–9 in *Rockhounding and Earth-Science Activities in Oklahoma, 1995 Workshop,* ed. Kenneth S. Johnson and Neil S. Suneson. Special Publication 96-5. Norman: Oklahoma Geological Survey, 1996.

Johnson, Kenneth S. *Maps Showing Principal Ground-water Resources and Recharge Areas in Oklahoma.* Oklahoma City: Oklahoma State Department of Health, 1983.

Johnson, Kenneth S. "Mineral Map of Oklahoma (Exclusive of Oil and Gas Fields)." Map GM-15. Norman: Oklahoma Geological Survey, 1969.

Johnson, Kenneth S. "Mountains, Streams, and Lakes of Oklahoma." *Oklahoma Geology Notes* 53 (1993): 180–88.

Johnson, Kenneth S., et al. *Earth Sciences and Mineral Resources of Oklahoma.* Educational Publication EP-9. Norman: Oklahoma Geological Survey, 2006.

Johnson, Kenneth S., Carl C. Branson, et al. *Geology and Earth Resources of Oklahoma.* Educational Publication 1. Norman: Oklahoma Geological Survey, 1972.

Johnson, Kenneth S., et al. *Geology of the Southern Mid-Continent.* Special Publication. Norman: Oklahoma Geological Survey, 1989.

Kagan, Hilde Heun, ed. *The American Heritage Pictorial Atlas of United States History.* New York: American Heritage, 1966.

Kappler, Charles J., comp. *Indian Affairs, Laws and Treaties.* Washington, D.C.: Government Printing Office, 1903–29.

Katz, Ephraim. *The Film Encyclopedia.* 4th ed., rev. Fred Klein and Ronald Dean Nolen. New York: HarperCollins, 2001.

Kelley, Leo. "Bamboo Bombers over Oklahoma: USAAF Pilot Training during World War II." *Chronicles of Oklahoma* 68, no. 4 (Winter 1990–91): 360–75.

Kennan, Clara B. "Neighbors in the Cherokee Strip." *Chronicles of Oklahoma* 27, no. 1 (Spring 1949): 76–88.

Kersey, Harry A., Jr. *The Seminole and Miccosukee Tribes: A Critical Bibliography.* Bloomington: Indiana University Press, 1987.

Kidwell, Clara Sue, and Charles Roberts. *The Choctaws: A Critical Bibliography.* Bloomington: Indiana University Press, 1980.

Kingsbury, Paul, ed. *The Encyclopedia of Country Music: The Ultimate Guide to the Music.* New York: Oxford University Press, 1998.

Lackey, Vinson. *The Chouteaus and the Founding of Salina.* Tulsa: Privately printed, 1961.

Landerdale, Virginia E. "Tullahassee Mission." *Chronicles of Oklahoma* 26, no. 3 (Fall 1948): 285–300.

Lanham, Edwin. *The Stricklands: A Novel.* Introduction by Lawrence R. Rodgers. Norman: University of Oklahoma Press, 2004.

Leckie, William H. *The Military Conquest of the Southern Plains Indians.* Norman: University of Oklahoma Press, 1963.

Lee, Victoria. *Distinguished Oklahomans.* Tulsa: Touch of Heart Publishing, 2002.

Lewis, Anna. "Camp Napoleon." *Chronicles of Oklahoma* 9, no. 4 (December 1931): 359–64.

Lewis, Anna. "Oklahoma as a Part of the Old Spanish Dominion, 1763–1803." *Chronicles of Oklahoma* 3, no. 1 (March 1925): 45–57.

Linenthal, Edward T. *The Unfinished Bombing: Oklahoma City in American Memory.* New York: Oxford University Press, 2001.

Littlefield, Daniel F., Jr. *Africans and Creeks: From the Colonial Period to the Civil War.* Westport, Conn.: Greenwood Press, 1979.

Littlefield, Daniel F., Jr. *Africans and Seminoles: From Removal to Emancipation.* Westport, Conn.: Greenwood Press, 1977.

Littlefield, Daniel F., Jr. *The Chickasaw Freemen: A People without a Country.* Westport, Conn.: Greenwood Press, 1980.

Litton, Gaston. *History of Oklahoma at the Golden Anniversary of Statehood.* New York: Lewis Historical Publishing, 1957.

Litton, Gaston L. "The Principal Chiefs of the Cherokee Nation." *Chronicles of Oklahoma* 15, no. 3 (September 1937): 253–70.

Livingston, Lilli Cockerille. *American Indian Ballerinas.* Norman: University of Oklahoma Press, 1997.

Logsdon, Guy, with Mary Rogers and Bill Jacobson. *Saddle Serenaders: Biographies of Western Musicians.* Salt Lake City, Utah: Gibbs Smith, 1995.

Luza, Kenneth V., and Kenneth S. Johnson. "Geologic Hazards in Oklahoma." *Oklahoma Geology Notes* 63 (2003): 52–72.

Mahnken, Norbert R. "Old Baptist Mission and Evan Jones." *Chronicles of Oklahoma* 67, no. 2 (Summer 1989): 174–93.

Mahon, John K. *History of the Second Seminole War.* Gainesville: University of Florida Press, 1967.

Malone, Bill C. *Country Music, U.S.A.* Rev. ed. Austin: University of Texas Press, 1985.

Malone, Henry T. *Cherokees of the Old South.* Athens: University of Georgia Press, 1956.

Mankiller, Wilma, and Michael Wallis. *Mankiller: A Chief and Her People.* New York: St. Martin's Griffin, 1993.

Marable, Mary Hays, and Elaine Boylan. *A Handbook of Oklahoma Writers.* Norman: University of Oklahoma Press, 1939.

Marriott, Alice. *The Ten Grandmothers.* Norman: University of Oklahoma Press, 1945.

Marsh, Ralph, with Gene Stipe. *A Gathering of Heroes.* Heavener, Okla.: Spring Mountain Press, 2000.

Martin, Lucille J. "A History of the Modoc Indians." *Chronicles of Oklahoma* 47, no. 4 (Winter 1969–70): 398–446.

Masterson, Vincent V. *The Katy Railroad and the Last Frontier.* Columbia: University of Missouri Press, 1952.

Mathews, John Joseph. *The Osages: Children of the Middle Waters.* Norman: University of Oklahoma Press, 1961.

Maxwell, Amos. "The Sequoyah Convention." *Chronicles of Oklahoma* 28, no. 2 (Summer 1950): 161–92.

McClure, Arthur F., and Ken D. Jones. *Heros, Heavies and Sagebrush: A Pictorial History of the "B" Western Players.* New York: A. S. Barnes, 1972.

McCoy, Doyle. *Roadside Flowers of Oklahoma.* Lawton, Okla.: C and J Printing Co., 1976.

McLoughlin, William G. *Cherokee Renascence in the New Republic.* Princeton, N.J.: Princeton University Press, 1986.

McLoughlin, William G. *Cherokees and Missionaries, 1789–1839.* New Haven, Conn.: Yale University Press, 1984.

McReynolds, Edwin C. *Oklahoma: A History of the Sooner State.* Norman: University of Oklahoma Press, 1954.

McReynolds, Edwin C. *The Seminoles.* Norman: University of Oklahoma Press, 1956.

Melvin, M. E. "Story of the Oklahoma Boundaries." *Chronicles of Oklahoma* 22, no. 4 (December 1944): 382–91.

Merrill, Perry H. *Roosevelt's Forest Army: A History of the Civilian Conservation Corps.* Montpelier, Vt.: Perry H. Merrill, 1981.

Milam, Joe B. "The Opening of the Cherokee Outlet." *Chronicles of Oklahoma* 9, no. 3 (September 1931): 268–86.

Miller, Lona Eaton. "Wheelock Mission." *Chronicles of Oklahoma* 29, no. 3 (Fall 1951): 314–23.

Miner, H. Craig. "Cherokee Sovereignty in the Gilded Age: The Outlet Question." *Chronicles of Oklahoma* 71, no. 2 (Summer 1993): 118–37.

Miner, H. Craig. *The Corporation and the Indian: Tribal Sovereignty and Industrial Civilization in Indian Territory, 1865–1907.* Columbia: University of Missouri Press, 1976.

Miner, H. Craig. "The Dream of a Native Cattle Industry in Indian Territory." In *Ranch and Range in Oklahoma,* ed. Jimmy M. Skaggs. Oklahoma City: Oklahoma Historical Society, 1978.

Miser, Hugh D. *Geologic Map of Oklahoma.* Norman: Oklahoma Geological Survey and U.S. Geological Survey, 1954.

Mitchell, Irene B. "Bloomfield Academy." *Chronicles of Oklahoma* 49, no. 4 (Winter 1971–72): 412–26.

Mix, Paul E. *The Life and Legend of Tom Mix.* New York: A. S. Barnes, 1972.

Mix, Paul E. *The Life of Tom Mix and the Ralston Straight Shooters' Manual.* St. Louis, Mo.: Ralston Purina, 1933.

Mooney, James. "Myths of the Cherokees," *Bureau of American Ethnology Annual Report, 1897–98,* part 1. Washington: Government Printing Office, 1900. (Reprint, *Historical Sketch of the Cherokees.* Chicago: Aldine Publishing, 1975.)

Morgan, Anne Hodges. "Oklahoma in Literature." Pp. 175–204 in *Oklahoma: New Views of the Forty-Sixth State,* ed. Anne Hodges Morgan and Wayne Morgan. Norman: University of Oklahoma Press, 1982.

Morgan, Anne Hodges, and Rennard Strickland. *Oklahoma Memories.* Norman: University of Oklahoma Press, 1981.

Morris, John W. *Geography of Oklahoma.* Oklahoma City: Harlow, 1961.

Morris, John W., ed. *Geography of Oklahoma.* Oklahoma City: Oklahoma Historical Society, 1977.

Morris, John W., Charles R. Goins, and Edwin C. McReynolds. *Historical Atlas of Oklahoma.* 3rd ed. Norman: University of Oklahoma Press, 1986.

Morris, Wayne. "Auguste Pierre Chouteau, Merchant Prince at the Three Forks of the Arkansas." *Chronicles of Oklahoma* 48, no. 2 (Summer 1970): 155–63.

Morrison, W. B. "Colbert Ferry on Red River, Chickasaw Nation, I.T." *Chronicles of Oklahoma* 16, no. 3 (September 1938): 302–14.

Morrison, W. B. *Military Posts and Camps in Oklahoma.* Oklahoma City: Harlow, 1936.

Morton, Ohland. "Early History of the Creek Indians." *Chronicles of Oklahoma* 9, no. 1 (March 1931): 17–26.

Murphy, Justin D. "Wheelock Female Seminary, 1842–1861: The Acculturation and Christianization of Young Choctaw Women." *Chronicles of Oklahoma* 69, no. 1 (Spring 1991): 48–61.

Myers, Arthur J. "History of the Boundaries of Oklahoma." *Oklahoma Geology Notes* 43 (1983).

Nall, Garry L. "King Cotton in Oklahoma, 1825–1939." In *Rural Oklahoma,* ed. Donald Edward Green. Oklahoma City: Oklahoma Historical Society, 1977.

Nelson, Guy. *Thunderbird: A History of the 45th Infantry Division.* Oklahoma City: 45th Infantry Division Association.

Nesbitt, Paul. "Battle of the Washita." *Chronicles of Oklahoma* 3, no. 1 (April 1925): 3–32.

Nuttall, Thomas. *Thomas Nuttall's Journal of Travels into the Arkansas Territory.* Vol. 13 of *Early Western Travels, 1748–1846,* 32 vols., ed. R. G. Thwaites. Cleveland: Arthur H. Clark, 1904–1907.

Nye, W. S., Captain. "The Battle of Wichita Village." *Chronicles of Oklahoma* 15, no. 2 (June 1937): 226–27.

Nye, Wilbur Sturtevant. *Carbine and Lance: The Story of Old Fort Sill.* Norman: University of Oklahoma Press, 1969.

O'Donnell, James H., III. *Southeastern Frontiers: Europeans, Africans, and American Indians, 1513–1840.* Bloomington: Indiana University Press, 1982.

Oklahoma Agricultural Statistics Service. *Oklahoma Agricultural Statistics 2000.* Oklahoma City: U.S. Department of Agriculture and Oklahoma Department of Agriculture, 2001.

Oklahoma Cattlemen's Association. "Range Roundup." *Oklahoma Cowman.*

Oklahoma Climatological Survey. *Monthly Summary.* Norman: University of Oklahoma, published monthly 1980–present.

Oklahoma Department of Libraries. *Oklahoma Almanac, 2005–2006.* Oklahoma City, 2005.

Oklahoma Department of Transportation, Survey Division. *Railroads of Oklahoma.* June 1870–April 1978.

Oklahoma Geological Survey. *Oklahoma Resources for Economic Development.* Special Publication 98-4. Norman.

Oklahoma State Board of Agriculture. *Report of the Oklahoma State Board of Agriculture to the Legislature of Oklahoma for the Years 1907 and 1908.* Oklahoma City, 1908.

Oklahoma State Planning Board. "A Compendium of Maps and Charts Pertaining to State Planning in Oklahoma." Report dated April 1936.

Oklahoma Water Resources Board. *Oklahoma Water Atlas.* Publication 135. Oklahoma City, 1990.

Parker, Mary Ann. "The Elusive Meridian." *Chronicles of Oklahoma* 6, no. 2 (Summer 1973): 150–58.

Penney, David W. *North American Indian Art.* New York: Thames and Hudson, 2004.

Phillips, George R., Frank J. Gibbs, and Wilbur R. Mattoon. *Forest Trees of Oklahoma and How to Know Them.* Oklahoma City: Forestry Division, State Board of Agriculture, 1973.

Perdue, Theda. *The Cherokee.* New York: Chelsea House, 1989.

Perdue, Theda. *Cherokee Women: Gender and Culture Change, 1700–1835.* Lincoln: University of Nebraska Press, 1999.

Perdue, Theda. *Nations Remembered: An Oral History of the Five Civilized Tribes, 1865–1907.* Westport, Conn.: Greenwood Press, 1980.

Perdue, Theda. *Nations Remembered: An Oral History of the Cherokees, Chicasaws, Choctaws, Creeks, and Seminoles in Oklahoma, 1865–1907.* Norman: University of Oklahoma Press, 1993.

Perdue, Theda. *Slavery and the Evolution of Cherokee Society, 1540–1866.* Knoxville: University of Tennessee Press, 1979.

Pierce, Earl B., and Rennard Strickland. *The Cherokee People.* Phoenix: Indian Tribal Series, 1973.

Porter, Kenneth W. *The Negro and the American Frontier.* New York: Arno Press, 1971.

Prucha, Francis Paul. "American Indian Policy in the Formative Years," in *The Trade and Intercourse Acts, 1790–1834.* Cambridge, Mass.: Harvard University Press, 1962.

Prucha, Francis Paul. *The Great Father: The United States Government and the American Indians.* 2 vols. Lincoln: University of Nebraska Press, 1984.

Ragland, Hobert D. "Some Firsts in Lincoln County." *Chronicles of Oklahoma* 29, no. 4 (Winter 1951–52): 419–28.

Records, Ralph H. "Recollections of April 19, 1892." *Chronicles of Oklahoma* 21, no. 1 (March 1943): 16–27.

Reese, Linda. *Women of Oklahoma, 1890–1920.* Norman: University of Oklahoma Press, 1997.

Reeves, Carolyn Keller, ed. *The Choctaw before Removal.* Jackson: University Press of Mississippi, 1985.

Reinking, Dan L., ed. *Oklahoma Breeding Bird Atlas.* Norman: University of Oklahoma Press, 2004.

Rister, Carl Coke. *Border Command: General Phil Sheridan in the West.* Norman: University of Oklahoma Press, 1944.

Rister, Carl Coke. *No Man's Land.* Norman: University of Oklahoma Press, 1948.

Rodgers, Lawrence R. "H. L. Mencken and the 'Oklahoma Style' of Literature." *Chronicles of Oklahoma* 78, no. 4 (Winter 2000–2001): 468–83.

Rosenthal, Cindy S. *When Women Lead: Integrative Leadership in State Legislatures.* New York: Oxford University Press, 1998.

Ross, Glen. *On Coon Mountain: Scenes from a Boyhood in the Oklahoma Hills.* Norman: University of Oklahoma Press, 1992.

Routh, E. C. "Early Missionaries to the Cherokees." *Chronicles of Oklahoma* 15, no. 4 (December 1937): 449–65.

Royce, Charles C. "The Cherokee Nation of Indians," pp. 121–378 in *Bureau of American Ethnology Annual Report, 1883–84.* Washington, D.C.: Government Printing Office, 1887. (Reprinted as *The Cherokee Nation of Indians,* Chicago: Aldine Publishing, 1975.)

Royce, Charles C., comp. "Indian Land Cessions in the United States." *Bureau of American Ethnology Annual Report, 1896–97,* part 2. Washington, D.C.: Government Printing Office.

Rucker, Alvin. "Initial Point in Oklahoma." *Chronicles of Oklahoma* 5, no. 3 (September 1927): 328–32.

Ruth, Kent, and Jim Argo. *Oklahoma Historical Tour Guide.* Ed. D. Ray Wilson. Carpentersville, Ill.: Crossroads Communications, 1992.

Savage, William W., Jr. *The Cherokee Strip Livestock Association: Federal Regulation and the Cattleman's Last Frontier.* Norman: University of Oklahoma Press, 1990.

Savage, William W., Jr. "Leasing the Cherokee Outlet: An Analysis of Indian Reaction." *Chronicles of Oklahoma* 46, no. 3 (Autumn 1968): 285–92.

Schrems, Suzanne H. "A Lasting Legacy: The Civilian Conservation Corps and the Development of the Oklahoma State Park System." *Chronicles of Oklahoma* 72, no. 4 (Winter 1994–95): 368–95.

Scott, Barbara Kerr, and Sally Soelle. *New Deal Art: The Oklahoma Experience, 1933–1943.* Lawton, Okla.: Cameron University, 1983.

Self, Nancy H. "The Building of the Railroads in the Cherokee Nation." *Chronicles of Oklahoma* 49, no. 2 (Summer 1971): 180–205.

Shadwick, Keith. *The Encyclopedia of Jazz and Blues.* Edison, N.J.: Chartwell Brooks, 2001.

Shirk, George H. *Oklahoma Place Names.* Norman: University of Oklahoma Press, 1965.

Shirley, Glenn. *Guardian of the Law: The Life and Times of William Matthew Tilghman, 1854–1924.* Austin, Tex.: Eakin Press, 1988.

Shirley, Glenn. *Heck Thomas: Frontier Marshal.* Norman: University of Oklahoma Press, 1981.

Shirley, Glenn. *Law West of Fort Smith: A History of Frontier Justice in the Indian Territory, 1834–1896.* Lincoln: University of Nebraska Press, 1968.

Shirley, Glenn. *West of Hell's Fringe: Crime, Criminals, and the Federal Peace Officer in Oklahoma Territory, 1889–1907.* Norman: University of Oklahoma Press, 1978.

Shoemaker, Arthur. "The Battle of Chustenahlah." *Chronicles of Oklahoma* 38, no. 2 (Summer 1960): 180–84.

Smith, Annick. *Big Bluestem: A Journey into the Tall Grass.* Photographs by Harvey Payne. Tulsa: Council Oak Books, 1996.

Smith, Chadwick, and Faye Teague. *The Response of the Cherokee Nation to the Cherokee Outlet Centennial Celebration: A Legal and Historical Analysis.* N.p.: Cherokee Nation, 1993.

Snider, L. C. *Geography of Oklahoma.* Norman: Geological Survey, 1917.

Spoehr, Alexander. "Oklahoma Seminole Towns." *Chronicles of Oklahoma* 19, no. 4 (December 1941): 377–80.

Southern, John H. *Farm Tenancy in Oklahoma.* Bulletin 239. Stillwater, Okla.: Agricultural Experiment Station, 1939.

Stambler, Irwin, and Grelun Landon. *Encyclopedia of Folk, Country, and Western Music.* New York: St. Martin's Press, 1969.

Stephens, Elizabeth P. *The Historical Geography of the Boundaries of Oklahoma.* Master's thesis, University of Oklahoma, 1964.

Sterling, Bryan B., and Frances N. Sterling. *Will Rogers and Wiley Post: Death at Barrow.* New York: M. Evans, 1993.

Stewart, Lowell O. *Public Land Surveys: History, Instructions, Methods.* Ames, Ia.: Collegiate Press, 1935.

Stewart, Roy P. *Born Grown: An Oklahoma City History.* Oklahoma City: Fidelity Bank, 1974.

Stouts, Joseph A. *Frontier Adventures: American Exploration of Oklahoma.* Oklahoma City: Oklahoma Historical Society, 1984.

Strickland, Rennard. *The Indians in Oklahoma.* Norman: University of Oklahoma Press, 1980.

Sutton, George Miksch. *Fifty Common Birds of Oklahoma and the Southern Great Plains.* Norman: University of Oklahoma Press, 1977.

Tahan. "The Battle of the Washita." *Chronicles of Oklahoma* 8, no. 3 (September 1930): 272–81.

Tennant, H. S. "The History of the Chisholm Trail." In "The Two Cattle Trails," *Chronicles of Oklahoma* 14, no. 1 (March 1936): 108–22.

Thomas, A. B. "Spanish Exploration of Oklahoma, 1599–1792." *Chronicles of Oklahoma* 6, no. 2 (June 1928): 186–213.

Thurman, Malvena, ed. *Women in Oklahoma: A Century of Change.* Oklahoma City: Oklahoma Historical Society, 1982.

Tomlin, Pinky, with Lynette Wert. *The Object of My Affection: An Autobiography.* Norman: University of Oklahoma Press, 1981.

Tortorelli, Robert L., Ellen J. Cooter, and James W. Schuelein. "Oklahoma Floods and Droughts," in *National Water Summary 1988–89: Hydrologic Events and Floods and Droughts.* USGS Water Supply Paper 2375. Denver, Colo.: U.S. Geological Survey, 1991.

Tulsa Ballet Theatre. "A Home of Our Own." Dedication booklet. Tulsa, Okla., 1992.

Turner, Alvin O. "Order and Disorder: The Opening of the Cherokee Outlet." *Chronicles of Oklahoma* 71, no. 2 (Summer 1993): 154–73.

Tyrl, Ronald J., Terrence G. Birdwell, and Ronald E. Masters. Illustrated by Bellamy Parks Jansen. *Field Guide to Oklahoma Plants: Commonly Encountered Prairie, Shrubland, and Forest Species.* Stillwater: Department of Plant and Soil Science, Oklahoma State University, 2002.

U.S. Adjutant General's Office. *Chronological List of Actions, & c., with Indians from January 15, 1837 to January, 1891.* Fort Collins, Colo.: Old Army Press, 1974.

U.S. Department of Commerce. *Climatological Data: Oklahoma.* Asheville, N.C.: National Climatic Data Center, published monthly 1896–present.

U.S. Department of Commerce. *Storm Data.* Asheville, N.C.: National Climatic Data Center, published monthly 1959–present.

U.S. Department of War. *The War of the Rebellion: A Compilation of the Official Records of the Union and Confederate Armies.* Washington, D.C.: Government Printing Office, 1880–1901.

U.S. Senate. *Report of the Select Committee to Investigate Matters Connected with Affairs in the Indian Territory.* Senate Report 5013. 59th Cong., 2nd sess.

Utley, Robert. *Frontiersmen in Blue: The United States Army and the Indian, 1848–1865.* Lincoln: University of Nebraska Press, 1981.

Van Riper, Guernsey. *Will Rogers: Young Cowboy.* Childhood of Famous Americans Series. Indianapolis: Bobbs-Merrill, 1951.

Van Zandt, Howard F. "The History of Camp Holmes and Choteau's Trading Post." *Chronicles of Oklahoma* 13, no. 3 (September 1935): 316–37.

Wallis, Michael. *The Real Wild West: The 101 Ranch and the Creation of the American West.* New York: St. Martin's Press, 1999.

Warde, Mary Jane. "Now the Wolf Has Come: The Civilian Civil War in Indian Territory." *Chronicles of Oklahoma* 71, no. 1 (Spring 1993): 64–87.

Wardell, Morris L. "A History of No Man's Land, or Old Beaver County." *Chronicles of Oklahoma* 35, no. 1 (Spring 1957): 11–33.

Wardell, Morris L. *A Political History of the Cherokee Nation, 1838–1907.* Norman: University of Oklahoma Press, 1938.

Wardell, Morris L. "Protestant Missions among the Osages." *Chronicles of Oklahoma* 2, no. 3 (September 1924): 285–97.

Warner, Richard S. "Barbed Wire and Nazilagers: PW Camps in Oklahoma." *Chronicles of Oklahoma* 64, no. 1 (Spring 1986): 37–68.

Webb, Charles E. *Distribution of Cotton Production in Oklahoma, 1907–1962.* Master's thesis, University of Oklahoma, 1963.

Webb, George W. *Chronological List of Engagements between the Regular Army of the United States and Various Tribes of Hostile Indians Which Occurred During the Years 1790 to 1898, Inclusive.* St. Joseph, Mo.: Wing Printing and Publishing, 1939.

Westbrook, Harriette Johnson. "The Chouteaus and Their Commercial Enterprises," parts 1 and 2. *Chronicles of Oklahoma* 11, no. 2 (June 1933): 786–97 and 11, no. 3 (September 1933): 942–66.

White, C. Albert. *A History of the Rectangular Survey System.* Washington, D.C.: U.S. Department of the Interior, Bureau of Land Management, 1984.

White, Carl Robe. "Experiences at the Opening of Oklahoma." *Chronicles of Oklahoma* 27, no. 1 (Spring 1949): 56–69.

White, James D. "Destined for Duty: The Life and Diary of Bishop Theophile Meerschaert." *Chronicles of Oklahoma* 71, no. 1 (Spring 1993): 4–41.

Williams, John, and Howard L. Meredith. *Bacone Indian University: A History.* Oklahoma City: Oklahoma Heritage Association, 1980.

Wills, Rosetta. *The King of Western Swing: Bob Wills Remembered.* New York: Billboard Books, 1998.

Winship, George Parker, ed. "The Coronado Expedition, 1540–1542." Pp. 341–593 in *Bureau of American Ethnology Fourteenth Annual Report,*– part 1. Washington, D.C.: 1892–93.

Woodward, Grace S. *The Cherokees.* Norman: University of Oklahoma Press, 1938.

Work Projects Administration. *The WPA Guide to 1930s Oklahoma.* Compiled by Writers' Program of the Work Projects Administration in the State of Oklahoma. Lawrence: University Press of Kansas, 1986.

Worster, Donald. *Dust Bowl: The Southern Great Plains in the 1930s.* New York: Oxford University Press, 1979.

Wright, Muriel H. "Additional Notes on Perryville, Choctaw Nation." *Chronicles of Oklahoma* 8, no. 2 (June 1930): 146–48.

Wright, Muriel H. "Brief Outline of the Choctaw and Chickasaw Nations in the Indian Territory, 1820 to 1860," *Chronicles of Oklahoma* 7, no. 4 (December 1929): 388–418.

Wright, Muriel H. "The Butterfield Overland Mail One Hundred Years Ago." *Chronicles of Oklahoma* 35, no. 1 (Spring 1957): 55–71.

Wright, Muriel H. *A Guide to the Indian Tribes of Oklahoma.* Norman: University of Oklahoma Press, 1951.

Wright, Muriel H. "Organization of Counties in the Choctaw and Chickasaw Nations." *Chronicles of Oklahoma* 8, no. 3 (September 1930): 315–34.

Contributors

James H. Anderson is Manager of Cartography for the Oklahoma Geological Survey at the University of Oklahoma.

David L. Boren is the only person in state history to have served as Governer of Oklahoma, as U.S. Senator from Oklahoma, and as a member of the Oklahoma House of Representatives and then to serve as President of the University of Oklahoma. He is the university's thirteenth president.

Dan Boyd is a certified petroleum geologist with the Oklahoma Geological Survey at the University of Oklahoma.

Robert L. Brooks is State Archaeologist and Director of the Oklahoma Archeological Survey at the University of Oklahoma.

Hans Butzer is Associate Professor of Architecture and Urban Design at the University of Oklahoma.

Josh Clough is a Ph.D. candidate in American Indian Studies at the University of Oklahoma.

Danney Goble is Professor of Letters at the University of Oklahoma.

Charles Robert Goins is Professor Emeritus of Regional and City Planning and Architecture at the University of Oklahoma.

Michael D. Green is Professor of American Studies and History at the University of North Carolina.

Arn Henderson is Professor Emeritus of Architecture at the University of Oklahoma.

Bruce W. Hoagland is Coordinator for the Oklahoma Natural Heritage Inventory and Associate Professor of Geography at the University of Oklahoma.

Howard L. Johnson is retired as Associate State Climatologist for the Oklahoma Climatological Survey at the University of Oklahoma.

Kenneth S. Johnson is Geologist Emeritus with the Oklahoma Geological Survey at the University of Oklahoma.

Guy W. Logsdon is a historian of Oklahoma and the American West and a folklorist, writer, and entertainer.

John R. Lovett is Assistant Curator for the Western History Collections, University of Oklahoma Libraries.

B. Byron Price is Director of the Charles M. Russell Center and holds the Charles Marion Russell Chair in the School of Art at the University of Oklahoma.

Linda W. Reese is Assistant Professor of History at East Central University in Ada, Oklahoma.

Lawrence R. Rodgers is Associate Dean of the College of Arts and Sciences and Professor of English at Kansas State University.

Berry Tramel is a sports columnist for *The Oklahoman.*

Alvin O. Turner is Dean of Humanities and Social Sciences at East Central University in Ada, Oklahoma.

Mary Jo Watson is Associate Dean of the Weitzenhoffer Family College of Fine Arts and Associate Professor of Art History at the University of Oklahoma.

Index

References to illustrations—including maps, legends, and photographs—appear in italics.